THE WAR AGAINST THE JEWS 1933–1945

Lucy S. Dawidowicz

BANTAM BOOKS
TORONTO · NEW YORK · LONDON · SYDNEY

*This low-priced Bantam Book
has been completely reset in a type face
designed for easy reading, and was printed
from new plates. It contains the complete
text of the original hard-cover edition.*
NOT ONE WORD HAS BEEN OMITTED.

THE WAR AGAINST THE JEWS 1933–1945

*A Bantam Book / published by arrangement with
Holt, Rinehart and Winston*

PRINTING HISTORY

Holt, Rinehart and Winston edition published May 1975
2nd printing . . . . . May 1975   3rd printing . . . . . . June 1975
Commentary Library edition published May 1975
History Book Club edition published June 1975
Book-of-the-Month Club edition published Fall 1975
Bantam edition / June 1976
2nd printing . . . . . . June 1976   5th printing . . . . . April 1979
3rd printing . . . . August 1976   6th printing . . . . March 1980
4th printing . September 1978   7th printing . September 1981

Maps by Vincent Kotschar.

ISBN 0-553-20534-X

Published simultaneously in the United States and Canada

PRINTED IN THE UNITED STATES OF AMERICA

16 15 14 13 12 11 10 9

IN MEMORY OF

TOBA (TOBTSHE) DAWIDOWICZ
WARSAW 1924–WARSAW GHETTO 1943

AND
ZAREK DAWIDOWICZ
WARSAW 1927–TREBLINKA 1942 (?)

TWO OF SIX MILLION

Contents

APPENDICES

MAPS

Europe under German Rule,
December 1942

Destruction of the European Jews

Number of Jews

3,500,000

3,000,000

2,500,000

2,000,000

1,500,000

1,000,000

500,000

0

NETHERLANDS

BELGIUM

PROTECTORATE OF
BOHEMIA AND
MORAVIA

GERMANY/
AUSTRIA

FRANCE

ITALY

White bars indicate the prewar
Jewish population for designated areas.

Black bars indicate the number of Jews
annihilated in designated areas.

BALTIC
STATES

SSR
WHITE
RUSSIA

RUSSIA
(RSFSR)

POLAND

SSR
UKRAINE

SLOVAKIA

HUNGARY

RUMANIA

YUGOSLAVIA

BULGARIA

GREECE

Acknowledgments

This book had its genesis in a course I developed at the suggestion of Rabbi David Mirsky, Dean of Stern College for Women, Yeshiva University. I am grateful to Dean Mirsky for facilitating this undertaking and for his confidence in its successful completion.

The immense scope of the subject required assistance in research and translation. I am grateful to the following foundations whose grants during the last five years enabled me to obtain that assistance: Atran Foundation, Inc., and its vice-president, Mr. Isaiah M. Minkoff; The Gustav Wurzweiler Foundation, Inc., and its president, Dr. Max Gruenewald; the John Slawson Fund for Research, Training and Education and Dr. John Slawson; The Lucius N. Littauer Foundation and its president, Mr. Harry Starr; the Memorial Foundation for Jewish Culture and its assistant executive director, Dr. Jerry Hochbaum.

I am indebted to Miss Dina Abramowicz, librarian of the YIVO Institute for Jewish Research, and to Mr. Harry J. Alderman, head of the Blaustein Library of the American Jewish Committee, for their unstinting helpfulness and expert advice. Mr. Ezekiel Lifschutz, archivist of the YIVO Institute for Jewish Research, now retired, was courteous and accommodating. Mr.

Samuel L. Haber, executive vice-chairman of the American Jewish Joint Distribution, kindly gave me permission to use that institution's archives and Mrs. Rose Klepfisz, JDC's archivist, cheerfully and knowledgeably guided me through these massive records. Mr. Milton Himmelfarb, director of the Information and Research Service of the American Jewish Committee, gave me permission to use the AJC's Records Center, and Mrs. Ruth Rauch, in charge of those records, gave me every assistance. Dr. Fred Grubel, secretary of the Leo Baeck Institute, was unfailingly helpful by giving me access to the Institute's unpublished collections and by sharing his wide store of knowledge in response to my many questions. Mr. Hillel Kempinski, in charge of the Franz Kursky Archives of the Jewish Labor Bund, and Mrs. Sylvia Landress, head of the Zionist Library and Archives, were generous in helping me locate various unpublished materials in their collections.

Dr. Hildegard von Kotze, archivist at the Institut für Zeitgeschichte in Munich, was most helpful in answering my inquiries and in providing me with copies of documents not available elsewhere. Mr. Robert Wolfe, specialist for modern European history, and Mr. John E. Taylor, assistant director of the modern military branch, both of the National Archives, were helpful in locating and providing me with copies of unpublished German documents which I requested. Mrs. H. Czarnocka, honorary secretary of the Studium Polski Podziemnej in London, helped to trace documents of interest to me. I am indebted also for valuable data to Mr. M. Mazor, director of the archives of the Centre de Documentation Juive Contemporaine in Paris; to Dr. Eloisa Ravenna, secretary of the Centro di Documentazione Ebraica Contemporanea in Milan; and to Mme. Luci Petrović, secretary of the Federation of Jewish Communities in Yugoslavia in Belgrade.

Dr. Isaiah Trunk and Dr. Lucjan Dobroszycki, both at the YIVO Institute, gave generously of their time and their vast fund of knowledge. Dr. Friedrich Brodnitz, Mrs. Chana Fryszdorf, Mr. Milton Himmelfarb,

Dr. Ismar Schorsch, and Dr. Trunk read portions of the manuscript and I benefited from their corrections and advice. For intellectual stimulation of a high order I thank Dr. Mortimer Ostow and the members of the ongoing Seminar on Jewish Response to Crisis, which he has conducted under the auspices of the Jewish Theological Seminary of America. My friend Rose Grundstein has encouraged me by her enthusiasm and dedication.

Above all, I owe this book to my husband Szymon, who gave me the courage to begin the work and the strength to complete it.

L.S.D.

The Subject:
Definitions and Contours

The annihilation of six million Jews, carried out by the German state under Adolf Hitler during World War II, has resisted understanding. The question persists: how could it have happened? That question embraces several questions, each charged with passion and moral judgment. They are:

1. How was it possible for a modern state to carry out the systematic murder of a whole people for no reason other than that they were Jews?
2. How was it possible for a whole people to allow itself to be destroyed?
3. How was it possible for the world to stand by without halting this destruction?

Part I of this book, "The Final Solution," attempts to answer the first question. Part II, "The Holocaust," attempts to answer the second. A partial answer or partial answers to the third question can be found in Appendix A, "The Fate of the Jews in Hitler's Europe."

"The Final Solution of the Jewish Question" was the code name assigned by the German bureaucracy to the annihilation of the Jews. The very composition of the code name, when analyzed, reveals its fundamental character and meaning to the Germans who invented and used it. The term "Jewish question," as first used during the early Enlightenment/Emancipation period in Western Europe, referred to the "question" or "problem" that the anomalous persistence of the Jews as a people posed to the new nation-states and the rising political nationalisms. The "Jewish question" was, at bottom, a euphemism whose verbal neutrality concealed the user's impatience with the singularity of this people that did not appear to conform to the new political demands of the state.

Since a question demands an answer and a problem a solution, various answers and solutions were propounded to the "Jewish question," by foes and even friends, that entailed the disappearance of the Jews as such—abandonment of the Jewish religion or its essential elements, of the Jewish language, Yiddish, of Jewish culture, Jewish uniqueness and separatism. The histories of Jewish emancipation and of European anti-Semitism are replete with proffered "solutions to the Jewish question." The classic illustration is the "solution" offered by Constantine Pobyedonostsev, chief adviser to Czar Alexander III, in 1881: one-third of the Jews were to emigrate, one-third to convert, and one-third to die of hunger.

To this concept that the National Socialists adopted they added one new element, embodied in the word "final." "Final" means definitive, completed, perfected, ultimate. "Final" reverberates with apocalyptic promise, bespeaking the Last Judgment, the End of Days, the last destruction before salvation, Armageddon. "The Final Solution of the Jewish Question" in the National Socialist conception was not just another anti-Semitic undertaking, but a metahistorical program devised with an eschatological perspective. It was part of a salvational ideology that envisaged the attainment of Heaven by bringing Hell on earth. "The Devil is loose," Friedrich Reck-Malleczewen noted in his diary on October 30, 1942. The most important event of our time, André Malraux said, was *"le retour de Satan,"* citing the German system of terror.

To attain its heavenly Hell on earth the German dictatorship launched a war that engulfed the whole world. Over 35 million people were killed, more than half of them civilians. On the battlefields 1 out of every 22 Russians was killed, 1 out of every 25 Germans, 1 out of every 150 Italians and Englishmen, and 1 out of every 200 Frenchmen. The human cost of 2,191 days of war surpassed the losses of any previous war in the world. That war brought death to nearly 6 million Jews, to 2 out of every 3 European Jews. Though one-third of them managed to survive, though the Jewish people and Judaism have outlived the Third Reich, the Germans nevertheless succeeded in irrecoverably destroying the life and culture of East European Jewry.

The Final Solution transcended the bounds of modern historical experience. Never before in modern history had one people made the killing of another the fulfillment of an ideology, in whose pursuit means were identical with ends. History has, to be sure, recorded terrible massacres and destruction that one people perpetrated against another, but all—however cruel and unjustifiable—were intended to achieve instrumental ends, being means to ends, not ends in themselves.

The German state, deciding that the Jews should not live, arrogated to itself the judgment as to whether a whole people had the right to existence, a judgment that no man and no state have the right to make. "Anyone who on the basis of such a judgment," said Karl Jaspers, "plans the organized slaughter of a people and participates in it, does something that is fundamentally different from all crimes that have existed in the past."

To carry out this judgment, designated as the Final Solution, the German dictatorship involved and engaged the entire bureaucratic and functional apparatus of the German state and the National Socialist movement and employed the best available technological means. The Final Solution destroyed the East European Jews. In doing so, it subverted fundamental moral principles and every system of law that had governed, however imperfectly, human society for millennia.

In writing the history of the Final Solution, I approached the subject from the inside as best I could. Here the Germans are the actors and their acts are viewed through the lenses of German documents. In dwelling on Hitler's ideas about the Jews and on the development of modern German anti-Semitism, I have tried to show the intellectual and historical origins of the Final Solution. Throughout I tried to demonstrate the mutual influences and interplay of ideology and action, belief and program, national character and political behavior.

Part II, "The Holocaust," describes the Jewish response to the Final Solution. "The Holocaust" is the term that Jews themselves have chosen to describe their fate during World War II. At the most superficial level, the word "holocaust" means a great destruction and devastation, but its etymological substratum interposes a specifically Jewish interpretation. The word derives from the Greek *holokauston,* the Septuagint's translation for the Hebrew *olah,* literally "what is brought up," rendered in English as "an offering made by fire unto the Lord," "burnt offering," or "whole burnt offering." The implication is unmistakable: once again in their history the Jews are victims, sacrifices.

The Holocaust, then, becomes another link in the historic chain of Jewish suffering. The very word summons up the remembrance of the Jews in 1096 during the First Crusade. The chronicles and liturgical poetry of those days, in a striking concurrence, evoke the image of the Akedah, the Binding—or sacrifice—of Isaac, as the prefiguration of their own ordeals. For the Jews the Holocaust did not transcend history, but was part of the recurrent pattern of persecution that has been the Jewish historic experience. Still, within the perspective of Jewish history, the Holocaust is the most massive and disastrous catastrophe since the earliest days of that history. Even at the time of the greatest Jewish national trauma, the destruction of the Second Temple, the physical survival of the Jews was not in such jeopardy as during the Holocaust. In 70 C.E. only about one-fourth of the Jews lived in Palestine, while the rest lived in the Diaspora. More Jews lived in Alexandria then than in Jerusalem. In 1939, in contrast, two-thirds of the world's Jews lived in Europe and three-fourths of them—half of all world Jewry— were concentrated in Eastern Europe.

The destruction of East European Jewry brought to an end the thousand-year-old culture of Ashkenazic Jewry that had originated in the Rhine Basin and that by 1939 was concentrated in Eastern Europe. It was a culture whose religious teachings and traditions defined its secular character and values. It was a culture whose language was Yiddish, the language in which Jewish males studied the Talmud, in which mothers sang lullabies and little children played games, in which merchants conducted business and preachers delivered sermons, in which shrews scolded and roughnecks cursed, in which young men courted their girls. Yiddish was a vehicle for a great religious and secular culture, and it generated a rich literature.

East European Jewry created a culture that venerated the *sefer*, the book of religious learning, but whose people laughed at themselves. It was a culture that put its people, familiar with poverty and hardship, on speaking terms with God. It was a culture unique in all Jewish history, and East European Ashkenazic Jewry, which fashioned that culture, was the wellspring of Jewish creativity for Jewish communities throughout the world.

Part II, "The Holocaust," opens with a chapter about the German Jews in their encounter with National Socialism in the first stage of its rule. Thereafter, Part II focuses on the experiences of the East European Jews, mainly in Poland and Lithuania, because they were the most numerous of all European Jews, because they constituted a unique civilization, and because Eastern Europe was the central locus of the Final Solution.

The primary task I set myself was to describe the responses of the organized Jewish community to the Final Solution in its several stages. I have stressed the role and functions of Jewish communal institutions and communal leadership at various levels in the reordered Jewish society under German occupation. To the best of my ability and within the limits set by the availability of sources, I have tried to delineate the varieties of Jewish communal policy as formulated and carried out in different communities and by different communal leaders at various levels, sometimes in harmony and sometimes at variance with each other, and to show wherever possible the responses of the masses to these policies. Consistently, I have used Jewish sources as the lenses through which to view the Jewish community and to analyze Jewish behavior.

One impediment was the inadequacy of Jewish documentation, despite its enormous quantity. Holocaust documents were composed under extreme persecution, and they are the quintessential products of external censorship and self-imposed restraints. Jewish official documents that have survived reflect the writers' awareness of the omnipresent Germans and their all-seeing eyes. The absence of vital subjects from the records may be explained by the predicament of terror and censorship; yet, lacking evidence to corroborate or disprove, the historian will never know with certainty whether that absence is a consequence of an institutional decision not to deal with such matters or whether it was merely a consequence of prudential policy not to mention such matters. The terror was so great that even private personal diaries, composed in Yiddish or Hebrew, were written circumspectly, with recourse to Scripture and the Talmud as a form of esoteric expression and self-imposed reticence.

Survivor documentation, on the other hand, frequently suffers from subjectivity, bitterness, and partisanship—commonplace and habitual defects of most historical records. These documents have a further shortcoming. For the most part, the experiences recounted by survivors bring to mind the adventures of Stendhal's Fabrizio del Dongo at the Battle of Waterloo. Like him, they are never quite certain what great events they are witness to. Like him, they have just missed seeing the Emperor—in their case, they have been too distant from communal responsibility to be able to describe with any authority those critical situations at which significant decisions were made and policies framed for the Jewish community.

With the liquidation of the ghettos, Jewish communal existence came to an end. Some 5, perhaps 10, percent of East European Jews lived a brief while longer in closed concentration/labor camps, but no formal Jewish communal institutions existed anymore. A minuscule number of Jews, atomized individuals, managed to survive even the death camps, but their story is not the history of the Jewish community. For this reason this book closes with the liquidation of the ghettos.

Appendix A, "The Fate of the Jews in Hitler's Europe," is an attempt to put on record the essential bare facts about the Jews in each European country. Each country is considered individually and its wartime status described. A sketch of that country's prewar Jewish population follows, and then the course of the Final Solution in the country is briefly recounted. It was my intention here to provide, in a kind of historical shorthand, a summary account of the fate of the European Jews during World War II and, at the same time, within the limits of the presentation, to enable the reader to distinguish those political, historical, social, and geographic factors that accounted for the different treatment accorded to the Jews in various countries.

This is not a value-free book. The very subject matter of the Final Solution precludes neutrality. In writing about a nation that transgressed the commandment "Thou shalt not murder," it is impossible to be what Charles Beard characterized as "a neutral mirror."

Whereas the Germans, in planning and executing the Final Solution, played the role of the Devil and his hosts, the Jews during the Holocaust were, alas, merely human, saints and sinners, imperfect earthlings. In writing about the Holocaust I have tried to avoid moral judgments, though I have not hesitated to describe demoralization. In discussing the deeds of the handful of Jewish leaders who have been charged by survivors and scholars with criminal behavior, I have been persuaded by Professor Herbert Butterfield's view that the historian can never quite know men from the inside, because he can never carry his investigation into the interiority of their minds and hearts, where "the final play of motive and the point of responsibility" are decided.

As best I could I have tried to present what actually happened. I strove to follow the two methods that Wilhelm von Humboldt perceived to be the historian's task in the approach to the historical truth: "The first is the exact, impartial, critical investigation of events; the second is the connecting of the events explored and the intuitive understanding of them which could not be reached by the first means."

PART I

THE
FINAL
SOLUTION

1

The Jews in Hitler's Mental World

"If at the beginning of the War and during the War," Hitler wrote in the last chapter of *Mein Kampf*, "twelve or fifteen thousand of these Hebrew corrupters of the people had been held under poison gas, as happened to hundreds of thousands of our very best German workers in the field, the sacrifice of millions at the front would not have been in vain."[1]

Did the idea of the Final Solution originate in this passage, germinating in Hitler's subconscious for some fifteen years before it was to sprout into practical reality? The idea of a mass annihilation of the Jews had already been adumbrated by apocalyptic-minded anti-Semites during the nineteenth century. Yet even the most fanatic and uncompromising anti-Semites, when confronted with political actualities and social realities, invariably settled for an aggregation of exclusionary measures. Hitler did not. He succeeded in transforming the apocalyptic idea into concrete political action. The mass murder of the Jews was the consummation of his fundamental beliefs and ideological conviction.

The nexus between idea and act has seldom been as evident in human history with such manifest con-

sistency as in the history of anti-Semitism. Jew-hatred
is one of those "unit-ideas," to use Arthur Lovejoy's
phrase, with "long life-histories of their own." Yet not
until Hitler's accession to power in Germany and his
dominion over Europe had the abstract idea of Jew-
hatred assumed so terrible a concrete and visible
reality. Nor had anti-Semitism ever before been so
obviously a product of a system of beliefs. For Hitler's
ideas about the Jews were the starting place for the
elaboration of a monstrous racial ideology that would
justify mass murder whose like history had not seen
before.

Only Hitler's followers took his ideas about the Jews
seriously. His opponents found them too preposterous
for serious consideration, too irrational and lunatic to
merit reasonable analysis and rebuttal. Today, looking
at his photographs, it seems easy to understand how
Hitler could have been underestimated, disparaged.
He was of medium height, with beady eyes and a
comic moustache. The unmanageable cowlick of his
pomaded hair became the burlesque symbol of unre-
strained passion. He was a strutter and a posturer,
"one of those men without qualities," wrote Konrad
Heiden, his face "without radiance."[2] Hermann Rauschning too characterized his look as lacking "the bril-
liance and sparkle of genuine animation." An authority
in "racial" biology described Hitler as he saw him in
1923: "Face and head: bad race, mongrel. Low, reced-
ing forehead, ugly nose, broad cheekbones, small eyes,
dark hair; facial expression, not of a man commanding
with full self-control, but betraying insane excitement.
Finally, an expression of blissful egotism."[3]

"A raw-vegetable Genghis Khan," wrote Friedrich
Percyval Reck-Malleczewen, observing Hitler without
his usual bodyguard in a Munich restaurant in 1932.
It would have been easy then, in the almost deserted
restaurant, to shoot Hitler. "If I had had an inkling of
the role this piece of filth was to play, and of the years
of suffering he was to make us endure, I would have
done it without a second thought. But I took him for
a character out of a comic strip, and did not shoot."[4]

A raving lunatic, a comic-strip character, a political absurdity. Yet this voice mesmerized millions, "a guttural thunder," according to Heiden, "the very epitome of power, firmness, command, and will." Was it the sheer physical quality of the voice that hypnotized them? Or was the charisma in the dark message of racial mastery and the rule of blood? Serious people, responsible people thought that Hitler's notions about the Jews were, at best, merely political bait for disgruntled masses, no more than ideological window dressing to cloak a naked drive for power. Yet precisely the reverse was true. Racial imperialism and the fanatic plan to destroy the Jews were the dominant passions behind the drive for power.

Hitler's ideas about the Jews were at the center of his mental world. They shaped his world view and his political ambitions, forming the matrix of his ideology and the ineradicable core of National Socialist doctrine. They determined the anti-Jewish policies of the German dictatorship from 1933 to 1945, and they furnished the authority for the murder of the Jews in Europe during World War II. Few ideas in world history achieved such fatal potency. If only because these ideas had such consequences, they deserve serious analysis despite their irrationality, historical falsehood, scientific sham, and moral loathsomeness.

Mein Kampf provides much of our knowledge about Hitler and his ideas. He wrote it in the prison at Landsberg, while serving a highly abbreviated term (November 11, 1923–December 20, 1924) of a five-year sentence for high treason in organizing the unsuccessful Munich Putsch. Graceless, prolix, disorganized, incoherent in parts, repetitious, *Mein Kampf* was written in the tradition of confessional biography, in which the hand of Destiny is clearly seen to be shaping the course of the writer's life. It is, above all, a self-aggrandizing document, in which the author is presented as intellectual nonpareil and political savior. Nothing was to detract from this image of Hitler, and consequently he suppressed mention of persons or events that molded and influenced him. As for his ideas, we can never really be confident that his descriptions in 1924 of the ideas he held in 1904 or 1908 or 1912 are honest, or whether he recreated his intellectual development swathed in legends. During his lifetime Hitler's champions and enemies furnished additional bits and pieces to the sketchy information about his early life. Subsequent scholarship has yielded a few more details to the portrait of the authentic Hitler. Still, much mystery surrounds his origins and early life.

Adolf Hitler was born April 20, 1889, in the town of Braunau, on the Inn River, at the Austro-German border, the fourth child of Alois Hitler and Klara, his third wife, twenty-three years his junior.[5] Alois (1837–1903) was the illegitimate son of Maria Anna Schicklgruber (1795–1847), in whose name he had been christened. The identity of Adolf Hitler's paternal grandfather has remained an unraveled historical mystery of more than passing interest, since it raised doubts about Adolf Hitler's pure "racial" ancestry. Nearly all the evidence is in dispute.

In 1842, when Alois was five years old, his mother married Johann Georg Hiedler (the family name variously spelled Hüttler, Hütler, Hitler). Alois, however, seems to have been brought up by Georg's younger brother, Johann Nepomuk, who, according to another version, was his real father. In 1876, when Georg was eighty-four years old, he formally acknowledged Alois, then thirty-nine, as his son, who, legitimated, took the name of his father, real or putative. Another version has it that with Georg long dead, Nepomuk managed to get the parish records changed, by bringing three witnesses to testify that they knew Georg had accepted Alois as his son.

A more fanciful version of Adolf Hitler's origins exists: the allegation that his paternal grandfather was Jewish. Its source was the confession by Hans Frank, governor general of German-occupied Poland, written while awaiting execution at Nuremberg. According to Frank, William Patrick Hitler, the son of Alois, Jr., Hitler's half-brother (by his father's second wife), had threatened in a letter to divulge Hitler's Jewish ancestry. Hitler asked Frank, then legal adviser to the NSDAP, confidentially to investigate the charge, which Frank claimed to have substantiated, that Maria Schicklgruber's child had been fathered by the nineteen-year-old son in a household, presumably Jewish, where she had been employed as a domestic. Post-1945 investigations of the local records indicate, however, that no Jews lived in that area at the time, and the story was probably groundless. Still, uncertainties about his own ancestry must have obsessed the man who made ancestry the measure of the Aryan man.

Adolf's father was a customs official in the Austrian civil service, and the family moved whenever his assignments were changed. Three years after Adolf's birth, they moved to Passau, another border town. In 1894, when Adolf was five years old, they moved to Leonding, a suburb of Linz, where they finally stayed. Alois retired the next year and spent his time buying and selling farms, strolling about the neighborhood, and socializing at the local tavern. His relations with his son Adolf were stormy and tense. An indifferent and indolent pupil, Adolf was, at his father's insistence, enrolled in the *Realschule* in Linz, a secondary school whose training would lead to a technical or business career. In sharp conflict with his father, Adolf wanted instead to become a painter, an artist. When Alois died in 1903, the pressure on Adolf ceased. Klara continued to draw her late husband's pension and Adolf continued his schooling.

The next year he was transferred out of the *Realschule* because of his poor scholastic record. He was enrolled in the *Staatsrealschule* at Steyr, where he boarded and which he left in 1905, with indifferent success, after completing four years of secondary school. The only two subjects in which he excelled were freehand drawing and gymnastics. He failed to take the final examinations and never received a diploma. Years later one of his teachers described him as lacking self-discipline, "being notoriously cantankerous, willful, arrogant, and bad-tempered." When he returned home from Steyr, his mother sold the house at Leonding and moved with Adolf to Linz proper. Living on her monthly widow's pension and the proceeds of the sale of the house, she supported Adolf, who seemed to have no thought of settling down or looking for work.

In *Mein Kampf*, Hitler minimized the influences on on him of his family, friends, and general milieu in Linz. He said he did not remember having heard the word "Jew" during his father's lifetime, characterizing Alois's views as "more or less cosmopolitan." There were just a few Jews in Linz, whom, Adolf said, he regarded merely as Germans of a different religion. He claimed that he "did not so much as suspect the existence of an organized opposition to the Jews." His boyhood friend August Kubizek remembered otherwise. Alois Hitler, he said, was a supporter of Georg von Schönerer, Pan-German nationalist and anti-Semite. One of Hitler's elementary school teachers was said to have been an open anti-Semite, and the *Realschule* had several teachers "with decided anti-Semitic views." According to Kubizek, Hitler himself was a confirmed anti-Semite as early as 1904. While attending the *Realschule* at Linz, he was reading the local anti-Semitic paper, *Linzer Fliegenden Blätter*. Furthermore, Linz was where Hitler discovered Wagner as composer and ideologue. He went to the theater to hear Wagner, and in Linz he discovered Wagner's prose writings and no doubt read *Jews in Music* and the grandiloquent *Decay and Regeneration*. Wagner, Hitler would later write, stands besides Frederick the Great and Martin Luther: "Whoever wants to understand National Socialist Germany must know Wagner."

He visited Vienna briefly in 1906 and then managed to convince his doting mother to finance a lengthier trip there to fulfill his ambition of entering the Academy of Fine Arts. In October 1907 he submitted his drawings to the academy, but they were rejected as unsatisfactory. He stayed in Vienna, living on money sent by his mother, and applied again the following year to the academy. This time he was not even admitted to the test. Meanwhile his mother had developed breast cancer and was rapidly succumbing to the disease. On December 21, 1908, she died and Hitler came home for the funeral. A few weeks later he left Linz for good and returned to Vienna, where he would live in anonymity for four cheerless years.

These years in Vienna are the most obscure in Hitler's life. After he spent his modest inheritance and orphan's pension, he had to move into a flophouse. He joined forces with a Reinhold Hanisch, a tramp in the same lodgings. Hitler painted postcards, copying views of Vienna, which Hanisch peddled about town. In 1910 Hitler thought he was being cheated by Hanisch and brought a suit against him. Hanisch was put in jail and that broke up the partnership. Very little is known of Hitler's life during the next three years in Vienna, except that he continued to live the same miserable marginal existence that he later described as the unhappiest years of his life.

In *Mein Kampf* he set down the record of how he wanted the development of his intellectual life to appear. Vienna, Hitler said, transformed him into an anti-Semite. "For me this was the time of the greatest spiritual upheaval I have ever had to go through. I had ceased to be a weak-kneed cosmopolitan and became an anti-Semite." The apprenticeship in anti-Semitism that he had served in Linz was glossed over. Hitler wanted his discovery of the "truth" to be wholly his own, untainted by any influence, especially a paternal one. Still, Vienna was far more decisive than Linz as the place where his ideas about Jews took shape and where he began to give serious attention to thoughts of race and racial biology.

Hitler dramatized his first confrontation with East European Jews: "Once, as I was strolling through the Inner City, I suddenly encountered an apparition in a black caftan and black hair locks. Is this a Jew? was my first thought." Observing the man, his next question was: "Is this a German?" To find an answer, he turned, "as always," to books: "I bought the first anti-Semitic pamphlets of my life." But he found the literature unsatisfying, for, he said, it presupposed knowledge or understanding of the Jewish question. Besides, the "dull and amazingly unscientific arguments" were unconvincing. Only his own study, his own experience, his own "slowly rising insights" brought him to an understanding of what the Jews were and of the need to combat them. That is, Hitler was saying, without the reinforcement of the then existent anti-Semitic movement, without prior influences from home, without benefiting from the plenitude of anti-Semitic literature then in the public domain, he himself mastered the "Jewish question" in the solitary genius of his mind. Vienna was for him, he wrote, "the hardest, though most thorough school" of his life, where he obtained the foundations for "a philosophy in general and a political view in particular," which remained with him for the rest of his life.

But outside influences were plainly at work upon him. In Vienna, in Hitler's time, anti-Semitic politics flourished, anti-Semitic organizations proliferated, anti-Semitic writing and propaganda poured forth in an unending stream. Despite his down-and-out flophouse existence, he was aware of much of the anti-Semitic doings. He was, for one, an avid, if unsystematic, reader. He tells us that he read the "so-called world press," the *Neue Freie Presse* and the *Wiener Tageblatt*. Impressed at first, he soon came to see in them, he claimed, the ugly manipulation by the Jews. The hostile attitude the Viennese press took toward Germany particularly vexed him. On this subject, he admitted, "I was forced to recognize that one of the anti-Semitic papers, the *Deutsches Volksblatt,* behaved more decently." The *Deutsches Volksblatt* was a popular Viennese paper whose appeal was derived from its anti-Semitism, anticapitalism, and antiliberalism. Hitler was familiar, then, with the anti-Semitic press. Perhaps he read it regularly. In fact, by his own admission, he bought and read anti-Semitic pamphlets.

Which ones? Of the superabundance of such writings in those days in Vienna he probably sampled a variety. We know that he was for a time fascinated by the publications of Lanz von Liebenfels, an eccentric occultist-racist.[6] Between 1907 and 1910 Lanz published a series of pamphlets called *Ostara: Briefbücherei der blonden Mannesrechtler* ("Newsletters of the Blond Champions of Man's Rights"), in which he depicted the struggle between the blond Aryan heroes and the dark, hairy ape-men representing the lower races. All human existence revolved around this struggle, whose central burden was to preserve the purity of Aryan women from the demonic sexuality of the ape-men. *Ostara* was available at many newsstands, and Hitler had picked up a copy at the corner tobacconist's and then began to buy it regularly. In 1909 he sought out Lanz to get back issues, which Lanz, flattered, provided free of charge.

The ape-men in *Ostara* were not always explicitly identified as Jews, perhaps because Lanz thought that the racial conflict as he depicted it was sufficiently lurid to gratify the erotic fantasies of his rootless, unemployed, down-and-out readers, most of whom, like Hitler, were unattached men. With regard to the Jews, Lanz wrote in an issue of *Ostara*: "We would never dream of preaching pogroms, because they will come without encouragement." Sterilization, the "castration knife," would, Lanz held, solve the Jewish problem. The swastika was regarded as a symbol of racial purity, and *Ostara* dwelt tirelessly on the swastika's origins and secret meanings. Practicing what he preached, Lanz hoisted the swastika over his castle, Burg Werfenstein, in 1907.

Besides *Ostara*, Lanz wrote pamphlets on race occultism, at least one of which was found in Hitler's private library: *Das Buch der Psalmen teutsch: Das Gebetbuch der Arisophen Rassenmystiker und Antisemiten* ("The Book of Germanic Psalms: Prayerbook of Ariosophic Race Mystics and Anti-Semites"). Another, *Das Gesetzbuch der Manu und die Rassenpflege* ("Manu's Book of Law and Race Cultivation"), published in 1908 and hence available to Hitler in those days, advocated that the "mongrelized breed" of Jews and other inferior beings be wiped from the face of the earth. These horror tales of race defilement and the lurid depiction of the perils confronting Aryan womanhood obviously gratified the young Hitler, feeding his fears and obsessions—personal, sexual, racial.* *Ostara's* influence—or its function as reinforcement—is evident in a much-quoted passage from *Mein Kampf*: "With satanic joy in his face, the black-haired Jewish youth lurks in wait for the unsuspecting girl whom he defiles with his blood, thus stealing her from her people."

Another racist pamphleteer whom Hitler read and perhaps also encountered was Guido von List, an indefatigable pseudoscholarly occultist. During the years that Hitler lived in Vienna, List published several works, in which he glorified the ancient Germanic past and extolled the Germanic wisdom in pagan nature which Christianity, regrettably, had enfeebled. The way to restore the true Germanic life force, List believed, was through the deciphering of ancient runic script and symbols. Like Lanz, List also regarded the swastika as one of the Teutonic mystic symbols. But unlike Lanz, List gave political expression to his racial and ritual occultism. He was associated with Georg von Schönerer's anti-Semitic Pan-German movement and wrote for its publication. His political mysticism envisioned a leader who would be reincarnated from the Teutonic warrior heroes. When that leader came, List promised, the Reich would be divided into *Gaue* (districts), each with its own *Gauleiter*—archaic terminology that the Nazis revived when they came to power.

Hitler's Vienna was the locus of two major political movements—Schönerer's Pan-Germans and Karl Lue-

---

* Some psychoanalysts have suggested that Hitler's hatred of the Jews was a projection of his self-hate and a consequence of guilt feelings for his dark and evil fantasies, and perhaps also for his putative Jewish ancestry. Still, not all self-haters became savage anti-Semites. People living in an anti-Semitic milieu—as Hitler did—already viewed Jews as diseased and filthy creatures, degenerate and corrupting, outsiders beyond fraternity or compassion. Since the society had already branded the Jews as loathsome pariahs, the Jews could then serve the symbolic and pathological needs of the obsessed and guilt-ridden.

ger's Christian Socials. By the time Hitler came to Vienna, Schönerer (1842–1921) was played out, but two decades earlier he had built the Pan-German movement into a significant force in and beyond Vienna, introducing anti-Semitism as a basic component in the ideology of Pan-Germanism.

Lueger was something else. For him, anti-Semitism had become the most successful of all political expedients, and his Christian Social party showed the greatest political viability of any anti-Semitic movement formed in Germany and Austria after the 1880s. The Viennese adored him and in election after election after 1895 returned him to the mayoralty (he did not take office till 1897 because both the Church and the Emperor refused to confirm his election).

In *Mein Kampf* Hitler discussed both Schönerer and Lueger at length and dismissed them both. Yet he confessed: "When I came to Vienna, my sympathies were fully and wholly on the side of the Pan-German tendency." Those sympathies had been formed in Linz, for when Hitler came to Vienna, Schönerer was then past sixty-five, a has-been, his movement torn by ideological differences and divided over tactics and strategy, impotent before Lueger's irresistible personality and pragmatic politics. But Schönerer had pioneered in legitimating anti-Semitism in Austrian politics. Still, Hitler is silent about any involvement on his part with the Pan-Germans. He devotes over twenty pages in *Mein Kampf* to the errors and misjudgments committed by the Pan-Germans. But he concedes, in one paltry sentence, that they were right on one point: that anti-Semitism of the Pan-German movement "was based on a correct understanding of the importance of the racial problem, and not on religious ideas." The laconism is understandable. Any elebration on the "correct" anti-Semitic doctrines of the Pan-German movement would expose Hitler's intellectual and ideological borrowings.

As for Karl Lueger's Christian Social movement, Hitler praised its tactics but condemned its "wrong" approach to anti-Semitism and its disinterest in German nationalism. Lueger, he believed, did not properly understand the "Jewish danger," and his anti-Semitism was flawed because it "was based on religious ideas instead of racial knowledge." That, Hitler thought, was no way to combat the Jews: "If the worst came to the worst, a splash of baptismal water could always save the business and the Jew at the same time." The Christian Socials, Hitler asserted, engaged in "sham anti-Semitism." Hitler had a point. Lueger, the master of pragmatic politics, regarded anti-Semitism primarily as a political tactic rather than an evangelistic doctrine. His classic statement that must have been familiar to Hitler was "*Wer Jude ist, das bestimme ich*" ("Who is a Jew, that I decide").

Hitler never mentions that he belonged to any political party or organization in Vienna. Yet, given his ideas, it seems strange that he did not seek out some kindred group, or even stumble upon one of the numerous societies that made anti-Semitism the center of their activity. As a matter of fact, Kubizek asserted that "one day in 1908," Hitler came into their room with the announcement: "Hey! Today I became a member of the anti-Semitic Bund and I enrolled you too." Perhaps indeed Hitler did drift into some small anti-Semitic group, composed of down-and-outers like himself, misfits and malcontents who gathered to talk about the vile conspiracies afoot in Vienna for which the Jews were responsible. Perhaps it was a group that failed to recognize or acknowledge Hitler's abilities. "In my little circle," Hitler writes in *Mein Kampf*, "I talked my tongue sore and my throat hoarse," but to no avail. But, he confesses, "speaking in the narrowest circles," he gained experience: "I learned to orate less."

But perhaps Hitler deliberately failed to mention any organizational affiliations he may have had because he wanted to preserve the classic legend of the man in the making, the political leader who reaches political maturity, while having protected his political virginity. "Today it is my conviction that in general . . . a man should not engage in public political activity before his thirtieth year," he wrote in *Mein Kampf*.

"Otherwise he runs the risk of either having to change his former position on essential questions, or . . . of clinging to a view which reason and conviction have long since discarded." Hitler was exactly thirty when he joined the *Deutsche Arbeiterpartei* in Munich in 1919.

What he "learned" about Jews in the Vienna period, as recorded in a brief span of ten pages of *Mein Kampf* ("Years of Study and Suffering in Vienna"), is a mere foreshadowing of the ideas to come. Images of the Jew as unclean predominate: "unclean dress," "physical uncleanness." Jews were at the heart of everything that was diseased. They were to blame for prostitution in Vienna and the white-slave traffic. (Psychoanalysts suggest here a projection of his guilt feelings about his sexual fantasies.) He had "discovered" that Jews dominated the liberal press in Vienna and the city's cultural and artistic life, that they were behind the Social Democratic movement—Marxism. Triumphantly he had at last found an answer to the original question he had posed about the Jew: "The Jew was no German."

With this intellectual baggage, the claptrap of the conventional anti-Semitism of the time, and deep fears of political democracy, Hitler left Vienna in May 1913 and came to Munich, the Mecca of Germandom.

He arrived in Munich, a rootless young man of twenty-four, without friends, without family, without career or occupation, in a restless search for his identity or, as he would have put it, his Destiny.

He found a room with a tailor's family in a working-class quarter of Munich and continued the same hand-to-mouth existence he had led in Vienna, peddling sketches and drawings. He continued the anti-Semitic racist "studies" he had begun in Vienna, reading the papers and pamphlets, "observing." He seems to have become more aggressive, more confident, speaking publicly in taverns and beer cellars. He had already cast himself as prophet: "In the years 1913 and 1914, I, for the first time in various circles which today in part faithfully support the National Socialist movement, expressed the conviction that the question of the future of the German nation was the question of destroying Marxism."

What various circles? Hitler makes them appear to have been more than a casual congregation of beer drinkers in a tavern. Did he perhaps belong to a National Socialist forerunner group? Of the various nationalist and anti-Semitic groups in Munich there were at least two proto-Nazi organizations he might have belonged to or frequented. The *Germanen- und Wälsungsorden* (Order of Teutons and Volsungs), founded in 1912 as a Masonic-style racist society, is a possibility. One of its offshoots or branches was called *Armanenorden*, and the inscription to Hitler found in a book in his private library supports the idea of such membership. It regarded its central function to be the struggle against the "secret Jewish conspiracy." The Germanenorden was replete with Teutonic vocabulary and symbols; its journal *Runen* was decorated with swastikas.

Another group that Hitler could have joined would have been the local Munich branch of Theodor Fritsch's *Reichshammerbund,* a minuscule network of nineteen discussion and propaganda groups throughout Germany, closely associated with the Germanenorden. As for Fritsch, he was the grand old man of anti-Semitic propaganda and it is inconceivable that Hitler could have failed to have read his classic work, *Antisemiten-Katechismus (Anti-Semites' Catechism)*, later entitled *Handbuch der Judenfrage,* which went through innumerable editions.

Still, if Hitler actually ever belonged to any group, he made no lasting associations. In later years no one came forward with reminiscences that could locate him in any specific anti-Semitic organization. Though *Mein Kampf* indicates that he had become more confident of himself, and had found places to frequent that were attuned to his ideas, he still appeared to have retained the characteristics of an eccentric loner.

The assassination of Ferdinand at Sarajevo unleashed World War I, and the war unleashed the pent-up nihilistic impulses that were raging within Hitler: "The sense of approaching catastrophe turned at last to longing: let Heaven at last give free rein to the fate which could no longer be thwarted."

On August 1, 1914, the declaration proclaiming war was read in Munich's Odeons Platz before a flag-waving, anthem-singing assembled mass. A photograph that later came to light showed Hitler in the crowd, eyes popping, mouth open, wildly exultant. Two days later, he submitted a petition to Ludwig III, the last king of Bavaria, to join a Bavarian regiment. The request was approved. "For me, as for every German, there now began the greatest and most unforgettable time of my earthly existence."*

He fought in France, was wounded, received the Iron Cross, Second Class, returned to the front, was wounded a second time. Then, fighting at the front again, he was promoted to lance corporal, and fought again in France. October 1918, blinded in a British gas attack, he was sent to a military hospital. That last year he received the Iron Cross, First Class, a decoration seldom given to a soldier of his low rank, though no one knows for what act of bravery it was presented. While at the hospital, he witnessed the Bavarian revolution of November 1918, led by Kurt Eisner, the overthrow of the monarchy, the armistice, and the creation, in weakness and indecision, of the Weimar Republic—in his mind, all the work of the Jews.

It was then, Hitler recollected, that he decided to go into politics. He returned to Munich, where the following April he saw the establishment of a Soviet republic, and then, within a month, its suppression in blood by the *Reichswehr*. He got a job as educational officer, the first real job he ever had, in the Press and Propaganda Office of the Political Department of the District Army Command in Munich. The department's

---

* Cf. Friedrich Meinecke, *The German Catastrophe:* "The exaltation of spirit experienced during the August days of 1914 . . . is one of the most precious, unforgettable memories of the highest sort" (p. 25).

function was to indoctrinate Reichswehr recruits on the dangers of radicalism. Hitler had become an employee in the very center of the military apparatus that would help undermine the new republic. He was called on to submit reports on various political organizations active in the Munich area. In 1919 he was assigned to cover a newly formed group called the *Deutsche Arbeiterpartei* (German Workers' party). He joined the group. On February 24, 1920, its name was changed to *Nationalsozialistische Deutsche Arbeiterpartei* (NSDAP), when the new twenty-five-point program that Hitler had drafted was adopted.

In the immediate postwar years in Munich Hitler's social life changed drastically from his prewar solitariness. He was in contact with several circles of likeminded people and those associations gave him certitude and reassurance. Under a variety of influences —people, books, and pamphlets—his ideas about race and about Jews crystallized. He had come to Munich with much of his anti-Jewish racist ideology already formed. He had emerged from the war still more politically paranoid, wildly blaming the Jews for the *Dolchstoss*, for that treacherous stab-in-the-back that made the Germans lose the war. Still, the influences in Munich were decisive, for they would make it possible for him to cast his ideas into one coherent system. One group with which he early came into contact was the Thule Society, a conspiratorial front for the postwar incarnation of the Germanenorden, which was involved in assassination attempts on Eisner and the leaders of the Munich Soviet. Besides counterrevolutionary violence, the Thule Society engaged in Volkist racist propaganda. Its members included Rudolf Hess, who was to become Hitler's most slavish follower; Karl Harrer, a cofounder of the Deutsche Arbeiterpartei; and Dietrich Eckart, an important influence on Hitler in those early Munich days.

Eckart (1868–1923) was the one man whom Hitler acknowledged as mentor and teacher, closing the second volume of *Mein Kampf* with a tribute to him: "That man, one of the best, who devoted his life to the awakening of his, our people, in his writings and his thoughts and finally in his deeds." Eckart, in his rootlessness and agitated mental state, was an elder version of Hitler, but was more Bohemian, addicted to alcohol and drugs. An unsuccessful playwright, he blamed the Jews for his failure. During the war he moved to Munich, barely managed to control his addictions, and became the bard of the Volkist movement. In 1919 he began publishing *Auf gut Deutsch*, a weekly replete with Volkist anti-Semitism, continuing until early 1921, when Hitler appointed him editor of the *Völkischer Beobachter*. One of Eckart's pamphlets, *Der Bolschewismus von Moses bis Lenin—Zwiegespräch zwischen Adolf Hitler und mir* ("Bolshevism from Moses to Lenin—Dialogue Between Adolf Hitler and Me"), published posthumously, has been adduced as an example of Eckart's influence on Hitler's ideas prior to *Mein Kampf*.

Eckart took Hitler under his wing, showed him the ropes, introduced him to influential and wealthy nationalists and proto-Nazis. In 1920 Eckart took Hitler with him on a flight to Berlin to join up with the rightwing Kapp Putsch, just before it collapsed. But Eckart's most lasting contribution to Hitler's intellectual development was merely coincidental. It was he who introduced Alfred Rosenberg to Hitler.

Rosenberg, the Baltic German whom Hitler would later ridicule and despise, enlarged Hitler's intellectual horizons, stretching his concepts beyond the borders of Germany. Rosenberg was one of those many Russian émigrés from the Bolshevik Revolution who imported into Western Europe the anti-Semitic notions of czarist Russia's Black Hundred ("beat the Jews and save Russia") and commingled the anti-Semitism of Russia's darkest reaction with the anti-Semitism of Germany's paranoid nationalism. Rosenberg was born into a family of middle-class German Balts in 1893, in Reval (Tallinn), a Hanseatic city that since the early eighteenth century had been part of the Russian empire. In 1910 he was admitted to the Institute of Technology in Riga, where he studied architecture. In 1915, when

the German front advanced, the institute was evacuated to Moscow, and Rosenberg went along with the
complement of faculty and students. In January 1918
he received his diploma and returned home. His
world collapsed when the revolution erupted. He
started his peregrinations and finally left Russia with
the retreating German army that had been in occupation.

When Rosenberg came to Munich, his interests were
no longer cultural, but political—the politics of reaction and counterrevolution. Like many another Russian
émigré, he had brought with him a booklet that utterly
possessed him: the *Protocols of the Elders of Zion.* An
implausible forgery concocted by the czarist secret
police at the turn of the century, it purported to dis-
close the secret plans of the so-called international
Jewish conspiracy for world domination. (It was "in-
comparably" done, Hitler was to write in *Mein Kampf.*)
The *Protocols* first appeared in German in 1920 and
was constantly being reprinted thereafter. Rosenberg
made something of a name for himself as a German
commentator on the *Protocols,* writing innumerable
articles and pamphlets on the subject.

His higher education, his penchant for wide-ranging
philosophic schemas, and the scope of his philosophic
reading admirably equipped Rosenberg for the role of
Hitler's intellectual mentor. From nineteenth-century
West European thought—Fichte, Schopenhauer, Nietzsche, Gobineau, and Houston Stewart Chamberlain—
Rosenberg took those ideas of nation, Volk, nationalism, race, the rise and fall of civilizations, and
conjoined them all with the crude and superstitious
anti-Semitic and anti-Bolshevik ideas that the Russian
émigrés had been nurtured on in their mother country.
Chamberlain, Rosenberg confessed years later, was
"the strongest positive impulse in my youth," and it is
no surprise that Rosenberg was said to have prepared,
for Hitler's easy study, excerpts from Chamberlain's
Die Grundlagen des neunzehnten Jahrhunderts (*Foundations of the Nineteenth Century*).

Russian-speaking and authoritative about Russian

culture and politics, Rosenberg became Hitler's mentor also on Russia and Bolshevism. He inducted Hitler into the domain of international relations and prepared him for the geopolitical concepts he would pick up from Rudolf Hess and Hess's teacher and friend, Karl Haushofer. Haushofer, general turned professor, likely introduced Hitler to the concept of "space as a factor of power," but Rosenberg elaborated the idea of *Lebensraum* (living space), which was to become a cornerstone of National Socialist ideology and one of the chief objectives of Germany's foreign policy. Those early days in Munich were no doubt Rosenberg's finest. Hitler would never again regard him so seriously.

While the international aspects of National Socialist ideology were still germinating within him, Hitler's general ideas about the Jews were fixed by 1920. In a letter, dated September 16, 1919, and written at the request of his military superior in the Press and Propaganda Office, in reply to one Adolf Gemlich, who asked for enlightenment on the Jewish question, Hitler set forth some of the ideas that in *Mein Kampf* he claimed to have already discovered in Vienna.[7] "Anti-Semitism as a political movement," he wrote, "cannot and should not be determined by emotional factors, but on the contrary by an understanding of the facts." The "facts," he continued, are that "in the first instance, Jewry is without question a race and not a religious fellowship." He then expatiated on the alleged Jewish single-minded pursuit of money and power, touching on the already classic anti-Semitic notion that Jews dominate, falsify, and exploit the press. "The effect of Jewry will be racial tuberculosis of nations." (In *Mein Kampf*, in the same context, he wrote: "It was no accident that man mastered the plague more easily than tuberculosis.")

From his analysis, Hitler concluded that anti-Semitism grounded merely in emotion would find its ultimate outlet in pogroms. That was not enough.

Rational anti-Semitism, however, must lead to a systematic legal opposition and elimination of the special

privileges which Jews hold, in contrast to the other
aliens living among us (aliens' legislation). Its final
objective must unswervingly be the removal [*Entfernung*] of the Jews altogether.

That paragraph carries, in the post-Auschwitz world,
a staggering freight. It prefigures the political realities
of the German dictatorship under Hitler, when the
Jews were deprived of all rights systematically and
"legally," and then "removed altogether," the ambiguity
of the word "removal" now more apparent than it was
in 1919.

Hitler made his first public speech at a meeting of
the Deutsche Arbeiterpartei on November 13, 1919, in
a Munich beer cellar, and soon began to attract large
audiences. Invariably he held forth on Germany's
defeat in the war, which he blamed on Jewish treachery. On April 29, 1920, the subject of his address was
"Jewry," and according to the summary in an army
political report, he concluded with a promise: "We
will carry on the struggle until the last Jew is removed
from the German Reich."

On August 13, 1920, he spoke at an NSDAP public
meeting in a large hall on the topic "Why Are We
Anti-Semites?" the text of which has recently been
published.[8] That speech differed in one respect from
Mein Kampf in that it was directed toward working
people and stressed the need for social and economic
reform. Exalting labor, Hitler followed an old anti-
Semitic tradition, asserting that Jews degraded and
exploited labor. His evidence was the Pentateuchal
injunction: "In the sweat of thy face shalt thou eat
bread," which he interpreted to mean that the Jews
regarded labor as "a curse from God." But in addressing himself to the subject of race and of Jews, the
speech laid out the basic concepts that he was to develop in *Mein Kampf*.

He emphasized the need for a political organization
to combat the Jews. It was not enough, he claimed, to
deprive them of their economic power. The campaign
for social reform must be accompanied by a struggle

against "the opponents of any social measures: Jewry."
The solution to the Jewish question must be "removal
[*Entfernung*] of the Jews from our nation, not because
we would begrudge them their existence—we con-
gratulate the rest of the world on their company—but
because the existence of our own nation is a thousand
times more important to us than that of an alien race."

During his enforced political inactivity in Landsberg prison, Hitler undertook to put his ideas together
in *Mein Kampf*, which was autobiography, ideological
doctrine, and party manual all in one. In *Mein Kampf*
he expounded on race as the central principle of
human existence and explicated the relationship, since
the start of time, between the two world adversaries—
the Aryans and the Jews. "The racial question," he
wrote, "gives the key not only to world history, but to
all human culture," for, he believed, "in the blood
alone resides the strength as well as the weakness of
man." All "great questions of the day" he held to be
momentary and derivative; only "the question of racial
preservation of the nation" was determinative, only
that was significant as a causal factor in the rise and
fall of civilization. An understanding of the "Jewish
problem" was a prerequisite for an understanding of
the racial problem. The "resurrection of Germany"
would never be achieved "without the clearest knowledge of the racial problem and hence of the Jewish
problem."

The "Aryan" race was the "bearer of human cultural
development" and, consequently, "human culture and
civilization" are inseparably bound up with the presence of the "Aryan." The "Aryans," therefore, by their
nature, their "blood," were chosen to rule the world.
The very existence of world civilization depended on
maintaining and safeguarding the purity of the "Aryan"
race:

*What we must fight for is to safeguard the existence
and reproduction of our race and our people, the
sustenance of our children and the purity of our blood,*

*the freedom and independence of the fatherland, so
that our people may mature for the fulfillment of the
mission allotted it by the creator of the universe.*

The state, according to Hitler, existed merely as a
means to an end—the preservation of the racial community. States that did not serve that purpose were
"misbegotten, monstrosities." The Volkist state "must
set race in the center of all life," for it is thus acting as
"the guardian of a millennial future." The mission of
the German people is the formation of such a Volkist
state, which will have *"the task, not only of assembling
and preserving the most valuable stocks of basic racial
elements in this people, but slowly and surely of raising them to a dominant position."*

But the obstacle, or threat, to the fulfillment of this
racial millennium is the Jew: "The mightiest counter-
part to the Aryan is represented by the Jew." In Hitler's system, the "Aryans" represented the perfection of
human existence, whereas the Jews were the embodiment of evil. *"Wer kennt den Jude, kennt den Teufel,"*
the saying went ("Whoever knows the Jew, knows the
Devil"). Indeed, Hitler wrote, the "vileness" of the Jew
is so gigantic "that no one need be surprised if among
our people the personification of the Devil as the
symbol of all evil assumes the living shape of the
Jews." The Jew as outsider, as the Other, had been
transformed into the ultimate evil.

The vileness of the Jew, he claimed, resided in the
blood of the race and was evident in the Jew's physical, mental, cultural being. This vileness, Hitler declared, had permeated nearly every aspect of modern
society. Over and over again he kept describing the
Jews in terms of filth and disease. "If the Jews were
alone in this world, they would stifle in filth and
offal." Jews, he asserted, were at the center of every
abscess, were "germ-carriers," poisoning the blood of
others, but preserving their own. The Jews were,
Hitler said, "a ferment of decomposition," quoting a
phrase used by Theodor Mommsen, which, out of
context, had become an anti-Semitic platitude. The

depiction of the Jews as the carriers of filth and disease and, hence, of death and destruction, goes back in the history of anti-Semitism to the Middle Ages, when Jews were accused of spreading the plague and poisoning the wells. As late as the seventeenth century, a pestilence in Vienna was readily explained: ". . . It is well known that such pestilential epidemics are caused by evil spirits, by Jews, by gravediggers, and by witches." Hitler accused the Jews particularly of sexual defilement and even blamed them for the presence of syphilis in postwar Germany. Nor did Hitler disregard cultural pollution: "Was there any form of filth or profligacy, particularly in cultural life, without at least one Jew involved in it?" The "poison" of the press allegedly controlled by the Jews "was able to penetrate the bloodstream of our people."

From the concept of the Jew as parasite, vampire, bloodsucker, contaminating the Aryan race, it was but a small step to the Jew as figurative bloodsucker in the financial and economic spheres: "The spider was slowly beginning to suck the blood out of the people's pores" through the war corporations. That image had its source in the leftist anti-Semitic stereotype of the mid- and late-nineteenth century.

How had the Jews succeeded in insinuating themselves into the body of the Aryan race? By gigantic fraud and deception, Hitler said, by "the first and greatest lie," that the Jews are "a religious community while actually they are a race—and what a race!" As Hitler saw it, "the Mosaic religion is nothing other than a doctrine for the preservation of the Jewish race." He believed that the Jews had no language or culture of their own, that they sapped and drained other cultures and races so as ultimately to destroy them. That way, Hitler maintained, the Jews would achieve dominion over the world: *"It is the inexorable Jew who struggles for his domination over the nations."*

The Jews had many conspiratorial techniques and vehicles for achieving world mastery, Hitler said, and in modern society these were Freemasonry, the press, democracy, parliamentarianism, the trade-union movement, Marxism, and Social Democracy. As for democracy, he held that "only the Jew can praise an institution which is as dirty and false as he himself." "The Jewish doctrine of Marxism," Hitler contended, rejects "the aristocratic principle of Nature." The goal of Marxism "is and remains the destruction of all non-Jewish national states." Marxism itself, Hitler believed, "systematically plans to hand the world over to the Jews."

He did not have to scour long for evidence. The best proof for his argument was what had happened in Russia, or rather to Russia. Hitler's association of the Jews with Russian Bolshevism—an idea fostered and insisted on by Rosenberg—was, in its delusional conclusion, more original than his other ideas about Jews and race that derived from the ample sources of European anti-Semitism and racial doctrine. That the Jews were the revolutionaries *par excellence,* the masterminds of the Bolshevik Revolution—that was nothing new. The reality of Leon Trotsky and the forgery of the *Protocols* documented that charge to the satisfaction of most anti-Semites. But Hitler went beyond this and "penetrated" beneath the surface of the conspiracy: *"In Russian Bolshevism we must see the attempt undertaken by the Jews in the twentieth century to achieve world domination."* All Russia, he believed, had somehow become captive of the Jews. Schooled by Rosenberg, Hitler had concluded that the Slavs were an inferior race, incapable of building a state. For centuries, Hitler explained, "Russia drew nourishment" from the "Germanic nucleus of its upper leading strata." But those strata, "exterminated and extinguished," were then replaced by the Jews. (A similar fate, he warned, faced Germany, unless it would show sufficient national will to resist.) Since the Russians, according to Hitler's view, could never by themselves shake off Jewish domination, the Russian empire must necessarily collapse. Having reached this point in the development of his ideas about Russia, Hitler then elaborated his doctrines of race and space that culminated in his foreign-policy program for a National

Socialist Germany. Spurning with contempt the suggestion that Germany ought to conclude an alliance with the Soviet Union, Hitler solemnly declared: *"The fight against Jewish world Bolshevization requires a clear attitude toward Soviet Russia. You cannot drive out the Devil with Beelzebub."* (That metaphor was one of Hitler's favorites all his life, but he used it expediently. In a speech on April 6, 1920, he was reported to have said that in order to achieve the National Socialist goal of extirpating the evil—the Jews, that is—root and branch, "every means is justified, even when we must ally ourselves with the Devil."⁹)

Mein Kampf is a vision of the apocalyptic conflict between the Aryans and the Jews, of the two world systems struggling for dominion. It was his own Manichaean version of the conflict between good and evil, between God and the Devil, Christ and the Antichrist. He saw himself as the Messiah who would bring deliverance from the Devil: "Hence today I believe that I am acting in accordance with the will of the Almighty Creator: *by defending myself against the Jew, I am fighting for the work of the Lord."* Some years later Hitler told Rauschning: "We are God's people." He repeated what he had written in *Mein Kampf*: "Two worlds face one another—the men of God and men of Satan! The Jew is the anti-man, the creature of another god. He must have come from another root of the human race. I set the Aryan and the Jew over and against each other."¹⁰

The Jews inhabited Hitler's mind. He believed that they were the source of all evil, misfortune, and tragedy, the single factor that, like some inexorable law of nature, explained the workings of the universe. The irregularities of war and famine, financial distress and sudden death, defeat and sinfulness—all could be explained by the presence of that single factor in the universe, a miscreation that disturbed the world's steady ascent toward well-being, affluence, success, victory. A savior was needed to come forth and slay the loathsome monster. In Hitler's obsessed mind, as in the delusive imaginings of the medieval millenarian sectarians, the Jews were the demonic hosts whom he had been given a divine mission to destroy.

All his life Hitler was seized by this obsession with the Jews. Even after he had murdered the Jews, he had still not exorcised his Jewish demons. At 4:00 A.M. on April 29, 1945, the last day of his life in the Berlin bunker, he finished dictating his political testament. His last words to the German people were: "Above all I charge the leaders of the nation and those under them to scrupulous observance of the laws of race and to merciless opposition to the universal poisoner of all peoples, international Jewry."[11]

The question continues to oppress us: how could a man with this poor baggage of deranged ideas and prejudices become Chancellor of Germany?* How was it possible that a state whose people and culture ranked high in the world's civilization should have entrusted its fate to this deluded man who believed that he had been chosen to lead a holy war against the Jews?

Many answers have been given and perhaps many are needed, for no single theory can satisfactorily explain Hitler's phenomenal success with the German people. They were mesmerized by his voice, and they responded to his message. Was it because their moral sense, at least with regard to the Jews, had become atrophied under the effect of generations of virulent anti-Semitism? Had the German people already become mithridatized by anti-Semitic poison, so that they had become immune even to Hitler's deadly brand? Was it because he spoke for them?

---

* Historians interested in Hitler's psychobiography put another question: what made Hitler an anti-Semite? Their search to establish the motivation for Hitler's anti-Semitism (which they look for in his personal life and psychology) may have a clinical interest for the psychoanalyst and titillate the general reader, but it seems to me irrelevant, bypassing more important historical and political questions. Thousands of Hitler's contemporaries in Central Europe were being shaped and developed as anti-Semites. Their psychological motivations are of relatively little interest to the historian, for they did not affect the course of history. Hitler's motivations—e.g., his putative Jewish origin—was not nearly as significant as his ideology and his program, that is, his beliefs and intentions.

2

Anti-Semitism in
Modern Germany

A line of anti-Semitic descent from Martin Luther to Adolf Hitler is easy to draw. Both Luther and Hitler were obsessed by a demonologized universe inhabited by Jews. "Know, Christian," wrote Luther, "that next to the devil thou hast no enemy more cruel, more venomous and violent than a true Jew." Hitler himself, in that early dialogue with Dietrich Eckart, asserted that the later Luther— that is, the violently anti-Semitic Luther—was the genuine Luther. Luther's protective authority was invoked by the Nazis when they came to power, and his anti-Semitic writings enjoyed a revival of popularity. To be sure, the similarities of Luther's anti-Jewish exhortations with modern racial anti-Semitism and even with Hitler's racial policies are not merely coincidental. They all derive from a common historic tradition of Jew-hatred, whose provenance can be traced back to Haman's advice to Ahasuerus. But modern German anti-Semitism had more recent roots than Luther and grew out of a different soil—not that German anti-Semitism was new; it drew part of its sustenance from Christian anti-Semitism, whose foundation had been laid by the Catholic Church and upon which Luther built. It was equally a product of

German nationalism. Modern German anti-Semitism
was the bastard child of the union of Christian anti-
Semitism with German nationalism.

German nationalism arose out of the ashes of German defeat in the Napoleonic wars. Fragmented, without nationhood, without political definition, lacking
military power and economic vitality, the Germans
searched for a shared identity that would restore the
self-esteem that the defeats by the French had
shattered. Since the real world, in its materiality, its
politics, economics, and the force of arms, could give
them no solace, they turned inward for self-definition,
in search of psychic and metaphysical values, qualities
of feeling and spirit. And they turned backward—to a
remote past of glory and mastery, to a past deep in the
womb of historic time, where they had once been
secure.

This German backward-lookingness had emerged
even before the Napoleonic wars, in the last quarter of
the eighteenth century as a reaction against the Enlightenment, especially its French and English protag-
onists. The Enlightenment represented the break with
the medieval world and its concepts of man's innate
sinfulness, whose only hope of salvation was through
divine providence. For this world view the Enlightenment substituted the idea of progress, of man's per-
fectibility through the attainment of knowledge, and
the theory that the universe was governed by reason.
This idea of progress was to catch hold particularly
among the French and the English, not only among
the philosophers and sociologists, but in political circles
as well.

In Germany these ideas spread too, but they were
soon aborted by Germany's dominant conservative
forces. The Holy Roman Empire, a paralytic, sclerotic,
thousand-year survival, managed to exist, propped up
by the strength of tradition and the inertia of apathy.[1]
The Germans preferred to retain their loyalties to the
past and resisted accommodation of their customs and
folkways to the enormous changes of modernity. Instead they romanticized the values and ideals of their

remote past. This commitment to the past explains the German preference for *Kultur* over *Zivilisation*. Culture was for them something innate, intrinsic, inherited, a tradition handed down from the past. Civilization was external, an artificial product of modernity, lacking the essence of a specific people, race, or culture.

Progress and enlightenment were associated not only with the French and English, but also with Jews. Invoking the universality of these concepts, Jews asked for emancipation, political equality. All France was astir over the pros and cons. The Alsatian Jews asked Moses Mendelssohn, then Europe's most eminent Jew, to help them. Believing that a plea for Jewish emancipation would have a better reception if presented by a Christian, Mendelssohn asked his friend Christian Wilhelm von Dohm (1751–1820), historian, political writer, and Prussian diplomat, to undertake the task. Dohm decided to extend his plea also on behalf of the German Jews. His work *Über die bürgerliche Verbesserung der Juden* (*On the Civic Betterment of the Jews*), Berlin, 1781, presented the case for granting Jews political equality. Its basic argument was the extraordinary notion that "the Jew is a human being even before he is a Jew." But the idea was too radical for the Germans.

Most participants in the ensuing public discussion disagreed with Dohm's belief that the Jews would become better citizens if the conditions under which they lived were improved. Adducing traditional medieval objections and citing Scripture or the Devil as evidence, some maintained that the Jews were unfit for emancipation and that there was no reason to think that things would change in the future. Others presented the argument of "Asiatic temperament": certain basic racial qualities inhered in Jews that were at variance with those of Germans. This fundamental difference between German and Jew was cited also, to the astonishment of Moses Mendelssohn, by Johann David Michaelis (1717–1791), an aged, prestigious scholar of biblical ("Old Testament") and Mosaic law at the University of Göttingen. Mendelssohn replied to Michaelis and other opponents of Jewish emancipation in classical terms: "Instead of using the expression 'Christians and Jews,' Herr Michaelis is continually served by 'Germans and Jews.' He refuses to recognize that the difference is in religion only and prefers to have us regarded as foreigners who must accept the conditions laid down to them by the owners of the land." Being himself a man of progress and enlightenment, he could not then, in 1783, foretell that the Germans could and would indeed choose another road.

The German response to the Enlightenment was an intimation of the future. From 1789 to 1815, the quarter-century between the French Revolution and the Congress of Vienna, the ethos of modern Germany took shape. The doctrines of the revolution were anathema to the princely, priestly, and knightly rulers of the German states and principalities. But the ideas had begun to infiltrate Germany, and within a few short years, as Napoleon's military success spread French influence across the face of Europe, French political domination of the German lands converted those ideas into political realities. German discomfiture with the new ideas of emancipation and equality turned into a deadly rancor both for the French and for the ideas and policies they had unleashed in Europe.

Wherever the French occupied German lands, Jews were the beneficiaries of the Rights of Man, winning emancipation in most of southern and western Germany. In some places under French command, the obligatory extension of equality to Jews enraged the Germans even more than French domination. Nevertheless, the trend toward emancipation reached even into the stronghold of Prussia. In 1812, as part of a sweeping program of legislative and economic reform, Minister Karl August von Hardenberg, himself under the influence of the ideas of 1789, persuaded the reluctant Frederick William III to grant the Jews citizenship and political rights.

Napoleon destroyed the Holy Roman Empire, that is, the shadow of it that had persisted. After Jena, in 1806, he reorganized the German lands, secularizing the ecclesiastical states and incorporating most of the free cities into territorial states. He hastened the demise of the medieval order of Free Imperial Knights, reorganized the six hundred myriad political units in a manageable number of middle-sized states, and formed a confederation of German states under French protection. (Ironically, that confederation would later provide a basis for German unification.) The formal bonds of historic empire that had linked the Germans to their Teutonic past had been destroyed. To compensate for the loss, for the humiliations at the hands of the French, for the fragmentation, the Germans began to forge a new nationalism that transcended the boundaries of the German states and the realities of their contemporary political life. That quarter-century, inaugurated by the French Revolution and closed by the Congress of Vienna, was the formative period in shaping German national character. From it emerged a national ethos that was to animate German cultural, social, and political life for well over a century.

To begin with, at the simplest and most obvious level, the Germans defined themselves in contrast to the French. What was French was un-German. Ernst Moritz Arndt (1769–1860), poet and pamphleteer, wrote of the war winter of 1812 that the German fatherland was located "where every Frenchman is called foe, and every German is called friend."[2] The great liberal ideas of the time—liberty, equality, fraternity—were French ideas, and Germans of that generation denounced liberal ideas as un-German. That outlook proved to be a durable one.

The philosopher Johann Gottlieb Fichte (1762–1814), in his *Reden an die deutsche Nation* (1808), admonished Germans to "have character and be German" (*"Charakter haben und Deutsch sein"*). His Gallophobia was equal to that of his contemporaries, but he excelled in his exaltation of Germanness. At a time when the Germans had been abjectly defeated, he con-

soled them with a messianic future: ". . . Among all
modern peoples it is you in whom the seed of human
perfection most decidedly lies, and you who are
charged with progress in human development. If you
perish in this your essential nature, then there perishes
together with you every hope of the whole human race
for salvation from the depths of its miseries."[3]

Called the father of German nationalism, Fichte has
also been called the father of modern German anti-
Semitism. His celebration of German nationalism was
matched by his denigration of Jews. In 1793 he had
argued against Jewish emancipation, characterizing
the Jews as a state within a state that would undermine the German nation. Jewish ideas were as obnox-
ious as French ideas. The only way in which he could
concede giving rights to Jews, he said, would be
"to cut off all their heads in one night, and to set new
ones on their shoulders, which should contain not a
single Jewish idea."

Similarly, Arndt, who had defined German specificity
by distinguishing the Germans from their external
enemy, the French, refined that uniqueness by further
distinguishing the Germans from an internal enemy—
the Jews. The Jews, beneficiaries of political emancipation that the French had thrust upon the unprepared
and unwilling Germans, became identified in the
German mind with the ideas and values of revolutionary France. They were not seen as true insiders.
In Christian feudal Germany, the Jews had been outsiders, and in the newly emergent idea of an ethnic,
national Germany, the Jews continued to be outsiders.

Arndt and his disciple, Friedrich Ludwig Jahn
(1778–1852), are credited with developing that particular concept of German nationalism associated with
the word "Volk." It is a word that has come to mean
more than simply "a people," more than the usual idea
of a people united by common traditions and cultural
heritage, language, territory, values, and morality.
"Volk," according to George Mosse, signified the union
of a group of people with a transcendental "essence,"
never specified, sometimes called "nature," "cosmos,"

"mythos." This essence, Mosse says, "was fused to man's innermost nature, and represented the source of his creativity, his depth of feeling, his individuality, and his unity with other members of the Volk."[4]

Jahn, a fiery German patriot who fought in the wars of liberation against Napoleon, in his book *Deutsches Volkstum* (*German Volkdom*), published in 1810, elaborated on the concept of Volk: "A state without Volk is nothing, a soulless artifice; a Volk without a state is nothing, a bodiless airy phantom, like the Gypsies and the Jews. Only state and Volk together can form a Reich, and such a Reich cannot be preserved without Volkdom."[5] (Is it mere coincidence that the two wandering peoples, Gypsies and Jews, against whom Jahn contrasted the "rooted" Germans, were precisely the two ethnic groups that Hitler consigned to the gas chambers?) In this work Jahn used the word *Volksthümlichkeit* (literally, "quality of Volkdom") to express his glorification of the simple people, the little folk, and the qualities associated with them—simplicity, naturalness, homespunness unspoiled by education and civilization.

According to Jahn, the Volk needed a state to house its soul and provide the means for its preservation. The German state was to serve some "larger" purpose—the preservation of the Volk and vehicle through which it could exercise its will. It was a Volkist idea that was to persist in Germany down to Hitler, who incorporated it into his ideology. The state was conceived as a kind of metahistorical entity that was identical with national spirit.

The "Christian" state had once been meant to serve "Christian" purposes, that is, the expansion of Christianity. The Volkist state approriated that purpose. The Jew, by definition an outsider in the "Christian" state, remained an outsider in the Volkist conception of the state. Indeed, the idea of a "Christian" country of which Jews were outsiders served as a transition to the idea of the Volkist state. Thus Christian Friedrich Rühs (1781–1820), who held the chair for history at the University of Berlin, denied the claims of the Jews to the rights of German citizenship, because "a foreign people cannot obtain the rights which Germans enjoy partly through being Christians. . . . Everything should be done to induce [the Jews] . . . to accept Christianity and through it to be led to a true acquisition of German ethnic characteristics and thus to effect the destruction of the Jewish people."[8]

Because Jews were loyal to their own "state within the state," Rühs said they could not be loyal to the Christian state. They could, therefore, be only its subjects, but not its citizens. (That distinction was to be made by Hitler—at first, with regard to the Jews, but later, when in his scheme of things they were not even entitled to the status of subjects, it was a distinction made between the Czechs in the Protectorate, who were subjects, in contrast to the Sudeten Germans, who were citizens.) The Jews, Rühs believed, as a tolerated alien group, should be excluded from holding public office, from the army, and from the guilds and corporations, that is, from institutions representing the economic as well as public and national life of the country. To identify this alien and hostile group within the German midst, Rühs proposed reviving the medieval yellow patch.

Emancipation was the consequence of revolution and of the political realization that all men, even Jews, were equal, but the concept of Volk was the consequence of counterrevolution and of a belief in superiority and inferiority among peoples, of difference and inequality. Out of the defeat inflicted upon them by the French, the Germans devised a notion of national, Volkist superiority to redeem their self-image. That self-image could not have been drawn without the Jew as antagonist.

The glorification of the natural man, the simple life, uncontaminated by the artificialities of civilization and the fetters of organized society, was a Romantic Rousseauist idea. The romanticization of the peasant as the natural man turned him into a receptacle of certain mystic qualities in his relationship to the land. The

Volkist conception turned these universal qualities into specifically German ones. The peasant, by virtue of his descent from Germanic-Teutonic stock and by virtue of the mysterious qualities of Germanness in the very soil he worked, became the embodiment not merely of natural man, but of Germanic man. The antagonist of Germanic man became the Jew, the embodiment of the urban man, the man of civilization. A money economy, for example, as the product of disintegrative civilization, was associated with Jews, who were buyers, sellers, and lenders. Whereas rootedness was an essential element of Volk, the Wandering Jew became the symbol of the flesh-and-blood Jews, condemned to eternal homelessness for having rejected the Messiah, whose fathers or forefathers had lived outside Germany, in other lands.

After Napoleon's defeat and the Congress of Vienna, the Germans took their revenge on the French and the Jews. The Congress of Vienna had provided for full civil and political rights "to differing parties of the Christian religion," but the "civil betterment" of the Jews was put off for further study. The Congress stated that Jews could retain such rights as they already had, but nearly everywhere in Germany the rights that the Jews had won were disavowed and rescinded. (Prussia was an exception: only some Jewish rights were abolished; most were retained.) A period of reaction set in, in which anti-Semitism was a major component.

A cyclical pattern in German political life began to emerge. The Congress of Vienna marked the first of four such cycles in subsequent German history that were to appear with startling regularity every two decades—long periods of reaction, repression, conservatism, and anti-Semitism following brief spells of liberalism and the expansion of rights. In all cycles the position of the Jews gradually improved, economically and educationally, even if their political rights were curtailed or denied. The changes in Jewish occupational or educational status did not appreciably decrease the deep hostility to them. The changes merely served to alter the specific arguments of anti-Semitic agitation.

The second cycle was defined by the short-lived Revolution of 1848 and the subsequent decade of reaction. The third cycle opened with the unification of Germany as a triumph of German liberalism that began to turn conservative, reactionary, and anti-Semitic in 1873. The fourth cycle, beginning after World War I, was marked by the simultaneity of both its liberal and its reactionary phases.

Not only did the German states abrogate Jewish rights from 1813 on, but the *furor teutonicus* that had found no satisfaction in the Congress of Vienna expressed itself in violent attacks and pogroms against the Jews. Peasants and burghers demonstrated and rioted in Bavaria, Württemberg, and elsewhere against Jewish rights. Some cities even attempted to banish the Jews altogether. But the most violent pogroms, whose like had not been witnessed in Europe since the Middle Ages, came with the "Hep! Hep!" movement, first erupting in Würzburg in 1819 and rapidly spreading throughout Germany. The origin of this movement was obscure, but it is generally conceded to have been an outburst of resentment against Metternich's repression of German nationalistic propaganda and activities. The movement called for "revenge" against the Jews, "who are living among us and who are increasing like locusts. . . . Our battlecry will be 'Hep! Hep! Hep! Death and destruction to all the Jews!'" It was the first major chapter in the history of German nationalism in which the Jews were marked as the enemy.

Meanwhile, hostility to the Jews began to emerge from the newly developing socialist movement. That anti-Jewish outlook had two sources: first, the atheist, anti-Christian bias condemning Judaism as the antecedent of Christianity, and second, the anticapitalist ideology that depicted the Jew as the embodiment of capitalism, the banker, the middleman, the parasitic profiteer. First to articulate this leftist anti-Semitism was Bruno Bauer (1809–1882), who in 1842 published an article on the Jewish question, which he supplemented and issued the following year as a separate book, *Die Judenfrage*. In this work he argued against political equality for the Jews. Orthodox Judaism was, in his view, an anachronistic phenomenon, whereas Reform Judaism was worthless; the Jews had never contributed to the civilization of the world—arguments that were later to become the stock-in-trade of the anti-Semitic right. Marx disputed Bauer's ideas on the ground that his view of the Jews as a religious group was distorted. The true Jewish religion, Marx argued, was *Schacher* (haggling, huckstering) and their god was money. Jews would first have to emancipate themselves from this "religion" of theirs; then their religious consciousness would disappear and human emancipation would be possible.

But despite the opposition to Jewish emancipation and the antipathy to Jews, the oncoming Revolution of 1848 heralded a growing liberalization in public opinion. When the National Assembly convened in Frankfurt and formulated a constitution, it included a section on "the fundamental rights of the German people," which declared that "the enjoyment of civil and political rights is neither dependent upon, nor restricted by, religious creed."[7] There was no question here of a bountiful bestowal of rights upon Jews by a graciously consenting ruler. The Jews were here equal beneficiaries of rights granted to all. The accomplishment was due to the overwhelmingly liberal character of the body. It was also the achievement of Gabriel Riesser (1806–1863), the notable advocate of Jewish emancipation during the previous two decades, who had been elected to the Frankfurt parliament. But within a year reaction set in. Bismarck was later to say that the great mistake of 1848–1849 was to think that the great questions of the day would be settled by "resolutions and majorities" rather than by "blood and iron." It was a judgment that bespoke the spirit that would later dominate German politics, where blood would erase resolutions and iron crush majorities.

For Jews 1848 was two-faced. The liberal constitu-

tion enacted a great principle that remained barely
fulfilled, for its implementation depended on the individual states. In the very heat of revolutionary ardor
counter-emancipatory trends came alive, and their
pressure on the state governments was irresistible.
When news of the revolution in Paris reached the
peasants in the Rhineland, they too revolted, seizing
land, destroying tax and tithe records, burning castles,
and pogromizing Jews. Revolutionary propaganda
called for wiping out the nobility, assassinating the
officials, establishing a republic, and expelling the Jews
from Germany. The popular agitation in many states
brought about restrictions of Jewish rights or failure
even to grant them. In Bavaria, for example, petitions
with eighty thousand signatures submitted to the
Chamber of Reich Counselors opposing Jewish emancipation succeeded in their purpose.

The liberals were too weak and too indecisive to
withstand the reaction of the next decade. (Weakness
and indecisiveness became hallmarks of German liberal
politics—in the late 1870s vis-à-vis Bismarck and, still
later, in the Weimar regime.) The Conservative party
was founded in 1848 as a vehicle for the counterrevolution, and the 1850s witnessed the expansion and
elaboration of an anti-Semitism that was not only
political, but also Volkist and racist. Then Wilhelm
Heinrich Riehl (1823–1897), historian and novelist,
began publishing his massive *Naturgeschichte des
Volkes als Grundlage einer deutschen Sozial-Politik
(The Natural History of the Volk as the Foundation of
a Germanic Sociopolitical System)*, idealizing pre-
capitalist German society, condemning contemporary
commercial and industrial developments. Then Paul de
Lagarde (1827–1891), later the Volkist patron saint
of the anti-Semitic movement, began his career with
an attack on Christianity and contemporary theology.
Eventually Lagarde would call for an expurgation of
the Jewish elements from Christianity and for its transformation into a Christian-Germanic faith.[8] The Germans, he believed, were too soft for the Jews to be
allowed to live together with them: "Every Jew is

proof of the enfeeblement of our national life and of the worthlessness of what we call the Christian religion."[9]

Lagarde, in another essay, was to write of Jews as vermin:

> One would need a heart as hard as crocodile hide not to feel sorry for the poor exploited Germans and—which is identical—not to hate the Jews and despise those who—out of humanity!—defend these Jews or who are too cowardly to trample this usurious vermin to death. With trichinae and bacilli one does not negotiate, nor are trichinae and bacilli to be educated; they are exterminated as quickly and thoroughly as possible.[10]

That imagery was to be repeated time and again until Hitler appropriated it and applied it with terrible literalness.

Meanwhile, the new "science" of race was developing, under the impetus of advances in anthropology and philology. Christian Lassen (1802–1871), a learned professor of ancient civilizations at the University of Bonn, in his *Indische Altertumskunde (Indian Antiquities)*, argued that among the Caucasians, only Semites and Aryans built up human civilizations. He counterposed one against the other: "History proves that Semites do not possess the harmony of psychical forces that distinguishes the Aryans." But the Semite has other qualities: he is "selfish and exclusive."

Then Arthur de Gobineau (1816–1882) became convinced that "the racial question overshadows all other problems of history, that it holds the key to them all, and that the inequality of the races from whose fusion a people is formed is enough to explain the whole course of its destiny." Though Gobineau's *Essai sur l'inégalité des races,* published in Paris 1853–1855, was not to be translated into German for another forty years, the idea of race as the determinant of the rise and fall of civilizations appeared among the German philologists and ethnologists and philosophers. Social degeneration, they believed, was caused by racial degeneration. Racial mixture, the dissipation of the pure racial blood, brought mediocrity and decline. Gobineau's basic scheme was to serve as a framework for the refinements of Chamberlain and other epigoni who saw the rise and fall of civilization as dependent on the preservation of the racial purity of the Germanic or Aryan race.

Richard Wagner (1813–1883), in his specifically Teutonic racialism and ferocious hatred of Jews, surpassed earlier Volkist anti-Semites. "Emancipation from the yoke of Judaism appears to us the foremost necessity," he wrote. He was to develop, in his music and journalism, the idea of a de-Judaized, hence de-Christianized, Germanic religion, in which the pagan Teutonic elements merged with, or displaced, the Christian ones.

The third cycle of liberalism/reaction came with the unification of Germany. Unification in itself represented a liberal turn in German history, if only in the modest sense that it abolished the particularism of the various states, introduced administrative uniformity, and erased the internal trade and tariff barriers. Bismarck needed liberals' support to achieve his ambitions, and in exchange he conceded universal political and civic rights. (In 1847, as a member of the Prussian Diet, he had opposed political rights for Jews.) The Reichstag of the North German Federation on July 3, 1869, voted such rights into law, abolishing all restrictions of civil and political rights because of religious creed and making participation in local, state, and federal government independent of religious creed.[11]

The unification of Germany introduced new facets to German anti-Semitism. The leaders of the liberals were Jews (Eduard Lasker and Ludwig Bamberger); both liberal parties (the National Liberal party and its split-off, the Progress party) and liberalism in general became the target of Volkist hostility and anti-Semitism. The unification of Germany and the creation of the nation-state forced the Germans into modernity. The nation-state was a concomitant of a new industrial, commercial, financial way of life that was changing the old bases of society and overturning that antiquated hierarchical order which, in Volkist minds, had become identified with the German Volkist past.

The expansive role of capital in the new state intensified charges that the Jews were using their newly acquired rights to exploit the Germans and manipulate their interests. The economic crisis of 1873 was adduced by the anti-Semites as further evidence that the Jews engaged in financial manipulations to undermine the country. Feverish and unchecked speculation had boomed in the wake of the spectacular growth of industry, railroad expansion, foreign trade, and banking that unification had stimulated and that the successful war against France had emboldened. Then, with the onset of a worldwide depression in 1873, came financial collapse in Germany. The crash was blamed on the Jews and the liberals, who were identified as Jews anyway.

In the next six years, the period of economic depression, a complete reorientation took place in German politics, with an authoritarian right turn by Bismarck. He no longer needed his liberal supporters; his Prussian conservatism and absolutism made him the natural enemy of the rising working class and its political spokesman, the Social Democratic party. The attack on both Jews and liberals began to gather momentum, from both right-wing Conservative sources and from populist agitators representing the "little people" in Germany who had indeed been severely affected by the financial disaster. The stereotype of the Jew as international financier became more common. Catholics joined in using the Jews and the liberals as the sticks with which to beat Bismarck and the government.

The first assault came from Wilhelm Marr, an unsuccessful journalist who blamed the Jews for his professional failure, and who is credited with having invented the word "anti-Semitism" (whose use in this context developed out of racial theories about the "Semitic" and "Aryan" races). His pamphlet *Der Sieg des Judentums über das Germanentum* ("The Victory of Jewry over Germandom"), published in 1873, became his first success, going through twelve editions in six years. Drawing on the ideas of race and Volkist nationalism, Marr argued that their "racial qualities" had enabled Jews not only to survive through the ages, but to become "the first major power in the West" in the nineteenth century. The Germanic state, he pessimistically concluded, had degenerated too far to withstand Jewish superiority.

Political anti-Semitism began in Berlin with Adolf Stöcker, though Stöcker did not actually begin with overt, explicit anti-Semitism. In 1878, in Berlin, where he was court preacher, he founded the Christian Social Workers' party. The name itself suggested the party's implicit anti-Semitic bias.* His purposes were to provide a political countervehicle to the Social Democratic party and to combat what he regarded as the dangerous and debilitating secularization and demoralization of society in the capital city. But the workers who came to Christian Social political rallies came only to mock and heckle.

The Progressives continued to hold their strength in Berlin in the election of 1878, but elsewhere in Germany they and the National Liberals lost about half their seats. Gains were made by the Conservatives and the Catholic Center party. That Reichstag gave Bismarck what he had previously been denied: passage of the "law against the pernicious pursuits of Social Democracy," which declared the Social Democratic party illegal and abolished freedom of speech, press, and assembly. (The law was extended four times, with the support of the National Liberals, and remained in force until 1890, when Bismarck resigned. It inaugu-

---

* The word "Christian" in a European organization's name indicated its anti-Semitic character. The classic illustration is Admiral Horthy's joyous embrace of the secretary of the American YMCA as the head of "such an important anti-Semitic organization."

rated a pattern that would be repeated in Germany's later history and showed how fragile was the new nation's commitment to political liberalism.)

Stöcker's failure to win support at a time when the whole country was making a right turn indicated to him that he was appealing to the wrong group. Indeed, the people at his meetings who shared his discontent with state and society were not workers, but members of the *Mittelstand,* which was then beginning to emerge as a political force in German society. Consisting of diverse elements whose economic interests and status drives were not necessarily common or consistent with each other—small farmers and peasants, artisans, small businessmen, lower echelons of officialdom, and lower levels of professionals—the Mittelstand shared a hostility to the rapidly burgeoning industrial urban society and to its political arrangements.

Farmers and peasants feared that industrialism would bring urbanization and destroy their land and way of life. Artisans feared that the factory system and mass production would render them and their crafts obsolete. Small businessmen were apprehensive that the national expansion of trade and a more rational organization of business would make them economically uncompetitive. The lower professionals, white-collar workers, and petty officials felt that their status was being lowered and that the old values they defended were being eroded, if not actually destroyed, by the emergent modern society. Only the workers and the industrialists, it appeared, were in harmony with contemporary economic and industrial developments.

In the next forty years the Mittelstand turned increasingly to the right. Its constituent groups shared an incredible susceptibility to political propaganda that blamed the Jews for the changes that were undermining their traditional ways of life. The "Jewish conspiracy" became the single and simple explanation for whatever had gone wrong in their world. To this audience, consequently, on September 19, 1879, at a

Christian Social meeting, Stöcker made his first anti-Semitic speech: "What We Demand of Modern Jewry."[12]

He began, as he put it, "in the spirit of Christian love." Modern Jewry, he declared, was "a great danger to German national life." He did not mean the Jewish religion as such, he claimed, though he characterized Orthodox Judaism as "a form of religion which is dead at its very core" and Reform Judaism as nothing more than "a pitiful remnant of the Age of Enlightenment." But modern Jews were "most certainly a force against religion," a destructive, secularizing, anti-Christian force, who, themselves not believing in Judaism, persisted in remaining Jewish. Using the platitudes of Volkist/racial anti-Semitism, Stöcker described the Jews as "a people within a people, a state within a state, a separate tribe within a foreign race," who pitted "their unbroken Semitic character against Teutonic nature, their rigid cult of law or their hatred of Christians against Christianity." Germans must protect themselves against the Jews. That protection could come only through "wise legislation." Stöcker's "wise" legislation included a number of general proposals and three explicitly anti-Semitic ones: (1) reintroduction of the denominational census "so as to find out the disproportion between Jewish capital and Christian labor"; (2) limiting the number of appointments of Jewish judges in proportion to the Jews in the population; (3) removing Jewish teachers from the elementary schools, while strengthening the schools' "Christian-Germanic spirit."

Stöcker's legislation originated out of both populist/leftist and rightist sources. The leftist proposals were those directed toward control of the credit system, the regulation of the stock exchange, easements (or complete abolition) of the mortgage system—measures designed to protect the peasant or small landholder, the small businessman, and the small investor from the manipulative power of big capital. They were implicitly anti-Semitic, since in the popular mind big capital was Jewish. The rightist proposals were explicitly anti-Semitic. With these proposals Stöcker, like many after him, succeeded in attracting followers from both the left and the right.

Eighteen-eighty was a watershed year, the start of a torrent of anti-Semitism that did not abate for nearly twenty years. It was as if all the quiet streams of prejudice conjoined in a massive flow of anti-Semitic hate, inundating the whole country. It began at the end of 1879, when Heinrich von Treitschke, National Liberal and prestigious professor of history at the University of Berlin, started a series of articles on the Jewish question in the *Preussische Jahrbücher,* which he edited. "Even in circles of the most highly educated, among men who would reject with disgust any ideas of ecclesiastical intolerance or national arrogance, there resounds as if from one mouth: *Die Juden sind unser Unglück!*"[13]

"The Jews are our misfortune"—the phrase was to ring down through later German generations. Heinrich Class, a leading anti-Semite a generation later, wrote that the phrase "became a part of my body and soul when I was twenty years old; it essentially influenced my later political work." Issued in pamphlet form, Treitschke's articles gave reinforcement and professorial authoritativeness to the anti-Semitic movement. Treitschke spoke, the anti-Semites said, "for thousands, perhaps millions of his countrymen."

In the fall of 1880 the "Anti-Semites' Petition" began to be circulated. Initiated by two schoolteachers (Ernst Henrici and Bernhard Förster, Nietzsche's brother-in-law) and a minor aristocrat (Max Liebermann von Sonnenberg), it was distributed with the help of a newly organized association of German students, explicitly organized as an anti-Semitic group. In the preamble, addressed to Bismarck, the petitioners asked for "the emancipation of the German people from a form of alien domination which it cannot endure for any length of time."[14] The Jew was depicted as the exploitative "master" of the laboring German people, who was gaining control of German urban and rural property and who would destroy the German father-land. Jews were an alien people, whose very feeling and thinking were completely alien to the German Volk. If the ideals of the Germanic Volk were not to be de-stroyed, if the German people were not to fall into the economic slavery of the Jews, steps would have to be taken to liberate the German people from this Jewish danger.

The following steps were proposed: (1) the im-migration of foreign Jews was to be restricted at the least, if not entirely prevented; (2) Jews were to be excluded from all government positions, and their appointment to the judiciary was to be subject to appropriate limitation; (3) the Christian character of the grammar school, even if attended by Jewish pupils, was to be strictly maintained and only Christian teach-ers admitted; in all higher schools the appointment of Jewish teachers could be made only in exceptional cases; (4) the census of the Jewish population was to be resumed.

While the petition was circulating (its center of strength was in Prussia, and especially Berlin), a Pro-gressive deputy asked the Minister of the Interior what the Prussian government intended to do about it. The interpellation was intended to elicit a condemnation, but the minister's *pro forma* reply that the government did not intend to abrogate Jewish rights was seen by the petitioners as an encouraging sign. When finally presented to Bismarck, in April 1881, the "Anti-Semites' Petition" had 225,000 signatures, mostly from Prussia, with 9,000 from Bavaria. Some 4,000 university stu-dents had signed it. (A counterpetition, circulated by liberal students, did poorly. At the University of Göt-tingen, for instance, the liberals received 180 signa-tures, compared with 400 for the "Anti-Semites' Peti-tion.")

At the time of the interpellation, Berthold Auerbach, the Jewish novelist who had been an ardent German nationalist and whose most successful work was the romantic idealization of the German peasant life of his *Schwarzwälder Dorfgeschichten* (*Black Forest Village*

Tales, 1848), was in despair. In a letter from Berlin, November 23, 1880, he wrote: "Living and working in vain! That is the crushing impression I have of this two-day debate in the House of Deputies. And if I tell myself again that it is perhaps not so bad, the horrible fact remains that such coarseness, such deceit, and such hatred are still possible."[15] A few months later, Leopold Zunz, then nearly eighty-seven years old, took another view, in a letter to a friend: "Thus I live, unconcerned about the anti-Jewish agitating swine-eaters: their din is a childish imitation of the Crusades, no longer in style. World literature today and in the newspaper press are more powerful than all the block-heads aping the Middle Ages."[16]

In 1880 Ernst Henrici, one of the organizers of the "Anti-Semites' Petition," founded a new anti-Semitic party, the *Soziale Reichspartei* (the Reich Social party), which, in contrast to Stöcker's Christian conservative anti-Semitism, disseminated a radical racist spirit: "If it is a question of racial characteristics, then both body and spirit must be kept in mind. . . . The religion of the Jews is a racial religion." Wherever Henrici spoke, he aroused masses to anti-Semitic violence. In Berlin his agitation at mass meetings around the "Anti-Semites' Petition" led to street brawls, attacks on Jews, window smashing, the hoodlums shouting *"Juden raus!"* In July 1881 he came to Neustettin, where he harangued the population with his anti-Semitic views. Serious anti-Jewish riots followed, and right after he left, the Neustettin synagogue was burned down. Henrici's party lasted barely two years, but he had succeeded in setting up a model for a radicalized political anti-Semitism.

In 1881 the *Deutsche Reformpartei,** patterned after Stöcker's party in Berlin, was founded in Dresden. Un-successful as a political party, it took on new life as a parapolitical organization, with the formation of *Re-*

---

* "Reform" was a word appropriated largely by the right and usually meant restrictions on free-trade policies. "Reform" movements often took on a populist, anti-Semitic coloration.

formvereine (reform unions) throughout Germany, groups in which anti-Semitism in all varieties flourished. By 1885 there were 52 such unions; by 1890, 136. The Reformvereine attracted members of the Mittelstand and provided an organizational framework of sorts for the burgeoning anti-Semitic movement. (The various leaders of the anti-Semitic movement tried, from time to time, to form a united organization, but their ideological differences, personal rivalries, and psychological instabilities conspired against them.)

The Vereine came under different intellectual influences in the anti-Semitic movement, from both the left and the right. In Westphalia, for instance, the branches were largely affected by the ideas of Eugen Karl Dühring, an anarchist with a strong following among the Social Democrats. A philosopher and an economist, he taught at the University of Berlin until his inability to get along with the university authorities forced his retirement in 1877. Like Marr and other malcontents, he attributed his failures to Jewish plotting. He had first propagated a proto-national type of socialism, but by 1881 the Jewish question had moved to the center of his mental universe, when he published *Die Judenfrage als Rassen- Sitten- und Kulturfrage* (*The Jewish Question as a Racial, Moral, and Cultural Question*). In this work he argued that the German spirit had sold itself to Judaism, that Germany's "social corruption" was the consequence of the parasitic Jews' settling in Germany and bringing about Germany's complete deterioration. Developing the crudest and most vicious racism, Dühring looked upon the Jews as a "counterrace" separated from all humanity, whom neither conversion nor assimilation could affect because their basic nature was evil and unchangeable. He shared the Wagnerian thesis that Christianity was a product of a "Hebraic orientalism," and that those who clung to the "entire" Christian tradition could not truly oppose Judaism or defend the "Nordic tradition." His influence among university students was substantial, beginning with his economic ideas and ending with his anti-Semitic racism.

The Leipzig branch of the Reformvereine was headed by Theodor Fritsch (1844–1933), a linchpin in the anti-Semitic movement, holding it together as political organizer, publisher, editor, author from its early political/nationalist stirrings in the 1880s until Hitler's accession to power. He bought up an unsuccessful anti-Semitic publishing house and in 1882 began to issue the *Antisemitische Correspondenz*. He was less interested in forming an anti-Semitic political party than in infusing all political parties with anti-Semitism.

Political anti-Semitism began also in Austria at this time. In Germany the concomitants to anti-Semitism were German nationalism and anti-modernity. In Austria the key element was Pan-Germanism, union with Germany and the preservation of the "German" character of "German" territory. The Austrian Germans stressed their Germanness to distinguish themselves from the East European nationalities in the Hapsburg Empire and to separate Cisleithan Austria from Transleithan Hungary. The doctrine of Pan-Germanism was first formulated by Georg von Schönerer and the university intellectuals who had supported him. Schönerer, in turn, acknowledged Dühring as teacher and master. Thus is tradition transmitted: Schönerer learned from Dühring, and Hitler learned from Schönerer.

Schönerer began his political career as a liberal in the *Reichsrat* in 1873, but he soon opted for a more radical economic program (his leftist heritage from Dühring) and a preference for German nationalism. In 1882 Schönerer and his followers formulated the so-called "Linz Program," which combined Pan-Germanism with a reform program that was part socialist and part romantically anti-industrialist. Anti-Semitism was scarcely apparent. But like Stöcker, Schönerer learned that anti-Semitism was the mainstay of the Mittelstand elements who supported him. He took his cue from the farmers and the craftsmen who saw the Jew as their enemy and regarded industrialism and urbanism as Jewish machinations. In 1885 Schönerer added one more point to the Linz Program that became the central one: "The removal of Jewish influence from all sections of public life is indispensable for carrying out the reforms aimed at." He introduced anti-Semitic motions in the Reichsrat, and in 1887 he sponsored a bill to restrict East European Jewish immigration into Austria. Anti-Semitism was to become the obverse side of Schönerer's German nationalism, the negative definition of his position, and as he lost his political footing and influence, both his nationalism and his anti-Semitism were to become, in the long years ahead, irrational obsessions colored by freakishness. His hatred of Jews and Catholics constituted also a rejection of Christianity; the pagan practices he adopted were no mere bizarre oddities, but reflected the longing for an idealized primitive world of German tribesmen in dark Teutonic forests. Though Hitler had much empathy for these hallucinated visions that Schönerer was propagating to his coteries of cultists, he despised Schönerer for abandoning himself to these arcane notions and failing to make political capital of such precious assets as German nationalism and anti-Semitism.

If Schönerer turned out to be a discredit to anti-Semitic politics in Austria, Karl Lueger (1844–1910) was its shining success. He made anti-Semitism politically viable, acceptable, and, finally, respectable. A master of pragmatic politics, an antinationalist and anti-Prussian, devoted to Emperor and empire, Lueger saw anti-Semitism mainly as a political expedient. In a few years Lueger's Christian Social party attained the political success that Schönerer had dreamed of, but never achieved.

Perhaps it was a matter of timing, for in Germany, too, that was the time when the anti-Semitic parties began to amass electoral strength. Within a decade they had succeeded in infecting all the major political parties, except the Social Democrats, with the poison of anti-Semitism. It began in 1887 when Otto Böckel was elected to the Reichstag as a deputy from a poor peasant constituency in Hesse, winning a long-held Conservative seat. A librarian who had made the collection of German folklore his hobby and had thus become familiar with peasant life, Böckel had a year earlier helped found a branch of the Reformvereine in Kassel and joined with Fritsch in an attempt to form an anti-Semitic alliance. He campaigned on a populist economic program, stirring the peasants with his fiery slogan: "Liberate yourselves from the Jewish middlemen!" Böckel believed that Jews were a racial group whose racial essence could not be affected by conversion or intermarriage and that Jews in Germany should never be allowed to have more than the rights of aliens, because they were by nature aliens. He argued that the Conservatives failed in their treatment of the Jewish question, which he regarded as the central "national question" in Germany. This "political" approach, with its unexpected success, threatened, above all, the Conservatives, who, then in a temporary alliance with the National Liberals, had soft-pedaled anti-Semitism. For the 1890 election Böckel organized the *Antisemitische Volkspartei* (Anti-Semitic People's party), whose program demanded "the repeal, by legal means, of Jewish emancipation" and "placing the Jews under alien legislation." His party won five seats in Hesse, his Conservative and other anti-Semitic rivals having withdrawn lest they split the vote.

Böckel was not an isolated phenomenon. In a by-election in 1892, in a rural district in eastern Germany, similarly without party backing or organization funds, Hermann Ahlwardt defeated his Conservative opponent. A schoolteacher who had advanced to school principal, his financial peccadilloes had entangled him in debts and scandals—though, using an ancient staple of anti-Semitic propaganda, he attributed these entirely to Jewish usurers. He was fired when found dipping into the school till. Then, in 1890, he published a book called *Der Verzweiflungskampf der arischen Völker mit den Judentum* (*The Despairing Struggle of the Aryan Peoples with Jewry*), in which he depicted the Jews as an octopus with claws in every sphere of German life. Two nasty anti-Semitic pamphlets followed, which brought him sentences of imprisonment for false charges, but having been meanwhile elected to the Reichstag, he enjoyed parliamentary immunity. His reckless rantings and his paranoia did not ensure his success in the Reichstag (eventually the anti-Semites came to regard him as a liability), but for years his constituency returned him to office, believing that he was a victim of nefarious Jewish power.

His racial anti-Semitism contained the familiar arguments drawn from the leftist, Volkist, and racist repertory. In a Reichstag address in 1895, supporting a bill to halt Jewish immigration into Germany, he analyzed Jewish "racial" qualities. The Jews were "beasts of prey" and "cholera bacilli." The only chance the Germans had to defend themselves was to "exterminate those beasts of prey," and the best way to start would be to keep them out of the country.[17]

After Ahlwardt's stunning success in 1892, the Conservatives drew what they thought was the appropriate conclusion: anti-Semitism was a legitimate political weapon to be used to attain political power. At their party convention at the end of that year, the Conservatives revised their party program to include not only implicitly anti-Semitic planks (for instance, "We demand Christian authority and Christian teachers for Christian pupils"), but also the explicit anti-Semitic statement "We fight the multifarious and obtrusive Jewish influence that decomposes our people's life." No greater gain could have been made, no greater respectability could have accrued to political anti-Semitism. No longer the possession of small splinter and sometimes crackpot parties, anti-Semitism had become the property of the most prestigious party of Imperial Germany.

The 1890s brought new vitality and organizational support to the anti-Semitic movement. The successes of populist racial anti-Semites had pushed the reluctant anti-Semitic "moderates" into the extremist camp, but even more significant for the solidification of political anti-Semitism was the anxiety engendered by the tremendous expansion of the Social Democratic movement. In 1890, the first election after the expiration of Bismarck's anti-Socialist law, the Social Democrats amassed over 1.4 million votes, winning 35 seats (they had previously held 11). Indeed, the only significant opposition to the rising tide of political anti-Semitism that was inundating Germany's political institutions came from industrial labor and from the Social Democratic party. "Anti-Semitism is the socialism of fools," August Bebel, the party's leader, had said when leftist, populist anti-Semitism threatened to infect the Socialist movement. The party continued firmly to resist anti-Semitism and succeeded in immunizing its members and supporters against it.

How did the Social Democrats succeed in warding off anti-Semitism, when everyone else, it seemed, succumbed so easily? For one thing, the party leadership early set a model for the ranks by its aggressive articulated opposition. In a generally authoritarian society, that authoritative denunciation of anti-Semitism must have had some effect. For another, the ideology of the Social Democratic movement interpreted all economic, social, and political phenomena in terms of an all-encompassing Marxist theory. Social Democrats did not need anti-Semitism, another all-embracing theory, to explain the great events of their lives. Finally, the Social Democrats, as industrial workers, had a stake in industrial urban society. With fewer romantic illusions about the primitive past, they had greater ambitions for a share in the comfort, convenience, and wealth that their labor was helping to produce. This modernist outlook, then, helped to render them impervious to anti-Semitism.

The Mittelstand, in contrast, viewed much of this expanding restless urban society through Volkist eyes and increasingly gave its support not only to conservative centrist parties (Conservative and Catholic Center parties), to Germany's expanding imperialism, but also to candidates representing a gamut of anti-Semitic opinion. From 1887, with Böckel's election, until the outbreak of World War I, about ninety anti-Semitic deputies were elected to the Reichstag. The various parties grouped and regrouped, for a while united, sometimes sponsored jointly by the Conservatives. In 1893, for example, candidates of anti-Semitic parties polled 263,000 votes, but if those who ran jointly on the Conservative line are added, the anti-Semitic vote was as high as 400,000. As for the anti-Semitic deputies, they were themselves the essence of the Mittelstand. Nearly all were Protestants, none were of the aristocracy (except for two chronic anti-Semites), and none from labor. Mostly they were small entrepreneurs and craftsmen who had experienced economic hardships, teachers, lower civil servants, white-collar employees, and lawyers—the same occupational groups that were also to provide support for the NSDAP after World War I. They all shared a sense of frustration, deep resentments—seldom rationally articulable—against "outside" forces that prevented their attainment of appropriate status or professional success. Cultists turned up in these movements, back-to-nature advocates, food faddists, occultists; all found a place in the anti-Semitic movement.

The year 1893 was the organizational highpoint for the Mittelstand. The *Alldeutscher Verband* (Pan-German League) was founded as a vehicle for the expression of middle-class nationalist imperialism and militarism, to cultivate "German national values all over the world." Under its first president, Professor Ernst Hasse, anti-Semitism was latent and secondary. In 1908, when Heinrich Class became president, the league became overtly anti-Semitic and closed its membership to Jews. At the turn of the century, its membership reached 20,000, with professors and university lecturers (over 5,000), small businessmen (4,900), teachers and civil servants (3,760), as the largest occupational groups.

Also founded in 1893 was the *Deutschnationaler*

Handlungsgehilfenverband (National Germanic League of Clerks), which started modestly with a group of 30 clerks in Hamburg; by 1913 it had nearly 150,000 members. The organization's constitution specified that "Jews or persons whose character is not blameless" could not become members. (The league was not only anti-Jewish, it was also anti-feminist, in an attempt to maintain white-collar employment as a male preserve.) Both the Alldeutscher Verband and the clerks' league functioned as political pressure groups, throwing their strength behind candidates of the various right-wing and anti-Semitic parties and raising funds for their candidates and organizations.

The third parapolitical Mittelstand organization founded in 1893, and probably the most influential, was the *Bund der Landwirte* (Agrarian League), which was to become a major force in right-wing politics and to transform the Conservative party. Though its leadership remained in the hands of relatively few big landowners, its rank-and-file members were small farmers. By the end of the decade, the Agrarian League had nearly 250,000 members. What held the diverse and sometimes divergent economic and social interests of the large-scale and small-scale farmers together was a German nationalism defined by anti-Semitism. At its first general assembly in 1894, the Agrarian League restricted its membership to Christians and announced itself as "an opponent of Jewry, which has become altogether too mighty in our country and has acquired a decisive say in the press, in trade, and on the exchanges." A year later the league's organ declared: "Agriculture and Jewry must fight to the death, until one or the other lies lifeless—or at least powerless—on the ground." It advocated boycotting Jewish stores, prohibiting social relations between Germans and Jews, and expelling Jews from Germany. In the Agrarian League, as in increasing numbers of German organizations and institutions, German nationalism and racist, Volkist anti-Semitism combined to form an effective, powerful political pressure group that radicalized German conservatism and made anti-Semitism a commonplace staple of any right-of-center political body.

The student organizations, the gymnastic and sports organizations (the *Deutsche Turnerschaft*, whose ancestry went back to Father Jahn, was not only Volkist nationalist but explicitly anti-Semitic), the youth and back-to-nature movements, though apolitical, added variety and density to political anti-Semitism, thriving as they did on irrationality, anti-intellectualism, race superiority, and race hate.

Anti-Semitic propaganda proliferated luxuriantly in the 1890s in the rich soil of political success and organizational abundance and grew into the twentieth century. In 1894 a society was formed by Gobineau's German translator, a disciple of Lagarde, to honor Gobineau and revive his work. The Wagner family circle gave the society its primary support, but when the Alldeutscher Verband became a supporting member of the Gobineau Society, a new union of racist Volkism and the Mittelstand was formed. Gobineau's work, as well as Houston Stewart Chamberlain's, became required reading for rightist German students. Julius Langbehn (1815–1907), a new Volkist prophet of discontent, having been exhorted by the tireless Fritsch to a hard anti-Semitic line, emerged with his dyspeptic version of cultural anti-Semitism. Langbehn saw to it that Lagarde's work was revived (a new edition appeared in 1891). Heinrich Class, whose pseudonymous book *Wenn Ich der Kaiser wär'* (*If I Were Kaiser*), in which he expounded his anti-Semitic theories, first published in 1912, went into five editions before war broke out, wrote of the impact on him of the works of Lagarde, Count Gobineau, and Houston Stewart Chamberlain: "At the end of the century, I plunged into them, and I do not know from which of these three great men I derived the most profit."[18]

At the turn of the century anti-Semitism had infected Germany. A book dealer found vast quantities of anti-Semitic literature in the libraries that he bought for resale. "Every year," he wrote, "tens of thousands of anti-Semitic pamphlets are sent free to all officials of the state and members of the upper ten thousand."[19]

The next cycle of anti-Semitism came with World War I. The elections of 1912 to the Reichstag had given a massive majority to the Progressives and Social Democrats. Political anti-Semitism, it seemed, was on the decline. But it erupted in the midst of the war, following the euphoria of patriotism at the outbreak of war, when even Jews had been included within the circle of national brotherhood.

By mid-1916 the war had begun to go badly. There were no military victories to compensate for the food shortages, the hardships, the wounded and the dead in battle. The Jews became the "explanation" for whatever was going wrong. The Jews, the accusations went, were not fighting for Germany. Those in the army had cushy jobs behind the front; Jews were profiteering out of the war, getting rich from the war corporations. Popular anti-Semitism once again rose to the surface. Just as this grumbling discontent was turning into a massive rumble, and under pressure of the officer corps, the war hero Field Marshal Paul von Hindenburg was appointed to replace the chief of the General Staff, who had been charged with the army's military failures. Another war hero, Erich Ludendorff, was appointed Hindenburg's aide (Ludendorff in reality exercised the authority and made Hindenburg's decisions). A few days after Ludendorff's appointment, the War Ministry ordered a religious census of the members of the armed forces, according to service at the front, in garrisons, or behind desks, and of the employees in the war corporations (war industry). In October, as if ignorant of these administrative measures, an anti-Semitic member of the Reichstag proposed that such a survey be made of the armed forces and a member of the Catholic Center party moved the same for the war corporations. The National Liberals, some forty years earlier accused of being the party of Jewry, went along with the proposal. Only the Progressives and Social Democrats were opposed. This coalition of authoritarian military leaders, anti-Semites, Catholic conservatives, and the components of the Mittelstand succeeded, without difficulty, in undermining the guarantee of equal rights of the Reichstag Act of 1869. The next two years of the war were marked by a crescendo of anti-Semitism, which Hitler epitomized in *Mein Kampf*: ". . . In the year 1916–17 nearly the whole production was under the control of Jewish finance. . . . The spider was slowly beginning to suck the blood out of the people's pores."

The Weimar Republic, born out of defeat and revolution, despair and hope, emerged with a new constitution that at long last gave the Jews complete equality. But at the very time that Jews had just begun to enjoy those political and civic rights for which they had been striving for a century, anti-Semitism burst forth in its most extravagant form. The Weimar Republic and its constitution had become an extreme example of the difference between the *pays légal* and the *pays réel*. The Jews now had the right to hold high public office (a few actually did), but they were also, in the minds of vast numbers of Germans, to blame for Germany's defeat, for the revolution, for the Munich Soviet, for the loss of the monarchy, for the passing of the past. They were the internal enemy. On February 24, 1920, just six months after the Weimar Constitution was enacted, the NSDAP issued its twenty-five-point program, which asserted that no Jew could ever be a member of the German Volk, that only persons of German blood could be regarded as members of the Volk and citizens of the German state. The *Deutschnationale Volkspartei* (DNVP; German National People's party), the postwar incarnation of the German right, was at its founding at the end of 1918, conservative, Christian, nationalist, though not yet anti-Semitic. But soon it was seized by the anti-Semitic madness, and in 1920 its party program took a stand "against the predominance of Jewry in government and public life." Parliamentary democracy survived in Germany for barely one decade, which witnessed the seemingly irresistible rise of the Nazis, the proliferation of anti-

Semitic associations and societies—as many as 430—
and of anti-Semitic periodicals—as many as 700. Anti-
Semitic bills were introduced with shameless regularity into state and national legislatures. The youth of
the country, especially the students at the universities,
were overwhelmingly anti-Semitic (in Berlin student
elections in 1921, two-thirds of the votes were cast for
anti-Semitic candidates). Violence often ruled the
streets, though Jews were not its only victims. After the
assassination of Catholic leftist leader Matthias Erz-
berger, the war veterans, the members of the Free
Corps, roaming the streets for victims and action, used
to sing:

> *Knallt ab den Walter Rathenau*
> *Die gottverdammte Judensau.*
> (Mow down Walter Rathenau,
> The goddamned Jewish sow.)

And they did. By 1926 even the strictest law-abiding
German Jews began to talk of learning how to develop
their bodies and defend themselves.[20]

There was no dearth of anti-Semitic propaganda.
Before the end of 1920 the *Protocols of the Elders of
Zion*, translated into German that year, had sold 120,000
copies. A Jewish reporter at that time wrote:

> In Berlin I attended several meetings which were en-
> tirely devoted to the Protocols. The speaker was usually
> a professor, a teacher, an editor, a lawyer or someone
> of that kind. The audience consisted of members of
> the educated class, civil servants, tradesmen, former
> officers, ladies, above all students, students of all
> faculties and years of seniority. . . . Passions were
> whipped up to the boiling point.[21]

It was a world intoxicated with hate, driven by
paranoia, enemies everywhere, the Jew lurking behind
each one. The Germans were in search of a mysterious
wholeness that would restore them to primeval hap-
piness, destroying the hostile milieu of urban industrial

civilization that the Jewish conspiracy had foisted on them.[22]

"*Deutschland erwache, Juda verrecke*" became a commonplace slogan. In 1923 the National Socialists had won 800,000 votes. In 1930 they had 6.5 million. In 1932 nearly 14 million voters out of 45 million voted for the NSDAP, in the last free election of the Weimar Republic.

National Socialism was the consummation toward which the omnifarious anti-Semitic movements had striven for 150 years.

3

Phase One:
Anti-Jewish Legislation,
1933–1935

On January 30, 1933, shortly before noon, Paul von Hindenburg, President of the German Republic, administered the oath of office to Adolf Hitler, whom he had decided just the day before to make Chancellor. Hitler swore the oath: "I will employ my strength for the welfare of the German people, protect the Constitution and laws of the German people, conscientiously discharge the duties imposed on me and conduct my affairs of office impartially and with justice to everyone." When Hitler uttered those words, he had already laid his plans to destroy the constitution and the laws he was swearing to protect. Exercising neither impartiality nor justice, he was about to conduct relentless war on his enemies —democracy, freedom, parliamentarianism, political pluralism, and, above all, the Jews, the embodiment of everything he hated.

In the elections of November 6, 1932, the NSDAP had received over 33 percent of the vote, a decrease from its high in 1930 of 37 percent. Still, the National Socialists did better than any other party. The left had fared worse, the Socialists getting 20 percent of the vote and the Communists 17 percent. The Catholic parties had 15 percent. The DNVP, the right-wing nationalist party that competed for votes with the NSDAP, got 9 percent. That election deepened the parliamentary crisis; the government was paralyzed. After months of political maneuvering, Hindenburg decided to form a government based on a coalition of conglomerate right-wing nationalist organizations whose common opposition to the principles of the Weimar Republic occasionally transcended their political and tactical differences—the NSDAP, DNVP, the *Stahlhelm* (a right-wing uniformed veterans' organization), right-wing Catholics, and miscellaneous right-wing independents. Hitler was awarded the chancellorship (this, Meinecke said at the time, "was not necessary"), and the National Socialists were given two other seats in the cabinet—Wilhelm Frick became Minister of the Interior and Hermann Göring, minister without portfolio (simultaneously Prussian Minister of the Interior).

Hitler had been appointed Chancellor under Article 48 of the Weimar Constitution, which granted the President the authority to invoke dictatorial power to protect the democratic order from overthrow, a clause originally inserted to ensure against a feared Communist revolution. Yet Hitler himself had repeatedly threatened to overthrow the Weimar Republic. His first official act was to convince Hindenburg and the Cabinet to dissolve the recalcitrant Reichstag and to order new elections on March 5. Hitler hoped by then to arrange to win a majority and have an incontestable "legal" mandate from the German people. In his first official proclamation he promised the Germans a "national awakening" and an end to the "shameful past" of Weimar. His direction was clear. He persuaded Hindenburg on February 4 to sign a decree that, under Article 48, authorized the Minister of the Interior and the police to prohibit public meetings and to suppress publications that they believed would endanger public security. Providing for prolonged periods of police detention, the decree was used right away against the Socialists, Communists, and other opponents of the NSDAP in the upcoming election campaign.

Hitler came to power legally, exploiting the letter of the law to subvert the law. Sensible people were sure that Hitler could not last long, that decency, rationality, and political order would—must—reassert themselves. No civilized nation, no rational people, it was held, could endure mass hysteria as a substitute for parliamentarianism, the rule of terror instead of the rule of law. But the Germans had entered upon a macabre era in which evil and irrationality would reign for twelve endless years, in which the whole nation would be suborned. The frenzy of mass meetings would replace the decision in the voting booth, the fluttering of flags would supplant political discussion. The rhythm of the goose step and the resonance of the Horst Wessel song, the crackling of terror in the streets and the bloodlust of massacres would define the political character of the Third Reich and describe its ambience. The Germans would live by two principles alone: rule by Führership and the dominion of race. They repudiated the Sixth Commandment.

On February 27 the Reichstag building was set afire. Marinus van der Lubbe, a deranged pyromaniacal Dutch Communist, was found on the spot. Until today no one knows for sure if van der Lubbe set the fire on his own initiative, whether he was a tool of the Communists or of the National Socialists conspiring to scapegoat the Communists. Whether by accident or by design, the fire gave Hitler the opportunity he needed. The very next day, over Hindenburg's signature, he issued a series of emergency decrees, the first phase in the process that would shortly undermine the constitution and destroy its guarantees of basic liberties. Described as measures to ward off "Communist acts of violence endangering the state," these decrees suspended all fundamental freedoms of speech, press, assembly, freedom from invasion of privacy (mail, telephone, telegram) and from house search without warrant. They gave the federal government the power to take over the state governments as needed to restore public security, and they imposed the death penalty—in place of life imprisonment—for treason, arson, railroad sabotage, and the like. Another set of decrees dealt with high treason, in a manner so deliberately ill-defined as to cover every possible form of dissidence, including the publication and dissemination of certain forms of printed matter.

In the next few days before the election, the NSDAP inundated the voters with propaganda about the imminent Communist revolution from which it had rescued Germany, but which still threatened. The terror had succeeded, but not quite enough. The National Socialists increased their vote to nearly 44 percent, but without a majority Hitler was forced to reaffirm a nationalist coalition with the DNVP, which had won a mere 8 percent of the votes.

Thereafter the Nazis began diligently to carry through their two-pronged assault of terror and pseudolegality against their opponents. The SA (*Sturmabteilung*—Storm Troops), the NSDAP's private army that had grown to 400,000—four times larger than the German army permitted under the Treaty of Versailles—accelerated its terror against Communists, Socialists, trade unionists, Jews. At the same time, Hitler began to lay plans to obtain the two-thirds vote at the first session of the newly elected Reichstag needed to pass an Enabling Act—a measure giving the government, without recourse to the Reichstag, the power to promulgate emergency legislation for a specific period of time. The session was set to open on March 21, marking the sixty-second anniversary of Bismarck's first Reichstag in a unified Germany. While Hitler was negotiating with the DNVP and the Catholic Centrists to get their support for the Enabling Act, his Storm Troppers and police were wrecking, burning, and looting Socialist and Communist party offices, assaulting, beating, and arresting

Socialist municipal officials and Socialist deputies. The Socialist newspaper *Reichsbanner* was suppressed in many German states.

The day before the Reichstag opened, the Cabinet approved the text of the Enabling Act as drafted by Frick. That same day, Heinrich Himmler, Reichsführer-SS (*Schutzstaffel*—Defense Corps, the most sinister of Nazi formations), then provisional police president of Munich, announced that arrangements had been completed for setting up the first concentration camp on the grounds of a former gunpowder factory in the area of Dachau, near Munich. It would serve, according to the *Völkischer Beobachter*, to concentrate "all Communist and, where necessary, *Reichsbanner* and Social Democrat officials . . . [who] cannot be allowed to remain free as they continue to agitate and to cause unrest."[1]

On the evening of March 21, 1933, the Reichstag opened with an elaborate ceremonial at the Potsdam Garrison Church, where Frederick the Great was enshrined. Hitler, in cutaway and top hat, with unaccustomed tact and modesty, paid formal homage to the aged President in his field marshal regalia. That very day the first prisoners were brought under SA guard to the Oranienburg concentration camp outside Berlin. In the next ten days some fifteen thousand persons were taken into "protective custody" in Prussia.

On March 23 the first working session of the Reichstag began, with all Communist deputies and twenty-six of the Socialist deputies missing—arrested or fled. Hitler had not yet convinced the Catholic Center to support the Enabling Act, and in his introductory address he tried to allay their anxieties over how he would use that authority. In the ensuing three-hour recess, the Centrists bitterly debated the question among themselves and decided finally to support the act. The vote was 441 for the bill, with all 94 Socialist deputies against. Standing in the chamber with outstretched arms in their party salute, the National Socialist deputies sang the Horst Wessel song.

The Enabling Act provided Hitler with the legal authority for dictatorship. It gave the government the power for four years to promulgate legislation, even if it deviated from the Constitution. (Under this authority, Hitler himself renewed the act in later years.) In less than eight weeks, Hitler had accomplished his "legal" revolution, having terrorized the Communists, as he soon would also the Socialists, and with cynical deceit, having promised the rightists and Centrists that he would restore legality and share power with them. But by early July the NSDAP alone remained in existence. The Communists and Social Democrats had been suppressed. Under Hitler's prodding, the DNVP, followed by the smaller parties and the Catholic Center, proclaimed their own suicide by self-dissolution. "The party has now become the state," Hitler declared on July 8, 1933. On July 14 a government decree legally solemnized the *fait accompli* and declared the NSDAP to be the only political party in Germany. Any attempt to maintain another party or form a new one would be punishable by three years of imprisonment, "if the action is not subject to a greater penalty according to other regulations"—those dealing with high treason, unmistakably.

After obtaining the Enabling Act, Hitler retired to Berchtesgaden. The question now uppermost in his mind concerned the Jews. On March 26 he summoned Goebbels, who had meanwhile become a member of the Cabinet as Minister of Public Enlightenment and Propaganda, and gave him instructions. Goebbels recorded that meeting in his diary:

We shall only be able to combat the falsehoods abroad if we get at those who originated them or at those Jews living in Germany who have thus far remained unmolested. We must, therefore, proceed to a large-scale boycott of all Jewish business in Germany. Perhaps the foreign Jews will think better of the matter when their racial comrades in Germany begin to get it in the neck.[2]

The organization of the anti-Jewish boycott showed Hitler's talent for rationalizing and politicizing raw anti-Semitism, channeling the passion for pogrom on the part of the rank-and-file anti-Semites into "meaningful" political action. Actually the boycott originated in the spontaneous violence of SA and Nazi hooligans against Jewish business and Jews in public life. Department stores, by Nazi definition "Jewish," were a particular target. (Back in 1920 the NSDAP program demanded "that the large stores shall be immediately communalized and rented cheaply to small tradespeople.") Police protection for Jewish stores was not available. On March 11, in a speech at Essen, Göring gave official sanction to the violence: "I will ruthlessly set the police at work wherever harm is being done to the German people. But I refuse to make the police the guardians of Jewish department stores." That same day in Breslau, after the SA had invaded a department store, the police came to stop them. The SA then broke into the courts, seizing Jewish judges and lawyers and dragging them through the streets. Again the police intervened, but local officials were in a quandary, not sure what they should do. Similar violence occurred in Braunschweig, Göttingen, Leipzig, Dresden, Chemnitz. In parts of Upper Hesse and Prussia, the SA had organized a series of boycotts against Jewish businesses and Jewish professionals. The German propaganda machine implicitly communicated the message: "German Jews are our hostages. We will hold on to them."[3]

The crescendo of violence and atrocities had meanwhile aroused world criticism. The strongest protests were being made on behalf of the Jews. There was talk, especially in the United States, of a boycott of German goods. In his characteristically improvisatory and opportunistic manner, Hitler had decided to exploit SA violence by branding the Jews as the enemies of Germany and the instigators of a worldwide campaign of lies and calumny to discredit the Reich. Even before Hitler had summoned Goebbels, he had already instructed his friend Julius Streicher, the notorious publisher of *Der Stürmer*, a perverted, vicious anti-Semitic paper, to organize a boycott committee.

Göring, too, had had his instructions. On March 26 he summoned the leaders of the Jewish organizations to his office. Clear, direct, and hostile, Göring told them that they would have to inform the Jews abroad to stop spreading atrocity stories about Germany and to halt the anti-German boycott campaign. Otherwise—as one communal leader later wrote— "otherwise pogrom."

The German Jews talked back. They called attention to the dangerous anti-Jewish agitation being carried on by the Nazi press, showing Göring a Nazi paper of Chemnitz, with a photograph of Jews being forced to wash streets under armed Nazi escort. They wanted to show other documents in their possession, but Göring impatiently replied that he had already punished all those guilty. (No one, of course, had been punished.) Finally, however, they had to promise, under threat, to contact Jewish organizations abroad and deny the atrocity reports. A plethora of cables, telegrams, and letters were issued by each Jewish institution in Germany to every contact abroad. Typical of the messages was a telegram, March 30, 1933, from the presidium of the Berlin *Gemeinde* (Jewish community) to the American Jewish Committee:

According to newspaper reports, atrocity and boycott propaganda against Germany is continuing overseas, apparently in part also by Jewish organizations. As Germans and Jews we must enter a decisive protest against this. The dissemination of untrue reports can only bring harm, affecting the reputation of our German fatherland, endangering the relations of the German Jews with their fellow citizens. Please try urgently to see to it that every atrocity and boycott propaganda report is halted.[4]

(The American Jewish organizations realized that these telegrams were sent under duress.)

On March 28, two days after Hitler's instructions, it was announced that a boycott of Jewish businesses was being called for April 1, by NSDAP leaders, who had organized a Central Committee for Defense Against Jewish Atrocity and Boycott Propaganda. The NSDAP issued instructions for the conduct of the boycott, whose enforcement became the responsibility of the SA, under supervision of the SS. All party units were to form local boycott committees—as a matter of fact, many had done this spontaneously weeks earlier. In one German town the Nazis placed an advertisement in the local paper, declaring that "international Jewry" was spreading "atrocity propaganda" against the Germans and that was why the boycott was being called. Three days later, a second advertisement appeared, with a list of specific businesses and individuals to be boycotted.[5] Party instructions were that teams of two SA and SS "protective guards" were to be stationed in front of Jewish stores to "inform" the public that these were Jewish establishments.

At his Cabinet meeting on March 29, Hitler explained that an organized boycott was necessary to control popular anti-Semitic outbreaks, but in an effort to calm the anxieties of the non-Nazis in the Cabinet who feared foreign repercussions, he promised that the boycott would last only one day. Formally, the boycott lasted three days, from Saturday, April 1, through Monday, April 3. Though the party instructions were to avoid violence, the police were advised not to interfere, and violence was activated all through Germany. A Jewish lawyer was said to have been lynched by a mob in Kiel.

On April 4 Goebbels announced that the boycott was over. He declared, with a regard for truth characteristic of a Minister of Propaganda, that it was a success since "with only a few exceptions . . . [the] outrageous foreign propaganda has been stopped."

Mass violence against Jewish business, in its prematurity, turned out to be politically and economically touchy. But the violence against Jews in public life—which Hans Kerrl, a National Socialist who had be-

come Prussian Minister of Justice, characterized as the
"self-help actions" of the people—offered few risks.
Weeks before the boycott, a combination of violence
and administrative action had already forced hundreds
of Jews from their positions as judges and lawyers in
the courts, journalists on newspapers, conductors and
musicians in orchestras, professors in universities. In
Breslau, for example, in the wake of the disorders of
March 11, the Department of Justice responded within
five days to the "wishes of the people" to "limit the
influence" of Jews in the administration of justice, by
reducing the number of Jewish lawyers attached to
the Breslau courts.

The dismissals of Jews from positions in government
and the professions accelerated through the month.
On March 25 the Bavarian Ministry of Justice ordered
that Jewish judges be replaced in criminal and disciplinary cases and that Jews be prohibited from serving as prosecutors. On March 31 Kerrl issued a statement to the effect that all persons in authority should
ask their Jewish judges to retire the following morning,
the day of the boycott. In case the Jews failed to
retire, they would be prevented by other means from
entering the courthouses. Similarly, Jewish state prosecutors should be retired and the number of Jewish
lawyers henceforth admitted to practice in the courts
would be limited to the proportion of Jews in the
population. Jews would no longer be eligible to serve
on juries. (A day earlier, Kerrl had sent one of his
legal assistants to Frankfurt to enlighten the judges
there about the upcoming Berlin procedures.)

The extent of these dismissals and forced resigna-
tions agitated even Hindenburg, whose compliance
with Hitler's wishes had hitherto been unhesitating.
What prompted Hindenburg to write to Hitler on
April 4 was neither conscience over legal niceties nor
compassion for Jews, but the honor of the German
army:

In the last few days a whole series of cases have been
reported to me in which war-wounded judges, lawyers,

and civil servants in the judiciary, with unblemished records of service, have been forcibly furloughed and will later be dismissed simply because they are of Jewish origin.

For me personally, revering those who died in the war and grateful to those who survived and to the wounded who suffered, such treatment of Jewish war veterans in the civil service is altogether intolerable. I am convinced that you, Herr Chancellor, share these human feelings and therefore I most sincerely urge you to concern yourself with this matter and to see to it that an honorable solution for the entire civil service is found. I believe that civil servants, judges, teachers, and lawyers who were wounded in the war or fought at the front, or are sons of those who died or had sons died in battle must—insofar as they have not given cause to be treated otherwise—be allowed to continue in their professions. If they were worthy to fight and bleed for Germany, then they should also be considered worthy to continue serving the fatherland in their professions.[6]

Hitler replied the next day, expatiating on the harmful effects of the Jewish presence in public life and the professions, and particularly on the deprivations suffered by German war veterans whom the Jews had displaced in the civil service. Nevertheless, taking into consideration the Marshal's "generous and humane" approach and his "noble motives," Hitler promised that Hindenburg's suggestions would be incorporated in a law on this question that was being prepared: "The solution of this problem will be carried out legally, and not by capricious acts."[7]

Anti-Jewish legislation was a familiar idea to the Nazis. From the earliest days of their parliamentary activity they had introduced anti-Jewish bills into the Reichstag and the state parliaments. In 1924, while Hitler was writing his memoirs in Landsberg, his party comrades had joined with like-minded groups in an election bloc and won thirty-two seats in the Reichstag. Frick held one, remaining in the Reichstag until he joined the Cabinet in 1933. On May 27, 1924, the Nazis introduced a motion "to place all members of the Jewish race under special legislation [*Sonderrecht*]." A few months later they proposed a bill to "exclude members of the Jewish race from all public offices in the Reich" and to "bring about their immediate removal from office." Frick, on July 17, 1925, addressed himself especially to the question of civil servants and proposed a bill, "Reduction of Personnel," which would dismiss from the civil service "the so-called officials of the revolution" and "members of the Jewish race." In explaining the motivation of his bill to the members of the Reichstag, Frick declared: "We deem it below our dignity to be governed by people of that race."[8]

In 1930, with 107 Nazis in the Reichstag, there was a spate of Nazi-initiated legislation, including a "socialist" measure to expropriate without indemnification the "bank and stock-exchange princes" for "the welfare of the German people as a whole." The same was to be done with the property of all East European Jews in Germany and of "persons of foreign race." That particular bill, introduced on October 14, 1930, turned the National Socialists into a national laughing stock. Hitler's financial backers, industrialists and bankers, were incensed at such radicalism. On their protest, Hitler then ordered his deputies to withdraw the bill. The Communists promptly reintroduced it, in its original Nazi wording; on Hitler's orders, the NSDAP deputies voted against their own bill.[9] But only the National Socialists laughed when, in 1938, Jewish property, private and communal, was expropriated without indemnification for "the welfare of the German people as a whole."

Some legislative proposals that the National Socialists sponsored were incorporated in the twenty-five-point program that Hitler had introduced at that memorable meeting of the Deutsche Arbeiterpartei on February 24, 1920. According to that program, Jews could not be citizens of Germany and hence could not hold public office. But the NSDAP program was itself derivative, drawing on a reservoir of anti-Semitic legislative proposals that had preceded it. The most influential, no doubt, was Heinrich Class's famous work, *Wenn Ich der Kaiser wär'*, in which these specific measures were enumerated:

All public offices, whether national, state, or municipal, salaried or honorary, are closed to Jews.

Jews are not admitted to serve in the army or navy.

Jews have neither an active nor a passive right to vote. The occupation of lawyer and teacher is forbidden to them, also the direction of theaters.

Newspapers on which Jews work must make that known; newspapers that may be called "German" are not permitted to be owned by Jews or to have Jewish managers or coworkers.

Banks that are not purely personal enterprises are not permitted to have any Jewish directors.

In the future rural property may not be owned by Jews or mortgaged by them.

As compensation for the protection that Jews enjoy as aliens, they must pay double the taxes that Germans pay.[10]

German anti-Semites regarded Class's book as "trailblazing," and his influence on the National Socialists was decisive. Paul Bang, in the early days a leading member of Class's Alldeutscher Verband and in 1933 State Secretary in the Ministry of Economy, regarded Class's book, which he called an "excellent treatise," as a "gold mine" of ideas.[11] On March 6, 1933, Bang sent a "personal" and unofficial letter to Hans Heinrich Lammers, secretary of the Reich Chancellery, suggesting that the time was ripe for "consciously Volkist" legislation. He proposed a law halting further East European Jewish immigration and another nullifying all name changes that had taken place since November 1, 1918. Lammers passed these recommendations on to Frick. He, for his part, had his own experts and thick files of draft bills on the "Jewish question."

In 1928, when the NSDAP was rapidly expanding, the party organization was divided into two sections: one whose task was to attack and undermine the Weimar regime, the second whose function was to plan for eventual takeover and the new state. Helmut Nicolai (1895–1951), a former official in the Prussian state government, was assigned to plan for the Ministry of the Interior. In the two years before the accession to power, he and his staff prepared memoranda and legislative proposals. An NSDAP memorandum of that time indicated the party's intentions: "If the NSDAP will receive an absolute majority, Jews will be deprived of their rights by legal means. If however, the NSDAP will attain power only through a coalition, the rights of German Jews will be undermined through administrative means."[12]

As a matter of fact, Nicolai had declared openly in 1932 that the NSDAP wanted to attain power legally and that it would respect the legal constitution: "But that does not mean that the NSDAP defends the spirit of equal law, like the present power-holders, whose 'system,' that is, Jewish-Roman legal ideas, we oppose."[13] Indeed, he went on to predict that the naturalization of Jews and "other people of alien race" would be rescinded when the "legitimate representation of the German Volk" came to power. All name changes, too, would be nullified, to prevent further racial contamination. The administration of justice would see to it that the courts and all government administration (civil service) would be "cleansed" of Jews.

Hitler's 1920 party program had demanded "that the Roman law which serves as a materialist ordering of the world shall be replaced by German Common Law." According to Nicolai, who was closely following party doctrine, "Jewish-Roman law" derived from the idea of a world state, which erased and eliminated national differences. In contraposition stood "Nordic, Teutonic, Germanic law," based on Volk and race. "When we utter the word 'race,'" said Nicolai, addressing German lawyers October 2, 1933, "we are sounding the *leitmotiv* of National Socialism and of the National Socialist state. There is absolutely nothing that we, that the new state, do not consider or appraise under the aspect of race."[14]

The legislation that Hitler's government began to enact sanctioned what violence had already accomplished to a considerable extent—the elimination of Jews from government service and public life. On April 7, two days after Hitler's letter to Hindenburg promising a "legal" solution to the "Jewish problem," the first anti-Jewish law in the Third Reich was promulgated. Eventually, some four hundred laws and decrees were enacted, inexorably leading to the destruction of the European Jews. The first decree, entitled "Law for the Restoration of the Professional Civil Service," authorized the elimination from the civil service of Jews and political opponents of the Nazi regime.[15] "Civil servants of non-Aryan descent must retire," and honorary officials "must be discharged." Hindenburg's objections were met in a paragraph exempting "officials who were already employed as civil servants on or before August 1, 1914, or who, during the World War, fought at the front for Germany or her allies, or whose fathers or sons were killed in action in the World War."

A companion law, promulgated at the same time, canceled the admission to the bar of lawyers of "non-Aryan" descent and denied permission to those already admitted to practice law, with the Hindenburg exemptions. In rapid succession came similar laws excluding Jews from posts as lay assessors, jurors, and commercial judges (April 7), patent lawyers (April 22), panel physicians in state social-insurance institutions (April 22), dentists and dental technicians associated with those institutions (June 2). On April 25 the Law Against the Overcrowding of German Schools and Institutions of Higher Learning was promulgated, limiting the attendance of "non-Aryan" Germans to a proportion to be "determined uniformly for the entire Reich territory." An accompanying executive decree set that ratio for the admission of new pupils at 1.5 percent until the proportion of "non-Aryans" would be reduced to a maximum of 5 percent. On May 6 the Law for the Restoration of the Professional Civil Service was extended to affect honorary professors, university lecturers, and notaries. With the promulgation of three more laws—the first forbidding the employment by government authorities of "non-Aryans" or of persons married to them (September 28, 1933); the second establishing a Reich Chamber of Culture (September 29, 1933), which saw to the exclusion of Jews from cultural and entertainment enterprises (art, literature, theater, motion pictures); and the third, the National Press Law (October 4, 1933), placing political newspapers under state supervision and applying the so-called Aryan paragraph to newspapermen—the Nazi regime had accomplished a cardinal objective toward which German professionals and academicians had striven as far back as 1847: the exclusion of Jews from public life, government, culture, and the professions.[16]

To simplify and clarify this procedure, a decree defining a "non-Aryan" was promulgated on April 11. A "non-Aryan" was anyone "descended from non-Aryan, especially Jewish, parents or grandparents." Descent was "non-Aryan" even if only one parent or grandparent was "non-Aryan": "This is to be assumed especially if one parent or grandparent was of Jewish faith." Thus, in cases of "racial" ambiguity, the religious affiliation would be decisive. Every civil servant had to prove "Aryan" descent, through submission of the appropriate documents—birth certificates and parents' marriage certificate. (Eventually, elaborate genealogical questionnaires had to be answered.) Finally, to deal with ambiguous or exceptional cases, the decree provided that "if Aryan descent is doubtful, an opinion must be obtained from the expert on racial research attached by the Reich Minister of the Interior."

The Nazi definition was simple: a Jew is a Jew is a Jew—that is, down to the third generation.* The files of the Ministry of the Interior probably bulged with legal formulas defining who was a Jew. Precedents in the anti-Semitic literature were abundant. Rudolf Jung, an Austrian Nazi, in the book *Der nationale Sozialismus*, first published in 1919, declared that proof of "German blood" must be furnished down to the third generation, meaning that all grandparents must be of "German blood." At about the same time, Gottfried zur Beek (Ludwig Müller) published, as a supplement to the German translation of the *Protocols of the Elders of Zion, a Deutsche Judenordnung* ("German Regulations for Jews"), with a somewhat more cumbersome definition: "All persons are considered as Jews whose ancestors belonged to a community of Mosaic faith until the issuance of the Edict on Jews of March 11, 1812, in Prussia,† or the equivalent laws in other states of the German Federation."[17]

Class had a more manageable definition: "A Jew is one who on January 18, 1871,‡ belonged to the Jewish religious community, as well as all offspring of persons who were then Jews, even if only one parent was or is Jewish." In practice, Class's definition worked out to three generations, according to his own illustration: "The grandchild, for example, of a Jewish convert to Protestantism in 1875, whose daughter married a non-Jew, for example, an officer, would be considered as a Jew."[18]

Three other laws were promulgated in 1933 that

---

* Hilberg cites a passage from Hellmut von Gerlach's *Von Rechts nach Links* (Zurich, 1937), which states that the anti-Semites in the Wilhelminian Reichstag did not propose any anti-Semitic legislation because they could not agree on a definition of who was a Jew. But Gerlach was wrong. Those deputies proposed many bills. The stumbling block was not in the definition of a Jew, but in the fact that such anti-Jewish draft legislation was transparently illegal under the North German Federation Reichstag Act of 1869 and the Weimar Constitution. The legislators of the Third Reich had no such problem.

† The reference is to Hardenberg's edict emancipating the Prussian Jews.

‡ The date of the founding of the German Empire, when Wilhelm I was inaugurated.

were taken from the standard anti-Semitic and Volkist treasury of legislative proposals. On April 21, a law was promulgated banning *shehita*, Jewish ritual slaughtering of animals for food. Anti-shehita agitation long predated the Nazis and was a staple of all anti-Semitic propaganda that depicted the procedure of shehita as brutal and inhumane. The Nazis preempted the issue. During the 1920s they sponsored an anti-shehita campaign in the state parliaments, and under their influence, Bavaria enacted an anti-shehita law in 1930. (No other legislation affecting the practice of Judaism was enacted.)

The Law on the Revocation of Naturalization and Annulment of German Citizenship, promulgated July 14, canceled, on Volkist grounds, naturalization of "undesirables," which had been granted during the lifetime of the Weimar Republic. The law's executive order (July 26) specified East European Jews as political undesirables, even if they had committed no offense. On September 29 the Hereditary Farm Law was issued, stipulating that only those farmers could inherit farm property who could prove that their ancestors had no Jewish blood as far back as 1800. This was evocative of the "Anti-Semites' Petition" of 1880, which had complained that rural land, "the most significant preservative basis of our political structure," was falling increasingly into Jewish hands.

By October 1933, a little more than six months since the Enabling Act had been passed, the National Socialists had succeeded in establishing a "uniquely German legal system," a phrase taken from a joyful pledge of support given to Hitler by the German Federation of Judges. With German thoroughness, the laws had seen to it that the Jews were dismissed from all positions in public life—government, professions, and all of Germany's social, educational, and cultural institutions. Both instrumental and affective purposes were served by the enactment of this legislation. For one thing, thousands of jobs became available. Furthermore, the ouster of the Jews brought high elation, solidified party loyalty, and augmented party strength.

What had begun as popular anti-Semitism, when the taste of victory had stimulated the taste for blood, now received complete legal sanction.

Hitler was consolidating his power. His will was transmitted through decrees; through the courts, whose judges had slavishly prostrated themselves before National Socialism; through the terror of the swaggering SA on the streets and the elitist SS in the concentration camps; and in the relentless flow of propaganda, in print, on the radio, and at the mass meetings. All sources of opposition had been crushed or had collapsed. Socialist and Communist leaders had been arrested or had fled. The Protestant clergy assented and gave their blessing. The Catholics were kept in line by the Concordat with the Vatican, ratified September 10, 1933; their religious rights and institutions were paid for by yielding political rights. Most professors and intellectuals, like most lawyers and judges, in an unparalleled abdication of mind and honor, submitted to the National Socialist state and enhanced it with their prestige. The army, scenting that it would be restored to grandeur and fully reactivated, climbed on the bandwagon.

The only dissatisfaction, it seemed, came from the SA, which had by the end of 1933 become a behemoth of four million, but whose leader, Ernst Röhm, felt unrewarded in the National Socialist state. Hitler began to regard the SA as a threat to his authority. Even though Röhm had been one of his old comrades from the Reichswehr days in Munich of 1919, Hitler did not hesitate to move against him. Over a period of months the SS and the army were readied, at Hitler's orders, to attack the SA. It was then that the SS emerged as the "elite" party military organization that would eventually dominate all Europe; it was then that the army smelled its great opportunity. On June 30, 1934, about two hundred SA men, including Röhm himself, were murdered with unspeakable brutality. The SA was finished as a major force in the German dictatorship and would henceforth exist under the shadow of the SS.

The ugly massacre was misunderstood within Germany and outside. Instead of seeing that Germany was being run, in Gerhart Ritter's characterization, by "a gang of criminals" who did not hesitate to shoot each other down with the vilest cruelty, many Germans believed that the purge of the SA represented Hitler's wish to halt the arbitrary terror of the SA in the streets and to restore a measure of legality to the country. After Hindenburg's death on August 2 and Hitler's "legal" merger of the chancellorship and the presidency, people hoped that things would somehow settle down. No significant anti-Jewish legislation was enacted during 1934, and that fact, too, reinforced the illusion that Jews might remain in Germany, albeit with limited rights.

Nineteen-thirty-five brought Hitler new triumphs that had repercussions on the Jews. The year opened with a plebiscite in the Saar, for which the Nazis had launched a propaganda campaign as far back as 1933. It paid off, when 90 percent of the voters supported reunion with Germany. That victory released some of Germany's restraints in international politics. On March 16 Hitler publicly repudiated those clauses of the Versailles Treaty that had disarmed Germany, and he announced the inauguration of compulsory universal military service in Germany. The European powers were dismayed, but using a formula that he would apply time and again with repeated success despite repeated deception, Hitler allayed their fears. In a major foreign-policy address on May 21, 1935, he offered to conclude bilateral nonaggression pacts with all Germany's neighbors and solemnly assured the world that he wanted only peace.

The mood in Germany was exuberant. German rearming and remilitarization had restored what the National Socialists liked to call German national honor. With an abundance of boisterous aggression to spend, in the absence of an external enemy, the Germans turned with renewed fervor against the internal enemy. Just as the Crusaders, who could not contain their passion for deliverance before they reached the Holy Land, struck the infidel in their midst, so too did the Germans. At the end of March 1935 acts of terror and boycotts of Jewish businesses were renewed. All local and national NSDAP party organizations and their associated institutions joined in a massive discharge of hate and violence. During the summer of 1935 Jews were prevented from going into cinemas, theaters, swimming pools, resorts. Small businesses were paralyzed by boycott and by violence, particularly in Berlin's main shopping street. Jewish newspapers were forced to suspend publication for periods of two or three months. But, precipitously, the party called a halt. The *Schwarze Korps,* organ of the SS, then editorialized: "The Jewish question is one of our people's most burning problems; it will not be solved by terror in the streets."

The records are not clear, but we can surmise that the violence against business was held to be premature. Besides, Hitler and most of his Cabinet increasingly showed a dislike of authentically spontaneous mob violence that was unpredictable and ungovernable. Though the party had become the state, the view of party leaders and Cabinet ministers differed sharply. At a conference called by Reichsbank President Hjalmar Schacht, August 20, 1935, of the heads of departments of the Ministry of Economy, the disagreement was overt and acrimonious.[19] Schacht condemned the "irresponsible Jew-baitings" because they diminished his ability to perform his duties effectively. He especially referred to repercussions abroad. Frick, who was present, had even drafted an order to the state governments demanding ruthless police intervention in "illegal actions" against the Jews. (The order was never issued because it was feared that it would be construed as capitulation to "international Jewry" and tantamount to admission of the extent of the terror, which had hitherto been officially minimized.) Despite the general tenor of the meeting, which favored legal measures to exclude the Jews from economic life, the NSDAP continued to justify "radical action" against them for "politico-emotional and abstract ideological considerations."

As once before in 1933, so now in 1935, the violence of anti-Semitism was channeled into law. On the occasion of the annual NSDAP congress in Nuremberg, new anti-Jewish laws, the so-called "Nuremberg Laws," were adopted unanimously by the Reichstag, on September 15, 1935. These laws legitimated racist anti-Semitism and turned the "purity of German blood" into a legal category. They forbade marriage and extramarital relations between Germans and Jews and disenfranchised those "subjects" or "nationals" of Germany who were not of German blood.

As with previous legislation, the Nuremberg Laws validated practices already in effect through administrative order or NSDAP pressure. As early as October 1933, the mayor of Mainz had instructed the Mainz Registry Office to inform him of every announcement of an impending marriage between a "person of German origin" and a "racial Jew." The information was to be transmitted to the regional NSDAP, which would then "suggest" that the German partner reconsider the marriage in view of the problems that would arise as a consequence. The Registry Office was also to point out to the German partner the difficulties that might ensue from such a marriage, with regard to employment and offspring.[20] The Mainz directives were not an isolated instance in Germany. The combined pressure of state and party, as delineated in the Mainz order, was being exerted wherever an impending "mixed" marriage became known in Germany. Mob law was not uncommon in forcing a halt to such marriages.

Nicolai, in his speech of October 2, 1933, had characterized the regulation of marriage for the purpose of maintaining the racial purity of Nordic stock as the "first legally creative act of the Nordic people." Even earlier, in June 1932, Göring, in a campaign speech, promised that not only would all Jews be removed from government offices and public life, but he specifically pledged also that the Nazis would not allow marriages between Germans and Jews. For years this racial/sexual prohibition had been a staple of Streicher's *Stürmer* and it can no doubt be traced back to racist pornographers like Lanz von Liebenfels whose writings had titillated Hitler in his early days. Fritsch's "Ten German Commandments of Lawful Self-Defense," in his *Antisemiten-Katechismus*, contained two "commandments" for maintaining racial purity, whose spirit the Nuremberg Laws later captured:

> Thou shalt keep thy blood pure. Consider it a crime to soil the noble Aryan breed of thy people by mingling it with the Jewish breed. For thou must know that Jewish blood is everlasting, putting the Jewish stamp on body and soul unto the farthest generations.
> Thou shalt have no social intercourse with the Jew. Avoid all contact and community with the Jew and keep him away from thyself and thy family, especially thy daughters, lest they suffer injury of body and soul.[21]

Nicolai had tried to legitimate Volkist racial legislation through tradition and claimed to base himself on the *Sachsenspiegel,* an authoritative legal code in northern Germany, circa 1230, which was allegedly purely Germanic, uninfluenced by Roman law. But the centrality of Volk and race in Nazi legal thought actually derived not from the *Sachsenspiegel,* but from *Mein Kampf.* There was one specific passage in which Hitler rambled on about purity and its importance in the light of the "syphilization" of the German people. This provided the rationale for National Socialist racial legislation: *"Blood sin and desecration of the race are the original sin in this world and the end of a humanity which surrenders to it."* In Hitler's mind, the "fight against syphilis" was associated with a campaign against prostitution and the restoration of the true purpose of marriage—offspring. Marriage, Hitler wrote, cannot be an end in itself, but "must serve the one higher goal, the increase and preservation of the species and race." Indeed, Hitler had already conceived of the state's regulating marriage for racial purposes in *Mein Kampf*: "*A folkish state must therefore begin by raising marriage from the level of continuous defilement of the race, and give it the consecration of an institution which is called upon to produce images of the Lord and not monstrosities halfway between man and ape.*" The ape-men of Lanz von Liebenfels' *Ostara* were apparently still vivid in Hitler's mind. Within a very short time after their accession to power, the Nazis began to promulgate laws whose purpose was to "increase and preserve" the German people biologically. On June 1, 1933, a Law for the Reduction of Unemployment was issued, whose Section 5, "Encouragement of Marriages," offered financial aid to needy young couples wishing to marry, with remittances of the loan for each child born. Candidates for such state aid had to submit certificates attesting to personal and "racial" health and also pass a test of political health, that is, loyalty to the Nazi state. This dual qualification of racial purity and political loyalty foreshadowed the qualifications for Reich citizenship as defined in the Nuremberg Laws.

On June 28, 1933, Frick spoke at the first meeting of the Council of Experts on Population and Race Policy: "Only when the State and the public-health authorities will strive to make the core of their responsibilities the provision for the yet unborn, then we can speak of a new era and of a reconstructed population and race policy." As a first step, he concentrated on the necessity of preventing those afflicted with serious hereditary diseases from reproducing themselves. A law to this effect was promulgated on July 14, legalizing sterilization for nine categories of people afflicted with hereditary disease. The law empowered so-called Hereditary Health Courts to carry out sterilization even against the will of the individual concerned.

Soon a host of institutions would come into being for racial breeding and purification. The preservation of German racial purity—"positve" eugenics—was as important an aspect of racial policy in National Socialist legislation as the exclusion of Jewish "impurity." The "euthanasia" program eventually followed as a logical consequence.

The disenfranchisement of the Jews embodied the most fundamental demand of every anti-Semitic movement from the start of the Emancipation. The NSDAP program of 1920 clearly related citizenship to race:

> Only those who are our fellow Germans [*Volksgenosse*] shall be citizens of our state. Only those who are of German blood can be considered as our fellow Germans regardless of creed. Hence no Jew can be regarded as a fellow German.
>
> Those who are not citizens of the state must live in Germany as foreigners and must be subject to the law of aliens.

Early in January 1934 Nicolai, now president of Magdeburg, published his ideas of appropriate draft legislation for citizenship in the National Socialist state. There were to be four categories: (1) full-blooded "Aryan" citizens, (2) foreigners residing in Germany, (3) Germans residing abroad, (4) Germans of alien blood, specifically Jews, Poles, and Gypsies. (The categories, except for Germans residing abroad, were all taken from Hitler's discussion of "Subjects and Citizens" in *Mein Kampf*.) The fourth category would have the protection of the state, but would not be allowed to hold public office, marry, or have sexual relations with, "Aryans."[22] That proposal was likely a product of Nicolai's apprentice years, before his accession to power, and similar draft bills must have bulked in the files of the Ministry of the Interior.

On July 27, 1935, just seven weeks before the promulgation of the Nuremberg Laws, Frick sent a memorandum to all states informing them that marriages between Aryans and non-Aryans would shortly be regulated by law. He instructed all registry offices to postpone not only such marriages, but even their announcement.[23] Still, nothing was done until Hitler decided, suddenly and unexpectedly, on September 13, that he wanted such legislation for the special ceremonial session of the Reichstag on September 15, to mark the festive closing of the party congress. The only law in preparation for that occasion was one forbidding the Jews to display the Nazi flag, which Hitler had thought of as a response to a demonstration in New York on July 26, 1935, when the swastika flag was ripped off the SS *Bremen*. Hitler now wanted something more spectacular and told Frick to prepare legislation regulating German-Jewish "blood" relationships.

Frick put Hans Pfundtner and Wilhelm Stuckart, his two top men in the Ministry, both then in Nuremberg, on the assignment. Needing the various draft bills in the files in Berlin, Stuckart telephoned Bernhard Lösener, the expert on "racial law" in the Ministry, and instructed him to fly to Nuremberg with the files.[24] Lösener arrived Saturday morning, September 14, and from then until about 3:00 A.M. on September 15, they composed drafts of bills that Frick then brought to Hitler for his consideration. Before long the Law for the Protection of German Blood and German Honor, whose basic provisions Hitler had outlined to Frick, was completed. Its preamble declared:

Imbued with the insight that the purity of German blood is prerequisite for the continued existence of the German people, and inspired by the inflexible will to ensure the existence of the German nation for all times, the Reichstag has unanimously adopted the following law, which is hereby promulgated.

The provisions were simplicity itself: marriage between Jews and "nationals of German kindred blood" was forbidden; extramarital relations between the two groups were forbidden. Jews were forbidden to employ female domestic help under forty-five years of age who were of "German or kindred blood."* Finally, Jews were forbidden to fly the German national colors, but could display "Jewish" colors.

Then Hitler asked them to prepare a basic Reich citizenship law. This took about an hour to prepare, and Hitler accepted the first draft. In line with Hitler's views in *Mein Kampf* and with the NSDAP program of 1920, this law gave the Jews a special status as subjects in Germany, reminiscent of a medieval Teutonic "law of aliens." The Reich Citizenship Law distinguished between a subject (*Staatsangehörige*) and a citizen of the Reich (*Reichsbürger*). A subject was anyone who enjoyed the protection of the Reich and was therefore obligated to it. A Reich citizen was a subject with "German or cognate blood" and acquired a "Reich certificate of citizenship," a reward that Hitler had already conceived in *Mein Kampf*.

The Reich Citizenship Law, as State Secretary Stuckart and his assistant, Hans Globke, explained in their commentary on German racial legislation, represented a revolutionary break from past concepts of individual rights and freedoms.[25] National Socialism, confronting the doctrines of the past on the equality of men, discovered that these doctrines did not take cognizance of the inequality of men, of their racial and national differences. Differences in rights and obligations should derive from racial differences, and that was the achievement of the Reich Citizenship Law. National Socialism conceived the state as the political instrument of the Volk. Consequently, citizenship was not a matter of individual rights but derived from membership in the Volk. "The recognition of the significance of blood and race for Volk and State," they wrote, "is one of the principal bases of the National Socialist world view." Yet even race did not suffice as a criterion for citizenship in this racial state.

---

* Psychoanalysts see in this a projection of Hitler's anxieties about his own origins, but the idea was commonplace in National Socialist ideology. A demand that Jews be forbidden to employ "Aryan" women as servants appeared, for instance, in Streicher's *Stürmer,* January 2, 1934.

Additionally, the Reich subject of German or cognate blood also had to prove by his conduct that he was "willing and able loyally to serve the German people and the Reich." Thus Reich citizenship was bestowed upon those both racially pure and politically subservient. *Kadavergehorsam* (slavish obedience) had long been regarded as an unfortunate German trait. Now it had its political reward. Yet the Reich Citizenship Law perpetrated a fantastic hoax upon the Germans. The Reich citizen was declared to be the "sole bearer of full political rights." But rights no longer existed in Germany. There were no political parties, no elections, no freedoms, no protection. The only right a citizen had was to give his assent—by shouting himself hoarse at mass rallies or by voting "*Ja*" in one of the five plebiscites that Hitler had substituted for political democracy. For unless the Reich citizen was *kadavergehorsam,* he would more likely be cadaver than citizen.

The Jews, however, were not hoaxed. The law and its thirteen supplementary decrees (the last published July 1, 1943) set the Jews apart from the Germans legally, politically, socially. Henceforth, they would be outside the protection of the state. Eventually, they would be completely at the mercy of the secret police, without access to law or courts. Indeed, the *Sachsenspiegel* had been far more humane in the protection it afforded the Jew as alien.

The centrality of "blood and race" that obsessed National Socialism was transformed with bureaucratic fastidiousness into legal racial categories. While drafting the Law for the Protection of German Blood and German Honor, the legal experts proposed certain distinctions among different categories of *Mischlinge,* the "mixed" offspring of Germans and Jews. Hitler had rejected these at the time, but left their legal clarification for supplementary decrees. After weeklong conferences of legal and racial experts (Hitler had himself called a meeting on this subject), the Ministry of the Interior finally arrived at a set of definitions of the different categories of Mischlinge.

The basic definition of a Jew, supplanting the definition of April 11, 1933, was published November 14, 1935, in the first supplementary decree to the Reich Citizenship Law. Later regulations defined categories of Mischlinge that did not come under the rubric of "Jew."

Briefly, the categories were: (1) Jew, (2) Mischling, first degree, and (3) Mischling, second degree. A Jew was anyone with at least three full Jewish grandparents. Also legally to be regarded as a Jew was someone who had two full Jewish grandparents and who belonged to the Jewish religious community when the law was promulgated September 15, 1935, or who joined later, or who was married to a Jew then or later, or (looking to the future) who was the offspring of a marriage contracted with a Jew after September 15, 1935, or who was born out of wedlock after July 31, 1936, the offspring of extramarital relations with a Jew. Anyone who was one-eighth or one-sixteenth Jewish—with one Jewish great-grandparent or great-great-grandparent—would be considered as of German blood.

More complicated was the status of the "part-Jews." A person with two Jewish grandparents, who did not otherwise fit into the group defined as Jews, that is, who was not affiliated with the Jewish religious community, who was not married to a Jew, etc., was designated as "Mischling, first degree." A person with only one Jewish grandparent was designated as "Mischling, second degree." For the time being, these distinctions affected marriage and offspring of that marriage. Within a few short years they were to decide between life or death.

The Nuremberg Laws completed the disenfranchisement of the Jews of Germany. The first stage of the National Socialist program had been achieved. Hitler himself, in introducing the laws to the Reichstag assembled at Nuremberg, hinted at a forthcoming change in anti-Jewish policy. The Law for the Protection of German Blood and German Honor, he said, was "an attempt to regulate by law a problem that, in the event of repeated failure, would have to be transferred by law to the National Socialist Party for final solution."[26]

During the next few years no substantial anti-Jewish legislation was enacted. Instead the SS, the most prestigious and dreaded branch of the National Socialist movement, increasingly began to assert its hegemony with regard to the Jews over all state and party institutions.

4

The SS: Instrument of the Final Solution

In 1936 a standard lecture for SS units contained the following passage: "The Jew is a parasite. Wherever he flourishes, the people die. . . . Elimination of the Jew from our community is to be regarded as an emergency defense measure."[1] The "right of emergency defense" was the title Hitler used for the last chapter of *Mein Kampf,* in which he had advocated the gassing of "twelve or fifteen thousand" Jews. The SS text reveals the emerging role of the SS as an expression of Hitler's will and as the central executing arm in the Final Solution of the Jewish Question.

The SS came into being early in 1925, by Hitler's order, as a select corps drawn from SA membership to serve as an efficient, elite, and completely dependable bodyguard for the party's leadership. The emphasis from the start was on loyalty, obedience, and discipline, but the SS remained insignificant in size and undistinguished in function until Hitler appointed Heinrich Himmler to head it and conferred upon him, in January 1929, the grandiose title of Reichsführer-SS. Himmler soon transformed the SS into an organization guided solely by the will of the Führer and that became, in Hans Buchheim's words, "the real and essen-

93

tial instrument of the Führer's authority."[2] Indeed,
Himmler came to regard himself as an instrument of
Hitler's will.

Himmler's name and title have come to evoke images
of a demonic evil contained within a frame of steely
iciness, rigor, and discipline, unloosed not in the
passion of rage or hate, but on calculation. Yet his
early life, shaped by familial authoritarianism, seemed
ordinary and dull, never suggestive of the sinister role
he would later assume.

Born in 1900 in Munich, the second son of middle-
class Catholic parents, Himmler had an unexceptional
youth. The diary that he started to keep in 1914 shows
him as pedantic, pedestrian, and unimaginative, already molded according to the parental tradition of
rigid self-discipline. When war broke out, he was
stricken with patriotic passion. At seventeen, when he
reached the age of eligibility, he applied to an officer
training program and was eventually admitted, but
while he was still in training the armistice was signed.
However, the cadets in training were not discharged
until after the military had suppressed the revolution,
dissolved its institutions, and regained political control. Here the young Himmler may have had his first
lessons in the uses of the military for political suppression.

Nineteen-nineteen was the critical year for Himmler
as it had been for Hitler. During his military training,
Himmler was no doubt indoctrinated in rightist-
nationalist politics. Surely there was talk about the
Dolchstoss, betrayal by the Jews, and the "Jewish"
role in the abortive Communist revolution that he
witnessed. It must have been an extraordinary revelation. In mid-1919, while recuperating from an illness
—he was always sickly and ailing—he read twenty-
eight books, some of which showed his newly developing interest in politics and war as well as in anti-
Semitism and anti-Masonry.[3] Of a tract replete with
anti-Semitic anecdotes, which drew lavishly from
the *Protocols of the Elders of Zion* and which depicted
Jews, Freemasons, and democrats as fomenters of

revolution, Himmler noted in his diary: "A book that explains everything and tells us whom we must fight against next time." He was to continue reading this kind of literature for the next few years.

Early in 1920 Himmler joined the *Einwohnerwehr,* a home-guard force, one of the many military and paramilitary groups formed by ex-soldiers reluctant to abandon military pursuits, whose nationalist bias intensified their discontent with Germany's new democratic government. Later that year, having decided that he would be a farmer, he enrolled in an agricultural training school and undertook to do his practical training on a farm. During this period, living in relative isolation, his nationalist political passion seemed to have been stilled, but shortly after his return to Munich at the end of 1921, he renewed his interest in rightist politics. He resumed his anti-Semitic reading, which now included Houston Stewart Chamberlain's booklet *Rasse und Nation,* of which he wrote in his diary: "It is true and one has the impression that it is objective, not just hate-filled anti-Semitism. Because of this it has more effect. These terrible Jews."

German racial notions began to absorb him. He had apparently renewed his contacts with the paramilitary and clandestine nationalist organizations then flourishing in Munich, and seemed eager to participate in their activities. When he completed agricultural school, he got a job just outside Munich with a nitrogen fertilizer company, reflecting, no doubt, a streak of coprophilia. While there, in the fall of 1922, he joined the *Reichsflagge,* one of the military groups under Ernst Röhm's leadership, and in August 1923, following Röhm, Himmler joined the NSDAP. The next month he quit his job and joined the Bavarian Reichswehr, fulfilling his boyhood warrior ambitions. In Hitler's attempted putsch that November, Himmler was the ensign bearer for Röhm's military formations. Although the ignominious failure of the putsch and the subsequent suppression of the rightist nationalist organizations (including the NSDAP) depressed

Himmler, they did not weaken the magnetism that drew him to rightist politics.

Early in 1924 he joined the *Nationalsozialistische Freiheitsbewegung* (NSFB; National Socialist Freedom Movement), headed by General Ludendorff and Gregor Strasser, one of the new Volkist organizations set up as a substitute for the banned NSDAP. He threw himself intensively into work for Volkist causes, speaking and writing. He stopped looking for work, lost touch with his old friends and his old way of life. But his reading habits and his literary taste persisted without change. About half the books he read were anti-Semitic or Volkist, or at the very least, elicited anti-Semitic comments that he set down in his diary. He discovered Fritsch's *Handbuch der Judenfrage,* in which "one can find all the relevant material. . . . If only some of the eternally blind could have it put before their eyes." He read avidly about Hitler and was deeply impressed by Eckart's *Der Bolschewismus von Moses bis Lenin,* which he promised himself to reread often. In 1924 Himmler wrote of Hitler that he "is truly a great man, and above all a genuine and pure one. His speeches are splendid works of Germandom and Aryanism."

About this time, too, Himmler discovered that his interest in agriculture could be brought into a racial context. He is believed to have come under the influence of the *Artamanen Bund,* a racialist utopian group that held that a nation could be kept vital and creative only through the existence of peasant communities of racial and national purity. This pseudomystical and occultist doctrine of "blood and soil" deeply affected him, but would not find an outlet until after he had attained sufficient confidence in himself and high rank in the Nazi party to indulge in such exercises. (Hitler, though himself attracted to occultist Volkism, had learned the lesson of Schönerer's failure and tried to discourage these tendencies within the party.)

In June 1924 Himmler finally found a job he wanted, one that would satisfy him ideologically and provide him with the political environment he had come to need. He became secretary and general assistant to Strasser, who was the NSFB Gauleiter for Lower Bavaria. Early in May 1925 the whole Strasser organization, lock, stock, and barrel, went over to the NSDAP, which Hitler had begun to rebuild after his release from Landsberg. Thus Himmler automatically became the NSDAP Deputy Gauleiter of Lower Bavaria. A year later, when Strasser became the party's propaganda leader, Himmler was once again made his deputy. In 1927 Himmler was appointed deputy leader of the SS, and finally, in 1929, at the age of twenty-nine, with the appointment as Reichs-führer-SS, he emerged at the top of the field in his chosen career—the professional Nazi.

As Reichsführer-SS Himmler was able to integrate his diverse compulsions and obsessions—with the military, the occult, racial nationalism, and anti-Semitism—and give them form and substance. The SS became a proving ground for Himmler's romantic, grandiose, and sinister ideas and offered scope for him to exercise his pedantry and his proclivities for spying and informing. It became the vehicle through which his meanness, hardness, and vindictiveness found deadly expression. His rigid sense of duty and obedience turned him into a zealot carrying out Hitler's murderous ideology with fanatical "idealism." No wonder the SS's most distinctive insignia was to become the death's-head.

The SS began, as its name, *Schutzstaffel* (Defense Corps), indicates, as an armed formation within the SA to protect the Führer, top party leaders, and party meetings. It also gathered confidential information about suspect party members. When Himmler took it over, the SS had 280 members, while the SA, its parent body and the party's paramilitary organization, had some 60,000 members. Himmler decided not just to expand the SS, but to convert it into an elite brotherhood selected according to racial criteria, permeated with a racial mystique, imbued with medieval, chivalric concepts (loyalty, honor, bravery, and the like), using the symbols and practicing the rituals of Teutonism.

The appeal to "elitism" succeeded in recruiting into the SS a broader variety of men than the down-and-outers who had joined the SA. By the end of 1930 the SS had nearly three thousand members. The enmity between the SS and SA had then become so intense that Hitler had to step in. Fearing that the SA was or might become disloyal to him, Hitler threw his support to the SS, making it independent of the SA and even giving permission for an SS black uniform to distinguish it from the SA's brown shirts. More important, Hitler expanded the SS's functions: "The task of the SS is primarily to carry out police duties within the party."[4] The SS was thenceforth to be Hitler's vigilant force, blindly dedicated to him, unflinching in its loyalty. On induction, the SS man swore an oath: "I swear to you, Adolf Hitler, as Führer and Chancellor of the German Reich, loyalty and valor. I pledge to you and to the superiors whom you will appoint obedience unto death, so help me God."

To ensure the high racial quality of SS recruits and also to lay the groundwork for Germany's future racial policy as he saw it, Himmler set up in 1931 a *Rasse- und Siedlungsamt* (RuSA; Race and Settlement Office), later *Rasse- und Siedlungshauptamt* (RuSHA; Race and Settlement Main Office). To head it he appointed Richard Walther Darré, the author of the "blood and soil" doctrine, who had strongly influenced Himmler some years before. The RuSA had as its primary function the physical and racial screening of prospective SS candidates. After Himmler's Betrothal and Marriage Order of December 31, 1931, the RuSA also investigated the racial genealogy of the prospective brides of SS members. SS members who married without permission of Himmler and the RuSA were expelled from the organization. The ultimate goal of this procedure was to form a racially superior stock from which Germany's future leadership would come.

(To encourage the bearing of racially valuable children, Himmler established within the SS in 1935 an organization called *Lebensborn*—Well of Life.)[5] This racial elite would have to return to the soil for its vitality. The RuSA conducted an intensive racial and ideological indoctrination program along these lines and Darré tried to encourage SS families to settle in rural areas. Although this rural settlement program was of no practical consequence, it prefigures the more fanatical program, on a wholesale scale, that Himmler embarked on during the war, involving population transfers and rural resettlement on a racial basis, carried out in characteristic SS fashion.

Himmler's SS grew rapidly. When the Nazis came to power, it had fifty thousand members. On the eve of the war, it had nearly a quarter of a million. Most of these men belonged to the *Allgemeine SS* (General SS), which, as it expanded, came to be organized in about thirty regional divisions. The Allgemeine SS spun off two other formations: the *Verfügungstruppe* (Reserve or Special Troops) and the *Totenkopfverbände* (Death's-Head Units).

The Verfügungstruppe originated out of political standby squads, which served as an auxiliary police force ready to go into action at any threat to Hitler, at any order from Himmler. (The most famous unit was the *Leibstandarte Adolf Hitler,* set up in March 1933.) Aware of the advantages of having his own military force, Himmler united these squads into the Verfügungstruppe, a sort of National Socialist army to be relied on in the event of treachery on the part of the regular army. In September 1934 it was accorded official status by a decree of the Defense Minister, permitting the SS to maintain "a standing armed force for such special internal political tasks as may be allotted to the SS by the Führer." By 1936 the Verfügungstruppe numbered ten thousand and even had its own cadet schools. Though service in the Verfügungstruppe under Nazi law counted as military service, the regular army resented it and until the outbreak of war refused to legitimate it as part of Germany's armed forces. On August 17, 1938, Hitler issued a secret directive clarifying the relationship between the Verfügungstruppe and the Wehrmacht in peacetime and in the event of war. The directive reaffirmed the military character of the Verfügungstruppe. In peacetime, under Himmler's command, its units—which belonged neither to the Wehrmacht nor the police, but were a permanent armed formation of the NSDAP exclusively at Hitler's disposal—were to be available for "internal political tasks." But in the event of mobilization, the Verfügungstruppe could be used by the commander-in-chief of the army, and though remaining a branch of the NSDAP, its units would then be subject to army instructions and military law.

The Totenkopfverbände originated from the guard unit at Dachau, the first concentration camp in National Socialist Germany. When the Nazis came to power, "deprivation of freedom in the form of protective custody" became the order of the day, and by March 1933 the prisons could no longer hold the thousands arrested in "preventive" measures to eliminate "threats from subversive elements."[6] Camps then were set up throughout Germany by Himmler in his capacity as head of the Bavarian police, the first at Dachau. By the summer of 1933 there were ten or more camps and detention centers, organized and operated by the SS, the SA, or the police, with over 25,000 inmates—Social Democrats, Communists, members of other opposition parties, journalists and writers (especially Jews), and various other "unpopular" categories.

In this early period, "wild improvisation," to use Martin Broszat's phrase, characterized the operation of the camps, but soon they came under Himmler's exclusive authority and were thenceforth removed from the control of the state's administrative and legal jurisdiction and operated outside the ordinary processes of law.

To reorganize the camps Himmler chose Theodor

Eicke, an SS Oberführer (brigadier general), whom he had once committed to a psychiatric clinic, then released in June 1933 for appointment as commandant at Dachau. Eiche's hardness, ruthlessness, ideological commitment, and his exemplary organization of the camp, especially his systematization of "disciplinary camp regulations," won him advancement in May 1934 to reorganize the other camps and standardize their procedures. Eicke distinguished himself a month later by personally shooting Röhm, an act for which he was rewarded on July 4, 1934, with a new title of *Inspekteur der Konzentrationslager und Führer der SS-Wachverbände* (inspector of concentration camps and commander of SS guard units) and, a week later, with a promotion in rank.

Eicke's reorganization led to consolidation of the smaller camps into larger ones with uniform procedures and administration. By March 1935 there were 7 camps, with a prison population under 10,000 (Dachau, the largest, had 2,500 inmates). The guard units were enlarged, organized in battalions, and given their chilling designation as Totenkopfverbände. Thereafter, funds for the operation of the concentration camps and for Eicke's armed-guard units came from the budget of the Ministry of the Interior. Though the number of prisoners in protective custody in the next two years declined and the small camps were closed down, two new camps were built with a capacity as large as Dachau's—Buchenwald and Sachsenhausen.

By the end of 1937 the Totenkopfverbände numbered five thousand men, in three formations that Himmler hoped to bring into his military establishment. But although the military had been forced to yield in some areas with regard to the Verfügungstruppe, they drew the line at the Totenkopfverbände, clearly an ideological organization that had no aspirations to acquire a spit-and-polish military character. After the war began, however, Himmler managed to bring some of Eicke's units into his SS army, and

along with the Verfügungstruppe, these also took part
in the military campaign in Poland. In mid-1940 the
Verfügungstruppe, augmented by Totenkopfverbände
units and police reinforcements, were redesignated as
the *Waffen-SS* (Armed SS).

High in the hierarchy of terror was the SS's *Sicherheitsdienst* (SD; Security Service). It grew into a
surveillance system that encompassed all Germany and
then all occupied Europe, an evil organizational eye
whose vigilance no one could escape. The SD was
originally established, in accordance with Hitler's
directive, in 1930, when the spy mania in the NSDAP
was rampant. A security service was wanted not just
to sniff out disloyalty and treachery in the tangle of
intraparty intrigue that threatened Hitler's leadership,
but also because the NSDAP was being infiltrated by
spies from opposition parties and by police agents of
the Weimar government. Himmler gave this new
intelligence-gathering agency a modest name—*Unter-
abteilung Ic* (Ic Subdivision), "Ic" being army code
for a section dealing with enemy intelligence. To head
this subdivision he appointed Reinhard Heydrich.

Heydrich, barely four years younger than Himmler,
had, like him, been too young for service in World War
I, but his patriotic military fervor found an outlet in
his imagination. Years later he claimed he had been
a runner in the *Freikorps* at fifteen.[7] But it is not unlikely that at sixteen he did belong to some military or
paramilitary group, perhaps a home-guard troop. During the war he is said to have developed "extreme
Volkist" ideas and turned into a "fanatic about pure
race." He joined, or tried to join, various Volkist,
nationalist organizations in the immediate postwar
years. He is said to have told a fellow cadet in the
German navy some years later that he had once been
a member of the *Deutsch-Völkische Schutz- und
Trutzbund* (German-Volkist Protective and Offensive
Alliance), an aggressively anti-Semitic rightist, nationalist group. He joined, he said, because in his home-

town of Halle his father was considered a Jew and
called "Jew Süss." This injured his pride and honor;
the only way to silence such talk, he thought, was to
be active in anti-Semitic circles. That was why he
joined the Schutz- und Trutzbund. The talk in Halle
then took a different tack: the elder Heydrich could
surely not be a Jew since his son was such a furious
anti-Semite.

The story of Heydrich's alleged Jewish ancestry
persisted during his lifetime and after. The genealogical facts are these: Heydrich's paternal grandmother
was married twice. By her first husband, Reinhold
Heydrich, she had many children, including Richard
Bruno Heydrich, Reinhard's father. After Reinhold's
death, she married a locksmith called Süss, an
Evangelical-Lutheran with impeccable "Aryan" credentials. In later years "Süss" was sometimes appended
to Bruno Heydrich's name. The Jewish attribution
came about because Süss was commonly regarded as a
Jewish surname (for example, in Lion Feuchtwanger's
novel *Jud Süss,* published in 1926). Whatever his
motivating impulse, Heydrich spent a good part of his
adolescent years in anti-Semitic and Volkist, nationalist circles where his identity as an uncompromising
anti-Semite and Nazi was shaped.

He became a naval cadet in 1922 and in a few
years had a promising career ahead of him. But early
in 1931 he was cashiered from the navy because of
scandals involving a woman. He then joined the Naval
SA, not that it offered the possibility of a career, but
presumably because of ideological compatibility and
the opportunity to continue to wear a military uniform. Since he was without a job or the possibility of
one, his sister cast about among friends and family for
useful contacts and found a leading SA officer, who
brought Heydrich to Himmler's attention.

In appearance Heydrich was the Nordic dream, the
"Blond Beast," once described as a "young evil god of
death." He was the embodiment of the SS ethos of
"hardness," a man of action, whose deeds were in-

tended to refute the gossip that he was of Jewish origin.* Hitler, in a eulogy at Heydrich's funeral, called him "the man with the iron heart." Ambitious, calculating, with an élan that the pedantic and cranky Himmler lacked, Heydrich was eventually to wield nearly as much power as Himmler himself. Indeed, within a year of his appointment, Heydrich rose rapidly to the rank of *Standartenführer* (colonel) and the Ic Subdivision emerged as the *Sicherheitsdienst* (SD) *des Reichsführers-SS* (Security Service of the Reichsführer-SS), foreshadowing the dreaded power it would exercise all over Europe.

The SD started out modestly. From Himmler's files and with a staff of three working in his own small apartment in Munich, Heydrich began to organize a card index of NSDAP opponents—those in the opposition parties, suspected spies within the Nazi party, antagonists in government posts, Jews and Catholics whose overt activities marked them as anti-Nazis. To combat these enemies (as well as to document and verify their enmity), Heydrich fashioned a network of espionage and counterespionage that in a short time enabled the SD to outdistance parallel and competing apparatuses in the NSDAP and in the SA.

After the Nazi accession to power, the demarcation between state and party became blurred and even erased. In a few years the SS and SD usurped most police functions and entangled them in their own networks. The process began on March 9, 1933, when Himmler was appointed acting police president of Munich and Heydrich was put in charge of political security. A week later the entire Bavarian political police came under Himmler's charge. Within the year Himmler had managed to become head of the political police in all the states except Prussia, where Göring

---

* In mid-1932 the rumors of Heydrich's putative Jewish ancestry led to a party investigation that finally validated his "Aryan" origins. Himmler is believed even to have discussed the matter with Hitler. They held that Heydrich's fear of being branded a Jew was so excessive that he would be everlastingly grateful to them for letting him hold his high position in the party.

maintained his authority over the Gestapo (*Geheime Staatspolizeiamt*—Secret State Police Office), established in April 1933. For some time Himmler tried to capture control of the Gestapo, and finally, in April 1934, the coveted Prussian police came into his hands. He then appointed Heydrich chief of the Gestapo. Now in control of all the police apparatus of the various German states, Himmler and Heydrich moved to consolidate their enhanced position in both party and state by undertaking to integrate the police organizations into the all-embracing network of the SS.[8]

On June 9, 1934, Hitler formalized the transfer of all NSDAP intelligence services to the SD, declaring that there was to be no other party intelligence or counterespionage service. The following month Hitler further rewarded the SS for "the great services" it had rendered in connection with the purge of the SA: "I hereby promote the SS to the status of independent organization within the framework of the NSDAP." Having attained primacy and autonomy within the party, Himmler and Heydrich moved to attain similar status in the government. After two years of a power struggle in which Frick, Göring, and the civil administrators of the Gestapo were engaged, Hitler settled the matter by issuing a decree on June 17, 1936,[9] which gave Himmler and Heydrich the authority they aspired to and which they had in fact in large measure already usurped. Himmler became, by decree, Reichsführer-SS and Chief of the German Police and could now operate autonomously, for it became impossible to disentangle his power as Reichsführer-SS from his authority as Chief of the German Police. The whole police apparatus was now centralized, nationalized, and Nazified, a part of the SS and an instrument of the Führer's will.

A few days later Himmler undertook a basic reorganization of the police, setting up two main departments: the Main Office of the *Ordnungspolizei* (Orpo; Regular Police), under Police General Kurt Daluege, and the Main Office of the *Sicherheitspolizei* (Sipo; Security Police), under Heydrich. Orpo comprised the uniformed urban and rural constabulary and the municipal police. Sipo consisted of the political police (Gestapo) and criminal police (Kripo). Thus the Gestapo, dealing with "enemies of the state," became separated from the regular police and was brought even closer to the party apparatus. The culmination of this process came with Himmler's decree of September 27, 1939, amalgamating Sipo and the SD into one organization under Heydrich, to be known as the *Reichssicherheitshauptamt* (RSHA; Reich Security Main Office). The merger of the state and party apparatuses was now "legally" complete, with Heydrich designated as Chief of Sipo and the SD (CSSD), a title paralleling Himmler's as Reichsführer-SS and Chief of the German Police. From a minuscule body of 280 men in 1929, Himmler had built the SS into a mammoth organization of nearly a quarter of a million men, whose myriad institutions operated even beyond the pseudolegality of the National Socialist state. In a few years this complex SS network would become the instrumentality for the annihilation of the Jews.

When the National Socialists came to power, the state took over the Jewish question and the SS remained satisfied for the time being to have its interest in the Jewish question lodged in Heydrich's card file in SD headquarters in Munich. Slowly the SD expanded in 1933, when two "specialists" were brought in, one for Catholic matters and one—a Major Walter Ilges—for "Jews and Freemasons." But in the first eighteen months after the accession to power the main thrust of SD activity was toward institutional expansion and consolidation of power. The SD's primary functions during that period were to assist Himmler in his drive to gain control of the police apparatuses in all the German states and to support, in the name of NSDAP security, the attack on the SA.

After June 1934, when the SA was eliminated as a contender for political power within the National Socialist movement, Heydrich began in earnest to expand the SD bureaucracy and simultaneously to pene-

trate the political police with SD personnel. The SD
Main Office in Munich was enlarged to three depart-
ments. Within the department known as *SD-Inland*
(domestic affairs), a separate desk for Jewish affairs
(coded II-112) was set up with SS-Untersturmführer
Leopold von Mildenstein in charge. Mildenstein hired
Adolf Eichmann at the end of 1934 as his expert on
Zionism, that niche in the bureaucracy coded II-1123.
About a year later an ambitious research program got
under way, with the gathering of data about prominent
Jews in Germany and abroad.[10] The Jewish press was
monitored. Studies were prepared about the ORT, a
worldwide Jewish organization promoting vocational
education and training, and the *Agudat Israel*, a worldwide organization of Orthodox Jews. Other studies
were under way and additional experts were put on.
Besides Eichmann, who specialized in Zionism, there
were desks for "assimilationists" and for "Orthodoxy
and philanthropy." (According to Eichmann, his colleagues were Dieter Wisliceny and Theodor Dannecker, both of whom were to become his dedicated
troubleshooters in organizing the deportation of the
European Jews.)

A somewhat similar setup existed in the Gestapo in
Berlin. In January 1934, when Göring still controlled
the Gestapo, a desk for matters concerning "émigrés,
Jews, Freemasons" was established in its Legal Department (coded II-F-2). It was directed by Karl
Hasselbacher, a young lawyer whose experience in
"Jewish" affairs had been obtained in the Ministry of
the Interior, working on the Law for the Restoration of
the Professional Civil Service.[11] After the Gestapo
came under SS jurisdiction in April 1934, it underwent
many changes, taking on, for one, a pseudomilitary
character with all the military titles and uniforms
brought in by the new staff from the SD and SS. A
thoroughgoing transformation was effected in the next
few months when the previous five departments were
consolidated into three, their staffs increased, and
their scope enlarged. Its new Main Office, coded II,
would become the keystone of the Gestapo. Its sub-

division II-1 dealt with "enemies of the state" and was
headed jointly by two officials whom Heydrich had
brought in from the Bavarian political police. (One,
Heinrich Müller, made a big career in the Gestapo
and later played a key role in the annihilation of the
Jews. To distinguish him from other Heinrich Müllers
in the Nazi galaxies, he became known as "Gestapo
Müller.") Subsection II-1-B handled religious associations, Jews, Freemasons, and émigrés, with Hasselbacher retaining charge of Jews, Masonic lodges, and
émigrés (expatriation and revocation of citizenship),
and enjoying the services of two assistants.

As soon as he could, Heydrich tried to turn his card
files and bureaucratic paperwork to practical effect.
Once he took over the Bavarian political police, he
began to exploit its apparatus for ideological purposes.
With regard to the Jews, his first act in this capacity
was his order of July 19, 1933, affecting all Jewish
organizations in Bavaria that were not purely religious
or did not serve purely charitable purposes. He forbade them to continue their activities and ordered
their property to be confiscated. Presumably he regarded such organizations as political and therefore
actually or potentially hostile to the National Socialist
state. Moreover, he may have felt that synagogues and
Jewish charitable agencies were useful inasmuch as
they segregated Jews from Germans. But the ban
on other organizations did not continue very long.
Heydrich had apparently concluded that police surveillance might serve his purposes better than suppression. Accordingly, in a decree dated March 20, 1934,
he lifted the ban on the *Reichsbund jüdischer Frontsoldaten* (Federal Union of Jewish War Veterans) and
various Jewish student and sports organizations, allowing them to meet and conduct business.[12] Now, however, they were forbidden to pursue any political
objectives and were subject to close police supervision.
The police were to be given a list of members, including the place and date of their birth and their
present residence (data that no doubt then found

their way into the SD files); new members had to be cleared by the police; police were to be informed of the resignation or expulsion of members. Orders by the police authorities about administration, activity, and sports exercises were to be strictly obeyed. All meetings were monitored. Thus Heydrich began to draw a tight net of police supervision over the Jewish community.

Police surveillance of Jewish organizations soon became a standard procedure all over Germany. In Prussia, before Heydrich's time, Gestapo surveillance over the Jews had been limited to "legal" and economic matters, but it did not take long before the system that Heydrich had innovated in Bavaria was introduced there. Agreements were worked out between the Gestapo and the SD arranging for joint activities as well as separate jurisdictions. Spying on the Jewish organizations was one such cooperative undertaking.

Surveillance was useful since it provided jobs for otherwise unemployed NSDAP members and it increased the activity of the SD bureaucracy. Although it fulfilled an expressive purpose though its exercise of terror over the Jewish community, surveillance in itself served no instrumental purpose for the National Socialists. It provided no "solution" to the Jewish question.

After the spate of violence, the boycott, and the enactment of the exclusionary legislation in 1933, neither the German state nor the NSDAP appeared to have a clear-cut policy with regard to the Jews. In fact, some government agencies continued to deal with Jews in a correct, even courteous manner, according to the rules and regulations that had prevailed in Weimar. Emigration, for example, was handled by the *Reichswanderungsamt* (Reich Office of Migration), within the Ministry of the Interior. It was staffed mostly by officials who were not National Socialists, but had, before 1933, been members of the Catholic Center and other nonleftist parties. These bureaucrats continued to operate up to 1938 not only according to

Weimar legality, but also with sympathetic understanding for the problems and priorities of the Jewish
organizations in trying to foster a systematic program
of emigration.[13]

Matters affecting Jews that were within the competence of the Ministry of Economy, also largely
staffed with old-line government officials, were handled
according to the habitual bureaucratic routine. A
paradoxical example was the successful appeal, after
initial prohibitions, by Jewish textile and clothing
factories to obtain government contracts to produce
goods for the armed services. The most significant instance of normal official procedures was the negotiations between the Ministry of Economy and the
Jewish Agency for Palestine, concluding in the so-
called "Haavara agreements" of August 1933. These
were, in essence, a compromise on the issue of emigrants' blocked accounts. Under this arrangement
Jews emigrating to Palestine deposited their assets in
special blocked accounts in Germany, held by a Jewish
trust company. Once in Palestine, the emigrant would
be paid off half the amount in Palestine pounds. The
other half was credited toward the purchase of
finished German goods by the Jewish Agency, which
paid half the cost in Palestine pounds. The Foreign
Office, too, was involved in the implementation of the
agreements over the years, and the officials there
manifested similar courtesy and correctness, and sometimes even more.[14]

The Haavara agreements were not regarded as an
ideological matter related to the Jewish question, but
rather as a matter of the German economy. The arrangement was seen as boosting German production
and German exports and discouraging a worldwide
Jewish boycott of German goods. Hitler appeared to
have no objections to the agreement, for he made a
neutral passing reference to it in a speech on October
24, 1933. As evidence that England was bad and Germany good, Hitler said that while England was
hindering Jewish settlement in Palestine, Germany

was aiding it, even to the extent of letting the emigrant take out of the country the currency required for the landing fee in Palestine.[15]

In 1934 it was widely held in Germany that the Jewish question had already been settled, though few people in the NSDAP leadership thought so. In the absence of clear-cut directives or guidelines, various ideas began to be bruited about in National Socialist circles about how to deal with the Jews. Goebbels, for one, seemed to be thinking along the lines of extending formal recognition of a ghettoized Jewish community. The idea no doubt derived from his experience with the *Kulturbund deutscher Juden,* an organization of Jewish actors, musicians, singers, and entertainers set up in 1933, after they had lost their jobs. The Kulturbund was formed to provide a means of livelihood for its members by arranging concerts, plays, and entertainment exclusively for the Jewish community. It was permitted to function under the supervision of a cultural commissar in Goebbels' Propaganda Ministry, who evolved a policy that Goebbels pridefully called "Jewish cultural autonomy." The Kulturbund was not only encouraged to perform the works of Jewish writers and composers, but was forbidden to perform works by Germans and "Aryans." This *de facto* situation may have given rise to the thought of formalizing it in a *de jure* arrangement applying to the entire Jewish community. At the end of 1934, another official in Goebbels' ministry, Hans Friedrich Blunck, then president of the *Reichsschrifttumskammer* (Reich Board of Literature), in an article in *Europäische Revue,* introduced that notion in a backhanded way. "The efforts of German literature," he wrote, "to achieve a concordat between the remaining Jewish population in the Reich and the government have been impeded again and again at the decisive moment by attacks from abroad."[16] Presumably that sentence was a sort of trial balloon. Though the response in the Jewish press indicated cautious interest in the proposal, nothing further came of the idea. It may have been suppressed at a higher level in the National Socialist hierarchy, perhaps even by an angered reaction from Hitler.

The SS, for its part, continued to cast about for ideas that would provide a long-range solution to the Jewish question. In mid-1934 an SS report on this very subject remarked, with disappointment, that the "armchair anti-Semites" were satisfied, now that the Jews had been pulled down a peg or two. It was consequently the responsibility of the party to devise an anti-Jewish policy that would "keep alive an awareness of the Jewish problem within the German people."[17] The unknown writer of the report rejected the exercise of further economic pressures on the Jews on the ground that that might arouse a foreign boycott of German goods. Next he explored the idea of mass Jewish emigration as an alternative, calling attention to the fact that among German Jews, only the Zionists advocated emigration and only they acknowledged that Jews could not truly be Germans. The reporter then proposed, as a desirable program, that the National Socialists give official preference to those Jewish organizations that promoted Jewish nationalism and separatism, while also encouraging those activities that prepared Jews for emigration.

Precisely such official encouragement was extended by the Bavarian political police, when Heydrich issued a directive to all police offices in the state on January 28, 1935: "The activity of the Zionist-oriented youth organizations that are engaged in the occupational restructuring of the Jews for agriculture and manual trades prior to their emigration to Palestine lies in the interest of the National Socialist state's leadership." These organizations, therefore, "are not to be treated with that strictness that it is necessary to apply to the members of the so-called German-Jewish organizations (assimilationists)."[18]

By spring, this approach had been legitimated, according to a directive of April 1935 that asserted that "the attempts of German-Jewish organizations to persuade Jews to remain in Germany" directly contradicted National Socialist principles and were to be prevented. The Jewish press, too, was to be monitored "to see that the more subtle forms of this propaganda are not disseminated."[19] One way the policy was executed was to deny permission to speakers to address public Jewish gatherings if they were known to advocate a Jewish presence in Germany. Persons who did express such views were often brought to the Gestapo for interrogation and threatened with detention in a concentration camp.

On May 15, 1935, the *Schwarze Korps*, official organ of the SS, supported this policy as the correct ideological posture for Nationalist Socialists. The Jews, it was argued, had to be separated into two categories—Zionists and assimilationists: "The Zionists adhere to a strict racial position and by emigrating to Palestine they are helping to build their own Jewish state." But the assimilationists were objectionably tenacious: "The assimilation-minded Jews deny their race and insist on their loyalty to Germany or claim to be Christians, because they have been baptized, in order to subvert National Socialist principles."[20]

The enactment of the Nuremberg Laws encouraged this approach. The Zionists and proponents of emigration to Palestine were less badgered in their activities by the police and the SD than the non-Zionists. Pressure was constantly exerted on Jewish communal leaders to pursue a policy of emigration, especially to Palestine. Removal of the Jews from Germany, *Entjudung* (de-Jewification) of Germany, seemed to have become the SS policy in the period between 1935 and 1938. Nevertheless, it was in no way official National Socialist policy and did not affect the routine bureaucratic procedures of the Reichswanderungsamt. The Haavara agreements were regarded with favor in SD circles as an incentive to Jewish emigration, but the *Auslandsorganisation*, the NSDAP branch dealing with Germans living abroad, strongly opposed it be-

cause it gave "valuable support for the formation of a
Jewish national state with the help of German
capital."²¹

Hitler issued no definitive statement in support of
the SS policy of encouraging the Zionists and emigration to Palestine, apart from that reference in his
speech in October 1933. Yet if Eichmann had read
Mein Kampf (at his trial he admitted he never had),
he would have seen that making a distinction between
Zionists and assimilationists was not likely to win
Hitler's approval. For Hitler had asserted that there
was no difference when he had studied them in
Vienna: "This apparent struggle between Zionistic and
liberal Jews disgusted me; for it was false through
and through, founded on lies." Furthermore, Hitler
had little regard for Palestine as a Jewish state. He
referred to Palestine only once in *Mein Kampf*, expressing the view that the Jews never intended to
build a state for the purpose of living there: ". . . All
they want is a central organization for their international world swindle, endowed with its own sovereign
rights and removed from the intervention of other
states: a haven for convicted scoundrels and a university for budding crooks."

The international complications of Jewish settlement in Palestine and of Arab opposition do not seem
to have become apparent to Hitler until 1937, when
Palestinian Arabs first turned to the Germans for help
against the Jewish settlement. In mid-1937 Foreign
Minister Konstantin von Neurath began to formulate a
policy on Palestine along the lines of *Mein Kampf*,
asserting that the creation of a Jewish state was not in
Germany's interest, because it would create a position
of power for "international Jewry somewhat like the
Vatican State for political Catholicism or Moscow for
the Comintern." Hitler was apparently undecided,
trying to reconcile the conflicting interests of his
ministries with his own ideological views. Though he
himself did not put anything down on paper, a government official reported in July 1937 that Hitler had
concluded that Jewish emigration should be con-

centrated on Palestine, because this would create "only *one* center of Jewish trouble in the world," which Germany could oppose by concerted counter-measures.[22] It may be no more than mere coincidence that about this time a Gestapo official who supervised Jewish organizations told a Jewish leader that the Gestapo did not like to have the Jews emigrate to America, but preferred Palestine, because "there we will catch up with you."[23]

By 1937 Eichmann had developed the idea that all matters relating to Jewish emigration should be centralized in one agency, and he adumbrated the idea of forced emigration, in actuality a policy of expulsion, as an expression of the German people's wrath against the Jews. That idea appealed to Heydrich, and in a short time it would become official policy.

The SD meanwhile still searched for an ideological or theoretical basis for an ongoing anti-Jewish policy for the National Socialist state. In a report of August 28, 1936, SS-Oberscharführer Schröder, Eichmann's superior at that time, described the work of his section with regard to the problem of arriving at an encompassing National Socialist definition of the concept of "Jewry as an enemy of the State and Party."[24] Schröder elaborated:

The Jew already as a person is a 100 percent enemy of National Socialism, as proven by the difference in his race and nationality. Wherever he tries to transmit his work, his influence, and his world outlook to the non-Jewish world, he discharges it in hostile ideologies, as we find it in Liberalism, especially in Freemasonry, in Marxism, and not least also in Christianity. These ideologies then accord with a broader concept of Jewish mentality.

He concluded that the correct method of combatting Jewry demanded sober judgment rather than the "fantastic notions of well-known, so-called anti-Semites," an idea reminiscent of Hitler's earliest statement on anti-Semitism, his letter to Gemlich in September 1919. Here, then, was the germ of the idea that the Jew, simply by being a Jew and thereby an enemy of the "Aryan" and hence of the National Socialist movement, would automatically become an enemy of the National Socialist state. The ideological concept was being transformed into a legal one.

Himmler, too, was developing the idea of the Jew as an enemy of the state, less in a legal sense than in a combative sense. Early in 1937, in a lecture to the Wehrmacht on the nature and purpose of the SS, he spelled out the idea that "the enemy in a war is an enemy not only in the military sense, but also an ideological enemy."[25] A few months earlier he described the methods with which the SS would defend Germany against this enemy:

> We shall unremittingly fulfill our task, to be the guarantors of the internal security of Germany, just as the Wehrmacht guarantees the safety of the honor, the greatness, and the peace of the Reich from the outside. We shall take care that never more in Germany, the heart of Europe, can the Jewish-Bolshevistic revolution of subhumans be kindled internally or by emissaries from abroad. Pitilessly we shall be a merciless executioner's sword for all these forces whose existence and doings we know . . . whether it be today, or in decades, or in centuries.[26]

Thus, at a time when talk of war was becoming the everyday rhetoric of National Socialist Germany, the SS, too, despite the careful paperwork of the SD, began increasingly to talk of war against the ideological enemy.

5

Foreign Policy,
Race, and War

The task of German foreign
policy, Hitler stated in *Mein Kampf,* was to "preserve,
promote, and sustain our people for the future." Because of the Dolchstoss, the sapping of Germany's
virility through betrayal, that task had to be executed
in two stages; the first, domestic policy, was "to restore," in Hitler's words, "to the nation its strength in
the form of a free power state." The second stage
entailed war and expansion into foreign territory. In
Hitler's view there was no division between domestic
and foreign policy. Domestic policy, he wrote, "must
furnish the Volkist instrument of strength" for the exercise of foreign policy, and that foreign policy, in
turn, would protect and sustain the Volkist instrument.

Hitler had spelled out his foreign-policy ideas and
plans in repetitive detail first in *Mein Kampf* and later,
in 1928, even more elaborately in a second manuscript, unpublished during his lifetime.* These ideological objectives as well as his broad strategical plans

---

* Found after the war, the manuscript was identified by Professor
Gerhard L. Weinberg and published, with his annotations, as *Hitlers
zweites Buch.* An English version is called *Hitler's Secret Book.*

remained essentially unchanged in the decade between the writing of *Mein Kampf* and his accession
to power. When Hitler became dictator of Germany,
his ideology and strategy both became the ends and
means of German foreign policy. "In political life
there are no principles of foreign policy," Hitler declared early in 1930. "The programmatic principle of
our party is its position on the racial problem, on
pacifism and internationalism. Foreign policy is only
a means to an end. In matters of foreign policy, I shall
not permit myself to be bound."[1] This was a cardinal
principle in his outlook. In *Mein Kampf* he argued
that since the goal of a state's diplomacy was to preserve its people, *"every road that leads to this is then
expedient. . . ."* Here were embodied the two integral
elements of policies he would pursue—unwavering
commitment to National Socialist ideology, and a
strategy combining opportunism, expediency, and improvisation.

The first stage of German foreign policy, Germany's
internal restoration, was to accomplish two ends. Germany first had to purge itself of its internal enemies,
and second, make itself strong. "Whoever wants to act
in the name of German honor today must first launch
a merciless war against the infernal defilers of German
honor," he wrote in his second book. He used the
language of war often in speaking of the Jews. The
National Socialist movement, he wrote in *Mein Kampf*,
"must call eternal wrath upon the head of the foul
enemy of mankind," the "inexorable Jew" seeking
domination over all nations. Only the sword, he held,
could stave off the enemy, in a process that "is and
remains a bloody one."

The application of the sword against the Jews
would come later, but the first step in this process was
purgation, which had been achieved with the promulgation of the laws of 1933 and the Nuremberg Laws.

The second means of restoring German virility was
remilitarization. The German people, now racially
purified, would have the will to war, but it needed the
means to make war, which the hated Versailles Treaty

had denied them. In his second book, Hitler declared
that "the first task of German domestic policy ought
to be that of giving the German people a military
organization suitable to its national strength." From
his very accession to power, Hitler began to build
according to this blueprint. On April 4, 1933, a National Defense Council was set up and began, in
secret, the process of military planning and German
rearmament. Six months later, Germany withdrew
from both the international disarmament conference
at Geneva and from the League of Nations. In November the German people enthusiastically affirmed
that policy in a plebiscite, while the nations participating in the disarmament negotiations, despite deep
misgivings about Germany's course, took no action
that would discourage or halt German remilitarization.
That passivity continued. Indeed, though the major
European powers protested Germany's restoration of
universal compulsory military service in 1935, Great
Britain—one of the protesters—rewarded Germany
with a naval agreement on June 18, establishing naval
parity betwen England and Germany. It was the first
of a long series of diplomatic and military acts of
appeasement that raised Germany's international
prestige and succeeded in strengthening the dictatorship at home.

German rearmament accelerated, though not yet
too openly lest France claim violations of the Locarno
Pact of 1925, which had reaffirmed the conditions of
the Versailles Treaty, stating that the Rhineland was
to remain demilitarized. But having prepared his
ground diplomatically as well as militarily, Hitler sent
German troops into the Rhineland on March 7, 1936,
while denouncing the Locarno Pact. Within a week
the flurry of crises was over. The British fear of risking
war had prevailed over French indecisiveness. Germany had achieved a stunning triumph without cost.
Hitler's gambles and his strategy of wile, bluff, and
outright deceit had succeeded, within three years, in
setting Germany on the path to war. In August 1936
Hitler drafted a memorandum, which became known

as the Four Year Plan, that was to put Germany on a war footing economically and militarily. Hitler felt that Germany was ready for "the reconquest of freedom for tomorrow."

In his scheme, war was inevitable. "War is life," Hitler said in 1932. "War is the origin of all things."[2] War would be the means to realize his quest for Lebensraum, a word that incorporated Hitler's ideas of racial supremacy into a pretentious geopolitical scheme. War, invasion, expansion, in National Socialist ideology, were not merely the expression of an imperialist drive for natural resources, exploitable markets in underdeveloped countries, or power over vast territories and numerous peoples (though they were that also); primarily they were instruments to serve national/racial survival. In *Mein Kampf* Hitler first expounded his theory of Lebensraum:

> *The foreign policy of the Volkist state must safeguard the existence on this planet of the race embodied in the state, by creating a healthy, viable natural relation between the nation's population and growth on the one hand and the quantity and quality of its soil on the other.*

Hitler's concepts about the basis of a state's physical existence and about population growth in relation to available agricultural land and food supply were derived from geopolitical ideas with which he became familiar in Landsberg. The basic idea was that of population pressure. While population grows, the amount of soil remains constant. Increasing soil productivity is not a satisfactory or long-range solution to relieve the pressure of population growth, Hitler believed. Nor could population control be a solution, for that would contravene the very purpose of the Volkist racial state. (Indeed, shortly after the Nazis came to power, birth-control centers were shut down, advertising for contraceptives was halted, and abortions became difficult to obtain.) The only satisfactory and fundamental way of eliminating the "intolerable"

relation betwen population and territory was war:
"The bread of freedom grows from the hardships of
war."

Germany was entitled to more land, not only because its people would have "the courage to take
possession of it, the strength to preserve it, and the
industry to put it to the plough," but because Germany
was the "mother of life," not just "some little nigger
nation or other." Furthermore, Germany's leaders were
justified in shedding even German blood to attain that
goal:

> . . . we National Socialists must hold unflinchingly to
> our aim in foreign policy, namely, *to secure for the
> German people the land and soil to which they are
> entitled on this earth.* And this action is the only one
> which, before God and our German posterity, would
> make any sacifice of blood seem justified. . . . The soil
> on which someday German generations of peasants can
> beget powerful sons will sanction the investment of the
> sons of today, and will someday acquit the responsible
> statesmen of blood-guilt and sacrifice of the people,
> even if they are persecuted by their contemporaries.

Where would the soil come from? There were, in
Hitler's plan, two sources—the "lost territories" and
"new soil." The "lost territories" were the lands that
would soon become part of Greater Germany—Austria
and western Czechoslovakia—and which would have
to be won back by war, *"back to the bosom of a common Reich, not by flaming protests, but by a mighty
sword."* But these territories would not solve Germany's problems. Only new soil would give Germany
"a path to life."

The new soil that would give Germany its Lebensraum could be "only in the East." Hitler spelled it out
in *Mein Kampf*: "If we speak of soil in Europe today,
we can primarily have in mind only *Russia* and her
vassal border states." The rationale for a German conquest of Russia was twofold. Using Rosenberg's ideas,
he advanced a historical claim of centuries-old Ger-

man colonization in Russia. But even more important
was the notion, assimilated also from Rosenberg, that
the Jews had taken control of Russia by means of
revolution and Bolshevism.

War for Lebensraum was thus associated in Hitler's
mind with war against the Jews, not alone in an
apocalyptic sense of a final struggle between Gog and
Magog, between Aryans and Jews, but also in a conventional sense. Back in 1927, Rudolf Hess wrote to a
friend that "in Hitler's opinion [world peace would]
. . . be realizable only when one power, the racially
best one, has attained complete and uncontested
supremacy."[3] That such supremacy could be achieved
only by war Hess did not spell out, but he clearly
articulated Hitler's view that this "great step" toward
world understanding was possible only "upon the solution of the Jewish question." War, the Jews, and racial
utopia were all interrelated in Hitler's mind. In 1935
he referred to war as a cover for planned murder,
when he told Gerhardt Wagner, the NSDAP's top
medical officer, "that if war came, he would pick up
and carry out this question of euthanasia," for then
"such a program could be put into effect more
smoothly and readily" and in the general upheaval
public oposition would be less likely.[4]

Often in discussing foreign-policy matters, Hitler
shuttled back and forth between a real world of
nations and armies and a phantasmagoric universe
ruled by the Jews. For instance, in 1935, shortly after
the Nuremberg party congress, Hitler had several
occasions to speak to small groups of party and government people. Consul General Fritz Wiedemann,
Hitler's adjutant, later recorded Hitler's plans at that
time with regard to the Jews: "Out of all the professions, ghetto, imprisoned in a territory where they can
disport themselves according to their nature, while the
German people looks on as one watches wild beasts."[5]
Though Wiedemann mentions no talk of war, Hitler
was already fantasizing of a time during or after the
war, when some territory, not precious German soil,
would be available for the internment of the Jews.

On September 24, 1935, nine days after the Nuremberg congress at which the Law for the Protection of German Blood and German Honor had been promulgated, Hitler called a closed meeting of party leaders, Reich officials, and Gauleiters to share his decisions with regard to racial determinations of the "half-Jews." Hitler spoke with considerable expertness, Bernhard Lösener noted, but then flabbergasted his listeners by breaking off, remarking that he needed to obtain further clarification on some points. He then turned to other subjects, alluding quite unmistakably to his war plans, saying that he still needed about four years to be ready.[6] Lösener thought he was rambling incoherently, but there could be no misunderstanding the associations in Hitler's mind between making fine racial distinctions among different categories of "half-Jews" and his plans for war.

At the end of August 1936, after the Olympic Games, Hitler went to Berchtesgaden, where he prepared his memorandum on the Four Year Plan. The body of the memorandum dealt with practical matters like saving foreign exchange, stepping up fuel production, mass-producing synthetic rubber, and increasing iron ore production so as to make Germany self-sufficient and ready for war within four years, but the ideological preamble on the need for war read like a chapter from *Mein Kampf*. The world, he stated, had been moving toward a new conflict, "the most extreme solution of which is called Bolshevism, whose essence and aim, however, is solely the elimination of those strata of mankind which have hitherto provided the leadership and their replacement by worldwide Jewry."[7] Since the victory of Bolshevism over Germany would lead to the annihilation of the German people, Hitler concluded: *"In face of the necessity of defense against this danger, all other considerations must recede into the background as being completely irrelevant."* Ideology had clearly superseded rational political and economic calculations. Hitler had decided on war against Bolshevism, which he had long regarded as a contrivance through which the Jews manipulated world power. Thus this holy war against Jewish Bolshevism would defeat the prime and ultimate enemy and win for the German people their Lebensraum.

The Four Year Plan also provided for the expropriation of all Jews when Germany went to war. The Reichstag was to pass a law "making the whole of Jewry liable for all damage inflicted by individual specimens of this community of criminals upon the German economy, and thus upon the German people." With this authority, Göring, as Plenipotentiary for the Four Year Plan, would, after the *Kristallnacht,* levy a billion-mark contribution on the Jews.

Hitler had the craft to plan and the patience to wait for the opportunity to carry out that plan. Even before he had come to power, he had devised his strategy. "We must be strong first," he said in Rauschning's company. "Everything else will follow in due course. I shall advance step by step. Never two steps at once."[8] Five years later, he made precisely the same point with regard to the Jews. On April 29, 1937, in a long speech before a regional NSDAP meeting, in which he addressed himself to the Jewish question, among others, he referred contemptuously to the insistent demands within the party for more action against the Jews. He reminded his listeners that he did not need pressure on this matter, being the original expert. Everything would be done in due time, within a total context, and at the opportune moment:

> Then: the final aim of our whole policy is quite clear for all of us. Always I am concerned only that I do not take any step from which I will perhaps have to retreat, and not to take any step that will harm us. I tell you that I always go to the outermost limits of risk, but never beyond. For this you need to have a nose more or less to smell out: "What can I still do?" Also in a struggle against an enemy. I do not summon an enemy with force to fight, I don't say: "Fight!" because I want to

fight. Instead I say, "I will destroy you! And now, Wisdom, help me, to maneuver you into the corner that you cannot fight back, and then you get the blow right in the heart." That's it.[9]

Preparations for war proceeded apace. In August 1936, about the time he was working on the Four Year Plan, the term of compulsory military service was extended from one year to two years. In October and November 1936 the Berlin-Rome-Tokyo Axis was forged. At the same time the Germans recognized the insurgent government of General Franco in Spain, openly supplying Franco's forces with matériel, experts, and even men. Germany and Japan also formed an explicitly anti-Soviet alliance, the Anti-Comintern Pact, and anti-Bolshevism thereafter became the central theme of the Nazi propagandists in and out of Germany. The whole Nazi apparatus became engaged in producing enormous quantities of deceitful and deliberately falsified propaganda describing Russia as the center of operations of the Elders of Zion. Goebbels and Rosenberg had major organizations devoted to anti-Communist propaganda and activities.

Yet none achieved Hitler's terrible potency. His speech at the NSDAP congress, on September 13, 1937, dwelled on the worldwide Bolshevik menace, using the themes he had developed in *Mein Kampf*: the preparation for world insurrection "without doubt originates from the authorities of Jewish Bolshevism in Moscow."[10] Having gained a foothold in Russia, the Jews would use it as the bridgehead in their quest for world domination. "I confirm only what is!" Hitler cried out with pathos. National Socialism had already "banished the Bolshevik world peril from the inner heart of Germany." Now it would protect the "community of European-culture nations" from "Jewish world Bolshevism." In a crescendo of hatred, the National Socialists depicted the "Jewish-Bolshevik world conspirators" as the primary enemy of mankind in a campaign that intended not only to justify the launching of the war, but to provide a continuous warrant in defense of both the conduct of the war and the execution of the Final Solution.

Hitler's plans for war were quite definite, when, on November 5, 1937, he called a select conference in the Reich Chancellery. His guests were Foreign Minister Konstantin von Neurath, a holdover from Hindenburg's Cabinet; War Minister Field Marshal Werner von Blomberg, another Hindenburg appointee; commander-in-chief of the army General Werner von Fritsch; commander-in-chief of the navy Admiral Erich Raeder; and Göring, in his capacity as commander-in-chief of the air force. All five were engaged in the business of war and/or foreign relations. Also present was Colonel Friedrich Hossbach, Hitler's army adjutant, who took minutes of the meeting.[11] Hitler began by stressing the high-level importance of the meeting and that in the event of his demise his statements were to be regarded as his "testamentary legacy." He then expatiated on German foreign policy as the means of racial preservation of the Volk through Lebensraum, just as he had set it forth in *Mein Kampf* and in his second book. The agenda for this meeting was Hitler's timetable for the conquest of Austria and Czechoslovakia. Of the possibilities for earlier or later deadlines that he presented, he obviously wanted the nearest, "even as early as 1938," asserting that the attack on Czechoslovakia must occur "with lightning speed."

The minutes are almost exclusively devoted to Hitler's presentation. The last three paragraphs barely reveal the shock of some of those present and the brief and hesitant discussion that followed. Blomberg, Fritsch, and Neurath, one reads between Hossbach's lines, disagreed with Hitler's political calculations and with his military assessments, cautiously wording their dissent. Their objections determined their fate, for Hitler had definitely made up his mind to go ahead in 1938. In less than three months Blomberg, Fritsch, and Neurath were removed from their positions (Blomberg and Fritsch by the most sordid and underhanded machinations).

Under the all-embracing cover of the Four Year Plan, Hitler planned 1938 as the decisive year to go ahead with the annexation of Austria and the invasion of Czechoslovakia—"Operation Green," whose military planning he ordered early in December 1937. His first spectacular success came on March 12, 1938, when he annexed Austria in an unresisted invasion. A month later, after an unprecedented show of terror and violence, the National Socialists held a plebiscite in which 99.75 percent of the voters supported union with Germany. The war fever then began to be fanned around the manufactured crisis of the Sudeten Germans in Czechoslovakia. The implications for the Jews in Germany grew more sinister, for their total expropriation and ultimate disposition had been awaiting the maturation of Hitler's war plans.

After the Four Year Plan had gone into operation, Hjalmar Schacht, Minister of Economy, had come into constant and bitter conflict with Göring. Schacht resigned late in 1937 and Göring, as Plenipotentiary for the Four Year Plan, assumed total control over all economic policies. When Walter Funk took over the Economy Ministry in February 1938, it had already been thoroughly reorganized by Göring, who continued to retain most of its authority. Freed from Schacht's legalisms and anxieties about unfavorable repercussions from abroad, and certainly acting under Hitler's orders, Göring turned his attention to the expropriation of the Jews.

The economic situation of the Jews had been continually deteriorating. By the end of 1937, Jewish professionals and civil servants, actors, musicians, and journalists, numbering tens of thousands, had lost their livelihood. Many Jews, workers and employees, had been dismissed from their jobs under pressure of rabid party and SA members. Shortly after Schacht's resignation, an "Aryan" organization was created whose purpose was to hasten the ouster of some twenty thousand Jews still employed in the clothing and leather industries. Innumerable small Jewish businesses were liquidated in the first two years of the regime, after experiencing boycotts and violence. "Voluntary" transfers of Jewish firms to "Aryan" purchasers usually involved smaller businesses; larger ones, especially those that brought large sums of foreign exchange into Germany, managed to continue to operate, partly because of Germany's pressing need for foreign currency and partly because of Schacht's resistance to taking formal action. According to official statistics, as of April 1938 nearly forty thousand Jewish firms were still doing business in Germany, many of them fulfilling crucial roles either in rearmament or in the import-export trade.

Early in January 1938 Göring initiated systematic planning for expropriation, declaring that first of all "it was necessary to have a legal definition of what constitutes a Jewish firm."[12] On March 26, speaking in Vienna (having not Austria, but Germany, in mind), Göring declared that "Aryanization" should not be impaired by wrong or stupid measures, but must be carried out "quite systematically, with full deliberation."[13]

The first decree, issued April 22, 1938, provided that any German engaged in an effort to camouflage the Jewish "character"—that is, ownership—of a business enterprise would be imprisoned or fined. (As a matter of fact, the district Gestapo office in Düsseldorf had concerned itself with such "camouflage" back in November 1936.) The next decree, issued April 26 over Göring and Frick's signatures, was the fundamental Decree Regarding the Reporting of Jewish Property. It provided that no later than June 30, 1938, every Jew had to report and assess his entire domestic and foreign property, except for personal and household goods, or if the total value of the property did not exceed five thousand Reichsmarks. A hint of things to come was contained in paragraph 7: "The Plenipotentiary for the Four Year Plan may take measures necessary to ensure that the use made of property subject to reporting will be in keeping with the interests of the German economy."[14]

The Third Decree to the Reich Citizenship Law, issued June 14, 1938, defined a Jewish business enterprise: "A business enterprise is considered Jewish if its owner is a Jew," by the standards of the Reich Citizenship Law. The "Jewish" character of large corporations or branch businesses was determined by fixed percentages of number of Jews or the amount of their capital in them. To make sure that no enterprise the government wanted to seize would escape the net, an enterprise was regarded as Jewish even "when it is under the dominant influence of Jews." In mid-June Frick began circulating drafts of a decree providing for compulsory "Aryanization" of Jewish businesses. On July 6 a decree was issued requiring the termination, no later than December 30, 1938, of Jewish businesses that rendered a variety of commercial services. On July 25 a decree forbade Jewish physicians (there were still about 4,000) from practicing as of September 30. (With permission from the Minister of the Interior, Jewish doctors could treat Jewish patients not as doctors, but as orderlies.) On September 27, 1938, Jewish lawyers (still about 1,700) were forbidden to practice law as of November 30.

"Voluntary" transfers of Jewish businesses to non-Jews continued in 1938 at a moderate pace of about fifty per month, despite an intensification of grass-roots street anti-Semitism by restless elements in the Nazi party and the SA. In August, at a meeting of party Gauleiters, Martin Bormann promised that Göring would make a "fundamental settlement of the Jewish question," which would fully satisfy the party's demands. In September, under the impact of both arbitrary and systematic violence, the number of "Aryanizations" rose to 235, and the same pace continued into October. In mid-October, at a meeting of German and Austrian senior civil servants, Göring spoke on the need of mobilizing all German armed forces and increasing military production for the com-

ing war. The time had come for an energetic handling
of the Jewish question, he said, and the Jews "must
be removed from the economy." But what must be
prevented, Göring said, was that "wild commissar
economy" that was developing in Austria, where over
3,500 party members, most of them without qualification, had become "commissars" over "Aryanized"
Jewish businesses. The solution of the Jewish question, Göring emphasized, was not intended as a
"charitable scheme for incompetent party members."
It was his firm conviction that Jewish property belonged to the Reich and not to individual party members who wanted to enrich themselves. (Göring, of
course, was permitted to enrich himself in the style of
an Eastern potentate, not only with industrial property
that had belonged to Jews, but also with European art
treasures.)

The war plans were synchronized also with plans to
put the Jews under the complete control of the police.
On January 5, 1938, a Law Regarding Changes of
Family Names and Given Names was promulgated,
which authorized the Minister of the Interior to issue
regulations about names and to order changes of
names that did not conform to those regulations. The
ominous character of the law became apparent only
on July 23, in a decree requiring all Jews to apply for
identification cards, which they would have to carry
with them at all times. On August 17, 1938, the Law
Regarding Changes of Family Names and Given
Names was issued, providing that as of January 1,
1939, all male Jews must assume the given name of
Israel and all female Jews the name of Sarah. Furthermore, Jews were forbidden to take as given names any
other than specifically designated "Jewish" given
names, as listed in an appendix to the decree. (More
than a hundred years before, the Prussian government prohibited Jews from using "Christian" given
names. Leopold Zunz, the founder of *Wissenschaft des
Judentums*, then wrote a scholarly paper, *Die Namen
der Juden*, showing that Christian and Jewish given
names had a common source in the Bible. His scholar-

ship was so persuasive that the Prussian government revised its restrictions to apply only to names associated with traditions of the New Testament.)

On October 5, 1938, a Law on Passports of Jews, signed by Werner Best, then head of the Sipo administrative office, required Jews to hand in their passports for foreign travel within two weeks; these would be reissued designating the holder as a Jew.

Other disquieting developments occurred. At the very outset of the year Himmler ordered the expulsion within ten days of all Jews in Germany who were Russian nationals, many of whom had been living in Germany since the Bolshevik Revolution.[15] On March 28 a decree was issued, signed by the Führer himself together with the Minister for Church Affairs and the Minister of the Interior, withdrawing from the Jewish religious communities and their central organizations (*Gemeinden*) their status as public legal bodies and subjecting them to government control. Following the decree a year earlier dissolving the B'nai B'rith, the Law Regarding the Legal Status of the Jewish Religious Communities was to prepare for the eventual centralization of all Jewish affairs in one organization that would be under the total control of the police.

Violence, too, had exploded again in the streets, no doubt a concomitant to the Austrian *Anschluss* and the war hysteria against Czechoslovakia. Attacks on the Jews and Jewish stores intensified. A Jewish journalist described the SA violence and havoc on Berlin's main shopping street: ". . . A gang of ten youngsters in Hitler Youth uniforms smashed the shop window and stormed into the shop, brandishing butcher knives and yelling: 'To hell with the Jewish rabble! Room for the Sudeten Germans!' "[16]

But far worse and more terrifying than the sporadic violence of the mobs and hoodlums was the expanding activity of the Gestapo and SS. On January 25, 1938, the Minister of the Interior issued a new order that extended the definition of "protective custody" to apply to "persons whose behavior endangers the existence and security of the Volk and the State."

Under the guidelines of another order the concentration camps were being given new functions, besides
detention of political opponents, as state reformatories
and labor camps for criminals and antisocials. Mass
Jewish arrests began late in May, and most of those
arrested were sent to Dachau. On June 1 Heydrich
issued instructions that between June 13 and 18 each
criminal police district was to take into "preventive
police detention at least two hundred male able-
bodied persons (antisocials) as well as all male Jews
with previous criminal records." They were to be sent
to Buchenwald.[17] The action was in implementation of
the Four Year Plan and the demands of the war
economy to put every able-bodied person to work.
This would provide the rationale for turning the concentration camps into forced-labor and then slave-
labor camps. The idea had a history going back to the
1923 Putsch. According to the draft constitution prepared then for the eventuality of takeover, concentration camps were to be established for "all persons
dangerous to security and useless eaters."[18]

The seizure of some 1,500 Jewish "antisocials"
served a different purpose. The police records of many
consisted of a parking violation or two. The Gestapo
was willing to release them only upon completion of
arrangements for their immediate emigration.[19] The
Gestapo had begun to coerce emigration along lines
that Eichmann had advocated a short while before.
After the Anschluss he had the opportunity to carry
out his ideas in real life in Vienna.

During the summer of 1938 Buchenwald, Dachau,
and Sachsenhausen began to be enlarged and provisions made for the exploitation of their prisoners'
labor. Prisoners at Dachau were ordered to sew Stars
of David on uniforms in preparation for a mass influx
of Jewish prisoners.[20]

The plans for war and for the expropriation of the
Jews, the directives providing for their identification,
the rash of police arrests, and the explosion of violence
all converged that summer of 1938 in a tidal wave of

terror. On September 12, at the Nuremberg party congress, Hitler was still sure that Operation Green would come off as planned on October 1, for he continued to promise the Sudeten Germans military assistance. But British Prime Minister Neville Chamberlain, the architect of appeasement, thwarted Hitler's bid for war with the Munich Conference of September 29, 1938. By awarding Hitler the Sudetenland, Chamberlain removed the pretext for Hitler's threatened invasion. Operation Green was called off. Instead, German troops marched only into the Sudetenland on October 1, in accordance with the Munich agreement. But Hitler did not abandon his original plans. Just three weeks later, in violation of that agreement, a new directive was issued to the armed forces for the dismemberment of Czechoslovakia.

The plan for war had, for the time being, misfired and with it the opportunity for taking drastic, but less visible, action against the Jews. But an unexpected opportunity for dealing with the Jews opened up with the assassination on November 7, 1938, of Ernst vom Rath, a third secretary in the German embassy in Paris, by a seventeen-year-old Polish Jewish student, Hershl Grynszpan. Grynszpan's parents, Polish Jews, who had lived in Hanover since 1914, had just been expelled from Germany. In March 1938 the Polish government, fearful that the Germans would soon expel Jews who were Polish nationals and return them to Poland, promulgated a denaturalization decree designed to annul the citizenship of Poles living abroad for more than five years unless they received a special stamp by Polish consular officials by October 31. Lacking that, they would be refused reentry to Poland. About fifty thousand Polish Jews were then resident in Germany. Overnight they became stateless when Polish officials refused to issue the requisite stamp. The German government soon learned that the Polish government was firm in its intention of barring the reentry of Jews. On October 28 the Gestapo, on orders from the Foreign Office, began rounding up

Polish Jews to transport them to the Polish border. Prevented from entering Poland, they were kept in appalling conditions in a no-man's-land on the Polish side at Zbąszyn, near Posen.* Grynszpan's parents had been among the first rounded up, and the son had become unsettled by their fate.

Hitler himself never uttered a word publicly on vom Rath's assassination or on the events of the Kristallnacht (night of glass). Yet those events could not have occurred without his approval. The incitement against the Jews began on November 8 with the first news report that vom Rath had been seriously wounded (he died two days later of his wounds) and an accompanying incendiary editorial in the *Völkischer Beobachter*. Goebbels called the signals, which were picked up by party and SA leaders all over Germany. In many small towns, meetings were called on November 8 or 9, at which the party leader and the local mayor agitated the assembled mob, which then went into action, setting fire to the local synagogues, destroying Jewish businesses and homes, and manhandling Jews.[21] At that moment in German history, with war fever running high and the Jews already clearly identified as enemies, the rank-and-file National Socialist was eager for a little action on his own. Many times in the past, the NSDAP had bridled these anti-Semitic enthusiasms in the interests of broader goals. Now Goebbels became the advocate of mob violence and the architect of a mob-action program.

Early in the evening of November 9, it was learned that vom Rath had died of his wounds. That very evening the NSDAP's leaders were congregating in the Old Town Hall in Munich for the anniversary celebration of the Munich Putsch. Hitler had dinner there with his old comrades and was seen in prolonged conversation with Goebbels. Hitler usually delivered the main speech on this occasion, but this evening he

---

* Eventually, under international pressure, Poland admitted its Jewish nationals.

left early. He had been overheard to say that "the SA should be allowed to have a fling."[22] Hitler had presumably decided, at Goebbels' suggestion, that "spontaneous" demonstrations, manifestly not initiated or organized by the party, were not to be discouraged.[23] His absence from the festivities was planned to exculpate him—and the government—from responsibility for the subsequent events. After Hitler left, Goebbels delivered an inflammatory exhortation to the assemblage, calling for "spontaneous" demonstrations. NSDAP members were used to such instructions from the party's earliest days, when it expediently served as the anonymous organizer of violent demonstrations. Now, the party members and SA men took Goebbels' hints as he intended them to be taken: Jewish blood was to flow for the death of vom Rath.

Three of Goebbels' colleagues in Hitler's cabinet were absent from the Munich celebration—Himmler, Heydrich, and Göring. Göring was then on a train to Berlin and learned only in the morning what had happened during the night. Himmler and Heydrich were both in Munich that evening, but not at the Old Town Tall, and were informed shortly before midnight about what was being planned. Long hostile to Goebbels, Himmler charged that his "lust for power" was behind this planned action. Himmler immediately checked with Hitler and then passed the word on to Heydrich: "The headquarters offices of the State Police are to conform to the wishes of the Propaganda offices." In the early hours of November 10, Heydrich issued a series of orders to all state police stations with instructions to deal ruthlessly with all looters, to guard against the spread of fires from burning Jewish buildings to non-Jewish property, and to see to it that foreigners, including Jews, not be molested. These orders also included instructions for the arrest in all districts of as many able-bodied male Jews, "especially rich ones," as could be accommodated in the space available for protective custody.[24] Thus the SS exploited Goebbels' plan for the sake of their own. These concentration-camp internees would have to buy their freedom by emigrating from Germany immediately upon release.

That night fires were ignited all over Germany, and the shattered plate glass that was to give the pogrom its name littered the streets of German towns and cities. (It was later estimated that the amount of plate glass destroyed equaled half the annual production of the plate-glass industry of Belgium, from which it had been imported.) Synagogues and Jewish institutions were burned to the ground. Over seven thousand Jewish businesses were destroyed. Nearly one hundred Jews were killed, and thousands more subjected to wanton violence and sadistic torments. David H. Buffum, American Consul General in Leipzig, in a report, November 21, 1938, to the State Department, described one of these sadistic amusements: "Having demolished dwellings and hurled most of the moveable effects to the streets, the insatiably sadistic perpetrators threw many of the trembling inmates into a small stream that flows through the Zoological Park, commanding horrified spectators to spit at them, defile them with mud and jeer at their plight." About thirty thousand Jewish men were arrested and incarcerated in Buchenwald, Dachau, and Sachsenhausen.

If the death of vom Rath had triggered Goebbels' pogrom, the pogrom itself provided the National Socialist government with the opportunity, short of actual war, to proceed with the total expropriation of the Jews and the complete removal of their freedom. Göring, in his capacity as Plenipotentiary for the Four Year Plan, took the initiative. in the next two days he conferred extensively with Hitler; he instructed Heydrich to prepare a report on the extent of the damage of Jewish property and to estimate the losses from looting of that property. On November 12 at 11:00 A.M. he convened a large meeting in his offices at the Reich Air Ministry, attended by top government and party people.[25] He opened the meeting by announcing that he had received a letter written on orders of the

Führer, requesting that "the Jewish question be now, once and for all, coordinated and solved one way or another." Furthermore, the Führer had asked him the day before by phone "to take coordinated action in the matter."

The business at hand was primarily an economic matter, and Göring deplored the demonstrations: "They don't harm the Jew but me, who is the final authority for coordinating the German economy." The purpose of the meeting was to involve all the competent agencies in taking the necessary measures "for the elimination of the Jew from the German economy." The measures, it appeared, had already been decided on. The meeting was to coordinate the procedures for confiscating Jewish businesses and factories. "We must agree," said Göring, "on a clear action that shall be profitable to the Reich." The elimination of the Jews altogether from the German economy was the chief topic of discussion. At one point Funk asked whether the Jewish stores should be reopened and Göring responded: "That is up to us to decide." Within a week Funk issued a circular letter to appropriate authorities declaring that Jewish businesses should not be reopened unless their management by non-Jews was assured.[26]

Goebbels asked about further legislation barring Jews from all public places—theaters, movies, beaches, resorts, and Pullman sleeping-car compartments—and expelling Jewish children still in German schools. Three days later, on November 15, the Ministry of Education issued an ordinance barring all Jewish children from the schools; two weeks later, on November 28, Heydrich issued a decree signed by the Minister of Interior giving various state and district authorities the right to impose curfew restrictions on the Jews. A month later the Führer himself approved Göring's proposal to forbid Jews access to most of the public places specified by Goebbels.[27]

A representative of the German insurance companies was then invited to report on compensation for damages caused by the demonstrations. After a lengthy discussion it was decided that the insurance companies had to pay the damages to retain their credibility. Where compensation was paid to Jews, the German government would arrange to confiscate those payments. Jews would also be made liable to repair the damages.

Heydrich then commented that even if Jews were eliminated from the economy, "the main problem, namely, to kick the Jew out of Germany, remains." He proposed forced emigration as successfully developed by his staff in Vienna. He also suggested making the Jews wear identifying insignia. Göring raised the question of ghettos, to which Heydrich objected; a ghetto "would remain the permanent hideout for criminals and also for epidemics and the like." But Göring favored the idea of the ghetto. (Hitler had mentioned the ghetto as a possibility back in 1935, and he may have spoken of it to Göring.) But the discussion trailed off into details of now to isolate Jews from "Aryans" in hospitals and public conveyances.

Göring had one more item on the agenda: what would the gentlemen present think if he would announce that Jewry should have to contribute one billion marks as a penalty? There were no objections and Göring remarked, "Incidentally, I'd like to say again that I would not like to be a Jew in Germany." Then, parroting his Führer's style, he closed the meeting with an ominous threat: "If in the near future the German Reich should come into conflict with foreign powers, it goes without saying that we in Germany should first of all let it come to a showdown with the Jews."

That same afternoon Göring issued the Decree on Eliminating the Jews from German Economic Life, which excluded Jews from retail stores, export mail-order firms, the calling of independent craftsman; from selling any goods or services anywhere; from serving as executive or manager of any firms; and from being a member of a cooperative.[28] At the same time he issued the Decree on the Penalty Payment by Jews

Who Are German Subjects, imposing the one-billion-mark contribution, because, according to the decree's preamble, the "hostile attitude of Jewry toward the German Volk and Reich, which does not shrink even from committing cowardly murder, necessitates determined resistance and harsh penalty."[29]

In his testimony at Nuremberg, Göring, trying to evade responsibility, claimed that the idea for the levy had been Goebbels', even though the idea for it had come from Hitler's Four Year Plan. The one-billion-mark payment had been intended, in Hitler's original memorandum and in Göring's decree, to relieve Germany's critical financial situation, particularly at that stage of its war preparations. Indeed, at a meeting of the Reich Defense Council, just six days later, with Göring in the chair, all ministers and state secretaries, all commanders-in-chief of the armed forces and chiefs of the General Staff present, Göring mentioned the "very critical situation of the Reich Exchequer" and said that relief had been attained "initially through the billion imposed on Jewry and through profits accruing to the Reich in the Aryanization of Jewish enterprises."[30]

On December 14 Göring sent a memorandum to the highest officials of the Reich, informing them that henceforth all decrees and other important directives touching on the Jewish question would have to go through his office and receive his approval, to assure the necessary centralization in dealing with the Jewish question, especially with regard to economic matters. All independent actions on the Jewish question, Göring emphasized, were to cease.[31]

Everything relating to the Jewish question, it seemed, had been disposed of, except the Jews themselves. On January 24, 1939, Göring gave Heydrich the power to take all measures for a stepped-up forced emigration of the German Jews, along the lines that Eichmann had pioneered in Vienna after the Anschluss. SS terror was rampant there, and the Jews were its primary target; thousands were rounded up and incarcerated in Dachau, Buchenwald, and a new camp at Mauthausen; other thousands were forced to clean streets and public latrines. Eichmann then offered "emigration" as an alternative to the terror. He set up the central organization that he had first proposed in 1937, a *Zentralstelle für jüdische Auswanderung* (Central Office for Jewish Emigration). For its successful operation, he demanded the reestablishment of the *Jüdische Kultusgemeinde* (Jewish Religious Community), which had been dissolved, and the release from detention of some Jewish communal leaders. With their cooperation, procured by terror, Eichmann began to process the forcible exit of Jews from Austria. The application of apposite doses of terror and blackmail, coupled with the centralization of bureaucratic procedures, so successfully speeded up "emigration" that in about six months after the Anschluss, 45,000 Jews had left Austria. Over 100,000 more would leave before war broke out.

Eichmann's activities were closely observed in Germany. The most serious drawback, from Göring's point of view, was the depletion of Jewish accounts abroad to finance emigration. All this was discussed at Göring's conference on November 12, 1938, at which Heydrich proposed to set up a similar procedure for the Reich, but without the "mistakes" to which Göring had alluded. To this Göring agreed on the spot. The directive, issued January 24, 1939, provided for the establishment of a *Reichszentrale für die jüdische Auswanderung* (Reich Central Office for Jewish Emigration), operating under Heydrich's direction. Its object was to promote the "emigration" of Jews from Germany "by every possible means." The directive further required that an "appropriate Jewish organization for the uniform preparation of emigration applications" be created. The "appropriate Jewish organization" was to be used in the same way that Eichmann had exploited the Jüdische Kultusgemeinde in Vienna.

Since the Jews were now deprived of all means of livelihood and all state benefits, and their children were barred from German schools, it was decided that the "appropriate Jewish organization" should also take over the tasks of welfare and education for the Jewish population. To this end, the Germans made use of the framework of the *Reichsvertretung der Juden in Deutschland* (Federal Representation of the Jews in Germany), a loose coordinating body representing the major German Jewish organizations that had been set up autonomously by the Jews in 1933. It was reconstituted, in the aftermath of the Kristallnacht, under a new name, *Reichsvereinigung der Juden in Deutschland* (Federal Union of the Jews in Germany), with three functions—emigration, education, and social welfare. The decree, formalizing the new organization, stipulated that it would be under the surveillance of the Ministry of the Interior, which meant the police.[32] (The decree was issued July 4, 1939, but the Reichsvereinigung was actually in operation under its new name and under Gestapo supervision as early as February.)[33]

The first working session of the Reichszentrale, under Heydrich's chairmanship, was held February 11, 1939, and began the process of concentrating all matters concerning Jewish emigration that had been handled by various ministries, in the hands of the police.[34] But the Reichszentrale did not have much of a life, for the outbreak of the war ended the possibilities of emigration, an eventuality that had surely not escaped Göring's attention. Gestapo Müller, whom Heydrich had first appointed to head the agency, gave up the post in October 1939, recommending Eichmann to succeed him. When Sipo and the SD were merged in October 1939 to become the RSHA, Eichmann was shifted from the SD bureaucracy to the political police (RSHA *Amt* IV), under Müller. He took over the desk for Emigration and Evacuation, coded IV-D-4, which in a later reorganization became Jewish Affairs and Evacuation Affairs, coded IV-B-4. From this office he would schedule, organize, and manage the deportation of the European Jews to the death camps. In 1938 "emigration" was a euphemism for "expulsion." Once war began, "evacuation" became a euphemism for "deportation," which, in turn, signified transportation to a place of death.

On January 21, 1939, Hitler told the Czech Foreign Minister Chvalkovsky: "We are going to destroy the Jews. They are not going to get away with what they did on November 9, 1918. The day of reckoning has come."[35] That was confidential, but on January 30, 1939, Hitler dilated on this theme when he addressed the Reichstag on the anniversary of his accession to power. The most salient passage of that long speech was two paragraphs to which Hitler himself would refer often during the war. They constituted his declaration of war against the Jews:

> And one more thing I would like now to state on this day memorable perhaps not only for us Germans. I have often been a prophet in my life and was generally laughed at. During my struggle for power, the Jews primarily received with laughter my prophecies that I would someday assume the leadership of the state and thereby of the entire Volk and then, among many other things, achieve a solution of the Jewish problem. I suppose that meanwhile the then resounding laughter of Jewry in Germany is now choking in their throats.
>
> Today I will be a prophet again: If international finance Jewry within Europe and abroad should succeed once more in plunging the peoples into a world war, then the consequence will be not the Bolshevization of the world and therewith a victory of Jewry, but on the contrary, the destruction of the Jewish race in Europe.[36]

6

Phase Two: From
Internal War to World War

Hitler's early invasions had been greeted with flowers, not guns. The entry of the German army into the Rhineland, then into Austria, and thereafter into the Sudetenland were adventures in diplomatic and military brinksmanship that had attained Hitler's goals without war. So, too, Germany's destruction of the Czech republic in mid-March 1939 proceeded without impediment. Hitler annexed Czechoslovakia's western provinces of Bohemia and Moravia as a German protectorate; the eastern province of Slovakia became a puppet state under the rule of Father Jozef Tiso, a right-wing Catholic priest and Slovak nationalist.

On March 15 Prime Minister Chamberlain, addressing the House of Commons, explained that in the light of Slovakia's self-proclaimed independence, Britain did not have to honor its treaty obligations to Czechoslovakia by coming to its assistance in the event of an act of unprovoked aggression. That was the kind of reaction that Hitler had contemptuously expected of the English, and it appeared to vindicate his strategy. But now Hitler miscalculated. Two days later, Chamberlain publicly admitted he had been deceived and disappointed, that the assurances that

Hitler had given in Munich in September 1938 had been worthless. (The annexation of the Sudetenland, Hitler had said then, would be "the last territorial claim" he would make in Europe.) Just two weeks later, on March 31, 1939, Chamberlain informed Parliament that the British government would come at once to Poland's aid "in the event of any action which clearly threatened Polish independence and which the Polish Government accordingly considered it vital to resist with their national forces." The French government, too, had authorized him to make it plain that on this question they took the same position as the British.

Hitler's rage at the Anglo-French stand and their agreement with Poland signed on April 6 still did not deter him from the course on which he had already embarked toward Poland's destruction. In March he had begun to make excessive demands of Poland—Danzig became the symbolic issue—and brash diplomatic maneuvers accompanied outrageous propaganda. On April 3 Hitler gave Field Marshal Wilhelm Keitel, Chief of the High Command of the armed forces, instructions to prepare Operation White, the invasion of Poland. In mid-April, addressing top military officers, Hitler argued that since Germany could not count on Poland's neutrality in case of a war with the Western powers, Germany must therefore first eliminate Poland through a lightning campaign (*Blitzkrieg*). He assured the officers that such an undertaking would not lead to another war.[1]

Just about this time a new diplomatic possibility unfolded that showed Hitler's capacity for opportunism, expediency, and deceit and that would, in addition, give impetus to Operation White. On April 17, for the first time since he had presented his credentials nearly a year ago, the Russian ambassador visited Ernst von Weizsäcker, then state secretary in the German Foreign Office. The Russians, it appeared, had contracted with the Czech Skoda Works for munitions and were now concerned about their delivery. The conversation then turned from trade to politics, and Weizsäcker recorded the position of the Soviet ambassador: "There exists for Russia no reason why she should not live with us on a normal footing. And from normal, the relations might become better and better."[2]

Though the Soviet Union appears to have taken the initiative for a German-Soviet rapprochement, it was Germany that more eagerly pursued the undercover negotiations. On April 28 Hitler denounced his 1934 agreement with Poland. That may have been intended to demonstrate to the Russians the German interest in coming to an understanding. The Russians then signified their interest on May 3 by suddenly dismissing Foreign Minister Maxim Litvinov. Litvinov embodied all that the Germans detested about Bolshevism—he was a Jew, a peace advocate, a supporter of the League of Nations, a friend of the Western democracies, and an opponent of Nazi Germany and its anti-Comintern Axis. Litvinov was replaced by Vyacheslav V. M. Molotov, the complete antithesis to Litvinov: a non-Jew, a close associate of Stalin's, a hard, ruthless man said to favor accommodation with Germany. With remarkable prescience the French ambassador in Berlin noted on May 7 that a fourth partition of Poland would surely be the basis of the German-Russian rapprochement.[3]

At a meeting on May 23, 1939, of his highest-ranking military officers to brief them on "the situation and political objectives," Hitler dilated, as usual, on racial and ideological matters as the basis for Germany's politics and then set forth his military strategy to attain both the racial and the political goals.[4] He said that while "the ideological problems" of the German people had been already solved, the question of German self-sufficiency still awaited solution. That was a question, he told them, not of Danzig but of Lebensraum: "If fate forces us into a showdown with the West it is good to possess a largish area in the East." The decision had to be to attack Poland at the first suitable opportunity. Possible accommodation with Russia was barely hinted at: "Economic relations with Russia are only possible if and when political relations have improved."

On May 30 the German Foreign Office instructed their ambassador in Moscow: "Contrary to the policy previously planned, we have now decided to undertake definite negotiations with the Soviet Union." Hitler had decided that in the event of Anglo-French intervention on behalf of Poland, it was the wiser strategy to protect his eastern flank. Once again, in the most backhanded way, he resorted to expediency and opportunism to advance his ideological and political goals. In fact, on the very eve of the invasion he admitted as much. General Franz Halder recorded Hitler's remarks at a meeting with top party people on August 28: "Soviet pact in many ways misunderstood by party. Pact with Satan so as to drive out the Devil."[5] (The metaphor was one he had used in the past, positively or negatively, as it suited his purpose.)

Everything was "go" for the Polish invasion. On June 23 Göring, as Plenipotentiary for the Four Year Plan, called a meeting of the Reich Defense Council to discuss manpower problems that war would impose on Germany. Funk was given the responsibility of deciding what kind of work could be assigned to war prisoners and to inmates of penitentiaries and concentration camps. Himmler promised that greater use would be made of the concentration camps during wartime, and Göring talked of employing foreign workers in Germany. The most extensive and inhumane network of forced and slave labor began to be organized.

The summer passed rapidly in the din of German threats against Poland, while official conversations with allies-soon-to-be-enemies concealed the simultaneous pursuit of secret negotiations with the Russians. Hitler had set August 26 as the start of Operation White (the Polish campaign was to be completed before the autumn rains) and therefore pressed vigorously to conclude an agreement with Russia before then. On August 19 Stalin informed the Politburo that he would sign a pact with Germany, and that same day a trade agreement between both countries was brought off. On August 23 Foreign Minister Ribbentrop arrived in Moscow and in the afternoon conferred with Stalin. In an extraordinary burst of energy, agreement on the text was reached later that day and the pact was signed after midnight. The pact, in its secret protocol, defined the spheres of influence of each signatory (Lithuania was in the German sphere; Latvia, Estonia, and Finland were in the Russian) and drew a demarcation line for the partition of Poland. Both parties obligated "themselves to desist from any act of violence, any aggressive action, and any attack on each other, either individually or jointly with other Powers."

On August 25 Britain signed a formal treaty with Poland, confirming the guarantees given on April 6. That day Hitler postponed Operation White to September 1, in the hope of eliminating British intervention, but he failed to detach the British from their commitment to Poland. Operation White was nonetheless ordered, and by 6:30 A.M. on September 1, 1939, German troops invaded Poland all along the frontier.

Later that morning Hitler addressed the Reichstag with self-justifying and belligerent rhetoric. Projecting upon the enemy his own intentions, he threatened: "Whoever fights with poison will be fought back with poison gas. Whoever deviates from the rules for the humane conduct of war can expect nothing else from us, but that we will take the same steps."[6] It was one of the few speeches in which he failed to mention Jews. (Was the passage just quoted an esoteric reference?) Yet later Hitler fixedly and repeatedly referred to *this* speech on *this* day as the speech in which he had threatened the Jews with destruction in the event of a war, though he had made *that* speech on January 30, 1939.* In his mind he associated his declaration of

---

* There were, to my knowledge, four such "slips."[7]

1. January 30, 1941: "And I should not like to forget the indica-

war on September 1, 1939, with his promise to destroy the Jews.

War and the annihilation of the Jews were interdependent. The disorder of war would provide Hitler with the cover for the unchecked commission of murder. He needed an arena for his operations where the restraints of common codes of morality and accepted rules of warfare would not extend. He had set into motion a twofold war—one that was traditional in its striving for resources and empire and that would be fought in traditional military style, and one that was unconventional inasmuch as its primary political objective was to attain National Socialist ideology and

---

tion that I had already given once, on September 1, 1939, in the German Reichstag. The indication, then, to wit, that if the rest of the world would be plunged into a general war by Jewry, then the whole of Jewry would have finished playing its role in Europe!

"They may still laugh today at that, exactly as they laughed at my prophecies. The coming months and years will prove that I also saw correctly here."

2. January 30, 1942: "We see our way clearly on the point that the war can end only in that either the Aryan peoples are annihilated or Jewry will disappear from Europe. On September 1, 1939, I declared in the German Reichstag—and I guard myself against premature prophecies—that this war would not end as the Jews imagine, namely, that the European-Aryan peoples will be annihilated, but on the contrary that the consequence of this war will be the destruction of Jewry."

3. September 30, 1942: "On September 1, 1939, I stated two things at the meeting then of the Reichstag:

"First, that after this war was already forced upon us, no force of arms and also no term would ever force us down, and second, that if Jewry would plot an international world war for the annihilation of the Aryan peoples of Europe, then not the Aryan peoples would be annihilated, but on the contrary Jewry. . . . The Jews laughed once also in Germany at my prophecies. I do not know if they are still laughing also today, or if their laughter has not already subsided. But I can also now only assert: Their laughter everywhere will subside. And I will be right also with these prophecies in the end."

4. November 8, 1942: "You will recall still that meeting of the Reichstag in which I declared: If Jewry perchance imagines that it can bring about an international world war for the annihilation of the European races, then the consequence will be not the annihilation of the European races, but on the contrary, it will be the annihilation of Jewry in Europe. I was always laughed at as a prophet. Of those who laughed then, countless ones no longer laugh today, and those who still laugh now will perhaps in a while also no longer do so."

that would be conducted in an innovative style of mass murder.

On September 3 Britain declared war on Germany, and a few hours later France followed suit. That same day Prime Minister Chamberlain broadcast the news. "It is evil things," he said, "we shall be fighting against, brute force, bad faith, injustice, oppression, and persecution. But against them I am certain that the right will prevail."

Poland was in no way a match for the Germans in the number of its fighting troops or in their equipment. Within a few days German air superiority had rendered Polish resistance ineffective. The German ground invasion moved so swiftly that the Russians, for their part, could barely keep up with them. On September 17, when the western half of Poland was in German hands except for Warsaw, which was holding out heroically against German besiegement, the Russians overran eastern Poland and occupied those areas agreed upon in the German-Soviet pact. On September 27, when Warsaw capitulated, the Polish campaign was over. The following day Ribbentrop and Molotov signed a German-Soviet Boundary and Friendship Treaty and a number of secret protocols adjusting the boundaries of the spheres of influence that had been defined in the agreement of August 23. They also issued a public declaration to that effect that they had now created "a firm foundation for a lasting peace in Eastern Europe," and called on England and France to end the state of war against Germany.[8]

The partition of Poland and its occupation* at last gave Hitler the opportunity to effect the racial programs that had obsessed him for two decades. On October 12, 1939, he issued a decree establishing a civil administration in Poland, called *Generalgouvernement,* with Hans Frank as Governor General. Frank

---

* See Appendix A for a brief account of the occupation and fate of the Jews in Poland.

would later describe himself to Curzio Malaparte as "the German King of Poland," a claim based more on vanity than on reality. Just three days before, on October 9, 1939, by secret decree Hitler had appointed Himmler Reich Commissar for the Strengthening of German Folkdom (RKFDV), a position that augmented his already vast authority as head of the SS with all its divisions and enterprises and that made him the *de facto* master and chthonian monarch of occupied Poland, in effect Hitler's plenipotentiary for racial empire. In the welter of conflicting jurisdictions in Poland—among the military, civil administration, labor supply, economic undertakings, and the SS— ideological interests, above all, the war against the Jews, became the province of the SS.

Racial policies to be pursued in Poland, according to Hitler's decree, were designed to eliminate the "harmful influence" of "alien" populations and to create new German colonies by resettlement. All non-Germans were to be expelled from those areas of Poland that would be integrated into Germany proper. As Hitler put it to Keitel on October 17, "the old and new Reich area" was to be "cleansed of Jews, Polacks and company."[9] A German racial "reclamation" project was put into operation, racially screening persons who claimed to be Germans or had Germanic features. Such persons were regarded as "racially valuable" and hence eligible for "re-Germanization." (Blond, Teutonic-looking Polish children were especially desirable.) These were sent to Germany to undergo the proper ideological indoctrination, while nearly a half-million racially pure Germans from the Reich were brought in to establish German peasant colonies in the areas from which the Poles had been expelled.

In the Generalgouvernement, however, as Hitler told Keitel, a "tough struggle for national existence [*Volkstumskampf*]" that "permits no legal restraints" would have to be conducted. The Generalgouvernement was to serve as a dumping ground for the Poles and Jews expelled from the parts of Poland that Germany annexed. The total number involved in this

Boundary of Poland up to September 1, 1939

Generalgouvernement of Poland after July 1941' (under German administration)

German-Russian border, September 1939–June 1941

Incorporated in the German Reich

Death camps (names underlined)

BALTIC SEA

LATVIA

Riga

LITHUANIA

Kovno

Vilna

REICHSKOMMISSARIAT OSTLAND Incorporated in

Danzig

EAST PRUSSIA

Minsk

GERMANY

WARTHELAND

Grodno

SOVIET UNION

Poznań

GENERALKOMMISSARIAT BIALYSTOK Białystok (quasi-incorporated with East Prussia)

Baranowicze

Chełmno

Treblinka

WARSAW

Brest Litovsk

Pinsk

Lodz

Sobibór

Breslau

Radom

Incorporated in REICHSKOMMISSARIAT UKRAINE

Czestochowa

Lublin (Majdanek)

Oświęcim (Auschwitz)

Bełzec

Cracow

Dubno

PROTECTORATE OF BOHEMIA AND MORAVIA

GENERALGOUVERNEMENT

Przemyśl

Lwów

Tarnopol

UKRAINE

SLOVAKIA

(added to Generalgouvernement in July 1941)

HUNGARY

Śniatyn

RUMANIA

The German Partition of Poland, 1939/41–1945

population transfer has been estimated at one million. The Polish leadership elite was to be killed, the Polish population to serve only as a source of labor for the Germans. The Jews were to be concentrated in a few large centers and then segregated from the non-Jewish population as a first step in a long-range plan that would end in their annihilation. The responsibility for this program was lodged with Himmler, and its execution entrusted to Heydrich and his SD striking force—*Einsatzgruppen* (special-duty groups).*

The Einsatzgruppen, as a paramilitary police force, were conceived of by Heydrich to provide a striking force for the political police and security intelligence. They were first used during the invasion of Austria, hunting down persons suspected of opposition to National Socialism. In connection with the planned invasion of Czechoslovakia, they were to follow, wherever possible, directly behind the advancing troops and take over all security, including also the security "of all enterprises necessary to the national economy and so, also to the war economy."[10] Their role was to become increasingly important as the war accelerated.

Six Einsatzgruppen were attached to the army during the military campaign in Poland. Their wholesale murder of Poles and their sadistic atrocities against Jews shocked some army generals. The generals' recoil from the sanguinary acts of the SS may be ascribed not to moral objections but instead to the Einsatzgruppen's deviations from army regulations and army discipline, and to the generals' desire to preserve the hegemony of the army. By September 1939 the army had been thoroughly ideologized, its men and officers indoctrinated in the teachings of National Socialism through the spoken and printed word. (Top-ranking officers usually got their ideological briefings directly from Hitler.) An army indoctrination booklet on "The

---

* *Einsatz* is a word with many meanings, most of them vague. In some usage it carries an overtone of self-sacrifice or dedication to duty, in the sense of "stake" (one stakes one's life for a meaningful outcome). "Special-duty groups" perhaps best renders the meaning; "striking force" too conveys some flavor of the German.

Jew in German History," published early in 1939, shows how thoroughly the army had adopted Nazi doctrine and, concomitantly, a double standard in combat.

> We Germans fight a twofold fight today. With regard to the non-Jewish peoples we want only to accomplish our vital interests. We respect them and conduct a chivalrous argument with them. But we fight world Jewry as one has to fight a poisonous parasite; we encounter in him not only the enemy of our people, but a plague of all peoples. The fight against Jewry is a moral fight for the purity and health of God-created humanity and for a new more just order in the world.[11]

The army's hostile reactions to the Einsatzgruppen served notice on Himmler and Heydrich that they had to convince the army of the top priority of their "political" tasks. On September 19 Heydrich conferred with army Quartermaster General Eduard Wagner, explaining that though the Einsatzgruppen chiefs were subordinated to army HQ, they received their instructions directly from him as Chief of the Security Police. Heydrich regarded the discussion as a "favorable outcome" in SD collaboration with the army.[12] Wagner passed on details of the conference to his superior, General Franz Halder, who recorded some laconic notes of the meeting in his diary:

> a. Missions [of the SD] must be known to the army. Liaison officers: Himmler army CC [General Walter von Brauchitsch].
> b. Cleaning out: Jewry, intelligentsia, clergy, nobility.
> c. Army demands: Cleanup after the withdrawal of the army and after the transfer to stable civil administration. . . .[13]

The SD did indeed get the better of the army, for the army had to be satisfied simply with knowing in advance about the special missions assigned to the SD. Furthermore, these "cleanup" missions against the

Jews and Polish elite groups would proceed as planned. The army asked Heydrich not to start these missions until after the Generalgouvernement was transferred to a civil administration, but this was of no avail. Two days after his meeting with Wagner, Heydrich, at a conference in Berlin, issued to his Einsatzgruppen chiefs his first major directive affecting the Polish Jews and that same day sent it out as an express letter.[14]

At that conference, a luncheon meeting, with fifteen SS officers present (including Eichmann, representing the Reichszentrale für die jüdische Auswanderung), Heydrich outlined the racial policies planned for Poland and the tasks of the Einsatzgruppen. They were instructed to prepare lists of top Polish leaders and also of those on the middle level of leadership—teachers, clergy, nobility, legionnaires. Those listed were clearly foredoomed. As for the Jews, the policy was to concentrate them in city ghettos "for a better possibility of control and later possibility of deportation." Jewish smallholders were to disapear. Jewish retailers could remain in rural areas only if they provided the army with supplies it required. A directive, Heydrich informed them, would be issued covering four points: (1) moving Jews as fast as possible into the cities; (2) transferring Jews out of the Reich into Poland; (3) moving the remaining 30,000 Gypsies also into Poland; (4) systematically ejecting the Jews from the German territories in freight cars.

Heydrich's directive, "The Jewish Question in the Occupied Territory," issued later that day, is a guidepost in the chronology of the Final Solution. It testifies that a master plan for annihilating the Jews had already been conceived, though only the preliminary stages were now to be implemented. Heydrich "once more" reminded the Einsatzgruppen chiefs that "the *planned overall measures* (i.e., the final aim) are to be kept strictly secret." He distinguished between "the final aim," requiring an extended period of time, and "the stages leading to the fulfillment of this final aim." The "final aim" is not mentioned further. (Eichmann, when confronted with the document at his trial, said right away that it could mean only "physical extermination.")[15] First, Heydrich described the task of expelling the Jews from the areas that were to be incorporated into the German Reich (Danzig, West Prussia, Posen, and Eastern Upper Silesia) and then of concentrating all the Polish Jews in a few urban areas. The aim should be, Heydrich emphasized, to establish as few concentration points as possible, and, "so as to facilitate subsequent measures," these concentration points should be at rail junctions or places located along railroad lines. At his conference Heydrich thought that this process would take three to four weeks. Actually, it took much longer, partly because of a temporary halt to meet army objections, but mainly because of the complexities involved in moving such vast numbers of people.

The second section, titled *Jüdische Ältestenräte* ("Councils of Jewish Elders"), prescribed that a Jewish council be established in each community to carry out the instructions of the Einsatzgruppen.* It was to consist of available "influential personalities and rabbis." The idea of a Jewish council headed by an "Eldest" (*Älteste*) probably derived from the practice in medieval Germany, when the internal affairs of the Jewish community were regulated by a so-called *Judenbischof*, "bishop of the Jews," in fact, chief rabbi. He was assisted by an advisory council of twelve *dayanim*, composing a Judenrat, all usually chosen or elected by the taxpaying members of the community and approved by the Emperor. Members of the council were called "Elders," and the chairman was designated the "Eldest." The practice persisted until the Reformation.

---

* The creation of a Jewish council, called "Judenrat," was proposed back in April 1933 in a draft Law to Regulate the Status of Jews (*Judengesetz*).[16] It was prepared by several persons, including Rudolf Diels, the first Gestapo chief, and by Dr. Johannes von Leers, a professor of history and "expert" on the Jews. The draft was submitted to Frick at that time, but never used. There is no evidence that Göring, then Diels's superior, or Heydrich ever knew of it.

The term "Judenrat" eventually became more common than "Ältestenrat," while "Älteste" was reserved for the council's chairman. This council, Heydrich stressed, was to be made *fully responsible,* in the literal sense of the word, for the exact and punctual execution of all directives issued or yet to be issued," and failure to do so would entail the "severest measures."

The functions assigned to the Jewish councils, though few, were onerous beyond the capacity of any nongovernmental agency: they were charged with the responsibility for carrying out the evacuation of the Jews from the countryside, for providing food supplies en route and housing in the cities of concentration. The Jewish councils were also to prepare censuses of the Jewish population in their jurisdiction, by age and principal occupational groups, which were intended, in time, to eliminate the nonworking populations— children and the old—and to indicate which occupations were needed by the army or the wartime economy.

Once the Jews were concentrated in a few large cities, Heydrich foresaw that for general reasons of security, it would probably be necessary to bar "Jews from certain sections of cities, or, for example, forbid them to leave the ghetto or go out after a designated evening hour."

Back on November 12, 1938, at Göring's conference, Heydrich had objected to Göring's proposal for ghettos on the grounds that they would harbor Jewish resistance, but now ghettos, which Hitler had already alluded to in 1935, were the obvious "solution" for concentrating the Jews during the preparations for the "final aim."

The third section of the directive, concerning the Jews in their economic and industrial capacities, indicated that these functions should be transferred to "Aryans" without impairing the "economic security" of the occupied territories. The army's needs were essential, Heydrich stressed, and Jewish-owner or Jewish-operated enterprises meeting the needs of the

army were to be tolerated only until "prompt Aryanization" could be accomplished.

The chiefs of the Einsatzgruppen were instructed to
report to Heydrich, with statistics, on their accomplishments in evacuating and concentrating the Jews and
in gathering the economic and industrial data required. To attain these goals Heydrich stated that he
expected "total deployment of all forces of the Security
Police and the Security Service," and to make sure
that all areas were covered he advised the Einsatzgruppen chiefs in adjoining territories to consult each
other. Copies of the directive were sent to the army,
the Plenipotentiary for the Four Year Plan, the departments of Interior, Food, Economy, as well as the heads
of the civil administration of the occupied territory.
The whole wartime German bureaucracy was thus informed and involved in the SS's plan to deal with the
"Jewish question in the occupied territory."

Some analysts have suggested that "the final aim" to
which Heydrich had alluded in his directive was, at
this time, not the planned annihilation of the Jews, but
the establishment of a vast Jewish reservation. Hitler
himself had mentioned that as a possibility back in
1935: the Jews would be "imprisoned in a territory
where they can disport themselves according to their
nature." From the start of the war, the Germans spread
reports that a "Jewish reservation" would be set up in
the Lublin district,[17] and indeed tens of thousands of
Jews from the newly annexed territories and from
Germany proper were sent there beginning in October
1939. The plan seemed even to have been approved by
Göring, Himmler, and Frank in early February 1940,
but it was canceled a month later, without explanation.
Meanwhile, another site for a reservation had been
bruited about—the French island of Madagascar. Certain Foreign Office and SS bureaucrats were enthusiastic about the idea, indefatigably drafting memoranda
on various aspects of the plan, ranging from problems
in international law to transportation. Even Himmler,
in a memorandum, "Some Thoughts on the Treatment
of Foreign Nationals in the East," that he submitted to

Hitler in May 1940, wrote: "I hope to see the concept of Jews completely obliterated with the possibility of a large migration of all the Jews to Africa or else in a colony."[18]

Yet everything we know of National Socialist ideology precludes our accepting the idea of a Jewish reservation as the last stage of the Final Solution. In the hierarchy of Nazi racial values, the Jews were bottom-most, slated for a crueler fate than the Slavs, a layer higher. The Slavs were *Untermenschen*, subhumans who, Himmler said, were to learn that to obey the Germans was a divine command. Hitler's "final" racial policy for the Slavs was "depopulation," which would prevent them from propagating, except to provide a continuous supply of slaves to serve the Germans. Hence, if justice was to be rendered according to the scale of National Socialist racial values, then clearly a more sanguineous fate than that of the Slavs was intended for the Jews. A reservation, whether in Lublin or Madagascar, could have been conceived of only as a transitional stage, comparable to ghettos as a means of concentration. Perhaps it was no mere coincidence that the first ghetto in Poland was established in Lodz in the spring of 1940, right after the Lublin plan was dropped.[19] Another enlightening datum on the purpose of a reservation can be derived from the report—surely a sick joke—that Philipp Bouhler, the head of Hitler's private chancellery, was slated to become governor of the Madagascar reservation. Bouhler headed the so-called "Euthanasia Program" (see below, p. 175), the first mass murder by gassing, experience that doubtless qualified him to run a reservation for Jews that would become truly their final destination. (Madagascar would have afforded the privacy that the Germans wanted for the Final Solution.)

By September 21, 1939, when Heydrich issued his instructions to his Einsatzgruppen chiefs, it seemed that the "final aim" was already envisaged, although the precise steps leading to its implementation were still to be formulated, planned, and executed. Poland was the launching area and testing laboratory not only for the execution of the Final Solution, but for all of Hitler's racial and imperial ambitions, but Russia would become the arena for the first encounter in the final struggle, the prelude to the millennium.

The plans to wage war against Russia were always in Hitler's thoughts. He told Keitel on October 17, 1939, that the area of Poland had military significance as an "advanced glacis" and could be used for troop deployment. Consequently, trains, highways, and communication lines were to be kept in order.[20] But first Hitler prepared the invasions of Western Europe as part of a grand strategy to consolidate the West under German dominion and thus free him for that decisive struggle in the East.

On October 9, 1939, just days after the end of the Polish campaign, he issued the first directive for Operation Yellow, the invasion of the Low Countries, but that plan had to be postponed, perhaps because of an attempted assassination on him. Spring invasions instead were set in motion—in April into Denmark and Norway, in May into the Netherlands, Belgium, and France.* With the surrender of the French on June 21, 1940, Hitler stood triumphant at the English Channel. On his agenda now was Operation Sea Lion, the invasion of Britain. All through the summer he issued directives for an invasion that was scheduled to take place on September 15, conditional on Germany's gaining air supremacy over England.

Meanwhile, Hitler vigilantly monitored Russia's moves in the East—its incorporation of the Baltic states into the Soviet Union, its threats against Finland and Bessarabia, its heavy troop concentrations in eastern Poland. Early in July he told the General Staff to draw plans for an offensive in the East, and the following month he ordered that Poland be readied as

---

* For the fate of the Jews in these countries, see Appendix A.

an assembly platform for an Eastern campaign and that the necessary roads, railroad lines, airfields, and military quarters be constructed.[21]

On September 15 the air battle for Britain reached its dramatic climax when the British air force succeeded in repelling Germany's massive and concentrated air attack over the Kent promontory. Two days later Hitler ordered Operation Sea Lion postponed indefinitely. But the plans for an Eastern campaign continued, and a war game was ordered in September to test campaign possibilities. Hitler proceeded, impelled more by ideology than strategy. On December 18, 1940, barely fifteen months after the conclusion of the German-Soviet Boundary and Friendship Treaty, Hitler issued the first directive for a German invasion of Russia: "The German armed forces must be prepared, even before the conclusion of the war against England, *to crush Soviet Russia in a rapid campaign* ('Operation Barbarossa')." According to this plan, preparations were to be concluded by mid-May, in time for an early summer invasion. (Fighting was expected to be over before the Russian winter set in.) Hitler's only other strategic plan, meanwhile, was to keep the British out of the Mediterranean, lest they interfere with his military movements in the East.

Preparations continued according to schedule, and in the middle of March German troops began to move eastward in readiness for the attack, then set for May 12.[22] On March 13, 1941, Field Marshal Keitel issued a top secret directive, in five copies, containing a series of "orders for special areas," in connection with Operation Barbarossa. Its main purpose was to define jurisdiction of competence and lines of authority in the areas of operation as they affected the armed forces, the SS, and the civil administration. One paragraph defined the role and function of the SS:

In the area of army operations the Reichsführer-SS will be entrusted, on behalf of the Führer, with *special tasks* for the preparation of the *political administration*

—tasks entailed by the final struggle that will have to be carried out between two opposing political systems. Within the framework of these tasks, the Reichsführer-SS will act independently and on his own responsibility. However, the executive power vested in the Supreme Commander of the army and in agencies acting under his orders will not be affected by this. The Reichsführer-SS is to see that operations are not disturbed by the execution of his tasks. Details are to be worked out directly between the High Command of the army and the Reichsführer-SS.[23]

The rhetoric about "tasks entailed by the final struggle that will have to be carried out between two opposing political systems" was one seldom encountered in military directives. It was the rhetoric of Hitler's racial eschatology, of the final struggle between the Aryan hosts and their Jewish-Bolshevik opponents. The whole paragraph was said to have been dictated by Hitler himself.[24] It was the authorization for Einsatzgruppen to kill the Jews in the territory that the army would first wrest from the enemy.

Keitel later claimed that he "had so stubbornly contested" the clause giving Himmler authority in the rear operational areas, but that his opposition was useless and he was overruled.[25] By clarifying the area of authority assigned to the SS and from the start obtaining Keitel's assent to the presence and activity of the SS Einsatzgruppen, both Hitler and Himmler assured themselves that the earlier conflicts between the army and the SS in Poland would not recur and that no impediment would arise to obstruct the program laid out for Einsatzgruppen.*

---

* Similar arrangements defining the relationships between the SS and the civil administration of the Eastern occupied territories were also provided for. On July 17, 1941, Hitler issued a decree establishing a civil administration upon completion of military operations. He appointed Alfred Rosenberg to the post of Reich Minister for the Occupied Eastern Territories. That decree—as well as another issued the same day signed by Hitler, Keitel, and Lammers—gave Himmler jurisdiction in that area over "police security" and within that sphere also the authority to give orders to the Reich commissioners who were

One more decision had been taken in the relentless course toward the annihilation of the Jews. Though the abundant documents of the German dictatorship have yielded no written order by Hitler to murder the Jews, it appears from the events as we know them now, that the decision for the practical implementation of the plan to kill the Jews was probably reached after December 18, 1940—when Hitler issued the first directive for Operation Barbarossa—and before March 1, 1941.

At about the same time that Operation Barbarossa was being planned to include procedures for the murder of the Jews in synchronization with the conquest of Russia, Himmler was initiating an even more sinister undertaking that would encompass the rest of Europe's Jews. On March 1, 1941, he visited Auschwitz, where he gave orders to Rudolf Höss, the camp commandant, for a tremendous expansion of the camp to accommodate 100,000 prisoners of war and 30,000 "peacetime" prisoners, 10,000 of whom would be assigned to the I. G. Farben synthetic-rubber factory.[26] The "prisoners of war" then in custody at Auschwitz, which served as a transit camp of sorts, had been arrested by the Security Police and could by no accepted standard be regarded as military prisoners. When Himmler spoke of providing accommodation for prisoners of war, he likely did not mean POWs in the traditional sense of captured men and officers of an enemy army, but rather ideological enemies, Jews and "Bolsheviks." Indeed, shortly after the invasion, on July 17, 1941, Heydrich issued a directive, in agreement with the army, giving his Einsatzkommandos authority to remove from prisoner-of-war camps in Russia "politically intolerable elements," including Soviet state officials, Communist party functionaries, and all Jews. That

subordinate to Rosenberg. Three-way conflicts among SS, army, and civil administration, as well as conflicts between Rosenberg and his staff, persisted throughout the occupation of Russia, as they did in the Generalgouvernement.

was one more example of the army's agreeableness to the SS's conducting ideological war in a military framework.

On March 30, 1941, Hitler met with his generals and top commanding officers assigned to the eastern front. After discussing at length the military and political situation, he then expatiated on his thesis about the inevitability of war with the Soviet Union. The slogan for his Russian policy, he told them, was "Destruction of Fighting Forces—Dissolution of State," in effect spelling out the strategy behind the March 13 order. Halder's elliptical diary entry conveys the brutal tone of Hitler's words:

> *Struggle between two opposing world outlooks.* Destructive decision on Bolshevism; is equal to social criminaldom. Communism extraordinary danger for future. We must disavow the point of view of soldierly comradeship. The Communist is not a comrade before and not a comrade after. It is a question of a war of destruction. If we don't conceive of it that way, then we will indeed beat the enemy, but in thirty years the Communist enemy will again confront us. We do not conduct war to conserve the enemy.
>
> Future political picture: Northern Russia will belong to Finland. Protectorates in the Baltic lands, the Ukraine, White Russia.
>
> Struggle against Russia: Destruction of the Bolshevik Commissars and the Communist intelligentsia. . . . The struggle must be conducted against the poison of decomposition. This is not a question of courts-martial. The leaders of the troops must know what is at stake. . . . In the East hardness is gentle for the future.[27]

According to Keitel, everyone appeared shocked, but no one protested. Hitler concluded: "I do not expect my generals to understand me, but I shall expect them to obey my orders."[28]

At that time—March 30, 1941—Operation Barbarossa was probably still scheduled for mid-May, but on March 26, 1941, a military coup had taken place in

Yugoslavia, overthrowing the government that had just formally joined the Tripartite Pact of Germany, Italy, and Japan. Fearing that the new government, supported by the revolutionary partisan movement, would jeopardize the success of Operation Barbarossa, Hitler had issued a directive on March 27 to invade Yugoslavia. To ensure Hungary's and Bulgaria's co-operation in that invasion, he offered them portions of Yugoslav territory to which they had revanchist claims, and he directed the German military to encourage internal tensions in Yugoslavia by dangling before the Croats the prospect of independence. Operation Barbarossa had to be postponed. After the capitulation of Yugoslavia on April 17, the Germans proceeded into Greece to bolster the collapsing Italian armed forces there. By the end of May all of Greece, including Crete, where British and Greek forces had offered resistance, was effectively under German control.*

Despite the Balkan military interlude, planning for Operation Barbarossa continued, especially with regard to the upcoming tasks of the SS and the Security Police and the efforts to legitimate them. On May 13 Hitler issued a decree that gave members of the armed forces a free hand in summary execution or "relentlessly" shooting down enemy civilians and which authorized "collective measures" to be taken against whole communities when individual culprits could not be identified. It promised protection to members of the armed forces and their "ancillary services" who engaged in such activities against enemy civilians, by guaranteeing that they "would not be subject to the constraint of prosecution even if the action is also a military crime or misdemeanor." A court-martial would be instituted only when required by military discipline or security.[29]

This unprecedented issuance of prepackaged immunity for acts normally subject to severe military discipline was followed up on June 6, 1941, by the heinous *Kommissarbefehl* (Commissar Order), signed

---

* For the fate of the Jews in these countries, see Appendix A.

by General Walter Warlimont, for the High Command
of the armed forces, "on the treatment of political
commissars."[30] The covering memorandum, thirty
copies of which were prepared, asked that the decree
be distributed only to the commanders of armies or
air force territorial command and that "its further
communication to lower commands follow by word of
mouth." The decree was an ideological justification of
Hitler's directive of May 13, specifically singling out
"political commissars" as symbols of the Bolshevik
regime. Its language indicated the extent to which the
German army had become indoctrinated with National
Socialist ideology and how far the war itself had become ideologized.

> In the struggle against Bolshevism, we must *not* assume
> that the enemy's conduct will be based on principles of
> humanity or of international law. In particular, hateful,
> cruel, and inhuman treatment of our prisoners is to be
> expected from *political commissars of all kinds* as the
> real carriers of resistance.
> The troops must be advised:
> 1. In this struggle consideration and respect for
> international law with regard to these elements are
> wrong. They are a danger for our own security and for
> the rapid pacification of conquered territory.
> 2. The originators of barbaric Asiatic methods of
> warfare are the political commissars. Accordingly
> measures must be taken against them *immediately* and
> with full severity. Accordingly, whether captured *in
> battle or offering resistance,* they are in principle to be
> disposed of by arms.

The regulations that followed specified that commissars were not to be treated as soldiers and that
the protection provided by international law for prisoners of war would not apply to them. They would be
segregated from other prisoners and "disposed of."
The Commissar Order was distributed only to top
officers, while ideological guidelines were prepared
for the troops. Thus an army HQ directive, "Guidelines for the Conduct of the Troops in Russia," issued

June 4, 1941, instructed the troops in National Socialist thinking and conduct:

1. *Bolshevism is the mortal enemy of the National Socialist German people. Germany's struggle is directed against this destructive ideology and its carriers.*

2. This struggle demands ruthless and energetic measures against *Bolshevik agitators, guerrillas, saboteurs, Jews,* and the complete elimination of every active or passive resistance.[31]

Once the German army had invaded Russia, the generals found it necessary to repeat these directives lest the men on the front forget their ideology on encountering the human reality of the enemy. On September 12, 1941, Keitel drafted a directive regarding "Jews in the newly occupied eastern territories," which repeated the language of the earlier guidelines: "The struggle against Bolshevism demands ruthless and energetic measures, above all against the Jews, the main carriers of Bolshevism."[32] Field Marshal Walter von Reichenau, commander-in-chief of the Sixth Army, issued a directive on October 10, 1941, whose ideological wording Hitler described as "excellent" and which Keitel ordered distributed as a model for all commanding generals. Reichenau's directive began:

With respect to the conduct of troops toward the Bolshevist system, vague ideas are still widely prevalent.

The most essential aim of the campaign against the Jewish-Bolshevist system is the complete crushing of its means of power and the extermination of Asiatic influence in the European region.

This poses tasks for the troops that go beyond the one-sided routine of conventional soldiering. In the Eastern region, the soldier is not merely a fighter according to the rules of the art of war, but also the bearer of an inexorable national idea and the avenger of all bestialities inflicted upon the German people and its racial kin.

Therefore the soldier must have *full* understanding

for the necessity of a severe but just atonement on Jewish subhumanity.* An additional aim in this is to nip in the bud any revolts in the rear of the army, which, as experience proves, have always been instigated by Jews.[33]

Given this extensive exposure of the regular troops to National Socialist propaganda, the ideological indoctrination of the newly organized Einsatzgruppen must have been even more intensive. The special task, transmitted orally, was to kill the Jews, to perform the mission entrusted to Himmler by the Führer, according to Keitel's directive of March 13, 1941. The Einsatzgruppen training program began in May 1941 at the recruitment centers in Pretzsch and Düben, in Saxony, where the three thousand men who were to form the four groups were assembled. The officers were recruited from the SS, the SD, the Gestapo, and Sipo. Men were drawn from these bodies too, but also from Kripo, the State Police (Stapo), Orpo, and the Waffen-SS. (Later, while at work, the Einsatzgruppen procured the services of Ukrainians, White Russians, Letts, and Lithuanians.) The size of the groups ranged from eight hundred to twelve hundred men. Besides basic military exercises, they were frequently briefed on their mission and exhorted to maintain the SS ethos of toughness. They learned from Heydrich, for example, that "Judaism in the East is the source of Bolshevism and must therefore be wiped out in accordance with the Führer's aims."[34]

The men who joined the Einsatzgruppen, in contrast to the ordinary Wehrmacht recruits, were already committed to National Socialist ideology and thoroughly imbued with the notion that Jews were Bolsheviks, and vice versa, and that the Jew-Bolshevik was the "mortal enemy" of the German people and the

---

* German original: *"Sühne am jüdischen Untermenschentum."* A strange use of the word *"Sühne,"* which seems to be applied in the sense of revenge or reprisal. The sense may be that the Jews are being made to atone for their "crimes," though atonement is normally an internal, subjective process and not performed by an outsider.

German state. Yet even so, every effort was made to indoctrinate the members of the Einsatzgruppen so that they could perform their "special tasks" with requisite zeal and efficiency. The reports of the Einsatzgruppen chiefs attest to the internalization of the ideology. There the platitudes of National Socialist doctrine are cited to support the statistics of killing: "The fight against vermin—that is, mainly the Jews and Communists," "the population of the Baltic countries had suffered very heavily under the government of Bolshevism and Jewry," "the terror of Jewish-Bolshevik dominion."[35]

The Einsatzgruppen performed their special tasks with staggering competence. When the German armed forces drove into Russia on June 22, 1941, in a line of attack extending from the Baltic to the Black Sea, with them, or right behind them, came the four Einsatzgruppen.[*][36] Einsatzgruppe A, assigned to Army Group North, operated in the Baltic countries; Einsatzgruppe B, assigned to Army Group Central, in White Russia and the territory farther east toward Moscow; Einsatzgruppe C, assigned to Army Group South, in the Ukraine, except for the southern portion, which, together with the Crimea, came under the jurisdiction of Einsatzgruppe D, assigned to the Eleventh Army. Their operational directives came from Heydrich's RSHA.

Russian resistance crumbled. In a brief span Hitler had won his Lebensraum and the unhindered possibility of creating his racial utopia. The Einsatzgruppen went to work. Their methods, combining guile, terror, and systematic savagery, must have been worked out at Pretzsch and Düben, for they are remarkably alike in widely separated geographic areas. Otto Ohlendorf, head of the RSHA Amt III (originally SD-Inland) and chief of Einsatzgruppe D, explained at Nuremberg how it was accomplished. Each Einsatzgruppe was divided into smaller units, commandos, led by a

---

[*] For an account of the occupation of the Soviet Union and the Baltic countries and the fate of the Jews, see Appendix A.

The Einsatzgruppen, 1941–1942

German-Soviet frontier as of September 1939
Paths of the Einsatzgruppen, July 1941–1942
Area occupied in German advance,
June 22, 1941–1942

Miles
0   100   200   300

CASPIAN SEA

CAUCASUS MTS.

FRONT LINE

EINSATZGRUPPE D

Stalingrad

Kislovodsk

Rostov

Krasnodar

Taganrog

BLACK SEA

Simferopol

CRIMEA

Kherson

Nikolayev

Odessa

Dnepropetrovsk

Kharkov

Poltava

Kursk

SOVIET

UNION

Moscow

Tula

EINSATZGRUPPE B

Orel

Bryansk

Gomel

Mogilev

EINSATZGRUPPE C

Kiev

Zhitomir

Rovne

Kamenets-
Podolski

Tarnopol

Cernăuţi

Lwow

GENERAL-
GOUVERNEMENT

Warsaw

Cracow

RUMANIA

Budapest

HUNGARY

SLOVAKIA

GERMANY

Lodz

Smolensk

Vitebsk

Minsk

Baranowicze

Pinsk

Brest Litovsk

Białystok

Bobruisk

Rzhev

FRONT LINE

Leningrad

Pskov

Ostrov

Polotsk

Daugavpils

Riga

Šiauliai

Kovno

Vilna

ESTONIA

Tallinn

FINLAND

LATVIA

LITHUANIA

BALTIC SEA

member of the SD, the Gestapo, or Kripo. The unit assigned to killing the Jews of a given place

> would enter a village or city and order the prominent Jewish citizens to call together all Jews for the purpose of resettlement. They were requested to hand over their valuables to the leader of the unit, and shortly before the execution to surrender their outer clothing. The men, women, and children were led to a place of execution which in most cases was located next to a more deeply excavated anti-tank ditch. Then they were shot, kneeling or standing, and the corpses thrown into the ditch.[37]

A report of December 1, 1941, by SS Colonel Jäger, who headed a commando in Einsatzgruppe A, described his procedures:

> The decision to free each district of Jews necessitated thorough preparation of each action as well as acquisition of information about local conditions. The Jews had to be collected in one or more towns and a ditch had to be dug at the right site for the right number. The marching distance from collecting points to the ditches averaged about 3 miles. The Jews were brought in groups of 500, separated by at least 1.2 miles, to the place of execution. The sort of difficulties and nerve-scraping work involved in all this is shown by an arbitrarily chosen example:
> In Rokiskis 3,208 people had to be transported 3 miles before they could be liquidated. . . .
> Vehicles are seldom available. Escapes, which were attempted here and there, were frustrated solely by my men at the risk of their lives. For example, 3 men of the Commando at Mariampole shot 38 escaping Jews and communist functionaries on a path in the woods, so that no one got away. Distances to and from actions were never less than 90–120 miles. Only careful planning enabled the Commandos to carry out up to 5 actions a week and at the same time continue the work in Kovno without interruption.
> Kovno itself, where trained Lithuanian [volunteers]

. . . are available in sufficient numbers, was comparatively speaking a shooting paradise.[38]

A report sent out from Warsaw in May 1942 by the Jewish Labor Bund, then underground, to the Polish government-in-exile in London was the first documentation to reach the West of the work of the Einsatzgruppen. Concerned primarily with the fate of the Jews in pre-1939 Poland, the report began:

From the day the Russo-German war broke out, the Germans undertook the physical extermination of the Jewish population on Polish territory, using for that purpose Ukrainians and Lithuanian Šiauliai.* It began first of all in Eastern Galicia in the summer months of 1941. Their method everywhere was as follows: Men from fourteen to sixty were rounded up in one place— a square or cemetery—where they were slaughtered, machine-gunned, or killed by hand grenades. They had to dig their own graves. Children in orphanages, inmates of old-age homes, and the hospitalized sick were shot, women were killed on the streets. In many towns Jews were taken away to an "unknown destination" and executed in the nearby woods. Thirty thousand Jews were murdered in Lwów, 15,000 in Stanisławów, 5,000 in Tarnopol, 2,000 in Złoczów, 4,000 in Brzeżany (the town had 18,000 Jews, now has 1,700). The same happened in Zborów, Kołomyja, Stryj, Sambor, Drohobycz, Zbaraż, Przemyślany, Kuty, Śniatyn, Zaleszczyki, Brody, Przemyśl, Rawa Ruska, and other places. . . . According to various estimates, the number of Jews bestially murdered in the Vilna regions and Lithuanian Kaunas is put at 300,000.[39]

At Nuremberg the International Military Tribunal concluded that of the approximately six million Jews murdered, two million were killed by the Einsatzgruppen and other units of the security police.

---

* Members of a paramilitary fascist police organization.

7

The Annihilation Camps:
Kingdom of Death

Sometime during that eventful summer of 1941, perhaps even as early as May, Himmler summoned Höss to Berlin and, in privacy, told him "that the Führer had given the order for a Final Solution of the Jewish Question," and that "we, the SS, must carry out that order."[1] Himmler had become the chief receiver and transmitter of Hitler's orders for the Final Solution and its operational principal, a role that he assumed with confidence and authority. In the late summer of 1941, addressing the assembled men of the Einsatzkommandos at Nikolayev, he "repeated to them the liquidation order, and pointed out that the leaders and men who were taking part in the liquidation bore no personal responsibility for the execution of this order. The responsibility was his alone, and the Führer's."[2] A year later, in a letter to one of his top SS officials who had just become liaison officer to Alfred Rosenberg, Himmler wrote: "The occupied Eastern territories are to become free of Jews. The execution of this very grave order has been placed on my shoulders by the Führer. No one can deny me the responsibility anyway."[3]

The murder of the Jews was clearly a "political/ideological" task that fell within the purview of the

NSDAP apparatus and especially its combat arm, the SS. But the success of the task depended on the cooperation of various state bureaucracies with mutually impinging jurisdictions. Consequently, Hitler transmitted his orders for the annihilation of the Jews not only to Himmler but also to Göring, who, as Plenipotentiary for the Four Year Plan, headed the state apparatus. Whereas Himmler was the responsible agent in carrying out the Final Solution, Göring served in effect mainly as an administrative conduit. It was he who authorized the involvement of the state apparatus in the Final Solution and legitimated it as a state undertaking. He did so by assigning the task of coordinating state and party agencies to Heydrich, who, as Chief of the Security Police and SD and head of the RSHA, represented the nexus of state and party. On July 31, 1941, Göring sent Heydrich the following directive:

> As supplement to the task that was entrusted to you in the decree dated January 24, 1939, namely, to solve the Jewish question by emigration and evacuation in the most favorable way possible, given present conditions, I herewith commission you to carry out all necessary preparations with regard to organizational, substantive, and financial viewpoints for a total solution of the Jewish question in the German sphere of influence in Europe.
>
> Insofar as the competencies of other central organizations are hereby affected, these are to be involved.*[4]

As a result, administrative responsibility for coordinating the Final Solution was given to Heydrich

---

* According to Eichmann's associate, Dieter Wisliceny, Himmler had written to Heydrich and to the Inspector of Concentration Camps, informing them that "the Führer had ordered the Final Solution of the Jewish Question" and that both "were entrusted with carrying out this so-called final solution" (*TMWC* 4:358–359). Wisliceny said that Eichmann showed him this order, dated April 1942, at the end of July 1942. But the Final Solution was long under way by then. Wisliceny may have been mistaken about the date or that order may have been an implementing rather than an initiating directive.

and was lodged in the RSHA's office IV-B-4, where Eichmann supervised "Jewish Affairs and Evacuation Affairs." Operational responsibility remained Himmler's. Back in March he had already instructed Höss to enlarge Auschwitz. Now, in the summer of 1941, when Himmler transmitted Hitler's order for the Final Solution, he told Höss that Auschwitz had been selected for that purpose because of its easy rail access, its isolation from populated areas, and the physical possibilities its location afforded for concealment and camouflage of its installations. Himmler said that Höss would get further instructions from Eichmann. At about the same time Himmler passed on similar instructions, specifically on the construction of Majdanek, to Odilo Globocnik, then SS and police leader in Lublin. Globocnik would soon become the head of a vast kingdom of death encompassing three annihilation camps—Bełżec, Majdanek, and Sobibór —and countless labor camps.

Some weeks later Eichmann came to Auschwitz and discussed with Höss various matters, such as scheduling the murder of the Jews and the techniques of killing to be used—some form of gassing. According to Höss, Eichmann mentioned "killing with showers of carbon monoxide while bathing, as was done with mental patients in some places in the Reich." Eichmann also told Höss "about the methods of killing people with exhaust gases in trucks, which had previously been used in the East." In September 1941 such a truck had been put at the disposal of Einsatzgruppe C, according to an affidavit by Paul Blobel who headed one of its units.

There was then no need for innovation, since the techniques of mass killing by gas had already been developed, under Hitler's close supervision, to carry out what was euphemistically entitled the "Euthanasia Program." That program, like the Final Solution, evolved from National Socialist ideology and from Hitler's fanatical ideas about racial health and racial eugenics, which he first spelled out in *Mein Kampf*.

Besides "positive eugenics," encouraging "racially

healthy" elements in the German population to breed, Hitler also fostered a program to destroy life and to prevent "the physically degenerate and mentally sick" from procreating. In *Mein Kampf* Hitler insisted that the Volkist state, using "the most modern medical means" at its disposal, "*must declare unfit for propagation all who are in any way visibly sick or who have inherited a disease and can therefore pass it on. . . .*" These notions of racial health that had become the stock of the National Socialist movement were incorporated into legislation in the National Socialist state. The actual program for killing was lodged in Hitler's private chancellery, from which its top staff was recruited. Its head, SS-Obergruppenführer Philipp Bouhler, an old party member, was appointed by Hitler to run the Euthanasia Program. SS-Oberführer Victor Brack, who served in Hitler's chancellery as liaison with the Health Department in the Ministry of the Interior, became Bouhler's deputy. Sharing the top responsibility with Bouhler was Karl Brandt, Hitler's personal physician since 1934. (Brandt's experience gained in killing the sick by gas apparently qualified him for appointment in 1942 as Plenipotentiary for Health and Medical Services.)

Hitler's chancellery had a department to handle various petitions for mercy. Late 1938 or early 1939 a request was received from the father of a deformed child, asking that the child be killed. Hitler turned the matter over to Brandt, instructing him to investigate. If the father's statement was true, Brandt was authorized to inform the physicians, in Hitler's name, to "carry out euthanasia." He was also to tell them that should they become involved in legal procedures as a consequence, these would be quashed on Hitler's orders. In fact, Hitler expressly informed the parents that he alone, not they, bore the responsibility for this action. He furthermore authorized Bouhler and Brandt to do the same in similar cases.[5]

In spring 1939 Hitler regularized this procedure of killing mentally deficient and physically deformed children through the establishment of the *Reichsaus-*

schuss zur wissenschaftlichen Erfassung von erb- und anlagebedingten schweren Leiden (Reich Committee for Scientific Research of Hereditary and Severe Constitutional Diseases).*

In compliance with a secret decree of the Ministry of the Interior, health departments, heads of children's clinics and hospitals, doctors, and midwives were to submit reports to the experts on the Reich committee regarding the presence of such children in their institutions. The experts then decided, case by case, whether to perform "euthanasia." To facilitate this program, twenty-one special children's departments were set up in as many hospitals. An estimated five thousand children were killed in this program, in operation until November 1944.

Having set in motion the official destruction of "racially valueless" children, Hitler next turned to the murder of the adult insane. In July 1939 he conferred on this with Hans Lammers, head of the Reich Chancellery, and with SS-Obergruppenführer Dr. Leonardo Conti, head of the Health Department in the Ministry of the Interior. At Nuremberg Lammers testified that Hitler had originally appointed Conti as head of the Euthanasia Program, but after learning that Conti had asked Lammers for official legitimation, something in writing, Hitler, enraged, replaced Conti with Bouhler, who willingly accepted oral orders. Also involved in the discussions was Dr. Herbert Linden, of the Health Department, who was commissioner of all the insane asylums in Germany. This program to kill the adult insane began to operate out of Bouhler's office in Hitler's chancellery at Tiergartenstrasse 4—hence its code name T-4.

After the occupation of Poland, Hitler discussed with his people the matter of a written authorization

---

* The names given to these institutions for killing, as well as the words used later to designate the killing of the Jews, were originally intended as camouflage to conceal from the general public these systematic programs of murder. This neutral bureaucratic terminology for various methods of murder no doubt later reinforced schizoid and delusional traits among the killers.

for these programs of "medical" murder, and at the end of October issued such an authorization, written on his personal stationery and predated September 1, 1939. (The association between war and other forms of killing was fixed in his mind.) The authorization read:

> Reichsleiter Bouhler and Dr. Brandt, M.D., are charged with the responsibility of enlarging the authority of certain physicians to be designated by name in such a manner that persons who, according to human judgment, are incurably sick may, upon the most serious evaluation of their medical condition, be accorded a mercy death.[6]

Of greater scope than the program to murder the deformed children, T-4 was an enterprise with more complex institutional arrangements. Three camouflaged front organizations were set up: (1) *Allgemeine Stiftung für Anstaltwesen* (General Foundation for Affairs of Insane Asylums), which employed the staff in the killing institutions; (2) *Reichsarbeitsgemeinschaft Heil- und Pflegeanstalten* (Reich Operative Team of Asylums and Nursing Homes), which distributed questionnaires to institutions regarding patients eligible for T-4 and obtained the appropriate judgments; and (3) *Gemeinnützige Krankentransportgesellschaft* (Public-Benefit Patient Transportation Society), which transported patients from their institutions to the killing centers. A significant portion of the personnel, medical and nonmedical, was drawn from the SS. Himmler himself was familiar with all these operations and apprised of problems.

Patients slated for killing were transferred first to a transit facility, called an "observation institution," of which there were five. They were then transferred to one of six "euthanasia" installations (at Bernburg, Brandenburg, Grafeneck, Hadamar, Hartheim, and Sonnenstein). Whereas the deformed children were put to death individually, usually by injection, these

six installations became the German dictatorship's
first laboratories for mass murder.[7]

A committee of physicians and medical experts,
headed by Brandt, were looking for a means of mass
killing that would disguise to the victims the fate in
store for them and deceive their families. Various
gases were experimented with.* At first carbon
monoxide was used, but cyanide gas—known by its
German trade name as Zyklon B—proved to be most
effective. Late in 1939 the first gas installation was set
up at Brandenburg, where Brandt, Bouhler, Brack,
and Company observed a test experiment, gassing four
insane male patients. Hitler was informed of the re-
sults and was said to have decided then that only
carbon monoxide was to be used.[8] Then the five other
installations were similarly equipped. The procedure
was pragmatically simple and convincingly deceptive.
In groups of twenty to thirty, the patients were
ushered into a chamber camouflaged as a shower
room. It was an ordinary room, fitted with sealproof
doors and windows, into which gas piping had been
laid. The compressed gas container and the regulating
equipment were located outside. Led into the chamber
on the pretext that they were to take showers, the
patients were gassed by the doctor on duty.

It did not take long before people learned what
was going on and watched for the heavy smoke to rise
from the crematory building, said to be visible over
Hadamar every day. In Grafeneck people began to
recognize the SS vans carrying the patients to the gas
chambers. Children seeing the bus in Hadamar would
shout: "There goes the murder-box again."[9] After more
than a year of rising public clamor in Germany, Hitler,
reluctant to "legalize" this operation, instructed Brandt
in August 1941 to "stall" this killing of mental patients.
It has been estimated that between 80,000 and 100,000
people were murdered under the auspices of T-4. But

---

* A historical curiosity, perhaps more than coincidental: Germany
was the first country to use poison gas in World War I.

before T-4 ground to a halt, it visibly demonstrated
the continuity between killing "racially valueless" elements within the German community proper and killing the racial enemy.

The T-4 experts also fathered the killings of "non-
Aryans" in the German concentration camps, known
under the code name "*Sonderbehandlung* [special
treatment] 14 f 13." Bouhler supplied Himmler with
"experts" to examine camp inmates—Jews and non-
Aryan Germans—who became too sick to work. In
practice, the "race" or the political records of the
victims sufficed for a murder decision. At first the
victims were transferred to the "euthanasia" stations
to be killed, but as the waiting lines grew very long,
every concentration camp installed a gas chamber of
its own. Before the Final Solution became operative,
thousands of Jews were murdered under the auspices
of 14 f 13.

Most of the manpower and even some of the apparatus of T-4 were transferred to the Final Solution
in a time sequence of such exquisite precision as to
suggest that Hitler yielded T-4 in preference to the
Final Solution. Globocnik, in charge of the annihilation of the Jews in the Generalgouvernement (code
name: Operation Reinhard), reported that Hitler's
private chancellery had provided ninety-two men to
staff Operation Reinhard.[10] One of these was Christian
Wirth, formerly chief of criminal police in Stuttgart,
who was transferred from Brandenburg to become
Globocnik's top aide. Another was SS-Oberführer
Oldenburg, who went from Hitler's chancellery to the
T-4 program to Globocnik.[11] Treblinka's first director
was Dr. Irmfried Eberl, also from Brandenburg, and
the nucleus of the first operative death camp at Chełmno was formed from a "Euthanasia Commando" in
Prussia.[12] Finally, in a burst of frugality, some of the
gas chambers in the T-4 program were dismantled,
shipped to, and reassembled at Bełżec, Majdanek, and
Treblinka.[13] In October 1941 Brack consulted Eichmann and members of Rosenberg's staff regarding the
construction of gassing facilities in the Russian occu-

pied territory.[14] Clearly, when Eichmann conferred with Höss in the summer of 1941, he was already familiar with the technical aspects of the T-4 program.

That summer of 1941 a new enterprise was launched —the construction of the *Vernichtungslager*—the annihilation camp. Two civilians from Hamburg came to Auschwitz that summer to teach the staff how to handle Zyklon B, and in September, in the notorious Block 11, the first gassings were carried out on 250 patients from the hospital and on 600 Russian prisoners of war, probably "Communists" and Jews whom Heydrich's Einsatzkommandos had taken out of the army's prisoner of war camps. Construction of Birkenau, which would become Auschwitz's killing center, got under way.

The first death camp to be completed was at Chełmno (Kulmhof in German), sixty kilometers from Lodz, intended for the Jews from the ghetto of Lodz. Chełmno began functioning on December 8, 1941, with mobile vans, using engine exhaust gases. (Gas trucks turned up at the same time to kill the Jews assembled in a makeshift camp in Semlin, Serbia, where the occupying German army had been embarrassingly efficient in rounding up the Jews for slaughter before annihilation facilities were ready.)

The next death camp to be completed was at Bełżec, near Lublin, at the end of 1941; it became operational in February 1942. Construction at Sobibór began in March 1942. The labor concentration camp Majdanek, near Lublin, which had been set up at the end of 1940, was transformed into an annihilation camp. Similarly, Treblinka, fifty miles from Warsaw, a labor camp since 1941, was turned into a death camp. In the second half of 1941, the technicians of death took over, building camouflaged gassing facilities. Different methods of gassing were experimented with—in mobile or permanent installations, using exhaust engine gases or Zyklon B. In the first half of 1942 both Majdanek and Treblinka joined the roster of functioning killing camps.

The mass killers by gas and the mass killers by shooting exchanged information, and in early fall 1941 the experts at Chełmno who had been schooled in the T-4 program dispatched a gas van to an Einsatzkommando in the Ukraine. In spring 1942 gas vans became more available to Einsatzgruppen, but whether or not they were used was a matter of individual taste. Höss, a man of schizophrenic sensibility, preferred gassing to shooting because he was "spared all these bloodbaths."[15] In contrast, an Einsatzkommando chief held that an execution by shooting was "more honorable for both parties than killing by means of a gas truck."[16]

These trials and experiments with mass-killing techniques were the subject of Heydrich's classic understatement, when he reported at the Wannsee Conference that "even now practical experience is being gathered that is of major significance in view of the coming Final Solution of the Jewish Question." The Wannsee Conference was held in a villa located in Am Grossen Wannsee in suburban Berlin, affording more privacy than RSHA headquarters, at which drinks and lunch were provided. It was originally called for December 9, 1941, but had to be postponed to January 20, 1942, after the Japanese attack on Pearl Harbor and America's declaration of war against Germany's Axis partner Japan. Heydrich called the conference for the purpose of effecting coordination among the various agencies with regard to the Final Solution, in accordance with Göring's directive of July 31, 1941, copies of which went out with the letters of invitation.

Heydrich chaired the meeting and did most of the talking to the thirteen persons present, representing both state and party apparatus.[17] The state agencies sent second-echelon men, deputies and State Secretaries, representing the civil administrations of the Occupied Eastern Territories and of the Generalgouvernement, the ministries of Interior, Justice, the Foreign Office, the Plenipotentiary for the Four Year Plan, the Reich Chancellery, and the Gestapo (Müller).

The party apparatus was represented by delegates from the NSDAP Chancellery, Himmler's RuSHA, and two Sipo/SD commanders, one representing the Generalgouvernement, the other both Latvia and Ostland (the Eastern occupied territories), the last already with extensive practical experience in mass killing, having just completed massacres in Riga affecting some 27,000 Jews. Eichmann, who had prepared the conference and done the administrative work connected with it, took the minutes.

Heydrich began with a lengthy review of Germany's policy toward the Jews, referring to the Reichszentrale under his direction, and the subsequent change in policy from "emigration" to "evacuation," in view of "the possibilities in the East." (In writing the minutes, Eichmann had obviously mastered the National Socialist technique of euphemism. With so much actual bloodletting, no wonder the vocabulary of murder was so bloodless.) Heydrich then presented a statistical review of the Jews in Europe—far from accurate, but so thorough that it included England, Ireland, Sweden, Switzerland, and Turkey—as an introduction to the first item on the agenda: how to proceed with the Final Solution in various foreign states. Some states posed difficulties, for they did not have adequate racial definitions, thus creating problems about eligibility for annihilation, while other states—Rumania was cited—were ready to sell citizenship protection to Jews. Heydrich outlined the general procedure in the Final Solution's "practical implementation," in which Europe was "to be combed through from west to east" for Jews, who would be evacuated "group by group, into so-called transit ghettos, to be transported from there farther to the East."

There would be a few exceptions—German Jews over sixty-five and those who had been seriously wounded in World War I or who had been distinguished for war service (reminiscent of Hindenburg's plea to Hitler in April 1933 on behalf of Jewish war veterans who were being thrown out of their civil-service positions). Heydrich had an "efficient solution." Jews in these categories were to be assigned to a ghetto for the aged. The site under consideration, he reported at Wannsee, was Theresienstadt, an old fortress town in Bohemia. In a few months Theresienstadt did indeed become a "model camp," the only one into which the Germans ever allowed foreign observers. It was a Potemkin village, purporting to be an autonomous Jewish community. Among its inmates were many prominent German Jews whose disappearance would prove embarrasing to the Germans in case of international inquiries about their welfare. In reality Theresienstadt was, for most of its inmates, just a stopping place before their final destination at Auschwitz.

In carrying out the Final Solution in countries occupied by the Germans or under German influence, Heydrich proposed that "the appropriate specialists in the Foreign Office confer with the competent official of the Security Police and the SD." He then remarked that "in Slovakia and Croatia the undertaking is no longer too difficult." (Most of the Jews had already been murdered by local initiative.) The appointment in Rumania of a Commissioner for Jewish Affairs would help, Heydrich thought, and in the near future the Germans should "impose an adviser on Jewish problems on the Hungarian government." In France, too, Heydrich foresaw no special difficulties. In this connection, the Foreign Office representative with the unlikely name of Martin Luther—like Eichmann, an eager-beaver fanatic on the "Jewish question"—cautioned that "thorough handling of this problem" would cause difficulties in a few countries, "such as the Nordic states," but that the Foreign Office saw "no great difficulties with respect to the Southeast and West of Europe."

The second, and final, item on the short agenda concerned the application of the Nuremberg Laws to various categories of partners in mixed marriages and of Mischlinge. For the time being, Heydrich said, the discussion was theoretical, but the basic problem was where to draw the line as to which categories of

Mischlinge could be exempted from the Final Solution. For example, a second-degree Mischling, a category normally classed with "persons of German blood," who had an "especially unfavorable appearance in racial terms" would now be classified as Jewish "on the strength of his exterior alone." Sterilization was proposed as an alternative, in some instances, to "evacuation."*

In the concluding discussion, the representative from Göring's Office for the Four Year Plan categorically stated that the Jews in essential war industries should not be evacuated as long as replacements for them were not available. Heydrich responded that they would not be evacuated anyway, according to instructions that he had already issued. But as a matter of fact, there had already been conflicts over killing Jews needed for the war economy and there would be more, the outcome usually favoring the SS point of view. State Secretary Dr. Bühler, representing Governor General Hans Frank of the Generalgouvernement, pressed for the solution of the "Jewish question" in his territory as speedily as possible.

The Wannsee Conference, like other high-level meetings involving the Final Solution, began with an ideological lecture, labeled in the minutes as a "brief review of the struggle conducted up to now against this enemy." But actually a spirit of administrative efficiency informed the proceedings at Wannsee, for the annihilation of the Jews had by now moved beyond ideology. The technical machinery for murder had been tested and was now under construction. A smooth functioning of the bureaucratic machinery had also to be assured. As a matter of fact, many basic administrative arrangements had already been worked out, for example, agreements between the Foreign Office and the RSHA, not unlike those between the

---

* Two more conferences were held, on March 6 and October 27, 1942, to discuss administrative practices with regard to forced sterilization and dissolution of mixed marriages. Both were under Eichmann's chairmanship.

SS and the army. In October 1939 Ribbentrop had given the RSHA the right to attach its intelligence agents to German diplomatic missions abroad, with the understanding that these agents were to be "solely devoted to serving the interests of the Reich." The Foreign Office soon discovered, as the army had in its case, that the RSHA was intruding on its jurisdiction, that the police attachés were interfering in the internal politics of the states in which they operated. A new Himmler-Ribbentrop agreement was drawn up on August 9, 1941, which specifically prohibited such interference unless covered by a special agreement. By October 1943 more than seventy police attachés or "experts" of one kind or another were attached to German missions in countries allied to Germany and in neutral countries.[18] In this way, the Foreign Office became an auxiliary to the SS in the murder of the Jews. Indeed, the functions performed by the Foreign Office in assisting the SS took precedence over the conventional Foreign Office operations. In all European countries the Foreign Office gave shelter and support to RSHA bureaucrats and SS agents whose business was the Final Solution, who intervened with the governments to enact anti-Jewish legislation, helped accelerate the concentration of the Jews and arrange the expropriation of their property, arranged for the exploitation of their labor, and, finally, speeded their deportation to the death camps.

Its technical problems having been mastered and its administrative matters arranged, the Final Solution entered its second operative stage—mass murder by gassing. Though the Einsatzgruppen were to continue to perform their "special tasks" in the East, most SS energies were now directed to bringing the Jews from all over Europe to the killing camps. Everywhere the deportations were accomplished by stratagem, terror, and force. "Resettlement for work in the East" was the fundamental lie used to deceive the Jews concerning their fate. To bolster the deception, the Germans usually permitted the Jews to take personal belongings with them. In the ghettos of Poland, where hunger ravaged the inmates, offers of bread and marmalade induced thousands of Jews to turn up voluntarily for "resettlement." "Resettlement" became the euphemism for the process of transporting Jews to the gas chambers.

The schedule prepared in the RSHA's IV-B-4 was put in motion in March 1942, when the first party of Slovakian Jews arrived at Auschwitz and when Jews from the ghetto of Lublin began to be deported to Bełżec. On March 27, 1942, Goebbels noted in his diary: "Beginning with Lublin, the Jews in the Generalgouvernement are now being evacuated eastward. The procedure is a pretty barbaric one and not to be described here more definitely. Not much will remain of the Jews."

On July 19 Himmler ordered that the "resettlement" of all the Jews of the Generalgouvernement be completed by the end of the year. Only those Jews still employed in five assembly camps (tightly closed forced-labor installations) would be allowed to remain, though not for very long. These measures, Himmler explained, were "necessary for the ethnic separation of races and peoples required in the context of the New Order of Europe, as well as in the interest of the security and purity of the German Reich and the spheres of its interest."[19]

Three days later, deportations began from the Warsaw ghetto to Treblinka, whose gas chambers had just been completed. In August the Jews from the ghetto of Lwów were sent to Bełżec. During the summer the Einsatzgruppen renewed their activity in White Russia, while Jews from France, Belgium, and Holland began to be deported to Auschwitz. In late summer the Jews from Croatia arrived in Auschwitz, followed by Dutch Jews. In November Norwegian Jews arrived in Auschwitz.

In February 1943 deportations began from the Bialystok ghetto, and that same month the remaining Jews in Berlin were deported. In March the Greek Jews began to arrive at Auschwitz. They were fol-

lowed by the Jews from Macedonia and Thrace. The
ghetto in Cracow was liquidated. Jews from Holland,
Luxembourg, Vienna, and Prague were sent to the
death camps.

On February 16, 1943, Himmler ordered the destruction of the Warsaw ghetto. The liquidation began on
April 19, setting off an uprising, which SS troops
quelled after about six weeks. In June the ghetto in
Lwów was liquidated. During the summer the Jews
from Upper Silesia and elsewhere in Poland were sent
to Auschwitz, and the ghetto in Bialystok was liquidated.

On June 21, 1943, Himmler ordered the liquidation
of the ghettos in the Ostland, allowing the survival
only of Jewish workers in a few labor concentration
camps. All others were to be destroyed. In September
the ghettos in Minsk, Lida, and Vilna were liquidated;
in the next two months the remainder of the White
Russian ghettos were liquidated and also the Riga
ghetto. In September and October Jews from southern
France and Rome were deported. In October the
Germans scheduled the deportation of the Danish
Jews, actually netting about four hundred. At the end
of the year about seven thousand Jews from northern
Italy were deported.

The deportation of Jews from Athens began in the
spring of 1944. In May and June the Hungarian Jews
began to be sent to Auschwitz. The Lodz ghetto was
liquidated in August and its seventy thousand inhabitants sent to Auschwitz. Deportations from Slovakia were renewed in September 1944; at the same
time the last transport of French Jews left for Auschwitz. In the last two months of 1944 the Jews from
Budapest were deported to concentrations camps near
Vienna.

The Final Solution had top priority, even at a time
of military exigencies. The need for railroads to transport Jews to their death often competed with the need
for railroads to transport soldiers and military supplies
to the front. Both received equal consideration. At a

meeting called by Governor General Frank with the SS police in Cracow on June 18, 1942, the question of transportation to remove the Jews was discussed. According to Frank's summary of the proceedings, Friedrich Wilhelm Krüger, higher SS and police leader* for the Generalgouvernement, Himmler's top agent in Poland, said:

> For the carrying out of such an action, the provision of adequate numbers of transport trains was necessary. Although a total railway ban had been ordered for the next 14 days, he had managed in negotiations with President Gerteis [of *Ostbahn*] to see to it that trains would be provided now and again for the deportation of the Jews. At the conclusion of the ban, the Jewish action would have to be carried out on an increased scale.[20]

At that time the Germans were preparing to launch a new summer offensive in southern Russia. They had committed 266 divisions—all their reserves—on the Eastern front. In preparation for the offensive, scheduled for early July, Gerteis, head of the Ostbahn, the Generalgouvernement's railroad system, declared a two-week embargo on all civilian traffic. Though Gerteis had been amenable to Krüger's persuasion to provide some transportation, this was not good enough for Himmler, who then moved the negotiations to a higher level. SS-Obergruppenführer Karl Wolff, the head of Himmler's personal staff, contacted Theodor Ganzenmüller, the new State Secretary for Transportation. On July 28 Wolff received a satisfactory report. "Since July 22," according to information that Ganzenmüller had received from the responsible people in Cracow, "a train with 5,000 Jews apiece has been

---

* *Höhere SS und Polizeiführer* (HSSPF; higher SS and police commanders), according to a decree promulgated November 13, 1937, were appointed by Himmler for wartime supervision of all SS forces operating in each military district. They were regarded as Himmler's plenipotentiaries in their districts.

Ostbahn — eastern railroad

leaving Warsaw via Malkinia for Treblinka every day; in addition, twice weekly a train with 5,000 Jews from Przemyśl to Bełżec."[21]

The following winter, Germany's military position had begun to deteriorate, but the top priority of the Final Solution remained unchanged. German troops, besieging Stalingrad, had been encircled by the Red Army. In mid-December 1942, the Germans sent in a fresh Panzer division in an effort to break up the Russian encirclement, and consequently a railroad embargo on civilian traffic had been imposed for one month beginning December 15. On December 4 Krüger asked Himmler to negotiate with the top people of the armed forces High Command and the Transport Ministry for trains to move the Jews. Because of the railroad embargo, Krüger wrote, "our master plan for Jewish resettlement is severely jeopardized."[22]

Himmler may have delegated Wolff to negotiate, or he may have decided to wait out the embargo. Finally, he appealed to Ganzenmüller on January 20, 1943, when the disaster at Stalingrad still necessitated extensive rail transport:

> One necessary condition for the pacification of the Generalgouvernement, of Bialystok and of Russian territories is the removal of all helpers of partisan bands and of persons suspected of partisan activities. In particular, the removal of Jews belongs under this head. So does the removal of Jews from the West, since we would otherwise have to reckon with an intensification of ambushes in those regions too.
>
> For this I need your help and your support. If I am to wind things up quickly, I must have more trains for transports. I know very well how taxing the situation is for the railroads and what demands are constantly made of you. Just the same, I must make this request of you: Help me get more trains.[23]

His plea succeeded, for in February 1943 trains were available to deport Jews from the Bialystok ghetto to Treblinka and from Berlin to Auschwitz. By

March the trains were carrying Jews from all over Europe to the death camps.

According to Dieter Wisliceny, transports of Jews from Greece to Auschwitz "commanded a sufficiently high priority to take precedence over other freight movements." Even when the Germans began evacuating Greece in July 1944 and rail transport was critically needed, the deportation of Jews continued on schedule.[24]

Hitler had embarked on an ideological war to achieve ideological/racial goals, but to win that war he needed also to fight a conventional war. Yet the rational interests of the latter often were sacrificed to the racial imperatives of the ideological war. This was especially evident in the treatment the Germans accorded the Poles, Russians, and Ukrainians, who, in Hitler's scheme of things, were *Untermenschen*. The Germans alienated larger numbers of them, especially the Ukrainians, many of whom subscribed to National Socialist philosophy in other respects and who willingly would have fought on the German side for the prize of national autonomy and independence from the Soviet Union. In the end, that manpower might have affected the outcome of the war. (For want of a nail was a kingdom lost?) The military constantly urged the use of Slavic formations, but Hitler opposed the idea on ideological grounds. Still, in a last-ditch effort to save the conventional war, he agreed to the presence of Slavs with the German fighting troops.[25]

No such concessions were ever made with regard to the Final Solution. Its categorical execution was accelerated at the very time when Hitler himself called a halt, because of wartime exigencies, to Himmler's grandiose racial plans. On January 12, 1943, Himmler ordered the expansion of *Generalplan Ost* (General Plan for the East), a fantastic plan to colonize Russia proper and the Ukraine with German settlements, written up at the end of 1941 in the RSHA. Himmler now wanted the Baltic countries, White Russia, and Crimea included as well. But in the wake of the calam-

ities that had befallen the Germans since the previous
November—the entrapment of Paulus's Sixth Army at
Stalingrad, the defeat inflicted by the British Eighth
Army on Rommel's army in North Africa, and, the
worst yet, the Anglo-American landings in French
Algeria and Morocco—Hitler became the realist. On
January 13 he grounded Himmler's schemes by issuing
an order for the complete suspension thenceforth of all
"preparations and plans for future peacetime projects."[26] But the Final Solution did not fall into this
category. Its completion was urgent and delays were
tolerated only on the few occasions when short-term
opportunities could be won.

The top war priority given to the Final Solution is
most evident in the handling of the acute wartime
shortage of labor. Rational considerations with regard
to the war economy demanded the use of all available
hands to produce armaments and provide essential
services to the army. In occupied areas where in prewar times Jews had dominated industry and trade, a
conflict erupted between the army, pursuing rational
interests, and the SS, unflinching in its commitment to
the Final Solution.

The conflict broke out first in the areas where the
Einsatzgruppen operated:

> Since a large part of the trades in Lithuania and Latvia
> are in Jewish hands and others carried on nearly exclu-
> sively by Jews (especially those of glaziers, plumbers,
> stove-builders, cobblers), many Jewish partisans are
> indispensable at present for repairing installations of
> vital importance for the reconstruction of towns de-
> stroyed and for work of military importance. Although
> the employers aim at replacing Jewish labor with
> Lithuanian or Latvian labor, it is not yet possible to
> displace all employed Jews, especially not in the larger
> towns.[27]

The civil administration opposed the "larger executions" in view of the labor problem, but the Einsatz-

gruppe chief responded "that it was a matter of carrying out basic orders."

According to a later report of the same Einsatzgruppe, the "definitive and fundamental elimination of the Jews" caused difficulties, because the Jews included "an extraordinarily high percentage of skilled workers," who were "indispensable because of the lack of replacements from other quarters in that area."[28] But a decision in principle had already been rendered, in response to an inquiry from a top official in the office of Heinrich Lohse, Reich Commissioner for Ostland. He had turned to the Reich Minister for the Occupied Eastern Territories for guidance regarding the liquidation of the Jews. Was it to take place "without regard to age and sex and economic interests (e.g., the Wehrmacht's in skilled workers in armament plants)?" The elimination of the Jews, he argued, "must be harmonized with the necessities of the war economy." The reply from Berlin on December 18, 1941, was succinct: "As a matter of principle, economic considerations should be overlooked in the solution of the problem."[29]

In Galicia, too, the deportation of the Jews had crippled the local war economy. The writer of a weekly situation report took it in stride. Since "the fundamental question, whether in the elimination of the Jews priority was to be given to political considerations over those of the war economy, was clearly decided at the highest authority in favor of the political factor," the lowering of economic achievement in the affected areas had to be accepted.[30] In Przemyśl, the Galician town from which Ganzenmüller was running trains twice weekly to Bełżec, the conflict between the ideological aim and economic considerations actually came to a physical clash. On July 27, 1942, when Jews began to be rounded up for deportation, the town's military commandant demanded exemptions for those Jews employed by the Wehrmacht. Upon the Gestapo's refusal, the army seized the bridges over the San River that connected both parts of the town, and even threatened to halt the departure of the deportation train. The local Gestapo called headquarters in Cracow, which then gave the Wehrmacht its exemptions.[31]

Another short-term postponement occurred in October 1942, when the RSHA had ordered the liquidation of the ghetto in Bialystok and of all other ghettos in the district. The head of the local Armaments Inspectorate, aware of the difficulty of obtaining replacements for the Jewish workers, appealed to the High Command in Berlin. He was supported by the local civil administrator, who adduced the deleterious effect that the elimination of the ghetto would have at the front. That intercession, too, succeeded—for a time.[32] All the ghettos in the area were liquidated, but the Bialystok ghetto remained unharmed for another four months, when part of its inmates were deported. A half-year later, in August 1943, it was totally liquidated.

The ideological decision to kill the Jews, it would appear, was occasionally susceptible to rational argument on behalf of the war economy. But the concessions seem to have been decided by the opportunism of geography and the confidence of the SS that their quarry was secure, regardless of the military situation. According to the geographic pattern that emerges, the exemption of certain groups of Jews from deportation or a halt in liquidating an entire ghetto within the Polish and Russian occupied territories lasted from three to six months, depending on the position of the westward-moving front. The longest deferment occurred in Lodz, in the so-called "Wartheland," which the Germans had incorporated into Germany proper.

In the Generalgouvernement the conflict between the army and the SS over the Jews sharpened after July 19, 1942, when Himmler ordered the "resettlement" of all the Jews in the Generalgouvernement by the end of the year. The officials of the High Command's Armaments Inspectorates attempted to get some concessions from Krüger, but he told them on August 14 that they could not expect to hold on to their Jewish workers until the end of the war. The orders were quite definite and valid for all of occupied Europe, and he presumed that "the reasons for them must be of a quite exceptional nature."[33] Although the SS made certain small concessions, such as separating the Jews employed in war industries from the rest of the ghetto, the basic order remained in effect. On September 5, 1942, Keitel added his authority to that of the SS and issued an order that all Jewish workers were to be replaced. General Kurt Ludwig Freiherr von Gienanth, commander of the military district of the Generalgouvernement, knew that getting replacements for Jewish workers was an unrealistic possibility. On September 18, 1942, he sent a memorandum to General Jodl, head of the High Command army operations, in which he pointed to the disastrous labor-supply situation in the Generalgouvernement, where Fritz Sauckel, Plenipotentiary for Labor Allocation, was siphoning off whatever Polish labor was still available for work in the Reich. Of the more than 1 million workers in war industries, over 300,000 were Jews, one-third of them skilled workers. Their immediate removal, Gienanth asserted, "would cause the Reich's war potential to be considerably reduced, and supplies to the front as well as to the troops in the General-gouvernement to be at least momentarily halted." Gienanth asked that the removal of the Jews be postponed until certain essential war production was completed, since he was prepared to accept the principle that the Jews were to be eliminated "as promptly as possible without impairing essential war work."[34]

There was no reply from Jodl, but Himmler issued a blistering memorandum on October 9. It was addressed to top members of his staff, with copies to the appropriate army officers, reiterating that portion of his decree of July 19, 1942, that ordered Jews still employed in war-industry shops (clothing, fur, shoes) to be assembled in concentration camps. The army was to submit its requisitions for clothing to the SS, which would guarantee uninterrupted delivery. Furthermore, Himmler had issued instructions "that steps

be ruthlessly taken against all those who think it their
business to intervene in the alleged interests of war
industry, and who in reality want only to support the
Jews and their businesses." (On September 30 Gienanth had been relieved of his command.) The consolidation of Jewish munitions workers into "a few
large Jewish concentration-camp enterprises" was the
next step, but, Himmler concluded, "even from there
the Jews are someday to disappear, in accordance with
the Führer's wishes."[35]

The next day the army High Command sent out
teletype instructions that "in agreement with the
Reichsführer-SS," it supported "the principle that the
Jews who are employed by the Wehrmacht for auxiliary military service and by the armament industry are
to be replaced by Aryan labor at once." The full text
of Himmler's directive was attached.[36] Once again
the German army's High Command had capitulated
to National Socialism and to the SS. Once again,
rationality was abandoned for the pursuit of ideology.

Lodz was just some seventy-five miles west of Warsaw, located in Wartheland, which was incorporated
in the Reich. It was governed by Gauleiter Arthur
Greiser, a man who could always spot the main chance
and who knew how to get on with Himmler. Before
the war Lodz had been Poland's major industrial
center, with the Jews preponderant as workers and
manufacturers. The ghetto perpetuated that tradition.
According to a report of the regional Armaments
Commission for February 1944, the largest armaments
establishment in the region was "the ghetto in which
80,000 Jews do 95 percent of the armaments work and
two-thirds of the textile production." The Jews were
"in the meantime" not being deported, the report
averred, because of "consideration for the importance
of armaments." That conclusion was only partly
justified. From late autumn 1943 until spring 1944,
Greiser, the SS, and the army were engaged in a
struggle for the ghetto. As a major war producer the
ghetto was a lucrative enterprise, and one that Greiser
wanted to retain. The SS wanted to turn the ghetto

into one of its closed labor camps and reap the profits. The army wanted to protect its own interests. This tug-of-war continued until the beginning of June 1944, when Himmler ordered the liquidation of the Lodz ghetto. Even at that late hour, the army mustered effort to counter the order. On June 5 Speer asked the regional Armaments Inspectorate for data on the ghetto as a productive enterprise, "to report, in the light of these figures, to the Führer." (On June 9 Greiser "dutifully" passed this information on to Himmler and, at the same time, sycophantically called attention to his completion of preparations to clear the ghetto.)[37] Meanwhile Anglo-American forces had landed on the Normandy beaches, and the Germans were now engaged in a two-front war. But the drastic change in their military situation permitted no accommodation with regard to the Final Solution. On June 23 the deportations from Lodz began, and by August 1944 the last seventy thousand Jews in the Lodz ghetto had been sent to Auschwitz.

As long as the Jews were permitted to live, their labor was extracted without reward or mercy. After their deportation, the Germans expropriated their remaining goods. "The wealth they had we have taken from them," said Himmler in his talk to SS leaders at Posen, October 4, 1943. Operation Reinhard systematized the disposition of the loot and the flow of proceeds from its sale into German hands. All cash proceeds in German notes were to be deposited to the Reichsbank account of the SS's *Wirtschafts- und Verwaltungshauptamt* (WVHA; Economic and Administrative Main Office), which managed the SS's economic enterprises and administered the concentration camps. Foreign currency (specie or paper), precious metals, jewelry, precious or semiprecious stones, pearls, dental gold, and scrap gold were to be delivered to the WVHA for immediate transmittal to the Reichsbank. All timepieces, alarm clocks, fountain pens, mechanical pencils, hand- or electric-operated shavers, pocket knives, scissors, flashlights, wallets, and purses were to be sent to a WVHA installation for cleaning and price estimation, and then forwarded, for sale, to the combat troops. Men's underwear, men's clothing, including footwear, were first to fill staff needs at the concentration camps and then to be sent, for sale, to the troops as an undertaking of the *Volksdeutsche Mittelstelle* (VOMI; Ethnic German Welfare Office). The proceeds were to go to the Reich. Women's clothing, underwear, and footwear and also children's clothing and underwear were to go to VOMI for cash. Pure silk underwear was assigned to the Ministry of Economy. Eiderdowns, quilts, blankets, dress materials, scarves, umbrellas, canes, thermos bottles, ear mufflers, baby carriages, combs, handbags, leather belts, shopping bags, tobacco pipes, sunglasses, mirrors, cutlery, knapsacks, leather and synthetic-material suitcases were to go to VOMI, with specific provisions for payment. Bed linens, sheets, pillowcases, handkerchiefs, washcloths, tablecloths were delivered to VOMI for cash. All kinds of eyeglasses and spectacles were assigned to the Public Health Office for sale. High-class furs, dressed or undressed, were to be delivered to WVHA; cheaper fur goods (neckpieces, hare and rabbit furs) were to be delivered to the Clothing Works of the Waffen-SS at Ravensbrück.

A provisional balance sheet of Operation Reinhard for the period April 1, 1942–December 15, 1943, showed that Reich income was augmented by about 180 million Reichsmarks from moneys and values in kind. On November 4, 1943, Globocnik, then on assignment in Trieste, submitted his final report to Himmler, closing out Operation Reinhard. The Generalgouvernement, he wrote, had been a special center of contagion that he tried to arrest. As justification for future history, Globocnik unctuously advised Himmler to call attention "to the elimination of this danger." He asked for some Iron Crosses to be awarded to members of his staff for their "special achievements of this difficult task." Himmler replied on November 30: "I express to you my thanks and my recognition for your great and unique merits that you acquired for the whole German people in the execution of Operation Reinhard."[38]

Arriving at Auschwitz, Bełżec, Chełmno, Majdanek, Sobibór, and Treblinka, the Jews encountered a standard procedure. At camps maintaining labor installations, like Auschwitz, 10 percent of the arrivals—those who looked fittest—were selected for work. The remainder were consigned to the gas chambers. They were instructed to undress; the women and girls had their hair cut. They were then marched between files of auxiliary police (Ukrainians usually) who hurried them along with whips, sticks, or guns, to the gas chambers. As in Operation T-4, these were identified as shower rooms. The Jews were rammed in, one person per square foot. The gassing lasted from ten to thirty minutes, depending on the facilities and techniques used. In Bełżec, according to an eyewitness, it took thirty-two minutes and "finally, all were dead," he wrote, "like pillars of basalt, still erect, not having any space to fall."[39] To make room for the next load, the bodies were right away tossed out, "blue, wet with sweat and urine, the legs covered with feces and menstrual blood." Later the bodies were burned, either in the open air or in crematoria. Himmler complained about the slowness of the proceedings. But no quicker or more secret method could be found. A worker at Auschwitz said that "the stench given off by the pyres contaminated the surrounding countryside. At night the red sky over Auschwitz could be seen for miles."[40]

The statistics of the death camps are only approximate. At Auschwitz, the largest mass-killing installation, many transports of deportees went directly from the detraining ramps to the gas chambers and were never statistically registered. On March 16, 1946, Höss made the following statement to two officers of the War Crimes Investigation Unit of the British Army of the Rhine: "I personally arranged on orders received from Himmler in May 1941 the gassing of two million persons between June–July 1941 and the end of 1943, during which time I was commandant of Auschwitz." Most victims at the death camps were Jews, but also all Gypsies and thousands of non-Jews—selected for particular reasons—were gassed.

Auschwitz	2,000,000
Bełżec	600,000
Chełmno	340,000
Majdanek	1,380,000
Sobibór	250,000
Treblinka	800,000
TOTAL	5,370,000

On October 4, 1943, Himmler addressed a body of SS-*Gruppenführer* (lieutenant-generals), in a long rambling speech about the SS. He spoke also about the annihilation of the Jews:

I also want to refer before you here, in complete frankness, to a really grave matter. Among ourselves, this once, it shall be uttered quite frankly; but in public we will never speak of it. . . .

I am referring to the evacuation of the Jews, the annihilation of the Jewish people. This is one of those things that are easily said. "The Jewish people is going to be annihilated," says every party member. "Sure, it's in our program, elimination of the Jews, annihilation—we'll take care of it." And then they all come trudging, eighty million worthy Germans, and each one has his one decent Jew. Sure, the others are swine, but this one is an A-1 Jew. Of all those who talk this way, not one has seen it happen, not one has been through it. Most of you must know what it means to see a hundred corpses lie side by side, or five hundred, or a thousand. To have stuck this out and—excepting cases of human weakness—to have kept our integrity, this is what has made us hard. In our history, this is an unwritten and never-to-be-written page of glory. . . .[41]

8

A Retrospective View

The Final Solution had its origins in Hitler's mind. In *Mein Kampf* he tells us that he decided on his war against the Jews in November 1918, when, at the military hospital in Pasewalk, he learned, in rapid succession, of the naval mutiny at Kiel, the revolution that forced the abdication of the Emperor, and finally the armistice. "Everything went black before my eyes," he wrote. In the ensuing "terrible days and even worse nights," while he pondered the meaning of these cataclysmic events, "my own fate became known to me." It was then that he made his decision:

> There is no making pacts with Jews; there can be only the hard: either—or.
> I, for my part, decided to go into politics.

Did Hitler really decide then, in November 1918, on the destruction of the Jews as his political goal? Or did the idea remain buried in his mind until it took shape in *Mein Kampf*, which he wrote in 1924? *Mein Kampf* was the basic treatise of Hitler's ideas, where he brought together the three essential components that formed the embryonic concept of the Final Solution. Each component originated in a politically common-

place notion that Hitler transformed into an inor-
dinately radical one. First, he turned political anti-
Semitism into a racial doctrine whose purpose was the
destruction of the Jews. Second, having defined Bolshevism as a Jewish conspiracy for world rule, he transformed anti-Bolshevism into a holy crusade to liberate
Russia from its allegedly Jewish masters. Third, using
race as a rationale, he transformed the imperialist drive
for autarky and world power into the concept of
Lebensraum. These three notions were consolidated
into a unified concept that became the theoretical,
ideational foundation of the Final Solution. In *Mein
Kampf* that concept appeared in its matured form and
remained a central tenet in Hitler's ideology from
which he never deviated. It was already then a fixed
idea, in both the everyday and psychiatric meaning of
the term, awaiting only the political opportunities for
its implementation.

If *Mein Kampf* is the *terminus ad quem* for the conception of the Final Solution, does its beginning indeed
go back to November 1918, as Hitler himself claimed?
It is a hazardous task to construct a chronology of the
evolution of this idea in Hitler's mind. The historical
evidence is sparse and no doubt would be inadmissible
as courtroom evidence. The very idea of the destruction of the Jews as a political goal demanded, when
Hitler first began to advocate it, camouflage and concealment. Its later consummation demanded, within
limits, secrecy. Consequently there is a paucity of
documents, and even those we have handicap the
search for definitive evidence because of the problem
of esoteric language.

How does one advocate publicly an idea or a program whose novelty lies in its utter radicalism? No
matter how anti-Semitic the Munich of 1919 and 1920
was, the explicit transformation of a slogan like "*Juda
verrecke*" into a practical political program would have
brought on the censorship of the local authorities and
discredited the incipient National Socialist movement
even among conventional anti-Semites. In this situation Hitler availed himself of a time-honored device—

the use of esoteric language. In all periods of history, when government or society has put limits on public discussion, those who wish to circumvent censorship resort to the use of esoteric language. Exoterically understood, the text is unexceptionable, but to the insiders who know how to interpret the words, the message is revolutionary and dangerous to the status quo.

Hitler complained in *Mein Kampf* that in the early days it was hard to get a hearing for the anti-Semitic point of view. "Our first attempts," he wrote, "to show the public the real enemy then seemed almost hopeless." He exaggerated, as usual, but the problem was that the National Socialists did not want to be dismissed "merely" as anti-Semites, single-minded crackpots without political solutions to contemporary problems. In the Reichswehr, where Hitler's oratorical talents and anti-Semitic presentations to the recruits were much admired by his superiors, there was anxiety that these speeches would be characterized as "anti-Jewish agitation." Instructions were consequently given for a cautious treatment and the avoidance of "plain references" to the Jews.[1]

The National Socialists in their public meetings seldom exercised such caution, for the word "Jew" occurs with obsessive repetitiveness. Still, according to the earliest reports of Hitler's speeches, the code words he used for Jews outnumbered the plain references: usury (usurers), profiteering (profiteers), exploiters, big capitalism (big capitalists), international big and/or loan capital, international money power, Communists, Social Democrats, November criminals, revolution criminals, aliens, foreigners. References to the press unmistakably were meant and interpreted as "Jewish" press. In one circumlocution, Hitler spoke of the fight "against the races [*sic*] who are the money representatives."[2]

The code words served to invest the crude anti-Semitic agitation of the National Socialists with the dignity of political argument and economic analysis. Simultaneously they served to depict for the insiders

the vast ramifications of the "Jewish conspiracy" and
to document the multifarious roles of the mythic Jew.
From the use of these code words, the insiders came
to learn that all of Germany's enemies were Jews or
tools of Jews.

Having defined the enemy exoterically and
esoterically, Hitler in his speeches began to indicate
how he would deal with that enemy. In those early
days his favorite words were *"Entfernung"* and
"Aufräumung," both meaning "removal," "elimination,"
"cleaning up." (In *Mein Kampf* he preferred to use
"Beseitigung," also meaning "removal," "elimination,"
but less ambiguous about its finality.) According to a
Reichswehr report of a meeting of April 27, 1920, Hitler in his closing remarks said: "We will carry on the
struggle until the last Jew is removed *[entfernt ist]*
from the German Reich." According to the Bavarian
police report, Hitler's conclusion that the NSDAP
would make a revolution that would "thoroughly clean
out *[aufräumen]* the Jew-rabble" received "protracted, stormy applause."[3]

Whether he used both words interchangeably or
whether the several reporters "interpreted" what they
heard, Hitler had resorted to language whose meaning
he intentionally made ambiguous, to be understood
both exoterically and esoterically. "Removal" or "elimination" could be understood to mean "expulsion," and
no doubt some of Hitler's listeners thought, if they
thought at all about specifics, that he planned to drive
the Jews out of Germany.

In this very early period only two documents are
extant that are authentically Hitler's, the direct
product of his hand and mind. These lend themselves
better to a probing of his meaning than the second-
hand reports of Reichswehr and police. The first document is his letter to Gemlich, written while he was
still working for the Reichswehr. Here, once more, is
that key passage:

Rational anti-Semitism, however, must lead to a systematic legal opposition and elimination *[Beseitigung]*

of the special privileges that Jews hold, in contrast to
the other aliens living among us (aliens' legislation). Its
final objective must unswervingly be the removal
[*Entfernung*] of the Jews altogether.

What Hitler is saying here is that a systematic program of anti-Semitism consists of two stages: a preliminary stage in which Jews are deprived of all rights,
and then the accomplishment of a "final objective"—
"removal of the Jews altogether." The phrase is obviously open to two interpretations. It was not that
Hitler was unable to express himself clearly and unequivocally. Rather he deliberately used a word that
could be interpreted two ways—one, vague and conventional; the other, specific and radical.

Such ambiguous usage persisted in the National
Socialist movement until the end, though its function
became somewhat different. Himmler, in his speech to
the SS-Gruppenführer on October 4, 1943, used the
word "*Ausschaltung,*" meaning "elimination," as
synonymous with "*Ausrottung,*" meaning "annihilation." There was no reason to invoke esoteric language
to that particular audience on that occasion at that late
date, but by then the political need for esoteric
language had given way to the psychological need for
euphemistic language.

In the second Hitler document, the text of his
speech of August 13, 1920, a typescript apparently
made from a stenographic record, with editorial eman-
dations in Hitler's own hand, "*Entfernung*" reappears
as a solution to the "Jewish question":

> Removal of the Jews from our nation, not because we
> would begrudge them their existence—we congratulate
> the rest of the whole world on their company [great
> merriment], but because the existence of our own na-
> tion is a thousand times more important to us than that
> of an alien race.

Here Hitler has introduced the very question of
whether the Jews are to live or die. The irony is heavy.

But precisely where does it begin? How did the inflections of his voice, his pauses, and emphases communicate his message? Does the irony begin with the phrase "not because we would begrudge them their existence"? Perhaps the party members are already responding to an inside joke, whereas the outsiders get the joke only at the next clause, which itself compounds the original ambiguity of the word "removal." Are the Jews to be expelled from Germany and thus forced upon other countries, or is Hitler referring to the Jews already living in other countries? The ambiguity is calculated. Nevertheless, Hitler posited an incontrovertible dichotomy: "their existence" versus "our existence."

The "either—or" that he had predicated in *Mein Kampf* was already evolving. In a speech on April 12, 1922, he said, referring to the "Jewish question": "Here, too, there can be no compromise—there are only two possibilities: either victory of the Aryan or annihilation of the Aryan and the victory of the Jew."[4] Hitler frequently used the rhetorical device of paired antitheses. Strictly, the construction should have read:

either victory of the Aryan [*and annihilation of the Jew*]
or
annihilation of the Aryan and the victory of the Jew.

The ellipsis of half of one pair was a signal to the cognoscenti of what he meant to say. Today we can appreciate a similar ellipsis in his famous prophecy of January 30, 1939:

Bolshevization of the world and a victory of the Jews
or
[*Aryanization of the world and*] *destruction of the Jewish race.*

In 1922 Hitler had to propagate the annihilation of the Jews in esoteric language. In 1939 he used the same technique to express his ambition for world dominion.

In the summer of 1922 a young man named Kurt Ludecke joined the National Socialist party and first met Hitler. Overwhelmed by both, he described his feelings at that time about the goals the movement had set for itself. These were his perceptions:

> The hugeness of the task and the absurdity of the hope swept over me. Its execution meant the liquidation of Jewry, of Rome, of liberalism with its tangled capitalistic connections; of Marxism, Bolshevism, Toryism— in short, an abrupt and complete break with the past and an assault on all existing world political forces.[5]

Hitler's goals had unmistakably been communicated, despite the handicaps of esoteric language. Within the movement, the destruction of the Jews seemed to have been accepted as a basic programmatic task, though the average National Socialist probably still thought of pogrom, despite Hitler's frequently expressed opposition to such "emotional" outbursts of anti-Semitism. Still, even in those early days of the movement, when plans were being laid for the Putsch and the takeover of political power, the Jews figured importantly in Nazi strategy. The destruction of the Jews was not just a matter of words, in esoteric language even then, but a deathly reality. Hermann Esser, one of Hitler's earliest party comrades, at an NSDAP meeting held in December 1922, at which plans for a forthcoming Putsch were discussed, mentioned the possibilities of foreign intervention on behalf of the Weimar Republic. That would not work, he said, for there would be "500,000 Jews as hostages carefully guarded, who will be ruthlessly dispatched, if even a single enemy crosses the German frontier." At the time of the Putsch, one battalion was assigned to keep the Jews from fleeing Munich, presumably to ensure their remaining as hostages.[6]

A draft constitution prepared by one of Hitler's associates in readiness for the NSDAP takeover provided, as a start, for the expropriation of "all movable and immovable property of the members of the

Jewish people."[7] Any attempt to circumvent expropriation was punishable by death. Concentration camps (*Sammellager*) were to be set up to "cleanse" the "cities, spas, and resort towns," especially "for the removal of all persons dangerous to security and useless eaters." Since these were to be the first steps during the transitional period while the NSDAP would be consolidating its power, it does not appear unlikely that still more Draconian measures were in store for the Jews.

In retrospect, it seems likely that Hitler had settled on his radical "either—or" anti-Semitism, as he formulated it in the Gemlich letter of 1919, already back in November 1918, as he claims in *Mein Kampf*. During the next few years Hitler's thinking remained geographically limited to Germany, albeit a "greater Germany." In his mind, the destruction of the Jews was the way to restore Germany to its virile Germandom. But once he encountered Alfred Rosenberg, Hitler's political horizons expanded; he began to see the Jews primarily as an international group whose destruction demanded an international policy.

This new approach is distinctly evident in his speech of July 28, 1922, delivered a month after Rathenau's assassination and upon Hitler's emergence from prison where he had served one month for breaking up an opposition meeting. The enforced leisure of prison had given him time to think, as later in Landsberg. Hitler now viewed his struggle against "Jewish world domination" in global terms:

> Today we all of us feel that two worlds are struggling with one another, and not alone in our country, but everywhere we look, in oppressed Russia, in Italy, in France, and England, etc. An inexorable struggle between the ideals of those who believe in a national people and the ideals of the intangible, supra-national international. . . .[8]

The content of this speech was a mostly familiar attack on the Jews and the "Jewish" conspiracy in which

"the stock-exchange Jew and the labor leader" together "pursue a single direction and a single aim."
The new factor was Hitler's global perspective: "How
long will it be before the whole world falls to
ruin . . . ?"

Rosenberg further showed Hitler the possibilities of
exploiting Russia as the political locus of international
Jewry, thus providing him with the eventual major
theater of operations for his war against world Jewry.
Under the influence of Rosenberg and the other Russian and Ukrainian émigrés with whom he associated
and with whom the National Socialist movement collaborated, Russia became a key element in Hitler's
thinking. The émigrés spoke constantly of the imperative need to invade Russia so as to liberate it from the
bondage of the "Jew-Bolsheviks." In the very first issue
of the *Völkischer Beobachter,* Rosenberg speculated
that the Soviet Union would shortly invade Poland
and argued that Germany should then intervene in
what he called "the eastern marches of Germany."
(Hitler was to use this idea in *Mein Kampf.*) Here, in
Rosenberg's mind, is the justification for Germany's
"liberation" of the Eastern territories from the "Jewish
Bolsheviks," which would simultaneously restore the
land to its original German owner. It was an idea that
Hitler and Himmler were to hold tenaciously for the
next twenty years. Thus, fitting piece by piece into a
large scheme, Hitler combined the annihilation of the
Jews with the destruction of Bolshevism, both of which
could be accomplished by an invasion of Russia. The
whole was supported in racial terms: the innate racial
perniciousness of the Jews and the innate racial
superiority of the Aryans whose culture justified their
need for Lebensraum.

Hitler probably derived the components for the idea
of Lebensraum from the impositions of the Versailles
Treaty. His earliest speeches all dwelled, in one way
or another, on the treaty, for which, as he saw it, the
Jews were responsible. He often referred to Germany's
lost colonies, the forfeiture of her merchant and fishing
fleets, the obligatory deliveries of coal to France and

the Low Countries, and the burdensome monetary payments. According to the Reichswehr report of a speech of December 10, 1919, on the "shame of the Versailles Treaty," Hitler spoke of Germany's need to import raw materials; according to the Bavarian police report, he complained that there was eighteen times more land for every Russian than for every German. (In that speech, he expressed the view that the Russian had a right to his land, a position he did not long hold.) In a speech on September 20, 1920, the racial justification for Lebensraum had already emerged. According to the Reichswehr report, Hitler said that Germany had a right to live, not only on the basis of its population, but also "on the basis of its culture." Thus, with the help of Rosenberg and eventually Haushofer, Hitler shaped his concept of Lebensraum, in which racial ideology became as vital as the imperialist drive.

Hitler wrote the first volume of *Mein Kampf* in Landsberg prison in 1924 and the second volume in 1925, when he was forbidden to engage in public speaking. The tone of the second is more aggressive and outspoken than that of the first;[9] Volume 2 is said to have benefited also from professional editorial assistance. The writing of *Mein Kampf* forced Hitler into a process of organizing his ideas in one all-embracing schema, however unsystematic and inchoate the final product. At its center was the war against the Jews that would culminate in their annihilation and the world supremacy of the Germans. The language, especially in the second volume, is no longer esoteric, but plainspoken. Though Hitler's hysteria and chiliastic rhetoric made the prose appear deceptively metaphorical, the words were meant to be taken literally. The destruction of the Jews is advocated time and again (all italics in original):

Only the elimination of the causes of our collapse, as well as the destruction of its beneficiaries, can create the premise for our outward fight for freedom.

> *. . . It is the inexorable Jew who struggles for his*
> *domination over nations.* No nation can remove this
> hand from its throat except by the sword. Only the
> assembled and concentrated might of a national passion
> rearing up in its strength can defy the international
> enslavement of peoples. Such a process is and remains
> a bloody one.

Writing about the failure of the 1923 Putsch, Hitler
accused the Weimar government of lacking sufficient
nationalism: "And in my opinion, it was then the very
first task of a truly national government to seek and
find the forces which were resolved to declare a war
of annihilation on Marxism and then to give these
forces a free road. . . ." Not only was the government
derelict in its task, Hitler argued, but so were all the
political parties, which "continued to bicker with the
Marxists only out of competitors' envy, without any
serious desire to annihilate them."

At the same time, Hitler kept projecting on the Jews
the very destructive ideas he held about them: "The
Jew would really devour the people of the earth,
would become their master," "the international world
Jew slowly but surely strangles us," "the Jew destroys
the racial foundations of our existence and thus destroys our people for all time."

He even argued retroactively for a "preventive" war
against the Jew in 1914–1918, which could have saved
Germany from defeat:

> It would have been the duty of a serious government,
> now that the German worker had found his way back to
> his nation [in August 1914], to exterminate mercilessly
> the agitators who were misleading the nation.

> If the best men were dying at the front, the least we
> could do was to wipe out the vermin.

> If at the beginning of the War and during the War
> twelve or fifteen thousand of these Hebrew corrupters
> of the people had been held under poison gas . . . the

sacrifice of millions at the front would not have been in vain. On the contrary: twelve thousand scoundrels eliminated in time might have saved the lives of a million real Germans, valuable for the future.

In the years between 1919 and 1925, the political climate had changed and Hitler now openly espoused his program of annihilation, without having to resort to concealment or camouflage. But only his followers took his words literally. Others, when they listened to Hitler or read *Mein Kampf*, dismissed his words as lunatic ravings. Yet these words were to become the blueprint for his policies when he came to power and would become, astonishingly, political and military reality.

Once Hitler adopted an ideological position, even a strategic one, he adhered to it with limpetlike fixity, fearful lest he be accused, if he changed his mind, of incertitude or capriciousness on "essential questions." He had long-range plans to realize his ideological goals, and the destruction of the Jews was at their center.

The grand design was in his head. He did not spell it out in concrete strategy. Nothing was written down. (On April 29, 1937, he advised NSDAP leaders: "Everything that can be discussed should *never* be put in writing, never!")[10] He even elevated his tactics of secrecy into a strategic principle: as few people as possible to know as little as possible as late as possible.[11]

The implementation of his plans was contingent on the opportunism of the moment or the expediency of delay. As head of both the German state and the National Socialist movement, he had to weigh the urgent passions of the little man in the party against the foreign-policy interests of the state, and to-balance his own desire for surprise attack with the state's readiness to mount one. Often he decided suddenly that the opportune occasion had arrived to carry out a specific aspect of his program, and then the practical work had quickly to be improvised.

In Hitler's schema, the removal of the Jews from posts in the state apparatus and from society's cultural and educational institutions represented, along with the remilitarization of Germany, the first phase of his program, the internal cleansing and healing of Germany. Whereas the anti-Jewish legislation of 1933 was for him merely the prerequisite for later stages of his program that would culminate in the Final Solution, this undoing of the emancipation of the German Jews represented for the conventional anti-Semites the attainment of their political ambitions. That was the time when the widest consensus existed in Germany with regard to anti-Semitism, when the values and goals of the conventional anti-Semites were identical and undistinguishable from those of the radical anti-Semites. That particular convergence made it easier for the conventional anti-Semites subsequently to acquiesce to the radical anti-Semitic program.

At the National Socialist party congress in Nuremberg in September 1935, Hitler introduced new anti-Jewish legislation, describing these laws as a repayment of a debt of gratitude to the National Socialist party, under whose aegis Germany had regained her freedom, and as the fulfillment of an important plank of the movement's program.[12] The Reich Citizenship Law, depriving the German Jews of the rights and protections of citizenship, marked the goal of conventional anti-Semitism—the total disenfranchisement of the Jews.

The Law for the Protection of German Blood and German Honor, on the other hand, even though it draw heavily upon a half-century's tradition of racist anti-Semitism, was a new departure. With its implementing decrees and with those of the Reich Citizenship Law, it initiated Hitler's program of radical anti-Semitism, with the process of identifying and isolating the Jews from the non-Jews, readying them, as it were, for their later fate.

The Nuremberg Laws were a watershed also in another respect, to which Hitler alluded ominously. In introducing the Law for the Protection of German Blood and German Honor, he said that it was "an attempt to regulate by law a problem which, in the event of repeated failure, would have to be transferred by law to the National Socialist party for final solution."* He was, it now appears, indicating that the state had come to the end of its competency in handling the Jewish question and that thenceforth all anti-Jewish measures would be carried out by the party. In this period, too, he spoke of sweeping plans for the Jews, involving ghettos and possibly a reservation, and on another occasion he talked of carrying out the "euthanasia" murder program once war came.

By the summer of 1936, Hitler believed that the first phase of his program—the internal domestic stage —was virtually completed and in August, having composed a memorandum on the Four Year Plan, he entered into preparations for the second phase—aggression and war. That memorandum, with its ideological justification for a war against "Jewish Bolshevism," transformed *Mein Kampf* into state policy. The doctrine of the party leader now became the plan for the state. The annihilation of the Jews, who are explicitly referred to as the power behind Bolshevism, is implicit in Hitler's familiar rhetorical construction (italicized in the original): *"For a victory of Bolshevism over Germany would not lead to a Versailles Treaty but to the final destruction, indeed to the annihilation, of the German people."*[13] As further clarification, Hitler specified that the Reichstag would have to pass a law expropriating the Jews. Thus the expropriation of the Jews had become, in Hitler's thinking, correlated with the advancement of his war plans. That decision explains why Hitler rejected the insistent demands of

---

* In his speech of April 27, 1920, Hitler was reported to have said, with regard to carrying out his planned anti-Jewish program: "First we try to carry it out kindly, and then, when that does not work, with ruthless violence."

the National Socialist movement between 1935 and 1938 to plunder Jewish property and possessions.

That decision explains also Hitler's apparent indifference to the unregulated pluralism with regard to the Jews that then flourished within state and party— the use of National Socialist law, arbitrary violence, normal bureaucratic procedures for normal migration coexisting with the SD's ideas of forced emigration. Hitler's toleration for such assorted "solutions" extended only until he was ready to put his war plans into operation.

Hitler appointed Göring to be his Plenipotentiary for the Four Year Plan and gave him a copy of that memorandum. They surely discussed aspects of this program, and Hitler must have shared his plans concerning the Jews. At least one other person also shared Hitler's confidences in this respect at this time—Heinrich Himmler. In the early summer of 1936 Himmler had, with Hitler's support, become Reichsführer-SS and Chief of the German Police, directly subordinate to Hitler and only to him. Hitler had by then already decided to hand over to the National Socialist movement the authority to "solve" the Jewish question. Himmler, then one of the most powerful figures in the party, had probably been inducted into the inmost circle and told of Hitler's plans for war and the destruction of the Jews—a task that would fall, at the proper time, within his jurisdiction.

How often and how specifically Hitler discussed his plans with Göring and Himmler no one knows. Yet they spoke, for instance, about ghettos as an interim measure, because Göring, at his post-Kristallnacht interministerial conference of November 12, 1938, proposed ghettos as a possible means of concentrating the Jews. (Heydrich's objections at that time indicate that he had not yet become privy to these plans.)

If the plans for dealing with the Jews were vague and nonspecific, so were the plans for military invasion, as the Hossbach protocal reveals. Hitler's military and diplomatic staffs were appalled to learn in November 1937 of Hitler's intentions to invade Austria and Czechoslovakia in 1938, not so much because of the suddenness with which they had to confront these plans, but because of lack of preparation. Their demurral, however, cost them their posts and careers, for Hitler remained inflexible, committed to his timetable. The Austrian invasion advanced smoothly, but Chamberlain's intervention in Czechoslovakia frustrated Hitler's plans. It appears that he had intended, under cover of the seizure of Czechoslovakia, to carry out the expropriation of the Jews, for the first National Socialist legislation in this area was issued early in 1938. Hitler no doubt counted on the general public upheaval over Czechoslovakia to muffle protests about robbing the Jews.

Thwarted by Chamberlain, but impatient to move ahead according to his schedule, Hitler took the first opportunity that would give him apparent justification to expropriate the Jews: the assassination of vom Rath. That opportunism proved doubly useful, for it gave the little Nazi a last chance for a fling. The pogrom and the expropriation were not really part of Hitler's new, radical anti-Semitism, but rather a reversion to medievalism, when Jews were subjected not only to violence, but to all sorts of taxes, fines, levies, exactions, amercements, and confiscations. In the Middle Ages complete expropriation went hand in hand with expulsion, and for the brief period that National Socialist pressure for Jewish emigration intensified following the Kristallnacht, Hitler seemed to be emulating Edward I and Philip the Fair. But pressure for emigration was, in Hitler's plans, only byplay. After the Kristallnacht the Jews in Germany became little more than hostages, perhaps no different from the way Hitler and Esser had envisaged the situation in 1923. The Reichszentrale, which Göring had instructed Heydrich to set up on January 24, 1939, effectively put the Jews at the mercy of the police and SD. (Probably then, Heydrich was made a party to the plan to destroy the Jews.)

On January 30, 1939, Hitler made his declaration of

war against the Jews, promising "the destruction of the Jewish race in Europe." The decision to proceed with this irreversible mission had already been taken. Thenceforth the Final Solution entered the stage of practical planning for implementation. Hitler's first opportunity to put into practice his ideas about killing the crippled and insane presented itself at this time, and shortly thereafter, on April 3, 1939, he instructed Keitel to start planning the invasion of Poland.

Hitler's gamble, then, was on a quick military victory in Poland, to be completed before Russia could gather wits or forces to act. Afterward he would consolidate his position, using Poland as the launching pad for his invasion of Russia. (The rapprochement with Russia, ideologically embarrassing but tactically expedient, did not at all affect his long-range plans, but merely eased his short-range military risks.) While planning the Polish invasion, Hitler, Himmler, and Heydrich worked out the first stage of the Final Solution, concentrating the Jews while consolidating the Polish gains. Heydrich's instructions to the chiefs of the Einsatzgruppen on September 21, 1939, are clear enough about present program and future intentions. The second, ultimate stage of the Final Solution was to be synchronized with the attack on Russia, when "Jewish Bolshevism" would be destroyed.

While the Jews in Poland were concentrated in ghettos and began to expire slowly of "natural" causes like hunger, disease, cold, exhaustion, the idea of systematically killing the Jews began to appear as an inevitable and even desirable development to a number of Germans not privy to the still-secret plans for the Final Solution. Thus SS-Brigadeführer Friedrich Übelhör, *Regierungspräsident* of Lodz (the top official in the civil administration of the district of Lodz), on December 10, 1939, in planning to establish a ghetto, already thought of its destruction:

The establishment of the ghetto is of course only a provisional measure. I reserve for myself the points in the time and the means with which the ghetto and thereby the city of Lodz will be cleansed of Jews. The end goal [*Endziel*] in any case must be that we burn out this pesthole without a remainder.[14]

Übelhör's hubris reveals that he knew nothing of the plans for the Final Solution, otherwise he would not likely have arrogated to himself a decision of the highest state and party priority.

A year later, on December 20, 1940, Governor Hans Frank addressed a Wehrmacht battalion stationed in Cracow. Remarking, as he often did, that their families must commiserate with them for having to serve in Poland, where there were so many lice and Jews, Frank said it would indeed be nice if they could write home and say that things with regard to lice and Jews had improved: "To be sure, in one year I can do away with neither all the lice nor all the Jews [merriment]. But in the course of time and, above all, if you help me, that will be made attainable."[15]

Still later, in July 1941, an official by the name of Höppner, in the city administration of Posen, sent Eichmann the official minutes of a discussion regarding the "Solution of the Jewish Question" in the Wartheland. One proposal read:

There is an imminent danger that not all the Jews can be supplied with food in the coming winter. We must seriously consider if it would not be more humane to finish off the Jews, insofar as they are not fit for labor mobilization, with some quick-acting means. In any case this would be more agreeable [*angenehmer*] than to let them die of hunger.

In his covering letter asking for Eichmann's comments, Höppner was optimistically categorical: "These things sound to some extent fantastic, but in my view absolutely practicable."[16] Eichmann, for his part, at precisely that time was working on the practicability of such fantastic ideas.

In December 1940 Operation Barbarossa entered the formal planning stage, and Hitler then no doubt explored with Himmler, and perhaps Heydrich, various practical possibilities for the last stage of the Final Solution. By February 1941 they had decided on a two-pronged attack against the Jews. In the active war zone, the Einsatzgruppen would coordinate their murder attack on the Jews with the military invasion. The rest of the European Jews in countries under German occupation or governed by rulers sympathetic to Germany would be brought to annihilation camps in or near the Generalgouvernement of Poland. (Himmler's visit to Auschwitz on March 1, 1941, was obviously exploratory, for he did not inform Höss then why Auschwitz was to be expanded.) All the decisions had been taken. The rest was a matter of technology, administrative clearance, and efficient operation. Through a maze of time Hitler's decision of November 1918 led to Operation Barbarossa. There never had been any ideological deviation or wavering determination. In the end only the question of opportunity mattered.

The Final Solution grew out of a matrix formed by traditional anti-Semitism, the paranoid delusions that seized Germany after World War I, and the emergence of Hitler and the National Socialist movement. Without Hitler, the charismatic political leader, who believed he had a mission to annihilate the Jews, the Final Solution would not have occurred. Without that assertive and enduring tradition of anti-Semitism by which the Germans sought self-definition, Hitler would not have had the fecund soil in which to grow his organization and spread its propaganda. Without the paranoid delusion of the Dolchstoss that masses of Germans shared in the wake of Germany's military defeat, political upheavals, economic distress, and humiliations of the Versailles Treaty, Hitler could not have transformed the German brand of conventional anti-Semitism into a radical doctrine of mass murder.

Anti-Semitism was the core of Hitler's system of beliefs and the central motivation for his policies. He believed himself to be the savior who would bring redemption to the German people through the an-

nihilation of the Jews, that people who embodied, in
his eyes, the Satanic hosts. When he spoke or wrote
about his "holy mission," he used words associated
with chiliastic prophecy (not only in the millennial
concept literally rendered as the "Thousand Year
Reich"), like "consecration," "salvation," "redemption," "resurrection," "God's will." The murder of the
Jews, in his fantasies, was commanded by divine
providence, and he was the chosen instrument for that
task. He referred often to his "mission," but nowhere
so explicitly as in *Mein Kampf*: "Hence today I believe
that I am acting in accordance with the will of the
Almighty Creator: *by defending myself against the
Jew, I am fighting for the work of the Lord.*" From
the moment he made his entrance on the historical
stage until his death in a Berlin bunker, this sense of
messianic mission never departed from him, nor could
any appeal to reason deflect him from pursuing his
murderous purpose.

Generations of anti-Semitism had prepared the Germans to accept Hitler as their redeemer. Layer upon
layer of anti-Semitism of all kinds—Christian church
teachings about the Jews, Volkist anti-Semitism. doctrines of racial superiority, economic theories about
the role of Jews in capitalism and commerce, and a
half-century of political anti-Semitism—were joined
with the solder of German nationalism, providing the
structural foundation upon which Hitler and the National Socialist movement built. Of the conglomerate
social, economic, and political appeals that the NSDAP
directed at the German people, its racial doctrine was
most attractive. Yet for the average National Socialist,
and still more for the party's fellow travelers, out of
the whole corpus of racial teachings, the anti-Jewish
doctrine had the greatest dynamic potency. The reports of early NSDAP meetings reveal, from the record
of audience responses, that violent attacks on the Jews
provided orgasmic outbursts and that Hitler was most
adept at getting the blood to tingle with his threats
against the Jews.[17] For the audience, the convolutions
of Hitler's ideology were, in the end, reduced in

significance to the timeworn slogan of German anti-Semitism: *"Juda verrecke."*[18]

The insecurities of post–World War I Germany and the anxieties they produced provided an emotional milieu in which irrationality and hysteria became routine and illusions became transformed into delusions. The delusional disorder assumed mass proportions. Germans, otherwise individually rational, yielded themselves to pathological fantasies about the Jews.[19] In that climate, where masses of Germans had lost the ability to distinguish between the real Jew and the mythic Jew of anti-Semitic invention, the chiliastic system of National Socialist beliefs could further influence their already distorted sense of reality. Belief in National Socialism was like belief in magic and witchcraft during the Middle Ages, similarly ruling and inflaming the minds of men.[20] In the Middle Ages private misfortunes and public calamities were attributed to witches and demons, whereas in modern Germany the Jews were regarded as the source of evil and disaster. A popular children's book of the time made it plain:

> *Ohne Lösung der Judenfrage*
> *Keine Erlösung der Menschheit.*[21]
> (Without solution of the Jewish question
> No salvation of mankind.)

In medieval days entire communities were seized with witchcraft hysteria, and in modern Germany the mass psychosis of anti-Semitism deranged a whole people. According to their system of beliefs, elimination of the Jews resembled medieval exorcism of the Devil. The accomplishment of both, it was variously held, would restore grace to the world.

German hysteria was rooted in fear. "That which drives the German to cruelty," wrote Curzio Malaparte, "to deeds most coldly, methodically and scientifically cruel, is fear."[22] That fear, which assumed pandemic proportions, operated through projection. What the Germans hated and feared most in them-

selves they projected onto the Jews, endowing the
Jews with those terrible and terrifying attributes they
tried to repress in themselves. The farther the image
of the Jew receded from reality, taking on the fantastic distortions of primeval hatred, the more abhorrent it became.

There were, fundamentally, two totally disparate
and mutually contradictory images of the Jew that
collided with each other in the paranoid propaganda
of National Socialist anti-Semitism, both inherited
from the recent and medieval treasury of anti-
Semitism. One was the image of the Jew as vermin, to
be rubbed out by the heel of the boot, to be exterminated. The other was the image of the Jew as the
mythic omnipotent superadversary, against whom war
on the greatest scale had to be conducted. The Jew
was, on the one hand, a germ, a bacillus, to be killed
without conscience. On the other hand, he was, in the
phrase Hitler repeatedly used, from *Mein Kampf* until
the end of the war, the "mortal enemy" (*Todfeind*),
to be killed in self-defense.

Also the counterimages that the Germans held of
themselves were dual and inconsistent. In one scenario,
the "Aryan" German was the wholesome, vigorous
superman, invulnerable to "Jewish" poison, who was
destined by innate racial superiority to rule the world.
According to the other scenario, however, the Germans saw themselves as latter-day Laocoöns in the
grip of a death struggle. In a paranoid vision, they
believed themselves to be innocent and aggrieved
victims, outwitted by the machinations of a super-
cunning and all-powerful antagonist, engaged in a
struggle for their very existence. It was a struggle, as
Hitler put it, of "either—or."

Once the illusory notions about "Jewish" power had
been transformed into delusions about a Jewish conspiracy to rule the world, the Germans became
possessed by the belief that mythic world Jewry was
committed to their destruction. Consequently, in the
deluded German mind, every Jewish man, woman, and
child became a panoplied warrior of a vast Satanic

fighting machine. The most concrete illustration of this delusion is the now familiar photograph taken from the collection attached to Stroop's report of the Warsaw ghetto uprising. It shows uniformed German SS men holding guns to a group of women and children; in the foreground is a frightened boy of about six, his hands up. This was the face of the enemy.

Hitler skillfully translated this mythic warfare into a real war in which the Germans engaged the real enemy along with the mythic enemy. On April 15, 1945, when six million Jews were already murdered, Hitler issued his last military order. He exhorted his soldiers to perform their utmost: "For the last time our mortal enemies the Jewish Bolsheviks have launched their massive forces to the attack. Their aim is to reduce Germany to ruins and to exterminate our people."[23]

In one sense the German war against the Jews fitted into Clausewitz's classical definition of war as a political act, the continuation of politics by other means. This was National Socialism's innovation, having transformed conventional anti-Semitism with its metaphoric imagery of combat into a literal war of annihilation. "True wars," said Himmler, "wars between races, are merciless and fought to the last man, until one side or the other is eliminated without trace."[24] But only the truly mad could have believed that it was war that they were waging against the Jews. For the Jews were a civilian population, dispersed among the European nations, having no country and no political power, and consequently none of the resources that even small nations could muster for war.

PART II

THE
HOLOCAUST

9

Between Freedom and Ghetto: The Jews in Germany, 1933–1938

Presiding over a meeting of Jewish communal organizations soon after the National Socialists had come to power, Leo Baeck, teacher, scholar, and rabbi extraordinary of Liberal Judaism, uttered prophetic words: "The thousand-year history of the German Jews has come to an end."[1] But most German Jews rejected his visionary judgment as a political verdict. They lived with a historical perspective that, like the tangle of all history, taught contradictory lessons. In the long perspective of Jewish history, in which anti-Semitism was a constant factor, National Socialist anti-Semitism seemed just a contemporary manifestation of the persecution that afflicted the Jews in all ages. In the shortened range of German Jewish history, however, National Socialism appeared as the latest passing cycle of reaction in the wake of dramatic progress. The German Jews had had to learn to live with anti-Semitism in the long run and to combat it in the short run.

Combat anti-Semitism they did as best they knew how. The *Centralverein deutscher Staatsbürger jüdischen Glaubens* (CV; Central Association of German

Citizens of Jewish Faith), founded in 1893 to defend
German Jewry, had been indefatigable in antidefama-
tion, refutation of anti-Semitic canards, apologetic
recitals of Jewish contributions to German culture and
civilization. But these tactics, which we, having
learned from their failures, belittle today, were not
their only strategy. Beginning in 1929, when National
Socialist victories threatened the republic, the CV
made alliances with the political parties on the center
and the left. It set up front organizations, some of
which used unorthodox methods not characteristic of
the staid Jewish organization. In 1930 the CV and the
Zionist Federation formed a joint committee for the
election campaign (that year about 65 percent of the
Jews voted for the *Deutsche Demokratische Partei,* or
DDP, and 30 percent for the left parties). The following year both organizations jointly mustered their
political influence, publicly appealing to Heinrich
Brüning, then Chancellor, to condemn anti-Semitism
and violence and, with the prestige of his office, to re-
assure the Jews as to their rights and place in Germany. That he refused to do so testifies not to a
Jewish failure to resist National Socialism, but to National Socialism's irresistibility to the Germans. In
1932, when the DDP had collapsed, about two-thirds
of the Jews voted for the Social Democrats. Every
democratic party received electoral and financial support from the Jews, the Social Democrats getting the
greatest share.[2]

The Jews were the one group in Germany that in-
vested most of their talents and resources in the defense of the Weimar Republic. True, there were Jews
whose dazzling success in business or a profession
blinded them to the encroaching blackness. True, there
were Jews in the leftist movements whose total aliena-
tion from Judaism and the Jewish community enabled
them to see Nazism only as the last gasp of a mori-
bund imperialist capitalism. But the organized Jewish
community—and the Jews who were their constituency
—knew that National Socialism in power would
threaten their status and rights as citizens of Germany.

But impotent in halting the National Socialist rise to power, the Jews in Germany evolved a basic strategy of survival that had served Jews in the past: a policy of holding on and holding out, of bargaining and negotiating. It was a strategy that appealed to most Jews during the first two years of the National Socialist regime.

The 500,000 Jews of Germany formed a remarkably homogeneous community. Well over 80 percent were natives and about as many were affiliated with the Liberal wing of Judaism, a modified form of Orthodoxy similar to Conservative Judaism in America. About one-third lived in Berlin, and nearly 40 percent more in other big cities. Over 60 percent were engaged in trade and commerce, about one-quarter in industry and manual trades, and one-eighth in public service and the professions, primarily law and medicine. Nearly half of the gainfully occupied were self-employed.[3] The Jews of each city were members of a Gemeinde, a communal organization based on religious association, in which each Jew was registered at birth. (There were over 1,300 Gemeinden.) The Gemeinde was a public body for whose upkeep the state was authorized to tax the affiliated Jewish members. The functions of the Gemeinde were to maintain religious institutions, promote religious education, and dispense philanthropy. The Gemeinden of each state (*Land*) belonged to an association.

The most representative secular organization of German Jewry was the CV, whose membership in 1933 of 70,000 probably comprised 60 percent of all Jewish families. The *Zionistische Vereinigung für Deutschland* (ZVfD; Zionist Federation of Germany), in contrast, had 10,000 members. The CV stood for the belongingness of the German Jews in Germany, not only in the civil polity, but also in German culture and society. The CV was ideologically anti-Zionist, but in the early 1920s some of its leaders joined the non-Zionist component of the Jewish Agency for Palestine. The CV generally supported practical, pragmatic

Zionism (Palestine as a place of refuge) rather than ideological Zionism (Palestine as the Jewish national home). Somewhat to the right of the CV stood the Reichsbund jüdischer Frontsoldaten (RjF; Federal Union of Jewish War Veterans), which shared the simple-minded patriotism of all veterans' groups. Its membership of 30,000 was consistently and vociferously anti-Zionist.

The modal German Jew, then, was native, metropolitan, a businessman or professional, Liberal in his practice of Judaism, centrist in his politics, with a more passionate attachment to Germany than to Jewishness. In contrast to this modal type, three minority groups stood out within the Jewish community: the Orthodox, the Zionists, and the *Ostjuden* (East European Jews). The Orthodox were about 15 percent of all German Jews. (An even smaller segment belonged to the Conservative movement, close to Orthodoxy in its religious observance, but nearer to Liberalism in its anti-Zionism.) The organization that spoke for them was the Agudat Israel. German Orthodox Jews were unique among European Orthodox Jews in that they shared with all German Jews a profound sense of German identity. Most had deep roots in Germany and grew up in the unique tradition of Samson Raphael Hirsch's neo-Orthodoxy: *Torah im derekh eretz*, the preservation of Torah within the world of modern secular culture. Their primary attachment was to Judaism, yet their German patriotism was sincere and meaningful.

The Zionists and the Ostjuden—to some extent, congruent—were the more conspicuous minorities among German Jews, for they challenged the central tenet of German Jewish existence—Jewish belongingness to Germany. During the life of the Weimar Republic most German Jews regarded Zionism as an alien doctrine: the son who left Judaism for Communism was less likely to be rejected than the one who chose Zionism. The ZVfD had originally consisted of a small circle of intellectuals and academicians, reinforced by the influx of Russian Zionists after the Bol-

shevik Revolution. Ostjuden—some 20 percent of Jews
in Germany—predominated among the Zionist rank
and file, their presence aggravating the reputation of
the Zionists as alien to the German Jewish community.
To be sure, by 1933 the acrimonious animosity that
had characterized the relations of the German and
East European Jews a decade earlier had evaporated,
but social distance still prevailed and political differences were marked.

On the very margins of the Jewish community,
beyond discourse with the modal or oppositional
groups within German Jewry, were the rightists and
the leftists. The *Verband nationaldeutscher Juden*
(Society of German Nationalist Jews), a minuscule
group founded in 1920, was dedicated to the basic
idea that Jews were indissolubly Germans except for a
formal tie to Judaism. On the left was the "red assimilation," which attracted some 10 percent of German Jewish youth. They were the cultural avantgarde,
the Weimar intellectuals, the Communists, the "homeless left" who congregated around *Die Weltbühne*, the
iconoclastic weekly Kurt Tucholsky edited in Berlin.

The National Socialist accession to power sent
tremors throughout this Jewish population from right
to left. On the one hand, panic and flight, despair and
suicide. On the other, steadfastness and solidarity,
courage and a stubborn will to resist. Immediately
after Hitler was appointed Chancellor, the CV issued a
statement, published February 2, 1933, in its organ
C-V Zeitung, defiantly challenging the National
Socialists: ". . . We are convinced that no one will dare
to violate our constitutional rights. Every adverse attempt will find us at our post ready for resolute defense." The CV advised its constituents: "Stand by
calmly."

In a matter of days and weeks, the shadowy nightmares of National Socialism became daylight realities.
Thousands upon thousands of Jews lost their livelihood; typists, clerks, and judges alike were ousted
from positions in the government; writers, actors,
musicians, teachers, and professors, men who had

earned the rewards of position and prestige, overnight
became outcasts. Hundreds of small Jewish communities throughout Germany became exposed to the
full fury of rank-and-file Nazism. The dissolution of
the Jewish settlement in Germany began in those
small, vulnerable communities, as their residents fled
to the larger cities. By October 1938, just before
Kristallnacht, over four hundred Jewish communities
—25 percent of all Jewish communities in Germany—
had been dissolved or were in the process of liquidation.[4]

Among some Jews who had staked their whole existence on identity with Germany, despair led to suicide. Between 1932 and 1934, nearly 350 Jews committed suicide, a rate 50 percent higher than in the
rest of the population. So sweeping was the epidemic
in the Rhineland in mid-1933 that the Gemeinde and
rabbinate of Cologne issued a public appeal:

> Under the shattering impact of the events of recent
> weeks, during which suicide claimed victim upon
> victim within our community, we turn to you, men and
> women of the Jewish community, with the appeal:
>   *Maintain your courage and will to live, preserve
> your confidence in God and in yourself!*
>   The fate which has befallen each one of us is a part
> of the great universal Jewish suffering: Let us bear it
> together and help one another fraternally! Advisory
> boards of our Gemeinde as well as the homes of all
> members of the undersigned bodies are open to you—
> come to us with your spiritual and material needs; we
> will advise and help you as much as we can.
>   Do not take the path into darkness from which there
> is no return. Think of those whom you must leave be-
> hind in all their sorrow and affliction; think of human
> and Jewish destiny; do not lose hope for a better
> future![5]

That first year the flight of panic was most marked.
Some 37,000 Jews fled Germany, the highest annual
figure in the subsequent record of Jewish emigration.[6]
First to flee were the leftists, for whom the only alter-

native in Germany was the concentration camp. Government and professional men whose accomplishments had won them international renown were also quick to leave, and some of the well-to-do businessmen calculated on the wisdom of leaving sooner rather than later. That the movement was flight rather than emigration is evident in the fact that three-fourths of the migrants fled not overseas, but elsewhere in Europe, about half returning to their native Poland or Czechoslovakia. Many fled unthinkingly, hoping to return soon with the anticipated collapse of the National Socialist regime. They were unprepared for life in a strange country, with a strange language and an alien culture, whether England, France, Italy, or Holland. Many returned after the Putsch in June 1934, thinking that legality had been restored to Germany. The emigration to America that year was small; as for the fewer than seven thousand who emigrated to Palestine in 1933, nearly all had been preparing for *aliya* years earlier.

Emigration was a traditional Jewish response to persecution, but in 1933 in Germany emigration—or flight—was an individual decision, not communal policy. Within the Jewish community, every organized group replied to National Socialism with resounding affirmations of the right of Jews to be German, to live in and love Germany. *Daseinrecht*, the right to maintain a Jewish presence in Germany, was construed as a legal right, a moral necessity, and a religious imperative by all Jewish organizations from Orthodox to Reform, right to left, Zionist and non-Zionist.

The *C-V Zeitung* on March 9, 1933, transmitted editorially the encouragement of "our countless friends in town and country." Their message was: "Germany will remain Germany and no one can rob us of our homeland and of our fatherland." Alfred Hirschberg, a veteran CV leader, exhorted the readers of the *C-V Zeitung*, on April 13, 1933, that "it is our aim to preserve within Germany a German-Jewish community, unbroken financially, physically, and spiritually."

Bruno Weil, CV vice-president, in one of his early speeches to the organization, transmitted a message of faith and hope in a German future for the Jews:

Fear? We have shown by a thousand martyrs that we have no fear of the deeds of human beings. Desperation? Even in the most trying times Jewry has never been desperate but was always strengthened by its faith in God and by the consciousness of its right. Faith? Yes. Faith in the inner strength which is born of the knowledge of events, and a clear conscience. Hope? Yes. The hope that coexistence through centuries with the German people will prove itself stronger than all prejudices.[7]

A youth leader, granting that the era that he defined as the "external Emancipation" had come to an end, argued that this had not affected "internal emancipation" which he defined as cultural sensibility and love for homeland. The time now required a renewal of the synthesis of Germandom and Jewry: holding on to one's German identity and acquiring also a Jewish one.[8]

The Zionists did not differ from the anti-Zionists or non-Zionists in respect to their deep attachment to Germany. An editorial, *"Jüdische Zwischenbilanz"* ("Jewish Trial Balance"), in the Zionist organ, *Jüdische Rundschau*, April 13, 1933, addressed itself to the profound identity of Jews with Germany: "The historical tie of centuries is not so easy to dissolve. Our avowal of Jewish peoplehood has never signified that we discarded, or could discard, anything that the German spirit bestowed upon us." Indeed, German culture had molded Zionist-minded Jews: "National Jewry, after its Jewish sources and values, learned from German writings what character and freedom are." Furthermore, even those thousands of German Jews who fled Germany would in their emigration continue to nurture German culture for years and decades: "Generations will remain faithful to what they received from the German spirit."

After the German army instituted the "Aryan" paragraph for officers and men on March 23, 1934, the Reichsbund jüdischer Frontsoldaten tried to assert its Daseinrecht by appealing to Hindenburg that no community should be deprived of the right and duty to defend the homeland. The Reichsbund declared that the Jews would remain in Germany and that just as they had fought for Germany before, so they would continue to do again.[9]

Joseph Lehmann, rabbi of the *Reformgemeinde* in Berlin, denied that the political changes of the spring of 1933 had affected "our position as Germans of the Jewish faith nor do they demand a change of our philosophy." Emigration could be a solution for some people, but most German Jews would struggle to retain their position and the "heritage of their German homeland."[10] Dasein, for Heinrich Stern, head of the Liberal Jews, was seen as a religious commandment, essential if the Jews were to achieve their universal mission to the world. Furthermore, he argued that fleeing from Germany was cowardly, just "because five painful months lie behind us and probably painful years of misjudgment, hate, and need lie ahead of us." Practically speaking, "we, as Jews, reaffirm a life in Germany and for Germany."[11]

Hans Joachim Schoeps, a young intellectual who organized the *Deutsche Vortrupp* (German Vanguard) in the spring of 1933, after the Jews were ejected from the "Aryan" youth movement, articulating a religious philosophy compounded of anti-Zionism, traditionalism, and messianic hope, believed that the Jew remaining in Germany fulfilled himself as Jew and German. Germany, wrote Schoeps, was more than merely a community of blood and race; it was also a community of fate and history. Consequently, "we are enclosed for all time as Prussian, Bavarian, Hessian, and Franconian Germans of Jewish faith and Jewish origin, because through acknowledgment of fate and history, we are actually and consciously German."[12] (In his memoirs written after the war, Schoeps describes his nightmarish remorse for not having advised

those hundreds of thousands who were later murdered
to flee right away at all costs.)

In all life and especially in times of crisis, as Freud
teaches us, the patterns of the past reemerge in a person's confrontation with the present and the future.
For most German Jews the first response to National
Socialism—insistence on their rootedness in Germany
and on their German identity—represented a recur-
rence of the Enlightenment/Emancipation syndrome.
The Jews once again ritually dredged up the nineteenth-century arguments, hoping these would serve
also in the twentieth century. As for the Orthodox,
they reverted to a far more ancient response to persecution and oppression: *mipnei chatoenu,* "because
of our sins," we have been punished. An editorial in
Der Israelit, organ of the Agudat Israel, April 7, 1933,
saw in National Socialism "the admonition of God to
all German Jews" to return to traditional Judaism.
Two weeks later another editorial declared that the
present "completely hopeless" political situation of the
Jews illuminated the "brittle condition of internal
decay," exemplified by mixed marriages, conversions,
birth control. Only *teshuva*—repentance, religious return—and adherence to the Torah could restore the
Jews.

The Zionists too responded according to pattern. In
the now celebrated editorial "Wear the Yellow Badge
with Pride," written on the occasion of the anti-Jewish
boycott of April 1, 1933, Robert Weltsch, editor-in-
chief of the *Jüdische Rundschau,* directed his animosity against the Zionists' internal antagonists—assimilationists and self-haters. If today, wrote Weltsch, the
Shield of David "is stained, it has not been entirely
the work of our enemies," for many were the "Jews
whose undignified self-mockery knew no bounds." The
Jews were themselves to blame:

> Jewry bears a great guilt because it failed to heed
> Theodor Herzl's call and even mocked it in some in-
> stances. The Jews refused to acknowledge that "the
> Jewish question still exists." They thought the only im-

portant thing was not to be recognized as Jews. Today we are being reproached with having betrayed the German people; the National Socialist press calls us the "enemies of the nation," and there is nothing we can do about it. It is not true that the Jews have betrayed Germany. If they have betrayed anything, they have betrayed themselves and Judaism.

Because the Jews did not display their Jewishness with pride, because they wanted to shirk the Jewish question, they must share the blame for the degradation of Jewry.[13]

Hardly an adequate response to National Socialism, the editorial nevertheless heartened the Jews, Zionist or not, with its message of self-affirmation and self-esteem. (Like Schoeps in this respect, Weltsch was later remorseful. On several occasions, he told friends that he deeply regretted having written that editorial, that instead of calling for Jewish pride, he should have exhorted the Jews to flee for their lives.) That Zionist effort to restore Jewish self-respect, coupled with the recurring shocks of the boycott and the anti-Jewish legislation, brought thousands of Jews into the Zionist movement, replacing those who had gone on aliya or returned to Poland. Most of the Zionist gains were registered by the fall of 1933. Thereafter, the early shock of National Socialism began to wear off, and Zionist membership growth slackened to a slow pace. By the end of 1935 membership stood at 22,500. The Zionist youth organization *Hehalutz*, numerically insignificant before 1933, within months turned into a mass movement with a membership of 15,000. Before 1933, the Zionists in Germany had over the years sent out about 2,000 Jews on aliya, a token of the movement's microdimensions. Sadly the ZVfD acknowledged in its report of 1936 that its new adherents joined not out of inner ideological conviction, but "under pressure of external circumstances."[14]

Most Jews looked to their religion and their community for comfort in their distress. In March 1933

the Rabbinical Union in Germany issued a statement
declaring that Judaism required no defense against
the attacks being made on it, for "the authentic spirit
of our religion speaks to whosoever will listen." The
Jews were exhorted to hold fast to their faith and conviction, to preserve their pride and keep up their
courage.[15] Appeals for Jewish return that were intellectually more challenging and Jewishly more profound were issued by Baeck and Martin Buber. Responding to the self-denigration of Jewish youth who
complained that the Jews had become mere objects in
history, Baeck expounded the idea that Jewry was a
living, effective subject of history and that the Jew
was, above all, the subject of his own history. Each
Jew, Baeck reasoned, had to discover himself and
thus renew his history.[16]

The most persuasive summoner to Jewish return
and Jewish self-awareness was Martin Buber, whose
lectures and writings in the first years of the German
dictatorship struck his Jewish audiences with the impact of revelation. "German Jews," he wrote in April
1933, "are confronted with Jewish world fate." How
were they to confront this crucial test, this ordeal by
fire? First, Buber said, the German Jew had to reorder
his system of personal existential values. Paramount
was the return to authenticity of self in all aspects and
relations, but above all in relation to God. In all his
work, Buber called for the diffusion of the Jewish
spirit and Jewish values throughout the whole person
and the whole community, not merely in one seg-
mented part of the individual's life or the community's
program.[17]

The synagogues became full to overflowing. They
were not only houses of prayer, but the locus of
solidarity and solace, the place that recompensed for
the loneliness outside. Jews felt secure and at home in
the company of other Jews in a Jewish setting. People
who had never been in a synagogue before came to
pray or, at the very least, to be with other Jews.[18]
Judaism flowered during those early years of National
Socialism in a spontaneous response to persecution.

The ritual of Judaism remained undisturbed, except for the prohibition of shehita, which went into effect December 7, 1933. The provision of ritually slaughtered meat became the chief concern of the *Reichszentrale für Schächtangelegenheiten* (Federal Central Agency for Matters of Ritual Slaughtering), which arranged for the purchase and importation, primarily from Denmark, of kosher beef and its distribution throughout Germany. Illegal shehita of poultry, which did not require public abattoirs, was commonly practiced despite threats of severe punishment. Eventually, as the Jewish community grew more impoverished and controls on the export of currency became tighter, the importation of kosher meat became a hardship. At one time two rabbis were sent to Holland to try to raise the necessary funds to import kosher meat for the Jewish sick in hospitals in Germany, whose medical recovery depended on meat diets.[19]

The vehicle through which the rabbi comforted his congregation, strengthened their self-esteem in the face of the external onslaught, was the sermon, which, according to Rabbi Joachim Prinz, then a young rabbi in Berlin, was "an attempt at collective therapy." Yet the watchful Gestapo was everywhere. (Police attended religious services and reported on the sermons.) The merest hint of criticism of the National Socialist regime could provoke a summons to the Gestapo. Thus, under censorship and persecution, an old means of discourse was revived, which Ernst Simon called the "New Midrash."[20] Haggadic Midrash —imaginative exegesis of the Bible with a moral or devotional purpose—had been, at least in part, a response to oppression, the exercise by a persecuted minority of an internal esoteric language that was not understood by the persecuting enemy. "Thus a sort of cryptic style developed which was interchanged with a smile between speaker and audience, presupposing and nourishing an intimate conspiratorial understanding." In Germany after 1933, the New Midrash sometimes created new parables on biblical, Talmudic, or even secular themes, but mostly it drew on the old

sources, infusing them with contemporary meaning
and topical allusion. The Psalms especially proved
immediately relevant in their timelessness. In 1936
Buber issued a selection of twenty-three Psalms entitled "Out of the Depths Have I Called Thee," published in a sequence that provided not only comfort
and consolation, but also an outlet for otherwise impotent rage:

> Be Thou my judge, O God, and plead my cause
>   against an ungodly nation;
> O deliver me from the deceitful and unjust man.

As always in times of persecution, the cycle of Jewish festivals assumed freshness and relevance. Passover, the festival of freedom marking the liberation
from Egypt, became a living reality. At Purim, during
the reading of the Scroll of Esther, Haman became
Hitler and the din of the noisemakers, the stomping
and booing traditionally accorded each mention of
Haman's name, surged through the synagogue. The
celebration of Hanukkah, which in Weimar Germany
had become a consolatory surrogate for Christmas, was
restored to commemoration of the Maccabean struggle
against the powerful armies of pagan Rome. The
Hanukkah Haftorah afforded rich opportunities for the
New Midrash: "Not by might, nor by power, but by
My spirit, saith the Lord of hosts."

The religious return was matched by a swelling interest in Jewish learning and in Jewish secular culture.
Buber's summons for renewal and authenticity elicited
a mass response. The desire for immersion in Jewish
living was both nurtured and satisfied by the Kulturbund deutscher Juden, founded on the initiative of
Kurt Singer, a physician with more than amateur
standing as musicologist, critic, choir director. The
idea for the Kulturbund was first broached in April
1933 as a vehicle to provide employment for the thousands of Jewish actors and musicians who were prevented from performing on the German stage and in

German concert halls.[21] Theatrical troupes, an orchestra and choir, and ensembles were organized from the membership of 19,000. Hundreds of artists and technicians were given full-time employment. In the first years of its existence, about 8,500 presentations were offered—operas, plays, concerts (orchestra, chamber music, choir, and soloists), lectures, recitations, cabaret performances, ballets, film showings, and art exhibits. Similar cultural associations began to be formed in other large communities. Jewish artists performed exclusively for Jewish audiences, and the content of the work performed was mostly Jewish. The walls of an invisible ghetto were beginning to rise around the German Jews.

When the news came on January 30, 1933, during a meeting discussing Jewish handicrafts, that Hitler had been named Chancellor, the chairman addressed the mixed conference of Liberals and Zionists: "A historical turning point has been reached. All differences among Jews have now become meaningless. We are all in the same danger."[22] Actually, the search for communal unity had begun long before, on the part of both the Gemeinden and the national organizations. Early in 1932 the association of Gemeinden in Prussia called an extraordinary conference to deal with the defense of Jewish rights. The Berlin Gemeinde independently convened a closed meeting of its delegates to discuss the political situation as it affected the Jews. By June 1932 a national association of all Gemeinden was approved provisionally, subject to ratification by the Land associations. Simultaneously, the national Jewish organizations (CV, ZVfD, B'nai B'rith, and welfare agencies) decided to form a joint committee for concerted action in defense of Jewish rights and for the eventuality of negotiating with government authorities "to ensure the honor, life, and economic existence of the Jewish population."

Yet neither the Gemeinden nor the national organizations managed to put together a central body before

January 30, 1933. In view of the urgency of the Jewish situation, the provisional national Gemeinde association on February 12 set up a five-man *Präsidium der Reichsvertretung der jüdischen Landesverbände Deutschlands* (Executive Board of the Federal Representation of the Jewish Land Associations of Germany), to function on an emergency basis. Representatives of the national organizations were soon coopted to the board, while negotiations continued to create a permanent representative body of men whose leadership would be accepted by the diverse movements among the German Jews.[23] Foundering on regional rivalries, the Reichsvertretung der jüdischen Landesverbände succeeded only in establishing the *Zentralausschuss der deutschen Juden für Hilfe und Aufbau* (Central Committee of German Jews for Relief and Reconstruction) on April 13, 1933. Intended to serve as a central conduit for funds from abroad for the mammoth tasks of welfare facing the Jewish community, it would become a major bolstering force at a time of precipitous decline.[24]

The idea of strong central leadership became even more urgent. There was a general feeling that the Jews needed one single organization that could represent them vis-à-vis the government, a role that demanded "dictatorial leadership."[25] At the initiative of three leaders of the Essen Gemeinde, a new try for communal unity began. Integral to this effort was the plan to put Leo Baeck at the head of the organization. He was the most prestigious Jew in Germany, whose *Essence of Judaism,* published in 1923 in answer to Adolf Harnack's *Essence of Christianity,* had elevated him to the role of spokesman for the Jews. A Liberal rabbi, a CV board member, and chairman of the Keren Hayesod, he was probably the only Jewish leader who could reconcile the internal differences within the community. Conducting their preliminary negotiations with tact and patience, the Essen Gemeinde leaders managed to subdue most of the regional animosities among the Gemeinden, especially

the distrust the Southerners felt for the Northerners
and the antipathy of all toward the Berliners. (Berlin,
with a third of Germany's Jews, regarded itself as a
super-Gemeinde. Its cultural big-town snobbishness
further exacerbated relations with the Gemeinden of
southern and eastern Germany.) At a preliminary
meeting convened in Essen on July 23, 1933, all the
regional Gemeinde associations were represented
along with the Berlin Gemeinde and all national organizations except the Zionists. The ZVfD had refused
to participate because its demand for two delegates
had been refused. Negotiations continued; the Zionists
were promised more representation on the executive
committee. The Berlin Gemeinde reluctantly relinquished its bid for control. Finally, on September 17,
1933, with Leo Baeck as its chairman, the *Reichsvertretung der deutschen Juden* (Federal Representation of German Jews) came into being. Co-chairman
was Otto Hirsch, a former government official in
Württemberg and a deeply committed Jew.

Communal unity on an intellectual level was pursued also by Martin Buber, who early in 1933 called
together a group of ranking Jewish communal and
intellectual leaders to discuss informally the problems
confronting German Jewry. The group was designated
as the Homburg Circle (the meeting was held at Bad
Homburg, near Frankfurt). A second meeting was
held on September 10, 1933. The extant minutes indicate a high level of intellectuality and abstraction.[26]
Plans for a third meeting never materialized.

The creation of the Reichsvertretung, nearly eight
months after the Nazis came to power, at last provided an instrument of Jewish solidarity. Yet the
solidarity was fragile and superficial, a valiant attempt
to cement a politically divided community. Though
everyone paid lip service to the idea of unity and
the need for it, conflicts over ideology and policy persisted. Few organizations were prepared to yield their
institutional sovereignty for the chimera of unity. The
CV appeared most sincere in its assiduous pursuit of

unity—perhaps because, speaking for the majority of German Jews, it was under less pressure to compromise, or perhaps, being more pragmatic and less ideological than other segments in the Jewish community, it was more willing to compromise.

Other organizations held fast to their basic commitments. The Reichsbund jüdischer Frontsoldaten sought to preserve its autonomy in matters affecting its constituency, even attempting independent negotiations with the National Socialist regime to obtain special status for Jewish war veterans. The Agudat Israel recognized only the "unity around the Torah." Rabbi Jacob Rosenheim, head of the Aguda, granted that cooperation in practical matters was possible, though he held that each political or religious grouping should approach its problems on its own, somewhat in the spirit of Lessing's words:

> Let each man zealously pursue where love,
> From prejudice and from corruption free,
> Shall lead him.[27]

In March 1934 the Aguda withdrew from the Reichsvertretung over differences in educational policy. In 1936 another Orthodox group, the *Vertretung der unabhängigen jüdischen Orthodoxie Deutschlands* (VUO; Representation of Independent Jewish Orthodoxy in Germany), concluded an agreement with the Reichsvertretung, which provided that it would speak for the VUO in all areas except religious-cultural matters.[28]

The Reichsvertretung was also used as a combat area by some of its constituents. The most serious disturbers of communal peace were the Berlin Gemeinde and the Zionists, each antagonistic to the other and both assaulting the Reichsvertretung in their bids for control. The Berlin leadership continued to argue from the strength of numbers, prestige, and experience. As for the Zionists, they were now, paradoxically, in the communal saddle. Each Nazi turn of the screw vindicated their ideological diagnosis of the Jewish predicament in the Diaspora. On that ground alone, besides an increasing membership, they felt that they deserved the decisive role in communal leadership.

The Reichsvertretung set itself the goal of representing all the Jews in Germany, and its primary aim —at least for the public record—was "a vigorous and honorable Jewish life on German soil within the German state."[29] This was to be accomplished by providing the Jews with possibilities for economic existence, by systematically planning and organizing emigration from Germany for those who had to or wanted to leave, and by defending the Jews against defamation. Education and culture, relief and welfare would soon become major functions.

From the start, the Reichsvertretung had conceived that its chief task would be to represent the Jews vis-à-vis the National Socialist regime, though no one knew how to do so or if it could be done at all. In the early months of its existence, the Reichsvertretung began to explore these possibilities, making new contacts or renewing old ones in various government ministries. That was a time of memoranda, submissions, petitions to the National Socialist government, attempts to establish a legal basis for Reichsvertretung activity, efforts to release Jews from "protective custody," and to protect them from violence and brutality.[30]

One of the earliest perilous dilemmas confronting the Jews involved the upcoming plebiscite of November 12, 1933. The plebiscite demanded a vote of approval for Hitler's domestic and foreign policies. What should Jews do? In the German dictatorship, absence from the polls would be regarded as opposition, treason. In small communities, where the Jews were visible and exposed, whether and how they voted would become a matter of local Nazi party or police interest. Yet how could they vote *"Ja"* for Germany's anti-Jewish policies? The Reichsvertretung inquiries at last yielded clarification. On November 3 the Reichsvertretung issued a statement:

> With the entire German people also we Jews as citizens are summoned to cast our votes on the foreign policy of the Reich government. They are required for Germany's equality among the nations, for the conciliation of the nations, and for the peace of the world. Despite all that we have had to undergo,
> The vote of the German Jews can be only Yes.[31]

The idea of approaching the regime for clarification as to the situation of the Jews was not exclusively the Reichsvertretung's. In the anarchy of autonomy that prevailed in the Jewish community, it was no surprise that about twelve different proposals were submitted to various government agencies by various Jewish organizations with a view to defining the position of the Jews in Germany.

On June 21, 1933, the ZVfD submitted a memorandum to the National Socialist government.[32] That memorandum proposed that the "new German state" recognize the Zionist movement as the most suitable Jewish group in the new Germany with which to deal, that Jewish status in Germany thenceforth be regulated on the basis of group status rather than individual rights,* and finally, that since emigration

---

* Minority rights for some Jews in Germany were under discussion in the League of Nations at just that time. A petition claiming deprivation of his rights had been presented to the League of Nations by one Franz Bernheim, from Upper Silesia, who had lost his job after the National Socialists came to power. In 1922, after part of Upper Silesia had been awarded to Germany in accordance with a plebiscite, Germany signed the Geneva Convention, thus placing national minorities in Upper Silesia under a system of international protection for a period of fifteen years. Under these terms the League of Nations discussed the Bernheim petition in May and June 1933; by September 1933 the German dictatorship formally agreed to fulfill its obligations under the convention. (Until the convention expired, in 1937, the Jews in Upper Silesia could hold office and work in the professions; shehita was permitted.) In September 1933 the League of Nations opened a general debate on minorities, which focused on the plight

would provide a solution to the Jewish question, it should therefore receive government assistance.

In presenting their proposals, the Zionists said that they were not concerned with the interests of individual Jews who had lost their economic and social positions, but rather with creating an opportunity for the existence of the whole group:

> On the foundation of the new state, which has established the principle of race, we wish so to fit in our community into the total structure that for us too, in the sphere assigned to us, fruitful activity for the Fatherland is possible.

This vague proposal for an apparent ghetto autonomy within the racial National Socialist state was followed by an exposition of emigration as a means of reducing the "pressure on the Jewish position in Germany," and thus as being in the interests of the German people. For this reason the Zionist movement hoped to win "the collaboration even of a government fundamentally hostile to Jews," and held out bait—in the event the Germans cooperated—that the Zionists would try to get the Jews abroad to call off the anti-German boycott. Finally, the memorandum argued that recognition of the Jews as a "national minority" might also benefit those Germans living abroad who wished to maintain their German identity.

The regime never responded to this memorandum, but the Zionists continued to pursue the idea of group rights for the Jews in Germany, from the start conceding individual rights and the achievements of the Emancipation.

The Reichsvertretung, for its part, refused to waive these rights. The Reichsvertretung wanted to discuss with, negotiate with, or petition the government for

of the German Jews. The international Jewish organizations submitted a memorandum asking, among other things, for the restoration of the rights of the Jews in Germany. But Germany refused to acknowledge the Jews as a national minority. The question became academic when Germany left the League of Nations in late October.[33]

alleviation of the present situation of the Jews. Proceeding slowly and cautiously, the Reichsvertretung on January 23, 1934, submitted a memorandum to that effect to each member of the Reich Cabinet. The submission was regarded as a trial balloon, to see whether it would elicit a response and thus provide a basis on which further discussions could be conducted.[34]

The Reichsvertretung memorandum first addressed itself to the ouster of Jews from employment in government, the professions, and business. The impoverishment and eventual pauperization of the Jews in Germany would, the argument went, affect their status as taxpayers. Consequently, the Reichsvertretung petitioned "that differential treatment as between Aryan and Jewish employed be discontinued in the future; that any pressure to displace or oust Jewish employees be checked."*

The second item concerned Jewish occupational structure, which the Reichsvertretung conceded was presently "unhealthy." To remedy that situation, the community was engaged in a program of vocational retraining. Consequently, the Reichsvertretung expressed the hope "that as a matter of principle no occupation be closed to Jews; that within the corporate state's reconstruction of manual trade and labor, agriculture and forestry, Jews, too, be afforded training and admission."

---

* An ambitious program had been elaborated on August 15, 1933, by Werner Senator, then head of the Zentralausschuss, for negotiations to be conducted with the government by the Reichsvertretung-to-be and the Zentralausschuss.[35] Senator believed that the economic problems confronting the Jews were too massive to be dealt with by voluntary organizations through infusions of relief and welfare. His draft guidelines included such points as the protection of the rights of Jews as citizens and taxpayers, the integral relationship between the economic life of the Jews and that of the whole country, the development of Jewish self-help through the development of a "buy Jewish" market, the development of a credit policy to help the middle class, occupational restructuring, and emigration. He also suggested that if quotas were being set, then "quota rights" should obtain, especially in the lower ranks of civil service. Senator returned to Israel in September, before the Reichsvertretung's work got far under way.

Occupational restructuring was then one of the few ideas on which Zionists and non-Zionists agreed.[36] According to Zionist dogma, Jewish occupational structure in the Diaspora was "abnormal," top-heavy in trade, commerce, and the professions, instead of widely based in agriculture and industry. The notion derived from the Enlightenment era, when it was argued by Jewish friend and foe alike that Jews had to engage in "useful" occupations before they deserved to be emancipated. Thereafter, criticism of the "abnormal" Jewish occupational structure became a staple of anti-Semitic propaganda. In 1933 German Jewish leadership, themselves professionals and businessmen, began advocating occupational restructuring as Jewish public policy to appease the National Socialists and at the same time to obtain new economic opportunities for Jews.

The third item in the Reichsvertretung memorandum dealt with emigration. It described the proportional decline in the past century of the Jewish population in Germany, thus drawing attention to the small space Jews occupied in the nation. Nevertheless, the memorandum continued, since many German Jews would have to emigrate, a systematically prepared and regulated emigration would be in German interests. Under conditions of a properly planned emigration, the emigrant would retain an attachment to his home country; his family and cultural ties would create "valuable economic connections with the old homeland." To that end, the Reichsvertretung requested the government to "support the work that we and competent organizations are doing for emigration to Palestine and other countries."

The final subject of the memorandum dealt with anti-Semitic agitation, prudently defined as "spiritual oppression," and substantially documented with appended materials. In deference to the racial premises of the state, the Reichsvertretung did not dispute "the alienness of its Jewish component." That much—but no more—was conceded. The charge of inferiority was repudiated, unacceptable to a "community that

values its honor and dignity." The influence of world
Jewish opinion and the implications for Germany
were raised, as if to suggest that the Jews had a bargaining point. The government was urged that "in the
future every defamation of Jewish group association
and origin be discontinued."

No response to this submission was ever received
from any quarter of the regime. Yet from time to time
the Reichsvertretung continued to submit appeals or
protests. The most quixotic no doubt was the two-
sentence telegram sent to Hitler himself, on May 3,
1934, protesting a special issue of *Der Stürmer* that
"with monstrous insults and horrifying statements"
accused the Jews of ritual murder. The Reichsvertretung solemnly swore: "Before God and man we raise
our voice in solemn protest against this unparalleled
desecration of our faith."[37]

While it soon became apparent that the role of the
Reichsvertretung as spokesman for the Jewish community vis-à-vis the regime was severely limited, it
became just as apparent that its role within the Jewish
community was growing to unprecedented responsibility and magnitude. The Reichsvertretung was becoming the community's primary instrument for support and sustenance, a Jewish self-government whose
functions far surpassed those of the medieval *kehilla*.

The existence of the Reichsvertretung was distinguished by paradoxes. It had been organized for unity,
yet it was beset by divisiveness from its origin to its
demise. Its public face was compliant and law-abiding, yet it engaged in conspiratorial activities. It supplied the worldwide press with documentation about
the plight of the Jews; it salvaged Jewish property
and funds from the rapacious state. It even provided
clandestine services and facilities that the German
dictatorship had officially denied to Jews. The *Hochschule für die Wissenschaft des Judentums*, for instance, was transformed in 1935 into a Jewish university after Jews had been banned from attending
German universities. Nazi authorities were told that
the Hochschule was, and they believed it to be, an

institution to train rabbis and teachers of Jewish religion.[38] While undertaking the systematic liquidation of the Jewish settlement in Germany, the Reichsvertretung found itself strengthening, even building, Jewish communal and cultural life. It tried resolutely to hold on to the achievements of the Emancipation, while in effect concurring in the ghettoization of the Jews. That paradox was especially evident in the area of general education.

After the Law Against the Overcrowding of German Schools was enacted on April 25, 1933, schooling had to be provided for thousands of Jewish youths who had been ousted from their schools and for thousands more in the elementary schools, where prejudice, hate, and hysteria had made their attendance untenable. The responsibility fell to the Reichsvertretung.

Before 1933 Jewish all-day schools had attracted a small proportion of Jewish children, mostly from Orthodox and/or East European backgrounds. In 1933 about ten thousand children—one-sixth of all Jewish children—attended thirty-five private Jewish schools, mostly on the elementary level.[39] Now, not by choice, most Jewish children began to attend all-Jewish schools.

As early as May 1933 Martin Buber had submitted a proposal to the Reichsvertretung for a program of Jewish education whose central postulate was that such an educational undertaking should be "not only formally but intrinsically Jewish," that it should "not merely remedy an external state of distress, but should also fill a great internal void in German Jewry by providing our youth with the firm stability of being united with the eternity of Judaism."[40] But Buber's educational philosophy was rejected. The guidelines for Jewish schools that the Reichsvertretung issued early in 1934 stipulated that the educational basis for the Jewish school was to be the dual Jewish/German experience to which each child living in Germany had been exposed. The coexistence of Jews and Germans as well as the tension between them was to be demonstrated in the classroom. Furthermore, the German subjects were "intended to demonstrate what Jewish being and Jewish thought owe to the German mind" and, reciprocally, "what Jewish minds and Jewish work have contributed to the fashioning of German culture."[41] The individual schools were free to work out the details of their curricula; eventually each school reflected the outlook of its teaching staff and of its pupils rather than the guidelines of the Reichsvertretung. In secondary schools, where students developed a consuming passion for Palestine, Frederick the Great and Goethe lost relevance. Zionist-oriented schools abandoned German history for Palestinian studies. Modern Hebrew was a required subject for those planning to emigrate to Palestine. Some schools stressed Judaism, Jewish history, and literature; others concentrated on vocational studies.

Tensions developed between teachers and pupils, between classroom and home. Many teachers in the newly organized Reichsvertretung schools who had taught in German secondary schools were poorly equipped in Jewish matters and retained a stubborn passion for things German. But others, jolted by the collapse of their German world, plunged into Jewish studies with the intensity of converts. That nationalist or religious intensity sometimes came into headlong conflict with children from assimilated homes, where Jewishness was lukewarm at best. But despite its tensions, inadequacies, and problems, the Jewish school offered the Jewish child shelter from the storm outside, warmth and love instead of rejection and hostility, simultaneously strengthening self-esteem.

Though Buber failed to influence the course of Jewish education, his success in Jewish adult education was spectacular. In November 1933, four years after Franz Rosenzweig's death had closed the Frankfurt *Lehrhaus*, the remarkable center of adult Jewish studies that he had founded in 1920, Buber reopened it, with a lecture on the tasks of Jewish adult education. A half-year later, the *Mittelstelle für jüdische Erwachsenenbildung* (Central Office for Jewish Adult Education), with Buber at its head, was set up within the Reichsvertretung. In an address at the founding conference, May 1934, Buber expatiated on the purpose of Jewish adult education: "No longer the equipment with knowledge, but the mobilization for existence." Through its grooming of individuals, Jewish adult education would, he said, "groom a community that will stand firm, that will prevail, that will guard the spark."[42]

A broad program evolved—lectures, discussions, courses, and community singing—which encompassed the gamut of religious and ideological thought. Subject matter included Bible (Buber's own special field), Semitic languages, medieval history, the philosophy of Plato, Kant, and Hume, general economic history, contemporary sociology, and study of the languages of emigration—English, Spanish, Hebrew.[43] The Mittelstelle trained the teachers from the German school system in Jewish subjects and the teachers in the Jewish school system in general and methodological matters.

The Mittelstelle and all its works constituted, in Ernst Simon's phrase, a bulwark of spiritual resistance. Yet some German Jews, in hindsight, came to regard this chapter of exaltation with self-reproach, because it had slowed down the process of dissolution. "A joint historic guilt," wrote a survivor of those times, rests on those who believed "that we had very, very much time."[44]

Vocational training and retraining, to accomplish the "occupational restructuring" of German Jews, consumed a major portion of Reichsvertretung resources, though probably no more than 25,000 persons benefited from the program. Not merely ideological appeasement of the Nazis, it was intended to provide a means of livelihood in the manual trades for the civil servants, professionals, and business people who had lost their jobs. To that end, training schools and workshops were set up to teach manual occupations, gardening, and agriculture. By 1937 there were sixteen training workshops for locksmiths, blacksmiths, tinsmiths, electricians, carpenters, etc., six in Berlin and the rest in other large cities, each with some hundred to two hundred young people enrolled. At thirty training centers, girls were prepared for work in Jewish hospitals, orphanages, homes for the aged, and public kitchens, and were taught cooking, laundering, housekeeping, sewing, dressmaking, tailoring. Thirty training centers for agriculture and gardening, mostly Zionist-operated, prepared young emigrants for Palestine. (One was non-Zionist; its trainees eventually settled as colonists in Argentina.) With each passing year it became clearer that the program benefited prospective emigrants more than unemployed civil servants.

Individual German Jews and the Jewish community were coming to the recognition that emigration was a more viable response to National Socialism than occupational restructuring. Emigration reflected the fluctuations of Nazi policies. In the first reaction of panic in 1933, some 37,000 Jews fled. With the apparent cessation of anti-Jewish legislation and the Putsch against the SA, emigration dropped to 23,000 in 1934 and to 21,000 in 1935. After the enactment of the Nuremberg Laws in September 1935, the figures rose to 25,000 in 1936, but fell once more in 1937 to 23,000, following the quiet that enveloped the 1936 Olympic Games.[45] Everyone scanned the political horizon for signs of change; an unexpected mildness in anti-Jewish policy or an inexplicable inconsistency was interpreted as a herald of change. Even Leo Baeck, who in 1933 had predicted the end of the thousand-year history of the German Jews, in 1934 dreamed that a military coup would soon overthrow Hitler. Once he remarked: "My idea is still this: I wake up one day and find on the billboards posters with the imprint: 'I have taken over executive power—General von . . .' "[46]

Other factors, too, practical and psychological, determined the statistics of emigration. In 1933 some 14,000 persons (besides the 37,000 who actually emigrated) applied for information about migration possibilities to the *Hilfsverein der deutschen Juden* (Welfare Association of the German Jews), the agency specializing in migrant assistance. The following quarter, however, the number of inquiries dropped, because, in the words of one communal official, "many have lost the courage and determination to leave because of the negative answers with reference to immigration, length of stay, and work possibilities in continental countries as well as overseas countries."[47]

The scarcity of visas for any country was the major obstacle. Not only was the number of visas insufficient for those who wanted to leave Germany, but many available visas were to countries where settlement was hazardous for the middle-aged, middle-class urban Jews of Germany, as for instance in some Central and South American countries, where hardy pioneers were called for. Altogether, emigration entailed a total transformation of one's life and culture. Observant Jews faced a particularly poignant dilemma if they received visas to Latin American countries, where few, if any, facilities existed for religious observance, burial, ritual slaughter, and ritual baths.[48] The alternative of remaining in Germany may have appeared less perilous.

Emigration to Palestine too was tightly controlled. Not only did the British limit the number of certificates, but the Zionist movement itself set up rigid standards for prospective immigrants. The Eighteenth Zionist Congress, in 1933, established, within the Jewish Agency for Palestine, a Central Bureau for the Settlement of German Jews, which, to begin with, excluded anti-Zionists as applicants for certificates.[49] Young people in good health, with some training for agricultural work or manual trades, and persons with capital were the preferred candidates for aliya, in a process where the needs and interests of Palestine took precedence over the strategy of rescue.[50] Systematic training and careful selection of candidates remained the chief characteristics of the migration until 1938. Indeed, the ZVfD opposed a plan of illegal migration to Palestine, approving it only after Kristallnacht.[51]

The search for places of refuge consumed the

Reichsvertretung and its subsidiary agencies. When the Evian Conference was convened in July 1938, the Reichsvertretung obtained permission from the German authorities to send a delegation.* They submitted to the conference and its individual delegations a memorandum that presented a grand plan for systematic emigration.[52]

For some Jews, lack of means hindered emigration, though the Hilfsverein could usually help. But there were some Jews for whom making money or protecting it had higher priority. Either business was too good to abandon or the estimated loss, around 1935, of 30 to 40 percent of property in transferring assets abroad was too great to endure. "Only business," wrote Kurt Tucholsky in a letter to Arnold Zweig, with bitter contempt because few Jewish businessmen had left Germany in 1933, reluctant to lose their profits. But now, in 1935, he wrote, "they slink out, gloomy, soundly thrashed, in shit up to their ears, bankrupt, their money robbed—*and without honor.*"[53]

Finally, age was the central and determining factor in emigration. From the start, all emigration programs —Reichsvertretung and Zionist—stressed the communal obligation to help the young people leave first of all. In late August 1934 a leading English Zionist who visited Berlin reported that Dr. Baeck had told him definitely that there was no place in Germany for the young Jews: "The only thing to do is to get them out."[54] Already in 1933 the German Jewish community was an aging community, which, in a century-old process of attrition through intermarriage, conversion, and a low birth rate, had twice as many persons over sixty in contrast to a population of normal growth.

---

* The Austrian Jews too sent a delegation, even though they were then already under closer Gestapo/SD surveillance than the German Jews. They worked closely with the Reichsvertretung delegation. Hans Habe's novel *The Mission*, written after the Eichmann trial, whose plot about a Gestapo plan to "sell" Jews which the Austrian Jews were to transmit at the Evian Conference, is pure fantasy, suggested no doubt by the negotiations between Eichmann and the Hungarian Jews in 1944. But in 1938 no such negotiations were undertaken, and no historical evidence exists for such a speculation.

This demographic characteristic affected the selection of migrants, for emigration was determined not only by necessity, but by the ability to build a new life and the availability of time for a fresh start. The selective process of emigration each year turned the remaining German Jewish population successively older. In June 1933, not quite half of German Jews were over forty; by September 1939 three-fourths were. In 1933 nearly 30 percent were under twenty-four; in 1939, only 13 percent were. Over 80 percent of the Jews under forty left Germany between 1933 and 1939, compared to half of those aged forty to sixty and a fourth of those over sixty.[55] By 1936 American Jewish philanthropic leaders worried that the Jewish community in Germany would become a gigantic old-age home whose inmates would have to be maintained by Jews abroad.[56]

Between January 1933 and November 1938, some 150,000 Jews—30 percent of the original population—left Germany. After Kristallnacht, under Gestapo pressure, nearly another 150,000 left.*

The year 1935 brought new misfortunes to the Jewish community as National Socialist anti-Jewish policy shifted into a higher gear. The isolation of the Jews became more confining, responsibilities of the Reichsvertretung multiplied, and internal dissension was aggravated, expressing the rage of impotence toward the outside foe. That January Heydrich issued a directive to the Bavarian political police stating that "the activity of the Zionist-oriented youth organizations that are engaged in the occupational restructuring of the Jews for agriculture and manual trades prior to their emigration to Palestine lies in the interest of the National Socialist state's leadership."† By early March Jewish organizations learned about that directive as well as about another that forbade propaganda urging Jews to remain in Germany.

---

* For the fate of those who remained, see Appendix A.
† See Chapter 4, p. 112, for context and sources.

On March 31 the ZVfD Executive Committee prepared a declaration that was adopted at the ZVfD
annual meeting on May 5, 1935. The declaration demanded a reorganization of the entire Jewish community at national and local levels, which would ensure recognition of the "due" influence of the Zionists.[57] Shortly thereafter the ZVfD turned the policy
statement into a demand for Zionist parity with non-
Zionists on the boards of the Reichsvertretung, its
institutions, and the Berlin Gemeinde. Officially the
Zionists justified their power bid with the argument
that history had vindicated the correctness of their
philosophy and that "the program which has been
accepted by the overwhelming majority of the Jews
residing in Germany can be realized only when it is
conducted by men who are inspired by Zionist
ideals."

Publicly no one attributed the Zionist power bid
to the Heydrich directive and to then current National Socialist policy favoring the Zionists, but the
connection did not pass unnoticed. The non-Zionists
were convinced that there was a connection and that
the Zionists themselves believed that the Gestapo
favored them over the non-Zionists.[58]

The Zionist demand for parity stunned the non-
Zionists. The C-V Zeitung of May 9, 1935, branded it
"unjustified, disruptive, and astonishing," an attempt
to turn present events in Germany to Zionist profit.
Nonetheless, the Zionists did eventually win parity,
perhaps because the Reichsvertretung feared Gestapo
intervention, perhaps because it had yielded to fatigue
and a sense of defeat.

The heaviest blow to the non-Zionists came with
the promulgation of the Nuremberg Laws. It then became clear as it had not been before that the Jewish
community had no future in Germany, that the pursuit of Daseinrecht was illusory. In 1933 the key
ideological difference between the Zionists and non-
Zionists was that the latter regarded emigration as "a"
solution and the former as "the" solution, though in
actual practice no real difference existed. But in 1935

the non-Zionists realized that emigration had become "the" solution. (Only extreme anti-Zionists continued, deep into 1937, to hold stubbornly to the conviction that a Jewish future in Germany was still possible.) After 1935 the ideological quarrel hinged on the destination of emigration, the Zionists insisting on Palestine exclusively and the non-Zionists searching the globe for any haven. The Zionist/non-Zionist difference became one of rigid ideology versus flexible pragmatism.

After the promulgation of the Nuremberg Laws, the Reichsvertretung reformulated its program in an attempt "to create a basis on which a tolerable relationship between the German and the Jewish people is possible," citing Hitler's words at Nuremberg as their frame of reference. The prerequisite for that tolerable relationship, the Reichsvertretung declared, was that a moral and economic existence be allowed the Jews and the Jewish communities in Germany through a halt of the defamation and the boycott against them.[59] Furthermore, in a courageous bid to retain control of the community and stave off increasing Gestapo intervention, the Reichsvertretung declared that any regulation of the life of the German Jews required "governmental recognition of an autonomous Jewish management."

The new program redefined the Reichsvertretung's most urgent tasks. First came Jewish education, to train the young "to become religiously secure, upright Jews, who will draw strength for meeting the heavy demands life will make of them from a conscious belongingness to the Jewish community." The second task was to further emigration to "Palestine above all" but also to other countries. The third task was care of the needy, the sick, and the aged. The fourth task entailed safeguarding the existing means of Jewish livelihood and providing aid to those without employment. The fifth item explicitly expressed the emotional identification of the Jewish community with Palestine, and the readiness on the part of the Reichsvertretung to establish institutional ties with the Jewish National Fund in Palestine. The heavy hand of the German dictatorship was evident: there were no longer any declarations of love or loyalty to Germany, its language or culture. The Jews had become completely isolated.

After the enactment of the Nuremberg Laws, Jews were no longer allowed to call themselves Germans. The Jewish organizations had to change their names so that they spoke for "Jews in Germany" rather than "German Jews." The Central Verein report, issued at the end of 1935, recorded its defeat. "Our relations with the German world around us have changed," the document commented drily. The new realities "have redefined our thoughts, feelings, and behavior. It would be undignified and foolish if we were not to comprehend this experience in its full significance."[60] The CV report was an institutional swan song, a melancholy statement of the defeat of its ideology not by Zionism, but by the victory of National Socialism. It attempted to draw up a balance sheet of the Emancipation, weighing the loss in Jewish content against the gains in individual achievement and creativity. It soberly recognized Palestine as a place of refuge, but adhered to its "historical Diaspora line."

The intrusion of the Gestapo in the Jewish community became ever more oppressive. Every public Jewish gathering was aware of the Gestapo's listening ear and watchful eye. Jewish organizations had to conduct their business in the presence of Gestapo agents. Documents were scrutinized or subject to scrutiny. For privacy, communal leaders resorted to meetings in each other's homes, at tea, lunch, dinner. They did not record all their transactions. For their constituencies, rabbis used to arrange local visiting, with small groups meeting periodically in one another's homes for religious study and discussion of current events.[61]

Any hint or suspicion of criticism of National Socialism and the German dictatorship brought immediate reprisals. Rabbis and communal leaders were summoned to the Gestapo for having spoken, or on suspicion of having spoken, forbidden words. If they were not arrested, they were prohibited from speaking publicly, preaching, or lecturing. Buber was banned from public speaking. Baeck was arrested again and again. In 1935, after the enactment of the Nuremberg Laws, he composed a prayer to be read from the pulpit as part of the Kol Nidre service. The Gestapo discovered the text, arrested him, and forbade the prayer to be used. The Nazis regarded the prayer as a revolutionary document, though it was written in the language of faith and tradition. It began in this way:

> In this hour every man in Israel stands erect before his Lord, the God of justice and mercy, to open his heart in prayer. Before God we will question our ways and search our deeds, the acts we have done and those we have left undone. We will publicly confess the sins we have committed and beg the Lord to pardon and forgive. Acknowledging our trespasses, individual and communal, let us despise the slanders and calumnies directed against us and our faith. Let us declare them lies, too mean and senseless for our reckoning.
>
> God is our refuge. Let us trust Him, our source of dignity and pride. Thank the Lord and praise Him for our destiny, for the honor and persistence with which we have endured and survived persecution.[62]

Censorship of the Jewish press went to extraordinary lengths. Subject to vague or nonsensical regulations, Jewish journals were given lists of prohibited subjects. (The German landscape was one.) Words and phrases were scanned for transgressive meanings. The word "blond" was banned in oral and written use, because it had become a code word for "Nazi." Periodicals were suspended arbitrarily for days or weeks, their licenses revoked, their writers and editors arrested. German censorship of Jewish cultural activities tightened and Jews were forbidden to perform works by "Aryan" writers and composers. Musicians who had once played Bach, Beethoven, and

Wagner now played, often to their personal distaste, East European Jewish folksongs.[63]

Above all, the Gestapo wanted to gain control of the Reichsvertretung or, failing that, other communal Jewish organizations. In pre-1938 days the Jewish community had not yet fallen wholly under the "legal" jurisdiction of the Gestapo as it would in post-1939 days. In their ambition to capture the Jews, the Gestapo tried to place a man they could trust on the Reichsvertretung Executive. Their man was Georg Kareski, a General Zionist suddenly turned Revisionist in the spring of 1933. To this day no one knows what hold the Gestapo had over Kareski or why he lent himself to the ugly drama.[64] Yet in spite of several forceful efforts by the Gestapo beginning in 1935, Kareski was rebuffed, partly by happenstance, but mainly because Jewish communal leaders resisted Gestapo pressure. (Later, in Eastern Europe, similar resistance brought certain death.) In June 1937, for the last time, the Gestapo tried to put Kareski on the Reichsvertretung Executive, but the rejection was unequivocal: in Max Gruenewald's lapidary phrase, "borrowed authority" had no place in Jewish life. Leo Baeck told the Gestapo: "You can force me to appoint Kareski as a member of the Executive of the Reichsvertretung. But you cannot force me to continue as president of the Reichsvertretung."

The National Socialist victory in 1933 had shaken the Jewish community, but within a few short months it had rallied, summoning an energy and will for organizational unity and fraternal solidarity and stimulating a powerful resurgence of Jewish identity. The wellsprings of this energy were the hope, faith, and belief that the German dictatorship would be short-lived or, at the very least, that a tolerable *modus vivendi* would be established. But after the Nuremberg Laws no such sanguine faith could be held. Morale began to decline, as the community became ever more impoverished by Nazi oppression, ever more enfeebled by emigration.

German Jewry had once been a prosperous community, contributing generously toward the needs of other Jewish communities less favorably situated, but with the growing Jewish impoverishment, the income of the Gemeinden from taxes—about 10 to 12 percent of income taxes—kept declining. (Actually not all Jews became impoverished: Jews in a host of businesses and industries, paradoxically, shared in the increasing prosperity of the National Socialist state.) Still, the sense of self-help was strong. To meet the costs of their communal programs, a system of voluntary monthly contributions was instituted under the name *Blaue Beitragskarte* (Blue Contribution Card), operated by volunteers on behalf of the Zentralausschuss. Though the contributions, scaled according to income, were small, the Blaue Beitragskarten raised respectable sums—in 1936, for instance, two million Reichsmarks. Still, that fell far short of the enormous needs. To close the gap, the American Jewish Joint Distribution Committee (JDC), the chief philanthropic organization of American Jews for overseas aid, and the Central British Fund, a comparable organization of British Jews, provided large amounts of money and goods. (On April 1, 1935, the Reichsvertretung took over most communal institutions in the field of relief and welfare, including the Zentralausschuss, and incorporated them into its structure.)

In 1936 about 20 percent of the Jewish population —83,761 persons out of 409,000—were in need. That year Jewish public kitchens dispensed 2,357,000 free meals. More than 75,000 persons, one-third of them in Berlin, received free matzot during Passover, the largest number of applicants for Passover relief in the history of Germany.[65] In 1937 the Reichsvertretung used most of its funds for emigration and preparation for emigration—5 million Reichsmarks out of a total of 7 million (about $1.7 million). Relief and economic aid were next in importance. The morale-building functions—schools, culture, religious life—were shrinking.

By January 1938 the Jewish situation had so de-

teriorated, the outlook had become so bleak, that even
Heinrich Stahl, president of the Berlin Gemeinde, the
most persistent advocate of Dasein, publicly declared:
"To those among our youth who have not yet decided
to emigrate, I say, there is no future for Jews in this
country. Whatever changes may be forthcoming for
us will probably not be for the better."[66]

Nineteen-thirty-eight was the last year that any
communal autonomy was exercised. The accelerated
confiscation of Jewish property and the final expulsion
of Jews from the economy began. The mass arrests of
June were followed by the mass expulsion of the
Ostjuden in October. A few days later, on Kristallnacht, the Jewish community of Germany went up in
flames. For months thereafter suicides accounted for
more than half the Jewish burials. All Jewish institutions were burned down or banned by order of the
Gestapo. The Jewish press was suppressed. The
Reichsvertretung was turned into the Reichsvereinigung with tasks of emigration, welfare, and education
assigned by the Gestapo. Its real function was to pre-
side over the final liquidation of German Jewry.

In March 1939 the *Jüdische Rundschau* reappeared
in Paris as the *Jüdische Welt Rundschau,* a new name
that bespoke the exile of German Jewry. Its first issue
contained an article by Martin Buber, "The End of
the German-Jewish Symbiosis," both eulogy and elegy
for that era: .

> I testify: it was the most extraordinary and meaning-
> ful circumstance. For the symbiosis of German and
> Jewish existence, as I experienced it in the four decades
> that I spent in Germany, was the first and the only one
> since the Spanish Era to receive the highest confirma-
> tion that history can bestow, confirmation through
> creativity. . . . But this symbiosis is at an end and it is
> not likely to return.

10

Death and Life in the East European Ghettos

With the German invasion of Poland on September 1, 1939, some two million Jews came under German rule. Two years later, when the Germans attacked the Soviet Union, some three million more Jews came under German dominion— the rest of the Jews of prewar Poland, all the Jews of Lithuania, Latvia, Estonia, and Soviet White Russia, and most of the Jews in the Ukraine, the Crimea, and Russia proper. These five million Jews lived in metropolitan industrial centers like Lodz and Warsaw, Kiev and Kharkov; in ancient historic cities like Cracow, Vilna, Lublin, and Riga; in provincial capitals like Kovno (Kaunas), Bailystok, Radom, Odessa, and Minsk. They lived in hundreds of county seats and market towns and were dispersed in thousands of villages. In prewar Poland, Jews had resided in over 16,000 localities.[1]

The East European Jewish settlement was massive and concentrated. The 350,000 Jews of prewar Warsaw equaled the whole Jewish population of prewar France. The 200,000 Jews of Lodz matched the number of Jews in all of Czechoslovakia. Kiev's Jewish population of 150,000 was nearly the size of the Netherlands' Jewish population. The 100,000 Jews of

Lwów (Lemberg) exceeded in number the combined Jewish populations of Belgium, Luxembourg,
Denmark, and Norway. Cracow's 56,000 Jews equaled
all of Italy's Jews; Vilna's prewar Jewish population
of 55,000 was greater than the Jewish population of
Bulgaria. The very numbers and density of East European Jewry determined their fate. In the past their
concentration had enriched their creativity. Under the
Germans it would hasten their doom.

The Jews of Eastern Europe remembered the last
war, its havoc and hunger, and the pogroms that had
drenched a wide swath of eastern Poland and the
Ukraine in Jewish blood. In 1939 Jews knew that they
would suffer the hardships that were the common
lot of war. They knew also that as Jews they would
endure still other afflictions at the hands of the Germans and even of the Poles among whom they had
lived for centuries more in tension than comradeship.

When German bombs rained down on Poland—on
Warsaw, Lwów, Piotrków, Bialystok, Radom, and
countless other nonmilitary targets in Poland—Jews
suffered along with everyone else, sharing in the
devastation of Polish cities. Warsaw underwent the
most massive destruction, as torrents of bombs turned
the city into a mass of craters, ruins, and ashes. On
September 16, the eve of Rosh Hashana, the Jewish
New Year, German planes bombed the dense Jewish
quarter, flying so low that there could be no mistak-
ing the deliberate intent.

When Warsaw came under siege, the Germans exploded some ten to thirty thousand shells daily on the
city.[2] Warsaw became a battle zone, with civilians
digging trenches to halt the advance of the German
tanks. Some 20,000 Polish Jews lost their lives during
the invasion and bombardments; Jewish homes, stores,
buildings, workshops, factories, and other installations
were destroyed, the losses estimated at 50,000 to
100,000 units. In Warsaw alone, about one-third of
Jewish-owned buildings were demolished and the
main centers of Jewish trade were reduced to rubble.[3]

All over Poland, the first response among Jews to the German invasion was flight. Thousands upon thousands of Jews set out on foot, on carts, in wagons, seeking refuge. Jews in small towns fled to the big cities; Jews in the metropolises fled to towns and villages. They moved eastward, toward Russia and Russian-held territory. Along the German-Russian demarcation line, territory passed back and forth between the Germans and Russians as border adjustments were made, the population surging forward and back, finally subsiding on the Russian side.

Jews, to be sure, were not the only people in flight. Thousands of Poles had taken to the roads and highways. On September 7, during the siege of Warsaw, the military, fearing that Warsaw would fall the next day, issued an order for all able-bodied men to leave the city. In the next few days, as many as 100,000 men set out eastward, large numbers of Jews and Jewish communal leaders among them. Since Hitler, in his declaration of war on September 1, had promised that he would "not war against women and children," the men, Poles and Jews alike, calculated that no harm would come to the womenfolk, whereas they, especially political and communal leaders, were endangered.

As soon as the Germans occupied Poland, their Einsatzgruppen began to direct a flow of human traffic that soon radically altered the age-old patterns of Jewish settlement in Poland. The Jews were driven from hundreds of localities in the Wartheland. They were expelled from thousands of small towns and villages throughout Poland and sent to nearby big cities. In Cracow, the ancient residence of the kings of Poland, the prewar Jewish population of 56,000 swelled to 68,000, as Jews in the neighboring small towns and villages fled to the big city. When Cracow was designated as the capital of the Generalgouvernement, Governor Frank ordered the "voluntary departure" of all Jews, except for those "economically indispensable." But only a few thousand—refugees from elsewhere—complied. After three months, the Germans took matters into their own hands: in one day they expelled 32,000 Jews.

In hundreds of small towns ancient Jewish communities were uprooted. The fate of the Jews of Aleksandrów, seven miles west of Lodz, was typical. Aleksandrów, one-fourth of whose twelve thousand residents were Jews, was the hosiery center of Poland. It was also the seat of the Aleksanderer *rebbe,* one of the most distinguished hasidic dynasties in all Poland, and the hasidim gave a special Jewish character to the town. The Germans entered Aleksandrów on September 7 and the next day burned down its synagogues. After three months of terror, arrests, shootings, expropriations, impressments into forced labor, the Jews were expelled on December 27, 1939. In the depths of the Polish winter, they were marched out on the highway, men, women, children, and infants, the hale and the halt, with the few belongings they were permitted to take in sacks and baby carriages, wheelbarrows and pushcarts, bicycles, and sleds. The nearest town was Glowno, on the border of the incorporated area and the Generalgouvernement, which most managed to reach. Wayworn, some eventually arrived in Lodz, others in Warsaw.[4]

Within a few months of the German occupation, thousands of Jewish settlements were erased from the map of Poland, their inhabitants ejected without notice, forbidden to take bare necessities, condemned to exposure, hunger, and homelessness. By the end of 1940, Warsaw had taken in 78,000 refugees from Lodz, Kalisz, and some 700 other places in the Wartheland. Piotrków's Jewish population swelled from 8,000 to nearly 12,000, with the accretion of refugees. Some 330,000 Jews—one-tenth of the Jews in Poland—became homeless refugees, beggars of bread and shelter, candidates for disease and death.

The very moment the Germans entered a town or city, they turned the Jews into outcasts of society. On entering Warsaw, the Germans agreed to distribute soup to the hungry population, having extracted one million zlotys from the municipal administration for that purpose. The agreement stipulated that all the hungry in the city, without exception, were to benefit. Yet immediately the Germans began to eject the Jews from the soup lines, calling upon the Poles on the line to do the same, "because the Jews deprive the Poles of their spoonful of soup."[5] It was interesting to observe, wrote an eyewitness, how quickly the brotherhood born under the continuous danger of death disappeared and how quickly the difference between rich and poor, Christian and Jew once again became apparent.[6]

Right away the Germans started to confiscate Jewish businesses and industry and to seal off Jewish retail stores for the disposal of either the military occupation or the SS. Sometimes Jewish shops were ordered to be opened only so that they could be plundered and robbed. In large manufacturing centers military trucks carried off the goods of Jewish factories and stores. In small communities Jews were ordered to bring in all their gold and jewelry under threat of death. Hostages were taken to enforce the extortion of large sums of money from the Jewish community, but were seldom released even after the contribution had been delivered.

Terror enveloped the Jews. The Germans reenacted the Kristallnacht in every town and city they invaded and occupied.[7] All over Poland synagogues went up in flames. (Those spared the fire were desecrated, turned into stables, garages, and public latrines.) Everywhere the Germans organized pogroms, rounding up the non-Jewish population to witness and learn how to mock, abuse, injure, and murder Jews. Unbridled killing and senseless violence became daily commonplaces for the Jews; the fear of sudden death became normal and habitual.

German terror in the Generalgouvernement in 1939 was wild and wanton. In the territory wrested from Russia in 1941, terror became systematic and massive. Within days of the German invasion, thousands upon thousands of Jews in Vilna, Kovno, Riga, Bialystok, Minsk, and hundreds of other towns, disappeared in raids carried out by Lithuanians, White Russians, and Ukrainians under German orders. It was said that the Jews were taken away for work. By mid-July a survivor here or there staggered back, physically maimed, psychically scarred, to report the mass executions of the Jews. In Bialystok some 7,000 Jews were killed by the Einsatzgruppen in July; in Kovno, some 6,000 to 7,000; in Vilna, 20,000 or more—nearly half the city's Jewish population—were swallowed up in the death pits at Ponary, a desolate village ten kilometers from Vilna. "How can one write about this? How can one assemble one's thoughts?" Herman Kruk asked in his diary on September 4, 1941, recording the eyewitness reports.[8] The reports were hard to believe; once believed, they were still harder to assimilate. They stunned the mind; they numbed sensibility. The Jews underwent a mass psychic occlusion, the normal flow of their emotions and energies shut off by shock and withdrawal, the business of their daily existence managed with a stringent economy of thought and feeling.

Everywhere the terror was aggravated by the sadism of the SS. In Częstochowa, on a frosty night in January 1940, the police surrounded a densely populated Jewish area, shouting "Juden raus!" Thousands of half-naked men and women were assembled in a large square and beaten to bleeding. Then they were kept standing for hours in the biting frost. Others— especially young girls—were taken into the synagogue now transformed into police headquarters, forced to undress, sexually shamed, and tortured.[9] In Kowel, which the Germans occupied a few days after the attack on Russia, they arrested a beloved hasidic rebbe, tortured him, and, in an act of mythic Chinese savagery, displayed his head for several days in the window of a main-street store.[10]

The refinements of cruelty were reserved especially for pious Jews and rabbis, whose traditional Jewish garb—hat and long coat—and whose beard and side-locks identified them as quintessentially Jewish. (In Germany the National Socialists had often failed to distinguish Jews from "Aryans" by "racial" features. During the High Holy Days of 1932, a Nazi gang, bent on anti-Jewish violence, mistakenly beat up "Aryans.")[11] The Germans deliberately chose observant Jews to force them to desecrate and destroy the sacred articles of Judaism, even to set fire to synagogues. In some places the Germans piled the Torah scrolls in the marketplace, compelling the Jews to set fire to the pile, dance around it, singing, "We rejoice that the shit is burning." Another German pleasure was "feeding" pork to pious Jews, usually in the presence of an invited audience. The most popular German game, played in countless variations, was "beards." In its simplest versions Germans seized bearded Jews and beat them. A more sophisticated entertainment involved plucking beards, hair by hair or in clumps. Sometimes Germans herded bearded Jews into barber shops, ordering them to be shaved and making them pay for the service. Sometimes the Germans themselves hacked off Jewish beards with bayonets, often along with parts of cheeks, chins, faces. In some places, Jews were assembled in the town square and shorn in a ceremony of mass mockery; elsewhere, beards were set afire.[12]

German terror was not exercised just in play, it was used also to extract work. Random seizures of Jews off the streets and even from their homes for forced labor began spontaneously, as it were, long before October 26, 1939, when Frank issued a decree making forced labor compulsory for all Jews aged fourteen through sixty.[13] Jews were seized to clean the streets of rubble, to scrub the floors in German residences, to haul and move, load and unload, to labor beyond fatigue. Sometimes they were released at the day's end and allowed to return home, but more likely they were kept for a week or two, incommunicado, unable to inform their families of their whereabouts or even of their very existence.[14]

As the Germans consolidated their position in

Poland, they set up labor camps outside the big cities, some of which—Treblinka and Majdanek—eventually became annihilation camps. Teams of forced laborers were assigned for periods of weeks and even months to construct these camps. After a stint of forest clearing, marsh draining, ditch digging, quarrying at these forced-labor installations, a normally robust man returned home sick, aged, and wasted. "Cursed Nazism now brings us physical slavery as well," observed Chaim Kaplan in his diary on September 14, 1940.[15]

In time, the SS was operating some 125 forced labor camps in the Generalgouvernement just for Jews, where terror, violence, and sadism ruled. Workers were wantonly shot or beaten to death. Those who tried to escape were shot. Some expired of exhaustion or hunger. Nearly all contracted disabilities or diseases endemic to their work. Underclothed and underfed, they became frostbitten, even to necrosis of parts of the face, fingers, and feet.[16] In the summer they suffered sunburn and severe blistering. Tendons, ligaments, muscles became swollen and inflamed under stress of unaccustomed labor. Heart muscles were seriously affected and coronary damage was a frequent affliction. Sites under construction had no dormitories. In one place the laborers used to march about ten kilometers to their place of work, where they toiled fourteen hours. Afterward, they trudged back those ten kilometers to the base camp, where they were rewarded with ten ounces of bread, some jam, and a plate of soup.[17]

Forced labor produced a new chapter in Yiddish folklore as dozens of songs, often plaintive and lachrymose, some bitter and ironic, were created to discharge the bitter accumulation of woe. Workers from Radom taken to the labor camp at Cieszanów used to lament:

> Work, brothers, work fast,
> If you don't, they'll lash your hide.

> Not many of us will manage to last—
> Before long we'll all have died.

Marching slave-labor brigades in the Libau ghetto used to sing:

> We are the ghetto Jews,
> The loneliest people on earth.
> Everything we had we lost,
> We have nothing left of worth.

To boost morale, the slave-labor brigades in the Kovno ghetto sang:

> We don't weep or grieve
> Even when you beat and lash us,
> But never for a moment believe
> That you will discourage and dash us.

> Jewish brigades,
> With rags for clothes
> March day in, day out
> And bravely bear their woes.[18]

On November 23, 1939, Frank issued an ordinance prescribing arm bands for all Jewish men and women in the Generalgouvernement over ten years of age—a white band, at least ten centimeters wide, with the Star of David, to be worn on the right sleeve of both inner and outer clothing. Jews were being concentrated and identified, so that none would escape the ever-tightening meshes of German control. On November 28, 1939, Frank issued a decree ordering the formation in each city of a Judenrat, whose membership roster was to be submitted to German officials for approval. In many places the decree came after the fact, for Heydrich's instructions to the chiefs of the Einsatzgruppen on September 21, 1939, had already been put in force. Frank's order specified that the Judenrat was obliged to accept German orders and was answerable for their conscientious execution. Furthermore, it stipulated that all Jews had to obey the directives that the Judenrat issued to implement German orders.

The next step was *de facto* ghettoization, soon to become *de jure*. One of the first ventures to establish a twentieth-century ghetto occurred in Warsaw, where a Judenrat had already been set up on Gestapo instructions since early October. A month later, on Saturday noon of November 4, 1939, the SS ordered Adam Czerniaków, chairman of the Warsaw Judenrat, to summon all twenty-four members to an emergency meeting at 4:00 P.M. At the appointed time, sixteen or seventeen had arrived and were waiting apprehensively. At 4:15, eight armed Gestapo officers burst in. After a roll call, the commanding officer gave those present half an hour to assemble all twenty-four members and all twenty-four alternates. People randomly available in the building and passersby were impressed to join the meeting. When the Gestapo officer returned, this time with some fifty men, he did not check credentials, but simply lined up the Judenrat members in one row and the putative "alternates" in another. He then read a decree supposedly issued by the army Command that ordered all Jews of Warsaw to move within three days into an area that was to be designated as a Jewish ghetto. The twenty-four alternates were then removed as hostages, with the warning that they would be shot if the Judenrat failed to comply with the order as specified.[19]

The Germans having left shortly before 7:00 P.M., the hour of curfew, the Judenrat decided to reconvene early next morning. Few slept that night and they returned the next morning tense and fatigued. Shmuel (Artur) Zygelboym, the representative of the socialist Jewish Labor Bund, held that the Judenrat had to refuse to carry out the order. How could they otherwise acquit themselves before the community and their children? But he received little support, for the majority feared that if they refused, the Germans would themselves forcibly carry out the ghettoization.

What then of their women and children? A sense of their tragic destiny possessed them. Men wept.

Still, agreeing that they must try to halt the establishment of a ghetto, they sent a delegation to General Neumann, the top military officer in Warsaw. Neumann, astonished at this information, denied that he had issued any such order and asked the Judenrat to withhold action until he had investigated the matter. A few hours later, the Gestapo summoned Czerniaków. Dr. Henryk Shoshkes, a member of the Judenrat, went along to give him moral support. The Gestapo officer was enraged because, by appealing to General Neumann, the Judenrat had circumvented his authority and disobeyed his warnings to deal only with the Gestapo. He savagely beat both men, while armed Gestapo men looked on. After Czerniaków apologized, the Gestapo officer, thus appeased, calmed down, even relenting sufficiently to negotiate minor expansions of the ghetto and concede a few streets to the Jews.

Meanwhile, though Warsaw had no newspapers and no radio,* news about the impending disaster swept through the Jewish community. Panic and terror seized the population. People with money and means started to look for apartments within the designated area. Thousands upon thousands of Jews besieged the offices of the kehilla, now Judenrat, pleading, weeping, clamoring for protection, for guidance, for instructions. Inside, the debate over the Judenrat's course of action continued. The Germans had not yet officially promulgated the order. On Monday, the day before the ghetto deadline, the crowds beleaguering the kehilla swelled to some ten thousand. Zygelboym decided to address them. First, Shoshkes described the situation as it then stood. Zygelboym thereupon exhorted his listeners to courage and dignity, calling on them to remain in their homes, to resist until they were forcibly moved. No one, he said, should go vol-

---

* The Germans confiscated all presses and radios; their possession was punishable by death.

untarily into a ghetto. Some in the crowd, probably a
following of Bundists, responded warmly, but the
record is silent about the reaction of the whole
populace.

Immediately thereafter, the Judenrat reconvened
its session, while some four hundred young men, assembled as couriers to inform and instruct the Jewish
population about the move into the ghetto, awaited
orders. Zygelboym once again advocated resistance,
but the majority held that failure to comply would
bring both ghettoization and reprisals. Zygelboym
then submitted his resignation. (Zygelboym's appeal
for passive resistance spelled the end of his career in
Warsaw. The Gestapo began to hunt for him. Two
months later, he fled Poland.)

Suddenly the ghetto order was withdrawn. No one
knows why—perhaps as the result of a confrontation
between the German army and the SS. But the SS
retreat was only *de jure,* because they had started
actually to circumscribe a ghetto. As early as October
barbed wire had enclosed the main streets of dense
Jewish population. In December 1939 the Judenrat
was compelled to set up large wooden signs, reading
"Danger: Epidemic Zone," at thirty-four street corners
leading into the heart of the Jewish quarter. In the
spring of 1940 these entries were walled up, restricting and hindering movement between the Jewish
quarter and the rest of Warsaw. The world of the
Warsaw Jews was becoming a prison.

Throughout Poland the Germans began to experiment with ghettos. The first try was in Piotrków in
October 1939, but the plan was abandoned then and
a ghetto was not established until as late as March
1942.[20] Detailed plans for a ghetto in Lodz were
ready in December 1939, approved in February 1940,
confirmed by Berlin in April; on May 1, 1940, the
Lodz ghetto, with over 160,000 Jews, was sealed off.
In Warsaw the ghetto walls began to be constructed
in the summer of 1940, and by November 1940 nearly
half a million Jews were enclosed and locked within
its walls and guarded gates. Warsaw and Lodz, with

the largest Jewish populations, were the most tightly, almost hermetically, sealed ghettos. Some ghettos had stone or brick walls; others had wooden fences with barbed wire entanglements. The Cracow ghetto was enclosed within walls in the form of Jewish tombstones, symbols of a terrifyingly literal character. Some ghettos, like Radom, Chełm, Kielce, with populations ranging from 15,000 to 25,000, were "open" ghettos, with access to other parts of town.

All ghettos eventually became "closed," rigidly circumscribed. On November 10, 1941, the governor for the district of Warsaw issued a proclamation instituting the death penalty for Jews illegally leaving the "Jewish residential districts" and also for those aiding such Jews or harboring them. Similar decrees were issued elsewhere in the Generalgouvernement. In the Eastern areas, ghettos were established soon after the first sweep of the Einsatzgruppen and were subject to the same regulations that obtained in the Generalgouvernement. In most communities there were actually two ghettos—the main ghetto and a so-called small or second ghetto, which served the Germans as a transit area.

The ghetto was an evil decree. Like sinners and criminals, Chaim Kaplan noted on November 13, 1940, "we are segregated and separated from the world and the fullness thereof, driven out of the society of the human race." Moving into the ghetto was everywhere a day of lamentation, a nightmare experience. Endless processions of weary men and women, babies in their arms, children at their sides, with bags, sacks, bedrolls on their backs and around their necks, the miserable remnants of their belongings loaded on carts, wheelbarrows, or makeshift conveyances, leftovers of their past life, artifacts of a vanishing civilization, pushing, shoving, screaming, groaning, shuffled into the ghettos.

Jewish historian Emanuel Ringelblum observed in his diary on November 8, 1940: "We are returning to the Middle Ages."[21] But his history was imprecise. The medieval ghetto had originated as a strategy for

Jewish existence and survival. During the Crusades
Jews petitioned for separate quarters within whose
walls they might better defend themselves. That
ghetto met the need for common protection as well as
for accessibility to Judaism's central institutions.
Later, when the church advocated the ghetto as a
means of separating Christians from Jews, the voluntary Jewish quarter was transformed into an obligatory ghetto, walled, its two gates guarded by
Christian gatekeepers who locked the inhabitants in
at night and during Christian festivals. Identifying
badges were then imposed on the Jews and their
pursuit of certain occupations and professions was
restricted, but the medieval ghetto, however crowded
and unsanitary, was not a prison. Every day Jews left
the ghetto to conduct their business outside; every day
Gentiles came into the ghetto to conduct their business. Social and economic intercourse between Jews
and Gentiles was unobstructed.

The only institution comparable to the Nazi ghetto
was the Nazi concentration camp, that "concentra-
tionary universe," where, in David Rousset's words,
"death lived among the concentrationees at every
hour of their existence."* Death bestrode the Nazi
ghetto and was its true master, exercising its dominion
through hunger, forced labor, and disease.

In August 1943, Zelig Kalmanovich (1881–1944),
scholar and writer, drafted a talk that was to have
been delivered on September 6, the second anniver-

---

* Clear distinction must be made between the Nazi ghettos and
the relocation centers established in the United States in 1942 to
intern the Japanese Americans who were evacuated from their homes
after Japan's attack on Pearl Harbor. The Japanese Americans were
housed in prisonlike barracks with primitive physical conditions, lacking the ordinary amenities of civilized life. Yet however severe the
physical hardships and however humiliating the stigma of disloyalty,
the internees never suffered hunger or epidemic disease, were not
impressed into forced labor, were never tortured, nor were any ever
deliberately killed by the authorities in sport or in earnest.

Even prison-of-war camps, with certain notable exceptions, fulfill
their international legal obligations to feed their inmates and provide
them with adequate medical care.

sary of the Vilna ghetto.²² The agglomeration of people in the ghetto, he wrote, could not be classified as a human collective that generates a sense of cohesion among its members. No one cherishes the ghetto, no one wants it to continue to exist: "On the contrary, the only desire that unites all the inhabitants of the ghetto from first to last is for the ghetto to disappear as rapidly as possible." Only one social institution, Kalmanovich wrote, was to a degree comparable to the ghetto—the prison. (Dostoevski, in *The House of the Dead*, noted that besides the loss of freedom, besides the forced labor, there is another torture in prison life—"compulsory life in common.") Yet even that comparison, Kalmanovich noted, was inadequate, because the prisoners, no matter how much they detest the prison, know they are there as punishment for having deviated from society's norms. This is not the situation of the Jew in the ghetto, who is incarcerated though innocent of any crime and, having broken no rules of human conduct, cannot fathom why he has been incarcerated.

The deprivation of freedom was universally felt. A thirteen-year-old boy in Vilna recorded in his diary the events of September 6, 1941, moving-day into the Vilna ghetto: "I feel that I have been robbed, my freedom is being robbed from me, and my home, and the familiar Vilna streets I love so much."²³

The isolation was compounded by the removal of telephones from private homes. (Radios had long since been confiscated.) Mail within the General-gouvernement and outside was erratic, undependable, and censored (letters had to be written in either Polish or German). Once the Jews were inside the ghetto, the Judenrat had to assume postal functions. Telegrams and cables could be sent only through the Judenrat and required Gestapo approval. Parcels of food and clothing were more often than not confiscated by the Germans before they ever reached the ghetto post office.²⁴

The ghetto's landscape sharpened the sense of isolation and imprisonment. The buildings huddled in a somber gray mass. In Warsaw the park in the former Jewish area had been excised from the ghetto, and just a few trees remained. The only other greenery were flowerpots and boxes on windowsills and balconies. Only one tree grew in the Vilna ghetto. A popular song sentimentalized:

> For them the square and boulevards,
> For me a place of misery.[25]

The ghettos were located in the oldest, most run-down parts of town, sometimes in outlying areas that lacked the basic facilities of the city proper—paved streets, lighting, adequate sewage, sanitation facilities. Ghetto dwellings were the most dilapidated, often in ruined and devastated condition because of bombings and shellings, looting, and wanton vandalism. The ghetto was congested, beggaring Baudelaire's vision of an ant-heap city. The air was fetid; the streets were filthy. A doctor in Vilna recorded some ghetto statistics: "About 25,000 persons live in our ghetto, in 72 buildings on 5 street sections. Comes to 1½–2 meters per person, narrow as the grave."[26] People lived so crowded together that they could no longer observe the normal conventions of privacy and modesty. The sense of shame vanished. Congestion bred noise. From the Warsaw ghetto a girl wrote: "My ears are filled with the deafening clamor of crowded streets and cries of people dying on the sidewalks. Even the quiet hours of the night are filled with the snoring and coughing of those who share the same apartment or, only too often, with the shots and screams coming from the streets!"[27]

In such congestion, keeping one's body and household clean posed Herculean tasks. In Vilna a young housewife, married to a doctor, vowed that she would never repeat "the idiotic words" that to be clean one needed only to want to be clean.[28] If you have never been poor, she wrote, you don't know that to be clean you need soap and fuel to heat water. If you get the

fuel, then you must decide whether to wash yourself
or cook the family's main meal, for in the communal
kitchen you can't have privacy for long. Moreover,
after ten hours of hard work, you don't have energy
to spare. As for keeping the room clean, if seven
people sleep on the floor at night, and cook and eat
there during the day, you have to keep scrubbing the
floor to keep it halfway clean.

Overcrowding precipitated the breakdown of sanitation. Three and four families lived in space adequate
for one. Toilets, running water, all plumbing and
sewage facilities were taxed beyond capacity and
beyond repair. The mephitic exhalations of latrines
and broken toilets poisoned the air. In the long win-
ters of bitter Polish cold, the water in the pipes froze.

Staying warm took priority over cleanliness. Fuel
was as scarce as disinfectants, and dearer. In Warsaw
coal was called "black pearls." In Lodz in January
1941 the Judenrat undertook a systematic program of
dismantling uninhabited places—stores, shops, fences
—to provide wood for fuel. Flocks of freezing ghetto
residents swarmed over the area, each with some
small saw or hammer. They descended on a building,
noted an observer, "like crows on a cadaver, like
jackals on a carcass. They demolished, they axed, they
sawed, walls collapsed, beams flew, plaster buried
people alive, but no one yielded his position."[29] In the
Lodz ghetto a man was arrested because he was
found to have concealed from the official housing
register the existence of another room in his apartment, which he had been dismantling for fuel.[30] In
Warsaw, Ringelblum wrote in his diary in mid-November 1941, "the most fearful sight is that of freezing children," standing "dumbly weeping in the street
with bare feet, bare knees, and torn clothing."

In December 1941 the Germans confiscated whatever furs could be taken from the Polish Jews. They
took men's and women's fur coats and fur linings, neck
pieces, fur collars, fur cuffs, skins, and sheepskins.[31]
The German army's troubles with the Red Army and

the Russian winter made the cold in the ghetto
tolerable. "I'd rather have Hitler in my furs," went a
ghetto joke, "than for me to be in his skin."

Hunger subjugated the ghetto. German policy was
to starve the Jews, and starvation stalked the great
ghettos of the Generalgouvernement. Special instructions issued November 4, 1941, by the German occupation authorities for feeding the civilian population
in the Occupied Eastern Territories[32] prescribed that
Jews were to receive half of the weekly maximum, in
grams, for a "population which does no work worth
mentioning," as follows:

Meat/meat products	none
Fat	70 [2½ oz.]
Bread	1,500 [3.3 lbs.]
Potatoes	2,000 [4.4 lbs.]

The average daily food ration provided about 1,100
calories per person—if it was all actually available.
Even that wretched pittance of food was sometimes
spoiled, stolen, or sold on the black market.

Bread and potatoes were basic subsistence. The
bread was, at best, rough and coarse, often stale,
sometimes moldy or compounded of foreign bodies,
like sand. "The bread is black and tastes like saw-
dust," Mary Berg wrote in her diary on February 28,
1941.[33] Its price rose and fell, according to supply and
demand. In prewar days it cost just groszy. In 1940
the price of a kilogram of bread hovered around 4
zlotys. In 1941 it fluctuated between 11 and 14.50
zlotys; by May 1942 it reached 15 zlotys.[34] Potatoes,
Chaim Kaplan noted, are "our whole life. When I am
alone in my room for a few moments of quiet, the
echo of that word continues in my ears. Even in my
dreams it visits me." Before the war, 100 kilograms of
potatoes had cost 30 zlotys. On November 27, 1940, it
had risen to 100 zlotys; a year later it reached 150
zlotys. In bad times, potato peelings substituted. In

Lodz, in May 1942, a person with a medical certificate could get 3 free kilograms of potato peelings daily from the public-kitchen division of the food department. The queues grew so long that the demand outran the supply.[35]

Horsemeat was sometimes available and fish on occasion, as Mary Berg noted on May 21, 1941: "Wagons full of stinking fish—tiny little fish in a state of decay." Also cabbage, beets, carrots, kohlrabi, turnips, radishes, horseradishes, and parsley could be had, usually in poor condition. In the big-city ghettos communal leaders instituted a campaign for home gardening under the auspices of Toporol (*Towarzystwo Popierania Rolnictwa*—Society for the Promotion of Agriculture), which gave courses in gardening and sold seeds. On March 30, 1942, Mary Berg observed that the seeds bought from Toporol were sprouting: "The little green radish leaves were the first to appear in the black ground. We have also planted onions, carrots, turnips, and other things." In Warsaw, Toporol planted flowers and vegetables in some two hundred yards. In the Lodz ghetto, small sections of a tenement yard were allocated as garden plots.

Hunger obsessed everyone. "A dybbuk has entered my belly. My belly talks, shouts, even has complaints and drives me mad," wrote Yehuda Elberg in his Warsaw ghetto diary.[36] "The gnawing devils of hunger," of Conrad's *Heart of Darkness*, attacked all ghetto residents, tormented their every waking moment. Everyone talked about food, at work, on the bread lines, or in the soup kitchen, exchanging recipes for concoctions that could be prepared from one or another item on the ration. "All became chemists, mixing this with that—just to turn out something."[37] Turnips sliced, cooked, mashed, mixed with mashed potatoes, flour, and seasoning became dumplings. Meat patties were made from ground horsemeat mixed with potatoes, rye flakes, a bit of flour, and seasonings, and fried in a drop of oil. In Vilna a factory produced "flour" and "starch" from potato peels, syrup and candy from potatoes.

The apportionment of one's bread ration required skill and art, for it had to last a week or ten days. How one managed depended not only on the tormenting pangs of hunger, but on strength of character, ability to postpone immediate gratification, and family responsibility. Elberg scored the loaf of his weekly ration to mark off each portion, for otherwise, "with the glutton that my belly is, the whole bread could disappear in a moment." Mary Berg told about an eleven-year-old girl who posed as a model in her art class, for whom the art students collected some small pieces of bread. She ate only a tiny piece, wrapping the rest in a bit of newspaper: "This will be for my little brother."

Hunger not only affected the belly, but injured the mind. People became coarsened, their manners less fastidious, their tastes less squeamish, their disgust for certain foods overcome by the intensity of their hunger. Hunger drove some to rapacity. To walk in the ghetto with an uncovered loaf of bread was neither prudent nor safe, for in a wink the bread could be snatched out of hand and whisked away.

Beggars lined the streets of the large ghettos, ubiquitous and commonplace, their doleful songs and plaintive laments filling the air. Children predominated among them, but also whole families begged, huddled together in rags, moaning and wailing. Some beggars in their desperation ignored the curfew and went out at night, crying for bread. "In the surrounding silence of night," Ringelblum observed, "the cries of the hungry beggar children are terribly insistent."

Offsetting the German policy of starving the Jews far exceeded the capacity of any welfare organization on the spot or even in wealthy America. Reporting, on September 24, 1940, on the hunger and disease in the ghetto of Lodz, a JDC official declared that it was imperative to set up soup kitchens to provide 100,000 warm midday meals, to prevent a complete catastrophe. The cost, estimated at 8 pfennig per person, would come to 8,000 Reichsmarks per day, or 240,000 Reichsmarks per month, which he said was then equivalent to $100,000 at the official rate of exchange. In the Warsaw ghetto a communal leader put the minimum budgetary needs for one person to survive at 5 zlotys per day, which, for a population of 400,000, would amount to 60 million zlotys per month. He did not count on charity, but calculated that to provide that amount of money, the ghetto would require a labor force of some 300,000 persons earning 8 zlotys per day—a utopian vision under those conditions.[38]

Only the illegal importation of food into the ghettos kept most Jews from dying of hunger. To be sure, the Germans prohibited the sale or gift of any type of food to Jews from outside the ghettos, such sale or gift punishable by heavy fines and impressment into forced-labor brigades, but the ghetto police often showed leniency in permitting contraband food to come in. If they were strict, or if German police were at hand, bribery helped induce leniency. The workers in labor brigades employed outside the ghetto used to bring in food, obtained by bartering clothing and household goods. In partly open ghettos peasants sometimes sold food at exorbitant prices. Children were the most numerous class of smugglers, small, spry, and, if caught, an object of pity for the policeman. A popular ghetto song eulogized the child smugglers:

Over the wall, through holes, and past the guard,
Through the wires, ruins, and fences,
Plucky, hungry, and determined,
I sneak through, dart like a cat.[39]

Smuggling was also big business, especially in the Warsaw ghetto, with half a million mouths to feed. Thousands of Jews made a living from smuggling, from the big operators who took big risks for big profits, down to the little peddler whose small supplies came from middlemen. Whole cows were smuggled into the Jewish cemetery adjoining the Catholic cemetery and later transported into the ghetto in hearses that had come from the ghetto with corpses for burial. Buildings bordering the ghetto, with entrances on the "Aryan" side and windows opening on the ghetto, became smugglers' nerve centers, operational headquarters for hoisting and lowering; small cranes, makeshift lifts, troughs, and pipes delivered grain, milk, cereal, vegetables, and even luxury products.⁴⁰

If not for the smugglers, the Germans would have succeeded in starving the ghetto to death. The ghetto's ingenuity and daring, the toughness of its brawling wagoners staved off massive hunger deaths. The greatest tribute to the smuggler appeared in a preface to a medical study on hunger in the Warsaw ghetto, prepared under the direction of Dr. Israel Milejkowski, who headed the Judenrat's Department of Hospitals. Writing in October 1942, when some 300,000 Warsaw Jews had already been deported to Treblinka, Milejkowski declared that because the smuggler had penetrated the ghetto walls, the ghetto's isolation had not succeeded in destroying the Jews. The smuggler played a paradoxical role in the ghetto: though smuggling demoralized the ghetto, the smuggler, "with his blood and sweat, gave us the possibility of existence and work in the ghetto."⁴¹

The smugglers became the arrivistes of the ghettos, as the old social structure collapsed. Rubinstein, the Warsaw ghetto's madman, incessantly shouted, "All are equal," but he was wrong. The ghetto was a great leveler, but it also created a new class of the well-to-do, whose means were acquired by illegal or unscrupulous means. (Many arose out of the prewar criminal ranks.) Smugglers, wheeler-dealers, swindlers, blackmailers, informers, rascals, bribe-takers, and knaves thrived in the cankered milieu of the ghetto, battening on its misery. Every ghetto had underworld operators who preyed on the populace, blackmailing because of furs withheld, secret radios, contraband goods, evasion of labor duty, forbidden activities. Their financial rewards were great and their risks of punishment few. Some strutted because of their riches or authority borrowed from the Gestapo, yet they were despised and ostracized by the Jewish community. A few even tried to buy status through charity and good deeds for the poor and pious.

This new class—smugglers, underworld, *nouveaux riches*—became the clientele for dozens of cafés, restaurants, and nightclubs that mushroomed in the ghetto. (Providentially, these gave a livelihood to actors, singers, musicians, and entertainers.) A shrill mood of *khaye sho* (the fleeting moment) and *carpe diem* spread in these circles, even reaching some segments of the respectable population, whose response to the deprivations of their ghetto prison was the pursuit of pleasure.[42] They passed their time dining, drinking, dancing. Yet even so stern a moralist as Chaim Kaplan defended frivolity. "It is almost a *mitzvah* to dance," he wrote on February 20, 1941. "Every dance is a protest against our oppressors."

In normal societies class and status derive from wealth, occupation, education, and family. In the ghetto, class was determined by occupation and personal property, both of which could buy food and provide security. (Status remained relatively stable: rabbis, scholars, doctors, political and communal leaders retained prestige and respect despite the precipitous decline in their material fortune.) Excluding illegal or criminal occupations, the top-ranking occupational categories in terms of food and security were officials and employees of the Judenräte, members of the Jewish police, foremen of labor brigades working outside the ghetto, and skilled workers. These people received larger food rations than the general public and higher wages; they were more secure from seizure for forced labor and for a while were exempt from deportation.

Personal property—furniture, household goods,

clothing, cash, jewelry, and other valuables—determined class. Wealth from real property, industrial investments, and bank holdings had been wiped out. The more personal property one had, the greater opportunities for sale or barter—to buy food or guarantee protection. The declassed well-to-do habituated the used-merchandise street markets near the entrances to the ghetto, selling their belongings. The sale of a dress could provide a kilo of bread; a carpet, a month's ration. During summer 1941, several thousand non-Jews daily used to come to buy in the street markets of the Warsaw ghetto; total sales were estimated at nearly a million zlotys daily.[43]

Some fifty thousand Central European Jews—from Germany, Austria, and Czechoslovakia—who were deported to ghettos in the Wartheland, the Generalgouvernement, and the Ostland (in especially large numbers to Lodz and Riga) added to the social differentiation. They arrived with good clothes and much personal property. In Lodz they cornered the black-market supply of bread, thus exacerbating their already tense relations in the ghetto with the resident Polish Jews, who also depended on that bread supply to stave off hunger.[44]

Hunger killed, but first it wrought disabling change —mental, psychological, and physical. Loss of weight and the disappearance of subcutaneous fat aged and withered its victims. Hunger destroyed the normal rhythm of existence, affected the physical capacity to work and the mental ability to think. Nutrition deficiencies caused anemia, suppressed the menses. Fatigue and dizziness, apathy and depression were part of the general sense of malaise. Nausea, vomiting, and diarrhea were the daily complaints of the hungry.

From September to December 1939, 4 Jews in Warsaw died of hunger; in 1940, 91 died; and in 1941, nearly 11,000.[45] Yet if hunger itself was not the big killer, it weakened and debilitated its victims so as to make them fall prey to countless other diseases.

When we had nothing to eat,
They gave us a turnip, they gave us a beet.
Here have some grub, have some fleas,
Have some typhus, die of disease.

Breeding on human misery, typhus is associated
with times of war, famine, and disaster, when people
are crowded together in abnormal conditions of filth,
cold, and hunger. The range of fatality varies from 5
to 25 percent. In the Warsaw ghetto the death toll
from typhus was estimated at 15 percent, even though
the Germans prevented proper treatment—basically,
maintenance of nutrition—and refused to allow the
necessary preventive measures to be taken and enforced. The relatively moderate death rate testifies to
the physical, indeed moral, stamina of the ghetto inhabitants. In the Warsaw ghetto alone, epidemic
typhus was believed to have affected between 100,000
and 150,000 persons, though the official figures were
barely over 15,000. The spread of disease was concealed from the Germans. Hospital cases of typhus
were recorded as "elevated fever" or pneumonia.
Mainly, the stricken were treated in their homes in a
massive clandestine operation, covering up the presence of the disease from German inspection teams
who periodically threatened to seal off the affected
areas.[46]

The most prevalent ghetto disease, typhus was
nevertheless not the most deadly. According to data
from the Lodz ghetto for 1940, 1941, and 1942, heart
disease alone accounted for about 30 percent of all
deaths, suggesting that the tensions and hardships of
life in a Nazi ghetto were more deadly than typhus.
Dysentery, tuberculosis, hunger, and diseases of the
digestive tract ranged next. Typhus as a cause of
death ranked eleventh or twelfth in a field of thirteen.[47]

Infants, the elderly, and above all, the refugees
succumbed with least resistance to hunger and disease. Forlorn and friendless in strange big cities, the

refugees were thrust upon the inadequate mercies of communities already overburdened with their own wants. Warsaw in 1941 sheltered some 130,000 refugees, nearly one-third of the ghetto population. Some lived on the streets, their very appearance shocking the passersby.[48]

Most refugees were housed in unused school buildings or other facilities never intended to be dormitories. The sheer numbers in these placements broke down the plumbing systems and, consequently, the possibilities of personal hygiene and public sanitation. In January 1942 a welfare report summarized the state of the refugees in the Warsaw ghetto: "Hunger, sickness, and want are their constant companions, and death is the only visitor in their homes."[49] The statistics of refugee mortality were staggering. They died in their bunks, expiring in nakedness and friendlessness. They died begging in the streets, their last entreaties frozen on their lips, their bodies lining the streets of the Warsaw ghetto. The tricycle-propelled hearses of the undertakers could not keep up with the accumulation of corpses. Covered with newspapers, stiff in the snow, they awaited Mottel Pinkert, the ghetto's chief undertaker, the true "king of corpses."

"More and more often at social gatherings we talk about life after death," wrote Halina Szwambaum from the Warsaw ghetto in June 1942. It was necessary to be prepared, she felt, "for the day when we shall have to admit that we have been defeated and must be gathered to Abraham's bosom."

In the ghettos death had become a ubiquitous intimate. Its ubiquity and its intimacy heightened the value of life. The preservation of life stood at the very center of Jewish tradition: "Ye shall therefore keep My statutes and Mine ordinances, which if a man do, he shall live by them." The text was interpreted to mean: "*Live* by them, and not die by them." During the Hadrianic persecutions, when Jewish martyrdom reached such high proportions as to imperil the survival of the Jews in Palestine, the preservation of life

him when the Messiah would come. Both brothers
dered awhile and then replied that great wars
ld be waged in 1915 and 1942, in both of which
Jews would suffer greatly. In one of these wars,
rebbes prophesied, the Jews would be delivered.[60]
olitical prophecy was a more substantial ghetto
le. In Warsaw, new words were put to an old
:

> Listen here, Haman you,
> Jews will live to settle scores.
> You will get your comeuppance.
> Jews have lived and will endure.
> But Haman, you will go to hell.[61]

Vilna, a popular song urged:

> Let's be joyous and tell our jokes,
> We'll hold a wake when Hitler chokes.[62]

olitical jokes reflected the indomitability of the
to spirit and became the weapon of the power-
Humor transformed the reality of power relations,
antasy permitting the Jew to triumph over his
ecutor. The joke afforded relief from the oppres-
of inferiority and from the tension of anxiety.
e in 1941, when the German army began to suffer
rses on the Russian front, anti-German jokes en-
ed the ghettos:

What's the difference between the sun and Hitler?"
he sun goes down in the West and Hitler in the East."

What's new?"
idn't you hear? They are confiscating chairs from the
ws."
What happened?"
itler got tired of standing outside Moscow and
ningrad."

tler appealed to the smugglers in the Warsaw ghetto

was deemed so important that the rabbis at Lydda
ruled that only with regard to three fundamental laws
—those prohibiting idolatry, unchastity, and murder
—should death be chosen over transgression.

The teachings of the religious tradition were incorporated in the folk wisdom: "A Jew lives with hope."
"While there's life, there's hope." "Even when the
slaughtering knife is at your throat, don't lose hope."
"As long as you draw breath, don't lose hope" or
"don't think of the grave." The religious teachings and
the folk wisdom, permeating every ghetto in Eastern
Europe, supplied the antidote to depression and despair. Everywhere the phrases "hold on" and "hold
out" epitomized the value of life and survival. In
Vilna a popular ghetto song exhorted:

> Moshe, hold on,
> Keep hold of yourself,
> Remember we must get out. . . .
>
> Moshe, hold on; hold on, Moshe—
> It isn't very long,
> The hour soon will toll. . . .[50]

The ration card represented access to life. The
Warsaw ghetto idiot used to admonish passersby:
"Don't give up your ration card." "Don't register your
ration card with Pinkert." Beggars used to sing a
ditty:

> I'm not giving up my ration card,
> Better times are coming.[51]

The rebbe of Żelechów, counseling his followers to
go into hiding, was alleged to have said: "Every Jew
who survives openly sanctifies God." Each Jewish
survivor, he declared, is a hero resisting the Nazis
because he refuses to extinguish his precious life.[52]
Rabbi Isaac Nissenbaum in the Warsaw ghetto was
reported to have said:

Now is the time for the sanctification of life [*kiddush
ha-hayim*] and not for the Sanctification of the Name

[*kiddush ha-shem*] through death. Once when our enemies demanded our soul, the Jew martyred his body for kiddush ha-shem. Today when the enemy demands the body, it is the Jew's obligation to defend himself, to preserve his life.[53]

The only gladdening aspect of the ghetto, one communal leader noted, was that "Jews cling so tenaciously to life, fight so stubbornly for life." As evidence he adduced "the trifling number of suicides in the ghetto," which he regarded as "a ray of hope that the Jewish masses in the ghetto will come through everything, survive this hell, and live to see better times."[54] In Lodz the daily statistics of death indicated a higher suicide rate among the assimilated German and Czech Jews than among the Polish Jews. The head of the Warsaw Judenrat's Statistical Office reported, with some astonishment, that the number of suicides in 1940–1942 was just 65 percent of the number in 1939.[55] Ringelblum attributed the low suicide rate to the exhortations against despair by communal leaders. Shakhne Zagan, leader of the Left Labor Zionists, Ringelblum's own party, for example, appropriated the motto that the Bratslaver hasidim in the ghetto had scrawled on the walls of their prayer house: "For the sake of Heaven, Jews, don't despair!"[56]

That summons to optimism, grounded in Judaism's eternal messianic hope, was shared by believer and nonbeliever. Salvation would come from one source or another. In the Chełm ghetto the Jews sang a Yiddish song, patterned on the Psalms, praying for salvation:

> O Look from heaven and behold,°
> Look down from the skies and see!
> For we have become as a derision,
> A derision among the nations. . . .

° Italicized lines were in the original biblical Hebrew.

Therefore we plead with You ever:
Now help us, Guardian of Israel,
Now take notice of our tears,
For still do we cry aloud, "Hear O Israel
O, take notice, Guardian of this nation.
Show all the peoples that You are our G
We have indeed none other, just You
Whose Name is One.[57]

In the Lodz ghetto, a hasid counseled pair "because salvation from God appea stant." In the ghetto of Stolin, the rebbe followers: "Don't despair, rally yourse Jews, and trust in God."[58]

In Bialystok, however, hope of deliv pinned on the Red Army:

> Alas, how bitter are the times,
> But deliverance is on its way;
> It's not so far away.
> The Red Army will come to free us
> It's not so far away.[59]

The "Partisans' Hymn," which first beca in the Vilna ghetto, epitomized the ultin charge against despair: "*Zog nit keyn mol dem letstn veg*"—"Never say you walk the

Religious people turned to superstition to buttress their hopes. They searched fo meanings in words and texts, looking for of the war's end and the Messiah's cc numerical value of the letters for the yea instance, equaled that for the word "Sal thus an omen for the good. A new body tales was fashioned in the style of the legends, foretelling deliverance. One story Warsaw ghetto recounted the adventu early hasidic rebbes, Rabbi Elimelekh (d. his brother, Rabbi Zusya (d. 1800). They return a favor to a man who had done th turn in their wanderings. His request wa

to help him get half a million German soldiers into
Moscow. They agreed, but in their own special way—
piece by piece, heads, hands, feet, each section
separately, little by little.

When furs were confiscated from the Jews in the
winter of 1941–1942, jokes and jingles coursed through
the ghetto:

> Against the Moscow frost and Moscow cold
> He's trying to save himself with Jewish furs and gold.

After the United States entered the war, a rhyming
jingle showed a new constellation of anti-Hitler allies:

> Hitler won't be able to cope
> With the English fleet
> And with the Russian sleet,
> With American dollars
> And Jewish smugglers.[63]

Like the inhabitants of Camus's plague city, the
ghetto Jews realized that they had no choice but to
come to terms with the days ahead in their prison
house. That realization was no mere passive recon-
ciliation with their lot. On the contrary, they enlisted
their whole historic experience in trying to transform
their environment. The commandment to preserve
life had generated a strategy of accommodation, a
tactic of adaptability, which centuries of powerlessness under oppressors had fashioned into a service-
able tradition. "Be pliable like a reed, not rigid like a
cedar," the Talmud says. Prohibited from pursuing
certain trades and occupations, Jews learned to survive in the interstices of the forbidden. Like grass
growing in the clefts of rock, Jews found means of
livelihood in the crevices of the economy, in marginal
areas overlooked or neglected by hostile authorities.
In the ghettos that tradition of accommodation stood
them in good stead. Necessity bred innovativeness.
There, within limits far more stringent than any past

tyrant had ever imposed, the Jews exercised their
ingenuity, manufacturing goods for sale, marketing
them inside the ghetto, smuggling them outside, producing and preparing food, making something out of
nothing.

Powerlessness had also taught Jews other strategies
of survival. Lacking weapons and military organization, they learned to use tricks of intelligence and
manipulation to prevail against their persecutors. They
learned not only to invent, but to circumvent; not
only to obey, but to evade; not only to submit, but to
outwit. Their tradition of defiance was devious rather
than direct, employing nerve instead of force. When
the Germans demanded electrical appliances or furs,
Jews in a silent boycott destroyed what they had or
gave them to Polish acquaintances. Ghetto Jews
evaded forced labor, in many ghettos even setting up
cooperative security systems within buildings to warn
against imminent seizures. En masse, Jews disobeyed
German decrees. In every ghetto hundreds were constantly being arrested for one transgression or another
—violating curfew, not wearing arm bands, smuggling, leaving the ghetto illegally.[64] Not even the severe
penalties discouraged them.

The solidarity of the family provided the biological
basis for the preservation of life and for Jewish continuity. Parental respect, filial obedience, obligations
of kinship, sanctity of the home—these were the elements in family life that gave security and stability to
the individual. In times of stress, the family became
the Jewish stronghold, the source of comfort and
moral strength. In the ghettos family relationships
deepened and broadened. Familial responsibility extended beyond the nuclear family to embrace grandparents, aunts and uncles, married brothers and
sisters. Families that had been separated became re-
united, preferring to share crowded ghetto lodgings
with each other rather than with strangers. They
shared not only housing and food, but hopes and
plans. The young and able-bodied worked for the old

and feeble. When the father was seized for forced labor, the onus of providing for the family fell on the mother. Parents and children divided responsibilities for maintaining the household, apportioning tasks as the hardships of the occasion demanded, no longer in accordance with fixed familial roles. When mothers worked, older children assumed household chores, queuing up for rations, cooking, cleaning. Younger children were sometimes taken along to workshops, where mothers could watch out for them and provide them with a bowlful of hot soup at midday. In the poorest families, with fewest resources, the children themselves undertook the perilous task of smuggling to feed the household.[65]

Some families, to be sure, became demoralized. Hunger drove some children or parents to steal food from each other. Some couples quarreled over property and belongings, their disputes coming under the jurisdiction of ghetto courts. But these were the exceptions. Though tensions and anxieties multiplied, devotion and mutual responsibiilty within the family kept pace. The stabilizing effect of the family showed up in the statistics. Divorce ceased, but all ghettos recorded a rash of marriages.[66] Marriages were sometimes the hurried decisions of young people who felt they had little time left; in some cases parents withdrew earlier objections to the match; sometimes marriages were conveniences for sharing cramped ghetto space or gaining the protection of labor cards. Widows and widowers married more frequently in the ghettos than in prewar days. The ghetto heightened emotional needs. At the very time when hunger and disease decreased sexual potency and desire, tenderness and affection supplanted passion.

On seeing two pregnant women in the Warsaw ghetto, an unknown diarist noted: "If in today's dark and pitiless times a Jewish woman can gather enough courage to bring a new Jewish being into the world and rear him, this is great heroism and daring. . . . At least symbolically these nameless Jewish heroines do not allow the total extinction of the Jews and of Jewry."[67]

The Jewish community was, of course, the extended Jewish family. In the ghettos most Jews felt a strong sense of Jewish identity, of belonging, of readiness to share Jewish fate. The proverb "What will befall all Jews, will befall each Jew" assumed new relevance. In the Lodz ghetto, German Jewish children presented a Hanukkah program in their school auditorium:

> Hunger, cold, and conflicts were forgotten. Shoemakers and tailors, physicians, lawyers, and pharmacists, all at once, we were one big family. That could not have happened in Berlin . . . but here, behind the barbed wire, something existed that united us all—our Jewishness. When they sang together, they forgot their suffering and misery; they were still alive and in song they praised God, who many times before had performed miracles. When they sang about the little lamp whose oil for one day lasted eight, the singers regained their courage and hope.[68]

At a seder in the Vilna ghetto, Kalmanovich recounted an anecdote. A child in a ghetto school learned, for the first time, the story of Jacob and Esau. He suddenly called out: "Teacher, we are the descendants of Jacob and they the descendants of Esau. Isn't that so? It's good that way. For I really want to belong to Jacob and not to Esau." Reflecting on the anecdote and its lesson for Jewish identity, Kalmanovich concluded that people, in the freedom of their imagination, could choose their own identity. That child chose freely to be a Jew.[69]

Even in the harsh realities of ghetto life, most Jews accepted their fate as Jews. The possibility of hiding out among non-Jews created problems rather than solutions. Living on false Polish identity papers outside the ghetto, wrote a woman in Vilna, "seems to me like treason against my own people. Here, in the worst, most awful moments, I am after all among my own. Never have I felt myself so strongly a Jew, never was I so united with my brothers as now. Intellectually I admit that hiding out among 'Aryans' is perhaps the best, perhaps the only solution. Emotionally, I consider it desertion."[70]

At bottom, Jews shared a deep faith in their ultimate survival and in the preservation of the Jewish people. Early in the war Chaim Kaplan observed: "Our existence as a people will not be destroyed. Individuals will be destroyed, but the Jewish community will live on."

11

The Official Community: From Kehilla to Judenrat

Upon entering the towns and cities of Poland in 1939 and of Russian-held territory in 1941, the German invaders ordered Jewish communal leaders to establish Jewish councils, Judenräte, in accordance with Heydrich's instructions of September 21, 1939.[1] Everywhere these Judenräte were formed out of the remnants of the prewar kehillot, the legally incorporated religious communities. These, like all political and communal structures, had been disrupted and shattered by the invasion, the bombardments and shellings, the mass flights and evacuations, and above all, by German terror. Only fragments remained of the institutions that had once regulated the country's political and social life.

In Warsaw, where the population held out longest against the Germans, a Jewish citizens' committee to replace the defunct kehilla was formed on September 11 to obtain help for the Jews from the makeshift municipality. The five-man committee, composed of Zionists and heads of the merchants' and artisans' associations, was legitimated by the city's president who, on September 23, appointed as the committee's head Adam Czerniaków, a former vice-chairman of the prewar government-appointed kehilla.[2] (In De-

cember 1936 the Polish government dissolved the
democratically elected Warsaw kehilla for acting
"beyond its competence"—that is, for opposing the
government's anti-Jewish politics—and appointed a
commissioner and an advisory council, which all
parties except the Aguda boycotted. Only a few of the
originally elected councilmen continued to serve.)

When the Russians occupied eastern Poland and the
Baltic countries, they arrested and subsequently
murdered many Jewish communal leaders whom they
regarded as anti-Soviet. When those territories were
incorporated into the USSR, the Jewish community as
a corporate entity ceased to exist. Jewish political
parties went underground, while Jewish service organizations—schools, hospitals, orphanages, libraries—
were taken over and operated by the government.

The Judenräte emerged from the diminished and
deficient pool of men who had once led and administered the now lapsed communal institutions.
Frank's decree of November 28, 1939, ordering the
establishment of Judenräte, provided that communities
with up to 10,000 inhabitants were to have a 12-mem-
ber council, larger communities a 24-member council.
In practice, however, the SS validated councils of
varying size. To run the thousand or so Judenräte
formed in the Generalgouvernement and the Eastern
occupied territories, no fewer than 10,000 men, and
probably many more, had to be coopted. Most had
served in prewar times as board or staff members of
local kehillot, social-welfare agencies, professional
associations, schools, cultural and religious organizations. The majority had been active in the various
Jewish parties, some having been elected to kehillot
or city councils on their party lists.

Many men active in communal service had reached
their positions through the conventional avenues of
access in the traditional community: family prestige,
wealth, Jewish learning, and dedication to the community through financial generosity and good works.
In addition, during the interwar period, new channels
for communal activity had opened up by way of the

political parties and professionalization of the social services. As a group, these communal activists were overwhelmingly middle class and professional, but included a growing segment of working-class people whom the political parties had elevated. Whether they had held paid or honorary positions, they were men of decency and integrity, imbued with the tradition of service to the community. "Do not withdraw from the community," the Talmud teaches. To be sure, some were tempted by the rewards of prestige and honor, but most regarded communal service as an obligation and responsibility. As a class, they were designated by the Yiddish term *"klal-tuers"* (literally, "community practitioners"). Today, somewhat indiscriminately, we call them all communal leaders. The problems to which they had addressed themselves in the past were mainly philanthropic and administrative. Few were leaders in the sense that they commanded a voluntary followership, a status achieved in the traditional community only by charismatic rabbis or illustrious Talmudic scholars. In the modern East European Jewish community such leadership was exercised only by the authoritative heads of the Jewish parties, a handful of men authentically dynamic and creative.

The German summons to form a Judenrat aroused deep misgivings and created imponderable dilemmas. Though the Germans declared that the Judenrat would have to carry out their orders, most Jews—leaders and masses alike—believed that the Judenrat would operate as a kehilla under a new set of ground rules. Many believed that the Jewish community required some kind of intermediary body to represent its interests vis-à-vis the occupying authorities, to plead and negotiate on its behalf. (In somewhat the same way, the German Jews had been motivated to create the Reichsvertretung in 1933.) Without such an institution to serve as spokesman for them, they felt that the Jews would fare worse under direct German control or—an equally dismal prospect—under the governance of Poles, Balts, or Ukrainians. When danger threatened, a Jewish body could—like the advocate of the Jews in premodern times, the *shtadlan*—intercede on their behalf, exercising tried and true methods to ward off that danger.

Other communal leaders were less confident, fearing that the Judenrat would have neither autonomy nor options, that it would become merely an instrument of German oppression. People were troubled, too, even in those early days of the occupation, that as members of Judenräte, they would become demoralized by the terror of their taskmasters. In the first days and weeks of German occupation, all had experienced that terror and witnessed the atrocities perpetrated by the Germans.[3]

Those who agreed to serve on the Judenräte did so with qualms and forebodings. Most who agreed to serve were prompted by Talmudical precepts, by *noblesse oblige*, a sense of responsibility that they could not or would not repudiate. In nearly every community, the German order to form a Judenrat was discussed and debated by the former communal leaders. In Lublin, in the fall of 1939, kehilla members were outspoken about their apprehension of dealing with the Germans. Having been elected to serve the kehilla in peacetime, some held that they had no mandate to serve in such uncertain times. Others argued that failure to accept their responsibility would expose the Jews to total lawlessness. If we reject our responsibility, they asked, whom will the Germans appoint in our stead? Finally, the argument of obligation to the Jewish community prevailed and the decision was taken to participate.[4]

In Vilna, a consultation of fifty-seven communal leaders was called on July 4, 1941, the very day the Germans ordered the Judenrat to be formed. At the meeting, chaired by the aged Dr. Gershon Gershuni, one of Vilna's most prestigious communal leaders, the atmosphere was heavy with dread. Gershuni was categorical: a Judenrat had to be formed, and whoever was selected had to accept the responsibility. He included himself, weeping at his words, and many

wept with him. There were few volunteers, and it was
decided that those chosen to serve must accept, considering themselves martyrs.[5]

In a small town near Vilna, the rabbi assembled the
Jews in the prayer house to select members for a
Judenrat in compliance with the German order. Since
no one was willing to assume the responsibility, the
candidates were chosen by lot.[6]

Every community had to make its decision swiftly,
under German pressure. There was neither time nor
opportunity for outside consultation, since communication and transportation were completely disrupted.
Local branches of nationwide parties or organizations
could not apply to headquarters for guidance and had
to determine their own policy. Eventually a general
pattern emerged, though it showed some local varia-
tion. Members of the middle-class parties—General
Zionists, Mizrachi, Revisionists, and Aguda—and the
several professional associations of merchants and
artisans assented to participation in the Judenräte as
board or staff members, though their parties did not
actually sanction such participation. In Warsaw, as
Chaim Kaplan noted, divided views prevailed among
his Zionist friends.

The left-wing parties, Right and Left Labor Zionists and Bundists, generally opposed participation on
political/ideological grounds. Distrusting the centrist
and rightist organizations, convinced that these would
not protect the interests of Jewish workers and of the
Jewish poor, the leftists preferred to stand aside.
Furthermore, they wanted to keep their political
hands clean from the taint of dealings with the Germans. There were occasional exceptions. In Piotrków,
for example, where Bundists had held leading positions in the prewar kehilla, they continued in the early
occupation period to hold those posts in the Judenrat.[7]

The reluctance on the part of communal leaders to
participate in the Judenrat was universal. In some
instances, when no candidates could be prevailed upon
to accept, the Germans themselves made random
appointments. In the absence of legitimate communal

leaders, a few unscrupulous individuals who had never served the community volunteered their services to the Germans.[8]

The two ambiguous cases involve Mordecai Chaim Rumkowski of Lodz and Moses Merin of Sosnowiec. Both later became strutting dictators in their wretched ghetto realms, megalomaniacs in the grip of rescue fantasies. Rumkowski, a childless widower and director of an orphanage, had been elected to the Lodz kehilla on the Zionist ticket. In 1937, when the Polish government took over the kehilla and put it under the control of the Aguda, the other parties instructed their members to resign. But Rumkowski, hungry for the prestige of office, stubbornly retained his seat, despite expulsion from his party. When the Germans burst into the kehilla offices in October 1939 and asked for the Älteste, Rumkowski, then sixty-three years old, responded, thinking they meant "oldest," not "Eldest." Another story has it that on learning that the Germans were trying to locate kehilla officers, Rumkowski voluntarily reported and offered his services.[9] Neither version can be substantiated.

When the Germans entered Sosnowiec in 1939, they arrested a sizable group of Jews, humiliating and beating them. In response to a German officer's inquiry about who among them were kehilla officials, Merin came forward, though the kehilla chairman, also present, did not. Merin, then in his late thirties, had been elected on the Revisionist ticket to the kehilla.[10] Whether he volunteered simply to escape further punishment, whether he calculated on improving his own situation, or whether he already dreamed of "power," no one knows.

The apprehensions about participating in the Judenräte were fulfilled to an extent never foreseen by even the most pessimistic of communal leaders. From the start, every order the Germans issued was enforced with relentless terror. Within days, or at the most, weeks, hundreds of Judenrat members were taken hostage, arrested, dispatched to labor camps, shot, or hanged. Hundreds of others needed no further inducement to flee for their lives.

In Będzin, the Germans levied a contribution on the Judenrat of 5 kilograms of gold and 20 kilograms of silver, taking 120 hostages as surety. Until the Judenrat delivered the contribution, the hostages were beaten and tortured. Thereafter, the Judenrat members fled, and no one in Będzin could be induced to hold office.[11] In Lwów, soon after taking office, the chairman of the Judenrat was arrested and subsequently killed for refusing to deliver several thousand Jews, ostensibly for forced labor.

In Częstochowa, within a short time, the Judenrat, originally composed mostly of former kehilla members, lost ten of them, including three rabbis, for sabotaging German orders. They were replaced by persons who had no previous record of communal service.[12] In October 1939 Rumkowski, officially named the Eldest of the Jews in Lodz, invited thirty leading members of various Jewish communal, philanthropic, and political organizations to form a consultative council. On November 7 the Gestapo arrested most of them, killing them then or later in concentration camps in Germany. A second advisory council was formed in February 1940, consisting of third-raters with no communal experience or responsibility.[13]

In Vilna, on July 26, 1941, the Germans demanded a contribution of 5 million rubles, 2 million to be paid the following morning. Otherwise Judenrat members would be shot. The news spread swiftly throughout town, and the Jews spontaneously began to raise the money. Men gave watches, women rings. By morning, 667,000 rubles, half a kilogram of gold, and some 200 watches had been collected, far short of the German quota. The Germans kept their word: two Judenrat members were shot. On September 2, a day of mass seizures, arrests, and killings, SS men entered the Judenrat offices and arrested 16 of the remaining 22 members. They were never seen again. That Judenrat was dissolved and a new one reconstituted, consisting of the 6 survivors, plus new members chosen by the Germans.[14]

In Warsaw, within three months of the formation of the Judenrat, 7 of its original 24 members fled abroad. On January 26, 1940, Czerniaków recorded that he had been summoned to the German police and ordered to pay 100,000 zlotys the next day. Otherwise 100 Jews would be shot. "Confronted with all this, I turned to the SS asking that I be relieved of my office, for in these abnormal circumstances I cannot lead the kehilla. They said, in response, that they would not recommend such a step." In a few cases Judenrat members resigned without penalty, but more often the Gestapo demanded custody of such persons.[15]

German terror coerced Jewish compliance. Council members who resisted German orders, even by temporization, were removed by terror, in a continuing process of deadly attrition. Their successors, alien to the tradition of Jewish communal service, learned from that experience the wisdom of compliance. Even where original members of original Judenräte continued to hold office and where their own persons were not threatened with death, the duress that the Germans exercised over the entire Jewish population was sufficient to ensure the Judenrat's submission to German orders.

From its inception, the Judenrat was looked upon as a reincarnation of the kehilla. Czerniaków's first draft of October 13, 1939, for organizing the Warsaw Judenrat was just a rehash of conventional kehilla departments: chancellery, welfare, rabbinate, education, cemetery, tax department, accounting, vital statistics. The kehilla's primary obligation had been to maintain the community's religious institutions (the rabbinate, *kashrut* and ritual slaughter, ritual baths, prayer houses). Social welfare concerns—care of the poor, the orphaned, the aged—came next, and then support of Jewish schools, maintenance of a cemetery and providing for Jewish burial, and administration of the Jewish hospital.[16]

In performing these functions, the kehilla had operated as a *Gemeinschaft* institution, serving the personal, religious, and communal needs of the solidary Jewish group, enhancing its cohesion, strengthening its morale, securing its survival. But the kehilla was an anomalous institution. Throughout its history in czarist Russia, it served also as an instrument of the state, obligated to carry out the regime's policies within the Jewish community, even though these policies were frequently oppressive and specifically anti-Jewish: excessive and punitive taxation, an iniquitous system of military conscription intended to effect conversion, harsh efforts to compel "modernization" of Judaism by forbidding traditional garb, and interference with traditional modes of Jewish education.[17] Traces of the kehilla's duality persisted in independent Poland, where the semifascist government meddled intrusively in kehilla affairs. Under German occupation that duality became even more distorted in the Judenrat, as its primary Gemeinschaft functions were curtailed.

The Judenrat underwent an even more significant metamorphosis. With ghettoization and the isolation of the Jews from the rest of society, the Judenrat had to assume functions normally associated with a municipality. New departments were created to provide housing, water and utilities, police, fire protection, a judiciary system of sorts, food production and distribution, fuel distribution, transportation, postal services, public health and sanitation, factory production and employment. The Judenrat was thus transformed into a formal *Gesellschaft* institution, providing general services on an impersonal basis. Its Gemeinschaft functions continued to shrink, with the notable exception of social-welfare services.

The dichotomization of Judenrat functions and roles evolved under contradictory pressures of German demands on the one hand, communal interests on the other. Agents of the oppressors, the Judenräte nevertheless regarded themselves as comforters of the oppressed. In their brief, wretched existence, they tried to reconcile their irreconcilable tasks.

To begin with, each Judenrat tried to make some
order out of the chaos engulfing its community. The first
task was to feed the hungry and heal the sick. At least
half the income of the Judenräte, often much more,
was spent on welfare and medical needs. In every
community public kitchens were organized under
Judenrat auspices. Some ghettos set up supplementary
food-ration depots for children; others had "tea
houses," which provided hot boiled water by the glass,
pitcher, or barrel. The Judenräte maintained hospitals,
clinics, first-aid stations, dental clinics, pharmacies,
inoculation centers, public baths, barber shops, disinfection stations, and public-health inspection teams.
They supported homes for the orphans and the aged,
shelters for the homeless, and they gave cash assistance
to the refugees. They sent supplementary food rations,
clothing, and fuel to the labor camps where the Jews
of their community were dragooned. For children they
provided day-care homes, residential centers, remedial
services.[18]

The needs were immense, their resources circumscribed. Judenrat officials, pleading as advocates of the
Jews, submitted memoranda to the German authorities, supplicated, humbled themselves. They appealed
for more food to feed their people, more space for the
ghetto, more medicines and medical facilities. They
petitioned for decrease in the forced-labor contingents,
for release of hostages, for news about prisoners held
incommunicado. They pleaded for a halt to harass-
ments and violence, for redress of grievances. Hazard-
ing SS reprisals, they exploited every available channel of authority—German military and civilian, Polish,
Balt, Ukrainian—in the hope of extracting supplies or
concessions, playing off one bureaucracy against another in the confused and conflicting jurisdictions.

Occasionally the petitions succeeded. Sometimes the
Germans yielded a street or two to enlarge the ghetto.
Sometimes they lowered their original assessments
against the ghetto, as in Bialystok, settling for 6 kilograms of gold instead of 25 and for half of their
demand for 5 million rubles.[19] But usually they re-

mained intractable. On January 26, 1940, Czerniaków was summoned by Orpo, the German regular police, and told that because a Volksdeutsch had been beaten, the Judenrat had to pay 100,000 zlotys the next day. Otherwise 100 Jews would be shot. Czerniaków appealed to the Gestapo to be released from the payment. They refused. He then tried to obtain a concession by asking to pay in installments. Again they refused. To salvage something, he asked to be relieved of supplying workers for snow removal. They remained implacable.

Flattery was applied to soften the Germans, but gifts and money were considered more effective. Bribery had long been a way of life in Eastern Europe, going back to czarist times, when it was built into the structure of the state bureaucracy. Among Jews bribery was used as leverage to obtain relief from persecution. An official who did not take a bribe used to be called a *roshe,* a villain. Ecclesiastes' cynicism that "money answereth all things" became the hope for many Judenräte. Some Judenräte maintained standing stocks of furniture, tableware, jewelry, and textiles to be available for emergencies. Bribes sometimes accomplished Jewish objectives: prisoners were sometimes released, hostages sometimes ransomed, forced laborers sometimes returned, harsh punishment sometimes mitigated, even death sentences sometimes commuted. But more often than not the insatiable maw of the German occupation swallowed the proffered gifts with few perceptible benefits to the Jewish population.[20]

In Warsaw, shortly after the occupation, random abductions by the Germans of large numbers of Jews for forced labor made venturing out on the street a perilous gamble. The fear of being dragooned aggravated the numerous other hardships and uncertainties of daily life. In an attempt to rule out at least one factor contributing to the chaos, Artur Zygelboym, the most radical member of Warsaw's first Judenrat, proposed that the Judenrat organize a labor pool from which a specific number of workers requisitioned by the Germans could be supplied. This sort of rational regulation of forced-labor recruitment would, it was anticipated, enable the Jewish populace to move about more freely, assured that they would not be waylaid and kidnapped if they went out for bread or to work. The Gestapo agreed to the proposal and asked for a daily contingent of two thousand workers. But the seizures did not cease. In response to the Judenrat's protests, the Gestapo replied that other German agencies were culpable. Nevertheless, the Gestapo now insisted on a labor quota as its prerogative.[21]

As the agency through which the Germans obtained forced laborers, every Judenrat set up a labor registry. To avoid a stint of forced labor, people paid to purchase substitutes. In time, procedures for buying exemptions became bureaucratized. The Judenrat used to collect fixed fees for exemptions for given time periods; that income was used partly to pay token wages to the forced laborers (the Germans paid nothing) and partly to replenish the Judenrat's ravaged treasury. In Lublin, for instance, in May 1940, nearly three thousand people paid sums ranging from fifteen to over fifty zlotys for labor substitutes. In the first year of the occupation, the Lublin Judenrat collected almost a half-million zlotys from these payments.[22]

The burden of forced labor consequently was borne disproportionately by the poor, though they benefited from the exemption fees, which were used to finance welfare programs. When the Jewish populace began to resist the labor draft, having learned the cost of forced labor to health and even life, the Judenrat began to seize people forcibly. The situation had a historical precedent. In the days of Czar Nicholas I, the Jewish community was required to supply very large numbers of Jewish youngsters as recruits for a twenty-five-year term in the Russian army. To make up the required quota, the kehilla, through its agents, used to kidnap orphans or children of the poor. That parallel with czarist times was not lost on the ghetto population.[23] On April 26, 1941, Ringelblum commented that "the melancholy tradition of kidnapping" that the Judenrat had revived was "like a projection of a picture out of the tragic past." More and more Jews who could not pay for exemptions refused to report for forced-labor duty. In Częstochowa, for example, when the Germans demanded a large contingent of laborers from the Judenrat, the Jewish police had to round up people forcibly. They managed to get eighty-two persons, detaining them overnight in a prayer house, but at night all but six succeeded in escaping.[24]

To provide the labor contingents demanded by the Germans, the Judenrat became increasingly coercive, for unless workers were forthcoming, the Judenrat and often the entire ghetto were threatened with worse consequences. In Bialystok, for instance, in September 1942, when the Judenrat failed to produce two hundred women workers requisitioned by the German Labor Office, Sipo (the German security police) took over, ordering all the ghetto unemployed to assemble in one spot the next morning. The fear that they would be deported or murdered prompted compliance, and two hundred workers came forward. Supplying forced laborers quickly ceased to be a means for the rational regulation of a labor pool as first conceived by Zygel-boym, but became only another means of appeasing the Germans. In the Judenrat's view, then, Jews who evaded forced-labor duty, who hid from the police summoning them, were not merely transgressing the rules that governed the ghetto, they were jeopardizing what little tranquillity may have prevailed in the ghetto at that time and perhaps even imperiling the ghetto's existence. Thus the Jewish populace and the Judenrat, each acting out of discordant interests and considerations, found themselves on a strategical collision course. The consensus that exists in a normal society concerning desirable and undesirable goals and standards had evaporated.

The most successful strategy the Judenräte devised was to use, or try to use, Jewish productivity to ensure Jewish existence. The entire economic structure that

had supported the Jewish population had collapsed.
Jewish stores and businesses, workshops and factories,
goods and supplies had been damaged in the bombings, then looted and robbed, and finally expropriated.
Ghettoization was the final blow, cutting off most
economic ties with the non-Jewish population. The
idea of ghetto industry, under the aegis of the Judenrat, as a means of restoring economic viability was first
advanced by Rumkowski in Lodz. On April 5, 1940,
shortly before the Lodz ghetto was sealed off, Rumkowski made a bid to the top German civil administrator: "I have forty thousand working hands in the
ghetto. This is my gold mine."[25] He offered to produce
finished goods for the Germans, if they would provide
the raw materials. His strategy was twofold. First, his
plan would provide work and income for the ghetto
population and thus bring about a measure of economic self-sufficiency. Second, he hoped to make the
Jews invaluable to the occupiers through the rational
exploitation of their labor, resourcefulness, and enterprise. A similar strategy was independently conceived
in 1941 by Ephraim Barash, head of the Judenrat in
the Bialystok ghetto.

Elsewhere, the idea of ghetto industry originated
out of the needs of the ghetto itself and of its inhabitants. Cooperatives in traditional Jewish trades were
set up by Judenräte in Lwów, Cracow, Radom, Siedlce,
for example, often in conjunction with remnant trade-
union groups or with ORT, the agency for vocational
training and rehabilitation: in men's and women's
clothing, shoes, hats, carpentry, brushes, bakeries.
(Bread baking became a key industry in all ghettos.)
The hasidim of Aleksandrów who had made their way
to Warsaw brought their expertness in hosiery manufacture and in 1941, with the help of the Judenrat and
of ORT, established a hosiery plant in Warsaw.[26]
Scrap collection and production of articles from
scrap furnished work for many Warsaw shops. These
undertakings, selling inside and outside the ghetto,
legally and illegally, provided a bare livelihood for
thousands of ghetto inhabitants.[27] Some Judenräte,

Vilna most notably, operated workshops to produce for the ghetto itself (food, vitamins, detergents, chemicals) and to provide it with needed services (laundry, disinfection, repair).

Bialystok, with about 40,000 Jews, had over 20 operating factories that produced a wide variety of finished goods, mostly for German military consumption. Lodz, with over 160,000 Jews, had at its peak 117 factories, workshops, and warehouses, producing for the Germans. In 1941 the industrial production of the Lodz ghetto brought in over 16 million Reichsmarks, paid out by the Germans mostly for slave wages, the balance as payments for the goods at noncompetitive rates. The value of the Warsaw ghetto's official export of industrial production during the first six months of 1942 was nearly 50 million zlotys. The illegal export, finished goods smuggled outside the ghetto and sold clandestinely, was estimated to be far higher.[28]

Ghetto industry brought some money to the ghetto and hence to the Judenräte. Their basic income was derived from taxation, and they taxed whatever they could: wages and earnings, even living quarters. There was a community tax, regular and emergency, a ration-card tax, a hospital tax, a sanitation tax, a labor-registry tax, a welfare tax, a cemetery tax. Special taxes were sometimes levied on the well-to-do, especially when the Judenräte required large sums to meet the extortionate German demands. Assessments were made by Judenrat committees, often in cooperation with representatives of professional groups and of tenement committees.[29]

Taxation, like forced labor, put the ghetto population in direct conflict with the Judenrat, for people resisted paying taxes. The Judenrat, dependent on tax moneys to support basic welfare services or to ransom the ghetto from some German threat, was compelled to enforce collection of taxes and even to apply sanctions against tax delinquents. The Jewish police, officially designated *Ordnungsdienst* (order service), was the Judenrat's instrument of enforcement. As a ghetto institution, the uniformed Jewish police exemplified the dynamics of degeneration that the Germans set in motion.

The Jewish police was an institution improvised by the Germans when they locked the Jews into ghettos. Initially police functions were to regulate the flow of pedestrian and vehicular traffic inside the ghettos and to maintain law and order. Like its parent organization, the Judenrat, the Jewish police came to serve dual and incompatible purposes; to protect the Jewish community while it was required to enforce German orders. Unlike the men who constituted the original Judenräte, most police recruits were not motivated by a sense of communal responsibility. Those who enrolled did so of their own volition and for their own advantage. The requirements for the police force were few: young, able-bodied men were wanted, preferably with military training. Few recruits had a record of communal service, in part because of their relative youthfulness. The only Jewish political party from which a sizable proportion of police was drawn was the Zionist Revisionists, perhaps because they put a high value on military training and militarism. For the most part, the left-wing parties interdicted their members from joining the police.

Some police chiefs and men were outsiders to the communities that they served, refugees or evacuees who found favor with the Germans, by whom they were appointed. Some were apostates. In Warsaw, the first police chief was Józef Andrzej Szeryński, formerly a colonel in the Polish police, a Catholic convert, reputedly an anti-Semite. He undoubtedly recruited police from his circle of apostate friends. (The Warsaw ghetto had a large population of converts to Catholicism, who were regarded as Jews under German racial law. They worshiped in two Catholic churches within ghetto limits.) On March 18, 1941, Ringelblum noted that a hundred apostates served in the police in visible positions. One of them, he added, was heard in church to have shouted "Down with the Jews."

To be sure, many ghettos had police chiefs and men who were kindhearted and community-minded. In Vilna and Kovno, as well as many small towns, the records indicate that such men played a substantial role, at least for a time, in the police. But they, too, like the Judenrat officials, were coerced by German terror into compliance. Charged with enforcing the isolation of the ghetto, the Jewish police at ghetto gates had to check people entering and leaving, examine their identity papers and permits, and search their persons and belongings for contraband. They were supervised by Polish guards and armed German police to ensure that they performed their tasks correctly and with appropriate strictness. Once a Jewish woman brought into the Warsaw ghetto a sack of potatoes, which a German guard on duty confiscated. According to Ringelblum's account, on April 17, 1941, a Jewish policeman asked the German to return the potatoes to the poor woman. To punish him for his audacity, the German guard knocked the policeman down, bayoneted him, and then shot him.

Another means the Germans used to control the Jewish police was by directly operating a collateral Jewish police apparatus in some large communities, which bypassed the Judenrat and offered more material inducement than did the Ordnungsdienst. The Germans encouraged members of the prewar Jewish underworld to set up informer and police agencies to do the dirtier work the Jewish police caviled at. Such groups existed in Lodz, Kovno, Lublin, and Warsaw. The largest operated in Warsaw, with a formidable German name: *Überwachungsstelle zur Bekämpfung des Schleichenhandels und der Preiswucherei im jüdischen Wohnbezirk* (Control Office to Combat Black-Marketing and Profiteering in the Jewish Residential District). Familiarly nicknamed by the Jews "the Thirteenth," from its location at 13 Leszno Street, it was headed by Abraham Ganzweich, a Polish Jew who had lived in Vienna before the war and may have then become entangled with the Gestapo. An inde-

pendent police force of about 300, elaborately uniformed, the Thirteenth served primarily as an intelligence agency for the Gestapo, though it also engaged
in social-welfare activities to win public legitimacy.
Formally dissolved by the Germans in the spring of
1942, about 200 of its staff were absorbed—at German
insistence—by the Jewish police.[30]

Before long, German terror set in motion a process
of negative selection among the Jewish police, eliminating the soft and irreproachable, leaving those who,
with a corroded instinct for self-preservation, were or
had become callous and ruthless, tenacious in their
will to perform the duties imposed on them.[31] Those
duties—ferreting out forced-labor dodgers, calling up
recalcitrant taxpayers, seizing smugglers and confiscating their illicit potatoes or onions—stiffened the resistance of the ghetto inhabitants, intent on their own
self-preservation. That resistance spurred the police
to greater efforts to perform their duty and to intem-
perate use of billy clubs, bludgeons, or rubber hoses.
Having lost legitimacy in the eyes of the ghetto, the
Jewish police could assert their authority only through
force. Instead of being the protectors of the ghetto
populace, they had become their assailants and adversaries.

The transformation from kehilla to Judenrat, from
Gemeinschaft to Gesellschaft institution, demanded
skills, expertness, and experience previously not in
plentiful supply in the East European Jewish community. Jews in Poland had, for the most part, been
excluded from the civil-service apparatus and therefore lacked experience in municipal administration.
To be sure, the centuries-long experience of admin-
istering kehillot stood the Jews in good stead, but it
could not satisfy the new needs. Consequently, many
outsiders came to fill important posts in the Judenräte.
In Warsaw key positions were given to apostates because many had had distinguished careers in public
service. German Jews filled some slots in the Lodz
Judenrat.

In Vilna, which had belonged to Poland before 1939 but had then become the capital of Soviet Lithuania, remaining nominally Lithuanian under the Germans, Lithuanian-speaking Jews from Kovno who knew their way around the Lithuanian bureaucracy took over responsible posts in the Judenrat. The most dramatic instance is that of Jacob Gens, a Revisionist from Kovno, formerly an officer in the Lithuanian army. He was first appointed police chief and then, with German support, usurped authority in the ghetto before the end of 1941. On July 10, 1942, the SS appointed Gens officially chief of the ghetto, dissolving the Judenrat for incompetence and dilatoriness.[32] The presence of outsiders, aliens by choice or geography, further eroded the Judenrat's Gemeinschaft character and reinforced the growing estrangement between it and the populace.

As the scope of their functions increased, the Judenräte enlarged their staffs to hypertrophy. Lodz maintained the largest apparatus, with nearly 13,000 people, about one-eighth of the ghetto population in August 1942. At its peak, the Warsaw Judenrat employed 6,000 persons, in contrast to the prewar kehilla's staff of 530. The Vilna Judenrat as of September 1942 employed over 1,500 people, then nearly 15 percent of its decimated population. In Lwów the Judenrat staff numbered about 4,000, nearly 5 percent of the Jewish population. The Bialystok Judenrat had 2,200 persons on its payroll, three times as large as necessary, by admission of Barash himself.[33] The very massiveness of the bureaucracy began to affect the spirit and character of the institution. The communal motivations and social impulses of the original Judenrat boards were often submerged in the administration of complex tasks performed by an unwieldy bureaucracy, in part inexperienced, in part alienated, all terrorized.

The Judenräte grew to behemoth proportions not only because their expanded and additional functions demanded more personnel, but also because the pressures of nepotism, favoritism, and patronage were irresistible. Employment in the Judenräte entailed advantages: higher pay, supplementary food rations, official exemption from forced-labor duty, more security than was available to the general population. Naturally, Judenrat officials used their positions to place their relatives on staff and payroll. Family connections became a route to security, a literal lifeline. Influence, knowing the right people, pull—or as it was referred to all through Europe, protection, *protektsye* —was the only way to get a good berth. "Vitamin P" was the most sought-after commodity to improve oneself. A person assigned to heavy-duty forced labor would habitually complain that he lacked Vitamin P.[34]

The use of influence was rampant everywhere, even in ghettos with a highly respected leadership. A member of the Kovno Judenrat once addressed a memorandum to its chairman, Dr. Elhanon Elkes, deploring widespread "protectionism." Elkes, in complete agreement, promptly issued an order to Judenrat personnel, forbidding the resort to nepotism and favoritism and setting up a control commission to enforce that order. Nonetheless, that evening, Dr. Elkes himself wrote a letter of recommendation for a distant relative, "a poor and helpless woman," who had applied to him for help.[35]

Favoritism in the Judenräte was widespread, but not always unethical or venal. (Barash in Bialystok, at a meeting on October 11, 1942, warned against favoritism, admitting that even he was guilty of practicing it.) Most Judenräte became sanctuaries for the comunity's intellectuals, its scholars, rabbis, writers, its creative stock. The Records and Archives Department of Warsaw's Judenrat was a refuge for Polish Jewry's outstanding historian, Meir Bałaban. Also Dr. Edmund Stein, Semitist and rector of the prestigious Institute for Judaistic Studies, was employed by the Warsaw Judenrat. In Lodz, historians, scholars, and writers were sheltered in the Judenrat's Statistical Office and Archives. In Vilna Gens readily agreed to a proposal made by communal leaders that Vilna's surviving intellectuals be put on the Judenrat's staff to ensure them some livelihood and security. In Częstochowa teachers exclusively constituted the Judenrat's street-cleaning brigade, work considered unexacting. Performed in the morning hours, this assignment gave teachers free afternoons to give private lessons, in the absence of official schools.[36]

The Judenrat bureaucracy had at its disposal a substantial part of the ghetto's resources: the distribution of food, the allocation of living quarters, the assignment of forced-labor duty. In a society that was all penalty and no amenity, abuses and malpractice in performing these functions multiplied. Hunger broke down traditional canons of morality; distress eroded ethical standards. People capitalized on the advantages of their positions. Those with access to the ghetto's food supply—warehouse workers, distributors, retailers, bakers, public-kitchen employees—took what could be taken. The stealing ranged from pilfering a loaf of bread or a sack of potatoes to large-scale thievery for profitable resale on the black market. To the hungry populace it always seemed that corrupt politicians and demoralized bureaucrats were stealing the food from the mouths of starving children, a persistent conviction in all cultures in times of disaster, but not always demonstrable. Yet, even in Lodz, where the hunger was great and the stealing prodigious, the proper distribution of the full food supply would not have appreciably alleviated the ghetto's famine. The tragic dilemma, as Ringelblum noted on May 30, 1942, was that the Germans simply did not allocate enough food to keep everyone alive.

Judenrat employees encountered another temptation: bribery. Any Judenrat employee who could provide an amenity—extra food or better housing—or an exemption from special taxes or forced-labor service was likely to be offered a bribe. Many refused to take bribes, yet even those who accepted were not always rascals, but good family men for whom the bribe might make the difference between their family's bare subsistence in the comfortless ghetto world and sufficiency.

The most corruptible and corrupted of the ghetto functionaries were the police. As in all societies, the police became corrupted by the populace. A bribe might win exemption from forced labor; a small present given *sub rosa* to a policeman might obviate paying a large sum in taxes to the Judenrat. The right kind of bribe could guarantee the success of a smuggling operation or release a member of the family from ghetto detention. Perhaps the police who took bribes and gave favors in return were more humane than the incorruptible ones, who carried out orders punctiliously. Still, the police thrived on the hardships of the ghetto, each new adversity providing new opprotunities for bribes and payoffs.

Every Judenrat tried to counteract these demoralizing and disintegrative tendencies within its staff. Disciplinary or "control" commissions were established that attempted to establish codes and standards for proper behavior. In Warsaw, according to Ringelblum, 700 policemen out of a force of 1,700 faced disciplinary trials. In Bialystok, Barash carried out a massive purge of the police in June 1942, because, as he put it, they promoted lawlessness rather than security in the ghetto.[37]

In Lublin, in the summer of 1942, the Judenrat adopted a set of bylaws governing newly created control and disciplinary commissions. The Control Commission was to supervise the Judenrat's functionaries. The Disciplinary Commission was to investigate complaints of violations of office, to fix penalties, and to allow for appeals. The Lublin approach was rigidly legalistic:

§1.   Members of the Judenrat, employees of the Judenrat, including members of the Ordnungsdienst, who fail to live up to their positions through any act, evasion, or negligence, and also by their conduct at work or away from it, demean the authority, seriousness, or trust of their position, shall be held responsible and incur disciplinary action.

§3.b.   A felony in the line of duty is a violation of official
        duty that brings injury both to the interests of the
        service and to the interests of the individual, or to
        the interests and reputation of the Council, or its
        institutions. A felony in the line of duty includes a
        number of misdemeanors or frequent recurrence of
        misdemeanors in the line of duty that give rise to
        especially grave consequences.[38]

From the beginning, the Jews regarded the Judenrat
as a legitimate successor to the kehilla, and in according
it their social validation, treated it with the same
mixture of grudging consent and sardonic contempt
that had been reserved for the traditional kehilla. As
it became increasingly apparent that the Germans
permitted the Judenräte neither latitude nor autonomy,
the Jews relinquished their consent and sanction.
Though they could exercise no political action to remove the the Judenräte, the populace's disapproval
was seen in the general reluctance to obey Judenrat
orders, in the evasion of obligations imposed by the
Judenrat, and the expressions of contempt for the
Judenrat heard in all ghettos from rich and poor, from
intellectuals and masses.

The most common epithet everywhere for the
Judenrat was *Judenverrat*, "betrayal of the Jews,"
"Jewish fraud" for "Jewish board." A popular couplet
ran through the Warsaw ghetto:

> When the chairman is a nitwit,
> The whole kehilla is a shit.[39]

A jingle heard all over Warsaw, which even Czerniaków
himself knew, went:

> Prexy Czerniaków, the fat pot,
> Gets his chicken soup hot.
> How so? Just dough!
> Money is a dandy thing.

> Madam Czerniaków is sure to get her hair done,
> She takes her tea with sugar and bun.

How so? Just dough!
Money is a dandy thing.

A riddle: "What is the difference between Czerniaków and Rumkowski?" The answer: "No difference. Both stink."

Chaim Kaplan, on October 27, 1940, characterized Czerniaków as a "nincompoop among nincompoops" and his advisers as "musclemen." On May 23, 1942, Kaplan was more caustic: "After the Nazi leech comes the Judenrat leech. . . . There is no end to the tales of its mischief and abominations."

"The Judenrat lived loathsomely and still more loathsomely did it die," noted Kruk in his diary on December 22, 1941, commemorating the time when Gens had gained control over the ghetto administration. Soon after, the Vilna ghetto Jews used to refer derisively to Gens as "King Jacob the First." A JDC report from Lodz, September 24, 1940, declared that the tragic situation of the Jews was, paradoxically, aggravated by "a certain Mr. Rumkowski," who was "despised and hated by every inhabitant of the ghetto."

Mordecai Tenenbaum, commandant of the Jewish resistance organization in Bialystok, once noted that Barash was "a decent man." He went on to say: "That is a great compliment for a chairman of a Judenrat. I knew three such decent men: Engineer Czerniaków, Dr. Brawer [of Grodno], and Barash is the third."[40]

Eventually the authority of the Judenrat came to rest exclusively on the naked coercive power of the Germans, the only wielders of power in the ghettos. The authority that the Germans delegated to the Judenräte was often divided among board members; complete responsibility for the operations of each department was lodged with its head. The Judenrat chairman generally coordinated the work of the departments, settling jurisdictional disputes and arbitrating personal and departmental conflicts. Such decentralized operations characterized the Judenräte in Warsaw, Lublin, Cracow, Lwów, and Kovno, to name some of the largest cities. Interpersonal relations of the board members varied. In Kovno, for instance, most Judenrat officers coexisted in mutual respect. On the Lublin Judenrat, in contrast, quarrels, rivalries, distrust, and tension marked the relationships. In none of these Judenräte did any dynamic or creative leaders emerge.

Four Judenräte were marked by strong, even dictatorial, leadership, with authority centralized in the hands of one man—Rumkowski in Lodz, Merin in Sosnowiec and Upper East Silesia, Gens in Vilna, and Barash in Bialystok. They were the policy and decision makers in their ghettos, the strategical thinkers on the ghetto's possibilities for survival. All, without doubt, by holding these posts of leadership, satisfied personal ambitions. Barash alone, by virtue of his past experience as head of the prewar Bialystok community, elicited wide respect from his colleagues and from the Jewish community at large.* He did not manifest the craving for office and the trappings of office that characterized Rumkowski, Merin, and Gens; nor did he have their crude megalomania.[41]

Rumkowski, the most original of the four, ruled Lodz by force of personality, tenacity of purpose, organizational intelligence, and political shrewdness, even outwitting the SS in its attempt to displace him. His presence and authority were felt everywhere in the ghetto. Every initiative on the part of political parties or individuals that he approved of, he appropriated and made officially his own. Whatever he disapproved of withered and died. He was mocked and despised, yet there was no one in all Lodz to unseat him.

---

* Barash and Bialystok Jewry for a brief while profited from the fact that Bialystok was the capital of the General Commissariat Bialystok, a separate administrative entity under Erich Koch, Gauleiter for East Prussia, who actively disliked Himmler and his racial resettlement policies.

No legitimate social order functioned in the ghettos of Eastern Europe. As the Judenräte, increasingly coerced by German terror, ceased to be regarded as authentic spokesmen for the Jews in the ghettos, countervailing organizations came into being to challenge the Judenräte's authority. Some eventually formed an alternative community, others a counter-community.

12

The Alternative Community

Like the kehilla before it, the Judenrat was only one institution in the complex web of associations that knit the East European Jews together. Despite the attempts by the Germans to impose a state of barbarism upon them, the Jews persisted in maintaining or in re-creating their organized society and their culture. The milieu in which the Germans confined them was that state of war or condition of insecurity which Hobbes epitomized: "No arts; no letters; no society; and which is worst of all, continual fear, and danger of violent death; and the life of man, solitary, poor, nasty, brutish, and short." Nevertheless, in nearly all the ghettos, the Jews conspired against the Germans to provide themselves with arts, letters, and society—above all, with the protection of community against man's solitariness and brutishness. Never was human life suspended.

The crisscrossing mesh of institutions enveloped the ghetto. Some, like the *bes-medrésh* (prayer house) and the *heder* (religious school), were rooted in traditional society. Others, like social-welfare organizations, cultural associations, and ideological movements, grew out of modern, urban Jewish life. Unlike the Judenrat and the kehilla before it, these multitudinous organizations were autonomous and voluntary, existing on

the basis of the free and uncoerced will of their constituents.

In the ghetto, just as in prewar normal society, these
institutions composed four functional groupings: social
welfare/communal; religious/congregational; educa-
tional/cultural; political/defense. In prewar Jewish
society, the functional religious and political groupings
had served as parallel or countervailing channels of
authority to the kehilla. In ghetto society, the welfare,
religious, educational, and cultural groupings emerged
as the Judenrat's rivals or underground components.
Some of the political groupings eventually formed an
adversary community.

Besides their functional purposes, the voluntary
Jewish organizations fulfilled more fundamental, if less
tangible, Jewish needs, creating community, enhancing group solidarity and social cohesion, reinforcing
belongingness and self-esteem. Membership in an
organization extended the periphery of family and
kinship circles and entitled one to whatever resources
the group could muster and whatever security it could
provide. Above all, the organization upheld morale
and combated the depression and despair to which
solitary individuals succumbed when confronted with
the insurmountable difficulties of ghetto existence.

The dislocations of war gave rise to a new network
of autonomous Jewish self-help associations. They
grew out of Warsaw's civil-defense tenement committees, *Obrona Przeciwlotnicza* (OPL; antiaircraft
defense), whose original functions during the German
invasion were to oversee blackout practices, provide
civilian shelter, organize fire protection and fire fighting, and render first aid. In the larger tenements in
Jewish neighborhoods, improvised health, welfare, and
food-distribution centers were organized for the
bombed-out and the refugees. Hundreds of meals,
prepared by housewives in the building, were provided out of funds collected from tenants. At the start,
the tenement committes operated independently, but
they soon came under the aegis of a Coordinating

Commission, formed on September 14, 1939, at the initiative of the JDC, with the participation of the leading Jewish welfare organizations of prewar Poland —TOZ (*Towarzystwo Ochrony Zdrowia*—Society for the Preservation of Health), and CENTOS (*Centrala Towarzystwa nad Sierotami*—National Society for the Care of Orphans). The Coordinating Commission became affiliated with a Polish citywide self-help committee.[1]

These self-help units continued their activities after the fall of Warsaw and into the German occupation. In January 1940, when the Germans ordered the Polish group to sever its relations with the Coordinating Commission, the Jewish group became an independent body, calling itself *Żydowska Samopomoc Społeczna* (ŻSS; Jewish Communal Self-Help).[2] Accredited under the Generalgouvernement's Department of Interior, in the division of *Bevölkerungswesen und Fürsorge*, with bylaws approved May 29, 1940, the ŻSS—and parallel Polish and Ukrainian agencies—operated throughout the Generalgouvernement in all fields of social welfare, authorized to unite existing welfare agencies, and to make contact, through the German Red Cross, with foreign organizations providing money and supplies.

All through German-occupied Poland ŻSS branches came into being, many already operating spontaneously as skeletons of the prewar service agencies. Within a year, the ŻSS had 118 branches, 38 in large cities. By the beginning of 1942, it had 412 branches. ŻSS personnel was recruited from the recognized social-service agencies and other communal institutions. Its founder and head was Michal Weichert (1890–1967), a man of many talents, trained in law, the theater, and literature. A teacher in a Jewish gymnasium in Warsaw, he served as legal adviser to the JDC and ORT, and enjoyed a career as journalist, actor, and director before the war. In mid-1942 the Germans dissolved the ŻSS, but later reconstituted it as the *Jüdische Unterstützungsstelle* (JUS; Jewish Relief Office). Technically still under the Interior Department's jurisdiction, JUS in fact fell under SS control. The Jewish underground thereafter regarded JUS in the same light as the Judenräte. (After the war, Weichert was tried in Poland on charges of collaboration, but was exonerated. He spent the last years of his life in Israel.)

ŻSS's basic strategy was to rescue what could be rescued. Once, early on, the German officer who headed the Bevölkerungswesen und Fürsorge division asked Weichert: "Don't you realize that you are on a sinking ship?"

"I know," Weichert replied, "but I think that one must rescue people even from a sinking ship."

Since the ŻSS was accredited to the German civil administration, it had access to supplementary supplies of food, clothing, and medicine that were not available to the Judenräte. Quantities were small, to be sure, but in the economy of scarcity prevailing in the ghettos, even small amounts extracted from the Germans were beyond price. The very fact that the ŻSS received supplies from the Germans heightened the contrast in the Jewish public mind between the Judenrat and the ŻSS. As one ŻSS official put it, it appeared that the Judenräte took from the Jews to give to the Germans, whereas the ŻSS took from the Germans to give to the Jews.[3]

ŻSS funding came largely from the JDC, which spent about $1 million a year in Poland until America's entry into the war, on December 7, 1941, halted the legal transfer of funds. Some moneys were obtained by voluntary donations, fund-raising drives, theater and concert benefits. (In one community, the local ŻSS raised a substantial sum in October 1941 by selling the opportunity to bless the *etrog* in the celebration of Succot.) ŻSS funding came also from the Judenräte, some of which subcontracted part or most of their welfare programs to the ŻSS.

The ŻSS network for the most part engaged in supplementary relief, providing supplies and assistance in operating public kitchen and supplementary food stations for children and the sick. In Warsaw alone, there were 145 public kitchens and 45 children's kitchens, serving 135,000 meals daily. ŻSS branches distributed clothing, gave cash relief. Obtaining and dispensing pharmaceutical supplies were two of its major achievements. The ŻSS focused much effort on child-care activities. About one-fourth of the 1.6 million Jews in the Generalgouvernement were children, on whom, as one CENTOS official put it, "all our hopes rest, our future, our survival." In Warsaw alone, 75 percent of the 100,000 children under fifteen were estimated to require some form of welfare.[4] According to a ŻSS report for July–October 1941, there were in the Generalgouvernement 26 residential centers with 2,734 children; 61 children's corners with 9,565 children; 122 public kitchens and nutrition centers serving over 47,000 children; 2 infant-care institutions with 1,725 babies; and 15 day-care centers for 6,413 children. Of the 30 orphanages and boarding institutions that CENTOS operated under the ŻSS, the most renowned was Warsaw's *Dom Sierot* (Orphans Home), under the direction of Dr. Janusz Korczak, pediatrician and pedagogue extraordinary.[5]

Relations between ŻSS branches and Judenräte were in some instances close and cordial, but more often marked by tension and friction. The ŻSS on occasion tried to draw the Judenräte into its network, with a view to giving the Judenräte German contacts independent of the SS. The top ŻSS officers, whose headquarters were located in Cracow, arranged a conference there on March 27–28, 1940, at which a delegation of the Warsaw Judenrat met with the head of the Bevölkerungswesen und Fürsorge division. But the attempted strategy of providing the Judenräte with greater maneuverability failed simply because the SS declared all other German agencies out of bounds for the Judenräte.

At an annual regional ŻSS conference held in Chełm, January 25–26, 1942, the subject of relations between the Judenräte and the ŻSS unexpectedly surfaced in the discussions. The participants included top members of the regional ŻSS, local ŻSS delegates, local Judenräte delegates, and physicians attached to

public-health departments of both ŻSS and Judenräte.[6]
The agenda dealt with such matters as epidemic control, public sanitation, child care, relief for new
arrivals, food supply, and financing. Tensions between
the self-help agencies and the Judenräte emerged out
of the hidden agenda, when a delegate from the
Chełm ŻSS remarked on the antagonism characterizing those relationships. Such antagonism, he observed,
harmed the interests of the populace. As a model of
sincere cooperation, he pointed to Chełm, where the
Judenrat provided a permanent monthly subsidy for
the ŻSS. In closing the meeting, the delegate from ŻSS
headquarters asked the Judenräte to support the ŻSS:
"I call for understanding, help, collaboration," he said,
"for you are both institutions of the Jewish population
and you must complement each other."

In Warsaw, relations were impaired by friction.
There the ŻSS branch, called *Żydowskie Towarzystwo
Opieki Społecznej* (ŻTOS; Jewish Society for Social
Welfare), was in a continual state of opposition to the
Judenrat. ŻTOS differed from most ŻSS branches by
virtue of its position of national hegemony. Not only
did it comprise most of the original personnel of the
Coordinating Commission from which the ŻSS developed, but it collaborated closely with the remnants
of the prewar national welfare institutions: TOZ,
CENTOS, ORT, Toporol, and *Centrala Kass Bezpro-
centowych* (CEKABE; Clearing House of Free Loan
Associations). When the Germans later forbade their
independent existence, CENTOS became the child-
welfare department of ŻTOS, and TOZ its public-
health and sanitation department.

ŻTOS developed into a mammoth organization,
rivaling the Judenrat in scope of program and size of
staff. It operated departments for refugee care, public
kitchens and food distribution, housing, clothing,
health, youth, art and theater, and journalism. ŻTOS
also helped religious institutions, even though many
observant Jews operated their own welfare agencies:
kitchens for their refugee communities and for their
students in clandestine *yeshivot*. (A committee called

Ezrat Harabanim [aid to rabbis] helped rabbis and Talmudic scholars, especially by ransoming them from forced-labor duty.)[7] At its peak, ŻTOS employed about three thousand persons, most of them with a record of Jewish communal service. As in the Judenräte, favoritism and patronage inflated the staff with communal elites and party veterans.

In its first year, ŻTOS aided nearly 35,000 families, over 113,000 persons, then about 30 percent of Warsaw's Jewish population. With the ceaseless influx of refugees, another 15,000 were added to ŻTOS welfare rolls within three months. Refugees accounted for about one-third of all welfare recipients. They themselves formed a unique self-help network within ŻTOS. Some sixty *landsmanshaftn*, associations of fellow townsmen, representing localities from which the Jews had been expelled, constituted a central committee of refugees whose members were usually former Judenrat officials of the dissolved communities. Thus the refugees themselves assumed the tasks of aiding their own and representing their cause in the councils of both ŻTOS and Judenrat.[8]

The most pivotal institution within ŻTOS was the network of tenement committees, whose like existed in no other ghetto. Having sprouted originally as civil-defense committees, they were assiduously cultivated by Emanuel Ringelblum in his role as head of ŻTOS's *Sekcja Pracy Społecznej* (SPS; Section for Communal Work). Intending to use these *ad hoc* tenement committees at first as a source of financial support for ŻTOS, Ringelblum assigned the task of organizing them into one centralized network to former staff members of *Keren Kayemet* (Jewish National Fund), the major fund-raising organization for Palestine. Since most tenement committees restricted their welfare activities to their own buildings and tenants, the SPS organizers undertook to widen their commitments. Though the tenement-committee activities remained confined to their own buildings, they were eventually drawn into a community-wide program of welfare and charity.[9]

Up to April 1940, 778 tenement committees had been organized. By September 1940, just a month before the Jews were forced into the ghetto, the number had grown to 2,000 with a committee membership of about 10,000. (Committees had 3, 5, or 7 members, depending on the number of tenants in the building.) With ghettoization, the committees had to be reorganized, adding to their roster new tenants who before then had lived outside the limits of the ghetto. In January 1942, 1,108 tenement committees operated in 6 precincts in the Warsaw ghetto, with committee membership estimated at 7,500.

All tenants paid dues, the sum determined at a public meeting. Well-to-do tenants were assessed according to their means. Campaigns for funds and materials were constantly under way: clothing and furniture collections; entertainments, concerts, and dances to raise money; benefits of every variety from low vaudeville to high culture. Some people gave voluntary donations; some offered loans. Mary Berg noted on April 4, 1941, that in her building a special kettle of soup was cooked every Friday for the children's hospital. She also mentioned the popular "spoon" campaigns, for which tenants were asked to contribute a spoonful of flour or sugar toward a general collection. Even the poor participated in helping others still poorer. Those who had nothing to give offered their labor.

Accredited to ŻTOS, the tenement committees were the only licit grassroots organizations in the ghetto. They were permitted to hold meetings and to conduct their business openly. Each was a microcosm of community, involving young and old in its operations, as donors or receivers. Women prepared food for the needy; the well helped the sick. Young people, especially activists in the Zionist and Bundist movements, provided the manpower for the committee's daily tasks and special activities: caring for the children in *ad hoc* nurseries, kindergartens, and makeshift classrooms, making the rounds for the collections, selling tickets, organizing entertainments, warning the

tenants about the arrival of police or SS. A protective
bulwark for their tenants, these committees became, as
Ringelblum put it, the forge of opposition to the
Judenrat.

Observant Jews in the prewar community accounted
for half, perhaps even more, of East European Jewry
—the Soviet Union excepted. Even though secularity
was becoming the dominant mode, the norms and
values of traditional Judaism still shaped the behavior
of the whole Jewish population. The observance of
Judaism had permeated all public aspects of Jewish
life. Keeping the Sabbath as a day of rest and abstain-
ing from forbidden foods were observances adhered to
by nearly the entire Jewish community. Judaism was
practiced in thousands of formal and informal groups:
synagogues, houses of prayer and houses of study,
yeshivot and *hedarim*, ritual baths and ritual-slaughter
abattoirs, religious courts, congregational bodies,
women's organizations, publishing houses and presses.
The political spokesman for this profusion of institutions was the Aguda.

The Germans, denying that Jews were a religious
group, had rendered the entire public existence of the
observant community illegal. Not only were observant
Jews singled out for German sport and persecution,
not only were most synagogues destroyed or desecrated, but all functions pertaining to the observance
of Judaism were outlawed: public and/or private
worship, religious study and religious teaching, shehita.
The entire enterprise of traditional Judaism was forced
underground. To be sure, some Aguda leaders were
on the boards or staffs of the Judenräte; some were
connected with ŻSS and ŻTOS. In Warsaw, for instance, Rabbi Samson Stockhammer functioned in all
three communal structures: in the Judenrat he represented the Rabbinical Council, which operated
clandestinely; in the ŻTOS he represented the observant community with regard to its welfare needs; perhaps most important, he headed the underground
organization of the religious community. Zisha Fried-

man, too, a prewar Aguda leader, worked in the Warsaw Judenrat, in ŻTOS, and in the underground.[10] Actually, most leaders of the religious community functioned clandestinely.

All through Poland Jews prayed in secret. On August 12, 1940, on the eve of Tisha B'Av, the fast-day commemorating the destruction of the Temple, Chaim Kaplan noted: "Public prayer in these dangerous times is a forbidden act. Anyone caught in this crime is doomed to severe punishment. If you will, it is even sabotage and anyone engaging in sabotage is subject to execution." But Jews prayed in thousands of secret *minyanim*, some six hundred in Warsaw alone. They prayed in cellars, attics, back rooms, behind drawn blinds, with men on guard. In Cracow, services were held in two prayer houses thanks to the cooperation of Jewish policemen who worshiped there and who warned the congregation when German police were to be expected.

In Lodz, public prayer was permitted in 1940. In Riga the Jews who had been deported from Germany were allowed to conduct public services, but the native Jews were prohibited. In Kovno and Vilna, public services were tolerated. On March 4, 1941, Frank issued a decree affecting the Generalgouvernement, permitting religious services to be held in private homes, synagogues, and prayer houses in observance of the Sabbath, the High Holy Days, and the three major festivals of Passover, Shevuot, and Succot. In practice, however, since German officials arbitrarily forbade worship or subjected the assembled Jews to humiliation and terror, most Jews continued to pray in seclusion.

Prayer took on new solemnity and urgency, with special petitionary prayers augmenting the regular service. In the Kovno ghetto it became customary after the morning and afternoon prayers to recite Psalms 130 ("Out of the depths have I called Thee, O Lord") and 142 ("With my voice I cry unto the Lord"). Also the petitionary and penitential prayers of the *Tahanun*, reserved normally for Mondays, Thursdays, and fast-days, used to be recited daily. Composed for the most part during the Crusades, these prayers now expressed a tragic immediacy. They were uttered to the accompaniment of weeping and lamentation, especially at the *"Shomer Yisrael"*: O Guardian of Israel, guard the remnant of Israel, and suffer not Israel to perish." Everywhere the rabbis called to penitence and prayer, since Jewish tradition regards these as indispensable for the redemption of all Israel.[11]

The calamitous march of events shook many pious Jews from their traditional moorings. Some rebelled. In one Warsaw congregation, the news that the Jews would be confined in a ghetto arrived just as the cantor was about to start *Neilah,* the closing service of Yom Kippur, when Jews pray importunately for salvation before the heavenly gates of mercy are closed. At once the cantor halted the service, saying that there was no point in praying when the gates of mercy were already locked. That was apparently no isolated incident, for Hillel Zeitlin (1872–1942), journalist, writer, philosopher, one of religious Jewry's charismatic leaders, admitted in 1941: "Characteristic is the rebellion against God, against Heaven, which is noticeable among many religious Jews who no longer wish to declare God's Judgment right."[12] A less severe judgment of the ghetto's religious moods was rendered at the same time by an unidentified communal leader: "The truly pious have become even more pious, for they understand and see God's Hand in everything. The unbelievers, in contrast, have become even more unbelieving. The vacillating, however, have taken to rebelling against God, conducting war against Him, spiting Heaven. These are the seemingly pious Jews who have suddenly begun eating pork and lard."[13]

Most observance of kashrut lapsed except among the exceptionally devout. Not only was shehita forbidden, but any sort of meat was seldom to be had in the ghettos. In the Vilna ghetto, four *shohatim* used to join up covertly with forced-labor brigades working outside the ghetto. With their ritual slaughtering knives concealed on their persons, they had clandestine contacts where they could slaughter poultry according to ritual. Then they risked getting back into the ghetto with their kosher contraband. In the Lodz ghetto only horsemeat was obtainable. Most observant Jews, driven by hunger, ate it, though it was not a permitted food. On February 23, 1941, during the great hunger, the rabbis in the Lodz ghetto ruled under the authority of the doctrine of *pikuakh nefesh* (saving an endangered life) that the consumption of nonkosher meat was permitted for pregnant women and persons in poor health.

In the Kovno ghetto the only food Jews in forced-labor brigades received for the whole day was soup made with horsemeat. Devout Jews abstained from eating it, but at least one rabbi ruled permissively for the sake of pikuakh nefesh. An observant Jew in the Warsaw ghetto once tried to explain to the director of a public kitchen that his heartache at transgressing kashrut would impair his health far more than the loss to his organism of a few grams of nonkosher food. For most observant Jews the suspension of kashrut was no easy accommodation. A sense of guilt and self-denigration pursued those who yielded to the demands of their hunger. For every mouthful of ritually impure food they consumed, devout Jews vowed that in the future, when they would once again be free to follow the Law as commanded by God, they would make up for their present transgressions.[14]

Observing kashrut during Passover was a formidable undertaking. The Germans grudgingly gave permission to bake matzot, but never in sufficient supply. In most ghettos pious Jews baked matzot illegally. One kilogram of matzo cost as much as 6 kilograms of bread in Vilna in 1943; yet, noted Herman Kruk, no household was without matzo. In Lodz in 1941 the 10-day ration allowed 2½ kilograms of matzo, whereas the bread ration was more generous. Some households, seeking to accommodate the observance of Passover to the prevailing hunger, compromised and took both bread and matzo rations. Beet juice, sweetened with saccharin, substituted for the seder's sacramental wine. "The only thing we had aplenty," commented one Jew, "was bitter herbs—not on the table, but in our hearts."

Like kashrut, the Sabbath was nearly impossible to observe. In Lodz, Warsaw, Vilna, and Kovno, the Sabbath was a permitted day of rest for brief periods or in certain communal institutions, but for the most part the Germans, with deliberate sadism, forced the Jews to work on Saturdays and the High Holy Days. When the Germans first entered Lodz, they compelled the rabbis to issue a ruling permitting Jewish shops to stay open on the Sabbath and Jewish festivals.[15] In Vilna the rabbis permitted Jews to work on the Sabbath, Yom Kippur, and other festivals for the sake of pikuakh nefesh. But they counseled Jews not to work if their lives would not be endangered by such a refusal. In the Kovno ghetto, pious Jews sought assignment in labor brigades that did not work on the Sabbath, even though that entailed forfeiting extra food rations or a chance for less strenuous or unpleasant work.[16]

After the Germans had forbidden ritual baths (*mikvaot*), rabbis in the Vilna ghetto ruled against performing weddings, since the brides could not take the prescribed bath. In Lodz, however, the rabbis gave permission, because weddings were often for the sake of pikuakh nefesh, when a woman without a work permit married a man who had one, and was thus exempted from deportation. In Warsaw the ritual baths were sealed and boarded up, but occasionally were used secretly. In 1940 a hasidic rebbe decided that he and his followers must immerse themselves in the ritual bath before Yom Kippur. Negotiations were conducted with the mikva's owner and it was agreed that at 5:00 A.M., when curfew ended, the mikva would be made accessible for one hour through a secret entry. The expedition, wrote a participant, "summons up for us a living picture of our ancestors in Spain during the Inquisition. . . . They surely never imagined that their descendants 400 years later would find themselves in a far worse situation . . . and would reenact the same procedures that they themselves had experienced."[17]

Hundreds of secret yeshivot and houses of study came into being in the Generalgouvernement and the occupied eastern territories. Warsaw's prewar yeshiva population of five thousand was greatly diminished by death and flight. Some boys abandoned religious study because they had to go to work, others because they succumbed to disbelief. In the Warsaw ghetto, some two hundred yeshiva students "learned" in at least eleven yeshivot. Most yeshiva students had no legal existence in the ghettos, since they were not registered with the Judenrat, and so were relieved of the onus of forced labor. But that meant that they had no ration cards. Some well-to-do families supplied they with food in quantity, as did some welfare agencies. Students took turns begging on the streets or soliciting food and money among people of means. A yeshiva student, found murdered in the Vilna ghetto in June 1942, had likely been buying food illicitly for the yeshiva from underworld persons with illegal stocks and may have inadvertently witnessed criminal dealings. Some people in the observant community did not approve of the clandestine yeshivot, for they felt that the students were separating themselves from the community and evading their responsibilities. But others believed, according to a venerable Jewish tradition, that by studying the Torah these yeshiva students were performing the most urgent and efficacious function of any in the ghettos to ensure the salvation of the Jews.[18]

When the Germans entered Poland, they closed down the Jewish schools and requisitioned their property. They further ordered the public schools to exclude all Jewish pupils. The Germans intended to deprive Jewish children of education, but they underestimated the place of education in the system of Jewish values. "And thou shalt teach them the statutes and the laws and shalt show them the way wherein they must walk." The survival of Jews and Judaism depended on the uninterrupted transmittal of the tradition from generation to generation. Within a half-year after the German invasion, some 180 underground hedarim and Talmud Torahs, with about 2,000 pupils, functioned in Warsaw. In Kovno, Vilna, Lublin, Lodz, and Cracow thousands of children received traditional instruction in Judaism privately or in secret schools.

General education, too, was a major commitment of the modern secular Jew, as the vehicle for upward mobility and achievement. Faced with the unprecedented wholesale proscription by the Germans of the entire Jewish educational enterprise, the pedagogic apparatus of the Jewish community rallied to thwart and outwit the Germans. All over Poland underground schools came into being. In Warsaw, with some 40,000 Jewish children between seven and fourteen, hundreds of informal classes of about 10 children each were organized, each group called a *komplet,* the Polish word to describe pupils studying together outside a formal classroom. These *komplety,* set up in public kitchens and private homes, were operated by CENTOS and the prewar Jewish school organizations, and were staffed by the teachers of the prewar schools. Meanwhile, in each community, the teachers, principals, and school administrators were pressing the Judenräte to get permission from the Germans to operate schools legally. (The ŻSS, too, intervened on behalf of the schools.)

In Warsaw, representatives of the diverse Jewish school networks, ranging from the traditionalist to the Zionist Hebraist and socialist Yiddishist, along with representatives of the Jewish teachers in the prewar Polish public schools, jointly formed a coordinating committee, despite their past competitiveness. This committee constituted the major pressure group exerting influence on the Judenrat for the legal reestablishment of the schools. Their status reinforced their cause. Eventually, when the Germans granted permission to reopen the schools, this coordinating committee assumed the responsibility for the educational curricula. It continued to represent and protect its professional interests vis-à-vis the Judenrat. The komplety that each organization operated became the nuclei of the official schools.[19]

Clandestine komplety flourished all over Poland. In Lublin, where about one hundred teachers staffed such groups, one komplet met in a basement shoemaker's shop, behind a makeshift partition. When a warning was given that Germans were about, the classroom disappeared. Books and papers were hidden, the partition removed, the children dispersed, and the teacher, one shoe off, became the shoemaker's customer.[20] Chaim Kaplan, a long-time Hebrew teacher, who organized komplety in his own home, described in his diary on February 15, 1941, the conditions of Jewish education under German barbarism:

> Jewish children learn in secret. In back rooms, on long benches near a table, little schoolchildren sit and learn what it's like to be Marranos. . . . In time of danger the children learn to hide their books. Jewish children are clever—when they set off to acquire forbidden learning, they hide their books and notebooks between their trousers and their stomachs, then button their jackets and coats.

The komplety attracted a relatively small proportion of the whole Jewish school-age population, but the pupils, especially those on the secondary level, responded with great seriousness to instruction. (Two underground Hebrew secondary schools functioned in the Warsaw ghetto.) "In prewar times we had never witnessed such studiousness as the pupils demonstrated in these komplety," wrote one teacher. "They went after their studies with zest, wanting to finish in one year a course of two or more years. No more dilly-dallying, no more excuses. They asked the teachers for more work."[21]

On August 31, 1940, Frank finally issued a decree giving the Judenräte in the Generalgouvernement the responsibility to provide elementary and vocational schools for the Jewish population. The Judenräte were also to train and prepare teachers.[22] Secondary and higher education were forbidden. But the decree was arbitrarily applied. German authorities in Warsaw, for instance, refused permission to open Jewish schools on the pretext that typhus would spread. In April, permission was finally given, on a highly restrictive basis; the schools did not begin to operate legally until October 1941.

In Lodz and Vilna the school systems operated under the aegis of the Judenrat, with a standard curriculum and Yiddish as the official language of instruction. (Polish was often the *de facto* language of instruction.) In the Lodz ghetto the schools existed barely two years, from May 1940 until 1942, and at their peak enrolled about 10,000 children in 45 schools. The Vilna ghetto maintained several elementary schools and a secondary school, with an enrollment of 2,000. Separate religious schools were operated under Orthodox auspices in both Lodz and Vilna.

In Warsaw 6 schools were opened in October 1941. Enrollments continued to increase. At the end of the school year, in June 1942, there were 19 schools with nearly 7,000 children. Most schools had 4 grades; some had 5 grades. The language of instruction was Yiddish, Hebrew, or Polish, though the last was officially forbidden. The curriculum included reading, writing, arithmetic, botany, Bible and Judaism, arts and crafts, and physical education. The Germans forbade the Jewish schools to teach history and geography, but Jewish history and the geography of Palestine were taught. Textbooks were seldom available and, if they were, hardly appropriate to the realities of the ghetto.

The secondary-school curriculum in Vilna included Yiddish, Hebrew, Jewish and general history, geography, biology, physics, mathematics, Latin, German (forbidden by the Germans), and drawing.[23]

Vocational courses in Warsaw alone attracted nearly four thousand students in the period from September 1940 to May 1941.[24] The trades for which training was offered in all cities—Warsaw, Kovno, Vilna, Lodz, Bialystok—included locksmithing, auto mechanics, electromechanics, optical tooling, turning and carpentry, drafting, dyeing, besides the familiar Jewish trades. In Warsaw and Kovno, vocational courses, besides giving the ghetto residents a chance to learn a trade that would give them some security, also provided a cover for forbidden higher education in some fields—nursing, pharmacy, chemistry, even some medical training, though, as Dr. Milejkowski pointed out, high quality could not be expected from such an undertaking.

Like the Jewish schools in Germany after 1933, the ghetto schools, legal or underground, formed a subcommunity of love and dedication that provided the ghetto children with shelter, physical warmth, medical and sanitary care, food, and emotional security. The ghetto schools erected walls against ghetto harshness and ugliness, and became tiny oases of joy and creativity in the bleak ghettos. Saturday, October 17, 1942, Yitzhok Rudashevski noted, was a boring day because there was no school: "I think to myself: what would be the case if we did not go to school, to the club, did not read books. We would die of dejection inside the ghetto walls."

The ghetto schools imparted a sense of Jewish identity, and by concentrating on Jewish subjects of study, reinforced Jewish solidarity. The world of Jewish culture and tradition helped to sustain them. The children learned to play, to sing, dance, and act. The schools themselves became bracing cultural centers for the whole ghetto. Dramatic, choral, and musical performances by schoolchildren, which proved particularly popular, were produced to raise funds for social-welfare programs, particularly on behalf of CENTOS. The sight and sound of the assembled children, neatly dressed, reciting poetry or singing songs in their appealingly childish voices, heartened the ghetto populace. These children, guarantors of survival beyond the ghetto, engendered high morale. In the summer of 1941 the Hebraist schools in Warsaw presented a dramatized version of Yitzhak Lamdan's classic narrative poem, "Masada." One could see, wrote the headmaster of a Hebrew school, not just the Masada of the past, but the resurrection of Masada's spirit in the Warsaw ghetto.[25]

In Vilna the literary circle of high-school students, under the direction of the young Yiddish poet Abram Sutzkever, prepared an exhibit and a public festival to commemorate Yehoash, Yiddish poet and translator of the Bible into Yiddish. The materials for the exhibit were smuggled into the ghetto from the Yiddish Scientific Institute (YIVO), where Zelig Kalmanovich, Sutzkever, and a task force of intellectuals worked, sorting the library of this famous research institute for the Germans. The Yehoash exhibit, which opened on March 14, 1943, young Rudashevski noted, was exceptionally beautiful. Visitors forgot that they were in a gloomy ghetto. The festival itself, wrote Rudashevski, was produced in a grand manner, in a mood of exaltation. On April 6, 1943, Sutzkever completed a poem, "Yehoash," about the undertaking:

> Death itself shrinks before this beauty.
> And drives back again
> His grimy smoking cauldron.[26]

Like bread and potatoes, education and culture sustained life in the ghetto. The ghetto's tastes in recreation ranged from low to high culture. Even before the ghetto, the conditions of curfew mothered new forms of recreation. Since people were forbidden to be out on the streets from 7:00 P.M. until 5:00 the following morning, those who lived in the same building or in adjoining buildings with a common courtyard used to visit one another, passing the long evening and night as best they could. Close friends often came to spend the night. Card playing, always a popular Jewish pastime, became still more popular. (Later, card players used to contribute a portion of the kitty to the local tenement committee.) One party of well-to-do card players devised the idea of a spot of entertainment as a break in the long-run card game. On November 8, 1939, they invited a popular Warsaw singing comedian to entertain them, having raised a large enough sum for his fee. They even set up a cloakroom and a refreshment bar. The idea spread to other buildings; the demand for entertainers grew so rapidly that impresarios could make a living by handling artists' bookings and fees.[27] Entertainers were in demand also in the mushrooming cafés and restaurants that catered to the ghetto *arrivistes* and underworld. The demand, in fact, surpassed the supply: amateurs were soon competing with professionals. The entertainment in private homes, cafés, and soon also in public kitchens consisted of variety acts, comic patter, song-and-dance routines, farce or satire on ghetto bureaucracy, and buffoonish or melodramatic one-acters. However poor the talent and trashy the content, this improvised entertainment heightened ghetto morale simply by releasing the audiences for a brief span from their day-to-day anxieties and transporting them into a more cheerful existence of prewar normality, even if tawdry or vulgar. For thousands of ghetto residents this entertainment was likely the first theatrical performance they had ever attended.

Warsaw's communal leaders, deploring the low culture of this burgeoning entertainment industry, organized in September 1940 a committee within ŻTOS whose dual function was to raise the cultural level of theatrical productions and to organize the nearly 500 actors, musicians, dancers, and artists in the ghetto, helping them find employment. ŻTOS thus obtained a percentage of the gate receipts for its welfare programs. In the first year of its existence the ŻTOS entertainment committee put on 1,814 programs, which yielded 32,500 zlotys in fees for the artists, over 30,000 zlotys for ŻTOS, apart from the funds that went directly to TOZ, CENTOS, and other institutions.

Eventually five theaters operated in the Warsaw ghetto, two performing in Yiddish and three in Polish, sometimes presenting serious drama, but more often

comedies and revues. Theaters operated also in Lodz
and Vilna. (In Vilna a large segment of the ghetto
populace disapproved. Their slogan was: "A graveyard
is no place for entertainment.")

In December 1940 a clandestine organization was
formed by Warsaw's Yiddishist elite to raise cultural
standards and also to elevate the status of Yiddish.
The presence of the converts in the ghetto was adduced as a cause for the apparent escalating preference
for Polish and the abandonment of Yiddish. Called
Yidishe kultur-organizatsye (YIKOR; Yiddish Cultural
Organization), the new group engaged in propaganda
on behalf of Yiddish, demanding that the Judenrat
use Yiddish officially, in addition to Polish and German. A pilot program to use Yiddish all the time was
set up by one tenement committee. The tenement
committees generally became the operational centers
for YIKOR activities. Nearly a hundred public meetings commemorating the Yiddish literary classicists
Mendele, Peretz, and Sholom Aleichem were held in
the larger buildings. YIKOR also set up series of well-
attended scholarly lectures and courses in Yiddish.[28]

Tekumah (revival), a Hebraist cultural organization,
was formed as an ideological counterforce to YIKOR,
though no real animosity between the two groups
existed. Tekumah served the interests of the Zionists
and Hebraists. One of its most impressive programs
celebrated Judah Halevi, twelfth-century Hebrew
poet and philosopher of Spain, some of whose poems
were read by Jacques Lewy, the Yiddish actor and
friend of Kafka. The main speaker, one of Tekumah's
most active lecturers, was Dr. Edmund Stein, rabbi,
historian, and outstanding Semitologist, president of
Warsaw's Institute of Judaic Studies. Stein himself
tried to maintain the highest levels of scholarship in
the ghetto. He lectured in a ghetto cellar for former
students of the institute on Socrates, Aristotle, Maimonides, and Saadia Gaon.[29]

The large ghettos had music too. Warsaw, Lodz,
Vilna, and Kovno had orchestras. The Lodz ghetto

symphony orchestra consisted of twenty-five professional players and ten amateurs. The Kovno ghetto
orchestra also had thirty-five players. (Strings, naturally, dominated.) Performances were given at least
once a week, sometimes more frequently. Forbidden
to play German music, Jewish musicians concentrated
on Mendelssohn, Meyerbeer, Halévy, Offenbach, and
the wide range of Yiddish and Hebrew art songs and
folksongs. In Vilna, where the Germans seemed less
interested in the ghetto repertoire, a largely amateur
orchestra at one concert performed Beethoven's
Leonore Overture No. 3, Chopin's piano concerto in E
minor, and Tchaikovsky's Fifth Symphony. The Kovno
ghetto had a mandolin orchestra, the Warsaw ghetto
several string quartets. Most ghettos had adult choral
groups, some affiliated with the political movements,
and children's choruses, organized in the schools.

The Kovno ghetto concert hall was in the renowned
yeshiva of Slobodka, whose buildings the Germans had
sequestered in 1941, used for shooting stray dogs, and
then abandoned. The ghetto police and workers
cleaned the premises and converted it into a small
concert hall. The first concert was held in August
1942, and as the orchestra's first strains wafted through
the halls, players and listeners alike wept. Their tragic
plight had not affected their ability to produce
music.[30]

A Viennese journalist, deported to Lodz, described
the audience at concerts in the House of Culture,
Rumkowski's gift to the ghetto. They have, he noted,
their favorite composers and favorite numbers. They
respond to Il Trovatore, Pagliacci, Rigoletto, Madama
Butterfly with smiling recognition and after the concert hum the melodies. "In this respect the ghetto
audience is not at all different from the frequenters of
European concert houses."[31]

In Warsaw, after the Germans shut down institutional libraries and bookstores, underground libraries
came into existence, with books circulated by courier
librarians. Halina Szwambaum was one: "In the

mornings, until 1 P.M., I am the 'lady from the library,' since people come to see me; between 1 P.M. and 9 P.M., I am the 'girl from the library,' since I run around town." Running around town meant going "to different apartments, up and down many flights of stairs, with a heavy briefcase."

In Częstochowa, where the Jewish Labor Bund had maintained a communal library of 20,000 volumes, the whole collection was secretly transferred in two days to a private home. That collection then became a secret library, serving more than 1,000 readers.[32]

In Lodz only one library was permitted to operate officially, with some 7,500 books and 4,000 subscribers. Several small circulating libraries functioned illicitly for a while. The German Jews maintained their own libraries; several political parties operated clandestine circulating libraries.

In the Vilna ghetto the *Mefitse haskalah* library was operated as the ghetto library by the Judenrat's Culture Department. Augmented by ownerless private collections, it had nearly 100,000 books and a peak membership in August 1942 of nearly 4,000 subscribers, almost a third of the ghetto population. The library circulated books (13,500 during March 1943), maintained a reading room (an average of 206 readers daily during March 1943), and also collected ghetto archival and folklore material.[33] On December 13, 1942, the library celebrated the circulation of the hundred-thousandth book with a program of speeches and music. Herman Kruk, the library's director, delivered a paper on ghetto reading and readers. Kalmanovich noted, no doubt from Kruk's statistics displayed in charts and diagrams on the platform, that 70.4 percent of the books read were Polish, 17.6 percent Yiddish, 2 percent Hebrew, the rest Russian and other languages.[34]

Besides the vast demand for narcotic literature—detective and adventure stories—fiction was most widely read. The most popular Polish novelists were Bolesław Prus, Henryk Sienkiewicz, Stefan Żeromski,

Andrzej Strug, and Eliza Orzeszkowa. The most widely read Yiddish writers were Y. L. Peretz and Sholem Asch; among Russian writers, Boris Pilniak, Ilya Ehrenburg, Maxim Gorki, and Mark Aldanov. The German Jews were more likely to read history and philosophy, but they read also Heine, Lion Feuchtwanger, and Emil Ludwig.[35] Observant Jews, too unlearned to study Talmud, turned to popular devotional literature. Lodz book dealers did a thriving business in such books, which, because of their sacred character, could not be used as waste. One of the most popular works in all ghettos was *En Yaakov*, a sixteenth-century collection of the haggadic material from the Talmud, systematically classified, which by the late nineteenth century had gone through some thirty editions. The other was *Hok le-yisroel*, a compendium of extracts from the Bible, Talmud, Zohar, and other sacred works, arranged for daily reading and study, also popular among the unlearned.[36]

The serious Jewish reader, Ringelblum noted on June 25, 1942, was fascinated by war writings: "People particularly enjoy descriptions of the year 1918 and the downfall of the Germans." The ghetto Jews read about Napoleon, delighting in accounts of the march on Moscow. For the same reason, Ringelblum remarked, Tolstoy's *War and Peace* was enormously popular in the ghetto. "In a word, being unable to take revenge on the enemy in reality, we are seeking it in fantasy, in literature."

Well-to-do women who borrowed books from the Vilna ghetto library devoured endless series of sentimental Russian novels. Schoolchildren requested Jules Verne's *The Tour of the World in Eighty Days* and Mark Twain's *The Prince and the Pauper* in Yiddish translations. Working people, who used the library in the evening, members of Zionist youth organizations, and refugees from Warsaw read novels with social content—for instance, Upton Sinclair and Theodore Dreiser, Ignazio Silone's *Bread and Wine*, Feuchtwanger's *The Jewish Wars*. Extremely popular was Franz Werfel's *Forty Days of Musa Dagh*, the novel about the annihilation of the Armenians by the Turks, which Werfel wrote in 1932.[37]

Reading was not only narcotic and escape, but also a discipline of mind, an attempt to retain the habits of a civilized existence. Reading about past wars and catastrophes involving other peoples and nations universalized the Jewish experience and transcended the misery within the ghetto walls.

At Emanuel Ringelblum's initiative and under his direction, a secret Jewish archive was established under the code name *Oneg Shabbat* (Pleasures of the Sabbath). Its purpose, as Ringelblum described it in his letter of May 20, 1944, was to gather "materials and documents relating to the martyrology of the Jews in Poland."[38] A large staff worked systematically to this end, stimulating the production of diaries, chronicles, all sorts of descriptive and analytic writings on every phase of Jewish life under German occupation—political, religious, economic, cultural. Photographs, posters, announcements, official reports, ghetto wit and humor, statistics—all became valuable documentation for Oneg Shabbat.*

In Lodz, Vilna, and Bialystok, too, groups of writers, intellectuals, and communal leaders gathered and prepared materials to document the Jewish experience under German rule. The idea of preserving a record for history and posterity inspired hundreds, perhaps thousands of Jews in the ghettos of Eastern Europe to keep diaries or accounts of their beleaguered existence. The diary became an expression of the will to live, the vehicle through which posthumousness, a modest form of immortality, would be conferred on them.

In his essay on the ghetto, Kalmanovich referred to the ghetto's social, educational, and cultural institutions as "the clear victory of spirit over matter." For the time that the ghetto Jews managed to cling to

---

* Much of the assembled material was buried in crates in the ghetto and uncovered after the war. Originals of the exhumed materials are in the Żydowski Instytut Historyczny in Warsaw; Yad Vashem in Jerusalem has copies of a great deal. Some material is also at the YIVO Archives in New York.

familiar cultural terrain, they triumphed over the Germans. The strategy of the communal leadership in the functional welfare, religious, educational, and cultural groupings was to hold back the tide of barbarism and create islands of civilization, normality, and decency. Operating under terror, amid hunger and disease, they succeeded in helping those they reached to retain and enrich their humanity.

13

The Countercommunity:
The Political Underground

"Real politics," Disraeli wrote, "are the possession and distribution of power." By that token the Jews in prewar Eastern Europe seldom engaged in real politics, for political power was not theirs to exercise or bestow. Jewish politics were both symbolic and visionary, with morality and messianism substituting for political and economic power. A minority fragmented by internal social, economic, and religious differences, the Jews through their political parties sought to win not power for themselves, but legitimacy as citizens of the states in which they lived. These parties fought for the equality and the rights denied to Jews, and through that political struggle instilled self-esteem in the Jew and inculcated respect for the Jew in the mind of the non-Jew. The Jewish parties defended the rights of Jews to work, to study, to pursue their own national culture, to be secure against defamation and violence. Jewish politics thus became more a matter of honor and dignity than the possession or distribution of power.

These Jewish parties, from the Aguda on the right to the Bund on the left, were not just political parties competing for office and political power. They were also ideological movements, seeking adherents and

believers. In the style of the political/ideological
movements of Central Europe, the Jewish parties
maintained dense networks of institutions and services
that provided for the members' needs and interests
from cradle to grave—kindergartens, schools, youth
groups, women's associations, charitable and loan
societies, cultural groups, medical care, and burial
services. They published daily newspapers, periodicals,
and books.

The German and Soviet invasions of Poland and
the Baltic countries in 1939 shattered this complex
political establishment. Jewish political leadership
became even more disabled than communal leadership.
Veteran party leaders fled the oncoming Germans.
Nazi and Communist police alike searched out Jewish
party leaders, arrested them, and then killed them.
The most notable instances under the Soviets were the
arrest and murder of the two Bundist leaders Henryk
Erlich and Viktor Alter.[1] In German-occupied Poland,
the Gestapo, armed with lists of Socialist councilmen
and deputies, rounded up dozens of political activists,
sometimes incarcerating them in concentration camps,
more often killing them right off.[2]

Flight, arrest, and murder depleted Jewish political
leadership from the start of the occupation, leaving
the parties for the most part in the hands of second-
and third-echelon activists. In the absence of party
veterans, of mature and experienced leaders, young
people in the parties began to move forward and make
their presence felt. In a short time the conflict between
youth and age in the Jewish parties would become
critical.

The political parties were outlawed. The parapolitical institutions and personnel of all parties provided
the infrastructure for the ghetto's alternative community, the refashioned functional groupings in welfare, religious observance, education, and culture,
which operated in the shadow of legality. Since the
parties could exist only clandestinely, the two great
parties of prewar Polish Jewry, the Aguda and the

General Zionists, as well as small parties like the Mizrachi, Folkists, and Revisionists, disintegrated as political entities. The Aguda leaders and masses, whose habitual prewar strategy had been political compliance in exchange for the unhindered observance of Judaism, now became engaged in a mass sacrificial endeavor to observe Judaism and to maintain the functional religious groups in the Jewish community. Their party apparatus totally collapsed.

As for the General Zionists, many of their ranking leaders were in the Judenräte, while their activists helped to sustain the functional educational and cultural groups. The substantial number of General Zionists in the Judenräte militated against their maintaining the party as an underground movement. For one thing, their energies were exhausted in the daily burdens of office. For another, they could never have reconciled the contradictory loyalties that such an arrangement would have demanded. In the General-gouvernement, the presence of the General Zionist movement in the Jewish political underground was upheld almost singlehandedly by Menahem Kirschenbaum, a member of the party's prewar central committee, who in the Warsaw ghetto held a top post in ŻTOS and operated from that vantage point.[3]

Only the left-wing parties and the socialist Zionist youth movements succeeded in maintaining their primary political character and in transforming their prewar apparatus—or its remnants—into functioning underground organizations. The largest of these was the Jewish Labor Bund, which in the 1930s had emerged as the major political Jewish organization on the municipal level and which controlled most of the Jewish trade unions. The Jewish section of the Communist party had been second in numerical strength before 1939, having commanded a substantial segment of Jewish support, controlling several trade unions and active fractions of some others. The Ribbentrop-Molotov agreements of August 1939 sharply diminished the party's following, but after Germany invaded

Russia in June 1941, Communist activity was revived under Soviet instructions. In early 1942 the *Polska Partia Robotnicza* (PPR; Polish Workers' Party), the Communist party in a new guise, made its appearance in the Generalgouvernement. Smaller and weaker than the Communists were the Labor Zionists, split into left and right wings. The larger party, the Left Labor Zionists, had fractions in several unions, though not controlling any. The Right Labor Zionists constituted the smallest of the left parties, their influence concentrated in Upper East Silesia.

The socialist Zionist youth movements included *Dror*, associated with the Labor Zionists; *Hashomer Hatzair*, whose pro-Sovietism brought it ideologically close to the Left Labor Zionists; *Hehalutz*, federation of Zionist pioneering (*halutz*) organizations; *Gordonia*, associated with *Hitachdut*, a Labor Zionist affiliate. Other halutz organizations were eventually accommodated within the leftist halutz sphere.

Despite sharp political differences with one another, these parties and organizations shared traits that gave them the viability for underground operation that the other parties lacked. They all had long cultivated attitudes and habits of challenge, defiance, and resistance of political authority. Under Poland's reactionary regime, they had learned how to cope with censorship and suppression and how to survive politically in opposition. That experience would serve them well. Furthermore, in normal times, the movement's ideology provided its members with profound satisfaction and confidence, for the party ideology postulated a world view that promised to solve all problems and bring an end to suffering and injustice. Under German occupation, party ideology was to become a gospel of salvation, the promise of survival. For the hard-core membership, the party insiders, the *aktiv*, as they were called, the movement was all, the surrogate for family and kinship. The left parties generated a mystique of fraternity that lifted each individual out of his narrow confines and linked him to a universal community of

brotherhood. The secular messianic vision of the left—
"We have been naught, we shall be all"—continued to
inspire its adherents, even in the bleakness of the
ghetto, with the radiant promise of the future.

Most parties maintained a visible, half-legal organizational identity in the web of public kitchens,
whose management in Warsaw, Lodz, and elsewhere,
was often assigned by the ŻSS or Judenrat, according
to party key.[4] These party kitchens, some located on
their former premises, functioned as meeting places
where members shared food, information, and com-
panionship. There the organization persisted, as movement rather than as party, for people did not congre-
gate for instrumental purposes, but were propelled by
their emotional attachment to the movement, by their
ties to the past and their traditions, by their convic-
tions about the luminous truth of the movement and its
goals.

Though an estimated two thousand members of
halutz groups in Poland had fled to Vilna in the fall of
1939, a few thousand still remained in the Generalgouvernement. Most managed to retain their *kibbutzim*, the training farms where they used to prepare
for aliya to Palestine. Kibbutzim operated in the suburbs of Warsaw, in Zagłębia, in Kielce, Lublin, Radom,
Hrubieszów, and Częstochowa. With Rumkowski's
cooperation, some twenty kibbutzim were established
in Lodz, with nearly a thousand members. In the kibbutzim the young Zionists engaged in agricultural
work and Zionist self-education. The members of the
kibbutzim were on the way to becoming elitists, having
distanced themselves from the teeming ghettos and
the masses of Jews. But by late 1941, when the Germans had ordered some kibbutzim closed, and when
Rumkowski and Merin, viewing the kibbutzim sus-
piciously, had withdrawn financial assistance, the
Zionist youth returned to the ghettos. There they confronted a vacuum in Zionist politics, for except for the
Left Labor Zionist movement in Warsaw and Często-

chowa and the Zionist public kitchens, no substantial political Zionist underground existed.[5] In a short time, the Zionist youth filled that vacuum.

The only underground political organization of significance soon after the German occupation was the Bund, with its center in Warsaw. Even during the siege of Warsaw, the Bund continued to issue its daily newspaper, setting and printing it by hand, after the destruction of the city's gas works. To serve those made homeless by the bombings and the incoming refugees, the Bund opened public kitchens.[6] Early in the German occupation, the Bund began to shape its underground activities. A relief commission was formed to operate the public kitchens and to distribute relief. Soon fourteen party kitchens and canteens—four just for children—were functioning. A Socialist Red Cross was set up to care for the sick, obtain pharmaceutical supplies, held persons in the forced-labor camps, and provide hideouts for party leaders wanted by the Germans. A trade-union commission was assigned to organize clandestine cells of fives or tens, by trade, drawn from the most reliable members of the prewar unions. A political commission undertook to reorganize the party and its youth division *Tsukunft*, in underground cells, with tight security provisions. A new party council and central committe were also put together.[7]

The Bund reactivated its prewar militia, which before the war had consisted of some three to four hundred men, schooled in the arts of defense, with a tiny arms arsenal at their command. The party militia had been formed in 1920, but its origins went back to the Bundist armed self-defense in czarist Russia that arose after the Kishenev pogrom of 1903. The Bund militia in interwar Poland, like similar defense units of political parties in Central Europe, was intended to protect party meetings from attack and disruption by opposition parties. As the major militia among the Jewish parties (the Left Labor Zionists also had a defense unit), the Bund militia functioned also as a pan-Jewish defense group in Poland against anti-Semitic violence and hooliganism.[8] The Tsukunft, too, maintained a defense arm, called *Tsukunft-shturem*. Reorganized in the ghetto, under stringent security, it started out in February 1941 with about thirty-five members in the seven cells.[9]

The first task of the parties and youth organizations was survival. "Even in those days," wrote a Dror member about his movement in the first months of German occupation in Vilna, "one of the most important tasks was to procure bread for the hungry." Wherever the JDC operated, its branches gave subsidies to the parties and to the haluts youth for their welfare activities. (Funds also came from the respective party headquarters abroad through underground channels, though these did not always prove dependable.) The ŻSS too provided significant welfare assistance and cover for political organizational activities. In Warsaw Ringelblum's key position in ŻTOS ensured posts for the Left Labor Zionists, to whose executive he belonged, and the use of various ŻTOS facilities to cloak party undertakings. In Cracow Aaron Liebeskind, leader of the Akiva haluts movement, was put in charge of the ŻSS's department of agricultural training so that he could travel in that capacity throughout the Generalgouvernement, ostensibly visiting the kibbutzim on official business.

In some ghettos—Bialystok, Kovno, Piotrków—one party or another enjoyed the support of the Judenräte, receiving both welfare aid and protection.

The parties first took care of their own, as a family looks after its members. Each party safeguarded its own constituency, its activists and loyal supporters. Its education and cultural apparatus continued to function in semilegal fashion. Warsaw was the locus for the parties' central committees, the stronghold of party operations. But throughout former Poland, now the Generalgouvernement and Ostland, were dozens of local and regional party branches, kibbutzim, and kindred organizations with which contact had to be renewed, which needed financial support, political guidance, and moral encouragement. Outlawed as corporate bodies, their people forbidden to travel, to use the telephone, their mail censored even if delivered, the parties devised a system of communication that depended exclusively on human intrepidity. Trusted party members, whose appearance and accents enabled them to pass as Poles, traveled across German-occupied Poland and Lithuania with forged papers, risking their lives to deliver news, money, organizational instructions, copies of the underground press to the communities they visited, and to bring back information. (The parties sometimes used couriers of the Polish underground movement.) They also operated, on a very limited scale, for a short time, underground railroads, that helped members escape from Poland. The Bund had a network of about thirty couriers. Among the couriers of the halutz organizations were a group of young women whose exploits became legendary. "They are a theme," Ringelblum noted, "that calls for the pen of a great writer."

Having provided for their own members, the parties then extended the periphery of their concern, to the limit that their resources permitted, moving from the private sphere, as it were, into the public. In the first two years of the war, the parties saw their function in the community at large primarily in terms of building and sustaining morale. Early in 1941 the Bund's Central Committee in the Warsaw ghetto sent a report to its New York organization, describing its functions as it then perceived them:

1. To strengthen the power of resistance and endurance of the Jewish masses in the face of the unheard-of terrible persecutions without parallel in human history. . . .

2. To inform the Jewish populace about the resistance and struggle against the occupant beyond the borders of the Jewish ghettos both in Poland and in all occupied countries.

3. To implant the firm conviction that though the Jewish masses may be persecuted, the majority will

nevertheless survive and live to see the conclusive defeat of the enemy.[10]

That hopefulness and that will to live permeated all the political groupings, despite their ideological differences. The Bundists looked to the Western Allies to defeat the Germans, whereas the Communists and the leftist Zionists looked to the Soviet Union. (England's policy in Palestine had alienated most Zionists; their distrust of England as mandatory power extended also to England as wartime ally.) All the leftist ideologies envisaged the defeat of the Germans, followed by revolutionary upheavals that would bring a new social order. In the first years of the German occupation, party people, habituated to the extravagant flow of rhetoric, often described the atrocities that the Germans committed against the Jews as "annihilation" and "destruction." But in fact no Jewish party, before early 1942, took political cognizance of Nazism as waging war specifically against the Jewish people. Thus, at a clandestine meeting in Warsaw in May 1940, the Bund's Central Committee adopted a policy statement setting forth their political hopes and expectations:

> Poland is our homeland, where we are entitled to equal citizenship rights, where our future lies. . . . Any other solutions offered, under present conditions, by Zionist or other Jewish groups, are wrong and utopian, as they always were. Together with the Polish working masses struggling underground, the Jewish people of Poland see no other means of survival, but the defeat of Hitlerism and the reconstruction of a free, independent, and Socialist Poland.[11]

On May 1, 1941, Dror issued a proclamation that avowed once more the movement's dual loyalty to Palestine and socialism and which held out the hope of the inevitable realization of a socialist Palestine:

> The struggle with the Hitlerite conqueror has temporarily separated us from Eretz Israel, but just as there

is no power in the world that can separate us from the struggle for a socialist world, thus nothing can separate us from the land of our ultimate hope. The building of Eretz Israel is undeniably connected with the collapse of capitalism; a socialist Eretz Israel will rise or fall with the success or failure of socialism.[12]

At the end of December 1943, a representative of the Left Labor Zionists, taking part in a clandestine meeting of the underground Polish Communist front, *Krajowa Rada Narodowa* (People's Home Council), spoke of victory with the political certitude of her party:

In the struggle for a new world of labor and of social justice, we are not isolated. The working masses of the whole world, with the heroic Red Army in the vanguard, are with us. Our struggle is their struggle; their victory shall be our victory. There can be no return to the past, no turning back to the past reactionary and fascist governments. The working masses, the invincible forces of progress and true democracy will prevail in this historic struggle.[13]

Maintaining the traditions of the movement became a conspiratorial activity, yet served to uphold morale. May Day 1940 in Lodz fell on the day the Jews were enclosed within the ghetto. That day Bundist activists visited as many members as they could locate, reminding them of May Day, distributing little red-ribbon boutonnieres, and passing the word: "Hold on and hold out." In January 1942 Dror proclaimed a fund-raising campaign in the Warsaw ghetto on behalf of the Jewish National Fund to be conducted according to Zionist tradition on the fifteenth day of Shevat, the New Year for Trees, the time for collections to aid Palestine's reforestation program.

Party ideology remained binding and the commitment of its adherents remained insusceptible to change even in the drastically altered conditions in which the Jews now lived. Just as before the war, each party continued to believe that it was the sole repository of political truth, that it held the key to a noble future. Any ideological deviation or political concession was regarded as a betrayal of principle. In conformity to the prewar pattern, some parties worked together on some undertakings, but these were mainly pragmatic ventures. A pan-Zionist interest prevailed, for instance, with regard to the halutz youth movements. On the left, Bundists and Left Labor Zionists jointly organized several strikes and demonstrations, as they had occasionally done before the war. But party sovereignty persisted along with ideological divisiveness. In a report of March 16, 1942, sent abroad, the Bund gave its version of the political disharmony in the ghettos:

> The Bund's and the Tsukunft's competitors show no concern for the fate of the land where they live. The Left Labor Zionists and the youngsters of the Hehalutz are prepared to relinquish their patrimony to the neighbor to the East [the USSR]. In addition, in their periodical writings, they dream of leaving for Palestine. They minimize the importance of the Allies for the future of their friends and our people. They tie their only hope to the USSR. The remaining former competitors [Aguda] passively await salvation.[14]

The Bund historically held the Marxist view of society in class conflict, its class-conscious bias denying the validity of national/ethnic group consciousness. Thus, according to the Bund, the Jewish working class had more in common with the Polish working class than with the Jewish bourgeoisie. While the Right Labor Zionists upheld Jewish group consciousness, at least until a Jewish state could be established, the Left Labor Zionists took the Marxist position. Thus the ingrained Marxist view of class conflict in the leftist Jewish parties undermined the concept of a common Jewish political interest.

The vehicle best suited to uphold party morale and to propagate the party's views was the underground

press. It was also the channel that gave the party
access to the larger society not only as spokesman for
its particular ideology, but as advocate for the
oppressed ghetto in its struggle for survival. Every
party published, though every publication was illegal.
The mere transmission of news was forbidden. The
penalty for possession of a radio was death. All printing equipment—typesetting machines and presses—
had been immediately confiscated by the Germans
when they invaded Poland, and by October 1939 all
publishing came under German control. Only the
Judenräte were permitted to retain some small printing apparatus.* Under these circumstances, the mere
dissemination of news—war news, political developments, diplomatic affairs, simple chronicles of events
inside Warsaw, inside Poland, in Europe, or worldwide—became a political function, a form of political
opposition to German tyranny. In Lodz an underground interparty group of about a dozen people
maintained an underground radio listening post for
five years. Their dissemination of foreign-broadcast
news acted as a massive antidote to ghetto apathy.

Some one hundred or more illegal bulletins and
newspapers were issued in the ghettos of the Generalgouvernement and in Ostland. Nearly half were published in Warsaw alone and eventually distributed in
the provinces by couriers.[15] Usually crudely duplicated
from typewritten texts, they consisted, on an average,
of some eight to twelve pages stapled together, in an
edition of a few hundred. According to a questionnaire
distributed among members of the Tsukunft, as
Henoch Rus noted in his record book on March 9,
1941, the *Yugnt-shtime*, monthly organ of the Tsukunft,

---

* In 1941 *Gazeta Żydowska* began to be published in Cracow as an
official "Jewish" periodical. Issued biweekly, ostensibly under the
supervision of the *Abteilung für Volksaufklärung und Propaganda*
(Department for Public Enlightenment and Propaganda) but actually
under Gestapo control, *Gazeta Żydowska* printed German news
bulletins, decrees affecting Jews, official information about the
activities of the Judenräte, and neutral filler material.

had some three to four thousand readers for its edition of three hundred. Other papers too averaged ten or more readers per copy.

In September 1939 the Warsaw Bundists had foresightedly removed two mimeograph machines from their headquarters and hidden them. These, plus some initial supplies of stencils, ink, and paper, constituted their underground printing establishment. Replacing the supplies became increasingly difficult. If a copy of an underground paper fell into German hands, the make of paper or printing ink could, if traced, expose the whole operation. Publishers of underground papers had to keep ahead of the Gestapo. In at least one instance, the Bund's counterintelligence saved the party press from falling into German hands. The machines and the paper were removed overnight. The next day, when the Gestapo arrived, they found a vacant apartment.[16] For purposes of security, underground publishers kept changing their papers' names, thus hoping to throw the Germans off the track. Illegal publications were sometimes backdated to prewar times to bedevil the Germans.

Security in issuing the paper, distributing it, even in reading it, became literally a matter of life or death. Instructions in the techniques of distributing the underground press were detailed in *Yugnt-shtime* of December 1940:

1. Who can be a reader? Not everyone can and not everyone should receive the *Yugnt-shtime*. He should be someone who is *known well* and is *reliable*. He should not be a shilly-shallier, nor a blabbermouth, nor a scatterbrain. It is foolishness and a crime to distribute the paper indiscriminately.

2. *Don't inquire!* Only you and the person who gives you the paper know from whom you get the paper. *No one else.* But you do not know from whom your distributor gets the paper. You should not know and should not ask.

3. *No substitutes!* No one should take your place in receiving or distributing the paper. You must do it yourself, alone. You are the one who is trusted.

4. *Don't make notes!* You must not make any notes, especially not addresses. Remember that if you must write something down, do it in code. Destroy your notes afterward.

5. *A clean apartment!* Don't procrastinate. If you receive the paper today, distribute it today. Don't let it accumulate in your place.

6. *Keep quiet!* About organizational work, the less said the better. Many are curious, among them those who are paid for their curiosity. If you happen to know more about the organization's work than others, keep quiet, because through your blabbing you can betray the movement. If you happen to know the names of leaders, keep quiet, never mention any name, for your blabbing can betray someone. This applies not only to the leaders of your organization, but to all underground workers. Don't talk in the street or in public institutions about the work, the illegal press. Remember, blabbing is a crime with regard to the movement.[17]

The instructions were practical and realistic. A month or two after they were issued, a seventeen-year-old Tsukunft activist was caught by the Gestapo with some issues of a party publication. He was imprisoned in Warsaw's dreaded Pawiak prison, where the Germans tortured him to make him reveal the names of the paper's editors. He died without mentioning a single name.[18]

All the underground papers devoted most of their space to military and political news about the war. The news was gathered from BBC broadcasts in many languages from London and also from Russian or underground stations in occupied countries. The Jewish underground parties thus managed to penetrate the wall of censorship erected by the Germans. The news which the underground press circulated in the ghettos helped to keep the Jews informed about major developments on the fronts and in political circles. The anti-Nazi editorials of the underground press articulated the hatred for the Germans that the silenced populace felt. All news about Allied victories and German defeats—scarce, to be sure, in the first years of the war—buttressed by editorial predictions of the ultimate defeat of the Germans, sustained the ghetto Jews and nourished their will to live. "The only thing that fortifies and encourages us to endure the dreadful tortures," wrote an unknown author in *Yugntshtime*, April 1941, "is the powerful belief that in the conflagration of the war fascism in all its forms will be destroyed forever." The Left Labor Zionist youth organ, *Yugntruf*, in March 1942, was confident that a new world would be born out of present suffering, in which "the persecuted and tortured will enjoy the life of a free people rooted in the soil of its homeland, Eretz Israel." A world without hope, says one of Malraux's characters, is suffocating.

In a vigorous campaign against apathy and depression, *Dror*, the movement's underground newspaper, addressed a series of letters to its readers: "At times you think that things have come to their end, that you are no longer capable of doing anything. You are mistaken if you think so. Do not let apathy and despair overpower you, or even influence you. Harness yourself to hard, intensive work, work as hard as you can."[19] The *Yugnt-shtime* exhorted its readers:

The very expression of apathy indicates submission to the enemy, which can cause our collapse morally and root out of our hearts the hatred for the invader. It can destroy the will to fight within us, it can undermine our resolution. . . . Our young people must walk head erect, despite the storms which threaten to destroy us.[20]

In March 1941, on the seventieth anniversary of the Paris Commune, Tsukunft issued a booklet *Di parizer komune*, whose essays and poems extolled the revolutionary commune and its leaders. An epigraph taken from Victor Hugo, "In the grave is the corpse,/The idea lives," suggested the immortality of the revolutionary idea. The comparison between the Warsaw ghetto and the Paris Commune was unmistakable.[21]

In the summer of 1940, *Dror* published a 114-page mimeographed booklet *Payn un gvure* ("Suffering and Heroism"), a literary and historical potpourri on Jewish martyrdom and resistance during the Crusades, the Chmielnitski massacres of 1648–1649, and the Ukrainian pogroms of 1917–1920. The introduction pleaded that its readers not abandon their faith in Western civilization and European culture because of Nazi barbarism, arguing that Nazism was a transitory phenomenon, a nightmare in mankind's history, induced by the profound social and economic contradictions of the political order. Therefore "we can conquer our own depression and not lose hope for a better future." The authors took pride in their tradition: "We are an old cultural people with a rich spiritual heritage from which we draw amply. We cannot and will not succumb, for we have survived similar hardships countless times in our 3,000-year-old history."[22]

The underground press enlarged and fed the animosities of the populace against the Judenräte and the police. Accusations of thievery, corruption, and bribery were leveled against the food, fuel, and housing departments of the Warsaw Judenrat time and again. The rhetoric flowed in abundance, though proof for the charges was scanty. That may not have mattered in the ghetto court of public opinion. The underground press, particularly the Bund's, presented itself as the defender of the poor against the Judenrat, which was depicted as the agent of the rich and influential. On February 1, 1942, a page-one editorial "'Führer' Mania in the Warsaw Ghetto," in the Bund's *Veker*, denounced the Judenrat in sweeping generalities for nepotism and exploitation of the populace. An editorial in the same issue asked rhetorically "What Has Happened to the Bread?" suggesting that the cut in the bread ration, which affected the poor and hungry, actually benefited the privileged.

In April 1941 the *Yugnt-shtime* attacked the Warsaw Judenrat in its role as kehilla successor:

> An especially sad chapter is the role of the kehilla. The Jewish folk masses always had a negative attitude toward this institution, and nowadays especially. . . . Taxes are levied equally on everyone; instead of taxing [just] the rich and the propertied, also the poor and unemployed are taxed.

The *Veker* of February 8, 1942, pursued the same line in its editorial "The Masses Pay—The Rich Rule." *Jutrzenka*, issued by Gordonia in the Warsaw ghetto, on March 14, 1942, charged the Judenrat with being "a tool in the hands of the Germans, traitors who will get their well-merited punishment." Every underground paper attacked the Jewish police, condemning them as "shameless blackmailers" and "thieves" who thrived on the misery of the poor, hard-working, decent populace.

The underground press intensified the popular hostility toward the Judenräte and the police, actively encouraging resistance to official orders. On May 23, 1942, *Dos fraye vort*, Bundist weekly succeeding the *Veker*, printed a news item to the effect that the German Labor Office in Warsaw was making night raids to ferret out skilled workers. The article advised: "Workers, hide and don't let yourselves be caught." Those unfortunate enough to "fall into the enemies' hands" were advised that "the slogan of the working class in all occupied lands is: *Work badly and slowly.*"

The parties and their press stimulated and organized sabotage in the ghetto factories. In the Lodz ghetto and elsewhere, "P.P.," standing for *pracujcie powoli,* "work slowly," became an underground code. Mysterious fires were a constant plague in the factories. Production was not only slowed down, but undermined deliberately. In Będzin, the Jewish underground even inserted revolutionary leaflets in clothing destined for German soldiers. Sabotage by the Jews working for the Germans was an important part of the program of the underground organizations. In Baranowicze, a team of Jews assigned to repair German trains on a local line was instructed to work slowly. The trains used to cross a wooded area controlled by Russian partisans, who usually managed to inflict some damage on the locomotives. The repair work was sabotaged so that seven of the nine locomotives on the line were always disabled.[23] Ghettos located along or near the perimeter of partisan operations, Vilna and Kovno, for instance, were usually extensively involved in systematic sabotage operations directed from the outside.

The most outspoken call to disobedience by the underground press came early in July 1942, after the Germans had shot 110 Warsaw ghetto Jews—90 men, 10 women, and 10 policemen—in reprisal for the increasing disobedience by the Jewish population to police regulations and for insubordination by the police in carrying out regulations. The 110 victims were taken at random from persons then being held in Pawiak prison on minor charges. An announcement explaining the shootings as an act of reprisal was issued over the signature of Heinz Auerswald, Warsaw ghetto commissar. The underground press responded with savage contempt. *Yedies,* a Hehalutz newspaper, asserted that the Jews would continue to disobey the German orders: "We will continue to evade every one of these cruel laws; we will continue to disobey all these draconic regulations."[24] On July 5, 1942, *Shturem,* the Bundist weekly under another new name, ran a lead editorial, "Honor to the Fallen." It was the most explicit call to disobedience that had appeared in the underground press:

> Let us not lament the victims, not weep, not wring our hands. They fell as soldiers at their posts. They were murdered because we Jews are a stiffnecked people, because we do not wish to expire "loyally" under the bloody German yoke, because we constantly break all regulations and laws which the cynical hangmen promulgate against us. The chief hangman Auerswald has announced in his placards that he murdered 110

Jews in reprisal for our rebelliousness, for our resistance to the Germans. The hangman may be sure that from now on we will disobey his Hitlerite laws still more. We do not fear the even greater punishment with which he threatens us. We have nothing more to lose—we can win everything. Auerswald's placard is the badge of honor of the struggling Jewish masses in the Warsaw ghetto.[25]

Overt opposition was inhibited by German terror, and the meager record testifies not to passivity, but to a healthy recognition by the Jewish parties of the real deployment of power in the ghettos. Self-discipline and the submission of the individual to the collective were the habitual posture prescribed for members of revolutionary organizations. Under German occupation, that posture became mandatory, for the relationship between discretion and valor was as the ratio of life to death. Civil disobedience as a strategy of political opposition can succeed only with a government ruled by conscience. In 1938, after Kristallnacht, when Gandhi advised the Jews in Germany to employ *Satyagraha,* the Indian version of passive resistance, he disclosed his inability to distinguish between English and German political morality. The Jews in Poland, with sharper political perceptions, made no such miscalculation.

In the first years of the occupation, the Jewish parties essayed several tests of strength. The first came at the end of March 1940 in Warsaw. Youthful Polish hooligans had charged Jewish neighborhoods, with cries of "Kill the Jews" and "We want a Poland without Jews." They stormed Jewish stores and even homes, robbing, looting, and beating up the Jews. The Germans stood by, observing and photographing. An emergency meeting of the Bund aktiv was called. In normal times, the Bund would have sent out its party and trade-union militia to fight off the pogromists, but now, under German occupation, the stakes had changed. The question that confronted the meeting hinged on the likelihood that the Germans would

intervene and declare all the Jews collectively responsible for any act of resistance undertaken by the Bund.
Consequently, the Jewish community would suffer
worse from German reprisals than from Polish pogroms.
Nevertheless, the Bund decided to fight back. Self-
discipline was invoked: the militia would use only iron
pipes and brass knuckles, forgoing knives and fire-
arms to minimize the risk of killing a Pole and calling
forth German retaliation.

The next day the pogromists encountered Jewish
resistance. Fighting took place in different parts of
town. Ambulances were called to carry off wounded
pogromists. Ringelblum even heard that a Pole had
been killed. At evening curfew the fighting halted, to
be renewed the following morning. That day, at last,
the Polish police were ordered to halt the fighting.[26]
The anticipated German reprisals did not materialize.

Other Jewish parties had opposed the Bund's action.
Most Jews feared that worse would come from such
audacious Jewish acts of resistance in those circumstances. While the underground movement and the
Jewish populace were clearly at one when the parties
vented contempt and hatred upon the Germans or the
Judenräte in their press, functioning expressively, the
divergence between party and mass was evident when
the party engaged in overt acts, functioning instru-
mentally, purposefully. Although the parties could
claim to speak for the people by articulating their feelings, they could not always claim to act for them,
simply because terror repressed the will to resist.

On some occasions, when hunger and misery grew
intolerable, the parties carried out demonstrations and
strikes with substantial popular support. To be sure,
spontaneity sparked some demonstrations, yet only
the underlying party organization could provide the
structure and formulate the goals for such actions. In
Lodz the Bund, the Left Labor Zionists, and the Jewish Communists, working together on an *ad hoc* basis,
succeeded in engaging in their activities some of the
more political-minded workers of the prewar, massive
trade-union movement. In the fall of 1940 the three

parties jointly convened a conference of some 130 factory delegates. The party leaders also used to meet with Rumkowski, representing the factory workers and defending their interests vis-à-vis the Judenrat. The ghetto was little more than six months old in January 1941, when hunger prevailed over terror and a series of demonstrations and strikes erupted. Workers demanded more food, an increase in the rations, higher wages, and even the rights of organization and representation. Rumkowski demanded unconditionally that the party leaders call off the strikes, which had broken out first among the cabinetmakers and then spread to the tailors and textile workers. Party and union leaders refused to accede to Rumkowski's demands, while he stubbornly withheld any concessions. Within a week the strikes collapsed, because some workers, unable to bear the hunger of their children, returned to the factories. In that encounter the parties could not sway Rumkowski, who, for his part, regarded the strikes as a threat to his authority. In that test of strength he demonstrated that he could subdue the ghetto without resorting to German force.[27] But unrest persisted throughout the ghetto. Children, organized by the Bund's juvenile organization SKIF, picketed in front of Rumkowski's home, shouting, "Rumkowski, you are our misfortune." So pervasive was the ferment within the ghetto that even the hasidim, the most passive element in the population, sent Rumkowski an ultimatum on January 29, 1941, to the effect that if their people did not get more bread and potatoes, they would organize a demonstration. For the next ten days they threatened to parade publicly with Torah scrolls to petition Rumkowski. The demonstration apparently never came off, probably because Rumkowski had summoned the rabbis and counterthreatened a bloody end to a demonstration with Torah scrolls. He reminded the rabbis that he himself had put up a fight with the Germans to keep the Torah scrolls.

In Bialystok about a hundred wagoners called a strike at the end of April 1942 against a mandatory registration of horses ordered by the Germans.[28] The action was likely spurred by the underground parties. The most spectacular demonstration occurred in the Częstochowa ghetto, where the Labor Zionists had established a labor council, whose function was to mediate between the five thousand workers in the ghetto and the Judenrat. Driven by hunger and anger, a thousand exhausted and emaciated workers convened in the labor council's public kitchen in December 1941 to hear their union leaders call on the Judenrat for increased bread rations and higher wages. One speaker, carried away by his cascading rhetoric, unexpectedly called for a protest demonstration against the Judenrat. The workers, impelled by passion, streamed down the street, swarmed into the Judenrat building, breaking down doors, smashing furniture, wrecking typewriters, assaulting the staff. Their violence communicated the anger they felt because of the hunger their families had to endure, and they demanded what was due to them as human beings. Order was finally restored by the labor council itself; a delegation was then selected from the workers to join the council executive in negotiating with the Judenrat. Finally, after hours of negotiations, during which the strikers barricaded the building, the Judenrat acceded to their demands.[29]

But German terror soon subdued both mass membership and party leadership with regard to overt acts like demonstrations and strikes. Not only did the populace fear the deadly German reprisals, but the parties dreaded decimation of their leadership and ranks. The Germans were always, from the first days of the occupation, on the lookout for Jewish political leaders and activists. They recruited paid agents from the Jewish underworld to help uncover party people and party hideouts. Survival became a question of security. The very existence of the party was at stake. Quite early, the Bund instituted a solemn oath for its members, demanding "loyalty unto death," a promise never to betray the organization. Each party suffered severe losses, as its activists were discovered. In 1941, in Lublin, a Bundist who had been distributing anti-

Nazi literature was caught by the Germans and publicly hanged.

Couriers were often apprehended, causing the collapse of an entire chain of contact or, even more seriously, jeopardizing a whole underground network. In May or June 1941 a Polish courier traveling on behalf of the Bund's central committee was arrested in Piotrków by the Gestapo. The documents found on her pointed to the party's organizations in a string of cities. Gestapo agents intensified their search for party activists in these places, one of which was Częstochowa. In mid-July a Bundist named Motek Kushnir, who headed the TOZ in Częstochowa, was warned minutes before the Germans arrived. He managed to escape from his office, but the Gestapo then seized five TOZ staff members and Kushnir's mother and brother, threatening to shoot them all if he did not turn himself in. The Bund's local committee decided, however, that Kushnir should remain in hiding for the time being. The Judenrat, which the Germans had involved, then warned the Bundists that the hostages would be shot. The party committee reconvened, debating whether they had the right or responsibility to decide about the life and death of other people. Kushnir, with the concurrence of the majority, decided to turn himself in. The party promised to do everything possible to release him. For weeks Kushnir was tortured by the Gestapo, but finally released at the end of September after the party succeeded in bribing a Gestapo agent with 35,000 zlotys and expensive goods to boot.[30]

The Germans continued their relentless hunt of party activists throughout the Generalgouvernement, driving the parties still deeper underground and forcing them to relinquish public activities. In the spring of 1942 the Germans carried out mass arrests and killings of groups of Jews in many ghettos (according to Ringelblum's information, in Cracow, Tarnów, Częstochowa, Radom, Kielce, Ostrowiec). These particular actions seemed directed against political activists, though the pattern was not consistent. In Warsaw, late Friday night, April 17, and long into the next morning, some fifty Jews were seized in their homes by the Gestapo and shot on the street. That night became known as "Bloody Friday." Most of those rounded up were printers and persons associated with the underground press. The rumor was spread in the ghetto that the slaughter had not been arbitrary, that the Germans were after persons involved in "politics" and in publishing illegal newspapers. Indeed, Czerniaków had summoned a Bundist leader to inform him that the Gestapo had indicated that these killings—"executions" was the term used—would continue as long as the underground press did. Czerniaków asked him to have the Bund desist from further publication, but the Bundist refused. His party later upheld his position.[31]

The murmurs in the ghetto grew louder and more voluble, spread probably by the Gestapo agents and picked up by a fearful populace, to the effect that the Socialists, the politicals, were causing the troubles in the ghetto. On April 30, 1942, an editorial in the Bundist *Veker*, "The Bloody Night," addressed itself to the killings and to the rumors:

Then let the dogs be silent who dare to bark on the graves of those who fell during the bloody Friday night in Warsaw. Let them not dishonor the peace of the martyrs. Let them not try to argue that it was the Socialists who brought on the misfortune. That Friday night in the Warsaw ghetto was only one *small* link in the *great* chain of the bestial murders of the Jews by Hitler.

The editorial then proceeded to analyze the recent course of events in the light of new insights. The Jewish political underground had come to see that the German atrocities against the Jews were not merely the destructive fallout of a fascist war against the capitalist order, but were part of a deliberate design to annihilate the Jews.

14

Who Shall Live, Who Shall Die

  Like a tornado the Einsatz-
gruppen swept through the Jewish settlements of
Eastern Europe in the summer of 1941, destroying
age-old communities in cyclonic upheaval. The German invasion found the Russians unprepared militarily and the civilian population disoriented and
demoralized. Exploiting the superstitious anti-Semitic
prejudices of the Lithuanians, Balts, and Ukrainians
and activating their accumulated hatred for the
Soviets, the Germans harnessed the violent energies
of these willing collaborators to round up and kill the
Jews. In Vilna and Kovno the Lithuanians roamed
the streets, capturing Jewish males, hauling them
away, purportedly for work. In Lwów the Germans
and Ukrainians, in house-to-house hunts for Jews, shot
them randomly on the spot. Belatedly avenging the
assassination—by a Jew back in 1926—of Semyon
Petlura, notorious anti-Semite and Ukrainian national
hero, the Ukrainians staged mammoth pogroms,
slaughtering thousands and carrying off other thousands of Jews to Einsatzgruppen headquarters.[1]
Within hours or days, those Jews who had been taken

away were machine-gunned en masse at some remote desolate area. The disaster was epic:

> There was everywhere terrible grief,
> Everywhere panic, and death in full many a form.

Jewish communal leaders appealed to the German military to halt the local pogromists and urged local Baltic or Ukrainian officials to restrain their people. Thousands of Jews besieged the quarters of German and local authorities to obtain the release of husbands, fathers, sons, brothers, to learn of their whereabouts, to send them food. To support their entreaties, the Jews offered gifts and bribes. Driven by anxiety, many Jews responded in panic and hysteria, in constant action and reaction. Others, with less psychic energy, succumbed to depression and apathy, paralyzed by fear. Still others, whose husbands or sons disappeared into the violent void, refused to believe that their men had been killed. In response to the strains and anxiety, they indulged in the comfort of wishful beliefs, convinced that husbands or sons had been taken away for work in some distant place, that surely they would return hale and whole after the war's end.

The wild spate of violence ebbed after a month. The Germans began to organize more systematic and disciplined programs of murder. In Kovno, for instance, in mid-August 1941, the Germans demanded from the Judenrat five hundred educated young men. When the Judenrat asked why these were wanted, they were told that the intellectuals would be assigned to classifying government archives and hence would be spared the heavy labor soon to become obligatory for all Jews. On that understanding, the Judenrat prepared a list. Volunteers, too, offered their services. In all, 534 young educated Jews were taken away and never seen again. Similar ruses were practiced in other cities in a deliberate plan to destroy the community's elite.

The German military, having taken over existing

industrial enterprises, began operating them to meet the needs of the German war effort. Airfields for supply and military purposes had to be enlarged and new ones constructed. The German army had to be supplied and its equipment kept in repair. Civil occupation facilities and military ones for the continuing campaign against Russia had to be erected. Each Jewish worker in these installations, factories, and workshops was issued an identity document, a *Schein*. Usually a white or colored card, identifying its holder as a skilled worker, it promised security from arbitrary seizure and deadly violence. Its aura of immunity transformed it into a symbol of life. Underlying the emotional significance that the Jews attached to the work card was the reasoned conclusion that, in order to wage war successfully, the Germans would have to make rational use of available manpower. Hence the Jews who provided the labor and the skills that the Germans needed would thus be assured of life. This conviction spurred Jews to seek work, registering with the Judenrat's labor office as skilled workers.

On September 15, 1941, just a month after the Kovno Jews had been enclosed in a ghetto, the Germans sealed off the ghetto. Working parties assigned to outside labor were not permitted to leave. The next day the Germans delivered 5,000 cards to the Judenrat, with orders that they were to be distributed to skilled workers. Signed by SS-Hauptsturmführer Jordan, specialist for Jewish affairs in the German administration of Kovno, these cards became known in the ghetto as "Jordan permits." Nearly 30,000 Jews then lived in the Kovno ghetto, some 6,000 to 7,000 having already been murdered by units of Einsatzgruppe A. The cards were entrusted to the Judenrat's labor office, whose officials, jointly with representatives of the various trades, began the distribution according to their registry. Several hours later, after many cards had been issued, a German official at an industrial enterprise telephoned to the Judenrat to make sure that "his" Jewish workers would receive what he described as their *Lebensscheins*—life permits. Instantly what had seemed to be mere administrative procedure turned into ultimate judgment as to who would live and, in consequence of the German decision, who would die.[2]

The Judenrat officers called an emergency meeting to confront the situation. What should they do? Among the proposals put forward was one to return all the cards to the Germans with a statement that the Judenrat could not and would not distribute them. Someone even suggested burning the cards. Since the whole Jewish community of Kovno appeared to be doomed, it was wrong to save one-sixth, just for the Germans to exploit them for German ends. "If we must die, let us all die together." Meanwhile, word about the significance of the Jordan permits spread rapidly. Panic swept the ghetto. A mob of thousands of Jews—mostly workers—swarmed to the Judenrat, broke in, searching for the cards, smashing doors, breaking furniture, shouting, "The cards belong to us." They seized the remaining cards, after Judenrat staff and Jewish policemen had already grabbed many for themselves.

All that night the Lithuanian police guarding the ghetto kept shooting, stirring even greater terror and panic among the trapped Jews. In the morning manned machine guns surrounded the ghetto. Armed Germans and Lithuanians ordered all the Jews in the small ghetto to assemble in the public square, lined up by families, in columns. A selection began and the holders of the Jordan permits were separated from the others. All at once a Gestapo official drove into the ghetto with a written message for the SS officer in charge of the selection. Upon reading it, he ordered his men back to their barracks. The Jews fled into their homes. Inexplicably the *Aktion** was called off.

Two days later, the Germans ordered the Kovno Judenrat to supply 1,000 men daily for heavy work at

---

* *Aktion*, meaning "activity" or "process," is one of those indeterminate German words used by the Nazis to refer to a killing procedure.

the airfield. The workers were available, for now everyone knew that work meant life. On September 26, German police surrounded part of the ghetto, and on the ground that Jews had shot a German policeman, removed about one thousand people—the old, the sick, and women whose husbands had disappeared during the first sweep of the Einsatz squads. They were all shot at the Ninth Fort, part of a massive fortress system built by the czars outside Kovno. The next week rumors were spread in town about a leprosy epidemic in the ghetto. A municipal medical commission came to investigate, finding nothing. Nevertheless, on October 4 the Germans once more surrounded the small ghetto. All persons with work documents, who were employed in specified enterprises or at the airport, were permitted to leave. All the others were taken to the Ninth Fort. The hospital was set afire, its patients and medical staff burned alive.

The ghetto lived in unbearable tension and constant mourning for the dead. After the seizure of many women without male support, convenience marriages became common. Anxiety enveloped the ghetto like a shroud. Rumors spread wildly; people were willing to believe anything, good or bad. They were tormented by the thought of recurring disaster, but no one could tell where, when, how, or even whether it would strike again. It was like living on a high-angle fault whose contractions and tensions set off a series of earthquakes. Everyone anticipated catastrophe.

On October 24, SS officers toured the ghetto, pausing for a while at a large square called Democrats Place. The next day, one of those officers, SS-Hauptscharführer Rauke, RSHA specialist in Jewish affairs, came to the Judenrat, politely explaining that the ghetto had great tasks to fulfill for the Wehrmacht. The SS, for its part, would undertake to provide the required food rations for persons engaged in heavy labor and their families, but it could not provide such rations for Jews unable to perform heavy work. These would have to be moved to the small ghetto. The Germans themselves would make the selection. Rauke then handed to the Judenrat chairman notices to be posted the next day, October 26, to the effect that on Tuesday, October 28, at 6:00 A.M., the entire ghetto population would have to assemble for a mass roll call at Democrats Place. Anyone found at home thereafter would be shot.

Once again the Judenrat convened in emergency session. In the light of recent events, they had little doubt about the eventual fate of the nonworking Jewish population. They decided first to check and verify Rauke's statements, seeking corroboration. The next day, learning nothing from several sources, they managed to secure a confidential meeting of their top officers with Rauke. Dr. Elkes, head of the Judenrat, suggested to him that if it was a matter of ensuring bigger food rations for the heavy workers, surely that distribution could be best entrusted to the Judenrat. Otherwise, what was the real purpose of this proposed roll call?

Rauke acted surprised that the Judenrat was worried by this order, for, he assured them, it was only a matter of administrative expediency. The Germans had thought of giving the Judenrat this responsibility, but knowing that Jews stick together, the Germans were afraid that the Judenrat would distribute the rations equally to all. Consequently, Rauke explained, since their economic interests were involved, the Germans preferred to handle the matter their way. Nothing further could be elicited from him. The Judenrat officers' report to the board did not ease their disquiet. Late into the evening they discussed the possible consequences if they refused to carry out the order. Would it be regarded as sabotage and thus bring even greater disaster to the ghetto? They reached a dead end in their thinking, unable to make a decision. At 11:00 P.M. they agreed to ask Kovno's Chief Rabbi, Abraham Dov Shapiro, to issue a ruling on the basis of *Halacha*, Jewish law.

Weakened by age and illness, shaken by the events of the recent past, Rabbi Shapiro was agitated even

more by the problem put to him. He asked for time to
study the Talmudic and rabbinic sources that addressed themselves to related problems. Sustained by
valerian, he pored over the texts all night. Late the
following morning, he ruled: if a community of Jews
is threatened by persecution, and some may be saved
by a specific action, then the leaders of the community have to muster the courage and the responsibility to rescue whosoever may be rescued. The
notices should therefore be posted.

October 28 dawned cold and overcast, as if, wrote
an observer, the sun was ashamed to show its face.
The 26,400 Jews of the Kovno ghetto assembled by
families as ordered, dazed and dulled by fear. Instructed by the police, they walked as if in a funeral
cortege, past Rauke, who, by a flick of his finger, indicated who was to go right, who left, who was to
live, who was to die. Small families and young people
were directed rightward, large families and older
people leftward. The procession lasted all day. Nearly
ten thousand people were segregated and sent for the
night into the desolate small ghetto. The next day
they were marched out in columns to the Ninth Fort
and shot. A few days later Jordan informed the
Judenrat that the Aktionen were over, but that the
Jews were expected to work in accordance with German orders and requirements.

The ghetto remained a place of mourning without
consolation, without joy or laughter, even without
tears. Drained of feeling, the survivors were psychically numbed. Fear alone thrived, embracing the
whole ghetto. The Deuteronomic text (28:66–67)
expressed the daily reality:

And thy life shall hang in doubt before thee; and thou
shalt fear night and day, and shalt have no assurance of
thy life. In the morning thou shalt say: "Would it were
even!" and at even thou shalt say: "Would it were
morning!" for the fear of thy heart which thou shalt
fear, and for the sight of thine eyes which thou shalt
see.[3]

Throughout the Diaspora, Halacha had guided Jews not only in ritual matters, but in all social, economic, political, and moral issues. In modern times, despite secularism's erosion of its authority, Halacha continued to retain its full validity for observant Jews in all aspects of their lives. It remained also a frame of reference even for nonobservant Jews at times when they confronted difficult and complex moral issues affecting the whole Jewish community. When the communal leaders of Kovno were faced with a problem involving the life and death of thousands of Jews, it was not unexpected that they sought the guidance of Halacha, hoping for ancient wisdom and ethical precepts to instruct them.

No Jewish community had ever before faced a comparable threat of annihilation. In their history the Jews had been subjected to the slaughter of many, enslavement, abduction of women or children, dire economic and religious sanctions. Those persecutions, reflecting the tensions between a hostile non-Jewish ruler and a local Jewish community, provided certain models in rabbinic teaching for the traditionally correct Jewish response. In the Talmud the basic case involved Joshua ben Levi, a third-century rabbi in Lydda, who had given refuge to a political fugitive. When the Roman authorities threatened to destroy Lydda and all its inhabitants, the rabbi presumably convinced the fugitive to surrender to the authorities. Thus Lydda and its people were saved.

Subsequent rabbinic tradition is both ambiguous and divided about Joshua ben Levi's role. The surrender to the authorities of a named individual wanted for a specific crime was generally permitted, whereas the surrender of an unspecified victim was forbidden, even if the whole community should perish as a consequence. Differences in rabbinic opinion even within these limits usually reflected contemporary political conditions. In times when the Jewish community was threatened with severe persecution, the rabbis, ruling leniently, approved of Joshua ben Levi's behavior and elaborated arguments to justify it. In times when persecution eased, the reasoning hardened.[4] Nearly a thousand years after Joshua ben Levi, Maimonides, addressing himself to this problem, wrote:

> . . . If heathens said to Israelites, "Surrender one of your number to us, that we may put him to death, otherwise, we will put all of you to death," they should all suffer death rather than surrender a single Israelite to them. But if they specified an individual, saying "Surrender that particular person to us, or else we will put all of you to death," they may give him up, provided that he was guilty of a capital crime. . . . If the individual specified has not incurred capital punishment, they should all suffer death rather than surrender a single Israelite to them.[5]

In many ghettos the rabbis wrestled with the Maimonides ruling, some accepting his authority, others citing variant readings of the text and different cases. Kovno's Chief Rabbi, Shapiro, was one of the few rabbis who rejected the Maimonides position, though he left no record of the legal precedents on which he based his decision. His conclusion—approving surrender of a part if thereby the rest could be saved—was shared by men who themselves knew little of the Jewish tradition. In Vilna, for example, during the Aktion of late October 1941, when Gens himself, as head of the Jewish police, directed the Jews to right or left, to life or death, the rabbis sent a delegation to tell him that he was contravening Jewish law. To support their position, they cited Maimonides. Gens, who knew little, if anything, of Jewish law, responded that it was justifiable to surrender a part if the others would thereby be saved.[6]

In Vilna over 20,000 of the 60,000 Jews vanished or were killed outright from the time the Einsatzgruppen entered the city until the Jews were enclosed in Vilna's ghetto on September 6, 1941. The mass shootings took place at Ponary, ten kilometers from town, inaccessible because the Germans restricted all civilian movement. For weeks no one in Vilna knew of the death pits at Ponary. Efforts to get news from non-Jews brought rumors and reports that a ghetto existed at Ponary, that Jews were seen working there. A few persons who survived the mass shootings returned to Vilna early in September, wounded, bloody, shocked and disoriented, with tales so harrowing that they were literally incredible. Doctors at a ghetto hospital thought that these patients were demented, their minds unhinged by personal problems.[7] Illusion was nourished by apprehension, for all the Jews were pervaded by the sense that disaster could strike momentarily, like a river cresting at floodtide.

Once the Jews were shut up within the walls of Vilna's large and small ghetto, more systematic seizures and killings began. Armed German and Lithuanian police would surround the ghetto, removing hundreds or thousands at a time. By mid-September another ten thousand Jews had vanished.[8] As in Kovno, Lwów, and elsewhere, the work card, the Schein, became the sole guarantee of security, the admission ticket to life. The Schein was the instrument with which the Germans screened the Jews, winnowing the "productive" from the "nonproductive."

Late in the day of Yom Kippur, October 1, 1941, the ghetto suddenly swarmed with German storm troops. Lithuanian militia drove thousands of Jews from their homes on the pretext that their identity cards had to be restamped at the ghetto gates. In the rapidly falling darkness, the Jews were herded through the narrow streets of old Vilna, the Jerusalem of Lithuania. It was an eerie, surrealistic procession, with thousands of Jews holding candles to light their way in the blacked-out town. Men, women, and children, clutching each other for comfort and assurance, shuffled along, some dazed and apathetic, others pushing and shoving, trying to break through the cordon of Jewish police and escape into the night. At the gate, some three thousand were taken away to Ponary. Thousands more were rounded up and spirited away in the next few days. Thereafter it became clear to all that Ponary meant death.

The Germans then undertook a new method of eliminating the Jews in mass. They gave the Judenrat three thousand yellow permits to be distributed to persons engaged in production essential to the German war effort. Some four hundred of these cards were allocated to employees of the Judenrat and other ghetto institutions. Each yellow-permit holder was entitled to protect his family, which, under German ground rules, was limited to husband, wife, and two children under sixteen.

In accordance with German war-economy priorities, quotas of workers entitled to yellow permits were assigned to each authorized factory and workshop. Upon the instructions of the German factory director, the Judenrat issued permits to those workers. A panic to register in the factories seized the ghetto. Jewish factory managers, with access to German directors, were besieged for protektsye. Jews gave gifts and bribes to be entered on a factory roster. Political activists exploited connections and prestige to save their leading members. The Judenrat's labor office, it was said, yielded to party pressure and also succumbed to bribery. The yellow permit became the most desirable of all possessions. "As precious as a yellow permit" became a new Yiddish coinage.

How the Judenrat managed the distribution of the four hundred yellow permits is unclear. Judenrat staff and members of the Jewish police received yellow permits. The German authorities apparently assigned quotas for various categories of ghetto employees: teachers in the ghetto schools, doctors, nurses, orderlies, public-kitchen staffs, sanitation workers, and the like. It is impossible to reconstruct on what general principles or by what expediencies the final allocation of permits was made. Ten permits were assigned for teachers, among whom the Communists were the single dominant group. They consequently exerted pressure to get permits for their people. The Germans had assigned only a few permits to ghetto medical personnel. A doctor in the Vilna ghetto, who years earlier had gone to medical school with a German who was now—coincidentally—the municipality's top medical officer, managed to wring from him a few more permits for medical personnel. Still, there were more doctors than yellow permits. A committee, consisting at least of two doctors and perhaps some members of the Judenrat, sat in session, deciding who among the candidates would get the yellow passport to life.[9]

The dilemmas about whom to save by means of the yellow permits did not cease with their distribution. Then came the problem of the three additional family members. Every yellow-permit holder tried to save those closest to him. Family bonds were the most fundamental and decisive factor in the choice. Yet never did the family undergo a more disintegrative experience. The yellow-permit holder who wanted to save his parents, his wife and children, his brothers and sisters, had to choose among them. In most cases, the decisions favored, as they would in modern Western societies, the nuclear family—wife and children—over parents, siblings, nieces, and nephews. If the yellow-permit holder was unmarried, widowed, or childless, he entered the next closest members of his family as wife or children, in whatever capacity would pass the German criterion. Nephews were entered as sons, fathers as husbands, wives as children, mothers as wives.

The Judenrat's labor office made sure that every holder of a yellow permit registered three family members to whom he was entitled. People without family were given fictive husbands, wives, and children. Names were changed; identity documents were reissued to conform to the individual's new status. The Judenrat canvassed the whole ghetto population to make certain that fully 12,000 persons would be covered, that no opportunity for life would be wastefully squandered. Nevertheless, in mid-October 1941, the Vilna ghetto held about 22,500 Jews, about 10,000 more than the permits could cover.

Those without yellow permits who could not get them officially, who could not buy authentic or even

forged ones, tried other means of saving themselves
or members of their families. Jews with non-Jewish
friends tried to hide out with them, at least for the
few days during which an Aktion was expected to
take place. Peasants in outlying areas could sometimes be prevailed upon, for large sums, to hide children or elderly parents. Here and there individual
Jews managed to obtain false papers, enabling them
to pass as Christians and live outside the ghetto. But
most people without yellow permits began to make
hiding places or to buy places in already prepared
hideouts for themselves or those whom they could
not otherwise protect. Hideouts became a ghetto
fever, an obsession, the cyclone cellars to protect
against the German disaster. Hideouts were located
in attics and cellars, behind blind walls. Some held
only one person; some held dozens. The hideout in
which young Rudashevski stayed was concealed in
the two upper stories of a three-story ghetto warehouse, entered through a hole in the wall of the adjoining apartment house: "The hole is blocked in-
geniously by a kitchen cupboard. One wall of the
cupboard serves at the same time as a little gate for
the hole. The hole is barricaded by stones." Bringing
bare necessities and a pillow, an imprisoned mass of
people bedded down in the inhospitable asylum for
the night.

The first major Aktion of the yellow permits took
place on October 24, after the permit holders and
their dependents were ordered to leave the ghetto for
their places of work. The remaining Jews were routed
from their homes, the Lithuanian police scouring the
buildings to uncover hideouts. "We are like animals
surrounded by the hunter," wrote Rudashevski.

> I feel the enemy under the boards I stand on. . . . They
> pound, tear, break. . . . Suddenly, somewhere upstairs,
> a baby starts crying. . . . We are lost. A desperate
> attempt to shove sugar into the baby's mouth doesn't
> help. They stop its mouth with pillows. Its mother
> weeps. In wild terror people demand that the baby be

strangled. The baby's wails grow louder; the Lithuanians pound more heavily against the walls.

The Lithuanians did not discover that hideout, but
elsewhere in the ghetto they found some 5,000 Jews
to send to Ponary. A few days later, another 2,500
Jews were dragged off from the small ghetto.

On November 2, while on night duty at a ghetto
first-aid station, a doctor was called out on an emergency. The patient was a Jewish policeman whose
legs had become paralyzed and his speech impaired. The doctor asked what had happened to him.
Another policeman, taking the doctor aside, told him
that the Jewish police had just been notified that a
three-day Aktion was to begin at dawn, that yellow-
permit holders and their families would be sent to
their places of work, and the remaining Jews would
be rounded up for Ponary. Under SS supervision, the
Jewish police would have to search out the concealed
Jews, blow up their hideouts. As soon as the Jewish
policeman heard these instructions, he had toppled
over and became paralyzed.[10] Most Jewish police,
however, terrorized by the fear of death—their own
and their family's—obeyed German orders. They
hunted Jews down, uncovering their hideouts, hand-
ing them over to the Lithuanians and Germans. A
new expression was coined in the Vilna ghetto: "You
can trust me, I'm not a ghetto policeman."

In those months of violence, the Vilna ghetto's
police chief, Jacob Gens, supplanted the Judenrat as
the ghetto's real head. During the selections, he himself checked the papers of the ghetto Jews as they
passed before him, three blue cards to one yellow
card. In October he participated in the Aktion that
removed about 150 old and paralyzed Jews from the
ghetto and in two Aktionen in December that delivered over 150 Jewish "criminals" to Ponary. Months
later, at a public meeting Gens exculpated himself:
"I, Gens, lead you to death, and I, Gens, want to save
Jews from death. I, Gens, order hideouts to be blown
up, and I, Gens, try to get certificates, work, and

benefits for the ghetto. I render the account of Jewish blood and not the account of Jewish honor." He went on: "When they ask me for a thousand Jews, I hand them over; for if we Jews will not give on our own, the Germans will come and take them by force. Then they will take not one thousand, but thousands. Thousands and the whole ghetto will be at their mercy. With hundreds, I save a thousand. With the thousands that I hand over, I save ten thousand." Finally, he attempted to vindicate himself before the bar of Jewish history and the verdict of future generations: "I will say: I did everything in order to save as many Jews as possible . . . to usher them into freedom. To ensure that at least a remnant of Jews survive, I myself had to lead Jews to death; and in order to have people emerge with a clean conscience, I had to befoul myself and act without conscience."[11]

The last of a series of small Aktionen took place on December 21, 1941. The next day the ghetto Jews awoke from fitful sleep to habitual daylight anxiety. But the Germans did not return again. The volcano ceased for a while its deadly eruptions. The Vilna ghetto, its population now about 12,500, entered a period of stability that was to last until April 1943. The survivors gathered up the remnant threads of their lives. Out of the wreckage of their institutions they began to rebuild the community. The normality that they reconstructed was external, part bulwark against the nightmares of the past, a grotesque ordinariness to combat memory. For the ghetto was haunted by 47,000 specters. Each survivor was burdened by an intolerable weight of guilt feelings, created by the circumstances of the yellow permits. Everyone who survived felt that his life had cost someone else's, a response common to survivors of all kinds of disasters. In Vilna the mathematics of survival were so simple and stark that self-reproach was the most common denominator.

The killing began in the Wartheland as it began to wind down in the Eastern territories. In the farming settlement at Heidemühle, comprising sixteen villages near Turek, the Germans in late September 1941 concentrated above five thousand Jews from six nearby towns. The displaced peasants were removed to adjacent villages. A Judenrat was organized and the Jews were set to lumbering in the woods, sowing and ploughing the fields. But premonitions of disaster soon began to pervade the Jewish community. On November 4 the Judenrat head convened the community's rabbis, informing them that the German district chief had ordered him to supply a list of all the Jews, each one to be designated as "fit" or "unfit," according to his capacity for work. Children under twelve and adults over sixty-five were to be designated as "unfit." The Judenrat head turned to the rabbis for guidance. The rabbis responded as to a community disaster, fasting, praying, and pondering the problem. On November 6 they ruled that "the law of the land is the law," even if an evil law. The list should, therefore, be submitted as ordered, but every Jew was to have the right to know which category he was assigned to.

The list began to be prepared. People used protektsye to get the records changed, to have one's children entered as older than they were, one's parents as younger. Bribery worked also on the German district officials; changes were constantly being made in the list. Panic intensified as the sense of imminent disaster overtook the community. The rabbis declared Mondays and Thursdays public fast-days; Jews recited psalms all day long, hoping to force God's intercession. The Judenrat head sent his parents away to another community, and others followed his example. Many Jews fled to other towns; some hid among the Polish peasants.

On December 8, 1941, at 2:00 A.M., hundreds of SS troops surrounded the settlement. In a house-to-house search, they routed the Jews from their beds and herded them all into one village. At 6:00 A.M. the Jews were marched out to a field, lined up, men and women separately. At 8:00 three German officers arrived and ordered the head of the Jewish police to read the names of the "unfit" from the official list. No one responded as he began the roll call. Those Jews had already fled. The silence hung heavy in the air. Then the German officer ordered the lines of men to file past, while another German officer directed the Jews to the right or left. About 1,100 Jews were sent leftward and marched off. In the next few days the Judenrat managed, through bribery and intercession, to rescue 400 of them. The rest were sent to Chełmno on December 13 and 14, 1941, just five days after its gas vans had begun to operate.[12]

On December 16, 1941, the German authorities told Rumkowski that 20,000 Jews would have to leave the Lodz ghetto. In his first public announcement on the subject four days later, Rumkowski said he had succeeded in reducing the number by half and had convinced the Germans to permit him to decide, "on the basis of internal autonomy," who was to leave the ghetto. Those to be transferred, he said, would probably be sent to small towns in the Generalgouvernement where the food shortage was less severe.[13]

To plan and organize the evacuation, Rumkowski right away called a conference of leading officials in his ghetto administration. Subsequently a Resettlement Commission was established, consisting of the head of the office of vital statistics, who was also in charge of new arrivals in the ghetto; commandant of the Jewish police; chairman of courts; commandant of the prison; head of the office of investigations; and director of penal administration. These men, under Rumkowski's imperious command, decided that the contingent of ten thousand deportees would consist of two categories: about two thousand recent arrivals, expelled from Włocławek and surrounding towns—only the old among them were to be exempted because of the hardships of deportation—and the rest to be taken from persons convicted of misdemeanors or felonies and sentenced, a category designated as "undesirables." The families of these persons were to be in-

cluded among the evacuees. To avoid subjectivity and
personal involvement, it was said, the lists would be
compiled on the basis of the official records of the
courts administration, investigations office, prison, and
penal administration.

That announcement on December 20, 1941, transformed the misery in the ghetto, a time of bitter cold
and savage hunger, into terror. Cold and hunger had
already turned thousands of law-abiding ghetto residents into "undesirables," because they had stolen
wood for fuel or potato peelings for food. "Criminals"
were now those who had been sentenced for violating
blackout regulations. People felt like trapped animals,
unable to extricate themselves. Though the deportation procedure provided an opportunity for appeal, in
practice only those with protektsye from Rumkowski or his associates managed to be exempted. People
who did not report for evacuation within three days
were cut off from food, since the supply depots were
instructed not to issue them rations. The deportees
were allowed to take with them personal possessions.
Their ghetto paper money, with Rumkowski's picture
on the bills, was exchanged for German Reichsmarks.[14]

The deportations got under way in mid-January
1942, when the first contingent of 1,292 poor and
ragged men, women, and children was sent off. On
January 17 Rumkowski made a speech, vindicating
himself:

Now, when we are deporting 10,000 people from the
ghetto, I cannot pass over this tragic subject in silence.
Unfortunately, in this respect, I received a ruthless
order, an order which I had to carry out in order to
prevent its being carried out by others. Within the
framework of my possibilities . . . I have tried to
mitigate the severity of the decree. I have settled the
matter so that *I assigned for deportation that portion
which was for the ghetto a suppurating abscess.* So the
list included the ousted operators of the underworld,
scum, and all sorts of persons harmful to the ghetto.[15]

The deportations lasted until January 29, 1942. But Rumkowski's success in satisfying the Germans with 10,000 Jews had been illusory. On February 22 the deportations were resumed. For the next 40 days nearly 1,000 Jews were daily deported to an unknown destination. After the Resettlement Commission ran out of "criminals" and "sentenced" undesirables, they tackled the records of the welfare recipients. About 80 percent of the 160,000 ghetto residents were then receiving assistance. To save their activists, the leaders of the political parties submitted the names of their people to the director of the Judenrat's welfare department, who then obliterated them from the welfare rolls. In a parallel effort, the director of the Judenrat's labor office placed party activists in factory jobs.[16]

The hierarchical ranking of categories for deportation—underworld elements, prostitutes, criminals, welfare recipients, nonworking people—must have originated with the Germans, because everywhere it prevailed. In Bialystok in September 1941, when the Germans ordered the Judenrat to expel 4,500 "unproductive" Jews to Prużana, Barash ordered lists to be compiled along the same lines. In Radom in 1940, when the Judenrat was compelled to reduce the ghetto population by one-third, lists were compiled first of "harmful" elements and then of "unproductive" ones.

Work became the fundamental principle justifying the Lodz ghetto's existence. Speaking on March 2, 1942, after the category of deportable "criminals" had been exhausted, Rumkowski said: "Wholly innocent people have begun to be deported because *a new principle was introduced: that only those people who work can remain in the ghetto!* On the other hand, those who don't yet have or have not gotten work *must leave the ghetto.* The order must be carried out, there is no choice."[17]

From February 22 to April 2, 1942, over 34,000 men and women were deported. April 2 was the first day of Passover, and pious Jews saw in this constellation a good omen. But the halt in the deportations, in April as in January, was no cessation, but only a pause. Later in April, Rumkowski issued orders requiring the unemployed, ten years old and up, to submit to examinations by a team of German doctors. Yet those orders were not pursued. Instead, Rumkowski announced at the end of April that starting May 4, 1942, the Jews from Germany, Luxembourg, Vienna, and Prague would be deported, except for the employed among them and the holders of the Iron Cross or other World War I decorations. Hitherto, those Jews as a group had been exempt from the deportations. A Czech Jew, himself an insider in the ghetto bureaucracy, speculated on Rumkowski's motives:

> Though in principle no distinction was made, the psychologist must after all understand: The compatriot is the true brother; the newcomer—a step-brother. He does not even understand the language of the ghetto. . . . If only the natives would have to be deported, the Chairman would have had to turn to his productive elements. . . . Who can blame a good father when he tries with all his might to spare his beloved child?[18]

From May 4 to May 15, 1942, 10,161 Central European Jews left Lodz in 12 transports. Even those eligible for exemption volunteered to leave, for the half-year they had spent in the ghetto, in hunger, cold, and abject misery, had deprived them of the will to live. They left almost readily, convinced that wherever they went, they would not be worse off than in the Lodz ghetto.[19]

Where did they think they were going? At first, because their ghetto money was being changed into Reichsmarks, the deportees thought they were going to work in Germany. Others speculated that their destination was the Generalgouvernement. People even heard rumors that the deportees had arrived in Warsaw. But the Lodz ghetto was so tightly sealed, a quarantined Jewish island in a hostile German milieu (substantial segments of native Poles had been displaced), that no news about Chełmno or Auschwitz seeped in. No one knew anything about the fate of the 55,000 deported Jews.[20]

In the summer of 1942 about 10,000 young, able-bodied Jews were brought into the Lodz ghetto from towns and villages in the Wartheland that were being emptied of Jews. A survivor from Brzeziny brought to a Lodz Bundist a postcard which he had received from the rabbi of Grabów. The rabbi wrote that he had spoken with three Jews who had escaped from Chełmno and told him what occurred there. That was the first news in Lodz of the death camps. The Bundists undertook to pass the information on to Rumkowski, with the advice that perhaps in the future he would bribe the Germans instead of obeying their orders. But Rumkowski, it was reported, when shown the postcard, said he had already had this information for some time. Zionists and Bundists alike decided that the news about Chełmno must be transmitted to their party headquarters in Warsaw. Couriers were sent out.[21]

All through the summer, rumors about a resumption of the deportations coursed through the Lodz ghetto, reaching a crescendo of anxiety in early September. The rumors were not groundless: the Germans were now demanding the sick, children under ten, and adults over sixty-five. Rumkowski reactivated his Resettlement Commission to prepare the lists. Sensitive to the horror of the undertaking, he tried to involve the communal and political leaders as his accomplices. He called a meeting of representatives of the political parties, informing them that Hans Biebow, German administrator of the Lodz ghetto, had threatened that if the full contingent of ten thousand children under ten were not provided, the whole ghetto would be deported. Biebow had, however, allowed Rumkowski a certain number of exemptions. He offered these to the party leaders in exchange for their cooperation. They, in turn, said that they would have to consult their committees. Rumkowski gave them until the following morning. That night the Bundists convened a meeting of twenty-one leading members, sixteen of whom were parents of small children. All but one, a mother, voted to reject Rumkowski's offer.[22]

But some were found in the ghetto who would round up other people's children to save their own. Besides the Jewish police, also members of the fire brigade and the so-called "White Guard"—teamsters of the food-supply department, so nicknamed because of their flour-coated smocks—volunteered to round up the old, the sick, and the children in return for their own family's immunity. From September 5 through September 12, an embargo (*Sperre*) was ordered on all movement in the Lodz ghetto. For the first day the streets were under the dominion of the Jewish police and their helpers, but thereafter the Germans took over, dissatisfied with the ineffectiveness of the Jewish police. The seizure of the old, the sick, and the children beggared fantasy.[23] Andromache's grief was ten thousand times multiplied in Lodz:

> O Greeks, you have found out ways to torture
> that are not Greek.
> A little child, all innocent of wrong—
> You wish to kill him.

The Trojan women had their Jewish counterparts:

> As a bird cries over her young,
> Women weep for husbands, for children,
> For the old, too, who gave them birth.

The first news of Chełmno had reached Warsaw long before the couriers from Lodz. At the end of 1941 or early 1942, two escaped Jews from Chełmno came to Warsaw, with an agonized account of the annihilation camp where Jews were being gassed to death. In ŻTOS offices, where they told their story, the listening communal leaders thought that these young men must have undergone such desolating experiences that they had become deranged. The ŻTOS staff actually recorded their report, but withheld distribution because of its implausibility, not wishing further to agitate the inhabitants of the Warsaw ghetto, whose existence was wretched enough without such tales.[24]

Meanwhile, news from Ostland was arriving in Warsaw. At the end of October 1941, a non-Jewish courier undertook a mission on behalf of Hehalutz in Warsaw to make contact with the movement in Bialystok, Vilna, and Lithuania. He brought back to Warsaw in mid-November the first news of the mass killings. At the end of December 1941 and early in January 1942, five couriers, members of Hashomer Hatzair and Hehalutz, arrived one by one in Warsaw from Bialystok and Vilna. They had come for money and arms to organize a resistance movement in their ghettos. In January they told a meeting of communal and underground political leaders that more than fifty thousand unsuspecting Jews had been taken away to death at Ponary. Those mass killings in Vilna, they were convinced, marked the start of the liquidation of all Polish Jewry. Consequently, they argued, preparations for active defense should begin right away. The older communal leaders did not agree. Some believed that the German killings in the Ostland were in reprisal for Jewish collaboration with the Soviets. Others declared that the Germans would never dare to undertake mass killing on such a scale in Warsaw, in the very heart of Europe.[25] Nothing much came of the meeting, though the young people got some money.

On January 25, 1942, the *Veker,* the Bundist underground paper, reported a new wave of deportations under way in the Wartheland. Ten thousand Jews had been sent out from Lodz, selected by "King" Rumkowski himself. "Where the deportees are sent is not known." In Kalisz, the article continued, where once more than fifteen thousand Jews lived, only one thousand skilled workers remained: "The rumors are

that the deportees are being killed." On February
1, 1942, the *Veker* published its first report about the
mass gassings: "From Koło, Izbica, Dąbie, Kłodawa
come dreadful reports about the brutal annihilation by
the crazed Hitlerites of the remaining scant Jewish
settlements. The Jews are expelled and put to death
in a murderous way. They are confined and killed
with gas."

The next week the *Veker* already knew the destination of the trains packed with Jews: Chełmno, eleven
kilometers from Koło and Dąbie. "There they are
crammed in, half-naked (men in shorts, women in
shifts), in hermetically sealed autos. In these autos
they are poisoned with gases. Jews who refused to
enter the autos were prodded with electrified bayonets."

These reports appeared on the third or last pages of
a four-page paper, as if the editors themselves had
misgivings about their authenticity, or regarded them
as inapplicable to Warsaw and the Generalgouvernement. News about the progress of the war and stories
about Judenrat corruption preempted the first pages.
In fact, just a week after the last report on Chełmno,
an editorial in the *Veker*, February 15, decried rumors coursing the Warsaw ghetto that 150,000 Jews
would be deported: "It is simply a crime to spread
these rumors. The nerves of the Jewish populace are
strained enough. By spreading these unfounded rumors, people are just doing the work of the Hitlerites
—they are psychologically undermining the Jewish
masses."

Authentic reports and exaggerated rumors alike
brought on generalized feelings of panic and hysteria.
In the face of an unparalleled threat to all Jews, at
once mysterious and incredible, the underground
movement responded ambiguously. To maintain
morale and contain panic it had to discount the reports, which were indeed hard to believe, but in order
to mobilize its followers and also the general populace
toward some eventual action to counter the threat
to the Jews, it was obligated to identify and locate

the danger confronting the community. The *Veker's* next issue, February 23, 1942, brought new details, now on the second page, about the killing procedure at Chełmno: "The 'execution' lasts fifteen minutes, accompanied by the roar of the motor which is set in operation to drown out the screams and groans of the tortured, defenseless victims. . . ."

The leftist Zionists, especially the halutz youth organizations, had meanwhile begun to think of active defense. To discuss such possibilities Hehalutz convened a meeting in mid-March 1942 of seven persons —two each from the Left Labor Zionists, the Right Labor Zionists, and the Bund, and one from Hehalutz.[26] Three of the participants, representing each of the parties, were over forty, party leaders of standing. The rest were younger in years and political experience. Yitzhak Zuckerman of Hehalutz analyzed the mass killings in Ostland and the Wartheland as the first step in the eventual annihilation of the Polish Jews. He proposed that a Jewish combat organization be established and arms procured.

Both Right and Left Labor Zionists were prepared to accept these proposals, but the Bundists disagreed.[27] The Bund's senior representative did not think that the Jews were the sole target of the Germans; the Poles too had suffered severe blows, their elite had been murdered, thousands had been incarcerated in labor camps. Furthermore, he held that the groups there assembled were too small, too weak, and altogether uninfluential—inside the ghetto and outside—to undertake any successful counteraction on their own. Determination of the ghetto's fate was far beyond the capacity or competence of the ghetto itself and depended on the Allied powers. Besides, Jewish resistance would be feasible and effective only in concert with Polish resistance. The creation of a joint Jewish combat organization seemed premature. For the time being, he declared, each organization should maintain or set up its own combat units, as the Bund had already done.

Nothing came of those deliberations. At about this

time, at the initiative of Jewish PPR members in the ghetto, a short-lived organization called the Anti-Fascist Bloc came into being.[28] Its constituent members, besides the PPR, were the Left and Right Labor Zionists and the Zionist youth organizations—Hehalutz, Hashomer Hatzair, Dror. Though they had no arms at all, the bloc members began to form combat units of fives, within each one's organization. When two PPR activists were arrested by the Gestapo and murdered in June, the whole apparatus of the PPR collapsed. The Bund meanwhile continued to train its own militia; in January 1942 the Tsukunft began to rebuild its youth militia, Tsukunftshturem. On April 12 the Tsukunft aktiv convened a meeting to discuss the organization of defense.[29]

In April the news about the first mass killings in the Generalgouvernement reached Warsaw. An underground paper, *Mitteylungen*, issued early in April in the Warsaw ghetto, carried a lead article about the deportations from Lublin, "The Jewish Population Under the Sign of Physical Annihilation":

> According to reliable information the Jews of Lublin and of the other towns in the Lublin district are being sent to the camp at Bełżec. . . . It is said . . . that the Jews at Bełżec are being killed the same way as at Chełmno, that is, poisoned by gas.[30]

In the Generalgouvernement the mass killings began in Lublin. Around midnight on March 16, 1942, without any prior warning, the German authorities delivered to the Lublin Judenrat's board orders to the effect that only those Jews with work permits stamped by the Security Police (Sipo) could remain with their families in Lublin. (The Judenrat had had no knowledge of this stamping procedure, which had been done at the factories.) Starting at noon on March 17, Jews with Sipo stamps would have to move from Ghetto A to Ghetto B, with their possessions. The Jews to be evacuated—fourteen hundred daily, the orders specified—were to assemble at designated places, taking with them fifteen kilograms of possessions, money and valuables. The Judenrat was ordered to transfer food supplies from Ghetto A to Ghetto B, to take care of various technical matters, and to provide immediate burial of the dead in the ghetto. The Jewish police were, according to these orders, put at the permanent disposition of the Judenrat, unless needed for other purposes by the Germans.[31]

Stunned and defeated, the Judenrat officers did as ordered. Only bribery offered itself as the one possibility of averting or ameliorating the disaster. Despite a difference of opinion among the Judenrat board as to the efficacy of bribery, two members undertook the task. They collected gold and jewels in large quantities, some obtained forcibly from recalcitrant Jews. The two Judenrat officials brought that royal ransom to the Gestapo. Both were arrested and never seen again.

The evacuation went on as planned. On March 19 a Judenrat official reported to ŻSS headquarters in Cracow: "There is no official news. The evacuees are apparently being sent to Bełżec, district of Zamość. I have not been able to have this confirmed." He did not know the nature of the facilities at Bełżec.

Two weeks later, on March 31, the Germans ordered a special meeting of the Judenrat convened, at which four SS officers were present and six Jews invited by the SS. The senior SS officer announced that the Sipo work permit was now invalid, that henceforth only holders of a J-identity card—"J" for "Jude" —could remain in Lublin. All the others would be deported. Furthermore, any person with a J-identity card who protected and concealed any Jew without one would be subject to deportation. The Judenrat roster would be cut from twenty-four to twelve members, but would include only six of those presently in office. Six new members had been appointed by the SS and had already been brought to the meeting. In a further stratagem of deceit, the SS officer assured the Judenrat chairman and his deputy, both to be deported, that they would, "by virtue of experience in this area," assume "administrative functions in the Judenrat and ŻSS in their new residence."

On May 9, after 30,000 Jews had been deported and only 4,000 remained in Lublin, the newly elevated Judenrat chairman wrote to ŻSS headquarters that he was holding 10,000 zlotys to be transferred to the evacuees. Complaining about his inability to get any information on their whereabouts from official German sources, he added: "After all, now that the evacuation has been completed, nobody can be interested in preventing people from sending parcels of food or clothing to members of their families who had been sent away without anything."

In Lwów, deportations got under way early in March. Unlike Lublin, where the Germans decided unilaterally who was to go and who to stay, the Lwów Judenrat officials had to participate in a German-dominated commission that determined priorities —antisocials, welfare recipients, unemployed—and procedures for the resettlement, ostensibly to Polesie. The Jewish police was assigned to round up the Jews to be evacuated. Thousands of Jews, trying to escape the dragnet, hid in attics, cellars, makeshift retreats. (Some Jews managed to stay in hiding for months, with the thought of revenge sustaining them. "Despite everything," wrote a woman in her diary after six months in a hideout, "I still believe in God and I ceaselessly invoke the God of Vengeance!") After three days, the German police and Ukrainians took over, dissatisfied with the meager accomplishments of the Jewish police. By April 1, 1942, when this Aktion had ended, over 15,000 Jews had been sent to Bełżec. It was months before anyone in Lwów realized that those Jews had not been resettled in villages in the East.[32]

In May the Germans began deporting the Jews from Upper East Silesia, where Moses Merin ruled a network of Judenräte, including those of the twin cities of Sosnowiec and Będzin. The Judenrat sent notices to selected Jews instructing them to appear within a few days for resettlement, with up to ten

kilograms of personal belongings. The notice assured
that no one would be harmed. About a thousand
people turned up of their own will. Shortly thereafter
the Germans asked for another transport, and the
Judenrat once again appealed for volunteers. This
time no one came. Merin then convened the rabbis
and communal leaders in his jurisdiction to ask for
their guidance.

The Gestapo, Merin told the meeting, wanted to
deport ten thousand Jews, but he had convinced them
of the usefulness of the Jews and the Gestapo lowered
their demand to five thousand. This figure, too, Merin
hoped, could be reduced. He himself held that the
Jews themselves should carry out the Gestapo's orders,
because they could then select whom to expel—first,
informers, thieves, undesirables; then, the insane, the
sick, and defective children. (The ranking had, no
doubt, been the German proposal.) If the Germans
themselves carried out the deportation, Merin argued,
they could likely send out the community's leading
citizens. Merin's attempted blackmail to involve the
communal leaders was transparent. That was a tactic
that Rumkowski and Gens also attempted, but Merin
had no more success than either of them. Most rabbis
held that Merin's position contravened Jewish law,
that no Jew had the right to deprive another of life.
One rabbi only, a notorious sycophant, used Jewish
law to legitimate Merin, by declaring the German
order as the lesser of two evils. Months later, Merin,
eager to justify himself in the eyes of the community,
claimed that he had saved some Jews instead of losing all: "Nobody will deny that, as a general, I have
won a great victory. If I have lost only 25 percent,
when I could have lost all, who can want better re-
sults?"[33]

All through the spring of 1942 fact and rumor
about the mysterious and terrifying mass deportations
in the Wartheland and the Generalgouvernement
filtered into Warsaw. Every ghetto Jew must have
heard something, even if he did not listen to the for-

bidden radio or read the illegal underground press. Many Jews in the Warsaw ghetto had encountered Jews who had escaped from the death camps and heard their tales of horror. The ghetto lived on the precipice of disaster. Any untoward event increased tension and anxiety, provoking near-panic.[34]

On April 29, 1942, Adam Czerniaków, head of Warsaw's Judenrat, noted in his diary that Auerswald, Warsaw ghetto commissar, had asked for population statistics by streets and buildings. That same day, another German official asked for ten maps of the ghetto. Czerniaków wondered whether a new decree, further delimiting the ghetto area, would be issued. On May 4 he noted that the *Transferstelle*, the German agency regulating the ghetto's economic affairs, had demanded a list of all workers in the ghetto, including also communal officials. "It occurs to me," he remarked, "that this must be related to the deportation of unproductive elements from Warsaw."

Rumors of an imminent deportation began to sweep the ghetto. The most reliable information originated from the despised and feared Jewish Gestapo agents, who spoke of 60,000 or 70,000 Jews, perhaps more, to be deported. The shooting of the 110 imprisoned Jews at the beginning of July aggravated the unrest in the ghetto. On July 18, Czerniaków noted, the ghetto was filled "with dire forebodings" and, on the next day, "with unimaginable panic." The arrival of 40 freight cars at a railroad siding was seen as hard evidence of impending doom. Czerniaków's headaches grew worse; he began to canvass the German officials for information. They denied that anything at all untoward was under way. On July 20 the Sipo officer assured him that the rumors were "rubbish" and "nonsense."

Before noon on July 21, 1942, Sipo men arrived at the Judenrat, rounded up the officials on hand, confining them in Czerniaków's office. Sipo asked for a list of the others. Soon some forty or more Judenrat officers and staff were arrested and taken away as hostages. Czerniaków was ordered to stay, but the SS set out to locate his wife and she too became a hostage.

At 7:30 the following morning, the small ghetto was surrounded by a detachment of special police. At 10:00 A.M., SS-Sturmbannführer Hans Höfle, whose title was resettlement commissioner for the Warsaw ghetto, appeared with his men at the Judenrat. They ordered the Jews to disconnect the telephone. Then they gave the Judenrat formal typed instructions for the deportations.[35] All Warsaw Jews, regardless of age and sex, were to be resetttled in the East, except for those employed by German enterprises, Judenrat staff, Jewish police, and Jewish hospital personnel, and their families. Those to be deported could take with them fifteen kilograms of personal property, valuables, and provisions for three days. The resettlement was to start within the hour.

The instructions further specified that the Judenrat was to be responsible for delivering six thousand Jews daily to the place of assembly. For this purpose the thousand-man Jewish police force was to be used. The Judenrat would be held responsible for protecting and inventorying property left behind, for maintaining the required level of productivity in the German enterprises, for promptly burying the dead. The Jewish population was to be informed that anyone leaving the ghetto without authorization would be shot, that any Jew committing an act intended to evade or interfere with resettlement measures would be shot, and that all Jews found in Warsaw at the conclusion of the resettlement who did not belong to the exempt categories would be shot. The instructions closed with the warning that if the Judenrat did not comply 100 percent, "an appropriate number of hostages, who will meanwhile have been taken, will be shot in each instance."

Czerniaków tried to salvage something, fighting a rearguard action. He asked for exemptions to be extended also to ŻSS employees, sanitation workers, and similar categories. Höfle agreed and a supplementary order was issued to that effect, equating those groups

with the Judenrat. Czerniaków asked also for the release of several hostages. "The most tragic problem"
he raised affected the children in the institutions. His
diary entry expressed hope that he might accomplish
something.

That afternoon, Jacob Leikin, the new head of the
Jewish police, told Czerniaków that glass had been
thrown at a police car. Should that recur, the Judenrat
hostages would be shot. Later, Höfle informed Czerniaków that his wife was free for the time being, but
if anything should go wrong with the evacuation, "she
would be the first to be shot as a hostage."

The next morning, July 23, 1942, Czerniaków continued his bargaining with Höfle's subordinate. He
won a few exemptions: vocational-school students
and husbands of working women. As for the orphans,
he was told to take that up with Höfle himself. But
Höfle would not be moved and Czerniaków, unable
to save the children, reached his breaking point. He
took the cyanide tablet that he had long kept ready
for that intolerable occasion, leaving two suicide
notes, one to his wife and one to his colleagues: "I
am powerless. My heart trembles in sorrow and compassion. I can no longer bear all this. My act will
prove to everyone what is the right thing to do."[36]

Chaim Kaplan, who had mocked and excoriated
Czerniaków in his lifetime, now eulogized him: "He
perpetuated his name by his death more than by his
life."[37]

The man who succeeded Czerniaków was nothing
more than a faceless tool of the Germans.

The day the deportations began, the ghetto's communal and underground political leaders convened an
emergency conference at ŻTOS headquarters.[38] The
twenty-odd participants included top ŻTOS and JDC
officials, spokesmen of the Aguda, General Zionists,
Right and Left Labor Zionists, Bund, PPR, Hashomer Hatzair, and Hehalutz. How were they to confront the new situation? Three points of view
emerged. The majority, whose views were expressed by
Zisha Friedman of the Aguda and Dr. Ignacy Schipper

(eminent Jewish historian and lifelong Labor Zionist), opposed resistance on the ground that German reprisals would wipe out the entire ghetto, whereas, according to available information, after some fifty to seventy thousand were deported, the situation would then become stabilized. A political antagonist summarized their arguments:

The conferees were impressed by what Zisha Friedman and Schipper said. Zisha Friedman believes in faith. "I believe in God and in a miracle. God will not let His people Israel be destroyed. We must wait and a miracle will occur. Fighting the Germans is senseless. The Germans can finish us off in numbered days as in Lublin. Things as they are can continue a long time. And a miracle will happen. My friends, you who look to the Allies, why are you in despair? You believe that the Allies will win. Or don't you believe that the Allies will bring you freedom? Those of you who look to the revolution and the Soviet Union believe that capitalism is at its end and that only the Red Army will bring you freedom. Then believe in your Red Army. My dear friends, endurance and faith, and then we will have freedom!"

Schipper did not approve of defense. Defense means destroying the entire Warsaw ghetto!!! "I believe that we can manage to save the core of the Warsaw ghetto. This is war and every people must make sacrifices. We too must make sacrifices to save the core of our people. Were I convinced that we would not succeed in saving the core of our people, I would have concluded otherwise."[39]

The leftist and halutz youth regarded the deportations as the beginning of the end of the Warsaw ghetto. The Jewish population, they argued, must be roused to resistance against the Germans. The Bund called for passive resistance; the populace should be urged to refuse to obey the Jewish police, to resist leaving voluntarily. The conferees reached no decision, except to meet again.

That day or the next the leftist groups—the members of the defunct Anti-Fascist Bloc and the Bund —agreed to form a united labor committee that would call the Jewish populace to passive resistance against the Jewish police. The committee would also monitor the course of the deportations so as to call for active resistance at the appropriate time. But the accelerating pace of the deportations and the crescendo of terror broke down communication among the six organizations; coordinated action was beyond possibility. Even to cross a street became a perilous undertaking while the SS ruled the ghetto. Each party strove to stay alive, to keep its own members alive and together, and if there was a glimmer of possibility, to engage in some activity—even communication. The Bund operated an underground workshop that produced counterfeit work permits, legitimating its members as employees of the Judenrat, ŻTOS, and other communal institutions whose personnel were exempt from deportations. They also issued leaflets calling on the Jews not to go voluntarily to the place of assembly. The resettlement, the leaflets said, was a snare and delusion, part of the continuing annihilation of the Jews throughout Poland.

On July 28 Hehalutz, at a meeting of its constituents—Hashomer Hatzair, Dror, and Akiva—decided to create a Jewish combat organization. Several activists were delegated to make contact with the Polish underground on the "Aryan" side of Warsaw to obtain arms for the ghetto. The whole arsenal of the new combat force then consisted of one gun. They did for their members what the Bund was doing for its, forging work identity papers. They too issued a leaflet declaring the resettlement meant death, that men should hide their wives and children and should themselves resist German orders. Hehalutz also decided to take action against the Jewish police and issued a death sentence against Józef Szeryński, whom they mistakenly believed still to be police chief. (Szeryński had been arrested in May 1942 by the Gestapo for stealing furs confiscated the previous winter from the ghetto Jews. He was released from arrest to assist in the deportations in a subordinate capacity.)

The same day, July 28, eight members of the Left Labor Zionist committee met. The head of the party, Shakhne Zagan, reported that "two SS officers had given their word of honor to the Judenrat that not one deported Jew had been killed; they are all sent to work." Work permits were the chief subject on the agenda. ŻTOS, it was reported, was legitimating several thousand additional people, and the Judenrat itself had "promised to legalize several hundred communal leaders by assigning them to its offices." But finally the meeting decided that legalizing party members in the workshops and factories would be more secure than ŻTOS or the Judenrat.

The resettlement began at the prisons and the refugee centers. No one in the ghetto could believe that those wasted and devitalized creatures could be really resettled in the East at hard work. In the absence of familiar cues to provide guidance in the uncertainty and confusion of these unprecedented events, anxiety and apprehension among the Jews intensified. To disarm the ghetto's panic, the Germans on July 24, 1942, directed the Judenrat to issue a notice: "In view of the false information circulating in the Jewish quarter in Warsaw in connection with the resettlement, the Judenrat in Warsaw has been empowered by the authorities to announce that the resettlement of the nonproductive population in the Jewish quarter actually will take place in the Eastern territories."[40]

Thereafter, rounding up the required contingent of six thousand Jews daily became routinized. SS formations patrolled the ghetto, shooting at random. A Jewish police formation, commanded by Sipo officers, blocked off all entrances and exits of designated buildings. The tenants were ordered down to the street for a check of documents. The Jewish police, meanwhile, scoured the apartments to uncover Jews in hiding. On the street a Sipo officer examined the documents, releasing persons with valid work permits. The others were loaded onto trucks and taken to the *Umschlagplatz*, the staging area. It consisted of two squares at the extreme northern boundary of the ghetto, adjoining a railroad siding. On one square stood the Jewish Hospital, whose personnel and patients had been transferred elsewhere in the ghetto, and which now had become an improvised barracks for thousands of Jews awaiting deportation, the old and the young, the rich and the poor, the apathetic and the hysterical, crowded together in the summer heat without adequate sanitary facilities, water, or medical aid.

When enough Jews had been assembled to load the trains, they were herded through an inspection team of two or more SS officers at the entry to the second square. A few hundred fit-looking men were separated and sent to transit labor camps. The rest, under the brutal goad of the Jewish police, were pushed into the waiting freight cars.

The diligence with which the Jewish police performed their work was generated by fear and dilated into viciousness. Every policeman's family—wife, children, and parents—had been exempted from deportation, but that exemption depended on slavish obedience to German authority. One policeman, trying to wrest a child from its father, responded to the father's plea: "What makes you think I'm human? Maybe I'm a wild beast. I have a wife and three children. If I don't deliver my five heads by five P.M., they'll take my children. Don't you see, I'm fighting for the life of my own kids?"[41]

Still the Jewish police—or some among them—were better than Germans or Ukrainians, because they could be bribed. For money or jewels they closed an official eye to Jews in hiding. For kingly ransoms they rescued people from the Umschlagplatz and took the risk of escorting them, with ostensible police protection, out of the danger zone.

The ghetto, though driven by fear of impending death or disaster, responded to the roundups with the logic of the situation. Everyone wanted to be "productive." Like trapped creatures, the Jews scurried back and forth to find a niche to safeguard themselves and their families. Possession of machines or tools—especially a sewing machine—became a lifeline. Long before 8:00 in the morning, when the roundups began, the Jews were besieging the shops and factories that promised safety.

Every regulative communal structure in the ghetto had collapsed. For the first time in its venerable history, Warsaw Jewry was without communal resources for maintaining or building morale, without communal leadership.[42] Only nuclear clusters of the political parties remained, isolated fragments of the welfare and religious communities. Apart from the handful of leaflets that the Bund and Hehalutz had managed to distribute, communication had completely broken down in the ghetto. The only source of news came from the German orders issued through the discredited, disorganized, and demoralized Judenrat. Rumors gripped the ghetto, displacing each other with lightning rapidity. People said: Only the poorest and the unemployed would be taken; the deportation would last just a few days; as soon as fifty thousand or so were deported, the ghetto would resume its old existence.

At the very start of the deportations, the stores closed down and the transaction of normal business halted. Formations of Ukrainian, Lithuanian, and Latvian auxiliary police surrounding the ghetto prevented the habitual illegal smuggling of food and barred the entry of Poles to buy and barter from the Jews. The scarcity sent food prices soaring far beyond ghetto inflation. A kilogram of bread, which in 1940 had cost 4 zlotys and 14 zlotys in May 1942, now cost 45 zlotys. A kilogram of potatoes cost 15 zlotys, a tenfold increase after 1941. Hunger became a daily concomitant of terror.

The Germans took advantage of the hunger. They announced that beginning July 29, for a period of three days, persons who reported voluntarily for resettlement would receive free three kilograms of bread and one kilogram of marmalade. Hunger drove thousands to the Umschlagplatz. Confronted with the hopelessness of their situation, unable to find work, unable to feed themselves or their children, fearful of the next day, these Jews accepted voluntary resettlement and the gift of bread as their solution. No left-wing leaflets warning that resettlement meant death carried weight against the rising hunger and spreading despair. Besides, many Jews regarded voluntary resettlement as a means of keeping the family together. Thousands calculated that it was better for their family to stay together in a new adversity than to be torn asunder in anguish or die of hunger.

The German ruse succeeded so well that the period of voluntary resettlement was extended twice. Now, too, relatives began to get postcards and letters from those deported, purportedly sent from Bialystok, Pinsk, Brześć—even from as far away as Smolensk. Actually written under duress at Treblinka, the messages were the same: the new places were satisfactory, they had work, the children had schools, they urged their relatives to join them. Those letters nourished the illusions that the Warsaw ghetto Jews spun about the fate of the deported. (The same thing happened in all the ghettos.) The wish to live, the inability to believe in one's own imminent death, the universal human faith in one's own immunity to disaster—all these factors conspired to make the Jews believe that resettlement, not death, was the fact. "At bottom," wrote Freud, "nobody believes in his own death." Not gullibility, or suggestibility, but universal human optimism encouraged them to believe in the deceptions that the Germans perpetrated. In the process of repressing and denying the overpowering threat that confronted them, perceptual distortion and skewed interpretation based on wishful thinking managed to reconcile the illogic and inconsistencies of their fears and hopes. Without accurate information, without corrective feedback from authoritative sources on the course of events, their isolation helped give credence to their distorted and distorting evaluation of their predicament. This mechanism of denial, this arming oneself against disquieting facts, was not pathological, but, as psychologists point out, a tool of adaptation, a means of coping with an intolerable situation in the absence of any possibility for defensive action. The alternative was despair, the quiet stunned reaction of the defeated.[43]

Every individual attempt to stand up to the Germans ended in death. The Jew who refused to budge when ordered, who spat at the German, who cursed him, who slapped his face, threw stones, or reached for a stick was shot on the spot. Thousands of such individual acts of resistance became nothing more than induced suicide. They left scarcely a record, except in the German statistics—more than five thousand shot to death—and a few poignant memories.

In August the Germans changed their techniques in rounding up Jews. Distrustful now of the Jewish police, the Germans demoted them, using increased numbers of Ukrainian, Lithuanian, and Latvian auxiliary police. Large SS formations, the so-called *Vernichtungskommando* (Annihilation Squad), buttressed by machine guns, took over. Their procedure was to rout the Jews out of the blockaded buildings —soon whole streets were blockaded—and herd them to the Umschlagplatz. In the first half of August, the small ghetto was liquidated, including its workshops and all its children's institutions, boarding homes, and orphanages.

A first-aid unit, run by the Judenrat, had been installed at the Umschlagplatz. A small place—two rooms with beds for the sick—it became a center of clandestine rescue activity. It was operated by Nahum Remba, a General Zionist long active in the kehilla and then Judenrat personnel secretary, aided by several nurses, known at the Umschlagplatz as the Rescue Brigade. Wearing a medic's coat, Remba used to scour the Umschlagplatz for persons to rescue— rabbis, communal leaders. They were taken into the first-aid station, held there until they could be returned safely to the ghetto. Remba saved hundreds of Jews, until the Germans and the Jewish police chief began to suspect him.[44]

When Janusz Korczak and the children of his orphanage came to the Umschlagplatz, Remba tried to save them too. As for Korczak, he long had been ready for death. When the Germans came that hot August morning and blockaded the orphanage, the two hundred children stood ready, washed and scrubbed from head to toe, dressed in clean clothes, each child holding a little bag with bread and a flask of water. They marched to the Umschlagplatz, Korczak at the head of the procession, hatless, his broken, bent body the orphans' bulwark, his nurses bringing up the rear. With armed German and Ukrainian police lining the streets, hurrying them forward, the children marched on. No one cried; no one tried to run away.[45]

Word of their coming had already preceded them to the Umschlagplatz. Remba settled the children back near a protecting wall, hoping to postpone their departure and perhaps so to rescue them. He urged Korczak to accompany him to the Judenrat to intervene in their behalf, but Korczak refused, not wishing to leave the children alone. (In the 1930s, he once explained to friends why he would not settle in Palestine: "If I left, I would never forgive myself. I detest desertion.") That day the trains were filling slowly and the order went out to load the children. "I will never forget that procession," wrote Remba. In contrast to the apathetic huddled masses who were herded into the freight cars, "all the children were lined up four in a row. Korczak at the head, eyes forward, holding a child with each hand, led the procession." Remba could not control himself, weeping for Jewish helplessness.[46]

German bestiality increased until "the Jews came to fear the Germans more than death." Pious Jews marched to the Umschlagplatz and into the waiting trains wrapped in their prayer shawls, reciting prayers and psalms, oblivious of the violence. *Kiddush ha-shem,* martyrdom for the glorification and sanctification of God, once more reasserted its place in Jewish tradition. For believing Jews the conviction that their sacrifice was required as a testimony to Almighty God was more comforting than the supposition that He had abandoned them altogether. To be sure, God's design was concealed from them, but they would remain steadfast in their faith. Morale was sustained by rabbis and pious Jews who, by their own resolute and exalted stance, provided a model of how Jews should encounter death. On the Umschlagplatz that August an elderly pious Jew exhorted the despondent masses, sunk in the misery and squalor of their surroundings: "Jews, don't despair! Don't you realize that we are going to meet the Messiah? If I had some liquor, I'd drink a toast."[47]

In the second half of August 1942, the Germans invalidated the old work permits, now requiring them to bear a Sipo stamp. The locale of roundups shifted from tenements to workshops. Dozens of productive enterprises that had been a sanctuary for Jewish workers were liquidated and thousands of skilled workers were carried off in a torrent of violence to the Umschlagplatz, regardless of German economic priorities. Even family dependents of workers with Sipo permits were no longer exempt from resettlement. By August 27, when the roundups halted for a brief respite, some 200,000 Warsaw ghetto Jews had been deported. The demographic structure of the ghetto was transformed. The family was disappearing. The age parameters of the ghetto were skewed: the old and the children were being erased from the statistics.

At that very time the young people in the fragmented underground parties—their veteran leaders were either killed or in hiding on the "Aryan" side—attempted to exercise some autonomy of action. The halutz groups set fire to abandoned ghetto buildings, and on August 20 one of their members made an attempt on Szeryński's life, but succeeded only in wounding him. The next day the halutz groups received, through the instrumentality of the PPR outside the ghetto, five guns and eight grenades. Then the halutzim ventured an unsuccessful attack on Germans and Ukrainians entering the ghetto. Two small parties of young people who had been sent into the woods to organize partisan units perished. On September 3, in two separate incidents, two leading members of their underground were arrested. The first arrest made it mandatory to transfer the tiny cache of weapons. But that venture too failed: the courier was caught; the arms were confiscated. Every attempt at resistance had ended in death or failure.

In mid-August the Bund, wanting to find out where the Jews were being transported, to verify rumors of death camps and to counteract the deceptive postcards, sent out a courier to learn the destination of the trains. A tall, blond, handsome man, the stereotypic "Aryan," Zalman Friedrich made contact with a Polish Socialist railway worker who knew the direction taken by the deportation trains. Friedrich reached Sokołów, where he learned that the Germans had constructed a new spur track to the village of Treblinka. The villagers knew of a large camp where dreadful things occurred, but little more. In Sokołów Friedrich met a bleeding and bruised escapee from Treblinka, who described in detail its killing installations and procedures. Friedrich made his way back to Warsaw with his news, but by the time he arrived, the Germans had returned to the ghetto in full fury.[48]

On September 5 the Germans issued an announcement that all Jews in the Warsaw ghetto, without exception, were to report the following morning for registration purposes, with food for two days and drinking utensils, within an area of seven square blocks located between the Umschlagplatz and Pawiak prison. Whoever did not comply would be shot. That whole day "passed with the oppressive sense of imminent death," wrote a Jewish teacher and scholar, now factory worker. "I would like to die in

peace and with the awareness that it must be so. . . .
I think there is no possibility of extricating ourselves
from the clutches of the wild beast and we are only
prolonging our death agony."[49]

The Germans called the Aktion an *Einkesselung,*
"encirclement." The Jews Yiddishized the word to
kesl, "cauldron." That roped-off area, surrounded by
armed police, was indeed a cauldron, its human mass
seething and churning, evoking the image of Dante's
Second Circle, where the blast of hell "never rests
from whirling . . . forever beating and hurling." The
encirclement lasted one week, with nearly 10,000
Jews deported every day. It ended on September 12,
1942, Rosh Hashana 5703. The *kesl* was a place of
anguish and terror, violence and resistance. Thousands still managed to summon the energy and the
will to live. In that week alone the German statistics
recorded that 2,648 Jews were shot to death. But
stupor and fatalism, a state of emotional catalepsy,
induced thousands of others to surrender passively to
German orders.

The ghetto was cut down to four tiny isolated en-
claves, separated from one another. The surviving
Jews lived at their factories or in hiding. Jewish home
life had been extinguished, the Jewish family obliterated. Of the more than 350,000 Jews in the Warsaw ghetto on July 22, 1942, no more than 45,000 or
so remained, about 60 percent between the ages of
twenty and thirty-nine.[50] German and Ukrainian
armed police patrolled the ghetto, shooting Jews on
sight. The streets were strewn with dead Jewish
bodies. On Yom Kippur the Germans carried out one
more roundup, perhaps only for sadistic gratification.
Over 2,000 Jews were taken that day, including some
600 Jewish policemen.

Emerging from the ashes of the Warsaw ghetto, a
new issue of a Bundist underground paper entitled
Oyf der vakh (On Guard) appeared on September
20. Its lead article, "The Annihilation of Warsaw Jews,"
warned the Jews: "Be on guard! Don't let yourself
be destroyed like sheep! Better to die with honor

than to be gassed in Treblinka!" Friedrich's report about Treblinka followed. In closing, it exhorted the survivors:

> Today every Jew should know the fate of those resettled. The same fate awaits the remaining few left in Warsaw. The conclusion then is: Don't let yourself be caught! Hide, don't let yourself be taken away, run away, don't be fooled by registrations, selections, numbers, and roll calls! Jews, help one another! Take care of the children! Help the illegals! The dishonorable traitors and helpers—the Jewish police—should be boycotted! Don't believe them, beware of them. Stand up against them!
>
> We are all soldiers on a terrible front!
>
> We must survive so that we can demand a reckoning for the tortured brothers and sisters, children and parents who were killed by the murderer's hand on the battlefield for freedom and humanity![51]

The report came too late for the 300,000 Warsaw Jews already deported. But it heralded the resistance to come.

15

"For Your Freedom and Ours"

"They were free. Their last links with everyday life were broken," wrote Gusta Dawidsohn, Akiva activist, in her diary, describing the halutz youth in Cracow after the deportations of June and October 1942, which took some 12,000 of the last 17,000 Jews in the ghetto. They "suddenly felt free to plunge into the maelstrom of underground work; it was a feeling of freedom which sprouted out of the rubble of shattered family life."[1]

In all the ghettos of the Generalgouvernement and the other occupied lands in Eastern Europe, in the wake of the great wave of killings or deportations, the youth of the Jewish political movements began to organize armed resistance to the Germans. Deprived of family, they had gained freedom and autonomy. Without families, they no longer had the care and anxiety for baby brothers, younger sisters, aging parents, no more the need to support or protect them. The possible consequences of rash acts held less terror now that the ghetto was no longer peopled by their families, now that the sense of familial responsibility no longer inhibited them.

The knowledge of the death camps and the sense of death's inevitability accelerated their resort to armed resistance. "One way or another," wrote Hersh Ber-linski, "lies death." Despair over Jewish powerlessness and revengefulness against the Germans had converted them to a new outlook. The political hopes and aspirations that had nourished the young people's will to live and which had provided both foundation and framework for their clandestine educational and cultural activities in the ghettos had been shattered by the realization that the Germans meant to destroy all Jews. In Bialystok, Mordecai Tenenbaum, Hehalutz activist and organizer of the Zionist youth underground, who called himself "the apostle of death," asked the Zionist youth at a meeting on February 19, 1943, whether there was any historic significance in any given person's remaining alive after the liquidation of three and a half million Polish Jews.[2] Mordecai Anielewicz, Hashomer Hatzair activist and eventually head of the Jewish combat organization in Warsaw, told Ringelblum of his deep regret that he and his comrades had "wasted" three years in educational and cultural work. Instead they should have learned how to use arms and schooled themselves in a spirit of revenge.[3]

The young people in the Zionist and Bundist movements, reared in the ideals of secular modernity, rejected the traditionalist values and modes of behavior that had sustained Diaspora existence for centuries. Contemptuous of the long tradition of Jewish accommodation, they sought ways—whether nationalist or socialist—to combat Jewish powerlessness. Like most modernists, they were fired by the medieval virtues of Christian chivalry that prescribed the defense of honor by arms. To modern secularists the Jewish tradition of martyrdom, kiddush ha-shem, was the epitome of the Diaspora fate against which they rebelled. To them, nonbelievers, martyrdom did not mean bearing witness to God, but merely signified Jewish helplessness, passivity in the face of destruction. The biblical passage in the liturgy that expressed readiness for martyrdom,

Nay, but for Thy sake are we killed all the day;
We are accounted as sheep for the slaughter [Ps. 44:23]

embodied values and an ideal that they repudiated.

The only question facing the Jews, Anielewicz told Ringelblum, was how to choose to die: "either like sheep for the slaughter or like men of honor." Among the Zionist youth in the resistance movement, "like sheep for the slaughter" became an epithet of ignominy, divorced from its original meaning of martyrdom as a meaningful option. These young Zionists, in their statements and proclamations, echoed the feelings of anger against Jewish passivity that Chaim Nachman Bialik had voiced in his poem *Be'ir hahareygah* ("The City of Slaughter"), written after the Kishenev pogrom of 1903:

Let them raise a fist against Me and demand revenge
    for their humiliation,
The humiliation of all generations from their first to last,
And let them break asunder with their fist the
    heavens and My throne.

Then, at the turn of the century, the emergent Bundist and Labor Zionist movements, in response to the pogroms erupting in the czarist empire, had forged a new instrument to protect the Jews, the *zelbshuts* (self-defense). Recruiting the robust and tough elements among Jews—carters, wagoners, teamsters, abattoir workers, even horse thieves—armed with knives, axes, poles, brass knuckles, clubs, switches, and thongs, the socialist Jews served notice on pogromists and indifferentists alike that the Jews would no longer be unresistant victims. They concluded what Machiavelli had long ago argued, that "among other evils which being unarmed brings you, it causes you to be despised."

The idea of self-defense had never been extinguished in the ghettos, but everyone—the young as well as the experienced—had realized in the earliest ghetto days that the SS was not comparable to a horde of drunken peasants or even a company of Cossack horsemen and that axes and knives, clubs and switches were no match for the war apparatus that the Germans commanded. Besides, everyone in the ghetto knew that even a limited armed action on a specific target would incur German reprisals whose cost to the ghetto in human life would surpass any benefit. But when it became clear to the underground that no option but death existed, the idea of resistance took on another aspect, becoming an affective undertaking rather than an instrumental one. Scarcely any of the young people seriously believed that resistance could save the remaining Jews in the ghetto, but all believed that by defying the Germans with whatever armed strength they could muster, they would redeem the honor of the Jews.

Resistance was thus not defense in the sense that the zelbshuts had been. It was instead an act of desperation, whose Jewish paradigm was the suicidal stand of the Zealots at Masada against Rome's imperial legions. Masada had been incorporated into modern Zionist myth under the influence of Yitzhak Lamdan's epic poem: "We have one treasure left—the daring after despair." Since hope for survival had been abandoned, one must die gloriously. Fatalism and the surrender to death haunted many young people in the ghettos. "We are going on the road to death, remember that," said Aaron Liebeskind, Akiva activist in Cracow. "Whoever desires still to live should not search for life here among us. We are at the end."[4]

One objective that joined all members of all parties in the underground was the passion for revenge on the Germans. Hatred for the Germans consumed them. The Zionist youth in Vilna issued an appeal: "Convey your hatred of the foe in every place and at every moment!" On March 1, 1943, a member of a Dror kibbutz in Bialystok wrote a letter to comrades in Palestine (which was never mailed), describing the production of hand grenades by the underground organization: "We'll kill our slaughterers; they will have to fall together with us." Above all, she admonished her overseas comrades: "We call you to vengeance, revenge without remorse or mercy. . . . Vengeance! This is our challenge to you, who have not suffered in Hitler's hell. This you are duty-bound to fulfill. Our scattered bones will not rest in peace, the scattered ashes of the crematoria will not lie still, until you have avenged us."[5]

As the young people plunged into the ramifications and implications of the idea of resistance, they began to define its objectives in more concrete terms than the rhetoric of despair or revenge allowed. In all ghettos, two lines of thought emerged. One view held that honor and vengeance demanded a last stand in the ghetto, a symbolic defense of the ghetto before its final liquidation by the Germans. The other view held that since no practical use could come of a defense in the ghetto, which was unsuitable terrain anyway for guerrilla warfare, Jewish resisters could make better use of their meager forces by joining up with the Russian partisans in the woods. That debate between the two points of view would continue in many ghettos until the very end.

The first resistance organization was set up in Vilna. It was sparked by a meeting on January 1, 1942, of about 150 young Zionists, who heard Abba Kovner, Hashomer Hatzair activist and poet, read a proclamation calling for self-defense: "Let's not allow ourselves to be led like sheep to the slaughter." It breathed with the resonance of Bialik in its condemnation of Jewish passivity and appealed to the youth of Vilna to redeem Jewish dignity and avenge the murder of Jews.[6] Within a short time thereafter, Hashomer Hatzair, *Hanoar Hazioni* (General Zionist youth), Revisionists, Bundists, and Communists formed the *Fareynikte partizaner organizatsye* (FPO; United Partisans Organization).[7]

In Warsaw, the halutz groups set about reactivating their combat organization in the relative quiet that followed the kesl. At a meeting early in October 1942 with the Left Labor Zionists to discuss formation of a

defense organization, two halutz youth leaders—
Anielewicz and Zuckerman—launched a bitter attack
on the Jewish political parties. The conflict between
the youth groups and the Left Labor Zionist party
focused specifically on whether the proposed combat
organization should have a dual executive apparatus—
political and military—or just military. The spokesmen
of the youth organizations feared that a political apparatus, controlled by veteran party leaders, would
inhibit freedom of military action. The parties, they
argued, had done nothing in the days before the
present calamity but talk. "The parties have no right
to dictate to us. Except for their youth organizations,
they won't do anything; they will only obstruct."[8]

The Left Labor Zionists responded with the argument that the political parties, and not the youth
organizations, had earned the confidence of the Jewish
masses. Even if the parties had made mistakes in the
past, they would still be the ones to determine the
shape of Jewish society in the future. "Don't think,
comrades, that just because you have two broken
revolvers, you can be hoity-toity and take no account
of anyone else." The Left Labor Zionists favored two
apparatuses, for "every armed undertaking in the ghetto
must be weighed and measured; we dare not permit
any reckless acts that might bring about a premature
liquidation of the Warsaw ghetto." Even if all the Jews
were to expire in the ghetto, the party still carried an
obligation for its acts to the Jews throughout the
world and its fraternal parties abroad. "We do not
want to be maligned in our graves for reckless acts
committed here." The Left Labor Zionist insistence
that the political parties oversee the combat organization finally prevailed. The organization was called
Żydowska Organizacja Bojowa (ŻOB; Jewish Combat
Organization).

When the young people in the ghettos began to
form their combat organizations, few gave thought to
the political and social requisites of an effective resistance movement: active support by an Allied gov-

ernment from the outside and assistance in—or, at the
very least, passive approval of—its activities by the
indigenous population within the area of operations.
Wherever these conditions were absent, Jewish resistance organizations foundered. Despite their courage
and readiness for self-sacrifice, the young people by
themselves were unable to win the confidence of the
Polish underground government, of the Soviet partisan
operation, and even of the Jewish populace in the
ghettos. For in those desperate times even more than
in normal times, trust and confidence reposed in men
and organizations whose past record of accomplishment had demonstrated their responsibility, integrity,
and ability to lead.

In Warsaw, the Polish capital and center of all
Polish underground organizations, some of the established Jewish parties continued to maintain a Jewish
political presence despite the decimation of their
ranks. A handful of surviving veteran leaders of the
central committees of the Bund, General Zionists, and
both Right and Left Labor Zionists, living on the
"Aryan" side under false identities, carried on. They
had the responsibility to sustain their parties and to
render whatever assistance could be given to the beleaguered Jews in the territory that had made up
Poland. Even more important was their function of
maintaining contact with the outside world—with the
Polish underground in the country, with the Polish
government-in-exile and with the Jewish representatives in the Polish National Council in London, with
their fraternal parties in Palestine and the United
States, and with Jewish listening posts in Switzerland
and Turkey. Since early 1942 the Polish National
Council in London had two Jewish members—Ignacy
Schwarzbart, a General Zionist, and Arthur Zygelboym, the Bundist who had fled Warsaw late in 1939.[9]
(Zygelboym took his life in London on May 12, 1943,
at the age of forty-eight.)*

---

* His farewell letter read:
   I cannot be silent. I cannot live while the remnants of the Jewish

The presence in Warsaw of acknowledged political leaders of Polish Jewry played a decisive role in the development of the resistance movement. One reason the halutz youth submitted to the political supervision of the adult parties was their realization that alone they could not succeed. They had been advised by friends in the prewar Polish scout movement, now associated with the underground Polish Home Army, that to get weapons from the Home Army they would need not merely the backing, but the full instrumentality, of a representative Jewish political body of weight and stature.

Confronted with the need for such political representation, the *de facto* combat organization then coopted, besides the Left Labor Zionists, also the General and Right Labor Zionists. These parties, together with the youth groups (Hehalutz, Hashomer Hatzair, Dror), constituted the *Żydowski Komitet Narodowy* (ŻKN; Jewish National Committee), which was to serve as the political arm of the combat organization. Adolf Berman, a veteran Left Labor Zionist, living on the "Aryan" side, became the authorized ŻKN representative to deal with the Polish civilian underground and Israel Chaim Vilner, a Hashomer Hatzair activist, was designated as ŻOB representative to the Polish military underground. The youth organizations also delegated some of their people throughout Poland to set up resistance groups in Bialystok, Będzin, Cracow, and Częstochowa.

Negotiations were conducted also with the Revisionists, who agreed to join both the ŻKN and ŻOB, though their membership was short-lived. They failed to maintain security among their members, and a more serious charge leveled against them was their uni-

---

population of Poland, of whom I am a representative, are perishing. My friends in the Warsaw ghetto died with weapons in their hands in the last heroic battle. It was not my destiny to die together with them but I belong to them and in their mass graves.

By my death I wish to make my final protest against the passivity with which the world is looking on and permitting the extermination of the Jewish people.

lateral contacts with right-wing Polish military groups outside the ghetto. They refused to share the weapons they had obtained and tried to bully their way to ŻOB leadership.[10] They later formed their own organization, *Żydowski Związek Wojskowy* (ŻZW; Jewish Military Union).

Negotiations with the Bund were more complex. The Bund, ready to join ŻOB, nevertheless insisted on maintaining its political autonomy and independence. In mid-October the Bund proposed as a solution to the organizational dilemma the formation of a coordinating committee, consisting of the Bund and the ŻKN, which would serve as the vehicle for overall political and communal representation. On October 20, general agreement was reached and the *Żydowski Komitet Koordynacyjny* (ŻKK; Jewish Coordinating Committee) was formed.[11] The ŻKK was to represent the Bund only in matters affecting Warsaw; with regard to the rest of Poland, the Bund retained its autonomy. (In May 1943, after the Warsaw ghetto rising, the Bund agreed to extend coordination over all Poland.) An understanding was also reached that political issues —presumably those of a general nature affecting Poland—would be handled independently by each party and excluded from coordination.[12] Negotiations with the Jewish Communists were protracted because they required instructions from the Warsaw Committee PPR, which eventually authorized participation in ŻOB and the ŻKK in matters limited to Warsaw alone.[13]

Within a few weeks formal bylaws for the ŻKK and ŻOB were drawn up, describing the purposes of the ŻKK as the defense of the ghetto in the event of a further effort by the Germans to deport the remaining Jews and the protection of the Jews in the ghetto from "the hirelings and flunkies of the occupant." (On October 29, ŻOB carried out its first successful "execution," killing Jacob Leikin, chief of the Jewish police.) The ŻKK was to supervise ŻOB and set its policies. ŻOB's basic combat units were to consist of six members each and a commander, organized according to places of work, and by parties or organizations. Every member of a combat unit was to be armed, the definition of arms extended to include "axes, knives, brass knuckles, caustic substances, incendiary materials, and others."[14]

At the time the ŻKK was being formed, Jan Karski, the liaison officer between the underground in Poland and the Polish government-in-exile, met with Leon Feiner, Bund leader on the "Aryan" side, and with an unidentified Zionist leader. Karski wanted to get information about the fate of the Jews, which he would bring to the Polish and Allied governments. At one point in their conversation, the Zionist said to him: "We are not going to die in slow torment, but fighting. We will declare war on Germany—the most hopeless declaration of war that has ever been made." Feiner, confirming these words, added: "We are organizing a defense of the ghetto, not because we think it can be defended, but to let the world see the hopelessness of our battle—as a demonstration and a reproach."[15]

The defense of the ghetto as the objective of Jewish resistance symbolized the isolation of the Jews in Eastern Europe. Resistance movements everywhere—maquis, guerrillas, partisans—were regarded as auxiliaries of the conventional armed forces on the battlefield, whose objective, within the limits of their capabilities, was to help the Allies and hinder the Germans. As irregular forces, they were to stage small-scale attacks on isolated or unprotected German installations, carry out diversions, disrupt communications, sabotage military facilities, and, if circumstances allowed, gather intelligence. Merely to enumerate these tasks is to demonstrate the disability of the Jews in the ghettos to perform them. Nevertheless, with regard to homefront operations, no substantial difference between the Jewish and European resistance movements existed. Both conducted activities to bolster morale, issuing underground papers and proclamations to provide information about Allied progress, and both condemned and executed spies and traitors in their midst.

No resistance movement in Europe was self-sufficient. None had substantial indigenous resources of arms or matériel. Nor could any resistance group operate independently to any advantage. To be useful militarily or politically, every resistance activity had to be fitted into an overall Allied strategy and synchronized into an overall Allied schedule. In the first years of the war, Great Britain was the sole support of all resistance movements in Europe, establishing for that purpose the Special Operations Executive, SOE. Until late 1942, when Russia regained the initiative on the Eastern front and reorganized the partisan movement on an expanded scale, London was the headquarters of the European resistance movement, where the governments-in-exile of the occupied countries served as liaisons to the British, pleading on behalf of their underground forces for military and financial assistance.[16]

A resistance organization, to receive aid, had to have the political backing of its government-in-exile and be able to render useful, if minor, military services to the Allies. The Soviet Union, for example, began in 1943 to back only such indigenous Communist resistance movements in the several East European countries as would provide it with postwar political footholds there. In Poland, the Home Army (*Armja Krajowa*), directed by the Polish government-in-exile and by its plenipotentiary (*Delegatura*) in Warsaw, was authorized to receive SOE assistance through a system of clandestine landings or drops. In all, nearly 500 flights provided the Home Army with some 600 tons of equipment—one-third of its total arms supply —and 40 million zlotys. The Soviet Union, for its part, through the PPR supported the People's Army (*Armja Ludowa*) with funds and matériel, on the calculation that it would establish the Communist presence in postwar Poland.

The surviving Polish Jews, imprisoned in ghettos and SS labor camps, did not fit into any conventional framework that would entitle them to aid from either Allied or Soviet channels. The Jewish resistance organizations in the ghettos had no access to areas where they could perform useful military tasks. Furthermore, their decimation rendered their postwar political importance or influence negligible.

The anomalous Jewish situation and unique objectives of Jewish resistance complicated the fundamental question of arms supply, without which resistance was mere rhetoric. ŻOB and the ŻKK applied for arms to the Home Army, which referred the appeal to the Delegatura, which, in turn, solicited the decision of London headquarters. The question was not just military, but political, and it was exacerbated by pandemic Polish anti-Semitism. In mid-November 1942, the Delegatura finally responded to the ŻOB request by expressing readiness to provide some arms if the resistance organizations would take a loyalty oath that in the event of war between Poland and the Soviet Union, they would not use those arms on the side of the Red Army. The ŻOB constituents gave their word, and at the end of November or at the very beginning of December, the Home Army delivered ten guns to ŻOB.[17]

On December 2, 1942, Henryk Wolinski, in charge of Jewish affairs for the Home Army's Chief Command, met with the two representatives of the ŻKK, Feiner of the Bund and Vilner for the ŻKN, who presented him with the bylaws of the coordinating committee. The political question as to the overall representation of the Jews in Warsaw was now clarified. The ŻKK representatives requested a larger supply of arms than the ten pieces already received, which, they said, did "not suffice to organize an armed resistance or any other action of a collective and non-individual character." They also wanted help in organizing the purchase of arms on the "Aryan" side and securing the services of instructors in military training. Most Jews who had been trained in the Polish army and could have served as instructors, they explained, were now with the Jewish police and hence untrustworthy. Wolinski forwarded a memorandum of this meeting and of the ŻKK requests to London with a lukewarm recommendation.[18] On the same application, General Stefan Rowecki, commander-in-chief of the Home Army, sent a splenetic and distrustful radio message to the Polish High Command in London on January 4, 1943:

> Too late Jews of various groupings, also Communists, appeal to us for arms, just as if we had full arsenals. As a trial I gave them a few pistols. I am not sure that they will use the weapons altogether. More weapons I will not give, because as you know we don't have them ourselves. We are awaiting a delivery. Inform us what connections our Jews have with London.[19]

The information relayed from London apparently proved satisfactory, because at the end of January—after ŻOB's armed challenge to the Germans in the Warsaw ghetto on January 18–22, 1943—the Home Army delivered to ŻOB 49 revolvers, 50 grenades, and a quantity of explosives. That delivery, along with the 10 guns received earlier, eventually made up about 10 percent of ŻOB's arsenal.[20]

The rest of their arms ŻOB—like combat organizations in other ghettos—bought at exorbitant cost and great peril from Poles and smuggled them into the ghetto. (In Galicia, where Italian soldiers were stationed, Jews used to buy arms from them.) Funds came from the political parties, which, through the Delegatura, received money from their fraternal parties abroad, from whatever resources still remained with the JDC, and—as the resistance movement gained in authority—from the Judenräte and their institutions. Barash, for instance, not only subsidized the resistance movement in Bialystok, but also sent money to Warsaw. Dr. Elkes in Kovno, with the support of several other members of the Judenrat, financed the purchase of arms for the local resistance organization and provided facilities for manufacturing grenades and explosives. In Warsaw the ŻKK set up a citizens' committee of JDC and party leaders who raised funds from private people with resources and who also demanded, and received, contributions from the Judenrat amounting to nearly one million zlotys.

ŻOB and the individual parties assigned couriers to the dangerous business of buying, testing, and smuggling arms. Both the ghetto and the "Aryan" city swarmed with police, blackmailers, informers, spies, and Gestapo agents looking for victims. Every courier was exposed to dangers and risks that tested to the utmost his or her ingenuity, daring, and courage.[21]

In each ghetto, organizing resistance presented a congeries of dilemmas even more complex and tangled than arms procurement.[22] Matters that on the surface appeared to be merely practical or technical—where to fight and when to fight—were actually a matter of life and death for the ghetto, however amputated it was at that stage. Decisions on such questions could not responsibly be taken without consulting the ghetto's legitimate leadership, whether it was the Judenrat, the alternative communal leadership, or the political underground.

As long as the ghetto leadership held that a possibility of survival for the ghetto existed—because the Red Army was approaching or because the ghetto worked efficiently for the German war economy—it could not support a policy of resistance. That was the case of the Lodz ghetto, where nearly ninety thousand Jews remained after the deportations of the children, the old, and the sick in September 1942. All through 1943, when nearly all ghettos in the Generalgouvernement and in Ostland were being liquidated, the Lodz ghetto seemed almost an island of serenity in a sea of blood. Its residents, working in the industrial enterprises that appeared to justify their existence, hoped that they would live to see the defeat of the Germans.

No armed resistance movement existed in Lodz. No contact was possible between Jews in the ghetto and Poles outside. The Bundists were cut off from contact with Polish Socialists; the Jewish Communists were isolated from their parent PPR. The ghetto was en-

veloped in political void. Its total imprisonment, which
rendered futile the smuggling even of contraband
food, turned the idea of smuggling arms into total
fantasy. The Lodz ghetto remained without guns, without weapons, without military resources.

The only strategy the underground parties evolved
was to protect their people until the moment of liberation. In February 1944, for instance, when the Germans asked for fifteen hundred able-bodied, skilled
artisans to be sent to Częstochowa, all party leaders—
Bundists, Communists, General Zionists, and Left
Labor Zionists—instructed and exhorted their party
activists to resist any effort to make them leave the
Lodz ghetto. The parties even undertook to hide some
of their people from seizure. Since those in hiding
forfeited their food rations, the Bund exacted from its
working members a contribution of bread and soup,
a sacrificial offering in a time of hunger.

On June 6, 1944, news of D-Day, the Allied invasion
of Normandy, stirred the Lodz ghetto to public embraces and tears of joy. No work was done in the
factories that day, as the Jews calculated their chances
of survival. But their bright hopes began to dim at the
end of June, when the Germans ordered a three-week
period of deportations, with two thousand Jews scheduled for weekly departure. Neither Rumkowski nor
the parties saw this action as the start of the ghetto's
liquidation. The parties still held to their policy of
protecting their members and managed to get them
exemptions. At that time, an interparty conference discussed the possibility of the ghetto's liquidation and
the question of active resistance. But without political
contacts and without arms, talk of resistance was mere
quixotism.

The deportations began in earnest on August 3,
1944, after Rumkowski announced that the entire
ghetto of Lodz, its workers and its industrial enterprises, were to be transferred elsewhere. The removal
procedure was scheduled by factories, and the workers
were instructed when to report at a railroad siding.
Few obeyed. The parties were advocating passive

resistance, noncompliance. Despite Rumkowski's pleas and Hans Biebow's threats, only hundreds instead of thousands came forward. Nor could the Jewish police dislodge them from their hideouts. Once again, as in the September 1942 Aktion, armed German formations intervened to accomplish what the Jewish police failed to do. Even so, for days on end, the Germans could not round up enough Jews to fill the trains. By the end of August the Germans finally depopulated the Lodz ghetto.

Several hundred Jews still remained in hiding. Among them was Dr. Daniel Weisskopf, who had operated a clandestine radio-listening service and engaged in other underground activities. On November 6, 1944, the bunker in which he and others were hiding was uncovered by an informer. Biebow himself was called to the scene. Weisskopf, a powerful man, attacked both the informer and Biebow, bloodying both. When he was about to strangle Biebow, a German policeman shot him. Weisskopf's last words were "Germans, your end is near."[23]

In ghettos where the Judenrat leadership was convinced that there was no chance for survival, cooperation with the resistance movement was likely. Some communal leaders took an intermediate position of giving the resistance organization moral and financial support, without subscribing to its outlook and program. One form of compromise between the ghetto and the resistance movement was the option in Eastern areas for the Jewish youth to join the Soviet partisan movement. That way they diminished the ghetto's jeopardy through disengagement while they, for their part, joined an irregular army to fight the Germans. The drawbacks were, however, not inconsiderable. The first thing the partisan—Jew or Gentile—learned, if he lived long enough, was that in defense of the Soviet Union no human cost was too high. Jews who joined the partisans suffered additional disabilities. For the most part city-dwellers, they were unfamiliar with life in the open. Some, after years of ghetto deprivation, lacked the physical stamina to sustain the hardships of nature. Few could read maps or repair guns. Dependent on the support of the local peasant population among whom they operated, they were exposed to rampant anti-Semitism and the danger of being turned over to the Germans. Even worse was the anti-Semitism that they encountered from the partisans themselves.[24]

Nevertheless, for those whose primary loyalty was to the Soviet Union, joining the partisans was the only viable option and the only cause worth dying for. For Jewish resisters without an organizational base in the ghetto and without ties to ghetto leadership, serving the PPR or the Soviet apparatus in whatever tasks were assigned to them was a desirable option, for it gave them opportunities to fight or kill Germans. In Cracow, for example, a small group of Zionist youths, isolated from the ghetto community, accepted the leadership of the PPR and under their orders carried out various strikes against German targets (setting fires, stealing weapons and uniforms from German military and police). On December 22, 1942, on PPR assignment, the Zionist resisters blew up two cafés in the heart of Cracow that were frequented by German officers, killing at least twenty, perhaps as many as fifty. The only reverberations in the ghetto from their daring act were the SS searches and threats. That same night about forty resisters were arrested. By February 1943 all members of the PPR and the Zionist combat units were arrested or killed. A month later the ghetto was liquidated without any attempt at an organized defense.[25]

In eastern Poland, where the Soviet partisan movement had by 1943 grown to considerable size and strength, joining the partisans offered the ghetto Jews, in addition to the opportunity of fighting Germans, also at least an even chance of survival under conditions of personal autonomy. In contrast, staying in the ghetto to fight at its ultimate liquidation meant certain death. Nevertheless, for those committed to the defense of the ghetto, to a last stand together with the remaining Jews, joining the partisans was viewed as betrayal, or at the least abandonment, of principle and community.

In Baranowicze these two outlooks collided in near-disaster. There the local combat organization had opted to fight in defense of the ghetto. But in a surprise action about forty members of the group, nearly all refugees from other towns and without ties or loyalty to the Jews of Baranowicze, seized the bunker in which the combat organization's arsenal was cached, planning to make off into the woods with the weapons. A tense confrontation prevented the flight, and only sheer accident saved the rebellious ringleader from being shot.[26]

In the Kovno ghetto a remarkable balance was struck between the Judenrat and the underground despite their divergent views on resistance. In September 1943 the ghetto came under the exclusive control of SS-Obersturmführer Wilhelm Goecke, whose task was to turn the ghetto into a labor concentration camp prior to its ultimate liquidation. Then the question of whether, when, and how the ghetto should defend itself became urgent. A resistance organization had been in the making for some time, but between late 1941 and early fall 1943 the youth in the Zionist underground had engaged mainly in cultural and educational activities. The Communists in the ghetto, trailed by the Hashomer Hatzair, were in contact with the Lithuanian Communist underground, making plans to form partisan bands. Goecke's arrival spurred the underground to decisiveness.

The Zionist combat organization, deeply tied to the ghetto by virtue of family and friends, at first rejected the plan to join the partisans. They favored making a last stand in the ghetto despite the contempt the Communists exhibited for notions of "dying with honor." But in coming to terms with the Judenrat's view of the ghetto's possibilities, the Zionists changed their plans. In the fall of 1943, the Judenrat leaders, especially Dr. Elkes, hoped that the ghetto could hold out for a few more months. The Allies had landed in Italy

and were fighting their way north; the Russians held
the initiative on the Eastern front and were driving
the Germans west. Given these military advantages,
which might in weeks or months cause the Germans
to retreat from Kovno, the Judenrat leaders believed
that nothing should be done to jeopardize the ghetto
and provoke the Germans to bring it to a premature
end. As for the aspiring resisters, the Judenrat felt that
their best chance for survival was to join the partisans.
To that end, the top officers of the Judenrat, using the
resources of ghetto institutions, provided the underground with money for arms, equipped them with
supplies, and encouraged them with moral support.

The youth, for their part, accepting the conclusion
that the ghetto was an unfavorable terrain for armed
defense and that an armed rising against the Germans
could not be imposed on a civilian population that
was unprepared and unwilling to fight, proposed instead a large-scale program to construct underground
bunkers in which the ghetto Jews could hide at the
time of the next Aktion. In the event that the Germans
uncovered the bunkers, which would be armed, the
Jews could defend themselves.

Bunkers were indeed constructed. At a subsequent
Aktion, a few thousand Jews were deported, but the
bunkers were not uncovered and the ghetto offered
no fight. Thereafter, general agreement prevailed that
the wisest course was to send the young people to the
partisans, despite the total disaster that had befallen
several earlier parties in the woods. The leaders of
the Judenrat equipped and outfitted some three hundred young people to leave the ghetto, hoping that
they would have at least an even chance to survive.[27]
The support that the Judenrat leaders of Kovno gave
the youthful resisters derived not so much from agreement with their instrumental goals as from paternal
solicitude and a sense that the young people, as their
heirs and successors, must be saved for the future.

When the Germans came to liquidate the Kovno
ghetto early in July 1944, the ghetto gave no resistance. Instead, a dramatic confrontation took place

between Dr. Elkes and Goecke. Elkes told Goecke that
he knew what the fate of the Kovno Jews would be—
the same fate that had befallen all the Jews of Europe.
Nothing, he said, would remain hidden from history.
Offering Goecke a chance to redeem himself, Elkes
asked him to save the ghetto. The Jews, he promised,
would know how to reward him after the war. Goecke
rejected the proposal on his honor as an SS officer.[28]

For the most part, ghetto Jews regarded the young
people who planned and plotted armed resistance as
irresponsible hotheads who would bring disaster upon
the whole ghetto. Skepticism and contempt marked
their attitude toward the handful of inexperienced
boys and girls who ventured to fight the Germans. In
some ghettos the populace responded with unvar-
nished fear and hatred to the would-be resisters, seeing
them as foolish fanatics or even raving lunatics.[29] In
Radoszkowice, a town in the district of Vilna with
about twelve hundred Jews, the ghetto populace
warned the newly formed underground that unless
the plans for resistance were abandoned, they would
denounce them to the Germans. Observant Jews even
assembled in the prayer house to excommunicate the
ten members of the resistance who intended to join
partisans in the woods.

In the Kobryń ghetto, when the young people began
to contact the partisans, their parents, as well as
Judenrat officials, advised them instead to safeguard
the ghetto's existence by working in the ghetto enterprises. In the Chmielnik ghetto, the influential Jews of
the community supported the Judenrat in efforts to
persuade the members of the underground of their
irresponsibility and to warn them of the misfortune
that they could bring upon the ghetto.[30] For the most
part, caution and prudence guided the ghetto populace
with regard to the danger of Germans reprisals. On
this matter, in contrast to others, a general consensus
existed between them and the Judenrat.

Tension between the Vilna ghetto population and
the resistance movement brought the ghetto to the

verge of civil strife. In late spring 1943, the FPO, whose strongest constituents had become the Communists and the Revisionists, in a strategy of expediency made contact with ghetto chief Gens. Aware that the Russians might soon rout the Germans from Vilna, Gens welcomed the opportunity for friends on the other side. After secret meetings between Gens and the FPO at which the defense of the ghetto was discussed, Gens in various small ways helped FPO members to procure and cache arms and to train in their use.[31] At the same time, through his habitual chicanery, he worked to undermine the FPO. Realizing the threat, the FPO adopted a policy decision that in case the ghetto authorities tried to harm it or any of its leaders, it would mobilize all its units for self-defense. That decision provoked deep opposition within the Bund, an FPO constituent, whose leaders held that any armed combat within the ghetto—except for the defense of the ghetto—would be an intolerable provocation.[32]

On June 26 the first test of strength between the FPO and Gens took place. Gens had ordered the arrest of Joseph Glazman, his former deputy, now FPO vice-commandant, one of the most popular figures in the Vilna ghetto. Arrested by the Jewish police, Glazman, handcuffed and chained, was being taken to a labor camp. Suddenly an armed FPO unit materialized near the ghetto gate, stopped the police vehicle, and freed Glazman. The dashing rescue of a ghetto hero, accomplished without gunfire or injury, was so widely admired in the ghetto that Gens did not dare to punish the FPO. Instead he negotiated with them, asking them to help save his prestige in the ghetto by having Glazman report voluntarily to the labor camp for one week. To avoid further confrontations, the FPO agreed, after receiving assurances about Glazman's safety.[33]

About a week later, in early July, the Gestapo learned from two arrested Lithuanian Communists about the existence of a Communist leader named Wittenberg in the Vilna ghetto. Itzik Wittenberg was the FPO commandant. Prewarned, he went into hiding. Several days later, Gens informed the FPO that he had bribed the Gestapo to forget about Wittenberg. On July 15, Wittenberg agreed to attend a meeting of the FPO staff with Gens. Around midnight, when the meeting with five top FPO staff members began, two Lithuanian policemen came in search of Wittenberg. Abba Kovner said no one by that name was present, but Gens pointed Wittenberg out and the Lithuanians led him away. On the street an FPO unit on alert attacked the Lithuanians, allowing Wittenberg to escape into the night and return to his hideout.

The next morning the Gestapo demanded Wittenberg from Gens. To coerce the FPO, Gens told them the Germans had issued an ultimatum to destroy the whole ghetto, if Wittenberg did not turn himself in. Gens then mobilized some four hundred toughs and ruffians, armed with sticks and bludgeons, to look for Wittenberg. The FPO, convinced that the end of the ghetto was at hand, issued the password for mobilization, opened its arsenal, and began to distribute arms to its members.

Addressing his thugs in front of the Judenrat building and the crowds that had swelled the street, Gens told them that the whole ghetto was imperiled just because of one person, and he referred to the FPO as the "snot-noses with their popguns." Panic swept the ghetto and the fear of imminent disaster made the ghetto populace turn their backs on the FPO. The sympathy generated by Glazman's release had dissipated.

The FPO was given a two-hour deadline to yield Wittenberg. The pressure from communal leaders weighed heavily on them. Confronted with the real possibility of having to fight the Jews in the ghetto, they could not decide what to do. (One FPO member proposed collective suicide as a solution.) The decision was made by Wittenberg's own party. The Communists in the ghetto demanded that the FPO surrender him and save the ghetto from civil strife. The FPO submitted and its staff went to search for Wittenberg, but the police found him first, disguised as a woman, trying to escape. He surrendered quietly and was taken to Gens's headquarters, where a Gestapo car had been waiting since early morning. The next day Wittenberg was dead.[34]

The FPO, under Gens's terror, began to flee to the partisans, but after the first escaping parties were caught in the woods by the Gestapo and slaughtered, the exodus halted. On September 1, 1943, when the Germans and the Estonian police entered the Vilna ghetto, the shrunken FPO, taken by surprise, tried to mobilize for defense, but half the units could not reach their arsenal and others simply fled. Some resisters waited at their preselected bit of ghetto terrain for the Germans to arrive, but no armed encounter of significance took place. The FPO did not impede the Germans in their work of rounding up some eight thousand Jews—about two-thirds of the ghetto—for deportation. That FPO failure convinced the members that their most prudent course would be to leave the remnant ghetto. Within days about two hundred young people succeeded in joining the partisans in the woods.[35]

In Bialystok Barash showed the same parental solicitude for the youthful resistance movement that Elkes demonstrated in Kovno. Indeed, the relations between Barash and Mordecai Tenenbaum, head of the combat organization, were mutually warm and trustful. Barash supported the resistance in Bialystok —and Warsaw as well—with funds, supplies, and secure locations for their clandestine operations, such as the manufacture of explosives and grenades. He shared information with Tenenbaum and advised him about how to extend the political base of the combat organization.[36]

After the initial wave of Einsatzgruppe killings in the summer of 1941 subsided, Bialystok was spared the subsequent killings and deportations that amputated the other ghettos in the East. In the fall of 1941 the population of the Bialystok ghetto stood at about forty thousand and remained at that figure until February 1943. Barash believed that Bialystok's productivity for the Wehrmacht guaranteed its continued existence, and he was confident that, in a contest with the SS, the Wehrmacht would defend the ghetto. Tenenbaum, less confident of the Germans, nevertheless yielded to Barash's evaluation of the ghetto's situation.

In late January 1943, when the combat organization was still in its formative stage, Barash was informed that the Germans planned an Aktion in Bialystok. On January 31, 1943, at a clandestine meeting of various underground party leaders with Barash and another Judenrat official, Tenenbaum asked for clarification on the underground's "limits of patience." For how long was resistance to be withheld and for what price? How many victims, he asked, would be sacrificed before a counterattack could be launched? The answer was that as long as a majority of the Bialystok Jews remained untouched, no armed resistance should be offered, lest it provoke greater catastrophe.

On the morning of February 4, Barash confided to Tenenbaum that the Germans had promised to take no more than three transports each of 2,100 Jews according to lists of the unemployed prepared by the Judenrat. That evening, a few hours before the scheduled roundups, Tenenbaum told his resistance organization: "We will sacrifice 6,300 Jews in order to save the 35,000 remaining." He had accepted Barash's view that the ghetto had a chance to survive: the Russians were now advancing and the situation at the front might bring a swift and radical change to the ghetto's fortunes. The roundups lasted a few days; about 9,000 Jews were taken. (The Jewish police, refusing to cooperate, had gone into hiding. The Germans themselves went from house to house, routing out Jews from bunkers.) Some days later, Tenenbaum told the members of Dror: "We are responsible for the lack of action. Those who come after us will judge us, to praise or condemn. We refrained from acting not out of weakness, but out of a sense of responsibility for 10 percent of Polish Jews."[37]

The working ghetto population believed Barash and trusted his assurances that productivity would ensure their survival. The deportations of the unemployed frightened them less than the shooting of a German policeman by a forty-year-old ghetto Jew, Abraham Melamed. In immediate reprisal the Germans shot 120 Jews on the street, even though they had ironclad work permits. Melamed had escaped. The Germans threatened to destroy the whole ghetto if he did not surrender. The Jewish police offered a reward of 10,000 Reichsmarks. Three days later, Melamed turned himself in "to save the ghetto." In the factories, Tenenbaum noted on February 7, was "joy." Though Melamed was not a member of the combat organization, the populace in Bialystok responded to his act of vengeance the same way the Vilna Jews did to the FPO and Wittenberg.

At the very time the Aktion was taking place, Tenenbaum was undergoing a profound personal transformation that may later have affected and impeded the operations of the combat organization. He began to sink into a state of melancholy and suicidal depression that differed markedly from the political despair and thirst for revenge that characterized the young people in the resistance movement. At the end of January 1943, Zvi Mersik, his closest friend in Bialystok, died of typhus. A few days later, on February 3, Tenenbaum learned from an issue of *Głos Warszawy*, an underground PPR paper, about the armed resistance in January in the Warsaw ghetto and of the high losses among the Jewish combatants. He assumed that his dearest friends in the halutz movement were killed. Meanwhile, he had not heard for over three weeks from his dearly beloved, Tema Schneiderman, a Dror activist and intrepid courier. He had had word that she had arrived in Warsaw early in January, bringing eighty thousand rubles from Barash for ŻOB, but no news thereafter. (Tema had in fact been killed in the

Warsaw fighting that January.) On that same February
3, overwhelmed by his losses, Tenenbaum confided to
his diary his wish to die, even in the face of his obligation to organize the resistance: "I do not want to wait.
I cannot. Cyanide. Quick and simple. . . . The dead
Mersik is with me. Also in life, yes, to be or not to be.
The eternal question. Eternal death."

The young people in the halutz movement were not,
however, dedicated to death, even though many were
committed to a last stand in the ghetto. Some clung
to the possibility of survival by joining the partisans in
the woods. On February 27, 1943, the Dror activists
discussed their options. Defense of the ghetto had its
advocates: "One thing remains for us. To organize the
collective act of resistance in the ghetto, at any cost, to
regard the ghetto as our Musa Dagh, to record a
proud chapter of Jewish Bialystok and of our movement." The counterview had its proponents: "It is
more important to remain alive than to kill five Germans. In a counteraction, everyone without doubt will
die. On the other hand, in the woods 40 to 50 percent
of our people will be saved. That will be our honor
and that will be our history." Tenenbaum summed up
the discussion: "We will do everything to get out as
many people as possible to partisan combat in the
woods. Every one of us who will be in the ghetto
during the action must respond with the first Jew
taken."[38] (He himself, as he noted in his diary after
a similar discussion with another youth group, was
"wandering after Tema's shadows.")

A short while later, the combat organization split
over this issue, the Communists and part of Hashomer
Hatzair opting to join the partisans; the other Zionists,
Revisionists, and the Bund choosing to make the last
stand in the ghetto.

The plan for resistance that Tenenbaum appeared to
have formulated early in 1943 remained in effect.
Whenever the Germans should come, combat units
located at the factories were to start the counterattack,
rallying the workers to join them in setting fire to the
installations and revenging themselves on the Ger-

mans. Leaflets were prepared in advance to explain to the populace that "resettlement" meant death in Treblinka. A proclamation drafted by Tenenbaum in mid-January exhorted: "Do not go to your death of your own free will! Fight for your lives to your last breath! We have nothing left but our honor—we can lose nothing else!"

In July rumors spread that the liquidation of the Bialystok ghetto was imminent. German commissions visited the ghetto, no doubt to decide about its life or death. Even Barash began to lose confidence, but nonetheless the Judenrat continued to encourage the populace about the possibility of survival. Then, without warning, at 2:00 A.M. on Monday, August 16, 1943, Gestapo forces surrounded the ghetto. An hour later several hundred fully armed SS troops entered the ghetto, occupying the sites of the factories and Judenrat headquarters. They informed Barash that the entire ghetto population, together with the factory equipment, would be evacuated to Lublin. By 5:00 A.M. notices were posted, instructing the Jews to assemble by 9:00 in a specified area with some personal belongings.

The combat organization was caught unprepared, not on the alert in the factories, but at home in bed. Once mobilized, the young people tried to rally the panicked Jews on the streets with speeches, with leaflets, shouting that resettlement meant death in Treblinka, calling on them to refuse to be evacuated. But to no avail. The ghetto populace streamed past them to the staging area, heedless of their appeals. The young people then set fire to the ghetto enclosures on the side leading into the woods, hoping thereby to create openings through which the Jews could flee. But once again the people did not respond. The 31,000 Jews of the Bialystok ghetto were sent to Treblinka and Majdanek.

The ghetto houses near the flaming enclosures began to burn. The Germans opened fire and the youthful combatants now returned fire. The terrain of their battle was a segment of the narrow, cramped ghetto streets, with low buildings that gave no cover and no vantage points for attack. To assault the Jewish resisters with their paltry weapons and homemade grenades, the Germans brought in tanks and the full equipment of a modern army. Yet the young people continued to fight in their isolation. Some managed to hold out, in hit-and-run attacks from bunkers, until August 20. Then some managed to escape to the woods. The partisans tried to rescue Tenenbaum, but he refused to leave the ghetto. His last words were said to be: "Jews, we have no arms. Grab sticks, set fire to the houses!"[39]

Everywhere the Germans employed lies, surprise, and stealth to liquidate the ghettos. Sudden encirclements at night or at dawn prevented organized combat groups from mobilizing and coordinating their units. In some places the precipitous confrontation generated spontaneous resistance, sparked by hate and the desire for revenge.[40] In a labor camp at Łuck, for instance, when the Germans came to liquidate the carpentry enterprise on December 12, 1942, they were greeted with gunfire. For over half a day the barricaded Jews succeeded in holding off the Germans despite German grenades tossed into the workshop. Finally the Germans resorted to setting fire to the whole building. In the adjoining buildings, in an act of collective suicide, over fifty Jews hung themselves rather than surrender.[41]

In Marcinkonis, a town with 370 Jews in the Grodno district, the Jewish police warned the Judenrat late at night on November 1, 1942, that the ghetto was being surrounded by an armed force. In the morning the Germans ordered the Judenrat to instruct all the Jews to pack their belongings to be resettled for work elsewhere. A small intrepid group tried to attack the German commissar in charge of the deportation, but when they could not get close enough to him, the head of the Judenrat shouted a warning: "Jews, if you want to live, run where you can. The game is up." Panic and pandemonium broke out, many Jews barehandedly attacking the Germans. At the end, 105 Jews were shot to death. Others flew into the woods. There was no one left to "resettle."[42]

In Tuczyn, a town with some 2,000 native Jews and a few hundred refugees from other towns, about 27 kilometers from Równe, the end came on September 23, 1942, when the Germans ordered all Jews to assemble at the ghetto gate the next morning. Two young men began to agitate the ghetto populace to disobey. Hundreds of Jews assembled spontaneously in the prayer house. Young people continued to exhort: "Resist!" "Don't go voluntarily!" "Don't you know that the mass pits are dug already?" Then someone shouted: "Set fire!" Everyone began to bring kerosene, in pitchers, kettles, jugs, cups, and glassware, from the ghetto, from the workshops that had employed them. That evening the Jews began to destroy their possessions lest they fall into German hands. As night fell, the fires began to glow, first here, then there. All at once the whole ghetto was aflame. The Germans and Ukrainians surrounding the ghetto, caught unawares, began shooting into the flames. In that confusion, about two thousand Jews managed to break through the ghetto enclosures, fleeing from the burning ghetto into the woods.[43]

Only in the Warsaw ghetto did Jewish resistance attain its objectives. After the kesl of September 1942 and the derailment of organized community activity, leadership passed from the Judenrat and the alternative community into the hands of the political and military underground—the ŻKK and ŻOB. Warsaw was unlike the Bialystok and Kovno ghettos, where the Judenräte retained the people's confidence until the very end and kept open channels of communication to inform and encourage the ghetto; it was also unlike Lublin and Cracow, where the deportations and the Judenräte's collapse left the survivors leaderless, adrift in a sea of chaos and fear. In the Warsaw ghetto the ŻKK and ŻOB filled the seat of leadership vacated by the impotent Judenrat and became figures of authority in the ghetto, providing the surviving fifty thousand Jews with information and direction, with cues for coping with unfamiliar situations, and with hope and morale, feeding the desire for revenge.

The mimeograph machine and the gun became the tools of leadership, the means by which the ŻKK and ŻOB established their legitimacy. ŻOB's leaflets furnished the ghetto Jews with an interpretation of the events they were witness to, explaining and uncovering German duplicity and trickery. They helped the populace to evolve a unified response to their predicament, as defined by ŻOB. ŻOB's guns executed Jewish traitors and Gestapo agents, thus enforcing its authority in the ghetto and demonstrating unequivocally that it had become the ghetto's defender against its internal and external enemies.

After the kesl thousands of Jews had gone underground, living illegally in the interstices of the ghetto segments, in hideouts and bunkers devised, with ingenuity and diversity, to conceal dozens and even hundreds of people for months on end. Some hideouts were equipped with electricity and radios. Some had running water provided by cunningly concealed piping; others had direct access to deep wells. Food stocks for weeks, even months, were laid in. Entrances were inventively camouflaged. Concealed doorways, blocked with sandbags or garbage or a piece of furniture, led to attics, cellars, and secret rooms. In constructing the bunkers, the Jews carved out passageways from one apartment to another, from attic to attic, from cellar to cellar. The ghetto soon became an enormous underground network of honeycombs connected by hundreds of invisible arteries, its inhabitants able to move about a square block without going outdoors.[44] Knowing that thousands of Jews eluded them, the Germans fabricated new lies to entice them out into the open. In late November 1942, the Germans declared that the Umschlagplatz had been liquidated and offered amnesty to the "illegals," holding out the offer of food and employment as bait. German factory directors promised visions of a good life. The Judenrat was asked to plan a six-month work program.

To these blandishments and lies ŻOB responded vigorously, exposing the duplicity. A ŻOB leaflet issued December 4, 1942, explained that the Germans aimed to destroy all the Jews by carrying out their annihilation in stages. The chief German tactic was the lie: "Let us therefore bravely look the truth straight in the face." The leaflet, taking up one by one each German assurance to the Jews of life and security, demonstrated German deceit and chicanery from the experience of the past: "Jews, citizens of the Warsaw ghetto, be on the alert, do not believe a single word or act of the SS bandits." Excoriating the Jewish agents and traitors in the ghetto, ŻOB called on the Jews to help one another, to show solidarity, and to prepare to defend themselves: "Remember that also you—the civilian Jewish population—are at the front in the fight for freedom and humanity."[45]

In the first half of January ŻOB issued an appeal to the ghetto populace not to believe the latest arrival of letters allegedly written by Jews deported from Warsaw, now supposedly in labor camps near Pinsk and Bobruisk. "Jewish masses, don't believe these stories. They are spread by Jews in the service of the Gestapo." This latest deceit, the leaflet warned, was just to facilitate the next deportation. The hour is approaching, ŻOB declared, when you must be prepared to resist. "No Jew should go to the trains. People who don't have the possibility of active opposition should offer passive resistance. That means they should hide."[46]

The first test came on January 18, 1943, when German troops, in a surprise move, surrounded the Warsaw ghetto. Neither the ŻKK nor ŻOB had any advance warning of the Aktion, nor did they have information about its planned size or scope. Fighting erupted spontaneously on the part of five ŻOB units, all isolated from one another and unable to communicate, but responding uniformly to the German threat to seize Jews for deportation. The ŻOB fighters killed or wounded about fifty Germans and seized some of their weapons, but their own losses were extensive. Nevertheless, after three days, the Germans halted the deportations, having taken a relatively small number of Jews. ŻOB's determined fighting and the abrupt departure of the Germans electrified the ghetto. The events confirmed the hopes: armed resistance could turn back the Germans. ŻOB popularity reached a new high. Bakers baked bread for them; leather workers fashioned holsters for their weapons. Even the smugglers and black marketeers supplied them with food and drink.

More than bread, ŻOB needed money—to buy arms to equip the combat groups. ŻOB began to "levy" taxes on the still well-to-do Jews in the ghetto, carrying out its threat to arrest recalcitrants. (ŻOB maintained its own "prison," where it held "tax-dodgers" and suspected Gestapo agents.) The Judenrat itself responded to ŻOB's appeals and contributed about a million zlotys. In true revolutionary tradition, ŻOB members also carried out bank expropriations. Two such acts took place in February 1943, one on the Judenrat treasury, yielding 70,000 zlotys, and the other on the ghetto bank, which brought in 100,000 zlotys.[47]

February 1943 was also a month for cleaning out Jewish Gestapo agents. In that month alone five of "the meanest scoundrels of society" were shot. A ŻOB leaflet, issued March 3, 1943, listed them by name, the dates of their execution, and the specific nature of their crimes. Warning that ŻOB had a complete list of others still working for the Germans, the leaflet warned that "unless they immediately cease their contemptible actions, they will all be shot!"[48]

The ŻKK, meanwhile, reorganized ŻOB after the January losses. Units of tens replaced the original fives or sixes. Organized by party, each unit consisted of at least eight men and no more than two women, with at least half the members required to have their own guns. In all, twenty-two combat units were formed. Half were associated with Hehalutz, and of these, five were Dror units, four Hashomer Hatzair, and one each Akiva and Gordonia. The Bund and PPR each had four units; the Right and Left Labor Zionists and the General Zionist youth each had one unit. After the January defense, ŻOB was besieged by eager applicants. There was no shortage of volunteers, only of arms. The Bund had a strict recruitment policy, maintaining, as it had in earlier times, tight security precautions, screening each applicant closely, rejecting many. The Bundists in ŻOB also rigorously adhered to regulations with regard to arms, turning away volunteers whose only weapons were sticks and stones.[49]

Morale in ŻOB was high. Few ŻOB members thought they were fighting to preserve their lives, yet none yielded to depression. Becoming a combatant, wrote a member, meant leaving behind the scramble for one's wretched existence, the sense of being pursued like an animal by the Germans. Joining ŻOB meant regaining one's humanity and sense of self-esteem. Belongingness enhanced morale. Responsibility for one's acts, for one's future no longer rested on the individual alone, but on the group. Every group had a leader to whom each member looked for guidance and authority. Responsibility for carrying out the group's aims was shared; personal and private interests were submerged and subordinated to the goals of the group. The interplay between leader and follower, between individual and group, forged new bonds and loyalties, which in turn strengthened and reinforced each individual member's morale and courage.[50]

After the abortive Aktion of January 18, the Jewish leaders were convinced that the Germans were preparing for the final liquidation of the Polish Jews. On January 21, 1943, ŻKN, using Delegatura facilities, sent a radio message via the Polish government-in-exile in London to Jewish leaders in New York:

We notify you of the greatest crime of all times, about the murder of millions of Jews in Poland. Poised at the brink of the annihilation of the still surviving Jews, we ask you:

1. Revenge against the Germans
2. Force the Hitlerites to halt the murders
3. Fight for our lives and our honor
4. Contact the neutral countries
5. Rescue 10,000 children through exchange
6. 500,000 dollars for purposes of aid.

Brothers—the remaining Jews in Poland live with the awareness that in the most terrible days of our history you did not come to our aid. Respond, at least in the last days of our life.[51]

On February 7 the underground Bund leaders sent a radio message to Zygelboym in the Polish parliament-in-exile in London:

In January the Germans began to liquidate the Warsaw ghetto. A few dozen Germans were thereby killed. Several hundred Jews were killed on the spot. . . . After three days the Aktion was halted. Six thousand were taken away. The liquidation is occurring throughout Poland. In mid-February they are to liquidate the Warsaw ghetto. Alert the whole world. Appeal to the Pope for official intervention and to the Allies to declare German war prisoners as hostages. We suffer terribly. The surviving 200,000 await annihilation. Only you can save us. The responsibility with regard to history will rest on you.[52]

In February the owners of the German industrial enterprises began to campaign among their workers to register for voluntary evacuation. At public meetings of workers, the German industrialists painted an incredibly idyllic Jewish future: "a paradisiac existence in beautiful bucolic surroundings, a life rich in magnificent amusements in leisure hours and days."[53] To give authenticity to the campaign, the SS remained behind the scenes, while Walter C. Többens, the owner of the largest ghetto enterprise, employing about 8,000 Jews, was officially put in charge of "resettlement." In March the first factories began to be liquidated. The night before the evacuation, a ŻOB unit ignited the Hallmann factory, where a thousand Jews had worked, destroying the raw materials and machinery packed for shipment. The next day only 25 workers showed up for voluntary removal. None of the 3,500 workers in the brush shops turned up for the scheduled evacuation. At the Schultz shops a ŻOB unit freed 60 Jews kept prisoners by the Germans. Increasingly ŻOB was seen by the ghetto Jews as their defender.

On March 14, ŻOB issued another proclamation calling on the Jews to resist the Germans, emphasizing that "voluntary resettlement" meant only the inevitable annihilation of the ghetto.[54] The leaflet was so effective in reinforcing the resistance of the workers that Többens was forced to reply. On March 20 he issued a leaflet, denying that any harm had come to the Jewish workers who were previously resettled. He tried to discredit ŻOB: "The ŻOB command cannot help you; they offer only empty promises." Többens even proposed a conference with ŻOB on the subject of "resettlement." The lack of success in effecting a voluntary evacuation prompted the Germans, who were then not ready to show force, to induce the Judenrat to invite ŻOB to a meeting, but that invitation, too, was rejected with contempt. The Judenrat chairman was said then to have told the Germans: "I have no power in the ghetto. Another authority rules here."[55]

The sense of urgency in the ghetto increased. Early in April both the Bund and the ŻKN dispatched another round of urgent radio appeals to London, Geneva, New York, and Jerusalem. "Storm heaven and earth," they cried, asking once again to alert the world to the annihilation of the Jews and swiftly to aid the survivors with money and to rescue them through exchange.[56]

At 2:00 A.M., Monday, April 19, 1943, armed German, Lettish, and Ukrainian patrols began to be deployed around the Warsaw ghetto. A half-hour later ŻOB received information about the German troop movements. By daylight ŻOB's units were mobilized. Nine units were located in the central ghetto, eight in the area of the Többens-Schultz workshops, and five in the area of the brush works. (Later, units of the Revisionist ŻZW participated in the fighting, as did also "wild" units, so nicknamed because they were unaffiliated.)

At 6:00 A.M. a contingent of two thousand heavily armed SS troops entered the central ghetto, with tanks, rapid-fire guns, and three trailers loaded with ammunition.[57] The ŻOB units were ready to confront them. The civilian ghetto populace was underground, hiding in their bunkers. ŻOB attacked the entering German columns. With incendiary bottles mass-produced in a secret ŻOB laboratory, they blew up German tanks and German troops. Shooting flared up in several areas. ŻOB units prevented German relief troops from entering the ghetto. By 5:00 P.M. the Germans, surprised and shocked by Jewish resistance, withdrew from the ghetto, having lost some two hundred dead and wounded.

"We were happy and laughing," said a ŻOB combatant. "When we threw our grenades and saw German blood on the streets of Warsaw, which had been flooded with so much Jewish blood and tears, a great joy possessed us." Everyone knew that the Germans would return, that the Germans would ultimately defeat ŻOB, that the Jews would soon be annihilated; yet after that day's fighting in the ghetto, people embraced and kissed each other.[58]

That April 19 marked the celebration of the first seder ushering in the festival of Passover. One of the combatants, searching for flashlight batteries, came into a rabbi's apartment where a seder was in progress. The room looked as if it had been struck by a pogrom. Only the wine goblets on the table suggested the festive occasion. The reading of the Haggada was punctuated by gunfire and shell bursts. The assembled Jews wept when the rabbi intoned: "Pour out Thy wrath upon the heathen nations that do not acknowledge Thee and upon the kingdoms that do not call upon Thy name; for they have devoured Jacob and laid waste his dwelling place."

Early the next day, April 20, the Germans, using the Judenrat as intermediary, issued an ultimatum to ŻOB, demanding that they lay down their arms by ten o'clock. But Lettish Waffen-SS reinforcements entering the ghetto were received with grenades and explosives. An electric mine killed about a hundred Germans of a three-hundred-man force. Corpses began to pile up in the streets. In the late afternoon the Germans brought in tanks and field artillery. Occupying several roofs, they set up heavy machine guns. Two Higher Police and SS officers appeared, again demanding that ŻOB units lay down their arms. If not, the entire area would be bombed. Once again, ŻOB's reply came from its guns. That very day, the Germans appealed to the ghetto Jews in hiding to volunteer for evacuation with the Többens and Schultz shops. But no one came forward.

The Germans began setting fire to ghetto buildings. ŻOB countered by igniting the warehouses of the *Werterfassung*, the agency in charge of expropriated Jewish property. Pillars of smoke began to rise over the ghetto. The Germans cut off the supply of electricity, gas, and water from the ghetto streets.

ŻOB fighters remained exultant, their morale high. On one roof they flew the red-and-white Polish flag alongside the Jewish blue-and-white banner. On another roof a ŻOB banner proclaimed: "We shall fight to the last." (PPR members, impelled by other loyalties, abandoned their units after two or three days of combat. Some managed to escape from the ghetto.)

On Wednesday, April 21, the Germans relied more on tanks, howitzers, and massive antiaircraft artillery. The ŻOB fighters shifted from offensive to defensive tactics. Increasingly the Germans resorted to fire, against which ŻOB had no weapons. Columns of smoke were visible for miles around Warsaw. The flames in the ghetto threatened to engulf all Warsaw.

By Thursday, April 22, the ghetto was enveloped in dense smoke. To dislodge the tens of thousands of

Jews hidden in bunkers and underground shelters, the Germans brought in flamethrowers. With listening devices and police dogs they hunted down the Jews. Emerging from their smoke-filled burning hideouts, the Jews, hands held over their heads, were marched to the Umschlagplatz. There the Ukrainians, beating and bullying them, loaded them on the waiting freight trains.[59]

The ghetto was a roaring sea of fire. ŻOB fighters regrouped their forces and began rescuing the Jews in the shelters, where thousands were being burned alive. People were seen silhouetted in the window frames of blazing buildings, sheathed in flames, like living torches.

On Friday, April 23, the fighting shifted northward in the ghetto. Többens, having dismantled his plant, was transporting it to Poniatowa and succeeded in taking with him some two thousand out of an estimated eight thousand workers. Fighting continued on the terrain of the brush works. On that day, Mordecai Anielewicz, ŻOB commandant, sent a letter to his friend Zuckerman, then on the "Aryan" side: "It is now quite clear to me that what took place exceeded all expectations." He asked Zuckerman to get rifles, hand grenades, machine guns, and explosives. Sooner or later, he believed, everyone would die. Still, he wrote, "the last wish of my life has been fulfilled. Jewish self-defense has become a fact. Jewish resistance and revenge have become realities."

That same day, the fifth day of the defense of Warsaw, ŻOB addressed a proclamation to the Polish population of Warsaw:

> Let it be known that every threshold in the ghetto has been and will continue to be a fortress, that we may all perish in this struggle, but we will not surrender; that, like you, we breathe with desire for revenge for all the crimes of our common foe.

Summoning up the remembrance of past Polish participation in struggles for freedom and liberation, the proclamation echoed the historic words of Poland's fight against tyranny everywhere: "A battle is being waged for your freedom as well as ours."[60]

From that day on, ŻOB fighters shifted to tactics of guerrilla warfare, leaving their bunkers at night to conduct hit-and-run assaults on German formations, to foray for weapons, and to spy out the situation. The sounds of gunfire and of grenade and mine explosions were deafening. Fires raged night and day.

No one had hoped to hold out that long. The ŻOB units, augmented by the Revisionists and the un-affiliated groups, all poorly equipped, numbered about a thousand combatants. According to the Home Army estimates, the Germans had some five thousand men and officers, massively equipped.[61]

Fighting became sporadic and isolated, in conse-quence of superior German fire power and dwindling Jewish ammunition supplies. The raging fires also limited access to the ghetto area. ŻOB forces became splintered and crippled. Meanwhile the Germans con-tinued to dismantle their more valuable plants for re-moval. On April 29, fighting continued at the Schultz factory, where ŻOB units and Jewish workers tried to halt the transfer of equipment.

There was almost no terrain left to fight on. The intense heat of the conflagrations had turned the pave-ment into a sticky pulp of tar. Food reserves had gone up in flames. The wells, so laboriously dug in the bunkers, were filled with rubble. All around, wrote a ghetto combatant, "the roar of the fire, the noise of falling walls. Outside the ghetto it was spring, but here a holocaust reigned."[62]

On May 8 the Germans surrounded the hideout of ŻOB headquarters. The civilians in the bunker sur-rendered, but the ŻOB fighters entrenched themselves, ready to fight the Germans. Instead, the Germans stopped up all the entrances and sent gas into the bunker. Over one hundred fighters were inside. One of them called out, "Let's not fall into their hands alive!" They began to kill themselves and each other, in a scene that must have rivaled the mass suicide at

Masada. Mordecai Anielewicz was among them. On May 10, about 75 ŻOB survivors made their way through the slime of Warsaw's sewers to escape, with the help of comrades on the "Aryan" side. The Warsaw ghetto became one huge cemetery.

In the Generalgouvernement the only Jews still surviving legally were those in the closed labor camps (for example, Płaszów near Cracow; Janów in Lwów; Skarzysko near Radom; Piotrków; Częstochowa). Other camps, including Trawniki and Poniatowa, where Többens and Schultz had been transferred, were liquidated by November 1943. There were also about 10,000 Jews in the forests, some trying to survive on their own in nature's hostile milieu, others attached to partisan groups, all hunted and driven. (In the Baltic, too, there were some 15,000 to 20,000 Jews in the woods.) About 30,000 Jews lived as "Aryans" in the cities—half in Warsaw—disguised, on false papers, exposed to denunciation and extortion by Polish blackmailers. Finally, about 20,000 Polish Jews were assembled in Vittel and Bergen-Belsen, in special camps for "foreigners"—Jews who, with money, influence, or by virtue of elite communal status had acquired Paraguayan or other citizenship and who were hoaxed into believing that they were being held for exchange.

The ŻKK tried to bring aid and comfort to as many of these Jews as they could reach through their own underground channels and couriers and, to a lesser extent, through the help of the *Rada Pomocy Żydom* (RPŻ; Council for Aid to Jews), a joint Polish-Jewish organization that had come into existence at the end of 1942 with the meager financial assistance of the Delegatura.[63] In a report sent by the ŻKN to Zionist leaders abroad, the underground leaders described the conditions under which they lived and worked: "We go about in disguises. We feel like tightrope aerialists performing over an abyss. Night and day we hover between life and death. Every day we work is a miracle. But we do not cease."[64]

Every day the number of surviving Jews dwindled.

In the cities, Polish police, blackmailers, spies, Gestapo agents, and Security Police hunted down Jews, especially Jewish leaders. In the forest, unfriendly peasants and anti-Semitic Polish, Ukrainian, or Russian partisans found it easier to destroy Jews than Germans. As for the labor camps and the camps at Vittel and Bergen-Belsen, the Germans liquidated them in rapid order. There were no Jewish communities anymore, no synagogues, no Jewish schools, no Jewish life to sustain. Blood-soaked debris of Yiddish and Hebrew books at the banks of the Vistula were all that remained of the thousand-year-old civilization of Jews in Poland.

"Our tasks now," Leon Feiner wrote in his report of November 15, 1943, "come down to this: at least to keep alive the remnants who have survived . . . so there will be some reserve for the future and witnesses to this crime."

16

Jewish Behavior
in Crisis and Extremity

Conventional wisdom tells us that the history of the past provides guidance for the strategy of the future, but Edmund Burke was closer to the truth when he wrote that "you can never plan the future by the past." The long Jewish past of persecution and disaster offered little that was instructive or relevant in the confrontation with the Final Solution. The Final Solution was a new phenomenon in human history.

Human perception is bound by the known and the familiar. To comprehend the strange and unfamiliar, the human mind proceeds from the reality of experience toward cognition by applying reason, logic, and analogy. People view the present and try to discern the outlines of the future through the prism of the past. The Jews, in their earliest encounters with the anti-Jewish policies of Hitler's Germany, saw their situation as a retroversion of their history, but in their ultimate encounter with the Final Solution, historical experience and even ideology failed them as explanation.

The responses of the Jewish community were determined not only by the experiences of the past, considered in the light of existing knowledge, but also by the dominant values of Jewish tradition and culture and by a modal national character and personality.[1] National character reflects the enduring formative influences of a people's culture and history. Through the processes of socialization during which the values of the group and patterns of behavior common to all its members are transmitted by family and 'peers, each individual's uniqueness is modified and seasoned by national characteristics.

Despite the recurrent cycles of disaster that marked their history, the Jews have been committed to a fundamental and abiding optimism grounded in the teachings of Judaism. All creation, Genesis declares, is good. Whatever God does, the tradition teaches, is for good. *Gam zu letova*—"This, too, is for the best" —which the Tanna Nahum of Gimzo used to say on any distressing occasion, was embodied in the folk wisdom, an expression of optimistic assent and acceptance of God's will.

The tradition teaches that the whole world depends on justice, that good is rewarded and evil punished. The universe is orderly and rational. Whatever exists and is done serves God's purpose and has meaning, though that meaning and purpose are not always revealed to men. In modern times, the liberal, progressive, radical, and nationalist ideologies that supplanted or supplemented traditional Judaism incorporated into their secular and sometimes explicitly irreligious doctrines the traditional Jewish optimistic view of man's goodness and of the eventual triumph of justice in a society of order and rationality.

The prime value that the Jews attached to life itself and to Jewish survival generated an activist tradition that influenced the behavior of the individual and the organized community. The pervasiveness of activism among Jews, especially in defense of their rights and their existence, derived from the exceptional responsibility that traditional Judaism places on every individual Jew. The obligations to preserve Judaism and the Jewish people have rested not on monarchs or prime ministers, nor on high priests, prophets, or rabbis, but on each Jewish man and each Jewish woman.

The tradition taught that everything must be done to remove any stumbling block that endangers life. The man who allows a broken ladder to stand in his house violates a precept of Jewish law. All through their history, in the observance of this precept, the Jews invoked the strategy of activism, using not one but all options open to them to save themselves from impending danger. Though they prayed to God, begging for His mercy and succor, they did not passively await deliverance. They applied for protection from one power against the assault of another; they sought refuge in temporary flight or undertook the hazards of permanent emigration. They made every effort to ransom hostages, to offer bribes and gifts to the oppressors. During the Crusades, the medieval pogroms, and the Ukrainian massacres of 1648–1649, the Jews within walled or fortified communities defended themselves against their assailants.[2]

The religious tradition prescribed patterns of behavior in conformity with ultimate values, but it was itself affected by the political condition of the Jews. The Talmud began to develop in the first traumatic period of Jewish powerlessness, after the destruction of the Second Temple. The rabbis addressed themselves not just to timeless pieties, but by indirection also to the political realities confronting them so as to evolve an appropriate posture and *modus vivendi* that would ensure Jewish survival. "Belong ever to the persecuted rather than to the persecutors," the Talmud taught. "God loves the persecuted and hates the persecutors." To compensate for lost national autonomy, the religious tradition elevated powerlessness into a positive Jewish value. It fostered submissiveness and cautioned against rash rebellion: "The Holy Spirit says, 'I adjure you that if the earthly kingdom decrees persecutions, you shall not rebel in all that it decrees against you, but you shall keep the king's command.'" (That advice suggests comparison with, for instance, the prudential policies of the French

resistance movement during World War II, which
regarded the price of active resistance to the Germans as too high in terms of human life and suffering.)

To facilitate their survival in powerlessness and to
lessen the impact of humiliation and suffering, the
Jews made virtues of self-discipline, prudence, mod-
eration, forgoing present gratification for eventual
benefit. They learned to practice nonviolent means of
resistance and to find ways of circumventing discrimination and deflecting persecution.

The European Jews discerned three stages in the
historical situation that confronted them after the National Socialists came to power. The first stage, disemancipation, corresponded with the first six years of
the German dictatorship and ended with Kristallnacht. Jews saw that period as a reversion to the pre-
Emancipation era, when the modern nation-state was
emerging and Jews were poised at the brink of
modernity.

The second stage, that of the ghetto and yellow
star, coincided with the German conquest and occupation of most European nations and with the establishment of German hegemony over nearly all the
others. The Jews saw that period as a fearful retro-
gression to the darkest days of the Middle Ages, when
they were the pariahs of society at the nadir of powerlessness.

The third stage, annihilation, unfolded with the
mass killings by the Einsatzgruppen in the second
half of 1941 and continued until the end of the war
with the operation of the death camps. That period
struck the Jews like a cataclysm of unparalleled proportions, a natural disaster without historical precedent or rational meaning.

With these perceptions of their situation, the Jews,
leaders and masses, evaluated German goals and intentions with regard to them. Their evaluations defined the choice of available strategies to cope with
changed circumstances. Like people anywhere, they

resorted to policies and tactics whose usefulness and effectiveness had been demonstrated by historical experience. Strategies were evaluated as to costs and benefits, the possible gains of one course of action weighed against its probable losses and in relation to available alternatives. Policy was always two-pronged: directed internally to strengthen the community and bolster its morale; directed outwardly, in dealings with the oppressor, to alleviate hardships and nullify persecutions.

Jewish communal leaders were confronted with imponderable tasks and unprecedented responsibility under German rule. In this time of crisis followed by extremity, they acted in accordance with their perceptions and evaluations and to the extent of their opportunities. During their lifetime they were judged for good or evil by their contemporaries on the basis of their successes and failures. After their demise, they— their acts as well as their persons—are still judged before the bar of history.

Responsibility means accountability or answerability for one's actions and their consequences. Historical responsibility is defined as an individual's answerability for committing or failing to commit acts that would have affected the outcome of any given situation.[3] A person charged with historical responsibility must have, besides the will and the capability to exercise it, also the opportunity to do or prevent something from being done that would have changed the course of events. Opportunity is determined by external circumstances and resources. The philosophers speak of the "'can' of opportunity," which is explained this way: "To have the opportunity to do something requires only that one be in a situation such that if, roughly speaking, one wanted to do it, it would be reasonable to expect that one would be successful in doing it if one were able to do it."[4]

In the first stage, most Jews and Jewish leaders in Germany foresaw their disemancipation at the hands of the National Socialist dictatorship. The severity of their pessimism was, however, mitigated by the unanimous Jewish view, shared by many liberal non-Jews, that the National Socialists could not long retain power. Jewish leadership first responded to disemancipation by conducting a policy of resistance in the posture of accommodation. After a century of struggle for equality, marked by cycles of advance and retreat, most Jews in Germany were not prepared to yield their rights without active effort to retain them. The general strategy was for the Jews to try to hold on and hold out, while their leaders, through official negotiations, backstairs bargaining, and petition, sought to protect the achievements of the Emancipation and the rights of the Jews to Dasein.

The community geared itself for emergency, retooling existing institutions for expanded, or altogether new, tasks. For the most part, unity on pragmatic goals was attained. In times of crisis people rally for the common good, and Jews perhaps even more so. In Jewish tradition, communal unity has a near-transcendental value, for according to one passage in the Talmud, the Second Temple was destroyed because of the baseless hatred of one Jew for another. The striving for unity later manifested itself in all Jewish communities under German occupation and duress.

Internal Jewish communal policy was directed toward building morale and organizing self-help. Despite the relentless vigilance of the National Socialists, Jewish leaders nevertheless found means of communicating with the rank-and-file community, providing cues and direction, counsel and encouragement. The external policy, the attempt to shore up the Jewish legal and economic position, was the first to fail. Without friends or allies, in a sea of torrential hostility, the Jews were deprived of resources and lacked opportunities to halt the course of disemancipation that the German dictatorship had set in motion. (Even the once influential Social Democratic party and the once massive German labor movement were completely powerless to defeat or deflect the Nazis.)

In the first years of the National Socialist regime the Jews demonstrated their defiance of the dictatorship by insisting on their rights, but by the last months of 1935, most Jews regarded the continued existence of a viable Jewish community in Germany as no more than a quixotic vision. Germany's foreign-policy successes indicated that National Socialism could no longer be regarded as a transient phenomenon in German history. The Nuremberg Laws had sealed disemancipation and presaged further, as yet unadumbrated, degradation. Reevaluating their situation, the Jews evolved a new strategy, to which all but the most stubborn adhered—the orderly dissolution of the Jewish community in Germany by a program of systematic emigration.

Kristallnacht and its consequences undid that Jewish strategy too. As Germany's anti-Jewish program entered a new phase of accelerated violence, an intensified sense of urgency entered Jewish evaluations of the deteriorating situation. The possibility of formulating communal policy on the basis of a limited range of available alternatives no longer existed. The knife was at the throat; Jewish leaders no longer had options. Thenceforth their strategy was shaped by German coercion.

In the postwar years, men who had held leading positions in the Jewish community in Germany expressed remorse for their underestimation of the threat that National Socialism posed to Jewish existence, for their unrealistic optimism, for their failure to foresee the outlines of the Final Solution. They blamed themselves for not having urged early and total emigration and for the consequent loss of thousands of lives. That self-recrimination bespeaks a refined sense of guilt rather than an assessment of historical responsibility. It does not take into account the " 'can' of opportunity." Had Hitler died or been assassinated in any of those years, had the English or French challenged Germany's violation of international treaties, then in the end Jewish policy would have been successful. With such alternatives, any call for the dis-

mantling of the Jewish community in Germany would
have appeared cowardly and hysterical.

The historical success or failure of any policy is
measured by the actual outcome of events, but that
success or failure is not determined by prescience or
wisdom, by right or wrong. The course of history, of
victory and defeat, is circumscribed by the fortuitous
confluence of resources and opportunity.

The second stage in the Jewish situation came with
the German invasion of Poland in September 1939. It
first appeared that the policy of disemancipation that
the Germans instituted right away was now coupled
with a policy of permanent pogrom. In Eastern Europe, where most Jews had experienced war, pogroms, and famine in their lifetime, where want and
deprivation had been Jewish familiars, the Jews,
trained by the habitude of suffering, viewed German
oppression in a historic perspective. Recurrent persecution was their portion. Nevertheless, with God's
help, they would, as they had done before in their
history, survive. Traditional Jewish optimism tempered
the grim reality of German rule by the universal expectation of a short-lived German occupation and a
rapid German military defeat. A world ruled by National Socialist Germany was inconceivable to the
Jews, whether they looked to God, the Red Army, or
the Allies for succor.

Within a few months, however, as the Germans began to separate the Jews physically from the rest of
the population, to identify them with Star of David
arm bands, and to isolate them in ghettos, the Jews
saw their situation as a reversion to the darkness of
the Middle Ages and they came to a new evaluation
of German policy. The Germans, they concluded,
were engaged in no random game of terror and persecution, but had embarked on a systematic program
to wipe them out through hunger and sickness, exploitation of their labor and plunder of their property.
Everywhere Jewish leadership rallied to resist this
German policy: to combat hunger and disease, to

prevent the physical extinction of the Jews. The idea of holding on and holding out became the fundamental Jewish policy. In Germany, holding on and holding out had applied to the legal and political rights of the Jews. In the East European ghettos, holding on and holding out meant the struggle for physical survival.

Every strategy that had availed them in past times of stress was tried. Though the continued state of war and the brute force of German rule prevented movement and emigration, huge masses of Jews in the early period of the occupation attempted flight, inside Poland and out. Everywhere Jews resorted to *shtadlanut*—intercession, petition, attempted bargaining—with German officials, indigenous functionaries, church leaders, and underground political authorities. Everywhere Jews used money and valuables to elicit favors or obtain remissions, to ransom their captives.

Against the devouring rapacity of the Germans, Jewish material resources, even when augmented by aid from American Jews, were piteously insufficient. Intangible spiritual resources were less vulnerable and more enduring—above all, communal solidarity. Everywhere, despite divisions by class and ideology, despite the conflict of generations between traditionalism and modernity, despite the cleavages between the nationalists and the universalists, every Jewish subcommunity rallied to help the Jews survive. The single goal that animated all Jewish leaders—whether they were in the official community, the alternative community, or the countercommunity, and despite the differences in their functions, outlooks, and policies—was to keep the Jews alive, to sustain them physically and morally.

The Jewish masses too rallied with energy, inventiveness, and optimism to face each cheerless day.*

---

* The will to live of Jews in the ghettos contrasted dramatically with the passivity and total resignation that characterized the Russian prisoners of war. Even ghetto Jews who encountered them at forced labor and who often risked their lives to give them bread were appalled at the transformation of human beings into wraiths of wretchedness.[5]

To be sure, thousands among millions of Jews succumbed to demoralization. There were those who, for the recompense of food, security, pleasure, or the illusion of authority, stole from or betrayed fellow Jews. But the overwhelming majority brought decency and fraternal solicitude to the ghetto. The traits of national character and the values that their culture had fashioned stood the Jews in the ghettos in good stead. They preserved their humanity by trying to carry on the daily routine of normal existence in a time of crisis—protecting the family, educating the children, feeding the hungry, caring for the sick, satisfying intellectual and cultural needs. "It is a great deal," says Camus, "to face destruction while cherishing the idea of a higher civilization."

The objectives of Jewish leaders and masses were congruent, though they differed, sometimes bitterly, invoking denunciation and recrimination, over the tactics and strategy to attain their common objectives. The Judenräte often missed opportunities and wasted resources, sometimes because of inexperience and inefficiency in operating large administrations under stressful conditions, sometimes because of the infiltration of corrupt and dishonest people into the ghetto bureaucracy. In many ghettos German terror so overwhelmed the Judenräte that their officials lost the ability for independent thought and became fearful of any initiative that might alleviate the ghetto's misery. Then there were a handful of leaders who, because of defects in personality—unrealized ambitions, vanity—were convinced that only their judgments and strategies were correct and would succeed while those of their critics were wrong and would fail.

For all their weaknesses, failings, and wrongdoings, these men—Rumkowski, Merin, Gens—were no traitors. The Jews had no Quislings, Lavals, or Vlasovs, no leaders who shared common goals and aspirations with the Germans.[6] The accusation that some Jewish leaders "cooperated" or "collaborated" with the Germans arises out of distortions of the historical record. Cooperation and collaboration with the Germans were policies voluntarily undertaken by leaders of nations that retained all or part of their independence and autonomy. In the ghettos of Poland, where German rule was total, where Hans Frank reigned as king, where Himmler's SS kept order, and where the German army operated the economy, Germany did not ask for or get either cooperation or collaboration. SS force and terror extracted compliance from the Jews and aimed to bring them to a state of unresisting submissiveness. Unlike Quisling, Laval, and Vlasov, no Jew—not even an underworld blackguard who sold information to the Gestapo—ever awaited German victory. No Jew ever hoped for a New Order in Europe. The officials of the Judenräte were coerced by German terror to submit and comply. To say that they "cooperated" or "collaborated" with the Germans is semantic confusion and historical misrepresentation.[7]

Could the course of events in the ghettos have been changed had there been fewer missed opportunities and wasted resources? In some ghettos, notably Lodz and Warsaw, more help—within the limits of the available means—might have been rendered to ease the misery of the poorest and most friendless. But the Germans never permitted the ghetto sufficient means to satisfy hunger and cure disease. Even if the ghetto bureaucracies had been more efficient, they could not have halted the course of events that the Germans actuated, simply because the Judenräte lacked the resources and opportunities necessary to thwart German plans. At a time when all Europe lay prostrate under German dominion, the Jews imprisoned within the ghettos had the least opportunity of any people or nation to determine their fate.

The third and final stage of the Jewish situation came with the deportations from the ghettos. The Jews realized that they now confronted even severer threats to their existence than before, though they had neither knowledge nor premonition of death. What they perceived was a major disruption of the wretched existence they had managed to maintain until then. The German strategy everywhere to facilitate the transportation of the Jews to the death camps consisted of lies and deception. The fundamental lie was that the Jews were being resettled for work in the Occupied Eastern Territories, that diligent and industrious Jews would continue to live unharmed in the ghetto.

Reluctant to uproot themselves from the familiar distress of the ghetto, most Jews believed that the future for those deported held nothing more than new hardships in strange and forlorn places. No Jewish official knew otherwise when the deportations began, for none was ever privy to German plans. No Judenrat official ever volunteered to deport Jews from the ghettos, even when they were deceived by German assurances. Everywhere the deportations were conducted under duress, even though Rumkowski and Merin appeared to take the responsibility upon themselves.

After information filtered into the ghetto about the mass shootings in the outdoors, about the operations of mobile death vans, about gassing installations in desolate camps, the first response everywhere was disbelief grounded in shock. Even the wanton and unconstrained killings and cruelties committed by the Germans had not prepared the Jews to grasp the facts of systematic mass murder.

Locked within their ghettos, under strict surveillance and unreined terror, the Jews had no opportunities of verifying the information that came to them, except by asking the Germans, who, unfailingly and unblinkingly, continued to lie. The Jews then tried to assess the possible authenticity of the reports in the light of experience and logic. The horror of an enterprise that would deliberately destroy human beings who were innocent of any wrongdoing was inconceivable. The senselessness of the undertaking further undermined the acceptance of the information. The Jews provided the German war industry with skilled labor, a precious wartime commodity. The

willful destruction of so valuable an asset was as inconceivable on rational grounds as systematic mass
murder was on experiential or moral grounds. These
evaluations were for the most part shared at all levels
of Jewish leadership and by the masses as well. The
information about the death camps was rejected all
over Europe, not only by the Jews, who, as the first
targets and victims, would be expected to disbelieve
most because the news threatened them most. In the
Netherlands, for instance, members of the Dutch resistance responded to the news—first relayed by Kurt
Gerstein—with such utter incredulity that they failed
to act on the information in any way, not even warning the Jews.[8]

During the first months of the deportations, in the
absence of reliable evidence that deportation meant
death, Judenrat officials did not communicate to the
community at large their disquiet and anxiety, fearful
of spreading panic and undermining morale. That
dilemma was described by Leo Baeck, writing about
his experiences in Theresienstadt in 1943. A camp in-
mate told Baeck, in the strictest confidence, that a
friend who had escaped from Auschwitz had secretly
visited him in the middle of the night. At Auschwitz,
the friend said, the Jews were gassed to death, except
for those assigned to slave labor. "So it was not just
a rumor," Baeck commented, "or, as I had hoped, the
illusion of a diseased imagination." He pondered his
responsibility as to whether he should inform the
Judenrat, of which he was an honorary member.
"Living in the expectation of death by gassing would
only be the harder," he reasoned. Furthermore, in an
exercise of denial, he thought that death was not
certain for all, since some people were selected for
slave labor. Perhaps not all transports were sent to
Auschwitz. "So," he concluded, "I came to the grave
decision to tell no one."[9]

Some Jewish leaders, like millions of the people
who looked to them for leadership, could not assimilate the information about the death camps. For
them, in Yeats's words, things fell apart, the center

could not hold. Their psychological solution lay in the denial of the information, the shocked retreat from reality, or in suicide. The paralysis of despair overtook many.

Would an alert, if issued, have changed the outcome of the deportations? Would it have saved lives? In Warsaw, the first warnings of the underground that resettlement meant death were unheeded by the ghetto populace. Without evidential corroboration and with noncompliance as the only alternative course of action, the populace rejected the warning, adapting to their situation by repressing and denying the information. Later, when the ghetto Jews in Warsaw and Lodz acted on warnings by hiding en masse, by passive resistance, the Germans managed to dislodge them from their hiding places in a relatively short time. (Whether the Jews were killed resisting deportation in the ghetto in full public view of non-Jews or in Treblinka or Auschwitz in relative privacy was, for the Germans, at bottom only a matter of public relations.) Even when Jewish leaders informed the community, the course of the Final Solution was not halted, but just retarded for a brief historic moment. In the small ghettos of eastern Poland and White Russia, where official leaders, often in concert with underground leaders, warned the ghetto of imminent liquidation, some Jews had opportunities to flee into the woods. But survival was a possibility only for the young and fit, those with the physical stamina and armed equipment that was their admission ticket to the partisans. It was unrealistic to expect that unarmed urban civilians could survive in the woods. Even the Gypsies, a people whose familiar milieu is the open country, were unable to elude the Germans in the very forests that they believed would be their refuge.[10]

Did Judenrat officials have opportunities or resources to prevent the Germans from carrying out the deportations? Were alternative courses of action available to them? In the light of our knowledge that

Hitler and his government would not permit rational considerations of maximal self-interest in the conduct of the war to interfere with the execution of the Final Solution, such questions about Jewish opportunities and resources to halt the Final Solution appear absurd.

Some Judenräte had no options at all, being simply confronted with accomplished facts of deportations that the Germans themselves organized and carried out. In other ghettos, however, Judenrat officials could be said to have had, in theory, a limited range of alternatives to unresisting compliance, even though in practice every alternative ended in death. In principle, their options were: noncompliance, attempted nullification of deportation, and attempted reduction of the size and scope of deportations in exchange for peaceable compliance.

Noncompliance, in the circumstances of the ghetto, meant either suicide or outright refusal to obey on the part of the Judenrat official. Refusal inevitably entailed being shot on the spot or immediate deportation. Suicide, not a characteristically Jewish response, was more common, because the man who took his life chose not to endanger the hostages taken by the Germans to assure Judenrat compliance. Confronted with Judenrat noncompliance, the Germans, at small cost, intensified the terror. They appointed a handful of demoralized Jews to carry out their orders and brought into the ghetto greater numbers of SS troops and Ukrainian and Baltic auxiliary police.

Some Judenräte attempted to nullify the deportations through the age-old strategy of bribery, but those who delivered the ransom disappeared forever, without deflecting the Germans from their course. In Kovno, when the Germans were already losing the war, even the offer of postwar protection did not dissuade the SS officer from completing the deportations. The strategy of rescue-through-work, pursued relentlessly by both Rumkowski and Barash, appeared to offer the greatest possibility of success. Their objectives were, so to speak, congruent with the tem-

porary interests of the German army, which they
were outfitting and supplying and which, consequently, tried to prolong the existence of the ghettos.
But if the Wehrmacht could not prevail against the
Führer and the SS, how reasonable is the expectation
that the Judenrat could have succeeded?

As German terror and the lack of Jewish opportunity rendered each strategy ineffectual and futile,
the only course left open to the Judenräte was the
strategy of desperation, to save what could be saved,
bargaining with the Devil. The Germans, to coerce
the Judenräte, threatened to destroy the whole ghetto
in case of noncompliance or even temporization. Occasionally proffering the carrot to temper the terror
of the stick, the Germans lyingly assured the Judenräte that once the Aktion in question was completed,
the ghetto survivors would be spared further affliction.

Could the history of human society or law provide
any guidance in such extremity? In desperation some
Jewish officials turned to Halacha for an answer, but
no legal code could provide any moral or practical
guidance for this ultimate dilemma.

Plain sense dictates that in a disaster one rescues
as many as can be rescued. The lifeboat cannot hold
all the passengers of the sinking ship, and the captain
decides who shall be saved. In the ghettos the
habitual rules of precedence for saving people from
disaster in predictable situations proved inappro-
priate. In preparing the list for the first deportation
from Lodz, Rumkowski, believing that the Jews were
being resettled for work, exempted the old among
the group slated for deportation, on the grounds that
the transfer would be too strenuous for them. But in
situations when the Jews themselves suspected that
the deportations meant death, the old volunteered so
as to spare the young, regarding themselves as the
most expendable sacrifice that the community could
make.[11]

The terminal decision to try to save some by
yielding up others was humanly inevitable in circum-

stances without choice or opportunity. German Communists incarcerated in Buchenwald, for instance, confronted precisely the same dilemma in precisely the same way. On April 7, 1945, as Allied forces were approaching Buchenwald, the SS commandant told the camp Eldest that unless the camp itself supplied three thousand men within a half-hour, the SS would use full force to assemble the next transport. Either eventuality, it was known, would mean the deaths of camp inmates, since the SS was erasing all evidence of the camp's existence. The underground Communist camp committee that represented the internal camp government, wishing to prevent the premature liquidation of the whole camp by adopting a stance of noncompliance, chose the lesser evil, taking upon itself the responsibility of selecting thousands of inmates whom they knew the Germans would destroy, while protecting others.[12]

That strange psychic process that afflicts the survivors of disaster, natural or man-made, with feelings of guilt, "existential guilt," just because they have survived and others have not, afflicted also the Jews who remained in the ghettos after the mass killings and the deportations. Even Judenrat officials, whose rescue strategy exposed them to the bitter accusations of the ghetto population, continuously and publicly rationalized their conduct not only to repudiate the charges, but to still their own nagging guilt feelings. The powerlessness of the Jews in their encounter with the Final Solution heightened their sense of guiltiness, for their own tradition placed upon each Jew the obligation for his own life and for the survival of the community. Zelig Kalmanovich spoke for all when he wrote in his diary of the imponderable dilemmas confronting the Jews in those days: "All are guilty, or perhaps more truly, all are innocent and holy."

Appendices

Appendix A

The Fate of the Jews in
Hitler's Europe: By Country

The following pages present a capsule account of the fate of the Jews in the European countries involved in World War II. The countries are grouped regionally, the presentation beginning with Western Europe and continuing eastward. The account of each country contains three sections: a brief description of the country's wartime status, a condensed characterization of the country's prewar Jewish population, and finally, a compressed chronology of the course of the Final Solution in that country.

Throughout Europe the fate of the Jews hinged first of all on each country's wartime status vis-à-vis Germany. Wherever German rule was total and supreme, the Jews were consigned to annihilation. In "Greater Germany" (Germany and Austria), in the Protectorate of Bohemia and Moravia, in occupied Poland, Russia, and in the Baltic countries, the Jews came directly under the jurisdiction of the SS. Their fate was determined.

In the other countries of Europe—allied to Germany, so-called neutrals, and those which, though invaded and occupied by the Germans, nevertheless retained some autonomy—the fate of the Jews depended on each country's commitment to civic equality and on its historical treatment of its Jewish population. Variations from country to country as to the fate of the Jews derived partly from differences in the degree of autonomy permitted by the Germans. German civil administration in the Netherlands and Norway, for example, was more rigorous than German military rule in Belgium.

Wherever indigenous political authority continued to exist, it buffered the Jews from the Germans. In some countries even indigenous political authorities who lacked a basic commitment to equal rights and who were traditionally anti-Semitic could at times be influenced by moral or religious appeals (Slovakia), persuaded by bribes (Rumania), or intimidated by threats of eventual punishment (Hungary) to protect the Jews from the long reach of the Germans. Some states, Vichy France and Bulgaria, for instance, were prepared to stand up to the Germans in order to protect their Jewish nationals, though ready to sacrifice foreign Jews within their jurisdiction.

Sometimes other factors contributed to the rescue of, or failure to rescue, Jews. The German occupation of Europe had turned the continent into a vast geographical trap from which few Jews could escape. For some Jews neutral Sweden's proximity to both Norway and Denmark was a providential geographic circumstance. The small size of a Jewish population also affected the feasibility of rescue or concealment, as in Italy and Denmark. But those factors were merely circumstantial. Denmark's dramatic rescue of its Jews and the overwhelming cooperation that the Italians gave their Jewish compatriots cannot be attributed merely to geography or population size, though these factors helped the undertakings to succeed, but are rather the consequence of the repudiation of anti-Semitism and the commitment to unconditional equality.

The Jews of Europe were socially and culturally diverse, some so acculturated that they had more in common with their fellow nationals than with Jews in other countries. Others remained separate from the non-Jewish population and separatist in their devotion to Jewish tradition. Ultimately the degree of acculturation proved to be without saliency in determining Jewish fate. The separatist Jews of Bulgaria were saved, while the acculturated Jews of Germany were not.

Still less salient to the outcome of the Final Solution was the role of the three Christian religions of Europe: Roman Catholicism, which regards itself as the universal church;

Protestantism, primarily the Lutheran, Evangelical, and Calvinist churches; and the Orthodox Church, which dominates Southeastern Europe. All yielded primacy to national politics in the countries in which they were located, subordinating the teachings of Christ to the national political tradition.

In Austria the Catholic bishops welcomed the Anschluss as enthusiastically as all Austrians. In Italy, in contrast, the Catholic hierarchy behaved like the Italians whose national aspirations had been kindled by the French Revolution and the libertarian tradition of the *Risorgimento*. In France the Catholic hierarchy was divided, as all the French were, either defending or attacking the French Revolution, torn between a republican egalitarian tradition and Bourbonism, still in conflict over Dreyfus.

In Bulgaria the Orthodox Church spoke up for the Jews, perhaps because secular political groups spoke up for the Jews. In Greece, however, the Orthodox Church was silent. As for the Protestant churches, their behavior conformed to the country in which they functioned. In Germany the Lutheran church abandoned Christian principles in subservience of the racial state. In the Netherlands the Calvinist church demonstrated its rigid conservatism by passivity and indifference to the situation of the Jews. In Denmark the extraordinary political defense of the Jews that the bishops of the Danish Evangelical Lutheran church demonstrated under German occupation reflected the Danish political ethos more than Christian doctrine.

At bottom, the success of the Final Solution throughout Europe depended on Germany's opportunities and resources to carry it out, that is, whether or not Germany had uncontested and supreme control of a country or territory. Elsewhere, the Final Solution was conditional upon a political tradition that held that all men were equal, that human life was valuable, and that the Jews were human beings entitled to life.

WESTERN EUROPE

France

On September 3, 1939, France declared war on Germany. After eight months of inaction (the "phony war"), France

was invaded from the north by Germany on May 17, 1940.
On June 10, Italy declared war on France and invaded from
the south. Paris was evacuated on June 13. Three days later,
Marshal Henri-Philippe Pétain took over as head of the
French government; the next day he asked the Germans for
an armistice. The armistice, signed at Compiègne, June 22,
1940, provided that French forces be disarmed and that
three-fifths of France be surrendered to German control.
One day later, General Charles de Gaulle, head of the
French National Committee in London, pledged continued
French resistance against Germany. Britain severed ties with
the Pétain regime. On June 24, France concluded an armistice with Italy, without yielding any significant concessions.

German-occupied France was divided into three different
jurisdictions. Northern France, the area around Lille, was
assigned to the military governor of Belgium. Alsace and
Lorraine were treated as quasi-incorporated areas in the
German Reich, each province governed by a Gauleiter.
The rest of the occupied zone was ruled by a succession of
military governors (General von Bockelberg, General Otto
von Stülpnagel, General Heinrich von Stülpnagel).

A French government was established in unoccupied
France on July 2, 1940, at Vichy, and a week later the parliament gave Marshal Pétain the power to establish an authoritarian regime, with Pierre Laval as vice-premier. That regime completely repudiated the Declaration of the Rights of
Man. On May 15, 1941, Pétain broadcast a pledge of cooperation with Germany. The question as to how much
collaboration the French should offer the Germans divided
the Vichy government. After the resignation of Admiral
Darlan and his supporters in April 1942, advocates for
minimal cooperation, Pierre Laval, the advocate of total collaborationism, became the virtual head of the French state.
In response to German demands, compulsory labor for all
men eighteen to sixty-five years old and unmarried women
twenty to thirty-four was instituted.

On November 8, 1942, the Allies landed 110,000 men on
the North African coast. Within three days, the Germans
occupied Vichy France. Italy occupied eight departments,
including Alpes-Maritimes and the area between Nice and
Grenoble, which came under German occupation the following year after Mussolini's overthrow. In response to harsher

conditions of German rule and intensified German terror, French resistance began to increase.

Allied forces landed on the coast of Normandy on June 6, 1944. Other Allied landings took place on the French Mediterranean coast on August 15, 1944. German forces in Paris capitulated on August 23–24, and French forces liberated the city. The administration of France was handed over to de Gaulle.

JEWS IN PREWAR FRANCE

Of a population of 45 million, the 350,000 Jews who resided in France just before the invasion were less than 1 percent. Of these, only some 150,000 were native-born. About 50,000 were refugees from Germany, Austria, and Czechoslovakia; some 25,000 had just fled from Belgium and Holland. The other foreign-born Jews were largely from Eastern Europe, having come to France during the 1920s and 1930s. The Jewish population was concentrated in Paris, Alsace-Lorraine, and eastern and northern departments.

The native-born French Jews were largely middle class, engaged in the professions, business, and commerce. The foreign-born were predominantly workers and small businessmen. The ready-to-wear clothing industry was largely Jewish. The Jewish working class was highly politicized and unionized.

Native- and foreign-born Jews were also differentiated socially. Native-born Jews were highly acculturated, associated with the Jewish community through the consistorial system, their Judaism expressed in lukewarm religious observance. Foreign-born Jews remained largely unacculturated, having transplanted from Eastern Europe their Jewish political affiliations (Bundists, Labor Zionists, Communists) and, for the most part, retaining the use of Yiddish. Distance rather than tension characterized the relationship between both Jewish communities.

Despite the considerable rise of anti-Semitism, native and German-imported, Jewish citizens enjoyed full civic equality and Jewish newcomers were well received. Léon Blum, head of the French Socialist party, had served as Premier of France.

JEWS IN WARTIME FRANCE

In the wake of the German invasion, France's rapid collapse, and the armistice, large numbers of Jews fled south. Relatively few Jews had lived in what became the unoccupied zone, but by mid-1940, 195,000 Jews lived there, of whom it was believed 145,000 were native-born, 20,000 East European Jews, and 30,000 Jewish refugees from Germany and Austria. The Jews in Alsace-Lorraine began to be expelled upon German occupation, and by November 1940 those still there were ordered out, their property confiscated. They themselves were dumped in the unoccupied zone. In occupied France some 120,000 Jews remained in Paris and in smaller communities in Nancy, Bordeaux, Bayonne, and also in new communities formed in Charente by Jews evacuated from Lorraine.

In the Unoccupied Zone: On August 27, 1940, the Vichy government annulled a decree of April 21, 1939, that punished slander and libel "toward a group of people who belong by origin to a particular race or a particular religion," thus providing a "legal" basis for its subsequent anti-Jewish legislation. On October 3, 1940, a major anti-Jewish statute was enacted that defined as Jews those persons who belonged to the Jewish religion or had more than two Jewish grandparents. It prohibited Jews from holding most public offices, banned them from the judiciary, teaching, the military, banking, real estate, and the media, and limited their presence in the professions.

A decree of October 4, 1940, authorized the internment of foreign Jews. Consequently, about 25,000 Jewish refugees from Germany and Austria, including some 7,500 German Jews whom the Germans had driven from Baden and the Palatinate into unoccupied France were interned at Gurs (later also at other camps). These internees were soon thereafter forced into labor brigades, and large numbers of them died of hunger, cold, and disease.

On March 20, 1941, a law was enacted creating a General Commissariat for Jewish Affairs, whose function was to implement existing decisions with regard to Jews, propose further legislation as needed, supervise the liquidation of Jewish property where "legally" prescribed in accordance with the needs of the national economy, and take all police measures with regard to the Jews. Xavier Vallat, long-time anti-Semite, was appointed Commissioner (replaced June 1942 by Darquier de Pellepoix). On June 2, 1941, a statute basing itself on measures enacted by the Germans in the occupied zone replaced the statute of October 1940. It defined the status of Jews more rigidly and set in motion the expropriation and "Aryanization" of Jewish property. A census of Jews and Jewish property was also decreed. The law of July 22, 1941, gave the General Commissioner wide powers in the process of expropriating Jewish property and business.

A decree enacted on November 29, 1941, established the *Union Générale des Israélites de France* (UGIF), whose officially stated purpose was to provide representation for all Jews vis-à-vis the state authorities, especially with regard to relief and social welfare. All existing Jewish organizations, excepting religious associations, were ordered dissolved and their property turned over to UGIF. Its board was to be administered by eighteen French-born Jews, nine in each zone, and to be under the authority of the General Commissariat for Jewish Affairs.

In the Occupied Zone: Jews in the occupied zone were subject to both the decrees of the German military government and the decrees of Vichy to the extent that the latter did not contravene the former. Responsibility for Jewish matters was lodged with the Foreign Office staff and the SS. Otto Abetz, German ambassador to Vichy, with two assistants in charge of Jewish affairs, was attached to the staff of the military governor, whose authority and manpower he needed to implement his orders. The SS, technically attached to Abetz, eventually took over responsibility for the anti-Jewish program. Obergruppenführer Karl-Albrecht Oberg supervised a series of "experts" on Jewish affairs, including Eichmann's assistant, Hauptsturmführer Theodor Dannecker.

On September 27, 1940, the Germans issued an ordinance that defined the status of Jews in racial terms, forbidding those who fled to return to the occupied zone, ordering a census of all Jews to be completed by October 20, 1940, and requiring public identification of Jewish businesses. On October 18, 1940, all Jewish enterprises had to be registered; their expropriation and "Aryanization" followed. The

French bureaucracy was used to implement these ordinances. On April 26, 1941, Jews were forbidden to engage in a wide variety of occupations, and their employment in positions in contact with the public was forbidden.

Under Dannecker's direction, Paris police compiled a card index of Jews in Paris, by name, street, occupation, and nationality. In May and August 1941, the roundups of Jews began: in the first roundup, 3,200 Jews, mostly Polish, were sent to camps at Pithiviers and Beaune la Rolande; in the second, 4,300 Jews, including 1,300 French natives, were sent to Drancy, which was to serve as the chief transit camp for Auschwitz. On December 12, 1941, 1,000 French Jewish lawyers and doctors were rounded up to be held for deportation to the East, as reprisal for an unsuccessful assassination attempt on a German air-force officer.

Decrees prescribing curfew, yellow-star arm bands and badges began to be issued in February 1942, while plans for deportation took shape. On March 28, 1942, the first deportation train left Drancy for Auschwitz. In Paris, on July 16–17, 12,884 non-French Jews, including women and children, were rounded up. Those without families were sent to Drancy. The remaining 9,000, including 4,000 children, were penned up in the vast sports stadium Vélodrome d'Hiver, where they spent a week in horrible conditions before being shipped off to Auschwitz. (Only 30 adults returned alive after the war; no child survived.)

Meanwhile the Germans were demanding that Laval hand over all foreign Jews in the unoccupied zone for deportation and that concerted action be taken in both zones against all Jews, French or foreign-born. On July 2, 1942, the Council of Ministers at Vichy decided, with Pétain's approval, to make a distinction in their zone between French and foreign Jews. French Jews would remain under the sovereignty and protection of the French government. In August 1942, fifteen thousand foreign Jews interned in camps in the unoccupied zone were handed over to the Germans for deportation. After November 11, 1942, when the Germans occupied all of France, they began to round up Jews in Marseilles. Many Jews then fled to the Italian occupation zone in southeastern France, where they remained in safety until September 1943, when the Germans also occupied that area (see Italy, p. 498). In the area of Nice, more than five thousand Jews, hunted down for over five months, were deported.

In the last months of the war, in addition to the deportations, mass executions also diminished the Jewish population. The accelerating activity of the resistance movement drove the Germans to ever severer reprisals, and Jews—mostly internees—were singled out as hostages and victims. Hundreds of Jews were executed under such circumstances.

In February 1944, Mercier du Paty de Clam, on the advice of a cousin highly placed in the underground, accepted the post of Commissioner General of Jewish Affairs, having been persuaded that the Commissariat was a good listening post and that he could do good by disorganizing its administration. In this he succeeded to a great extent and was consequently replaced on June 1, 1944.

On August 24, right after the liberation of Paris, Drancy was liberated. The number of Jews who were deported, executed by the Germans, or who perished in internment camps is estimated at 90,000, most of them foreign-born.

Belgium

On May 10, 1940, Germany, which had in 1937 guaranteed Belgium's neutrality, invaded that country without warning. On May 27–28, upon order of King Leopold III, the Belgian army capitulated. The royal family remained in residence, but the Belgian Cabinet formed a government-in-exile in London and continued to wage war against Germany.

Belgium was put under German military occupation and was ruled by a military governor, General Alexander von Falkenhausen. (The Belgian districts of Eupen, Malmédy, and Moresnet were incorporated into the Reich by decree on May 18, 1940.) The actual administration of the country continued to be exercised largely by the Belgian civil service acting under the secretaries-general (heads of government departments), most of whom became compliant accessories of German policy. Also the Rexists, the native Belgian fascist movement, collaborated actively with the Germans. The overwhelming majority of the population, especially the French-speaking Walloons, had no Nazi sympathies and displayed considerable solidarity with the Jews. Resistance and sabotage increased to such an extent that the Germans sought to establish tighter control over the Belgian population. In July 1944, the German military government was changed to a civilian administration under a Reich Commissioner and the post combined the authority of the Wehrmacht and the Higher SS and Police.

Early in September 1944, British and American troops, with the support of a Belgian underground army, liberated Brussels and most of Belgium. In December 1944 the Germans counterattacked, swept into the Ardennes region, and succeeded in penetrating deep into Belgium. After a series of costly counterattacks (Battle of the Bulge), the Allied forces destroyed and routed the Germans on January 16, 1945.

THE JEWS IN PREWAR BELGIUM

Before the German invasion, about 90,000 Jews lived in Belgium, 1 percent of the total population. Of these, 15,000 were refugees from Germany and most of the others were themselves immigrants, predominantly from Eastern Europe, or children of such immigrants. Most Jews lived in Antwerp (55,000) and Brussels (30,000), with the rest in Charleroi, Liège, and Ghent.

About three-fourths of the gainfully occupied were self-employed; the rest were workers. They were well represented in the clothing industry, small businesses, and retail trade. The diamond trade in Antwerp was largely in Jewish hands. The production of fine leather goods was also a Jewish specialty.

Jewish communal and cultural life was a combination of the French consistorial system and the East European mode. The Jews in Brussels were on the whole an acculturated group. Antwerp was a center of both Orthodoxy and Yiddish secular culture. Besides two day schools that enjoyed government subsidy, many afternoon Jewish schools were operated there under Orthodox and secular auspices.

Despite their relatively recent arrival in Belgium, Jews were well received. In 1938 the Belgian government had allocated a grant of six million francs toward the relief of German Jewish refugees. In elections that year the Rexists and other fascist and semifascist groups were spectacularly rejected at the polls.

THE JEWS IN WARTIME BELGIUM

In October 1940, six months after German occupation, anti-Jewish policies began to be promulgated. On October 23, 1940, shehita was abolished. A decree issued on October 28, 1940, defined Jews according to German racial standards and ordered their registration. Another decree on that date excluded Jews from public service, schools, law, press and other media. Jewish businesses were required to be registered. The registration, completed later, showed 42,000 Jews in Belgium, only a few thousand of them native-born. Well over 20,000 were in hiding, and an estimated 25,000 Jews had fled to France, from which most were subsequently deported.

Economic measures against Jews and their property were enacted on May 31, 1941, setting in motion the "Aryanization" of Jewish property and the rapid impoverishment of the Jews. In July 1941 the Jews had to declare their real estate holdings; orders were issued forbidding banks to accept deposits from Jews; 7,600 Jewish firms still in existence were ordered closed. By mid-1942, Jewish property was completely "Aryanized."

The process of isolating the Jews began in the fall of 1941, when Jews became subject to curfew, were forbidden to travel outside the major cities where they were concentrated, and were prohibited from using the parks or strolling in the streets of Antwerp. As of December 31, 1941, Jewish children were excluded from the public schools. In the spring of 1942 decrees issued in Antwerp compelled Jews into forced-labor brigades for *Organisation Todt*. On June 6, 1942, Jews were forced to wear the Star of David arm bands.

On November 25, 1941, the Germans ordered the organization of a Judenrat. A Jewish committee had meanwhile been organized, headed by Dr. Salomon Ullmann, head of Jewish chaplains in the Belgian army. This *ad hoc* body became the *Association des Juifs en Belgique* (AJB), to which all Jews were subject. Its initial tasks were to provide social services and organize the education of Jewish children, but it soon was forced to transmit German orders. A Jewish underground organization, *Comité de Défense des Juifs,* affiliated with the Belgian resistance movement, was active and tried to counteract the AJB.

Early in 1942 deportations began. Queen Elizabeth and Cardinal van Roey had asked protection for the few thousand Jews of Belgian nationality. Falkenhausen agreed to exempt them, but the promise was not fully kept. About a thousand Jews of Belgian nationality were actually deported. According to German records, 25,437 Jews were deported to Auschwitz via the transit camp at Malines from mid-1942 through mid-1944. Several thousand were sent to Lodz and deported from there. Considerable numbers of Jews died in Belgium of hunger, disease, or overwork in labor and transit camps or as victims of random shootings and terror. In sum, about 40,000 of the 65,000 Jews who had remained in Belgium perished. At liberation, about 20,000 Jews were found in Belgium, 6,000 of them German and Austrian refugees, 8,000 Polish Jews, the rest Belgian and Dutch nationals.

Luxembourg

The Grand Duchy of Luxembourg, a 1,000-square-mile triangle bordering on Belgium, France, and Germany, with a population of 300,000, was invaded, in violation of its neutrality, by Germany on May 9–10, 1940. Grand Duchess Charlotte and the Cabinet fled, establishing a government-in-exile in London. The German military occupation was succeeded in August 1940 by a Chief of Civil Administration, Gustav Simon, head of the adjoining Gau of Koblenz-Trier. Two years later he announced that Luxembourg, as a "Germanic" state, would be incorporated into the Reich and, to drive the lesson home, he issued an order for military conscription. The ensuing general strike in the capital city was suppressed with severity, and its many participants were deported.

In September 1944 Allied armies liberated Luxembourg.

JEWS IN PREWAR LUXEMBOURG

In 1935 about 3,000 Jews lived in Luxembourg, 1 percent of the total population. It was an ancient Jewish community that had been reconstituted in 1791 after the French Revolution. About two-thirds of the Jews lived in the capital, the remainder in smaller cities. Additionally, 1,500 German Jews had found refuge in the country. The Luxembourgian Jews enjoyed complete equality and prosperity. The Jewish community was organized in the consistorial system, with Robert Serebrenik as Chief Rabbi.

JEWS IN WARTIME LUXEMBOURG

When the Germans invaded Luxembourg, over 1,000 Jews fled or were evacuated by French troops. With the German occupation, the local Volksdeutsche emerged to take active part in anti-Jewish persecutions. On September 5, 1940, the major body of anti-Jewish legislation was issued. Jews were ghettoized in communal quarters, compelled to wear arm bands, assigned to forced labor, and expropriated. A policy of expulsion and deportation was put into effect early, since Luxembourg was to be incorporated into the Reich. Under the leadership of Rabbi Serebrenik and the Consistory, about 2,500 Jews were evacuated, through illegal channels, to unoccupied France and Portugal in the period between August 8, 1940, and October 15, 1941. Thereafter the possibility of voluntary departure ceased to exist. From October 1941 through April 1943, approximately 800 Jews were deported to Lodz, Auschwitz, and Theresienstadt.

After liberation, about 400 Jews were found to have survived in Luxembourg.

The Netherlands

On May 10, 1940, the Germans invaded the Netherlands without warning. Dutch resistance crumbled, and Rotterdam surrendered on May 13. Several hours later, its entire center was wantonly destroyed by German air bombardment. The government, headed by Queen Wilhelmina, fled to London, where it continued to exist in exile. On May 14 the Netherlands capitulated to the Germans.

The Netherlands, slated for eventual incorporation into the Reich as a "Germanic" state, was governed by a civilian German administrator, a Reich Commissioner, the Austrian

Artur Seyss-Inquart, appointed on May 18, 1940. He suspended the Dutch parliament and Council of State, subordinating the Dutch civil service, under the secretaries-general, to his rule. Important posts were assigned to Dutch Nazis, who became prominent in the country's governance.

On February 25, 1941, a general strike broke out in Amsterdam, Hilversum, and Zaandam, paralyzing transport and industry. The strike was brutally suppressed in three days by the German army, and martial law was imposed. The Dutch population was heavily fined, and the Germans succeeded in stifling further overt resistance in the Netherlands during the occupation.

In September 1944 Allied airborne forces attempted only partially successful landings at Arnhem and Eindhoven, liberating part of southern Holland, while the Germans continued to retain the rest of Holland. Starvation and German terror, including the vengeful bombing of Rotterdam and Amsterdam, were the lot of the Dutch until May 6, 1945, when the country was liberated by the Allies and Queen Wilhelmina returned to her throne.

JEWS IN PREWAR NETHERLANDS

Just before the German invasion, 140,000 Jews lived in Holland, 110,000 of them Dutch and 30,000 refugees from Germany and Austria. Nearly 60 percent, 80,000 Jews, lived in Amsterdam alone.

About half the Dutch Jews were engaged in trade and commerce, many in second-hand and street trade. Ten percent were in the diamond industry, 20 percent in other manufacturing, 5 percent in the professions. Jews played a significant role in the political and cultural life of the country.

The 5,000 Dutch Sephardic Jews were organized in a union of two communities, one with 4,500 members in Amsterdam, and the others in The Hague. The largest Ashkenazic communities were in Amsterdam, The Hague, and Rotterdam. Both Sephardic and Ashkenazic groups maintained, besides their synagogues, religious schools and charitable organizations that provided a variety of social services, especially valuable for the refugees. Over twenty Jewish newspapers and periodicals, nearly all in the Dutch language, were published.

The Dutch Jews enjoyed full civic equality, and many of their religious and welfare institutions received government subventions. Although most Dutch Jews, especially the middle classes and professionals, were highly acculturated, Jewish communal and cultural life managed to survive, despite the low birth rate and the high intermarriage rate.

THE JEWS IN WARTIME NETHERLANDS

The first anti-Jewish decree, enacted on August 31, 1940, abolished shehita. A decree of October 22, 1940, required the registration of a wide range of business enterprises, owned or operated wholly or in part by Jews or in which Jews had financial interests, Jews being defined in racial terms. Other anti-Jewish decrees, along the German pattern, followed. On January 10, 1941, a decree ordered all Jews to register within a set period with local branches of the Census Office; failure to do so was punishable with five years' imprisonment and/or confiscation of property. The statistics, submitted by the Census Office on August 27, 1941, showed 160,820 registrations, 140,552 of them Jews, 14,549 "half-Jews," and 5,719 "quarter-Jews."

On February 12, 1941, the *Joodsche Raad* (Jewish Council) was formed under duress amid a series of violent incidents between Jews and Dutch Nazis, occurring mostly in Amsterdam's old Jewish section. Hans Rauter, Higher SS and Police Leader, Seyss-Inquart's Commissioner for Security and Police, sealed off the area, summoned several of Amsterdam's Jewish leaders, and demanded the formation of a Jewish Council, which would be required to preserve order in the Jewish quarter.

A week later, in south Amsterdam, a more prosperous section where one-fourth of Amsterdam's Jews lived, another violent incident occurred between a German police patrol and Jews. A few days thereafter, the Germans seized 400 Jews, twenty to thirty-five years old, who were eventually deported to Mauthausen. The seizure and deportation were among the factors that led to the general strike on February 25, 1941. (The SS then threatened the Jews with further reprisals unless the strike was called off.)

On March 12, 1941, the Germans began the process of

"Aryanizing" Jewish property, and a decree of May 21, 1942, authorized complete expropriation, except for items like wedding rings and gold teeth.

The Germans placed all Jewish organizations under the authority of the Joodsche Raad on March 18, 1941. Decrees were then issued prohibiting Jews from traveling, dismissing them from the civil service, cultural posts, and the stock exchange, barring them from public parks. On August 29, 1941, Jewish children were barred from public schools and vocational schools.

In the spring of 1941 a *Zentralstelle für jüdische Auswanderung* (Central Office for Jewish Emigration), under SS-Hauptsturmführer Ferdinand aus der Funten, was charged with rounding up the Jews and deporting them. The Joodsche Raad was made subordinate to the Zentralstelle.

In January 1942 forced-labor camps for Jews were set up. Meanwhile the Dutch Jews began to be concentrated in Amsterdam. On April 29, 1942, the identifying Jewish star was introduced. Jews were further restricted in their occupational activities. Curfew was introduced.

In July 1942, deportations began, continuing through September 1943. Two transit camps, Westerbork and Vught, were set up where Jews were concentrated until schedules permitted their entrainment to Auschwitz. On September 29, 1943, in the last major roundup, about 5,000 Jews, including the heads of the Joodsche Raad, were deported via Westerbork. Only small protected categories of Jews still remained, including diamond workers and Jewish partners in mixed marriages. Most of these were deported early in 1944.

Some 110,000 Jews were deported to Auschwitz, Sobibór, and, in smaller numbers, to other camps. About 5,000 survived the death camps. Seventy-five percent of Dutch Jewry perished.

Italy

Though politically and ideologically close to Germany, Italy decided, at the start of the war, to maintain her neutrality, but on June 10, 1940, Italy declared war both on Great Britain and on collapsing France, which it invaded from the south. On September 27, 1940, Italy, Germany, and Japan concluded a three-power pact, Italy thus becoming a full partner in Germany's war. On October 28, 1940, Italy attacked Greece, but, driven back, required military help from Germany. In April 1941, Italy occupied the largest, but least populated, part of Greece and also littoral Yugoslavia. On June 22, 1941, Italy joined Germany in declaring war on Russia, and Italian forces joined the invasion. On December 11, 1941, Italy declared war on the United States. After the Allied invasion of North Africa, Italy joined Germany on November 11, 1942, in occupying the hitherto unoccupied zone of France. Italy took over eight departments in southeastern France, including Nice.

As the tide of war turned against Germany and with the Allied invasion of Sicily on July 10, 1943, Italy underwent internal upheaval. The Fascist Grand Council and King Victor Emmanuel forced Mussolini to resign. A new government was established under Marshal Pietro Badoglio on July 25, 1943; three days later he dissolved the Fascist party and put Mussolini under arrest. On September 3, 1943, the Allies invaded southern Italy, and on September 8 the Badoglio government surrendered to them. The Germans, however, were prepared for these maneuvers: they rescued Mussolini and proclaimed him the head of a newly established National Fascist government, later known as the Italian Social Republic. With great dispatch the Germans occupied Italy, as well as all Italian-held territory in southeastern France, littoral Yugoslavia, and Greece. Mussolini's neo-Fascist government notwithstanding, rule of Italy remained in the hands of the German military governor, Gruppenführer Otto Wächter, and two German plenipotentiaries, Rudolf Rahn of the Foreign Office and Obergruppenführer Karl Wolff, general of the Waffen-SS.

In February 1944 the Allies returned part of southern Italy to Italian jurisdiction. Fighting moved north. The Allies landed on the Italian coast south of Rome in June 1944, and by mid-August, with the capture of Florence, they controlled Italy as far north as a line running from Livorno to Ancona, but until the very end of the war the industrial north remained in German hands.

On April 28, 1945, Mussolini was captured and shot. Early in May the Germans in Italy capitulated.

JEWS IN PREWAR ITALY

In 1938 some 57,000 Jews lived in Italy, about one-tenth of 1 percent of the Italian population. About 10,000 were refugees from Germany and Austria. Most Jews lived in large cities: Rome (13,700), Milan (8,000), Trieste (5,000), Turin (3,700), Florence (2,800), Genoa (2,700), Venice (2,000), Livorno (1,750), and Ancona (1,000).

An old Jewish community, the Italian Jews since Emancipation had been fully accepted socially and economically into Italian society. Jews were predominantly middle and upper middle class, engaged in trade and commerce, with more than one-quarter of the gainfully employed in the professions. Pockets of Jewish poverty remained, especially in the old ghetto of Rome, where several thousand Jews continued to live in slums, eking out a living from street trade and sometimes beggary.

The observance of Judaism, except among the poor, was in decline; the rate of intermarriage on the rise. (In the 1930s, 30 percent of the Jews who married wed non-Jews.) The major cities had synagogues and other institutions that provided basic or minimal services in terms of ritual and Jewish education. Zionism existed as a cultural influence rather than a political movement.

Anti-Semitism was not a serious threat to the Italian Jews, even during the early years of the Fascist regime. Three laws, passed in the period from October 1930 to November 1931, provided for the reorganization of the Jewish community under a new civil code that strengthened its status and influence. The individual Jewish communities were to provide for the ritual and educational needs of the community through an annual registration fee. All communities were represented in the *Unione delle Comunità Israelitiche Italiane*.

After Hitler's accession to power, Italy became a place of refuge for German, and later Austrian, Jews. By 1938 over 10,000 Jewish refugees were in Italy. Under increasing pressure from Hitler, Mussolini acceded to the views of those in his government who felt that Italy should move closer to Germany. Though Nazi anti-Semitism was not to the Italian taste, a series of anti-Jewish laws was enacted in November 1938 that defined the Jews, though not entirely on a racial basis, and excluded them from civil service, army service,

Fascist party membership, and ownership of enterprises employing large numbers of Italians. All naturalizations obtained after January 1, 1919, were nullified and all foreign and denaturalized Jews were ordered to leave Italy by March 1939. (By late 1941 more than seven thousand Jews, most of them denaturalized Italians, had emigrated.) A decree of June 29, 1939, restricted Jewish professionals to practice only among Jewish clients and patients. Marriages between Jews and Italians were forbidden. Limitations were put on property ownership, especially agricultural land. This legislation impoverished the once prosperous Jewish community. Over 10 percent emigrated; another 10 percent apostatized.

JEWS IN WARTIME ITALY

Whatever hardships the Italian Jews had to undergo from the end of 1938 on, their situation was enviable in contrast to those Jews who lived under direct German occupation. The Italians remained unresponsive to German demands to deport Jews. In Italy proper and in all areas occupied by Italy, the Jews remained safe from deportation, though they were subject to harsh legislation and deprivation. When the Germans occupied Italy, only about forty thousand Jews still remained.

With the German occupation in September 1943, Jews became subject to deportation. The first action took place in October 1943 in Rome, where the Germans managed to round up over one thousand of the eight thousand Roman Jews and deport them to Auschwitz. Most of the other Jews of Rome had fled or gone into hiding.

The Italian puppet regime issued a police order on November 30, 1943, stipulating that all Jews should be sent to concentration camps and their property confiscated for the state. Up north Jews fled and went into hiding, but the Italian police, in their hunt for Jews, managed to send more than seven thousand to camps at Fossoli di Carpi (near Modena) and Bolzano, which served as assembly centers for deportation to Auschwitz and Birkenau. Many Jews were incarcerated in Italian prisons, the most notorious being San Vittorio in Milan, where torture and murder were common. About eight thousand Italian Jews were annihilated.

NORTHERN EUROPE

Norway

Norway sought to maintain neutrality when war broke out, but on April 8–9, 1940, Germany invaded Norway with sea- and airborne forces. The Norwegians offered resistance and were reinforced by Anglo-French forces that had managed to land on the Norwegian coast, but by June 9, superior German forces crushed all resistance. King Haakon VII and his Cabinet escaped to London, forming a government-in-exile.

Norway became a Reich Commissariat under the rule of Josef Terboven, who was directly responsible to Hitler. On September 25, 1940, Terboven declared the King dethroned, the government abolished, and all political parties dissolved except the pro-Nazi *Nasjonal Samling* (National Unity party), headed by former Norwegian Minister of War Vidkun Quisling. On February 1, 1942, Terboven rewarded Quisling for his services to Germany by appointing him Minister-President. Within the week Quisling abolished the Norwegian constitution and made himself dictator. Norway's long border with Sweden, which offered avenues of escape, and an active resistance movement, strengthened from London, helped to mitigate the hardships of German occupation and Quisling rule.

In May 1945 the Germans surrendered in Norway. Quisling was arrested, tried, sentenced to death in September, and executed October 24, 1945.

JEWS IN PREWAR NORWAY

In a population of nearly 3 million, about 1,800 Jews lived in Norway, of whom 300 were refugees from Central Europe. Over 1,000 Jews lived in Oslo and about 300 in Trondheim. The Jews were integrated in all aspects of Norwegian life. The low estate of anti-Semitism is evident in the fact that in 1936 Quisling's Nasjonal Samling vote dropped from 2.23 percent to 1.83 percent of the total vote.

JEWS IN WARTIME NORWAY

Even before Reich Commissar Terboven had decreed the expropriation of the Jews, Quisling's storm troopers began a campaign of terror against them, seizing their businesses for personal profit. No specific anti-Jewish legislation along German lines was enacted, but anti-Jewish policies were carried out within the framework of Terboven's enactments. In July 1941 all commercial establishments were told to submit lists of their employees, indicating their religion. In November an inventory of Jewish-owned real estate was requested from the provincial governors. In June 1942, Jewish businesses were placed under the control of commissioners.

Beginning on March 1, 1942, passports and identity cards had to be marked "Jew." The chief of the Norwegian State Secretariat, Fugelsand, the intermediary between the German authorities and the Nasjonal Samling, was put in charge of a "racial department" to implement the anti-Jewish orders. Jews were interned in labor camps set up in northern Norway. In September 1942 extensive roundups of Jews began.

On October 23, 1942, a Quisling frontier guard was assassinated. Two of the assassins were identified as Jews. This served as a pretext for Quisling to order the confiscation of all property owned by Jews in Norway. In addition, a further hunt for Jews got under way. Where heads of families could not be found, women and children were taken as hostages. At least half the Norwegian Jews were interned or imprisoned. In November one boatload of victims was sent by sea from Oslo to Stettin. In February 1943 another boatload of Jews, who had been interned in concentration camps, sailed. In all, about eight hundred Jews were deported, most to Auschwitz, a smaller number to slave-labor camps in Germany. Only twenty-three of the deported Jews survived.

Some nine hundred Jews, about half the Jewish population, managed to evade arrest and internment. With the help of the Norwegian resistance movement they fled over the border to Sweden. Norway became emptied of Jews.

Denmark

On April 9, 1940, Germany invaded neutral Denmark. Cecil von Renthe-Fink, German minister in Copenhagen, in demanding Denmark's capitulation without resistance, declared officially that Germany had no intention, then or in the future, of encroaching on Denmark's territorial integrity or political independence. Denmark accepted German occupation.

King Christian X remained on the throne and the Danish army, navy, and police remained undisturbed. A government appointed by the King and responsible to parliament continued to function, and parliament continued to exercise its legislative functions. In June 1940, Erik Scavenius, known for his pro-German sympathies, was appointed Foreign Minister and exercised considerable influence over ailing Prime Minister Thorvald Stauning. (After Stauning's death, Scavenius became Prime Minister in November 1942.) Notwithstanding various political concessions to the Germans, the Danes continued to maintain a democratic parliamentary government and an independent policy.

In fall 1942 Hitler changed his policy toward Denmark, intending to incorporate it into Germany. Leading German personnel in Denmark were changed; career diplomat Renthe-Fink was replaced by SS-Obergruppenführer Karl Werner Best, acting as Reich Plenipotentiary. The new Wehrmacht commanding general planned to disband the Danish army and establish military rule in Denmark.

The Danes stiffened against German demands, and even Scavenius opposed German efforts to take over rule of Denmark. Sabotage and resistance within the country increased and reached their climax in August 1943. The German army then entered Copenhagen, disarmed the Danish army, imprisoned the King, and declared the Danish government dissolved. A state of emergency and martial law were declared. Though the emergency was officially lifted October 6, 1943, in effect conditions remained the same, with Danish sabotage and resistance intensifying against the Germans. In July 1944, with news of the attempted assassination on Hitler, general strikes swept Denmark. Until liberation, in May 1945, the Danes remained in a veritable state of war against the occupying Germans.

JEWS IN PREWAR DENMARK

About 8,000 Jews, .2 percent of the total population, lived in Denmark at the time of the German occupation. Some 6,500 were Danish Jews (including 1,300 offspring of mixed marriages), consisting of old Danish families and also of East European Jews who had settled in Denmark before and after World War I. About 1,500 were recent refugees from Germany, Austria, and Czechoslovakia. The old Jewish families had been thoroughly integrated into Danish social, political, and economic life. The later settlers brought with them Zionist and Jewish cultural concerns that helped to revivify Jewish communal life in Denmark. Anti-Semitism, despite extensive imports from Germany, was limited to small, extremist groups.

JEWS IN WARTIME DENMARK

Despite efforts by Himmler and other top Germans to convince the Danes that the Jews were an alien element, Jews remained under the protection of the Danish government. No anti-Jewish legislation was enacted and no Jewish property was expropriated. No Jews were ousted from government posts.

After Denmark came under martial law, Best tried to deport the Danish Jews. His plans, confided to a German shipping industrialist, were reported on September 28 to Danish Social Democratic leaders. The Germans had scheduled the roundup of the Jews for October 1, 1943, but in an extraordinary operation involving the whole Danish people and the agreement of the Swedish government, nearly all Danish Jews were hidden and then ferried across to Sweden, where they remained in safety until the end of the war. The Germans managed to round up some four hundred Jews, whom they sent to Theresienstadt.

The internment of the Danish Jews in Theresienstadt agitated the Danish government, which repeatedly requested permission to inspect the camp. In June 1944 such permission was granted, and the visit was made by delegates of the Danish Red Cross. As a consequence of persistent Danish interest in the deported Jews, none was sent to Auschwitz. At the end of the war, fifty-one had died in Theresienstadt of natural causes.

Finland

When war broke out, Finland announced its neutrality, but on November 30, 1939, Finland was invaded by the Soviet Union. When the Soviet-Finnish war was concluded in

March 1940, Finland had to yield territory and make other political concessions to Russia. On June 22, 1941, Finland joined Germany in attacking the Soviet Union. Finland provided a base of operations for the Germans, but was never actually occupied by the Germans, except in the northern regions.

There were two thousand Jews in Finland. In a visit to Helsinki in July 1942, Himmler attempted to induce the Finns to deport the Jews, but Finnish Foreign Minister Rolf Witting refused to give the matter any consideration.

In September 1944, Finland capitulated to Russia and then had to fight the Germans to force them to evacuate Finland.

CENTRAL EUROPE

Germany and Austria

JEWS IN PREWAR GERMANY

When the Nazis seized power in 1933, 500,000 Jews, or about 1 percent of the population, lived in Germany. Subject to terror and an accelerating process of discrimination, isolation, and expropriation, conducted under guise of legality, nearly 150,000 Jews, 30 percent of the 1933 population, emigrated by November 1938.

The pogrom of November 10, 1938 (Kristallnacht), and the subsequent German policy of forced emigration hastened the exit of another 150,000 Jews. The outbreak of war severely limited the availability of transportation and in effect halted further departures.

With the enactment of the Tenth Decree Supplementing the Reich Citizenship Law, July 4, 1939, the Germans set up the Reichsvereinigung der Juden in Deutschland, subject to the authority of the Gestapo and replacing all autonomous Jewish communal organizations.

JEWS IN PREWAR AUSTRIA

At the time of the Anschluss, March 12, 1938, 185,000 Jews lived in Austria, 170,000 in Vienna alone. In August

1938, responsibility for Jewish emigration was charged to the Zentralstelle für die jüdische Auswanderung, operated by the Gestapo. Under the pressure of terror, some 20,000 Jews left Austria by the time war broke out. Another 6,000 left by the end of 1939. Nearly all remaining Jews in Austria were concentrated in Vienna, where the Israelitische Kultusgemeinde remained the only Jewish organization. The provincial Jewish communities ceased to exist.

JEWS IN THE WARTIME GREATER REICH (GERMANY AND AUSTRIA)

In 1940 the Germans began to deport Jews into the Generalgouvernement of Poland, also evicting some 7,500 Jews from Baden and the Palatinate, whom they dumped into France. On September 1, 1941, a police decree was issued compelling all Jews over six years of age to wear an identifying Star of David. In October 1941 general deportations began to major ghettos in the territory of Poland (Lodz, Warsaw, Lublin) and also as far east as Riga and Minsk. Over 40,000 Reich Jews, regarded as "privileged" deportees, were sent to Theresienstadt. At the end of 1942, the Kultusgemeinde in Vienna was dissolved and a Council of Elders set up in its place. By that time, 150,000 Jews had been deported from the Greater Reich.

Early in 1943, 20,000 more Jews were deported, including the munitions workers in Berlin who until then had been protected. In May 1943 Berlin was declared free of Jews. On June 10, 1943, the Reichsvereinigung was dissolved, its members having been deported, and on July 1, 1943, under the 13th Decree Supplementing the Reich Citizenship Law, any Jews still in the Reich were to be denied protection of the courts and were to be surrendered to Gestapo jurisdiction.

When the war ended, the 28,000 Jews surviving in Germany and in Austria were, for the most part, Jews only by National Socialist racial standards.

Czechoslovakia
The Protectorate of Bohemia and Moravia

On March 13, 1939, having decided to take the two western provinces of Bohemia and Moravia, Hitler summoned two

Slovak nationalist and pro-German leaders, Father Jozef Tiso and Ferdinand Durcansky, and told them to proclaim Slovak independence or suffer occupation. The next day the provincial diet in Bratislava voted to secede from Czechoslovakia and form a separate state, a decision that the Germans used to justify their invasion of Czechoslovakia on March 15. By afternoon, the Germans concluded the occupation without encountering resistance. The provinces of Bohemia and Moravia were declared a Protectorate, a joint, autonomous part of the Reich, whose German inhabitants would become Reich citizens, while the Czech inhabitants were designated as Protectorate nationals. The former Czech head of state, given the title of State President, was responsible to a Reich Protector, who was the factual ruler of the country. To this post of Reich Protector Hitler appointed Konstantin von Neurath, a career diplomat and a former German Foreign Minister, who took over his duties on April 16, 1939.

The Czech army was demobilized; its arms and ammunition were seized by the Germans. Through policies of political harshness and economic exploitation, the Germans established themselves as masters, but political and economic unrest continued to disturb the country. Blaming Neurath, Hitler in late September 1941 appointed as Deputy Protector Reinhard Heydrich, chief of the Reich Security Main Office, who immediately introduced rule by terror and succeeded in breaking Czech resistance.

On May 27, 1942, Heydrich's car was bombed and he was severely injured, dying of his wounds on June 4. The assassination had been planned and directed by the Czech government-in-exile in cooperation with the British Special Operations Executive, an agency for underground warfare, in the hope of reanimating Czech resistance. The brutal reprisals that the Germans exacted—the destruction of the village of Lidice and all its male inhabitants—stilled further Czech opposition.

On May 5, 1945, Czech resisters unsuccessfully tried to oust the Germans. On May 11 the Russians entered Prague.

JEWS IN PREWAR BOHEMIA AND MORAVIA

About 118,000 Jews lived in the provinces of Bohemia and Moravia, amounting to one-third of all Czech Jews. Half the gainfully occupied were engaged in trade and commerce, 20 percent were in industry and handicrafts, about 10 percent in the professions. In the Czechoslovak republic, Jews enjoyed full civic and religious freedom. There had always been some anti-Semitism, though no violence. The Jewish religious community maintained a modest network of religious and educational institutions. Zionism attracted a substantial interest.

About 26,000 Jews emigrated between March 15, 1939, and the outbreak of the war, leaving some 90,000 Jews in the Protectorate.

JEWS IN WARTIME BOHEMIA AND MORAVIA

On June 21, 1939, the Reich Protector issued a comprehensive decree placing Jews under German jurisdiction, defining the status of Jews in accordance with German legislation, and setting in motion the isolation of Jews and the expropriation of their property. A Zentralstelle für die jüdische Auswanderung was established by decree on March 5, 1940, similar to the one in Vienna and, like it, subordinate to the one in Berlin. Run by the Gestapo, it was given complete authority over the Jewish community, using the Kultusgemeinde of Prague as its channel for transmitting orders. All subsequent anti-Jewish legislation enacted in the Protectorate conformed to German laws. All new Reich legislation (for example, the introduction of the identifying yellow Star of David in September 1941) was applicable to the Protectorate.

In October 1939 the first deportations of Czech Jews to Poland took place. In the fall of 1941 the Germans established a central ghetto for Protectorate Jews at Theresienstadt (Terezin), formerly a Czech garrison town. This ghetto was to serve two functions, that of a "model" camp to which privileged categories of Reich Jews would be sent and also as a transit camp from which to deport Czech Jews to the death camps in Poland. In 1942 alone, about 55,000 Jews from the Protectorate were sent to Theresienstadt, and most were later deported to Auschwitz and other death camps.

About 10,000 Jews from Bohemia and Moravia survived.

Slovakia

In March 1939 Slovakia was declared an independent state, with Father Jozef Tiso, a Catholic priest, as Prime Minister, and with the Hlinka People's party, a right-wing Catholic nationalist group, as the only legal party. Slovakia had to adhere to the German-Italian-Japanese axis, to provide rail and road access to the Germans to the east, and after the German attack on Russia, also to provide fighting troops. In October 1939 Tiso was elected President; pro-Nazi Voytech Tuka became Prime Minister; Sano Mach, head of the Hlinka Guard, became Minister of the Interior, and Ferdinand Durcansky, Foreign Minister.

For the first two years of the war, Slovakia enjoyed significant benefits from its new status, such as increased trade and help in industrial, development, but after the German defeat at Stalingrad and the turning of the tide of the war, Slovak sentiment among both government and people became noticeably less pro-German. At the beginning of 1944, when the Soviet army stood at the frontiers of Ruthenia, young Slovaks began to be more responsive to the appeals for resistance issued by the Czech government-in-exile. Soldiers in the Slovak army began to desert to join resistance groups in the mountains. Popular opposition grew. Open fighting broke out in August 1944. Tiso then proclaimed martial law and total mobilization. The Slovak uprising gave the Germans the pretext they needed to occupy the country. Serious fighting between the Slovak partisans and the Germans continued through October, when the Germans succeeded in crushing the resistance. The Russian advance through Slovakia began in January 1945, but it was not before April 1945 that Slovakia was liberated from German occupation.

JEWS IN PREWAR SLOVAKIA

In 1938 about 135,000 Jews lived in Slovakia, of whom 40,000 lived in the territory ceded to Hungary (Ruthenia and Subcarpathia). About 5,000 emigrated voluntarily before the war, leaving about 90,000 Jews, 3 percent of the population. Slovakia was poorer and far less industrialized than the historic Czech crown provinces of Bohemia and Moravia, and so were its Jews. They were engaged mostly in retail trade and handicrafts, servicing the peasantry.

The small segment of well-to-do Jews spoke Hungarian and were assimilated, maintaining religious congregations of a somewhat lukewarm character. Most other Jews were highly traditional, among whom Hasidic rebbes enjoyed huge followings.

During the life of the Czechoslovak Republic, Jews enjoyed full civic and religious rights, even though anti-Semitism, particularly among the predominantly peasant population, was widespread.

JEWS IN WARTIME SLOVAKIA

In April 1939 the new Slovak state began to enact anti-Jewish legislation, defining the status of a Jew along religious rather than racial lines (Slovakia was a Catholic country, ruled by a priest and a Catholic party). In rapid succession came a series of decrees excluding and restricting Jews in various professions and occupations. Anti-Semitic violence on the part of the Hlinka Guard accompanied the administrative anti-Semitism.

In August 1940 SS-Hauptsturmführer Dieter Wisliceny, Eichmann's representative from the Reich Security Main Office, arrived in Bratislava as an adviser on Jewish affairs. The Hlinka Guard and the *Freiwillige Schutzstaffel* (Slovak volunteers in the SS) were reorganized on the model of the SS and given the responsibility of carrying out anti-Jewish measures.

On September 26, 1940, a new decree established the *Ústredna Židov* (Center of Jews) as the only authority permitted to represent the Jews, responsible to the Central Economy Office (under the Minister of the Interior) and obliged to transmit its instructions to the Jews.

On September 9, 1941, the Slovak government promulgated a major body of anti-Jewish legislation, containing 270 articles, redefining the Jews as a racial group, requiring them to wear the identifying yellow Star of David, making them liable to forced labor, and evicting them from specified towns and districts.

Plans for deportation began late in 1941; in March 1942 five assembly points for deportees were set up, and despite intensive efforts on the part of Jewish communal leaders to halt them, deportations continued unabated from March through August 1942. By then, only 25,000 Jews remained in Slovakia. Three more transports left in September and October. Some 58,000 Jews, 75 percent of Slovak Jews, had been deported, mostly to Auschwitz.

Further deportations were put off, partly through the intervention of the Catholic church and partly through a strategy of bribery and promises of financial profit that the Jewish leaders used in negotiations with Slovaks and with Wisliceny himself.

After the Slovak national uprising in 1944, the SS took 19,000 prisoners, of whom 5,000 were Jews. Under the subsequent German occupation, 13,500 more Jews were deported. No more than 5,000 Slovakian Jews remained in the country in hiding or on Aryan papers. About 10,000 of those deported in 1944 survived and returned to Slovakia.

Hungary

Hungary's policies before and during the war can best be understood in the light of her revanchist goals. In November 1938 Hungary joined Germany in the dismemberment of Czechoslovakia, annexing some Slovakian districts and a part of Subcarpathian Ruthenia. In March 1939, when Slovakia declared itself an independent state, Hungary occupied the rest of Ruthenia. In August 1940, Hungary received northern Transylvania from Rumania under the Vienna Award. As repayment, Hungary joined the Tripartite Pact on November 20, 1940. On April 1941, Hungary occupied the Bačka basin in northeastern Yugoslavia.

On June 22, 1941, Hungarian forces joined the Germans in invading Russia, though Hungarian military participation was less than wholehearted, with Regent Nicholas Horthy resisting German demands for Hungary's general mobilization. In March 1942, Horthy replaced Hungary's pro-German Prime Minister Laszlo Bardossy with Miklos Kallay, who sought to disentangle Hungary from the war. Hungarian losses on the Russian front and Hungary's preoccupation with her traditional enemy, Rumania, accelerated Hungarian troop withdrawals from the front, to the extent permitted by Germany.

In early 1943, Hungary appeared, in Hitler's eyes, to be acting more like a neutral than a German ally. Consequently, in April 1943 Hitler summoned Horthy to his headquarters in Klessheim Castle near Salzburg and criticized him for Kallay's policies, both as to Hungary's obligations to Germany and as to the need to eliminate Hungary's Jews. Kallay, however, continued his policies and on August 1943 broadcast a peace speech, following the overthrow of Mussolini in Italy, Hungary's traditional ally.

In March 1944, with the war going badly for Germany, Hitler again summoned Horthy and members of his cabinet to Klessheim (Kallay refused to join them). Hitler confronted Horthy with what he regarded as Hungary's treachery, declaring that Germany had to occupy Hungary. Horthy was held incommunicado for a day; when he returned home on March 19, the German occupation of Hungary had been completed. On March 22 a new Hungarian government was formed under Prime Minister General Dome Sztojay, formerly the Hungarian minister in Berlin. The real rulers in Hungary thenceforth were the SS and Reich Plenipotentiary Edmund Veesenmayer. All political parties and trade unions, with their press, were suppressed. The Sztojay government could not, however, maintain itself because of overt opposition from the right—the Hungarian National Socialists and the Fascist Arrow Cross, under Ferenc Szalasi. Rumania's surrender to Russia in August 1944 and the stunning defeat of the Germans at that time by Russian and Rumanian forces shook Hungary. Sztojay resigned on August 30; Horthy replaced him with General Geza Lakatos, in an effort to restore more Hungarian autonomy. In October 1944, Russian forces crossed into Hungary. The Budapest radio announced that Horthy was asking the Russians for an armistice. The German SS under Veesenmayer reacted swiftly on October 16, by kidnapping Horthy's son and holding him under threats. They thereby forced Horthy to appoint Arrow Cross Chief Szalasi as Prime Minister. Szalasi canceled the armistice, but the Hungarian commander-in-chief and his chief of staff went over to the Russians. By November 1944 the Russians had overrun two-thirds of Hungary and had reached Budapest's outskirts. Budapest remained under Russian siege until February 1945, though the Hungarians had signed an armistice a month earlier. Finally, by April 4, 1945, no more Germans remained in Hungary.

JEWS IN PREWAR HUNGARY

In 1930, 445,000 Jews lived in Hungary, about 5 percent of the population. Half lived in Budapest, where they made up 20 percent of the population, and in two other large cities. The rest of the Jewish population was dispersed; there were 24 communities with about 1,000 Jews each and 180 with fewer than 1,000 Jews each.

In a country with a landed aristocracy and a large peasantry, the Jews were distinctively middle class. Of gainfully employed Jews, 38 percent were self-employed businessmen in industry (including small craftsmen), commerce, and banking, and also professionals; 28 percent were salaried (white-collar employees mainly in commerce, banking, and industry); and 33 percent were wage earners (workers), though predominantly in commercial enterprises.

Most Jews in Budapest were highly acculturated, in contrast to the Jews in the small towns where Orthodoxy prevailed. There were three national religious Jewish communities: the Neologs (somewhat similar to Reform Jews), the Orthodox, and a smaller organization called "Status Quo Ante Jewish Communities," who stood somewhere between them. Intermarriage and baptismal ratés were quite high; in 1938 there were 35,000 baptized Jews in Hungary. Conversions, the declining birth rate, and continuing emigration as a consequence of Hungary's anti-Semitic policies reduced the size of the Jewish population in Hungary, estimated at about 400,000 in 1939.

Hungarian Jews had been emancipated in 1867, but resentments on the part of the non-Jewish population—because of the territorial losses after World War I, chaotic economic conditions, and the abortive Communist dictatorship of Bela Kun—were vented on the Jews. Horthy came to power as a blaze of pogroms raged in Hungary, particularly in the provinces. The violence was followed by various administrative measures eliminating most Jews from public service and restricting their admission into universities. From 1924 to 1933, under the conservative regime of Count Stephen Bethlen as Prime Minister, the situation of the Jews somewhat stabilized, but in the mid-1930s, under the impact of National Socialism in Germany and its Hungarian admirers, anti-Semitism intensified.

On May 24, 1938, a month after Hitler's annexation of Austria, the Hungarian parliament, in an effort to appease Hitler and prevent seizure of power by the Hungarian Nazis, enacted its first anti-Jewish law, prepared by the Horthy government, despite the bitter opposition of the Smallholders and Socialist parties and Bethlen's conservative followers. The law limited employment of Jews in private business firms to 20 percent. A year later, a more far-reaching anti-Jewish law was passed, defining the status of Jews, barring them from leading positions in the media, prohibiting the issuance of new trade licenses to them or the renewal of old ones. The law also barred further admission of Jews to the professions until their share fell to below 6 percent. It authorized the government to expropriate, with compensation, Jewish landed property. Jews could no longer acquire Hungarian citizenship by naturalization, marriage, or adoption. Voting rights of nonnative Jews or those whose forebears were not permanently resident before 1868 were canceled.

JEWS IN WARTIME HUNGARY

After Munich and the Vienna Awards, Hungary added another 250,000 to its Jewish population of 400,000: 75,000 Jews in former Slovakian territory, 25,000 in the Bačka basin of Yugoslavia, and 150,000 in Transylvania, for a total of 650,000 Jews in Greater Hungary. There were, besides, some 100,000 Christians, who were regarded as "racial" Jews and subject to anti-Jewish laws. (In August 1941 a more stringent law was enacted, defining who was a Jew.)

In August 1941 the Hungarian government rounded up some 17,000 stateless Jews in its annexed Ruthenian territory and pushed them over the border to Kamenets-Podolsk in the German-held Ukraine, but the Germans complained that the Jews disrupted their military communications. After the Hungarians drew off several thousand to be used as slave laborers, the German Einsatzkommandos massacred the remaining 11,000. Several thousand Yugoslav Jews in Bačka were also massacred by the Hungarian occupying forces at Novi Sad.

No further deportations took place, and when the Kallay government took over in March 1942, Jews were subject only to tightening employment restrictions, forced-labor conscription, and more extensive expropriations. Some 16,000 Jews from Austria, Slovakia, and Poland even found refuge in Hungary and were not handed over to the Germans. At the end of 1942, Kallay rejected German demands to introduce yellow badges for Jews and deport them to Poland. In May 1943 Kallay, in a public speech, rejected "resettlement" of the Jews as a "final solution," so long as the Germans were giving no satisfactory answer about where the Jews were being resettled.

The virtual German occupation of Hungary in March 1944 and the installation of the pro-German Sztojay government drastically transformed the situation of the Hungarian Jews. On March 19, the very day of the German takeover, Eichmann himself came to Budapest with a battery of SS officers in charge of Jewish affairs. Eichmann ordered the Jewish community leaders to appear for a conference the next day, when they were told to establish a Judenrat, which would have to carry out German orders. Meanwhile, on March 29, new anti-Jewish legislation was enacted, forcing Jews entirely out of the professions, ordering the registration of their property, and arranging for its almost instant expropriation. The yellow star was introduced, and the Jews were concentrated in designated places.

To carry out the deportations of the Jews, Eichmann divided Hungary into six zones: Zone I, Carpathians; II, Transylvania; III, northern Hungary; IV, southern Hungary east of the Danube; V, Transdanubia, including the suburbs of Budapest; VI, Budapest proper.

With the participation of a *Sondereinsatzkommando* (special-duty commando) that Eichmann had brought from Mauthausen and with the help of the Hungarian police, the Germans began to round up the Jews, concentrating them within the designated zones, and deporting them in rapid order. By June 7, Zones I and II had been cleared of nearly 290,000 Jews. By June 30, over 92,000 Jews were deported from Zones III and IV. By July 7, over 437,000 Jews, including some 50,000 from Budapest, had been deported to Auschwitz.

Meanwhile, the Jewish relief committee in Budapest, following up earlier initiatives of Slovakian Jews, began negotiations with SS-Hauptsturmführer Dieter Wisliceny about ransoming the remaining Hungarian Jews from deportation. On behalf of the Jewish relief committee, Joel Brand was sent to Turkey to contact the Allies about the possibilities of exchanging goods for Jewish lives. Negotiations were protracted and complex, but Eichmann never halted the deportation trains. Finally, nothing substantial developed in the rescue of the Jews, except for one train-load of Hungarian Jews who were saved.

In July 1944, after news about the Hungarian deportations had been sent abroad, various high-level interventions on behalf of the Jews began to dismay the Hungarians. Horthy ordered the deportations halted. When the pro-German government was toppled in August, the new Prime Minister Lakatos then asked the Germans to remove Eichmann's Sondereinsatzkommando. Some anti-Jewish restrictions began to be lifted, but after the German coup in October 1944, with Arrow Cross leader Szalasi as Prime Minister, the Jews again fell into German hands for deportation. By October 26 some 35,000 Jewish men and women had been rounded up, but since Auschwitz was then being liquidated, these Jews were to be used as slave laborers. The exigencies of war rendered railroad transportation impossible, and so the Germans marched off 27,000 Jews on a terrible trek of over 100 miles to Austria. But Szalasi soon stopped these marches because of the high death rate.

Some 160,000 Jews remained in Budapest, subject to terror and murder at the hands of the Arrow Cross, suffering cold, hunger, and disease in their ghettolike quarters, under the rain of Russian bombardment. About 20,000 died that winter. On February 14, 1945, the Russians took Budapest.

Over 450,000 Jews, 70 percent of the Jews of Greater Hungary, were deported, were murdered, or died under German occupation. Within the boundaries of lesser (pre-1938) Hungary, about half the Jews were annihilated. Some 144,000 survived in Budapest, including 50,000 "racial" Jews, and about 50,000 to 60,000 survived in the provinces.

SOUTHEASTERN EUROPE

Rumania

When war broke out, Rumania was under Carol II's dictatorial government. In 1938, threatened by the spectacular rise to power of the Nazilike Iron Guard, which he himself had earlier encouraged, Carol had dissolved all parties and concentrated power in his own hands. His domestic policies aimed to check the expanding power of the Iron Guard, and

in foreign affairs he tried to keep Rumania neutral between
the Allies and the Axis, though leaning closer to the Axis.
The collapse of Poland and then of France led Carol to sever
his Anglo-French ties on July 1, 1940, and proclaim a reorientation of Rumania's foreign policy as a "neutral ally"
of the Axis. Three days earlier, the Soviet Union, having occupied half of prewar Poland, demanded the cession of
northern Bucovina and all of Bessarabia, to which Rumania,
on Germany's advice, promptly acceded. Then, to satisfy
the revanchist ambitions of its neighbors, Rumania was
forced by Germany and Italy to cede the northern part of
Transylvania to Hungary as part of the Vienna Awards of
August 30, 1940. A week later, Rumania ceded southern
Dobruja to Bulgaria.

Carol's policies having brought humiliation to Rumania,
the Iron Guard accused him of treachery, and he was de-
posed, in a bloodless coup in September 1940, by a military
group under General Ion Antonescu, long associated with
the Iron Guard. Carol was exiled; his son, Michael I, became
king, with Antonescu as *conducator* (leader) of Rumania.
All political parties and movements except the Iron Guard
were outlawed. Some 120,000 German troops entered Rumania as a "military advisory mission," to "protect" Rumania's oil-fields, and in November Rumania joined the Axis.

The Antonescu coalition was torn by violent conflict between the army and the Iron Guard. After a bloody clash
between them in January 1941 in Bucharest, in which the
Iron Guard carried out a terrible massacre of the Jews and
its other "enemies," the army won complete control of the
country, which was then ruled by a military dictatorship
under Antonescu. Rumanian armed forces joined German
forces and participated in the invasion of Russia in June
1941. Rumanian army units and Rumanian police also took
part in Einsatzgruppe D. To compensate for its other territorial losses, Rumania recaptured Bucovina and Bessarabia
from the Soviet Union and took also a portion of the south-
western Ukraine.

So long as the progress of the war favored Germany and
its allies, the Rumanians supported it, but when the tide
turned, particularly with the heavy casualties suffered by
the Rumanian army in the Battle of Stalingrad, Antonescu
faced considerable domestic opposition. In April 1944 the
Red Army recaptured Bucovina, Bessarabia, and Odessa; in

August the Russians entered Moldavia, in rump Rumania. On August 23, 1944, Michael arrested Antonescu, took over the government, and surrendered to the Russians.

THE JEWS IN PREWAR RUMANIA

The Jewish population of prewar Rumania was 757,000 with the largest concentrations in Bessarabia, Moldavia, Walachia, Crishana-Maramuresh, Bucovina, and Transylvania. (In August 1940 some 150,000 Jews in Transylvania came under Hungarian rule, as a consequence of the Vienna Awards.) Though Jews made up 4 percent of the Rumanian population, they formed 25 to 35 percent of the urban populations in Moldavia, Bessarabia, and Bucovina. Two-thirds of the Jews lived in urban centers, the rest in villages.

Over 40 percent of the Jewish labor force were engaged in industry and crafts, another 40 percent in trade and commerce, and 3 percent were in the professions and civil service.

Rumania never lived up to its obligations undertaken after World War I to recognize all Jews living in its territory as Rumanian nationals, and it intensified its attacks on the rights of Jews in the interbellum period. In 1938 a special decree, "Revision of Citizenship," stripped a substantial number of Rumanian Jews of their citizenship. Severe economic discrimination and violent anti-Semitism terrorized the Jewish population.

Assimilation was strong among Jews in the provinces of the Old Kingdom of Rumania, especially Walachia, but among the denser communities in Bucovina and Bessarabia, Jews were culturally separatist, with Yiddish as the predominant language and flourishing movements for Jewish cultural autonomy and Zionism. The Federation of the Unions of Jewish Communities, consisting of religious and provincial bodies, was the central Jewish organization, with the authority to tax its constituents.

JEWS IN WARTIME RUMANIA

In August 1940, under Carol, the government enacted an anti-Jewish statute, based on the Italian model, which for the most part codified existing legislation. Jews were expelled from the cultural life of the country and from all government service, including the army. They were not permitted to be on the boards of commercial or industrial corporations and were prohibited from buying immovable property without the consent of the government. In October 1940, under Antonescu's coalition regime, anti-Jewish legislation was enacted providing for the "Rumanianization" of Jewish property. A month later, a similar law affecting Jewish industrial and agricultural property was enacted. Subsequent decrees expelled Jews from all gainful employment. Jews were made liable for forced labor, without pay, instead of military service. Radu Lecca, Commissar for Jewish Questions in Antonescu's government, handled the problems of ghettoization and deportation, while economic despoliation of the Jews was in the jurisdiction of the Labor Minister.

This administrative anti-Semitism was, from the start, accompanied by pogroms and violence. In January 1941, during the fighting between the Iron Guard and Antonescu's army supporters, a massacre took place in Bucharest, in which about 170 Jews were murdered in an especially abhorrent manner.

With the invasion of the Soviet Union and the recapture of northern Bucovina and Bessarabia, unbridled plunder and murder of Jews were authorized by the Rumanian army's high command. The first major wartime pogroms occurred in Iaşi in June 1941, organized by special Rumanian troops assigned to rounding up, deporting, and murdering Jews. Thereafter, thousands of Jews were packed in cattle cars on the pretext that they were signaling to Russian planes, and shipped off without food or water, to no particular destination. Those who did not die of suffocation were shot. About 8,000 died. In and around Czernowitz (Cernauti) and Storojinetz, 12,000 Jews were killed; in Bessarabia, over 200,000. Rumanian army units working with Einsatzgruppe D in southern Russia dismayed the Germans with their passion for killing and their disregard for disposal of the corpses.

In August 1941 the Rumanians began to expel Bessarabian Jews across the Dniester, in territory under German military occupation. The Germans resisted having this area become a dumping ground for unwanted Jews, but then agreed that Transnistria, the area between the Dniester and the Bug rivers, could serve as a reservation for Rumanian Jews. By mid-November 1941 over 120,000 Jews had been deported there, and by late 1942, according to a conservative estimate, some 200,000 Rumanian Jews had been shipped to Transnistria, nearly two-thirds of whom had already died of hunger and epidemics. By September 1943, only some 50,000 Rumanian Jews remained alive in Transnistria, along with 25,000 to 30,000 Russian Jews, native inhabitants of that area.

On December 16, 1941, the government dissolved the Federation of the Unions of the Jewish Communities, setting up instead, in Bucharest, the Center for Rumanian Jews (*Centrala Evreilor din Romania*), as the "sole body authorized to represent the interests of the Jewish community of Rumania." Its functions were to fulfill government demands on the Jewish community, fund the still existing network of Jewish elementary and high schools, and aid the needy, including those in Transnistria. Dr. W. Filderman, for many years chairman of the Federation and indefatigable in his efforts on behalf of Rumanian Jews, was shunted aside and replaced by two government-appointed officials.

Early in the summer of 1942 Eichmann's representative, SS Hauptsturmführer Gustav Richter, operating out of the German legation in Bucharest, reached an understanding with the Rumanian government regarding the deportation of the Rumanian Jews to Lublin, but the Rumanians changed their minds a few months later. Lecca, having been snubbed by the SS while in Berlin, became less cooperative. Dr. Filderman, meanwhile, though no longer officially head of the Jewish community, submitted several urgent memoranda to the Minister of the Interior, pointing out that though Hungary had not deported its Jews, it had actually profited from its alliance with Germany by receiving Rumanian territory. Other interventions, by Jews and non-Jews, against deporting the Jews finally led to Rumania's definite repudiation of the plan. Nevertheless, Rumania continued to oppress the remaining Jewish population by labor exploitation and expropriation.

At the end of 1942, Antonescu informed the Germans that instead of deporting the Jews to Poland, he would allow them to buy their way out and emigrate to Palestine. In 1943 negotiations began between Rumanian Jewish leaders and the government about the possibilities of emigration via Bulgaria and Turkey to Palestine and regarding improvement of conditions in Transnistria. Nothing significant emerged from the emigration scheme, but during 1942 substantial relief provided by Jewish groups helped to improve the lot of the survivors in Transnistria. German military reversals also influenced Antonescu's decision. In December 1943 the first group of Jews returned to Rumania from Transnistria, and early in 1944 about 1,500 Jewish orphans were repatriated from there. Between April 1944, when the Russians recaptured Bucovina, Bessarabia, and Odessa, and late August, when Rumania surrendered, the situation of the surviving Jews in Rumania remained precarious. It turned out, however, that the Germans, in retreat through Rumania, no longer had the means to continue rounding up the Jews.

In Transnistria only some 50,000 survived out of the 300,000 Bessarabian and Bucovinian Jews. Some 50,000 had been deported to Siberia during the first Russian occupation, and their fate is not known. Most of the others were in the path of Einsatzgruppe D. Except for the 8,000 to 10,000 Jews murdered at Iaşi in 1941 and other thousands killed in pogroms, about 300,000 Jews in Rumania survived, most of them in Old Rumania proper.

Bulgaria

When war broke out in September 1939, Bulgaria remained neutral. Bulgaria's only interest in the war was the possibility it offered to attain its revanchist goals: the return of territory from Rumania, Greece, and Yugoslavia that it had been forced to cede after World War I. In June 1940, when the Soviet Union demanded from Rumania northern Bucovina and Bessarabia, Bulgaria also pressed its claim for the return of Dobruja, some three thousand square miles in southeast Rumania. Acceding to Germany's advice, Rumania yielded the territory on September 7, 1940.

In March 1941, when Germany needed passage through Bulgaria to come to Italy's aid in Greece, Bulgaria joined the Axis and demanded, in return for Germany's right of passage, a restoration of its "historic frontiers," by the annexation of western Thrace from Greece and Serbian Macedonia from Yugoslavia.

Though some German troops remained stationed in Bulgaria, Germany never actively intervened in its internal administration. Bulgaria declared war on the United States on

December 13, 1941, in accordance with its membership in the Axis, but never declared war on the Soviet Union. Bulgarian troops moved beyond the borders of Old Bulgaria only into those areas of Yugoslavia and Greece that became part of Greater Bulgaria. On September 5, 1944, the Soviet Union declared war on Bulgaria, and three days later Bulgaria asked for an armistice. On September 8 the Soviet armies moved into Bulgaria, which then declared war on Germany.

THE JEWS IN PREWAR BULGARIA

About 50,000 Jews lived in Old Bulgaria, less than 1 percent in a total population of over 6 million. An urban group, 55 percent of Bulgarian Jews lived in Sofia, where they constituted 9 percent of the population. The majority were largely self-employed in commerce and trade. Those in manufacturing and crafts were engaged in the traditional Jewish occupations of tailoring, shoemaking, brush making, tinsmithing. About 15 percent of the gainfully employed Jews were in the professions or civil service.

The Jewish community enjoyed complete civic and political equality, first guaranteed under the Congress of Berlin in 1878. The constitution of Trnovo of 1879 provided religious freedom and full equality for all citizens. Under a law of 1880 the synagogue was recognized as the local unit of the Jewish religious community; the Chief Rabbi, recognized by the state as the head of Bulgarian Jewry and authorized to represent it in relations with the government, was paid by the state. The Central Consistory served as an advisory body. Early in the twentieth century, however, as a consequence of a process of secularization and democratization, the Zionists gained control of the local communities and subordinated the Rabbi to the Central Consistory in national matters. Out of special taxes the Jews maintained an extensive network of religious, communal, and educational institutions (including courts to settle religious and family disputes). Economically and politically integrated in the life of the country, the Jews nevertheless remained communally and culturally segregated, and the majority of Jewish children attended Jewish schools.

While anti-Semitism had erupted violently occasionally

in Turkish times, from the start of the twentieth century until the rise of Nazism in Germany, Jews enjoyed a period of tranquillity and physical security in Bulgaria, relatively free of discrimination. With the expansion of German economic and political influence in the Balkans, an anti-Semitic movement began to take shape in the 1930s. Students returning from German universities and White Russian émigrés spread anti-Semitic propaganda in Bulgaria, yet their effect was limited. In 1937 a Jewish journalist succeeded in gathering statements against anti-Semitism from sixty influential Bulgarian notables, including sixteen former premiers and Cabinet members.

THE JEWS IN WARTIME BULGARIA

With the appointment in February 1940 of Bogdan Filov as Premier, Bulgarian policy shifted in a pro-German direction. The Jews became the first victims. In July 1940 the government announced its intention to introduce anti-Jewish legislation and officially forewarned the representatives of the Jewish communities. The Law for the Protection of the Nation, passed by the Sobranie (parliament) on December 24, 1940, and its first implementing executive order, published on February 17, 1941, defined persons of Jewish origin as any person with at least one Jewish parent. It differed from the German definition in that it exempted certain converts from the racial definition. Consequently, mixed marriages increased sharply in 1940, most doubtless convenience marriages, and hundreds of "mercy baptisms" were performed. Also exempted from the legislation were Jews who had been war volunteers, war invalids, or decorated war veterans.

The law restricted Jewish rights and social relations, along the lines of German anti-Jewish legislation. Jews had to be registered, had to use Jewish first names, were forbidden to have Bulgarian-sounding names. Barred from military service, they had to serve instead in labor squads in the army. The government could exclude them from certain types of employment, expel them from certain towns, or confine them in others. Jews could not own or rent real estate or houses in rural communities and had to sell such property within a year. All other property had to be registered with the government. Legislative additions and revisions continued to be issued through 1942, affecting also some 14,000 Jews in Greater Bulgaria—8,000 Macedonian Jews in the territory wrested from Yugoslavia and 6,000 in annexed Thrace. These Jews were not given Bulgarian citizenship, but were subject to the disabilities of the Bulgarian Jews.

A special tax on Jewish-held property was enacted in July 1941. Jews were then also subject to curfew; telephones and radios were removed from their homes and offices.

In June 1942, at the initiative of the Minister of the Interior, Peter Gabrovski, the Sobranie was asked to delegate to the Cabinet the authority to "solve the Jewish question." Gabrovski's consultant, Alexander Belev, a German-trained lawyer, proposed to "solve the question" by expelling all Jews from Bulgaria and confiscating their property. Over the outspoken protests of a minority, the Sobranie voted blanket authorization to the Cabinet. On August 28, 1942, a Commissariat for Jewish Affairs was established in the Ministry of the Interior, and on September 3 Belev was appointed its head. This agency in charge of Jewish affairs was the link with the German officials in charge of carrying out the Final Solution in Bulgaria. That month Bulgarian Foreign Minister Ivan Vladimir Popov concluded a secret agreement with German Ambassador Beckerle, surrendering to German jurisdiction those Bulgarian citizens who were Jewish and residing in German-occupied countries.

The Star of David was introduced in September 1943. Orders were issued to expel unemployed Jews from the cities, to confiscate Jewish property, and to assign Jews to special quarters in Sofia. Encouraged by these developments, the SS began to press to deport the Jews from Bulgaria, and in January 1943 SS-Obersturmführer Theodor Dannecker, Eichmann's assistant, arrived in Sofia to begin concrete negotiations to this end. In February 1943 an oral agreement was reached between Dannecker and Belev to the effect that twenty thousand Jews, mostly from the newly annexed territories, would be deported in March, and that the Jews should first be concentrated in temporary camps near railway stations and allowed to carry enough food and clothing for ten to fifteen days. On February 3 Belev telegraphed all local representatives of the Commissariat for Jewish Affairs to draw up lists of Jews in their areas by family, sex, age, and occupation and clearly showing the addresses. On February 22, 1943, the agreement between Belev and Dannecker was signed, and preparations to deport the Jews were begun even before the Cabinet confirmed the agreement on March 2. The Thracian and Macedonian Jews began to be rounded up, and instructions were issued to prepare deporting Jews from Bulgaria proper.

On March 6, news leaked out in Kyustendil, a town some fifty miles from Sofia, that a camp was to be set up nearby for the Jews who would be deported by the Germans "to the East." The Kyustendil Jewish community notified the Jewish Consistory in Sofia and also the town's leading citizens, including Dimiter Peshev, a deputy and vice-president of the Sobranie. On March 9 Peshev and his friends went to Gabrovski, who, under personal threat from them, the same day countermanded the deportation orders affecting the Jews of Old Bulgaria, but the deportation of the Macedonian and Thracian Jews remained in force. A total of 11,384 of these Jews were sent to Treblinka and other death camps.

Peshev's protests and opposition succeeded in halting the deportation of the Bulgarian Jews, though as a consequence he himself was dismissed as vice-president. The Germans continued to exert pressure to deport the Jews, but the counterpressure of Bulgarian opinion, especially of the Bulgarian Orthodox Church, restrained the government from compliance. King Boris, too, was opposed to deporting any but "Communist elements."

In May 1943 King Boris ordered the resettlement of the Sofia Jews in provincial towns, despite protests by Jews and Bulgarians. That dispersal appeared to be Boris's acceptance of an alternative to the German proposal to deport the Jews to Poland.

Boris died on August 28, 1943; the changing face of the war and the Allied invasion of Italy shook up Bulgaria. A new Cabinet formed in September under Dobri Boshilov, though pro-German, tried to establish a more independent stance for Bulgaria. Gabrovski and Belev were dropped from the Cabinet, and a more liberal attitude toward the Jews was taken. The Jews were allowed to return to Sofia from time to time to take care of their affairs. In response to German pressure for deportations, the Bulgarians responded that German insistence on deportation would make the government less favorably inclined to Germany. In the summer of 1944 Nikolas Balabanov, Bulgarian minister in Istanbul, was engaged in negotiations with Ira Hirschmann of the United States War Refugee Board (WRB) regarding the evacuation of Jews to Palestine via Turkey. In August 1944 Balabanov wrote to the WRB that the Bulgarian government regretted its anti-Jewish measures and would abolish them "at an opportune moment." On August 24 the Commissariat for Jewish Affairs was abolished, and the Jews were free to engage in any occupation. On August 29 the Cabinet voted to abolish all anti-Jewish legislation; the decree was published September 5, 1944, three days before the Soviet army entered Bulgaria. The fifty thousand Bulgarian Jews were spared.

Yugoslavia

When war broke out Yugoslavia, under the regency of Prince Paul, had remained neutral, but on March 25, 1941, it joined the Axis. The next day Paul was overthrown in a bloodless coup, and the new government announced that Yugoslavia would remain neutral, though in fact it was anti-German. On March 27 Hitler, outraged at the coup, issued a directive calling for the invasion of Yugoslavia. That invasion began on April 6, when German forces, along with their Italian, Bulgarian, and Hungarian allies, entered Yugoslavia. The government capitulated on April 17, though guerrilla forces continued their resistance.

Yugoslavia was partitioned. Serbian Macedonia was ceded by the Germans to Bulgaria. Bačka, the northeastern basin between the Danube and the Tisza, was annexed by Hungary. The Italians occupied most of the Dalmatian coast and the islands. Old Serbia, with Belgrade as its capital, came under German military rule, with a local puppet government established in August 1941. Virtual rule of the country was in the hands of the German Chief of the Administrative Staff at the Military Commander Headquarters, State Councilor Harald Turner.

Croatia declared its independence on April 10, 1941, and a puppet government was established in Zagreb, under Ante Pavelić, leader of the Ustachi, a Croat nationalist terrorist organization. Notwithstanding this "independence," Italian forces remained in part of Croatian territory and German troops occupied all important Croatian towns outside the Italian zone.

Ustachi terror and brutality alienated many Croats from support of the Pavelić regime, and the partisans, particularly those under the leadership of Josip Broz, called Tito, made considerable gains among the population, in Serbia as well. Pavelić's influence continued to decline as that of the partisans grew, though severe tensions existed between different partisan organizations. German reprisals against the partisans were extremely harsh.

By early 1944 the partisan movement, supplied by both the British and the Russians, kept gaining ground. In September 1944 the Germans began to retreat; on October 20, 1944, Russian troops and Yugoslav partisans ousted the Germans from Belgrade. In Croatia Pavelić managed to hold on with his desperate Ustachi remnants until May 4, 1945, when the last German troops left.

JEWS IN PREWAR YUGOSLAVIA

Some 76,000 Jews, .4 percent of the total population, lived in Yugoslavia before the German occupation. About 25,000 were Sephardic Jews, whose ancestors had come from Spain in the fifteenth and sixteenth centuries. About 51,000 were Ashkenazim, most of whose forebears had come in the eighteenth and nineteenth centuries from Central Europe, primarily the Hapsburg Empire. The Sephardim were organized in 37 religious communities, the Ashkenazim in 77.

In a country where 75 percent of the population was engaged in agriculture, the Jews formed a middle-class element that was concentrated in retail trade, commerce, industry, and handicrafts. The Jews in Serbia and Croatia were on the whole well-to-do, while those in the other provinces were poorer.

Besides their well-organized religious communities (114 in 103 places), which enjoyed government recognition and support, the Yugoslav Jews maintained welfare, educational, and cultural institutions and conducted a variety of Zionist activities. The religious communities were the focal point of Jewish social life.

Jews enjoyed full civic and religious rights in Yugoslavia. Anti-Semitism had had no tradition in Serbia, but during the 1930s it began to seep in from Croatia, which had long been virulently anti-Semitic. German influence and Yugoslavia's pro-German policies intensified the anti-Semitic climate. The one Jew in the Yugoslav Senate was expelled in 1938, and the Prime Minister asked the Regent to appoint a non-Jew in his stead. In October 1940 two anti-Jewish laws were adopted, one limiting the access of Jews to secondary and higher education, the other halting the issuance of licenses for Jewish businesses and restricting the renewal of others. Though not widely enforced by local authorities, no serious opposition was offered to their enactment.

JEWS IN WARTIME YUGOSLAVIA

Serbia: Of the twelve thousand Jews in Old Serbia, over eight thousand lived in Belgrade, where, within a week of occupation, the Germans began to register them and introduce the identifying Star of David badge. In May 1941 the Jews were ordered into forced-labor brigades. On May 31 the military commander issued anti-Jewish regulations defining Jews, ordering the registration of their property, and removing them from the economic life of the country. "Aryanization" of Jewish property began in July.

Anti-Jewish violence on the part of the German troops and Volksdeutsche was widespread, particularly in Banat, from which the Jews were expelled and brought to Belgrade. In August 1941 the German army carried out a mass internment of adult male Jews, setting up one camp on the outskirts of Belgrade, another at Niš (for Jews in eastern and southern Serbia), and a third at Šabac. Since the death camps were not yet ready, the Germans undertook to shoot the interned Jews en masse and by mid-November had murdered about five thousand male Jews. In December they interned women and children and then shot them too. The few hundred surviving Jews in hiding were hunted down by Serbian collaborators and turned over to the Germans. By mid-1942 the Germans in Serbia had succeeded in "solving the Jewish question."

Croatia: Over thirty thousand Jews lived in Croatia, ten thousand of them in Bosnia and Herzegovina. Standard anti-Jewish legislation was introduced right after Pavelić's government was set up, defining the status of Jews, requiring the registration of Jewish property, ordering identifying badges for Jews and Jewish businesses. Jews were also ordered to pay heavy levies. Forced labor was introduced within the month. Under a decree of June 26, 1941, and one of November 23, 1941, mass arrests and internments of Jews were ordered.

By October 1941 most Jews in Croatia, Bosnia, and Herzegovina were engaged in forced labor, languishing in camps, or had already been shot. In August 1942 some 9,000 Jews were deported, most of them to Auschwitz. Smaller groups were deported in 1943 and 1944, including many who had found refuge in the Italian zone, which had, after September 1943, come under German control.

Jewish losses for all of Yugoslavia are estimated at about sixty thousand.

Greece

Greece remained neutral when war broke out. In October 1940 Italy attacked Greece, but with British reinforcements that had landed in Crete, the Greeks managed to force the Italians back into Albania. The Germans then began mustering troops to help the Italians. Though the Greeks permitted a British expeditionary force to land in March 1941, superior German forces invading in April broke Greek resistance. The British were evacuated; King George II and his government fled. Italy occupied most of Greek territory, while the Germans occupied Macedonia and eastern Thrace. Bulgaria, having provided land transit for German troops into Greece, was rewarded with western Thrace. In May 1941 the Germans invaded Crete and drove the British out.

The Germans installed a puppet Prime Minister in Athens whose jurisdiction included both the German and Italian zones. Germany itself maintained a military government in Greece, with Max Merten, counselor to the military governor, in charge of civilian affairs. Conditions of famine intensified resistance in Greece; the Greek resistance movement received support from both the English and the Russians. Greek collaborationists were unable to win popular support and despite the severe reprisals by the occupying forces against the guerrillas, opposition continued. From 1943 on, economic and administrative life in Greece was seriously disrupted by sabotage and resistance activities.

In September 1943, after the Badoglio government in Italy surrendered to the invading Allied forces, German troops occupied Italian-held Greece and extended their military rule over all of Greece. In October 1944, British troops, having landed in Greece, worked with the Greek resistance movement to drive out the retreating Germans. Under Russian pressure, Bulgaria relinquished Thracian Greece.

JEWS IN PREWAR GREECE

The Jewish population in prewar Greece was close to 76,000, .9 percent of the total population. In Salonika, the most eminent Sephardic settlement in Europe, dating back to the fifteenth century, the 55,000 Jews made up over 20 percent of the city's population. The Jews, merchants and craftsmen in a land of peasants and soldiers, had once made Salonika a great city of trade, commerce, and industry. The Salonikan Jewish community in the late 1930s still retained most of its unique economic functions in trade, commerce, and industry, though it was no longer as prosperous as it once had been.

Under a statute of 1920, Greek Jews were organized in twenty-four religious communities, maintaining religious and educational institutions (Salonika had forty synagogues, named after once-famous Jewish communities of Spain). They supported their own social-welfare institutions. Two daily newspapers were published in Ladino.

During the period of stormy strife of the Greek republic (1924–1935), overt anti-Semitism—propaganda and violence—became commonplace. The restoration of the monarchy and the subsequent dictatorship under Metaxas (1936–1941), with its heavy censorship and control, suppressed popular political agitation, including anti-Semitism.

Nearly thirteen thousand Jews fought in the Greek army at the time of the German invasion.

JEWS IN WARTIME GREECE

After suppressing the Ladino newspapers and confiscating the Jewish community's financial assets and records, the Germans appointed Saby Saltiel, a former communal official, as President of Jews in Salonika. Jews were evicted from their homes, humiliated, arrested, and taken as hostages. No formal legislation was enacted until July 1942, when Jews were made liable for forced labor; about ten thousand were rounded up for forced-labor battalions. The terrible conditions in malaria-infested swamps, which caused high mortality among the internees (12 percent), prompted the Jewish community to offer to exempt the Jews for ransom. After lengthy negotiations, Merten agreed to accept 2.5 billion drachmas (then about $100,000). At the same time, Jewish property and Jewish businesses were being despoiled and confiscated.

In December 1942 the Germans appointed Rabbi Zvi Koretz head of the Jewish community. In February 1943, Dieter Wisliceny, Eichmann's deputy, arrived in Salonika to set in motion the machinery for deportation. The Jews were ordered to wear Star of David badges and to move into ghettos, which were in fact segregated areas. They were subjected to a wide variety of other restrictions.

Deportations began in March 1943 from Salonika and Thrace; at the same time the Bulgarians were assisting the Germans in deporting the Greek Jews from the territory they had annexed. By mid-May some 45,000 Jews from Salonika had been deported.

At the end of September 1943, when all of Greece came under German military rule, SS General Jürgen Stroop took over the SS command in Athens. On October 3, 1943, he issued a general anti-Jewish regulation, defining the Jews and ordering them to register. Jews who did not report to the Germans within five days would be shot, and any Greek providing shelter to Jews would be shot without trial. Early in 1944 the deportations of Jews from Athens began and the Germans began to round up the Jews on the islands of Corfu, Crete, Rhodes, and elsewhere.

Over sixty thousand Greek Jews were annihilated, most having been deported to Auschwitz.

EASTERN EUROPE

Poland

World War II began on September 1, 1939, when Germany invaded Poland. German forces, estimated at 1.7 million men, highly mechanized and motorized with superior air power, easily overwhelmed the outnumbered and inadequately equipped Polish forces. On September 17, Russia, with whom Germany had concluded a nonaggression pact on August 23, 1939, sent her troops into Poland from the east, and on September 19 the German and Russian armies met near Brest Litovsk. On September 27, after destructive bombing, Warsaw surrendered and Polish military opposition crumbled. The next day Germany and Russia divided Poland.

The Russians occupied over 77,000 square miles of eastern Poland, with a population of over 13 million. Germany gained an area of 73,000 square miles, with a population of 22 million. Germany annexed Danzig outright and incorporated into the Greater Reich also 32,000 square miles of territory between East Prussia and Silesia. The western portion was divided into two districts (Gauen): Danzig–West Prussia (under Gauleiter Albert Forster) and Warthe (under Gauleiter Arthur Greiser). The remaining 39,000 square miles were designated as Generalgouvernement of Poland, and placed under German civil administration, with Hans Frank as Governor General, appointed November 8, 1939, and headquarters in Cracow. The Generalgouvernement was divided into four districts, each with its own governor (Cracow, Lublin, Radom, Warsaw), and categorized as "Nebenland," adjunct of the Reich.

The Germans, determined to carry out their racial policies, began massive deportations of Jews and Poles from the incorporated territories. Thousands of Poles were executed, other thousands were sent to Germany as slave laborers, still others were pushed into the Generalgouvernement. In the Generalgouvernement, Poles were allowed the barest forms of local self-government, with only the town and village communes in the hands of Polish officials, but real authority was lodged with the German *Kreishauptmann,* the principal district official. The Polish police apparatus remained intact, but was subordinated to German police authority. Certain Polish civil courts were allowed to continue. All other governmental and public functions were taken over by the Germans, from agriculture and industry through education and the press. Though the civil administration under Governor Frank supposedly exercised absolute power, the German army controlled war production in the Generalgouvernement, and the SS and police exercised a wide variety of functions related to racial policy, war production, finances, and security. The Germans ruthlessly exploited Poland's economic resources, from raw materials to corporation securities.

The German invasion of the Soviet Union on June 22, 1941, brought Russian-occupied Poland under German rule. The Polish district of Łomża and part of Grodno, between East Prussia to the north and the Generalgouvernement to the south—designated as Generalkommissariat Bialystok, with Bialystok as its headquarters city—became a quasi-incorporated district of the Reich, attached to East Prussia. Northeastern Poland, along with the Baltic countries and White Russia, was included in the Reichskommissariat Ostland (see the Soviet Union, p. 537). East central Poland, the district of Volhynia, became part of the Reichskommissariat Ukraine. Galicia in southeastern Poland became the fifth district of the Generalgouvernement (Lwów).

The Polish government-in-exile, formed in Paris on September 30, 1939, and eventually transferred to London, maintained close contact with underground Polish patriotic groups, including the clandestine Polish Home Army. Polish prisoners of war in the Soviet Union were allowed to form a corps under General Władysław Anders to fight with the Allies.

In July 1944, Soviet troops entered eastern Poland and a provisional Polish government was established. The following month, as the Red Army neared Warsaw, Polish underground forces, led by General Tadeusz Bor and under the control of the Polish government-in-exile, rose against the German occupation forces. The Red Army, on the far side of the Vistula, failed to come to their support, and after bitter fighting, the uprising was suppressed by the Germans on October 2, 1944. The last German forces were finally expelled from Poland early in 1945. The Poles suffered great losses during the fighting and bombardments in 1939 and then in 1944. Some 2.5 million Poles were sent to Germany as forced laborers.

JEWS IN PREWAR POLAND

About 3.3 million Jews lived in Poland before the outbreak of the war, nearly 10 percent of the total Polish population. More than three-fourths of the Polish Jews lived in cities and towns, constituting 27 percent of Poland's urban population. About 40 percent were engaged in industry and handicrafts, over a third in trade and commerce, about 6 percent in the professions. The clothing industry was largely in Jewish hands. The worldwide economic depression in the 1920s and 1930s and the active anti-Semitic policies of the Polish government combined to keep the economic level of the Jewish community low. Except for a thin stratum of wealthy and upper-middle-class Jews, the preponderant majority were lower-middle-class workers, small businessmen, and a proletariat, employed or unemployed.

The republic of Poland had come into being in 1919, after its representatives had signed a treaty with the Allied powers, promising to guarantee the civil and political equality of its minorities, to safeguard their rights as citizens, and in addition, to extend to all minorities the right to establish their own educational, religious, charitable, and social institutions. From the start these guarantees were never fully implemented, and in 1934 they were completely renounced. Pogroms marked the inauguration of Poland's independence and were a recurring phenomenon in the twenty years of independent Poland. Universities and professional schools introduced a *numerus clausus* system for Jews. The government's growing control of economic life was accompanied by discriminatory regulations and restrictive practices that succeeded in impoverishing the Jewish community. The rise of Nazism in Germany and, following Marshal Piłsudski's death in 1935, Poland's accelerating fascist course brought near-disaster to the Jewish community. A torrent of anti-Semitic legislation, brutal pogroms, and an official government policy of "evacuating" the Jews from Poland overwhelmed them. In 1938 laws were enacted withdrawing Polish citizenship from Jews resident abroad.

Despite the increasingly hostile atmosphere, the Polish Jews managed to maintain a vital community, with a vast network of religious, educational, philanthropic, social, and cultural institutions, without comparison elsewhere in Europe. Besides kehillot, which served the community's religious, welfare, and educational needs, Polish Jews were also organized in a range of political parties. These parties put up candidates, whenever democratic elections were conducted, for the Sejm (parliament), city councils, and the kehillot. With the increasing impoverishment of the Jewish community, Jewish voters shifted their support in municipal and kehilla elections in the late 1930s from the Zionist parties, which had enjoyed a majority or plurality of votes, to the Bund, which in the elections of 1938 and 1939 won an outright majority in many large cities.

JEWS IN WARTIME POLAND

With the German occupation, the Jews became isolated from the Poles. In accordance with Heydrich's instructions of September 21, 1939, to the leaders of the Einsatzgruppen, the Jews were expelled from most of the territories to be incorporated, except for Lodz. In the Generalgouvernement, Jews were expelled from small towns and villages and were forced to make their way to the large cities where they were being concentrated. (About 300,000 Jews fled into Soviet-occupied Poland.) In these larger cities, the Germans ordered the Jews to set up Jewish councils (Judenräte) to govern the Jewish communities in accordance with German instructions. A series of ordinances streamed from Governor Frank whose purpose was to isolate the Jews from the Poles and subject them to special treatment. Jews were required to wear identifying arm bands; they were subject to seizure for forced labor in camps and other German installations being constructed. They were forbidden access to certain sections of the city; they were allotted smaller food rations than the Polish population. They were subject to arbitrary terror and violence; most synagogues were destroyed; thousands of Jews were killed at random. This first period of German occupation lasted about six months.

The next period was ghettoization. The first major ghetto in which Jews were enclosed was in Lodz, on May 1, 1940. Jews were sealed within the Warsaw ghetto in November 1940. By April 1941 most Jews in the Generalgouvernement were ghettoized. After Galicia was taken by the Germans in July 1941, Jews there were subjected to the same process, and by the end of the year ghettoization was completed. During this period Jews endured hunger, disease, and impressment into forced-labor brigades. It is estimated that at least a half-million Jews died as a result of this policy of annihilation from "natural causes" and of random terror.

The third stage in German anti-Jewish policy began at the end of 1941, when the death camps became operational. In December the deportation from the Wartheland to Chełmno began. In March the Jews of Lublin began to be deported to Bełżec. From July to September 1942, over 300,000 Jews were deported from Warsaw to Treblinka. Only those engaged in what German military authorities designated as essential war production were exempt from deportation. Himmler, however, ordered all Jewish workers to be replaced with Poles and all ghettos to be destroyed by the end of 1942. The process took somewhat longer. In March 1943 the Cracow ghetto was liquidated. In April the Germans undertook to liquidate the Warsaw ghetto and encountered armed resistance from the Jews. In mid-May the Warsaw ghetto was liquidated. The Lwów ghetto was liquidated in June 1943. The Lodz ghetto lasted longest—until August 1944, when the last 70,000 Jewish workers were deported.

Some Jews remained in slave-labor installations and in hiding. Some took part in the Warsaw uprising under General Bor of August 1944.

When the war ended, some 50,000 to 70,000 Polish Jews were found to have survived—in Poland, in the Polish army, and in camps in Germany. About 180,000 or so were repatriated from the Soviet Union. Three million Polish Jews had been killed.

Soviet Union
(Including Latvia, Lithuania, Estonia)

On September 28, 1939, when Germany and Russia divided Poland, Russia also concluded pacts with Latvia, Lithuania, and Estonia, obtaining from them rights to military bases. Russia ceded Vilna, which had been part of Poland, to Lithuania, whose historic capital it had been.

On June 28, 1940, Russia occupied Bessarabia and north Bucovina, which Rumania had ceded to it under pressure. In July 1940 the three Baltic states were incorporated into the Soviet Union as individual republics and occupied by Russia. Russia's harsh policy and the deportations of large numbers of the population whom Soviet leaders regarded as political opponents intensified popular hostility to Russian occupation and rule. Consequently, in most areas from the

Baltic north to the Ukrainian south, which the Germans occupied following the invasion on June 22, 1941, they were generally well received by the local populations.

Through 1941 and 1942 the Germans advanced eastward to Leningrad (under siege from August 1941 to January 1943) in the north, Moscow, in a line south to Voronezh following the Don River to Stalingrad, and then toward the Black Sea. While the eastern portion of this territory remained a military area and subject to military administration, the western sector of German-held Russian territory, including that part of Poland earlier occupied by Russia, came under German civilian administration. Hitler appointed Alfred Rosenberg to be Reich Minister for the Occupied Eastern Territories. The Baltic countries and White Russia were incorporated into a Reich Commissariat for the Ostland, with Heinrich Lohse as Reich Commissioner, and each of the units (Latvia, Lithuania, Estonia, White Russia) with its own commissioner. To the south was the Reich Commissariat for the Ukraine, reaching as far north as Brest Litovsk and south to the Black Sea, with Erich Koch as Reich Commissioner. Jurisdictional and bureaucratic conflict in both commissariats was frequent, for besides the rivalry between Rosenberg and the two Reich Commissioners, control was variously vested in the Wehrmacht, the SS, with Göring as Plenipotentiary for the Four Year Plan, or Sauckel as Plenipotentiary for Labor Recruitment.

The Baltic countries, whose populations the Germans regarded as racially assimilable, were given a limited degree of autonomy, in contrast to the Ukraine, which was under tight German rule because its people were regarded as racially inferior. Ukrainian nationalists, disappointed by the failure of the Germans to recognize their separatist aspirations, became less enthusiastic about cooperating with the German occupation. The partisan movement, growing in both Ostland and the Ukraine, was reorganized in a military hierarchy commanded from Moscow by Red Army officers.

In January 1943, when the siege of Leningrad was lifted, the Red Army began its counterattack, which, despite reverses and heavy losses, continued to force the Germans back. By late 1944 the Germans had retreated from Russian territory.

THE JEWS IN PREWAR USSR AND BALTIC COUNTRIES

USSR: According to the 1939 census, there were over 3 million Jews in the Soviet Union, about one-half in the Ukraine, nearly a million in Russia proper (RSFSR), 375,000 in White Russia, with the balance in the Asiatic USSR. A relatively small number (20,000) lived in the so-called Jewish autonomous region of Biro-Bidzhan.

More than 70 percent of Soviet Jews were wage earners (industrial workers) or salaried (white-collar and professional employees) of the state or state enterprises). A substantial proportion had higher education.

After the Bolshevik Revolution, the traditional religious and communal organizations of the Jewish community were suppressed, as were also the modern Jewish national movements, Zionist and Bundist. The only form of Jewish culture permitted to the Jews was a Yiddish version of Bolshevik culture. Until the mid-1930s Yiddish schools and the publication of Yiddish books, periodicals, and newspapers were permitted, but during the Great Purge these institutions were liquidated.

Jews enjoyed equal civic status in the Soviet Union, but popular anti-Semitism continued to exist, especially in the Ukraine.

Lithuania: Some 155,000 Jews made up 8 percent of the Lithuanian population. Less than half the gainfully occupied Jews were engaged in retail trade and commerce, about 40 percent were in industry and handicraft, 10 percent in farming, 9 percent in the professions.

Though Lithuania had under the terms of the Paris peace treaty granting it sovereignty, obligated itself to guarantee civic, religious, and cultural rights to its minorities, it failed to live up to this commitment. The Jews, nevertheless, maintained a rich and varied communal life, supporting internationally renowned yeshivot as well as excellent Yiddish and Hebrew secular school systems, and a diversified press. A range of Jewish political parties defended Jewish interests in the Lithuanian parliament, in the municipalities, and in public.

Jews suffered discrimination in higher education and in

employment in various professions. The rise in nationalistic feeling, engendered by Lithuanian sovereignty, and the urbanization of part of the population led to intensified anti-Semitism against Jews in business and industry.

Latvia: The more than 93,000 Jews in Latvia were less than 5 percent of the total population. On the whole somewhat more prosperous than the Lithuanian Jews, Latvian Jews played an important role in expanding Latvia's industry. They were engaged in the production of textiles, paper, leather, tobacco and matches, flour, and yeast, and in the importation of crude oil and coal. A small proportion were in banking and in the professions.

Because of the cross-cultural influences in Latvia, many Jews identified with German or Russian culture. Over 50 percent of the Jewish school children were enrolled in schools with Russian as the language of instruction, 13 percent were in German-language schools, over 30 percent in Yiddish or Hebrew schools, while only 3 percent attended Lettish-language schools. Jewish political parties, from the Aguda to the Bund, with Zionist and middle-class parties in the center, represented Jewish group interests in the Latvian assembly. They could accomplish little, however, in the face of the accelerating fascist trend of the country during the 1930s, the suppression of parliamentary government, and the abolition of school autonomy in 1934. Anti-Semitism was rampant in the streets and in economic life.

Estonia: There were only about 5,000 Jews in Estonia, less than a half of 1 percent of the population. About half lived in the capital city of Tallinn (Reval). They were engaged in trade and industry, about 10 percent were in the professions. Jewish religious and educational institutions existed in a considerable variety, considering the small Jewish population. Anti-Semitism was negligible.

JEWS IN WARTIME USSR

After the Soviet occupation of eastern Poland, about 300,000 Jews fled from Nazi-held Poland eastward. During the period of Soviet occupation of the Baltic countries, about 10,000 politically suspect Jews (along with non-Jews) were deported to slave-labor camps in Siberia and elsewhere deep in Russia. Thousands of Polish Jews who refused to give up their Polish citizenship were also sent to forced-labor camps.

With the German invasion of Russia on June 22, 1941, a few thousand young Jews in the Baltic countries joined the Red Army and another few thousand managed to flee into Russia. Most Jews in the Baltic, White Russia, the Ukraine, Bessarabia, and the Crimea were caught by the German invasion, which advanced too rapidly to permit large-scale flight or systematic evacuation.

Hard upon the invading German army came the Einsatzgruppen, rounding up Jews, murdering thousands upon thousands in mass shootings at execution pits. As the Einsatzgruppen advanced, the German civilian administration moved in and set up ghettos for the remaining population in the larger Jewish cities (Vilna, Kovno, Shavli, Riga, Dvinsk, Minsk, Mohilev, Zhitomir, Berdichev) and ordered Judenräte to be organized. In some places, where massacres proceeded so rapidly, ghettos were no longer needed. In Kiev in September 1941, for instance, over 33,000 Jews were shot in two days at a ravine in outlying Babi Yar. By the end of October 1941, German statistics showed that a quarter of a million Jews had been slaughtered in the Baltic and White Russia. The Baltic and Ukrainian populations collaborated voluntarily with the Germans in murdering the Jews.

During intermittent periods between mass killings, Jews in the ghettos were exploited for slave labor and subjected to hunger and disease. In the summer of 1943 the Germans began to liquidate the surviving remnants of the ghettos (Bialystok in August; Minsk, Lida, Vilna in September; Riga in November). The ghettos in Kovno and Shavli existed until July 1944.

In most ghettos some form of resistance was organized and numbers of Jews managed to escape to join the partisan movement.

Jewish losses were well over 1 million, perhaps as high as 1.3 million. In the Baltic, about 90 percent of the Jews were killed. Losses in Russia proper were about 100,000. In White Russia about 66 percent and in the Ukraine about 60 percent of the Jews were annihilated.

Appendix B

The Final Solution
in Figures

No one can establish with certitude the exact number of Jews murdered in the course of the Final Solution. The first estimate, made at the Nuremberg trials in 1945, of 5.7 million Jews killed has been shown by subsequent censuses and statistical analyses to have been remarkably accurate. The data of the 1959 census in the Soviet Union confirm the staggering Jewish losses during World War II.

The Jewish population figures for each country in the following table are estimates of the population within the country's borders at the time the Final Solution began to be carried out.

ESTIMATED NUMBER OF JEWS KILLED
IN THE FINAL SOLUTION

Country	Estimated pre–Final Solution Population	Estimated Jewish Population Annihilated	
		Number	Percent
Poland	3,300,000	3,000,000	90
Baltic countries	253,000	228,000	90
Germany/Austria	240,000	210,000	90
Protectorate	90,000	80,000	89
Slovakia	90,000	75,000	83
Greece	70,000	54,000	77
The Netherlands	140,000	105,000	75
Hungary	650,000	450,000	70
SSR White Russia	375,000	245,000	65
SSR Ukraine*	1,500,000	900,000	60
Belgium	65,000	40,000	60
Yugoslavia	43,000	26,000	60
Rumania	600,000	300,000	50
Norway	1,800	900	50
France	350,000	90,000	26
Bulgaria	64,000	14,000	22
Italy	40,000	8,000	20
Luxembourg	5,000	1,000	20
Russia (RSFSR)*	975,000	107,000	11
Denmark	8,000	—	—
Finland	2,000	—	—
Total	8,861,800	5,933,900	67

* The Germans did not occupy all the territory of this republic.

Notes

The following abbreviations have been used:

AJC-RC	American Jewish Committee, Records Center
AJDC-A	American Joint Distribution Committee, Archives
AJYB	*American Jewish Year Book*
Blfg	*Bleter far geshikhte*
BŻIH	*Biuletyn Żydowskiego Instytutu Historycznego*
DGFP	*Documents on German Foreign Policy*
IMT	International Military Tribunal, Nuremberg
JLB-A	Jewish Labor Bund, Archives
JSS	*Jewish Social Studies*
LBI-A	Leo Baeck Institute, Archives
LBI, YB	Leo Baeck Institute, *Year Book*
NCA	*Nazi Conspiracy and Aggression*
TMWC	*Trial of the Major War Criminals*
TWC	*Trials of War Criminals*
VfZ	*Vierteljahrshefte für Zeitgeschichte*
Y-A	YIVO Institute for Jewish Research, Archives
YiAn	*Yivo Annual of Jewish Social Science*
Yibl	*Yivo-Bleter*
YVS	*Yad Vashem Studies*

1. THE JEWS IN HITLER'S MENTAL WORLD

1. All quotations from *Mein Kampf* are from Ralph Manheim's translation (Houghton Mifflin). Because of the extensive use of this book and also of Hitler's *Secret Book*, no page references have been given. Italics in quotations from *Mein Kampf* are in the original.

2. Heiden, *Der Fuehrer*, p. 34.

3. Heiden, *Der Fuehrer*, p. 190.

4. Friedrich P. Reck-Malleczewen, *Diary of a Man in Despair*, p. 27.

5. For Hitler's early life, I have relied heavily on F. Bradley Smith's splendid study, *Adolf Hitler: His Family, Childhood and Youth.*

6. Wilfried Daim, *Der Mann, der Hitler die Ideen Gab*, passim; William A. Jenks, *Vienna and the Young Hitler*, passim.

7. Text in Ernst Deuerlein, "Hitlers Eintritt in die Politik und die Reichswehr," *VfZ* 7 (1959):203–205. Subsequent quotations from Hitler's early speeches are taken from the documents published here.

8. Reginald H. Phelps, "Hitlers 'Grundlegende' Rede über den Antisemitismus," *VfZ* 16 (1968):390–420. The introduction contains an excellent analysis of the sources in conventional German anti-Semitism from which Hitler derived his ideas.

9. Reginald H. Phelps, "Hitler als Parteiredner im Jahre 1920," *VfZ* 11 (1963):277–278.

10. Rauschning, *Hitler Speaks*, p. 238.

11. Adolf Hitler, "My Political Testament," *NCA*, 6, Doc. 3569-PS, pp. 258–263.

2. ANTI-SEMITISM IN MODERN GERMANY

1. For background on Germany I am indebted to the brilliant work by the late Klaus Epstein, *The Genesis of German Conservatism.*

2. Cited in George G. Iggers, *The German Conception of History: The National Tradition of Historical Thought from Herder to the Present* (Middletown, Conn., 1968), p. 41.

3. Johann Gottlieb Fichte, *Reden an die deutsche Nation* (Berlin, 1808), p. 488.

4. Mosse, *The Crisis of German Ideology*, p. 4.

5. Quoted in Kohn, *The Mind of Modern Germany*, p. 88.

6. Quoted in Adler, *The Jews in Germany*, p. 41.

7. Quoted in Ernest Hamburger, "One Hundred Years

of Emancipation," in LBI, *YB* 14, p. 11.

8. For more on the anti-Christian aspect of anti-Semitism, see Uriel Tal, *Religious and Anti-religious Roots of Modern Anti-Semitism.*

9. Quoted in Stern, *The Politics of Cultural Despair*, p. 61.

10. Quoted in the German original in Alex Bein, "Modern Anti-Semitism and Its Effect on the Jewish Question," *YVS* 3 (1959):14.

11. Hamburger, "One Hundred Years of Emancipation," p. 15.

12. Massing, *Rehearsal for Destruction*, pp. 278–287.

13. Heinrich von Treitschke, "Unsere Aussichten," in Boehlich, ed., *Der Berliner Antisemitismusstreit*, p. 113.

14. Text published in Reventlow, *Judas Kampf und Niederlage in Deutschland*, pp. 342–344; an English translation in Dawidowicz, *Holocaust Reader.*

15. Quoted in Leschnitzer, *The Magic Background of Modern Anti-Semitism*, p. 219.

16. Nahum N. Glatzer, *Leopold Zunz: Jude-Deutscher-Europäer* (Tübingen, 1964), p. 470. Dr. Fred Grubel called this letter to my attention.

17. Massing, *Rehearsal for Destruction*, pp. 300–305.

18. Quoted in Stern, *The Politics of Cultural Despair*, p. 91.

19. Mosse, *The Crisis of German Ideology*, p. 144.

20. Mosse, *The Crisis of German Ideology*, p. 268.

21. Quoted in Cohn, *Warrant for Genocide*, p. 136.

22. Cf. Peter Gay, *Weimar Culture*, especially Chapter 3.

3. PHASE ONE: ANTI-JEWISH LEGISLATION, 1933–1935

1. Quoted in Martin Broszat, "The Concentration Camps: 1933–1945," in Buchheim et al., *Anatomy of the SS State*, p. 405.

2. Joseph Goebbels, *My Part in Germany's Fight* (London, 1935), pp. 269–270.

3. Ernst Herzfeld, "Meine Letzten Jahre in Deutschland, 1933–1938," LBI-A, Memoir Collection, p. 4.

4. AJC-RC, "Jews in Germany, 1933."

5. Allen, *The Nazi Seizure of Power*, pp. 210–211.

6. *Dokumente der deutschen Politik und Geschichte*, 4:147–148.

7. *DGFP*, Series C, 1, Doc. No. 141, pp. 253–255.

8. Pfundter, ed., *Dr. Wilhelm Frick und sein Ministerium*, pp. 180–181.

9. Heiden, *Der Fuehrer*, pp. 403-404, 407.

10. Fryman [Class], *Wenn ich der Kaiser wär'*, p. 76.

11. Bracher, Sauer, Schulz, *Die nationalsozialistische Machtergreifung*, p. 280.

12. Schleunes, *The Twisted Road to Auschwitz*, p. 70. Originally a doctoral dissertation, this study attempts to trace the evolution of Nazi Germany's anti-Jewish policies up to 1938. Schleunes found much interesting archival material, but failed to place it in any intelligible framework. His only reference to *Mein Kampf* is to dismiss it as an inadequate "reflection" of German-Jewish relations.

13. Nicolai, *Die rassengesetzliche Staatslehre*, p. 51.

14. Nicolai, *Rasse und Recht*, p. 5.

15. All laws are cited from Hoche, ed., *Die Gesetzgebung Adolf Hitlers*. For an English translation of selected laws, see Dawidowicz, *Holocaust Reader*.

16. Cf. Salo W. Baron, "The Impact of the Revolution of 1848 on Jewish Emancipation," *JSS* 11 (1949):210.

17. Gottfried zur Beek, *Die Geheimnisse der Weisen von Zion*, p. 236.

18. Fryman, *Wenn ich der Kaiser wär'*, pp. 75-76.

19. *DGFP*, Series C, 4:568-570.

20. Kommission zur Erforschung . . . , *Dokumente zur Geschichte der Frankfurter Juden 1933-1945*, pp. 216-217.

21. "The Racists' Decalogue," in Massing, *Rehearsal for Destruction*, pp. 306-307.

22. *AJYB* 36:174.

23. Kommission zur Erforschung . . . , *Dokumente zur Geschichte der Frankfurter Juden 1933-1945*, pp. 217-218.

24. Cf. Bernhard Lösener, "Das Reichsministerium des Innern und die Judengesetzgebung," *VfZ* 9 (1961).

25. Stuckart and Globke, *Kommentare zur deutschen Rassengesetzgebung*, 1:12-13.

26. Domarus, *Hitler: Reden und Proklamationen*, 1:537.

4. THE SS: INSTRUMENT OF THE FINAL SOLUTION

1. Quoted in Höhne, *The Order of the Death's Head*, p. 327.

2. Buchheim, "The SS—Instrument of Domination," *Anatomy of the SS State*, pp. 139-140.

3. Smith, *Heinrich Himm-*

ler, pp. 72–76, 91–92, 121–124, 141–148. The passages that follow in the text are drawn from this excellent study of the young Himmler.

4. Höhne, *The Order of the Death's Head*, p. 59.

5. See Larry V. Thompson, "*Lebensborn* and the Eugenics Policy of the Reichsführer-SS," *Central European History* 4 (1971):54–77.

6. Martin Broszat, "The Concentration Camps: 1933–1945," in Buchheim et al., *Anatomy of the SS State*, p. 402. The following pages in the text are based on this study.

7. Aronson, *Reinhard Heydrich und die Frühgeschichte von Gestapo und SD*, is the best source for biographical data on Heydrich. I have drawn from this excellent book for the material of Heydrich and also for the early history of the SD.

8. Höhne, *The Order of the Death's Head*, pp. 170 ff. The following section of the text is based largely on this well-documented journalistic account of the SS and on the scholarly study by Buchheim, cited in note 2.

9. Domarus, *Hitler: Reden und Proklamationen*, 1:624–625.

10. "Report of SS-Oberscharführer Schröder on the Status of Projects in II-112,"

August 28, 1936, in Aronson, *Reinhard Heydrich*, pp. 327–328.

11. Aronson, *Reinhard Heydrich*, pp. 174–177.

12. The text is published in Hans Mommsen, "Der nationalsozialistische Polizeistaat und die Judenverfolgung vor 1938," *VfZ* 10 (1962):77–78.

13. Arthur Prinz, "The Role of the Gestapo in Obstructing and Promoting Jewish Emigration," *YVS* 2 (1958):205–208.

14. DGFP, Series C, 1:661–662, 732–736. See also Ernst Marcus, "The German Foreign Office and the Palestine Question in the Period 1933–1939," *YVS* 2 (1958):179–204.

15. R. Melka, "Nazi Germany and the Palestine Question," *Middle Eastern Studies* 5 (1969):221.

16. Quoted in Hans Lamm, "Über die innere und äussere Entwicklung des deutschen Judentums im Dritten Reich," p. 47.

17. Quoted in Schleunes, *The Twisted Road to Auschwitz*, pp. 177–178, from a document in the Himmler records at the National Archives. Unfortunately Schleunes has not indicated in which SS division the report was prepared.

18. Mommsen, "Der nationalsozialistische Polizeistaat," pp. 78–79.

19. Schleunes, *The Twisted*

Road to Auschwitz, p. 193. The directive has not been identified as to departmental origin, city, or jurisdiction and lacks the exact date.

20. Schleunes, *The Twisted Road to Auschwitz*, p. 194.

21. Melka, "Nazi Germany and the Palestine Question," p. 222.

22. Melka, "Nazi Germany and the Palestine Question," pp. 222–223.

23. Interview with Dr. Max Gruenewald, New York, February 1, 1973.

24. See note 10.

25. *TMWC*, 29, Doc. 1992 [A]-PS, pp. 206–234.

26. Himmler, *Die Schutz-staffel als antibolschewistische Kampforganisation*, p. 29.

5. FOREIGN POLICY, RACE, AND WAR

1. Quoted in Heiden, *Der Fuehrer*, p. 415.

2. Rauschning, *The Voice of Destruction*, p. 6.

3. G. Weinberg, "National Socialist Organization and Foreign Policy Aims in 1927," *Journal of Modern History* 36 (1964):434.

4. Mitscherlich and Mielke, *Doctors of Infamy*, p. 91.

5. Helmut Krausnick, "Judenverfolgung," in Buchheim et al., *Anatomie des SS-Staates*, 2:325. This passage was egregiously mistranslated in the English version. The mistake has, unfortunately, been perpetuated in Bracher, *The German Dictatorship* (p. 336), and in the article "Ghetto" in the *Encyclopedia Judaica*.

6. Bernhard Lösener, "Das Reichsministerium des Innern und die Judengesetzgebung," *VfZ* 9 (1961):281.

7. *DGFP*, Series C, 5:853–862.

8. Rauschning, *The Voice of Destruction*, p. 28.

9. Text in Kotze and Krausnick, *Es spricht der Führer*, pp. 147–148.

10. Domarus, *Hitler: Reden und Proklamationen*, 1:727–728.

11. *NCA*, 3, Doc. 386-PS, pp. 295–305; Domarus, *Hitler*, 1:748–756.

12. Quoted in Schleunes, *The Twisted Road to Auschwitz*, p. 219.

13. Quoted in Genschel, *Die Verdrängung der Juden aus der Wirtschaft im Dritten Reich*, p. 150.

14. Hoche, ed., *Die Gesetzgebung Adolf Hitlers*, 27:323. For an English translation, see Dawidowicz, *Holocaust Reader*.

15. *DGFP*, Series D, 1:900–901.

16. Fromm, *Blood and Banquets*, p. 274.

17. Martin Broszat, "The

Concentration Camps: 1933–1945," in Buchheim et al., *Anatomy of the SS State*, pp. 453–455.

18. Gordon, *Hitler and the Beer Hall Putsch*, pp. 266–267.

19. Arthur Prinz, "The Role of the Gestapo in Obstructing and Promoting Jewish Emigration," YVS 2 (1958):211.

20. Kochan, *Pogrom: 10 November 1938*, p. 34.

21. Graml, *Der 9. November 1938: "Reichskristallnacht,"* pp. 17–22.

22. Kochan, *Pogrom*, p. 51.

23. *TMWC*, 32, Doc. 3063-PS, pp. 20–29.

24. *TMWC*, 31, Doc. 3051-PS, pp. 515–519.

25. *TMWC*, 28, Doc. 1816-PS, pp. 499–540; also *NCA* 4: 425–457.

26. Kommission zur Erforschung . . . , *Dokumente zur Geschichte der Frankfurter Juden 1933–1945*, pp. 196–198.

27. *NCA*, 3, Doc. 841-PS, 606–608.

28. Text in Genschel, *Die Verdrängung der Juden*, p. 300; also IMT Docs. 1662-PS and 2875-PS (identical texts).

29. Genschel, *Die Verdrängung der Juden*, p. 299; also IMT Doc. 1412-PS. For an English translation, see Dawidowicz, *Holocaust Reader*.

30. *TMWC*, 32, Doc. 3575-PS, 411–415.

31. *Dokumente zur Geschichte der Frankfurter Juden*, p. 198.

32. Hoche, *Gesetzebung*, 32:69–72.

33. Shaul Esh, "The Establishment of the 'Reichsvereinigung der Juden in Deutschland' and its Main Activities," YVS 7 (1968):19–38.

34. *DGFP*, Series D, 5: 933–936.

35. Quoted in Krausnick, "The Persecution of the Jews," in Buchheim et al., *Anatomy of the SS State*, p. 44.

36. Domarus, *Hitler*, 2: 1058.

6. PHASE TWO: FROM INTERNAL WAR TO WORLD WAR

1. Goerlitz, *History of the German General Staff 1657–1945*, p. 345.

2. Sontag and Beddie, *Nazi-Soviet Relations: 1939–1941*, pp. 1–2.

3. Churchill, *The Gathering Storm*, p. 370.

4. *DGFP*, Series D, 6, No. 433, pp. 574–580.

5. Halder, *Kriegstagebuch 1939–1942*, 1:38.

6. Domarus, *Hitler: Reden und Proklamationen,* 2:1315.

7. Domarus, *Hitler,* in order, pp. 1663, 1828–1829, 1920, 1937.

8. *DGFP,* Series D, 8:164–167.

9. Broszat, *Nationalsozialistische Polenpolitik 1939–1945,* p. 22; *TMWC,* 26, Doc. 864-PS, 377–383.

10. *TMWC,* 20:211–219.

11. Quoted in Messerschmidt, *Die Wehrmacht im NS-Staat,* p. 354.

12. Minutes dated September 21, 1939, of Heydrich's staff meeting, Berlin, September 19, 1939; copy from the Institut für Zeitgeschichte.

13. Halder, *Kriegstagebuch,* 1:79.

14. Minutes dated September 27, 1939, of Heydrich staff conference with Einsatzgruppen chiefs, September 21, 1939. Copy from the Institut für Zeitgeschichte; express letter of Heydrich to chiefs of Einsatzgruppen regarding the "Jewish question in the occupied territory," September 21, 1939 (IMT Doc. 3363-PS), full German text in *Yibl* (1947), pp. 163–168; English text in Dawidowicz, *Holocaust Reader.* The army was informed of these plans on September 20; see Halder, *Kriegstagebuch,* 1:81–82.

15. Arendt, *Eichmann in Jerusalem,* pp. 77–78.

16. Shaul Esh, "Tachnit-av lehakikat hanazim neged hayehudim," *Ha'aretz,* April 1, 1963, p. 7.

17. The most thorough discussion and analysis of the so-called Lublin reservation is Philip Friedman, "The Lublin Reservation and the Madagascar Plan," *YiAn,* Vol. 8.

18. H. Kr., "Denkschrift Himmlers über die Behandlung der Fremdvölkischen im Osten," *VfZ* 5 (1957):197.

19. I. Trunk, "Shtudye tsu der geshikhte fun yidn in varteland," *Blfg* 2 (1949):81.

20. IMT Doc. 864-PS (see note 9, above). Keitel briefed his generals on this conference. Cf. Halder, *Kriegstagebuch,* 1:107.

21. Goerlitz, *History of the German General Staff 1657–1945,* pp. 380, 385.

22. Görlitz, ed., *The Memoirs of Field-Marshal Keitel,* p. 137.

23. *TMWC,* 26, Doc. 447-PS, pp. 53–58; English text in Dawidowicz, *Holocaust Reader.*

24. Warlimont, *Inside Hitler's Headquarters 1939–1945,* pp. 150–152, 608.

25. Görlitz, ed., *Memoirs of Keitel,* p. 136.

26. Höss, *Commandant of Auschwitz,* pp. 125–126, 231–232.

27. Halder, *Kriegstagebuch,* 2:336–337.

28. Keitel, in Görlitz, ed., *Memoirs of Keitel,* p. 136.

29. IMT Doc. C-050, in Jacobsen, "Kommissarbefehl . . . ," in Buchheim et al., *Anatomie des SS-Staates*, 2: 216–218.

30. Jacobsen, "Kommissarbefehl . . . ," 2:225–227; IMT Doc. NOKW 1076.

31. IMT Doc. NOKW 1692, in Jacobsen, "Kommissarbefehl . . . ," 2:223.

32. IMT Doc. 878-PS, in Jacobsen, "Kommissarbefehl . . . ," 2:250; *NCA* 3:636.

33. *TMWC*, 35, Doc. D-411, pp. 81–85; English text in Dawidowicz, *Holocaust Reader*.

34. Höhne, *The Order of the Death's Head*, p. 358.

35. *TMWC*, 38 Doc. L-180, pp. 670–717; *TMWC*, 30, IMT Doc. 2271-PS, p. 73.

36. The fullest sources regarding the operations of the Einsatzgruppen in Russia are *TWC*, 4, *Case No. 9, Einsatzgruppen Case;* Hilberg, *The Destruction of the European Jews;* Reitlinger, *The Final Solution.*

37. Affidavit by Otto Ohlendorf, November 5, 1945, *NCA,* 5, Doc. 2620-PS, p. 342.

38. Jäger report, Einsatzkommando No. 3, Kovno, December 1, 1941, in Hilberg, *Documents of Destruction*, pp. 56–57. Photostat of the original document, held by the USSR, in the Institut für Zeitgeschichte, Munich.

39. Y-A, "Raport Bundu w sprawie prześladowań Żydów," May 1942; for an English translation, see Dawidowicz, *Holocaust Reader.*

7. THE ANNIHILATION CAMPS: KINGDOM OF DEATH

1. Höss testimony, *TMWC* 2:398, 416. See also his autobiography, *Commandant of Auschwitz*, pp. 160, 205.

2. Ohlendorf's testimony, *TMWC* 4:318; also his testimony in Einsatzgruppen Case, p. 251.

3. Letter to Gottlob Berger, July 28, 1942 (NO-626), in Heiber, ed., *Reichsführer!*, p. 134. Similiar admissions appear in *The Memoirs of Doctor Felix Kersten* (New York, 1947), pp. 174–175, 234. See also the affidavits by Konrad Morgen, July 13 and July 19, SS-65, SS-67, *TMWC* 42:551–565, quoting Reich Physician-SS Dr. Ernst Robert Grawitz to the effect that Hitler had given Himmler the order and the responsibility to destroy the Jews.

4. *TMWC*, 26, Doc. 710-PS, pp. 266–267; English text in Dawidowicz, *Holocaust Reader.*

5. Klaus Dörner, "National-sozialismus und Lebensvernichtung," *VfZ* 15 (1967): 140. I have relied heavily on this splendid study about bio-racial killing.

6. *TWC*, Case No. 1, *The Medical Case*, 1, Doc. 630-PS, p. 848.

7. *TWC*, Case No. 1, *The Medical Case*, 1, testimony of Victor Brack, pp. 843–844.

8. *TWC*, Case No. 1, *The Medical Case*, 1, p. 877.

9. *TWC*, Case No. 1, *The Medical Case*, 1, Himmler to Brack, December 19, 1940 (Doc. NO-018), p. 856; letter dated August 13, 1941, from the Bishop of Limburg to the Minister of Justice (Doc. 615-PS), pp. 845–847.

10. Helmut Krausnick, "The Persecution of the Jews," in Buchheim et al., *Anatomy of the SS State*, p. 97. See also *TWC*, *The Medical Case*, 1, Doc. NO-205, pp. 721–722. Brack, in a letter to Himmler, June 23, 1942, advocating mass sterilization of two to three million Jews still fit to work, wrote:

On the instructions of Reichsleiter Bouhler I placed some of my men—already some time ago—at the disposal of Brigade-führer Globocnik to execute his special mission. On his renewed request I have now transferred additional personnel. On this occasion, Brigadeführer Globocnik stated his opinion that the whole Jewish action should be completed as quickly as possible so that one would not get caught in the middle of it one day if some difficulties should necessitate a halt of the action.

11. Höss, *Commandant of Auschwitz*, p. 262.

12. Henkys, *Die national-sozialistischen Gewaltverbrechen*, pp. 64, 95, 245, 246.

13. Mitscherlich and Mielke, *Doctors of Infamy*, p. 114.

14. *TWC*, *The Medical Case*, 1, Docs. NO-365 and NO-997, pp. 870–871, 887–888, draft letters from Rosenberg's Ministry for the Occupied Eastern Territories, October 1941.

15. Höss, *Commandant of Auschwitz*, p. 163.

16. Affidavit of Karl Rudolf Werner Braune, *TWC* 4:215.

17. Minutes of the Wannsee Conference, IMT Doc. NG-2586-G, *TWC*, Case No. 11, *Ministries Case;* German original published in full in Kempner, *Eichmann und Komplizen*, pp. 133–147; English text in Dawidowicz, *Holocaust Reader*.

18. Seabury, *The Wilhelmstrasse*, pp. 126, 128–129.

19. Himmler to Krüger, July 19, 1942, NO-5574; English text in Dawidowicz, *Holocaust Reader*.

20. Piotrowski, ed., *Hans Frank's Diary*, pp. 256–257.

21. Krausnick, "The Persecution of the Jews," p. 104; Berenstein et al., *Eksterminacja Żydów*, No. 157, p. 297; Eichmann trial document 1253, Ganzenmüller to Wolf [*sic*], July 28, 1942.

22. Quoted in Hilberg, *The Destruction of the European Jews*, p. 314.

23. IMT Doc. NO-2405; Berenstein et al., *Eksterminacja Żydów*, p. 320.

24. *NCA*, 8, Dieter Wisliceny, Affidavit C, November 29, 1945, pp. 612–613. For more, see correspondence of Edmund Veesenmayer, Reich Plenipotentiary in Hungary, with Eichmann et al., on the need for railroad cars, in Randolph Braham, ed., *The Destruction of Hungarian Jewry*, 1:346–351, 367–371.

25. For more on how these racial policies in the occupied Eastern areas were applied and their cost in military terms, see the impressive work by Dallin, *German Rule in Russia;* also Koehl, *RKFDV*. Two interesting documents are IMT Doc. 2220-PS, a memorandum by HSSPF Lieutenant General Krüger, April 12, 1943, on failures in the administration policy of the Generalgouvernement, *NCA* 4:855–860; and IMT Doc. 054-PS, a memorandum of October 7, 1942, on the mistreatment of Ukrainian workers in Germany and the impact on the occupied population, *NCA* 3:90–99.

26. Helmut Heiber, "Der Generalplan Ost," *VfZ* 6 (1958):291–292.

27. *TMWC*, 38, Doc. L-180, p. 986.

28. *TMWC*, 30, Doc. 2271-PS, p. 76.

29. *TMWC*, 32, Doc. 3663-PS, pp. 435–436; English text in Dawidowicz, *Holocaust Reader*.

30. Lageberichte, Distrikt Galizien, August 29, 1942, in Philip Friedman, "Hurban yehude lvov betkufat 1941–1944," in N. M. Gelber, ed., *Lvov: Entziklopedya shel galuyot* (Jerusalem, 1956), pp. 745–746.

31. M. Shatner, "Khurbn pshemishl," in Menczer, ed., *Przemyśl Memorial Book* (Sefer *Pshemishl*), p. 512.

32. Cf. A. Eisenbach, "Di felkeroysrotung-politik fun daytshn imperyalizm . . . ," *Blfg* 3 (July–December 1950): 44–46.

33. Quoted in Krausnick, "The Persecution of the Jews," p. 107; in the German edition, 2:424–425.

34. Krausnick, "The Persecution of the Jews," pp. 108–110; in German edition, 2: 426–428; the English translation is neither accurate nor complete. For a full English version, see Dawidowicz, *Holocaust Reader*.

35. Doc. NO-1611, Himmler to Pohl, Krüger, Globocnik; English text in Dawidowicz, *Holocaust Reader*.

36. Doc. NOKW-134, National Archives.

37. National Archives, T-77, Roll 620, Wi/ID1.26; Roll 621, Wi/ID1.13; MA 285, pp. 2927–2928.

38. For documents relating to Operation Reinhard, see Schnabel, *Macht ohne Moral*,

pp. 441–457. See also *TMWC*, 34, Doc. 4024-PS, pp. 58–92.

39. Deposition of Kurt Gerstein, *Le Monde juif*, 19, January–March 1964; English text in Dawidowicz, *Holocaust Reader*.

40. Quoted in Naumann, *Auschwitz*, pp. 177–178.

41. *TMWC*, 29, Doc. 1919-PS, pp. 110–173; excerpts in English translation in Dawidowicz, *Holocaust Reader*.

8. A RETROSPECTIVE VIEW

1. E. Deuerlein, "Hitlers Eintritt in die Politik . . . ," *VfZ* 7 (1959):199.

2. The Reichswehr reports of Hitler's speeches were published by Deuerlein, "Hitlers Eintritt"; the Bavarian police reports were published by Reginald H. Phelps, "Hitler als Parteiredner," *VfZ*, Vol. II (1963).

3. Deuerlein, "Hitlers Eintritt," p. 212; Phelps, "Hitler als Parteiredner," p. 301. Deuerlein's document dates the meeting April 29, 1920; Phelps has corrected this.

4. Baynes, ed., *The Speeches of Adolf Hitler*, 1:14.

5. Ludecke, *I Knew Hitler*, p. 72.

6. Gordon, *Hitler and the Beer Hall Putsch*, pp. 265–307.

7. Bayerisches Hauptstaats-

archiv München, Abt. II, Geheimes Staatsarchiv, MA 103 476, pp. 1169–1179. I am indebted to Professor Harold J. Gordon, Jr., for his helpfulness in providing the documentation that enabled me to obtain a copy of the constitution. Paragraph 14 (p. 1173) provided for the expropriation of the Jews; Paragraph 14a expropriated those "who profited from the distress of the German people during the war," a fine legal category; Paragraph 15 provided the death penalty for evasion of expropriation; Paragraph 16 (p. 1174) provided for the roundup of persons and the establishment of concentration camps.

8. Quoted in Heiden, *Der Fuehrer*, p. 118.

9. Professor Jäckel, in his

incisive book, *Hitler's Weltan-schauung*, argues that Hitler first advocated the physical liquidation of the Jews in *Mein Kampf*. One piece of evidence that he adduces in support of his view is a statement that Hitler made in an interview while in Landsberg, to the effect that his past methods in fighting the Jews had been too soft and "that in the future the most severe methods of fighting will have to be used" (p. 57). Actually Hitler had always stressed the need for the most ruthless methods in confronting the enemy. If indeed he meant anything specific at this time, he may have been referring to tactics rather than goals.

10. Kotze and Krausnick, *Es spricht der Führer*, p. 154.

11. *DGFP*, Series D, 6:580.

12. Domarus, ed., *Hitler: Reden und Proklamationen*, 1: 537.

13. *DGFP*, Series C, 5:855.

14. Blumental et al., *Dokumenty i Materiały*, 3:31.

15. *TMWC* 29:415.

16. Blumental et al., *Dokumenty i Materiały*, 3:192; text in *Biuletyn Głównej Komisji Badania Zbrodni Niemieckich* (*Hitlerowskich*) *w Polsce*, Warsaw, Vol. 13, Document 28, pp. 27F–29F.

17. Cf. Deuerlein, "Hitlers Eintritt"; and Phelps, "Hitler als Parteiredner," pp. 274–330.

18. Abel, *The Nazi Movement: Why Hitler Came to Power*, pp. 155–156. This book is primarily an analysis of six hundred autobiographies written by members of the NSDAP in 1934.

19. For a penetrating psychoanalytic study, see Ernst Simmel, "Anti-Semitism and Mass Psychopathology," in his *Anti-Semitism: A Social Disease* (New York, 1946). Also suggestive is Martin Wangh, "National Socialism and the Genocide of the Jews," *International Journal of Psycho-Analysis* 45 (1964):386–395. A pioneering study of the psychological origins of the National Socialist movement is Peter Loewenberg, "The Psychohistorical Origins of the Nazi Youth Cohort," *American Historical Review* 76 (December 1971):1457–1502.

20. For more on the relationship between witchcraft and modern anti-Semitism, see Leschnitzer, *The Magic Background of Modern Anti-Semitism*, and Joshua Trachtenberg, *The Devil and the Jews* (Cleveland and New York, 1961). For perspective on National Socialist anti-Semitism in the light of medieval millenarians, see Norman Cohn, *The Pursuit of the Millennium* (New York, 1961).

21. Ernst Hiemer, *Der Giftpilz* (Nuremberg, 1938).

22. Curzio Malaparte, *Kaputt* (New York, 1946), p. 91.

23. Trevor-Roper, ed., *Hitler's War Directives*, p. 212.

24. Quoted in Buchheim, "Command and Compliance," *Anatomy of the SS State*, p. 338.

9. BETWEEN FREEDOM AND GHETTO: THE JEWS IN GERMANY, 1933–1938

1. The sources differ as to the occasion; some refer to a meeting of the Gemeinden, April 13, 1933; others cite the first meeting of the Reichsvertretung in September 1933.

2. The authority on Jewish defense during the Weimar Republic is Arnold Paucker, whose study "Der jüdische Abwehrkampf," in Mosse and Paucker, eds., *Entscheidungsjahr 1932*, pp. 405–499, was later expanded into a book, *Der jüdische Abwehrkampf in den letzten Jahren der Weimarer Republik* (Hamburg, 1968). See also his "Jewish Defence Against Nazism in the Weimar Republic," *The Wiener Library Bulletin* 26 (1972):21–31.

3. Esra Bennathan, "Die demographische und wirtschaftliche Struktur der Juden," in Mosse and Paucker, *Entscheidungsjahr 1932*, pp. 87–131.

4. Hilde Ottenheimer, "The Disappearance of Jewish Communities in Germany, 1900–1938," *JSS* 3 (1941):191.

5. *AJYB*, 39:336–337; 36:158–160; Zvi Asaria, *Die Juden in Köln* (Cologne, 1959), p. 332.

6. Werner Rosenstock, "Exodus 1933–1939," LBI, *YB* 1 (1956):373–390.

7. Bruno Weil, *Der Weg der deutschen Juden* (Berlin, 1935); English translation quoted from AJC Office Report, February 21, 1935, AJC-RC, "Jews in Germany 1935."

8. Heinz Kellermann, "Ende der Emanzipation?", *Der Morgen* 9 (August 1933):173–177.

9. Messerschmidt, *Die Wehrmacht im NS-Staat*, p. 45; Leo Lowenstein, "Die Linie des Reichsbundes jüdischer Frontsoldaten," in *Wille und Weg des deutschen Judentums*, pp. 7–11.

10. Quoted in Wolfgang Hamburger, "The Reactions of Reform Jews to the Nazi Rule," in Strauss and Grossman, *Gegenwart im Rückblick*, pp. 154, 160–162.

11. Heinrich Stern, "Die inneren Voraussetzungen für Hilfe und Aufbau in deutschen Judentum," *Der Morgen* 9 (August 1933):165–172.

12. Hans Joachim Schoeps, "Der Deutsche Vortrupp—der

Ort geschichtlicher Besinnung," in *Wille und Weg*, p. 55; Schoeps, "Wir gehen einen deutschen Weg," *C-V Zeitung*, July 13, 1933, p. 275; Schoeps, *Die letzten dreissig Jahre*, p. 101.

13. *Jüdische Rundschau*, April 4, 1933; quoted from the English translation by Harry Zohn in Nahum N. Glatzer, *The Dynamics of Emancipation* (Boston, 1965), pp. 104–108; also in Dawidowicz, *Holocaust Reader*.

14. *3 Jahre Zionistische Bewegung*, passim.

15. "Eine Erklärung der deutschen Rabbiner," *Gemeindeblatt der Synagogen-Gemeinde zu Köln a/Rh.*, March 31, 1933, reproduced in Asaria, *Die Juden in Köln*, p. 329.

16. Leo Baeck, "Das Judentum in der Gegenwart," *Der Morgen* 8 (1933):237–240.

17. Martin Buber, *Die Stunde und die Erkenntnis: Reden und Aufsätze*, especially "Das Erste" and "Erkenntnis tut Not."

18. Ernst Simon, "Von Palestina nach Deutschland: Eindrücke und Besinnung einer jüdischen Reise," *Der Morgen* 10 (1934):115; Joachim Prinz, "A Rabbi under the Hitler Regime," in Strauss and Grossman, *Gegenwart im Rückblick*, pp. 231–238; Max Gruenewald, "Education and Culture of the German Jews

under Nazi Rule," *Jewish Review* 5 (1948):81.

19. Willy Mainz, in Ball-Kaduri, *Das Leben der Juden in Deutschland im Jahre 1933*, pp. 133–134; Isi Jacob Eisner, "Reminiscences of the Berlin Rabbinical Seminary," LBI, *YB* 12 (1967):46–47; Michael L. Munk, "Austrittsbewegung und Berliner Adass Jisroel-Gemeinde 1869–1939," in Strauss and Grossman, *Gegenwart im Rückblick*, pp. 146–147; Yehiel Jacob Weinberg, *Seride Esh* (Jerusalem, 1961), pp. 3–7; conversation with Dr. Alexander Altmann, February 8, 1973; interview with Josef Kalter, February 5, 1973.

20. Ernst Simon, "Jewish Adult Education in Nazi Germany as Spiritual Resistance," LBI, *YB* 1 (1956):92.

21. Herbert Freeden, "A Jewish Theatre under the Swastika," LBI, *YB* 1 (1956): 142–162.

22. Ball-Kaduri, *Das Leben der Juden*, p. 34.

23. Dr. [Julius] Blau, *Zur Geschichte der Reichsvertretung* (Frankfurt/M, December 1937), typescript, LBI-A; Max Gruenewald, "The Beginning of the 'Reichsvertretung,'" LBI, *YB* 1 (1956):51–67; Hugo Hahn, "Die Gründung der Reichsvertretung," in Tramer, *In zwei Welten*, pp. 97–105; Kurt Lowenstein, "Die innerjüdische Reaktion auf die Krise der deutschen Demo-

kratie," in Mosse and Paucker, *Entscheidungsjahr 1932*, pp. 401–403; *AJYB* 34 (1932–1933):58–59; K. Y. Ball-Kaduri, "The National Representation of Jews in Germany," *YVS* 2 (1959):159–178; Ernst Herzfeld, "Meine letzten Jahre in Deutschland, 1933–1938," LBI-A, Memoir Collection.

24. Friedrich Brodnitz, "Zentralausschuss der deutschen Juden für Hilfe und Aufbau," *Der Morgen* 8 (1933): 276–279; the JDC Archives contain a wealth of correspondence and reports of the Zentralausschuss and also a complete file of its newsletter, *Informationsblätter*.

25. AJDC-A, "Germany: General and Emergency, 1933": "Bemerkungen zu einem wirtschaftlichen Verhandlungsprogramm," proposed by Dr. Werner Senator, August 15, 1933 (3 pp.); "Entwurf von Thesen betr. Wirtschaftsfragen der deutschen Juden," attached; Werner Senator, on letterhead of Jewish Agency for Palestine, Jerusalem, October 1, 1933, to J. C. Hyman, AJDC, New York (3 pp).

26. These minutes (7 typescript pp.), as well as related documents of less substantive interest, are in the Martin Buber Archives (Ms. Var. 350), at the Jewish National and University Library, Jerusalem.

27. At the second meeting

of the Homburg Circle; see note 26.

28. *AJYB* 36:179, 182; *Informationsblätter*, March–April 1936, p. 25.

29. Otto Hirsch, "Die Reichsvertretung der deutschen Juden," *Der Morgen* 9 (1934): 437–439.

30. Notes by Julius Brodnitz, in Ernst Herzfeld, "Meine letzten Jahre," pp. 17–18.

31. Published as an announcement of the Reichsvertretung, *Jüdische Rundschau*, November 3, 1933.

32. Franz Meyer, "Bemerkungen zu den 'Zwei Denkschriften,' " in Tramer, *In zwei Welten*, pp. 114–127, gives the complete text of the document (pp. 120–123). For an English translation, see Dawidowicz, *Holocaust Reader*. Apart from attributing its authorship to Georg Landauer, a ZVfD leader, Meyer does not give any information about the document, except to say that it was given to him in the strictest confidence.

33. Nathan Feinberg, "Jewish Political Activities against the Nazi Regime," in Conference on Manifestations of Jewish Resistance, *Jewish Resistance During the Holocaust: Proceedings*, pp. 74–93; see also Oscar I. Janowsky and Melvin M. Fagen, *International Aspects of German Racial Policies* (New York, 1937).

34. *AJYB* 36:175; interview

with Dr. Friedrich Brodnitz, February 27, 1973; the text of the memorandum is published in Franz Meyer, "Bemerkungen," in Tramer, *In zwei Welten*, pp. 124–127; for an English translation, see Dawidowicz, *Holocaust Reader*.

35. See note 25.

36. A. Szanto, "Economic Aid in the Nazi Era," LBI, *YB* 4 (1959):208–219; Rudolph Stahl, "Vocational Retraining of Jews in Nazi Germany 1933–1938," *JSS* 1 (1939): 169–194.

37. *Sonderbeilage zur Jüdisch-liberale Zeitung*, No. 35/36; LBI-A, "Reichsvertretung," AR-C.A. 103, 31/221. Ernst Herzfeld, in "Meine letzten Jahre," characterized the protest as quixotic.

38. Richard Fuchs, "The 'Hochschule für die Wissenschaft des Judentums' in the Period of Nazi Rule," LBI, *YB* 12 (1967):3–31.

39. Cf. Colodner, *Jewish Education in Germany under the Nazis*, passim.

40. Buber, *Die Stunde und die Erkenntnis*, pp. 128–130; an English translation in Dawidowicz, *Holocaust Reader*.

41. Fritz Friedlander, "Trials and Tribulations of Jewish Education in Nazi Germany," LBI, *YB* 3 (1958):191–192.

42. "Jüdische Erwachsenenbildung," in Buber, *Die Stunde und die Erkenntnis*, pp. 111–112; an English translation

in Dawidowicz, *Holocaust Reader*.

43. Ernst Simon, "Jewish Adult Education," passim.

44. Georg Lubinsky, quoted in Ball-Kaduri, "The National Representation of Jews in Germany," *YVS* 2 (1959):174.

45. Rosenstock, "Exodus 1933–1939."

46. Ball-Kaduri, *Vor der Katastrophe*, p. 42.

47. Translation of a memo by officers of the Hilfsverein der deutschen Juden, Berlin, April 1934, to Dr. B. Kahn, AJDC-A, "Germany: General and Emergency: Emigration 1933–1937."

48. Cf. "Die Agudas Jisroel und die Auswanderung," *Der Israelit*, November 18, 1937.

49. Central Bureau for the Settlement of German Jews (JAFP), *Report to the XIXth Zionist Congress and to the IVth Council of the Jewish Agency in Lucerne*, London, July 1935, pp. 6, 21.

50. Landauer, *Der Zionismus im Wandel*, pp. 13–46 and passim.

51. Yisrael Gutman, in Conference on Manifestations of Jewish Resistance, *Jewish Resistance*, p. 115.

52. The text of the memorandum is published in S. Adler-Rudel, "The Evian Conference on the Refugee Question," LBI, *YB* 13 (1968): 261–271.

53. Ball-Kaduri, *Vor der*

Katastrophe, pp. 41–42; Kurt R. Grossman, "Deutsche Juden auf der Linken," in Strauss and Grossman, *Gegenwart im Rückblick*, pp. 86–105. Grossman published the full text of Tucholsky's letter of December 5, 1935. For more on Tucholsky, see Poor, *Kurt Tucholsky and the Ordeal of Germany*, esp. pp. 221–223.

54. "Confidential Notes of a Brief Visit to Berlin by Dr. Selig Brodetsky, August 29–September 2, 1934" (3 pp.), AJC-RC, "Germany, Jews, 1934."

55. Genschel, *Die Verdrängung der Juden aus der Wirtschaft im Dritten Reich*, p. 263; Reichsvertretung der Juden in Deutschland, *Arbeitsbericht für das Jahr 1938* (processed), AJDC-A.

56. *Arbeitsbericht des Zentralausschusses für Hilfe und Aufbau bei der Reichsvertretung der Juden in Deutschland für das Jahr 1936* (processed), p. 163.

57. *3 Jahre Zionistische Bewegung*, pp. 31, 43–44.

58. Ernst Herzfeld, "Meine letzten Jahre," p. 30.

59. "Das Programm der Reichsvertretung," *C-V Zeitung*, September 26, 1935; an English translation in Dawidowicz, *Holocaust Reader*.

60. Jüdischer Central-Verein, *Aufgaben/Satzung/Organisation*, Berlin, [1935]; an

English translation in Dawidowicz, *Holocaust Reader*.

61. This practice was inaugurated by Rabbi Max Gruenewald in Mannheim.

62. Leo Baeck, "A People Stands Before Its God," in Boehm, ed., *We Survived* (Santa Barbara, Cal., 1966), pp. 285–286.

63. Cf. Ludwig Misch, "Memoirs," LBI-A.

64. Most of this narrative is found in Freeden, *Jüdisches Theater in Nazi-deutschland*, pp. 58–65; also, interviews with Dr. Friedrich Brodnitz, February 27, 1973, and Dr. Max Gruenewald, February 1, 1973; Kurt Jacob Ball-Kaduri, "Leo Baeck and Contemporary History," YVS 6 (1967):121–129; Max Gruenewald, "About the Reichsvertretung der deutschen Juden," in YIVO Colloquium, *Imposed Jewish Governing Bodies under Nazi Rule*, pp. 42–54; *AJYB* 38:324–325, and 40:203; *Mitteilungsblatt der Hitachduth Olej Germania*, October, I, and December, I, 1937.

65. "Erwerbt die Beitragskarte für Hilfe und Aufbau," *Informationsblätter*, May 22, 1933; confidential informal statement on the JDC budget for European Jewish relief in 1937, presented by Dr. Bernard Kahn, December 3, 1936 (12 pp.), AJDC-A, "Germany: General and Emergency";

Arbeitsbericht des Zentralaus-schusses für Hilfe und Aufbau ... 1936, p. 13; Kurt Alexander, "Die Reichsvertretung der deutschen Juden," in Reich-mann, ed., *Festschrift zum 80. Geburtstag von Rabbiner Dr. Leo Baeck*, p. 80; *AJYB* 38: 325.

66. *AJYB* 40:204.

10. DEATH AND LIFE IN THE EAST EUROPEAN GHETTOS

1. Yad Washem, *Blackbook of Localities Whose Jewish Population Was Exterminated by the Nazis*, p. xi and passim.

2. Zygelboym, *Zygelboym-bukh*, pp. 107–115; Julien Bryan, *Siege* (New York, 1940), p. 36.

3. Y-A, "Di arbet fun der dzhoynttsentrale in poyln far di 13 milkhomekhadoshim (september 1939–oktober 1940)," pp. 3–4.

4. Blumenthal, *Aleksander*, passim.

5. "Der onheyb," *Zygel-boym-bukh*, pp. 116–117.

6. "Report of Mr. [H.] Szoszkies [Shoshkes] on the Situation in Warsaw," in "Report on Mr. Szoszkies' Visit to JDC Office, Paris, December 5, 1939," AJDC-A, "Poland: General and Emergency: Po-groms 1940."

7. Central Commission . . . , *German Crimes in Poland*, Vol. 1, is the best single source for this documentation. Also, all memorial books of Jewish com-munities contain descriptions of similar crimes. For docu-mentation on Polish participa-tion, see E. Ringelblum, "Sto-sunki polsko-żydowskie w czasie II wojny światowej," *BŻIH* 28 (October–December 1958):3–37.

8. Herman Kruk, *Togbukh fun vilner geto*, p. 55. Kruk was a member of the Bund in War-saw, who had fled to Vilna at the outbreak of the war and remained there until his death in a slave-labor camp in Es-tonia in September 1944.

9. Brenner, *Vidershtand un umkum in tshenstokhover geto*, pp. 8–9.

10. Baler, ed., *Pinkes Kovel*, p. 84.

11. Moritz Goldstein, "Ger-man Jewry's Dilemma before 1914," LBI, *YB* 2 (1957):240.

12. Huberband, *Kiddush ha-shem*, pp. 84–87.

13. English translations of some of Frank's ordinances in Dawidowicz, *Holocaust Reader*.

14. *Zygelboym-bukh*, pp. 142–150.

15. Chaim A. Kaplan, *Scroll of Agony*, p. 195. Kaplan was

a Hebrew educator and writer. He was deported from Warsaw in 1942.

16. Jacob Nochimovski, "Meditsinishe unterzukhungen baym arbetsamt fun kovner geto," *Fun letstn khurbn* 10 (December 1948):28–37.

17. Mordecai Lenski, "Problems of Disease in the Warsaw Ghetto," *YVS* 3:283–293.

18. "Fun undzer lider-zamlung," *Fun letstn khurbn* 7 (May 1948):95–96.

19. Accounts of this meeting and its immediate consequences, varying in minor details, are in Mendelsohn, *The Polish Jews Behind the Nazi Ghetto Walls*, pp. 6–7; *Zygelboym-bukh*, pp. 125–136; "Report to Mr. [H.] Szoszkies" (note 6); Shoshkes, *Bleter fun a getotog-bukh*, pp. 11–20.

20. Philip Friedman, "The Jewish Ghettos of the Nazi Era," *JSS*, Vol. 16, 1954, passim.

21. Ringelblum, *Notes from the Warsaw Ghetto*, p. 82.

22. Zelig Kalmanovich, "Der gayst fun geto," *Yibl* 30 (1947):169–172.

23. Rudashevski, *The Diary of the Vilna Ghetto*, p. 32.

24. Ruta Sakowska, "Łączność pocztowa warszawskiego getta," *BŻIH* 45/46 (January–June 1963):94–109.

25. Kaczerginski, ed., *Dos gezang fun vilner geto*, p. 19.

26. Extract from the diary

of Dr. Lazar Epstein, *Yad Vashem News* 3 (1971):15.

27. Halina Szwambaum, "Four Letters from the Warsaw Ghetto," *Commentary* 31 (1961):491.

28. Alexandra Solowiejczyk, "Dray fertl yor unter di daytshn in vilne," *Yibl* 30 (1947):59–93. The paraphrased passage is on p. 89.

29. Quoted in Isaiah Trunk, *Lodzher geto*, p. 149.

30. Trunk, *Lodzher geto*, p. 337; Dąbrowska and Dobroszycki, *Kronika getta łódzkiego*, 1:11–12, 72–73.

31. Czerniaków, *Yoman geto varsha*, p. 254; excerpts in English translation in Dawidowicz, *Holocaust Reader*.

32. NCA, 3, Doc. 1189-PS, p. 833.

33. Berg, *Warsaw Ghetto: A Diary*, p. 53.

34. Based on entries in the Chaim Kaplan and Ringelblum diaries.

35. Dąbrowska and Dobroszycki, *Kronika*, 1:563–564.

36. Yehuda Elberg, "Erev shabes in a varshever hoyf (fun mayn getotogbukh)," *Di goldene keyt* 74 (1971):142.

37. S. Glube, "Maykholim in lodzh," *Fun letstn khurbn* 9 (September 1948): 78–81.

38. A. Rosen, [reply to a questionnaire], *Blfg* 1 (August–December 1948):195–200.

39. "The Little Smuggler,"

translated from the Polish original of Henryka Lazawert; the complete poem in English in Dawidowicz, *Holocaust Reader*.

40. Smuggling in the Warsaw ghetto was best described by Opoczynski, *Reportazhn fun varshever geto*, pp. 62–74; an English translation in Dawidowicz, *Holocaust Reader*. See also Goldstein, *The Stars Bear Witness*, pp. 76–78; Abraham M. Karmi, "The Jewish Cemetery in Occupied Warsaw," *Yad Vashem Bulletin* 16 (February 1965):42–47.

41. Apfelbaum, ed., *Maladie de famine: recherches cliniques sur la famine exécutées dans le ghetto de Varsovie en 1942*, pp. 10–11.

42. The best single source that describes this demoralized society in Warsaw is Jonas Turkow, *Azoy iz es geven*, pp. 133–178, 195–246, and passim; see also Ringelblum, *Ksovim*, passim.

43. "Ankete vegn farbroykh in varshever geto," *Blfg* 2 (January–December 1949): 273–289; P. Tykocinski, "Voluvke," *Blfg* 1 (August–December 1948):203–210; Dworzecki, *Yerushelayim delite in kamf un umkum*, pp. 156–157; Samuel Gringauz, "The Ghetto As an Experiment of Social Organization (Three Years of Kovno Ghetto)," *JSS* 11 (1949):13.

44. Isaiah Trunk, "Mayreveyropeishe yidn in di mizrekheyropeishe getos," *Di goldene keyt* 15 (1953):80–102; Dąbrowska and Dobroszycki, *Kronika*, 1:517–520; Kaufmann, *Die Vernichtung der Juden Lettlands*, passim.

45. Apfelbaum, *Maladie de famine*, pp. 112–113. See also Falstein, *The Martyrdom of Jewish Physicians in Poland*, pp. 190–192, 200–295.

46. Lenski, "Problems of Disease," pp. 288–290; Isaiah Trunk, "Epidemics and Mortality in the Warsaw Ghetto, 1939–1942," *YiAn* 8:82–122.

47. Calculated from the data in Trunk, *Lodzher geto*, pp. 222–223.

48. Ruta Pups-Sakowska, "Opieka nad uchodźcami i przesiedleńcami żydowskimi w Warszawie w latach okupacji hitlerowskiej," *BŻIH* 65/66 (1968):73–104.

49. Y-A, Wasser Collection, "January [1942] Report of the Refugee 'Town' Dzika and Niska"; English translation in Dawidowicz, *Holocaust Reader*.

50. Dworzecki, *Yerushelayim delite*, pp. 295–458 and passim. See also Dworzecki, "The Day-to-Day Stand of the Jews," in Conference on the Manifestations of Jewish Resistance, *Jewish Resistance*, pp. 152–181.

51. Y-A, Wasser Collection, "Folklore."

52. Unger, *Sefer kedoshim*, p. 181. This book, like most accounts of religious life during the Holocaust, is unreliable as a documentary source. Many such works are little more than contemporary exercises in mythmaking or hagiography. The efforts to reconstruct conversations long after the event should be regarded with great skepticism. This literature is on the whole shoddy. See Hersh Wasser on Hillel Seidman, *Blfg* 1 (January–March 1948):186–197.

53. Eck, *Hatoim bedarke hamavet*, p. 36.

54. A. Einhorn [reply to a questionnaire], *Blfg* 1 (April–June 1948):121.

55. Seidman, *Togbukh fun varshever geto*, p. 149.

56. Ringelblum, *Ksovim fun geto*, 2:117.

57. Bakalchuk-Felin, ed., *Yizkorbukh Khelem*, pp. 589–590.

58. Peter Schindler, "Responses of Hassidic Leaders and Hassidim During the Holocaust . . . ," pp. 90, 163.

59. Y-A, Wasser Collection, "Folk Songs." For an English translation of the whole poem, see Dawidowicz, *Holocaust Reader*.

60. Y-A, Wasser Collection, "Folklore" (9 pp.). Ms., titled "Hosofe tsu: Remozim fun geule."

61. N. Blumenthal, "Verter un vertlekh fun der khurbntkufe," *Yidishe shprakh* 22 (1962):30.

62. Kaczerginski, ed., *Lider fun getos un lagern*, p. 324.

63. Y-A, Wasser Collection, "Folklore," apparently collected by S. Lehman, late 1941.

64. Y-A, Sutzkever-Kaczerginski Collection, No. 305, Statistisher Amt in vilner geto: politsey-amt, "Tetikeyt fun di politsey-revirn far dem ershtn halbn yor 1942."

65. Mark Dvorjetski [Dworzecki], "Adjustment of Detainees to Camp and Ghetto Life," *YVS* 5 (1963):193–220, and "Der mentsh in tehom," *Di goldene keyt* 74 (1971): 73–82; Gringauz, "The Ghetto As an Experiment," *JSS* 11 (1949):17; interview with Isaac Orenstein, May 10, 1973; Rudashevski, *Diary of the Vilna Ghetto*, passim.

66. Cf. Huberband, *Kiddush hashem*, pp. 92–93.

67. Y-A, Wasser Collection, No. 32–6, handwritten ms., pp. 3–27, entries June 27, 1942–July 10, 1942.

68. LBI-A, Memoir Collection, Ruth Alton (Tauber), "Litzmannstadt (Lodz Ghetto)."

69. Zelig Kalmanovich, "A togbukh in vilner gheto," *Yibl*

35 (1951):60–61. For excerpts in English translation, see Dawidowicz, *Holocaust Reader*.

70. Solowiejczyk, "Dray fertl yor," *Yibl* 30 (1947):77. Cf. Henia Karmel-Wolfe, *The Baders of Jacob Street* (Lippincott, 1970), in which her heroine, Halina Bader, returns "home" to the Cracow ghetto, rather than live disguised as an "Aryan."

11. THE OFFICIAL COMMUNITY: FROM KEHILLA TO JUDENRAT

1. Cf. Isaiah Trunk, *Judenrat*, a comprehensive study of the Judenräte in Eastern Europe. I have relied heavily on its extensive documentation.

2. "Report of Mr. [H.] Szoszkies [Shoshkes] on the Situation in Warsaw," in "Report on Mr. Szoszkies' Visit to JDC Office, Paris, December 5, 1939," AJDC-A, Poland: General and Emergency: Pogroms 1940; Shmaryahu Ellenberg, "My Meetings with Adam Cherniakow," *Yad Vashem Bulletin* 16 (February 1965):50–54; A. Hartglass, "How Did Cherniakov Become Head of the Warsaw Judenrat?" *Yad Vashem Bulletin* 15 (August 1964):4–7; Czerniaków, *Yoman geto varsha*, pp. 2–6. It appears that Czerniaków extracted that appointment on his own, without the consent of the other committee members.

3. A summary of the arguments pro and con participating in the Judenrat is in Gar, *Umkum fun der yidisher kovne*, pp. 288–294.

4. Blumenthal, *Teudot mi-geto lublin*, p. 40.

5. Herman Kruk, *Togbukh fun vilner geto*, pp. 8–12.

6. Trunk, *Judenrat*, p. 19.

7. Dworzecki, *Yerushelayim delite*, pp. 41–42; Kruk, *Togbukh*, pp. 169–170; Celemenski, *Mitn farshnitenem folk*, pp. 76–77, 100–104.

8. Trunk, *Judenrat*, p. 16.

9. Jasni, *Di geshikhte fun yidn in lodzh*, passim; Solomon F. Bloom, "Dictator of the Lodz Ghetto," *Commentary* 7 (1949):111–112; Jacob Nirenberg, "Di geshikhte fun lodzher geto," in Jewish Labor Bund, *In di yorn fun yidishn khurbn*, pp. 235–236.

10. Trunk, *Judenrat*, pp. 25–26; Philip Friedman, "Two 'Saviors' Who Failed," *Commentary* 26 (1958):479–491.

11. David Liwer, "Khurbn Bendin," in Stein, ed., *Pinkes Bendin*, p. 186.

12. Brenner, *Vidershtand un umkum in tshenstokhover geto*, p. 15.

13. Trunk, *Lodzher geto*, pp. 30–31, 63, 362.

14. Kruk, *Togbukh*, pp. 46–48, 69; Dworzecki, *Yerushelayim delite*, pp. 44, 71.

15. Trunk, *Judenrat*, pp. 318–319.

16. For more on the interwar kehilla in Poland, see Jacob Lestchinsky, "Economic Aspects of Jewish Community Organization in Independent Poland," *JSS* 9 (1947):319–337; and Ruta Sakowska, "Z dziejów gminy żydowskiej w Warszawie 1918–1939," *Studia Warszawskie*, Vol. 14, 1973.

17. Cf. Isaac Levitats, *The Jewish Community in Russia, 1772–1844* (New York, 1943).

18. Trunk, *Judenrat*, pp. 115–142; see also M. Merin to JDC, February 24, 1941, AJDC-A, and Y-A, report of the Department of Social Welfare, Vilna Ghetto Judenrat, April 1945, both in English translation in Dawidowicz, *Holocaust Reader*.

19. Blumenthal, *Darko shel yudenrat*, p. 67; excerpts in English translation in Dawidowicz, *Holocaust Reader*.

20. Trunk, *Judenrat*, pp. 388–400.

21. Zygelboym, *Zygelboymbukh*, pp. 142–150.

22. Blumenthal, *Teudot mi geto lublin*, pp. 164–165, 207–209, and passim. For excerpts in English translation, see Dawidowicz, *Holocaust Reader*.

23. Cf. Celemenski, *Mitn farshnitenem folk*, p. 75.

24. Brenner, *Vidershtand un umkum*, p. 32.

25. Trunk, *Judenrat*, p. 401, and *Lodzher geto*, p. 437.

26. Peretz Opoczynski, "Di shopn," *Blfg* 7 (October–December 1954):89.

27. E. Ringelblum, "Stosunki polskożydowskie w czasie II wojny światowej," *BŻIH*, 28 (October–December 1958):3–37.

28. Trunk, *Lodzher geto*, pp. 50, 87–88, and *Judenrat*, pp. 76–90. See also J. Winkler, "Dos geto kemft kegn virtshaftlekher farknekhtung," *Blfg* 1 (August–December 1948):3–40.

29. Trunk, *Judenrat*, pp. 237–247.

30. Abraham Rosenberg, "Dos 'draytsentl' (a tsushtayer tsum problem fun kolaboratsionizm in varshever geto)," *Blfg* 5 (January–June 1952):187–225 and 5 (July–September 1952):116–148.

31. For more on the police, see Trunk, *Judenrat*, pp. 474–527, 586–587; William Glicksman, "Daily Record Sheet of the Jewish Police (District I) in the Czestochowa Ghetto (1941–1942)," *YVS* 6:331–357.

32. Kruk, *Togbukh*, pp. 74–75, 304–305.

33. Trunk, *Judenrat*, pp. 50–53.

34. I. Kaplan, *Dos folksmoyl in natsi-klem*, pp. 34–35.

35. Samuel Gringauz, "The

Ghetto as an Experiment of Jewish Social Organization (Three Years of Kovno Ghetto)," *JSS* 11 (1949):10.

36. Eck, *Hatoim bedarke hamavet*, p. 83.

37. Blumenthal, *Darko shel yudenrat*, pp. 195–201.

38. Blumenthal, *Teudot mi-geto lublin*, pp. 365–368; the complete text in English, see Dawidowicz, *Holocaust Reader*.

39. Y-A, Wasser Collection, "Folklore II."

40. Neustadt, *Khurbn un oyfshtand fun di yidn in varshe*, 2:357–358.

41. For portraits of Rumkowski, see Tabaksblatt, *Khurbn lodzh*, pp. 27–29, 164–171; Solomon F. Bloom, "Dictator of the Lodz Ghetto," *Commentary* 7 (1949):111–112; Saul Bellow, *Mr. Sammler's Planet* (New York, 1970), pp. 230–233. For portraits of Gens and Merin, see Philip Friedman, "Two 'Saviors' Who Failed," *Commentary* 26 (1958):479–491.

12. THE ALTERNATIVE COMMUNITY

1. Ruta Sakowska, "Komitety domowe w getcie warszawskim," *BŻIH* 61 (January–March 1967):59–86.

2. I have drawn heavily for information of the ŻSS, in all its mutations, from Michael Weichert, *Yidishe aleynhilf*, and Sakowska, "Komitety domowe."

3. Quoted in Trunk, *Judenrat*, p. 339.

4. A. Berman, "O losie dzieci z zakładów opiekuńczych w getcie warszawskim," *BŻIH* 28 (October–December 1958):65–78.

5. L. Bursztyn, "Odezwy Janusza Korczaka z lat okupacji," *BŻIH* 45/46 (1963): 262–266. For an English trans-lation of three of these documents, see Dawidowicz, *Holocaust Reader*. For Korczak's biography and writings, see *Selected Works of Janusz Korczak*, and Olczak, *Mister Doctor: The Life of Janusz Korczak*. Of exceptional insight and beauty is Aaron Zeitlin's poem in prose "Yanush Kortshaks letster gang," in *Vayterdike lider fun khurbn un lider fun gloybn un Yanush Kortshaks letster gang* (New York, 1970).

6. Minutes of the conference translated into Yiddish from the Polish original, in Bakalshuk-Felin, ed., *Yizkor-bukh khelem*, pp. 601–619.

7. There is no systematic

compilation of data about the participation of rabbis and observant Jews in welfare institutions. See individual biographies in Lewin, *Ele ezkra.* Also of interest is Hersh Wasser's review of Hillel Seidman's *Togbukh fun varshever geto,* in *Blfg* 1 (January–March, 1948), especially pp. 186–188.

8. Jonas Turkow, *Azoy iz es geven,* pp. 61–87; Menachem Linder, "A yor yisa," *Blfg* 1 (April–June 1948):3–13; Wasser, review of Seidman's *Togbukh;* Ruta Pups-Sakowska, "Opieka nad uchodżcami i przesiedleńcami żydowskimi w Warszawie w latach okupacji hitlerowskiej," *BŻIH* 65/66 (1968):80–83.

9. Eck, *Hatoim bedarke hamavet,* pp. 20–27; Sakowska, "Komitety domowe...," *BŻIH* 61 (1967):64–66; Chaim Kaplan, *Scroll of Agony,* pp. 227–229, 259; Peretz Opoczynski, "Di tragedye fun a hoyz-komitet," *Blfg* 14 (1961):171–179.

10. Neustadt, *Khurbn un oyfshtand fun di yidn in varshe,* 2:688–689, 598–599.

11. Trunk, *Judenrat,* pp. 187–196; Dworzecki, *Yerushelayim delite in kamf un umkum,* pp. 288–292; Y-A, Vilna Archives, No. 577a; Oshry, *Khurbn lite,* pp. 104–108.

12. Hillel Zeitlin, [response to a questionnaire], *Blfg* 1 (April–June 1948):111–114.

For an English translation, see Dawidowicz, *Holocaust Reader.*

13. [Response to a questionnaire], *Blfg* 1 (August–December 1948):201–202.

14. Trunk, *Lodzher geto,* p. 455; for an English translation, see Dawidowicz, *Holocaust Reader;* Oshry, *Khurbn lite,* p. 143; Rachel Auerbach, "Bagegenishn mit Pole Elster," in *Dray—Ondenbukh,* p. 57.

15. Mentioned in *Min hametzar,* literary supplement to *Hamispar,* underground Hebrew newspaper issued irregularly in Lodz, No. 1, July 8, 1941; the entire issue, along with other fragments, published in *Dappim leheker hashoa vehamered,* Part 1, pp. 115–139.

16. Rabbi Elhanon Person, "Dos religyeze lebn in kovner geto," *Fun letstn khurbn* 9 (September 1948):44.

17. Y-A, Wasser Collection, [Huberband], "Der marsh in mikve arayn." For more on ritual baths, see Huberband, *Kiddush ha-shem,* pp. 88–92.

18. Huberband, *Kiddush ha-shem,* pp. 75–114; Person, "Dos religyeze lebn," p. 44.

19. Ruta Sakowska, "O szkolnictwie i tajnym nauczaniu w getcie warszawskim," *BŻIH* 55 (July–September 1965):57–84.

20. Nahman Korn, "Dertsi-

yung-problemen un kinder-elnt in geto: zikhroynes," in Litvin and Lerman, eds., *Dos bukh fun lublin,* pp. 503–508.

21. Anna Natanblut, "Di shuln in varshever geto," *Yibl* 30 (1947):173–187.

22. "Verordnung über das jüdische Schulwesen im Generalgouvernement," *Verordnungsblatt für das Generalgouvernement,* 1, No. 51 (September 11, 1940):258.

23. Rudashevski, *The Diary of the Vilna Ghetto,* pp. 117, 135.

24. Esther Goldhar-Mark, "Dos yidishe fakh- un hekhere shulvezn in varshe in der tsayt fun der daytsher okupatsye," *Blfg* 2 (1949):175–206.

25. Zylberberg, *A Warsaw Diary,* pp. 34–35.

26. Rudashevski, *Diary,* pp. 134–135; Sutzkever, *Lider fun geto,* pp. 24–25.

27. Turkow, *Azoy iz es geven,* pp. 195–196. Turkow provides the fullest account of entertainment and cultural activities in the Warsaw ghetto, pp. 195–246.

28. Y-A, Wasser Collection, "Yidishe kultur-organizatsye—yikor"; Emanuel Ringelblum, "Cultural Work of the Jewish Underground in Poland," report written Warsaw, May 20, 1944, *Newsletter of the YIVO* 5 (November 1944):1, 6–8; Turkow, *Azoy iz es geven,* pp.

247–255; Ringelblum, *Ksovim fun geto,* 2:164–168.

29. Eck, *Hatoim bedarke hamavet,* pp. 40–41; Neustadt, *Khurbn un oyfshtand,* pp. 309, 692–693.

30. J. Gurevich, "Kovner geto-orkester," *Fun letstn khurbn* 9 (September 1948): 52–58.

31. Oscar Rosenfeld, "Konzert im Kulturhaus," in Trunk, *Lodzher geto,* pp. 447–450.

32. M. Kushnir, in Jewish Labor Bund, *In di yorn fun yidishn khurbn,* p. 308.

33. Y-A, Sutzkever-Kaczerginsky Collection, "Report of the Culture Department for March 1943." English translation in Dawidowicz, *Holocaust Reader.*

34. References to the library celebration are found in the diaries of Kalmanovich, Kruk, and Rudashevski, all entered December 13, 1942; a parallel set of statistics for the last three months of 1941 appears in Kruk, *Togbukh,* p. 131.

35. Trunk, *Lodzher geto,* p. 401.

36. "Lomdim ve-korim," *Min hametzar,* in *Dappim,* p. 130.

37. Dina Abramovich, "Vilner getobiblyotek," in Sudarsky et al., eds., *Lite,* pp. 1671–1678.

38. For more on Oneg Shabbat, see Ringelblum, *Ksovim fun geto,* 2:76–102.

13. THE COUNTERCOMMUNITY: THE POLITICAL UNDERGROUND

1. Cf. Lucy S. Dawidowicz, "Two of Stalin's Victims," *Commentary* 12 (December 1951):614–616.

2. A straightforward account of political activity in the ghettos can be found in Isaiah Trunk, "Dos politishe lebn in di getos," in his *Geshtaltn un gesheyenishn*, pp. 132–172.

3. Neustadt, *Khurbn un oyfshtand fun di yidn in varshe*, 2:634–635.

4. Rachel Auerbach, "Bagegenishn mit Pole Elster," in *Dray—Ondenbukh*, p. 54; Tabaksblatt, *Khurbn lodzh*, pp. 90–99.

5. Cf. Israel Gutman, "Youth Movements in the Underground and the Ghetto Revolts," in Conference on Manifestations of Jewish Resistance, *Jewish Resistance*, pp. 260–284. For more on the activities of Zionist youth, see Tenenbaum-Tamaroff, *Dappim min hadleka*, pp. 112–126; "Korespondentsya pnimit," *Dappim leheker hashoa vehamered*, 1: 148–156; Bronia Klibanski, "The Underground Archives of the Bialystok Ghetto Founded by Mersik and Tenenbaum," *YVS* 2 (1958):295–329.

6. Zygelboym, *Zygelboymbukh*, pp. 107–115; Goldstein, *The Stars Bear Witness*, pp. 31–32.

7. Goldstein, *The Stars Bear Witness*, pp. 42–55; Jewish Labor Bund, *In di yorn fun yidishn khurbn*, pp. 329–339.

8. A fascinating account of this aspect of Bund history that also illuminates a whole chapter of Jewish social history is Bernard Goldstein, *20 yor in varshever bund 1919–1939* (New York, 1960).

9. JLB-A, record book kept by Henoch Rus, activist in Tsukunft, January 1941–June 1942. I am grateful to Mr. Hillel Kempinski for making this document available to me.

10. Only portions of this document were published in "A briv fun varshe," *Undzer tsayt*, July 1941, pp. 10–13. No date was given; the report was probably written at the end of 1940 or early 1941.

11. Quoted in *The Ghetto Speaks* (American Representation of the Bund), No. 1, August 1, 1942.

12. Quoted in J. Kermish, "The Land of Israel in the Life of the Ghetto As Reflected in the Illegal Warsaw Ghetto Press," *YVS* 5:112–113.

13. "Deklaratsye funem farband fun yidishe arbeter geleyent durkh Pola Elster . . . ," in *Dray*, pp. 110–111.

14. "List Bundu," March 16, 1942, Y-A from original in the archives of Studium Polski Podziemnej, London; an En-

glish translation in Dawidowicz, *Holocaust Reader*. Party rivalries have done great disservice to the historical record. Every party tried to magnify its role and belittle that of its opponents during the occupation and long after. Ringelblum, for instance, a highly partisan Left Labor Zionist, has fewer than a dozen references to the Bund, mostly negative comments about a few individuals. Politics was Ringelblum's life, coloring his whole account of Jewish life in the ghetto, despite his historical commitment.

15. No satisfactory work on the underground press has yet been done. Very inadequate is Joseph Kermish, "On the Underground Press in the Warsaw Ghetto," YVS 1 (1957):85–123; a listing of the Bundist underground press appears in H. Kempinski, "Di untererdishe prese fun 'Bund' in varshever geto," *Undzer tsayt*, March 1949, pp. 28–30.

16. Goldstein, *The Stars Bear Witness*, pp. 44–45, 88–89.

17. JLB-A, *Yugnt-shtime*, No. 3, December 1940.

18. Celemenski, *Mitn farshnitenem folk*, pp. 69–70.

19. Quoted in Joseph Kermish, "The Land of Israel . . . ," YVS 5 (1963):125.

20. Quoted in Joseph Kermish, "On the Underground Press in the Warsaw Ghetto," YVS 1 (1957):103–105.

21. Abrasha Blum, ed., *Di parizer komune: zamlbukh* (Warsaw, 1948).

22. *Payn un gvure in dem yidishn over in likht fun der kegnvart*, Munich, 1947. Reprinted from the mimeographed original published in 1940.

23. E. Lidowski, "Vidershtand-organizatsye," in *Baranovitsh: sefer zikaron*, pp. 472–473.

24. Chaim Kaplan, *Scroll of Agony*, pp. 306–307; Czerniaków, *Yoman geto varsha*, pp. 315–316; Kermish, "On the Underground Press," YVS 1: 110–111.

25. Copies of much of the Bundist press are in the Franz Kursky Archives of the Jewish Labor Bund in New York, which also has a few issues of other party papers. No copy of Auerswald's placard, referred to in the cited editorial, appears to be extant.

26. Goldstein, *The Stars Bear Witness*, pp. 51–53; Ringelblum, *Ksovim fun geto*, 1: 105–106. Chaim Kaplan, *Scroll of Agony*, pp. 134–135, describes the pogroms, but apparently did not hear of the Jewish counterattack. Ringelblum reports also that when pogromists attempted to attack the Judenrat building, members of the labor brigades drove them off (p. 107).

27. Tabaksblatt, *Khurbn lodzh,* pp. 100–101; Jacob Nirenberg, "Di geshikhte fun lodzher geto," in Jewish Labor Bund, *In di yorn fun yidishn khurbn,* pp. 227–230; Frank, *Togbukh fun lodzher geto,* pp. 24–29; "Podziemne życie polityczne w getcie łódzkim (1940–1944)," *BŻIH,* No. 54, 1965, passim.

28. Trunk, *Judenrat,* p. 532.

29. Zvi Rosenwein, "Der hungershtrayk in tshensto-

khover geto," in Singer, ed., *Tshenstokhov,* pp. 47–51.

30. Brenner, *Vidershtand un umkum in tshenstokhover geto,* pp. 60–63; M. Kushnir, "Di tetikeyt fun 'Bund' in der tsayt fun der hitleristisher okupatsye in tshenstokhov," in Jewish Labor Bund, *In di yorn,* pp. 306–315.

31. Goldstein, *The Stars Bear Witness,* pp. 103–104; cf. Ringelblum, *Ksovim fun geto,* 1:354.

14. WHO SHALL LIVE, WHO SHALL DIE

1. On Vilna, see Tzippora Birman's letter, March 1, 1943, "Appendix One," to Bronia Klibanski, "The Underground Archives of the Bialystok Ghetto Founded by Mersik and Tenenbaum," *YVS,* Vol. 2, especially pp. 308–309. On Kovno, see Samuel Gringauz, "Khurbn kovno," *Fun letstn khurbn,* No. 7, May 1948, especially pp. 10–15, On Lwów, see Rubinsztajnowa, "Pamiętnik ze Lwowa," *BŻIH,* No. 61, January–March 1967, especially pp. 89–91.

2. This incident and also those that follow in the text are recounted in different variations by Gringauz, "Khurbn kovno" and Jacob Goldberg, "Bletlekh fun kovner eltestnrat," both in *Fun letstn khurbn,* No. 7, May 1948; Garfunkel, *Kovno hayehudit behurbana;*

Gar, *Umkum fun der yidisher kovne.*

3. Garfunkel, *Kovno,* pp. 74–79. See also Braun and Levin, *Toledoteha shel mahteret,* pp. 45–48.

4. See David Daube, *Collaboration With Tyranny in Rabbinic Law* (London, 1965), a brilliant and elegant elucidation of this question. I have very roughly summarized a few points of Dr. Daube's learned and sophisticated work.

5. Maimonides, *Mishneh Torah: The Book of Knowledge,* trans. Moses Hyamson (Jerusalem, 1965), Chapter 5, Precepts, p. 40b.

6. Dworzecki, *Yerushelayim delite in kamf un umkum,* p. 294.

7. Cf. Balberyszski, *Shtarker fun ayzn,* pp. 207–208;

Dworzecki, *Yerushelayim delite*, pp. 53–55.

8. For a contemporary statistical record, see Kruk, *Togbukh fun vilner geto*, pp. 258–
261.

9. Very little has been written on the distribution of yellow permits. Unfortunately the
entries in Kruk's diary from
October 2 through December
21, 1941, consisting of some
100 manuscript pages, are
missing. Kalmanovich made no
entries during this period. Mr.
Shlomo Kovarsky, a survivor
of the Vilna ghetto and an active member of its resistance
movement, provided some information that helped me reconstruct the procedure. See
also Dworzecki, *Yerushelayim
delite*, p. 102; Balberyszski,
Shtarker fun ayzn.

10. Dworzecki, *Yerushe-
layim delite*, pp. 108–109.

11. Dworzecki, p. 308.
Dworzecki presents the Gens
text as if it were verbatim,
though it is clearly a reconstruction from memory. No
such talk by Gens is mentioned
by either Kruk or Kalmanovich, nor do they refer to that
specific occasion mentioned by
Dworzecki. Kalmanovich, in
his diary entry of October 25,
1941, cites a talk by Gens in a
similar vein. Justifying himself
and the Vilna ghetto police for
carrying out an Aktion in a
nearby town, Gens said: "To
be sure, our hands are stained

with the blood of our brethren,
but we had to take upon ourselves this dreadful task. We
are clean before the bar of history."

12. S. Glube, "Di din-toyre,"
Fun letstn khurbn 6 (August
1947):44–47.

13. Dąbrowska and Dobro-
szycki, "Biuletyn z 20 grudnia
1941 (sobota)," *Kronika getta
łódzkiego*, pp. 323–329.

14. J. Nirenberg, in *Jewish
Labor Bund, In di yorn fun
yidishn khurbn*, pp. 253–257.

15. Dąbrowska and Dobro-
szycki, "Biuletyn Nr. 7, za okres
od 14 do 31 stycznia 1942,"
Kronika, p. 398. Italics in original.

16. Tabaksblatt, *Khurbn
lodzh,* p. 103.

17. Dąbrowska and Dobro-
szycki, *Kronika,* p. 440. Italics
in original.

18. Quoted in Trunk, *Lo-
dzher geto*, pp. 258–259.

19. Trunk, *Lodzher geto,*
pp. 260–261.

20. Dąbrowska and Dobro-
szycki, "Biuletyn Nr. 9: za mi-
esiąc luty 1942," *Kronika*, pp.
402–403; Barbara Beatus, "O
genezie rozwoju i działalności
Lewicy Związkowej w getcie
łódzkim," *BŻIH* 54 (April–
June 1965):49.

21. Nirenberg, in *Jewish
Labor Bund, In di yorn fun
yidishn umkum*, pp. 260–262;
Tabaksblatt, *Khurbn lodzh,*
pp. 103–104.

22. Y-A, Mordecai Gold-

stein, oral interview, transcript
(7 pp.). Cf. also Nirenberg, in
Jewish Labor Bund, *In di yorn
fun yidishn khurbn.*

23. A lengthy journalistic
contemporary account of these
September deportations is Y-A,
Joseph Zelkowicz, "In yene
koshmarne teg," 74-page typescript. Extracts in English
in Dawidowicz, *Holocaust
Reader.*

24. Jonas Turkow, *Azoy iz
es geven,* p. 257.

25. Y-A, "Powstanie i rozwój Ż.O.B.," report written in
Warsaw, March 1944, and
sent through underground
channels to London, May
1944. Its author, or major
author, is Yitzhak Zuckerman
(orig. Cukierman), a member
of the high command of *Żydowska Organizacja Bojowa—
ŻOB.* For an English translation, see Dawidowicz, *Holocaust Reader.* This conference
with the couriers from Vilna
and Bialystok is mentioned also
by one of the surviving couriers, Chayke Grossman, in her
memoirs, *Anshe hamahteret.*
Mordecai Tenenbaum, who
came to Warsaw in January
1942 and remained there until
October, in his letter to his
comrades in Palestine, written in Bialystok, April 1943
(*Dappim min hadleka,* pp.
127–128), refers to a meeting
in April. What appears to have
remained in his memory was
a combination of the March

meeting and one held July 22,
1942.

26. Three reports of that
March 1942 conference exist.
One is Zuckerman's "Pow-
stanie i rozwój Ż.O.B," cited
above. The second is Hersh
Berlinski's memoirs, published
in *Dray,* pp. 154–187, written
late 1943 into 1944. Discrep-
ancies exist between both
texts as to dates, persons involved, and minor matters. A
third report by Elihu Gutkow-
ski is very brief and in part in-
decipherable. The original is
in the archives of kibbutz Lohamei hagetaot.

27. It is extremely difficult
to reconstruct the views of
Mauricy Orzech, the Bund's
senior representative, since
they have come down to us
only in the reports of his political opponents—Zuckerman,
Berlinski, Tenenbaum, Grossman. See also Neustadt,
*Khurbn un oyfshtand fun di
yidn in varshe,* pp. 132–133,
and Cukierman [Zuckerman],
"Powstanie żydowskie," *Nasze
Słowo* 3 (April 19, 1948):5-
10.

28. According to Zucker-
man, the Anti-Fascist Bloc was
formed at the initiative of the
Left Labor Zionists. Ber Mark,
Blfg 4 (January 1941):64, attributes its founding to the
PPR.

29. JLB-A, Henoch Rus
record book, "Protocol No. 1,

January 8, 1942; Protocol No. 9, April 12, 1942."

30. Y-A, Wasser Collection, 60.7. The issue is dated 1942 and numbered "1." The latest date mentioned in the text is March 27, 1942.

31. N. Blumenthal, *Teudot migeto lublin*, passim; T. Brustin-Bernstein, Ida Rappaport-Glickstein, and Hertz Goldberg, in Litvin and Lerman, *Dos bukh fun lublin*, pp. 363–364, 396, and 484–485, respectively.

32. Rubinsztajnowa, "Pamiętnik ze Lwowa," *BŻIH*, No. 61, January–March 1967; Philip Friedman, "Hurban yehude lvov bitkufat 1941–1944," in N. M. Gelber, ed., *Lvov: Entziklopedya shel galuyot* (Jerusalem, 1956), passim.

33. David Liwer, "Khurbn Bendin," in Stein, ed., *Pinkes Bendin*, pp. 188–189; Trunk, *Judenrat*, pp. 422–423, 425–426. A widely used source for Merin speeches and conversations is Pawel Wiederman, *Plowa Bestia* (Munich, 1948). Employed in the Judenrat, Wiederman was a keen observer. His memoirs, however, record alleged conversations verbatim at which he was not present, and whose contents he could not possibly have known. At best his evidence is hearsay; it is probably highly colored.

34. Cf. Abraham Lewin, "Funem geto-togbukh," *Blfg*

5 (October–December 1952): 22–68.

35. The text of Höfle's order to the Warsaw Judenrat is published in Berenstein, Eisenbach, and Rutkowski, eds., *Eksterminacja Żydów*, pp. 300–302; an English translation in Dawidowicz, *Holocaust Reader*.

36. Joseph Kermish, "Introduction," in Adam Czerniaków, *Yoman geto varsha*, p. xix.

37. Suicide under such circumstances occurred elsewhere. Cf. Jacob Frum, "Lomzher geto un ir sof," in Sabotka, ed., *Lomzhe: Ir oyfkum un untergang*, pp. 286–289.

38. This account of the meeting of July 22, 1942, and of subsequent underground activities is based on a variety of reports, which, though somewhat inconsistent and contradictory, furnish an outline of the events. The sources are "Powstanie i rozwój Ż.O.B." (see note 25); Hersh Berlinski, memoirs in *Dray*, pp. 154–187; A. Berman, "O ruchu oporu w getcie warszawskim (Refleksje)," *BŻIH* 29 (January–March 1957):40–57; Y-A, report by Leon Feiner (Berezowski), August 31, 1942, to Artur Zygelboym, Bundist representative in the Polish National Council in London; Goldstein, *Finf yor in varshever geto*, pp. 245–250.

39. Berlinski, in *Dray*, pp. 159–160.

40. Much of this account of the deportation from Warsaw is based on an underground report sent by the *Żydowski Komitet Narodowy* from the Warsaw ghetto, November 15, 1942, to Jewish organizations in Jerusalem, London, and New York. Many official documents were appended. An English translation was issued in mimeographed form by the World Jewish Congress, *Extermination of Polish Jewry: Reports Based on Official Documents*. A Yiddish translation of most of the document is in Neustadt, *Khurbn un oyfshtand fun di yidn in varshe*, pp. 78–96. A compelling description of the deportations is also in Turkow, *Azoy iz es geven*, pp. 282–394.

41. Donat, *The Holocaust Kingdom*, pp. 80–81.

42. In *Eichmann in Jerusalem*, Arendt writes: ". . . if the Jewish people had really been unorganized and leaderless, there would have been chaos and plenty of misery, but the total number of victims would hardly have been between four and a half and six million people" (p. 125). This extraordinary argument on behalf of chaos derives from total ignorance of the historical evidence. The Germans managed with amazing facility to deport over a quarter of a million Jews from the Warsaw ghetto at this time precisely because the Jews of Warsaw were "unorganized and leaderless."

43. The small body of scientific literature on human response to disaster sheds light on Jewish behavior during the deportations. Robert Jay Lifton, *Death in Life: Survivors of Hiroshima* (New York, 1967), is suggestive, especially for his concept of "psychic closing off." Other works I have found instructive include Harold Basowitz et al., *Anxiety and Stress: An Interdisciplinary Study of a Life Situation* (New York, 1955); Herman Feifel, ed., *The Meaning of Death* (New York, 1965); William H. Form and Charles P. Loomis, "The Persistence and Emergence of Social Cultural Systems in Disasters," *American Sociological Review* 21 (April 1956):180–185; George H. Grosser et al., eds., *The Threat of Impending Disaster: Contribution to the Psychology of Stress* (Cambridge, Mass., 1964); Bradford B. Hudson, "Anxiety in Response to the Unfamiliar," *Journal of Social Issues* 10 (1954):53–60; F. P. Kilpatrick, "Problems of Perception in Extreme Situations," *Human Organization* 16 (1957):20–22; Henry Krystal, ed., *Massive Psychic Trauma* (New York, 1968); Eugene E. Levitt, *The Psychology of*

Anxiety (New York, 1967); Richard S. Lazarus, *Psychological Stress and the Coping Process* (New York, 1966); Joost A. M. Meerloo, *Patterns of Panic* (New York, 1950); New York Academy of Medicine, *Panic and Morale: Conference Transactions* (New York, 1958); Neil J. Smelser, *Theory of Collective Behavior* (New York, 1965); Martha Wolfenstein, *Disaster: A Psychological Essay* (Glencoe, Ill., 1957).

44. Turkow, *Azoy iz es geven*, pp. 298–302.

45. [Yehoshua Perle], "Khurbn varshe," *Blfg* 4 (July–September 1951): 119–121.

46. This only surviving fragment of Remba's memoirs is recorded by Ringelblum, *Ksovim fun geto*, 2:213–214.

47. Seidman, *Togbukh fun varshever geto*, p. 77. Such attitudes and incidents were recorded all over Eastern Europe. See especially *Zeszyty oświęcimskie, II: Rękopisy członków sonderkommando* (1971), pp. 108–115; a description by a Jew who worked in an Auschwitz *Sonderkommando*. He mentions that pious Jews from Poland and Hungary drank toasts with brandy brought specially for the occasion, danced and sang before entering the gas chambers, because they were going to meet the Messiah.

48. Goldstein, *The Stars Bear Witness*, pp. 117–118. No source indicates when Friedrich set out. My reconstruction conforms with the surmises of Vladka Meed and Chana Fryshdorf, survivors of the Bundist underground with whom I talked.

49. Abraham Lewin, "Togbukh fun varshever geto," *Blfg* 7 (April 1954):76.

50. [Author unknown], "Struktura demograficzna ludności żydowskiej pozostałej w Warszawie," *BŻIH* 37 (January–March 1961): 98–105.

51. JLB-A, *Oyf der vakh*, September 20, 1942. Friedrich's report was subsequently published in *Undzer tsayt*, September 1952, pp. 32–35.

15. "FOR YOUR FREEDOM AND OURS"

1. Dawidsohn-Draengerowa, *Pamiętnik Justyny*, pp. 86–87. Excerpts in an English translation in Dawidowicz, *Holocaust Reader*. For an account of Jews in Cracow during the German occupation, see Dora Agatshtein Dormond, in Bauminger et al., *Sefer Kroke*, pp. 389–401.

2. Tenenbaum - Tamaroff, *Dappim min hadleka*, p. 91.

3. Ringelblum, *Ksovim fun geto*, 2:147–149.

4. Dawidsohn-Draengerowa, *Pamiętnik Justyny*, p. 101.

5. Tzippora Birman's letter, "Appendix One," to Bronia Klibanski, "The Underground Archives of the Bialystok Ghetto Founded by Mersik and Tenenbaum," *YVS*, 2:322–324.

6. Y-A, Sutzkever-Kaczerginsky Collection, "Lomir zikh nisht lozn firn vi shof tsu der shkhitel" (5 pp. typescript), dated "Vilna, in the ghetto, 1/1/1942." An English translation in Dawidowicz, *Holocaust Reader*. Cf. Abba Kovner, "Di letste oyfn moyer," *Di goldene keyt*, Vol. 46, 1963.

7. Y-A, Sutzkever-Kaczerginsky Collection, Nisl Reznik, "Geshikhte fun F.P.O.," March 12, 1944 (typescript, 11 pp.).

8. The only source for this discussion is Berlinski's memoirs, in *Dray*, pp. 169–171.

9. For more on the Polish government-in-exile and its origins, see Karski, *Story of a Secret State*, especially pp. 124–134.

10. Yitzhak Zuckerman, in a 5-page typed Yiddish letter, December 31, 1972, in response to a series of questions I put to him about the organization of, and political relaships within, ŻOB; later cited as Zuckerman, "Tshuves."

11. Edelman, *The Ghetto Fights*, p. 28. This memoir is, on the whole, unreliable for dates. Nevertheless, Zuckerman ("Tshuves") also puts the date of the establishment of the ŻKK at the end of October 1942.

12. Y-A, Report B, "Sprawozdanie za czas od 1 Lipca 1943r. Do 15 list. 1943r," Warsaw, November 15, 1943, from Berezowski [Leon Feiner], for the Central Committee of the Bund in Poland, to Dr. Emanuel Scherer, its representative in London. Dr. Feiner cites a section of the ŻKK bylaws that does not appear in the version that has survived (see note 14). In his report, which included an explanation of the function of the ŻKK, Feiner wrote: "'Political issues,' so states Paragraph 2 of the Coordinating Commission's bylaws, 'being settled independently by each of the coordinating parties in accordance with their ideology, are excluded from coordination.'" It is possible that this paragraph was introduced in a revised ŻKK statute about July 1943.

13. Not all reports mention the participation of the PPR. Two explanations are possible. (1) The ŻKK leaders may have been reluctant to include the PPR in reports that went to or via the Home Army and the Polish government-in-exile, both of which regarded the PPR—quite correctly—as an agent of the Soviet Union and disloyal to them. (2) By

late 1943, when the Bund and the ŻKN were sending reports abroad, the PPR no longer played any role in the underground remnant Jewish community.

14. The original text from the Central Archives of the Polish Home Ministry is published as "Aneks 2" to Bernard Mark, "Statut Żydowskiej Organizacji Bojowej," *BŻIH* 39 (July–September 1961):59–60. A full English translation in Dawidowicz, *Holocaust Reader*.

15. Karski, *Story of a Secret State*, pp. 328–329.

16. Michel, *The Shadow War*, pp. 52 ff. Chapters dealing with the military and political organization of West European resistance, especially French resistance, appear reliable. The section on Jewish resistance, however, betrays ignorance of a high order. The material on Polish resistance is sketchy and imprecise.

17. The only source regarding the Delegatura's demand for a loyalty oath is Berlinski. As for the date of the arms delivery, most sources indicate late December, but according to the evidence of Henryk Wolinski's memorandum (see note 18), those ten pieces must have been delivered by December 3, 1942.

18. The original text from the Central Archives of the Polish Home Ministry is pub-

lished as "Aneks I" to Bernard Mark, "Statut Żydowskiej Organizacji Bojowej," *BŻIH* 39 (July–September 1961):58–59. A full English translation in Dawidowicz, *Holocaust Reader*.

19. This text is the version received in London, January 7, 1943, and published by Adam Ciołkosz, "Bróń dla getta warszawy," *Zeszyty Historyczne Instytut Literacki* (Paris, 1969), p. 22. A variant text, "Too late Jews of various Communist groupings" etc., appeared in a Yiddish translation in Ber Mark, *Dokumentn un materyaln vegn oyfshtand in varshever geto* (1953). Mark used a copy of the document as transmitted, Ciołkosz a document as received. Whether the discrepancy is based on Mark's honest rendering of the text or whether it is a political falsification, I cannot judge. Neither version establishes General Rowecki as a friend of the Jews.

20. Edelman, *The Ghetto Fights*, p. 31; Y. Zuckerman, "Di yidishe kamforganizatsye un der poylisher untergrunt," *Payn un gvure* (New York, 1959), p. 32; an English version of Zuckerman's letter to the commander-in-chief of the Home Army, November 26, 1943, requesting aid for ŻOB and recapitulating what aid had been given, appears in *Extermination and Resistance*,

pp. 14–19. See also Y. Zucker-man, "Twenty-Five Years After the Warsaw Ghetto Revolt," in Conference on Manifestations of Jewish Resistance, *Jewish Resistance*, p. 30.

21. The best account of the perils of buying and smuggling arms is Meed, *On Both Sides of the Wall*. See also Klin, *Mitn malekh-hamoves untern orem*.

22. For a somewhat rhetorical presentation of these dilemmas, see Yitzhak Zuckerman (Cukierman), "Powstanie żydowskie," *Nasze Słowo* 3 (April 19, 1948):6.

23. Trunk, *Lodzher Geto*, pp. 282–308, 327–334, 464–471; Jacob Nirenberg, in Jewish Labor Bund, *In di yorn fun yidishn khurbn*, pp. 281–294.

24. The fairly rich Yiddish and Hebrew literature on Jews among the Soviet partisans deals extensively with the hazards and hardships they encountered and with the anti-Semitism that poisoned most relations. The Russians eventually broke up all the Jewish partisan bands and dispersed their members in non-Jewish groups. The Jewish partisans were beyond the reach of Jewish communal policy as shaped in the ghettos and were, for the most part, prevented by their Soviet superiors from using the partisan organization as an instrument of Jewish vengeance.

25. Cf. Neustadt, *Khurbn un oyfshtand fun di yidn in*

varshe, pp. 148–149, 423–425, 485–487, 491–494; Aaron Nirenstein, "Vidershtand fun yidn in kroke unter der hitleristisher okupatsye," *Blfg* 5 (January–June 1952):226–263.

26. Eliezer Lidowski, "Vidershtand-organizatsye," in *Baranovitsh: sefer zikaron*, cols. 475–479.

27. Samuel Gringauz, "Khurbn kovne," *Fun letstn khurbn* 8 (June 1948):27–38; Braun and Levin, *Toledoteha shel mahteret*, pp. 73–74, 129–248; Sarah Neshomit, "Beginnings of the Partisan Movement in the Kaunas Ghetto," *Extermination and Resistance*, pp. 129–139; Rahi Ben-Eliezer, "Kamfs-bavegung in kovner geto," *Fun letstn khurbn* 10 (December 1948):3–15.

28. Garfunkel, *Kovno hayehudit behurbana*, pp. 194–195. The author reconstructed the dialogue between Elkes and Goecke from the report of a communal leader who was present at the confrontation.

29. L. Brenner, *Vidershtand un umkum in tshenstokhover geto*, p. 116.

30. Trunk, *Judenrat*, pp. 457–458.

31. Niusia Dlugi, "Der Vitenberg-tog in vilner geto," *Yibl* 30 (1947):192–193.

32. Kruk, *Togbukh fun vilner geto*, pp. 563–564, 569–570, 573–574.

33. Kruk, *Togbukh*, pp.

582–586; Kalmanovich, "A togbukh in vilner geto," *Yibl* 35 (1951):56. See also Reznik, "Geshikhte fun F.P.O."; Niusia Dlugi, *Yibl* 30 (1947): 194–195.

34. Reznik, "Geshikhte fun F.P.O."; S. Kaczerginski, [7th notebook of wartime diary, Yiddish, entry dated July 27, 1943], handwritten ms., Y-A, Sutzkever-Kaczerginski Collection; Brayne As, Shimon Palewski, Zenia Berkon, "Der Vitenberg-tog in vilner geto," *Yibl* 30 (1947):200–213. All accounts differ in many details.

35. Reznik, "Geshikhte fun F.P.O.," pp. 9–11.

36. Tenenbaum's diary, *Dappin min hadleka,* reveals the close relations between Barash and Tenenbaum and their mutual regard.

37. Tenenbaum, *Dappin min hadleka,* pp. 67–68, 81.

38. Minutes of this meeting, found after the war, were first published in Kaczerginski, *Khurbn vilne,* pp. 315–322; an English translation appeared in *Commentary* 8 (February 1949):105–109. A somewhat altered translation in Dawidowicz, *Holocaust Reader.*

39. For more on the resistance in the Bialystok ghetto, see Reisner, *Der umkum fun bialystoker yidntum,* pp. 162–169; Ber Mark, *Der oyfshtand in bialystoker geto,* passim; Chayke Grossman, *Anshe hamahteret;* Kantorowicz, *Di yidishe vidershtand-bavegung in poyln,* pp. 284–295.

40. Cf. Joshua Vermut, "Mayne iberlebungen," in Meltzer, ed., *Sefer Horodenka,* pp. 296–297.

41. A. Zigelboym-Savitski, "Der oyfshtand in geto," in Shtrachman, ed., *Sefer Lutsk,* pp. 517–518.

42. Leyb Koniuchowsky, "Der umkum fun martsinkantser yidn," *Yibl* 37 (1953): 222–224.

43. Mendel Mann, "Der oyfshtand in tutshiner geto," *Fun letstn khurbn* 9 (September 1948):59–66.

44. Cf. Donat, *The Holocaust Kingdom,* pp. 111–112.

45. Original Yiddish text published in Mark, ed., *Oyfshtand in varshever geto: naye dergentste oyflage un dokumentn-zamlung* (1963), pp. 197–200. An English translation in Dawidowicz, *Holocaust Reader.*

46. "Oyfrufn," *Blfg* 4 (January–March 1951):83–84.

47. Hersh Berlinski, "Zikhroynes," *Dray,* pp. 188–191.

48. Text in Bernard Mark, "Aneks 3: Statut Żydowskiej Organizacji Bojowej," *BŻIH* 39 (July–September 1961): 61–62. An English translation in Dawidowicz, *Holocaust Reader.*

49. Chana Krystal-Fryshdorf, "Iberlebungen beysn oyfshtand," *Undzer tsayt,* April–May 1949, pp. 17–18; Y.

Zuckerman, "Powstanie i rozwój Ż.O.B."

50. Chana Krystal-Fryshdorf, "Iberlebungen in getooyfshtand," *Undzer tsayt*, April–May 1958, pp. 22–23.

51. Y-A, coded radio message, No. 15, sent from Warsaw January 21, 1943. The message addressed to Stephen Wise of the American Jewish Congress, Nahum Goldmann of the World Jewish Congress, and George Backer, then of the AJDC.

52. Y-A, coded radio message No. 59, sent from Warsaw February 7, 1943, by Leon Feiner (Berezowski) and Mauricy Orzech (Janczyn). The cryptic remarks about the January armed defense were not understood. On February 10, Zygelboym, via radio, asked for further information, which Feiner provided in a later radio message.

53. Zuckerman, "Powstanie i rozwój Ż.O.B."

54. The leaflet issued to counteract Többens' appeals was printed on a mimeograph machine brought at great risk from the brush works area of the ghetto. For an account of that transfer and the attempt to return it, see Krystal-Fryshdorf, *Undzer tsayt*, April–May 1949, pp. 19–20.

55. Zuckerman, "Powstanie i rozwój Ż.O.B."

56. Y-A, coded radiograms, No. 67, sent from Warsaw April 6, 1943, by ŻKN to the Zionist Executive in London and Jerusalem; No. 67a, sent by David Guzik of the JDC in Warsaw to JDC in New York; No. 67D, to Dr. Schwartzbart in London, Dr. Silberstein of Vaad Hatzala in Geneva, and M. Neustadt in Tel Aviv, signed by Zionist party leaders in Warsaw; No. 70, submitted April 13, 1943, by Feiner and dispatched April 17, 1943, to Zygelboym in London.

57. The following account of the defense of the Warsaw ghetto is based on Zuckerman, "Powstanie i rozwój Ż.O.B.," ŻOB/ŻKK daily communiqués and situation reports, in "Getto w Walce," *Przełom*, No. 17, April 19, 1948 (excerpts in English in Philip Friedman, *Martyrs and Fighters*, New York, 1954); Y-A, coded radio messages sent by ŻKK to London; reports of individual participants—Sholem Grajek, Simha Rathauser, Toviah Borzykowski—in Neustadt, *Khurbn un oyfshtand*, pp. 264–292.

58. Zivia Lubetkin Zuckerman, testimony at the Eichmann trial, quoted in Gideon Hausner, *Justice in Jerusalem* (New York, 1966), p. 223.

59. Y-A, Abraham Hersh, eyewitness report.

60. The text of the appeal was written by Samsonowicz, a Bund activist on the "Aryan" side, on behalf of ŻKK and

ŻOB. An English translation in Dawidowicz, *Holocaust Reader*. Cf. Meed, *On Both Sides of the Wall*, p. 183.

61. Cf. Stefan Krakowski, "Stosunek sił w powstaniu w getcie warszawskim," *BŻIH* 62 (1967):23–41. Stroop's report very likely understated, for professional and ideological reasons, the number of troops involved.

62. Ziviah Lubetkin, "The Last Days of the Warsaw Ghetto," *Commentary* 3 (May 1947):401–411.

63. Y-A, Report A, June 22, 1943, and Report B, November 15, 1943, sent by Leon Feiner, on behalf of the Central Committee of the Bund in Poland to the Bund representative in the Polish parliament-in-exile in London. Original in Polish;

a Yiddish translation of most of the document in: Jewish Labor Bund, *In di yorn fun yidishn khurbn*. Also, Y-A, "Sprawozdanie z działalności Rady Pomocy Żydom," October 23, 1943. An English translation is in Władysław Bartoszewski and Sofia Lewin, eds., *Righteous Among the Nations: How Poles Helped the Jews, 1939–1945* (London, 1969), a complacently tendentious and self-serving work.

64. Y-A, report, in the original Polish, of the ŻKN, sent from Warsaw, May 24, 1944, signed by Dr. A. Berman [Borowski], Yitzhak Zuckerman [Antek], and three others. An English translation in World Jewish Congress, *Extermination of Polish Jewry: Reports Based on Official Documents*.

16. JEWISH BEHAVIOR IN CRISIS AND EXTREMITY

1. Cf. Rabbi Yehoshua Moshe Aaronson, "The Story of the House of Bondage in Konin," in *Extermination and Resistance*, pp. 110–116.

2. Cf. Jacob Katz, *Exclusiveness and Tolerance: Studies in Jewish-Gentile Relations in Medieval and Modern Times* (Oxford, 1961), especially pp. 86–87; Rabbi Nathan Hanover, *Abyss of Despair* (*Yeven Metzulah*), trans. Abraham J. Mesch (New York, 1950).

Raul Hilberg, whose knowl-

edge of Jewish history is not equal to his rashness in generalizing about it, has flawed his otherwise valuable work with uninformed comments and distorted conclusions about Jewish behavior, especially in pp. 662–669, but also elsewhere (e.g., pp. 145–146, 154–156, 206–208, 315–322, 328–329). His deficiency in Jewish history is especially evident on pp. 145–146, his description of what he presumes were the kehilla's functions.

3. See Robert Stover, "Responsibility for the Cold War —A Case Study in Historical Responsibility," *History and Theory* 11 (1972):145–178. This excellent article clarifies and isolates the elements of historical responsibility.

4. Bruce Aune, "Can," *The Encyclopedia of Philosophy*, quoted in Stover, "Responsibility for the Cold War," p. 153.

5. Abba Kovner, "The Miracle Born of Despair," in Hashomer Hatzair, *The Massacre of European Jewry*, p. 225; Z. Levinbook, "Umkum fun baranovitsher yidntum," in *Baranovitsh: sefer zikaron*, p. 571; Alexander Dallin, *German Rule in Russia*, p. 427.

6. For more on collaboration, see Robert Aron, *The Vichy Regime 1940–44* (Boston, 1969), passim; Stanley Hoffmann, "Collaborationism in France during World War II," *The Journal of Modern History* 40 (September 1968): 375–395; John A. Armstrong, "Collaborationism in World War II: The Integral Nationalist Variant in Eastern Eurrope," *The Journal of Modern History* 40 (September 1968): 396–410.

7. The most egregious example is Hannah Arendt, *Eichmann in Jerusalem*, in which she flatly states: "Wherever Jews lived, there were recognized Jewish leaders, and this leadership, almost without exception, cooperated in one way or another, for one reason or another [*sic*], with the Nazis" (p. 125). Miss Arendt's penchant for grand philosophic schemata flourishes on her disdain for historical evidence. One would have expected, nevertheless, that the expert on totalitarian terror in its philosophic aspect would have recognized the phenomenon of totalitarian terror in its historical reality.

8. Cf. Louis de Jong, "The Netherlands and Auschwitz," *YVS* 7:39–55. Jong's conclusive findings about disbelief in and rejection of the information of the death camps and the failure of the Dutch underground to inform the Jewish Council has nevertheless not halted him and others from accusing the leaders of the Jewish Council of "collaboration" with the Germans.

9. Leo Baeck, "A People Stands Before Its God," in Boehm, ed., *We Survived*, p. 293.

10. Jan Yoors, *Crossing* (New York, 1971), passim.

11. Cf. Z. Kalmanovich, "A Diary of the Nazi Ghetto in Vilna," *YiAn* 8:33.

12. Benedikt Kautsky, *Teufel und Verdammte* (Zurich, 1946), pp. 292–294.

Sources

It would be impracticable and immodest to attempt to present a full bibliography of the Final Solution and the Holocaust. The general reader interested in pursuing these subjects can obtain useful bibliographies from the Jewish Book Council of America (15 East 26th Street, New York, N.Y. 10010) or from the Anti-Defamation League of B'nai B'rith (315 Lexington Avenue, New York, N.Y. 10016). A magisterial bibliographical work is the Bibliographical Series issued jointly by the Yad Washem Martyrs' and Heroes' Memorial Authority in Jerusalem and the YIVO Institute for Jewish Research in New York. Since the publication in 1960 of the first volume, *Guide to Jewish History Under Nazi Impact,* edited by Jacob Robinson and Philip Friedman, eleven more volumes have appeared: four devoted to writings in Yiddish, five to Hebrew works, and one to the Hungarian Jewish catastrophe. The latest volume (1973) is *The Holocaust and After: Sources and Literature in English,* edited by Jacob Robinson with the assistance of Mrs. Philip Friedman.

The German documents captured by the Allied armies at the war's end have provided an incomparable historical record, which, with regard to volume and accessibility, has been unique in the annals of scholarship. The very volume of the documents has posed unprecedented problems, for no individual can in his lifetime possibly master these sources. The National Archives and the American Historical Association jointly have published sixty-seven volumes of *Guides to German Records Microfilmed at Alexandria, Va.* For my work I have limited myself mainly to published German documents. The most important series of these publications are:

International Military Tribunal. *Trial of the Major War Criminals*

Before the International Military Tribunal: Official Text. 42 vols. Nuremberg, 1947–1949. (Blue series)

Nuernberg Military Tribunals. *Trials of War Criminals Before the Nuernberg Military Tribunals Under Control Council Law No. 10.* 15 vols. Washington, D.C., 1949–1953. (Green series)

Office of the United States Chief of Counsel for the Prosecution of Axis Criminality. *Nazi Conspiracy and Aggression.* 11 vols. Washington, D.C., 1946–48. (Red series)

United Nations War Crimes Commission. *Law Reports of Trials of War Criminals.* 15 vols. London, 1947–1949.

Documents on German Foreign Policy 1918–1945. Series C, 1933–1937, 5 vols.; Series D, 1937–1941, 13 vols. Washington, D.C. 1957–1967.

Blumenthal, Nachman, Borwicz, Michal, Friedman, Filip, eds. *Dokumenty i Materiały.* 3 vols. Lodz, 1946.

In writing about the Holocaust, I had access to several archival collections; the most important were at the YIVO Institute for Jewish Research, New York. Among these were the Sutzkever-Kaczerginski Collection on the Vilna ghetto; the Wasser Collection, largely, but not exclusively, on the Warsaw ghetto; and the Zonabend Collection on the Lodz ghetto. The Archives of the American Jewish Joint Distribution Committee and the Franz Kursky Archives of the Jewish Labor Bund provided me with extremely valuable documentation. For more circumscribed topics I used unpublished materials at the Zionist Archives, the Leo Baeck Institute, and the Records Center of the American Jewish Committee, all in New York.

The spate of *yizkor* books, unique commemorative collections in Yiddish and/or Hebrew devoted to individual communities, renders the researcher's task even more laborious in separating the documentary wheat from the epitaphic chaff. The flow of memoirs, too, forces the researcher into a rigorous process of selection. I have limited the following list of sources to those published works that I regard as most useful. In the interest of brevity I have listed only a few basic sources for both appendices. A complete listing of the mass of articles and studies for each country would be disproportionate to the text and too specialized for most readers.

I have excluded all periodical and serial articles from the list of sources, though many appear in the notes. Several periodicals and serials, frequently cited in the notes, should be mentioned here because they are fundamental documentary sources.

American Jewish Year Book, published by the American Jewish Committee, 1899–date.

Biuletyn Żydowskiego Instytutu Historycznego, published

quarterly by the Żydowski Instytut Historyczny w Polsce, Warsaw, 1950–date.

Bleter far geshikhte, published quarterly, now irregularly, by the Żydowski Instytut Historyczny w Polsce, Warsaw, 1948–date.

Fun letstn khurbn, published by the Central Historical Commission of the Central Committee of the Liberated Jews in the U.S. Zone, Munich, 10 issues, 1946–1948.

Vierteljahrshefte für Zeitgeschichte, published quarterly by the Institut für Zeitgeschichte, Munich, 1953–date.

Yad Washem Studies on the European Jewish Catastrophe and Resistance, published irregularly by the Yad Washem Remembrance Authority, Jerusalem, 1957–date.

Year Book, published by the Leo Baeck Institute, London, Jerusalem, and New York, 1956–date.

YIVO Annual of Jewish Social Science, published by the YIVO Institute for Jewish Research, New York, 1946–date.

Yivo-bleter, published irregularly by the YIVO Institute for Jewish Research, New York, 1931–date.

PART I: THE FINAL SOLUTION

Abel, Theodore. *The Nazi Movement: Why Hitler Came to Power*. New York, 1966.

Allen, William Sheridan. *The Nazi Seizure of Power: The Experience of a Single German Town 1930–1935*. Chicago, 1965.

Arendt, Hannah. *Eichmann in Jerusalem: A Report on the Banality of Evil*. Rev. and enl. ed. New York, 1965.

———. *The Origins of Totalitarianism*. New York, 1958.

Aronson, Shlomo. *Reinhard Heydrich und die Frühgeschichte von Gestapo und SD*. Stuttgart, 1971.

Baynes, Norman H., ed. *The Speeches of Adolf Hitler, April 1922–August 1939*. 2 vols. London, 1942.

Beek, Gottfried zur (Ludwig Müller). *Die Geheimnisse der Weisen von Zion*. 5th ed. Berlin, 1920.

Berenstein, T., Eisenbach, A., Rutkowski, A., eds. *Eksterminacja Żydów na Ziemiach Polskich w Okresie Okupacji Hitlerowskiej: Zbiór Dokumentów*. Warsaw, 1957.

Best, Werner. *Die deutsche Polizei*. Darmstadt, 1941.

Bidess, Michael D. *Father of Racist Ideology: The Social and Political Thought of Count Gobineau*. New York, 1970.

———, ed. *Gobineau: Selected Political Writings*. London, 1970.

Blau, Bruno. *Das Ausnahmerecht für die Juden in Deutschland 1933–1945*. 2nd ed. Dusseldorf, 1954.

Boehlich, Walter, ed. *Der Berliner Antisemitismusstreit*. Frankfurt, 1965.

Boelcke, Willi A., ed. *The Secret Conferences of Dr. Goebbels: The Nazi Propaganda War 1939–1943.* New York, 1970.

Bracher, Karl Dietrich. *The German Dictatorship: The Origins, Structure, and Effects of National Socialism.* New York, 1970.

Bracher, Karl Dietrich, Sauer, Wolfgang, and Schulz, Gerhard. *Die nationalsozialistische Machtergreifung.* 2nd ed. Cologne, 1962.

Briffault, Herma, ed. *The Memoirs of Doctor Felix Kersten.* New York, 1947.

Broszat, Martin. *Nationalsozialistische Polenpolitik 1939–1945.* Stuttgart, 1961.

————, ed. *Studien zur Geschichte der Konzentrationslager.* Stuttgart, 1970.

Buchheim, Hans, et al. *Anatomy of the SS State.* New York, 1968. (*Anatomie des SS-Staates.* 2 vols. Olten und Freiburg im Breisgau, 1965.)

Bullock, Alan. *Hitler, A Study in Tyranny.* Rev. ed. New York, 1964.

Cecil, Robert. *The Myth of the Master Race: Alfred Rosenberg and Nazi Ideology.* London, 1972.

Central Commission for Investigation of German Crimes in Poland. *German Crimes in Poland.* 2 vols. Warsaw, 1946–1947.

Churchill, Winston. *The Gathering Storm.* New York, 1948.

Cohen, Elie A. *Human Behavior in the Concentration Camp.* New York, 1953.

Cohn, Norman. *Warrant for Genocide: The Myth of the Jewish World-conspiracy and the Protocols of the Elders of Zion.* New York, 1967.

Council for Protection of Fight and Martyrdom Monuments. *Treblinka.* Warsaw, n.d.

Crankshaw, Edward. *The Gestapo: Instrument of Tyranny.* New York, 1956.

Dahrendorf, Ralf. *Society and Democracy in Germany.* New York, 1967.

Daim, Wilfried. *Der Mann, der Hitler die Ideen gab: Von den religiosen Verirrungen eines Sektierers zum Rassenwahn des Diktators.* Munich, 1958.

Dallin, Alexander. *German Rule in Russia, 1941–1945: A Study of Occupation Policies.* New York, 1957.

Delarue, Jacques. *The Gestapo: A History of Horror.* New York, 1964.

Dicks, Henry V. *Licensed Mass Murder: A Socio-psychological Study of Some SS Killers.* London, 1972.

Dokumente der deutschen Politik und Geschichte. 4 vols. Berlin, n.d.

Domarus, Max, ed. *Hitler: Reden und Proklamationen, 1932–1945.* 2 vols. Würzburg, 1962.

Eisenbach, Artur. *Operation Reinhard: Mass Extermination of the Jewish Population in Poland*. Poznan, 1962.

Epstein, Klaus. *The Genesis of German Conservatism*. Princeton, N.J., 1966.

Fest, Joachim C. *The Face of the Third Reich: Portraits of the Nazi Leadership*. New York, 1970.

Frick, Wilhelm. *Die Nationalsozialisten im Reichstag 1924–1931*. 2nd enl. ed. Munich, 1932.

Frick, Wilhelm, and Gütt, Arthur. *Nordisches Gedankengut im Dritten Reich: Drei Vorträge*. Munich [1936].

Friedländer, Saul. *Kurt Gerstein: The Ambiguity of Good*. New York, 1969.

Fritsch, Theodor. *Handbuch der Judenfrage: Die wichtigsten Tatsachen zur Beurteilung des jüdischen Volkes*. 53rd ed. Leipzig, 1933.

Fromm, Bella. *Blood and Banquets: A Berlin Social Diary*. New York, 1944.

Fryman, Daniel (Class, Heinrich). *Wenn ich der Kaiser wär': Politische Wahrheiten und Notwendigkeiten*. 5th enl. ed. Leipzig, 1914.

Gay, Peter. *Weimar Culture: The Outsider as Insider*. New York, 1968.

Genschel, Helmut. *Die Verdrängung der Juden aus der Wirtschaft im Dritten Reich*. Göttingen, 1966.

Goerlitz, Walter. *History of the German General Staff 1657–1945*. New York, 1953.

Gordon, Harold J., Jr. *Hitler and the Beer Hall Putsch*. Princeton, N.J., 1972.

Görlitz, Walter, ed. *The Memoirs of Field-Marshal Keitel*. New York, 1966.

Graml, Hermann. *Der 9. November 1938: "Reichskristallnacht."* 3rd ed. Bonn, 1955.

Grossman, W. *Die Hölle von Treblinka*. Moscow, 1946.

Halder, Generaloberst (Franz), *Kriegstagebuch 1939–1942*. Edited by Hans-Adolf Jacobsen. Stuttgart, 1962–1964.

Heiber, Helmut, ed. *Reichsführer! . . . : Briefe an und von Himmler*. Stuttgart, 1968.

Heiden, Konrad. *Der Fuehrer: Hitler's Rise to Power*. Boston, 1969.

———. *A History of National Socialism*. New York, 1935.

Henkys, Reinhard. *Die nationalsozialistischen Gewaltverbrechen: Geschichte und Gericht*. Stuttgart, 1964.

Hilberg, Raul. *The Destruction of the European Jews*. Chicago, 1967.

———. *Documents of Destruction: Germany and Jewry 1933–1945*. Chicago, 1971.

Hillgruber, Andreas. *Hitlers Strategie: Politik und Kriegsführung 1940–1941*. Frankfurt, 1965.

Himmler, Heinrich. *Die Schutzstaffel als antibolschewistische Kampforganisation.* Munich, 1936.

Hitler, Adolf. *Mien Kampf.* Translated by Ralph Manheim. Boston, 1943.

Hitler's Secret Book. Introduction by Telford Taylor. New York, 1961.

Hitler's Secret Conversations 1941–1944. Introduction by H. R. Trevor-Roper. New York, 1953.

Hoche, Werner, ed. *Die Gesetzgebung Adolf Hitlers.* 33 vols. Berlin, 1933–1939.

Hoess, Rudolf. *Commandant of Auschwitz: The Autobiography of Rudolf Hoess.* Cleveland and New York, 1960.

Höhne, Heinz. *The Order of the Death's Head: The Story of Hitler's SS.* New York, 1970.

Die Hölle von Maidanek: Bericht der ausserordentlichen polnisch-sowjetischen Kommission zur Untersuchung der von den Deutschen im Vernichtungslager Maidanek in der Stadt Lublin begangenen Verbrechen. Zurich, 1945.

Hull, David Stewart. *Film in the Third Reich: A Study of the German Cinema 1933–1945.* Berkeley, Cal., 1969.

Jäckel, Eberhard. *Hitler's Weltanschauung: A Blueprint for Power.* Middletown, Conn., 1972.

Jacobsen, Hans-Adolf. *Nationalsozialistische Aussenpolitik 1933–1938.* Frankfurt, 1968.

Jenks, William A. *Vienna and the Young Hitler.* New York, 1960.

Kempner, Robert M. W. *Eichmann und Komplizen.* Zurich, 1961.

Kessel, Joseph. *The Man with the Miraculous Hands.* New York, 1961.

Kochan, Lionel. *Pogrom: 10 November 1938.* London, 1957.

Koehl, Robert L. *RKFVD: German Resettlement and Population Policy 1939–1945.* Cambridge, Mass., 1957.

Kogon, Eugen. *The Theory and Practice of Hell: The Concentration Camps and the System Behind Them.* New York [1950].

Kohn, Hans. *The Mind of Germany: The Education of a Nation.* New York, 1960.

Kommission zur Erforschung der Geschichte der Frankfurter Juden. *Dokumente zur Geschichte der Frankfurter Juden 1933–1945.* Frankfurt, 1963.

Kotze, Hildegard von, and Krausnick, Helmut. *Es spricht der Führer.* Gütersloh, 1966.

Kraus, Ota, and Kulka, Erich. *The Death Factory: Documents on Auschwitz.* Oxford and London, 1966.

Lamm, Hans. "Über die innere und äussere Entwicklung des deutschen Judentums im Dritten Reich." Doctoral dissertation. Erlangen, 1951.

Langer, Walter C. *The Mind of Adolf Hitler: The Secret Wartime Report.* New York, 1972.

Laqueur, Walter. *Russia and Germany: A Century of Conflict.* Boston, 1967.

Lebovics, Herman. *Social Conservatism and the Middle Classes in Germany: 1914–1933.* Princeton, N.J., 1969.

Leschnitzer, Adolf. *The Magic Background of Modern Anti-Semitism: An Analysis of the German-Jewish Relationship.* New York, 1956.

Lochner, Louis P., ed. *The Goebbels Diaries 1942–1943.* New York, 1948.

Ludecke, Kurt. *I Knew Hitler: The Story of a Nazi Who Escaped the Blood Purge.* New York, 1937.

McRandle, James H. *The Track of the Wolf: Essays on National Socialism and Its Leader, Adolf Hitler.* Evanston, Ill., 1965.

Manvell, Roger, and Fraenkel, Heinrich. *Himmler.* New York, 1965.

Maser, Werner. *Hitler's Mein Kampf: An Analysis.* London, 1970.

Massing, Paul W. *Rehearsal for Destruction: A Study of Political Anti-Semitism in Imperial Germany.* New York, 1949.

Meinecke, Friedrich. *The German Catastrophe: Reflections and Recollections.* Boston, 1963.

Messerschmidt, Manfred. *Die Wehrmacht im NS-Staat: Zeit der Indoktrination.* Hamburg, 1969.

Mitscherlich, Alexander, and Mielke, Fred. *Doctors of Infamy: The Story of the Nazi Medical Crimes.* New York, 1949.

Mosse, George L. *The Crisis of German Ideology: Intellectual Origins of the Third Reich.* New York, 1964.

Naumann, Bernd. *Auschwitz: A Report on the Proceedings Against Robert Karl Ludwig Mulka and Others Before the Court at Frankfurt.* London, 1966.

Neumann, Franz. *Behemoth: The Structure and Practice of National Socialism 1933–1944.* New York, 1944.

Neusüss-Hunkel, Ermenhild. *Die SS.* Hanover, 1956.

Nicolai, Helmut. *Die rassengesetzliche Staatslehre: Grundzüge einer nationalsozialistischen Rechtsphilosophie.* Munich, 1932.

—————. *Rasse und Recht: Vortag gehalten auf dem deutschen Juristentage des Bundes nationalsozialistischer deutscher Juristen am 2 October 1933 in Leipzig.* Berlin, 1933.

Niewyk, Donald L. *Socialist, Anti-Semite, and Jew: German Social Democracy Confronts the Problem of Anti-Semitism 1918–1933.* Baton Rouge, 1971.

Nolte, Ernst. *The Three Faces of Fascism: Action Française, Italian Fascism, and National Socialism.* New York, 1966.

Norton, Donald Hawley. "Karl Haushofer and His Influence on Nazi Ideology and German Foreign Policy, 1919–1945." Doctoral dissertation. Clark University, 1965.

Olden, Rudolf. *Hitler.* Amsterdam, 1935.

O'Neill, Robert J. *The German Army and the Nazi Party, 1933–1939.* New York, 1966.

Orlow, Dietrich. *A History of the Nazi Party 1919–1933.* Pittsburgh, Pa., 1969.

Pfundter, Hans, ed. *Dr. Wilhelm Frick und sein Ministerium: Aus Anlass des 60. Geburtstage des Reichs- und preussischen Ministers der Innern, Dr. Wilhelm Frick am 12. März 1937.* Berlin, 1937.

Pinson, Koppel S., ed. *Essays on Antisemitism.* 2nd rev. and enl. ed. New York, 1946.

Piotrowski, Stanislaw, ed. *Hans Frank's Diary.* Warsaw, 1961.

Pulzer, Peter G. J. *The Rise of Political Anti-Semitism in Germany and Austria.* New York, 1964.

Rauschning, Hermann. *Hitler Speaks: A Series of Political Conversations with Adolf Hitler on His Real Aims.* London, 1939.

————. *The Revolution of Nihilism: Warning to the West.* New York, 1939.

————. *The Voice of Destruction.* New York, 1940.

Reck-Malleczewen, Friedrich Percyval. *Diary of a Man in Despair.* New York, 1970.

Reichmann, Eva G. *Hostages of Civilisation: The Social Sources of National Socialist Anti-Semitism.* Boston, 1951.

Reitlinger, Gerald. *The Final Solution: The Attempt to Exterminate the Jews of Europe.* 2nd rev. and enl. ed. New York, 1961.

————. *The SS: Alibi of a Nation 1922–1945.* London, 1956.

Reventlow, Ernst. *Judas Kampf und Niederlage in Deutschland: 150 Jahre Judenfrage.* Berlin, 1937.

Ringer, Fritz K. *The Decline of the German Mandarins: The German Academic Community, 1890–1933.* Cambridge, Mass., 1968.

Robertson, E. M. *Hitler's Pre-War Policy and Military Plans 1933–1939.* New York, 1967.

Rogger, Hans, and Weber, Eugen, eds. *The European Right: A Historical Profile.* Berkeley, Cal., 1965.

Rosenberg, Alfred. *Der Zukunftsweg einer deutschen Aussenpolitik.* Munich, 1927.

Schellenberg, Walter. *The Schellenberg Memoirs.* London, 1957.

Schleunes, Karl A. *The Twisted Road to Auschwitz: Nazi Policy Toward German Jews 1933–1939.* Urbana, Ill., 1970.

Schnabel, Reimund. *Macht ohne Moral: Eine Dokumentation über die SS.* Frankfurt, 1957.

Schubert, Günter. *Anfänge nationalsozialistischer Aussenpolitik.* Cologne, 1963.

Seabury, Paul. *The Wilhelmstrasse: A Study of German Diplomats Under the Nazi Regime.* Berkeley and Los Angeles, Cal., 1954.

Smith, Bradley F. *Adolf Hitler: His Family, Childhood, and Youth.* Stanford, Cal., 1967.

————. *Heinrich Himmler: A Nazi in the Making 1900–1926.* Stanford, Cal., 1971.

Sontag, Raymond James, and Beddie, James Stuart. *Nazi-Soviet Relations: 1939–1941.* New York, 1948.

Stein, George H. *The Waffen SS.* Ithaca, N.Y., 1966.

Sterling, Eleanore. *Judenhass: Die Anfänge des politischen Antisemitismus in Deutschland (1815–1850).* Frankfurt, 1969. (Rev. ed. of *Er ist wie du*, Munich, 1956.)

Stern, Fritz. *The Politics of Cultural Despair: A Study in the Rise of the Germanic Ideology.* Berkeley and Los Angeles, Cal., 1961.

Stuckart, Wilhelm, and Globke, Hans. *Kommentare zur deutschen Rassengesetzgebung.* Munich and Berlin, 1936.

Tal, Uriel. *Religious and Anti-religious Roots of Modern Anti-Semitism.* New York, 1971.

Taylor, Telford. *Sword and Swastika: Generals and Nazis in the Third Reich.* New York, 1952.

Trevor-Roper, H. R. *The Last Days of Hitler.* New York, 1947.

————, ed. *Hitler's War Directives 1939–1945.* London, 1964.

Warlimont, Walter. *Inside Hitler's Headquarters 1939–1945.* New York, 1964.

Weinberg, Gerhard L. *The Foreign Policy of Hitler's Germany: Diplomatic Revolution in Europe 1933–36.* Chicago, 1971.

Weinryb, Bernard Dov. *Jewish Emancipation Under Attack: Legal Recession Until the Present War.* New York, 1942.

Weizsäcker, Ernst von. *Memoirs of Ernst von Weizsäcker.* London, 1951.

Wheaton, Eliot Barculo. *The Nazi Revolution 1933–1935: Prelude to Calamity.* New York, 1969.

Wormser-Migot, Olga. *Le Système concentrationnaire Nazi (1933–1945).* Paris, 1968.

PART II: THE HOLOCAUST

Adler, H. G. *The Jews in Germany: From the Enlightenment to National Socialism.* Notre Dame, Ind., 1969.

Adler-Rudel, S. *Ostjuden in Deutschland 1880–1940.* Tübingen, 1959.

Apfelbaum, Emil, ed. *Maladie de famine: recherches cliniques sur la famine exécutées dans le ghetto de Varsovie en 1942.* Warsaw, 1946.

Auerbach, Rachela. *Der yidisher oyfshtand: Varshe 1943.* Warsaw, 1948.

Avtichi, Aryeh, ed. *Rovne: sefer zikaron.* Tel Aviv, 1956.

Bakalchuk-Felin, Melech, ed. *Yizkor-bukh Khelem.* Johannesburg, 1954.

Balberyszski, M. *Shtarker fun ayzn.* Tel Aviv, 1967.

Baler, Bezalel, ed. *Pinkes Kovel.* Buenos Aires, 1951.

Ball-Kaduri, Kurt Jakob. *Das Leben der Juden in Deutschland im Jahre 1933: Ein Zeitbild.* Frankfurt, 1963.

————. *Vor der Katastrophe: Juden in Deutschland.* Tel Aviv, 1967.

Baranovitsh: sefer zikaron. Tel Aviv, 1953.

Bauminger, Aryeh, Bossak, Meir, Gelber, N. M., eds. *Sefer Kroke.* Jerusalem, 1959.

Berg, Mary. *Warsaw Ghetto: A Diary.* New York, 1945.

Bickel, Shlomo, ed. *Pinkes Kolomey: geshikhte, zikhroynes, geshtaltn, khurbn.* New York, 1957.

Blum, Abrasha, ed. *Di parizer komune: zamlbukh dershinen in 1941 in varshever geto.* Warsaw, 1948.

Blumenthal, Nachman, ed. *Aleksander.* Tel Aviv, 1968.

————. *Darko shel yudenrat: teudot migeto byalistok.* Jerusalem, 1962.

————. *Teudot migeto lublin.* Jerusalem, 1967.

Bochner, Mordecai. *Sefer khzhanov: lebn un umkum fun a yidish shtetl.* Munich and Regensburg, 1949.

Borzykowski, Tuvia. *Between Tumbling Walls.* Beit Lohamei Hagetaot, Israel, 1972.

————. *Tsvishn falndike vent.* Warsaw, 1949.

Braun, Zvi A., and Levin, Dov. *Toledoteha shel mahteret: He-Irgun haloham shel yehudei Kovno bemilhamet ha-olam ha-shinaya.* Jerusalem, 1962.

Brenner, L. *Vidershtand un umkum in tshenstokhover geto.* [Warsaw, 1951.]

Buber, Martin. *Die Stunde und die Erkenntnis: Reden und Aufsätze 1933–1935.* Berlin, 1936.

Celemenski, Jacob. *Mitn farshnitenem folk.* New York, 1963.

Colodner, Solomon. *Jewish Education in Germany Under the Nazis.* New York, 1964.

Conference on Manifestations of Jewish Resistance. *Jewish Resistance During the Holocaust: Proceedings.* Jerusalem, 1971.

Czerniaków, Adam. *Yoman geto varsha: 6.9.1939–23.7.1942.* Jerusalem, 1968.

Dąbrowska, Danuta, and Dobroszycki, Lucjan. *Kronika getta łódzkiego.* Vol. 1: January 1941–May 1942. Lodz, 1965.

Dappim leheker hashoa vehamered. Part 1. Tel Aviv, 1947.

Dawidsohn-Draengerowa, Gusta. *Pamiętnik Justyny.* Cracow, 1946.

Donat, Alexander. *The Holocaust Kingdom.* New York, 1965.

Dray—Ondenkbukh: Pole Elster, Hersh Berlinski, Eliyohu Erlich. Tel Aviv, 1966.

3 Jahre Zionistische Bewegung in Deutschland. Sonderdruck des Berichtes der Zionistische Vereinigung für Deutschland an den XXV Delegierntag. Berlin, 1936.

Dworzecki, M. *Yerushelayim delite in kamf un umkum.* Paris, 1948.

Eck, Nathan. *Hatoim bedarke hamavet.* Jerusalem, 1960.

Edelman, Marek. *The Ghetto Fights.* New York, 1946.

Extermination and Resistance: Historical Records and Source Material. Vol. 1. Kibbutz Lohamei Haghettaot, Israel, 1958.

Falstein, Louis, ed. *The Martyrdom of Jewish Physicians in Poland.* New York, 1963.

Frank, Shlomo. *Togbukh fun lodzher geto.* Buenos Aires, 1958.

Freeden, Herbert. *Jüdisches Theater in Nazideutschland.* Tübingen, 1964.

Freier, Recha. *Let the Children Come: The Early History of Youth Aliyah.* London, 1961.

Gar, Joseph. *Umkum fun der yidisher kovne.* Munich, 1948.

Garfunkel, L. *Kovno hayehudit behurbana.* Jerusalem, 1959.

Geto in flamen: zamlbukh. New York, 1944.

Goldstein, Bernard. *Finf yor in varshever geto.* New York, 1947.

———. *The Stars Bear Witness.* New York, 1949.

Grossman, Chayke. *Anshe hamahteret.* Israel, 1950.

Grossman, Mendel. *With a Camera in the Ghetto.* Ghetto Fighters' House, Israel, 1970.

Hashomer Hatzair. *The Massacre of European Jewry: An Anthology.* Israel, 1963.

Huberband, Simeon. *Kiddush ha-shem: ktavim miyome hashoa.* Tel Aviv, 1969.

Jasni, A. Wolf. *Di geshikhte fun yidn in lodzh: in di yorn fun der daytsher yidn-oysrotung.* 2 vols. Tel Aviv, 1960, 1966.

———, ed. *Sefer Klobutsk: Yizkor-bukh fun der farpaynikter klobutsker kehile.* Tel Aviv, 1960.

Jewish Labor Bund. *In di yorn fun yidishn khurbn: di shtim fun untererdishn bund.* New York, 1948.

Kaczerginski, S. *Khurbn vilne: Umkum fun di yidn in vilne un vilner gegnt.* New York, 1947.

———. *Partizaner geyen!* 2nd enl. ed. Bamberg, 1948.

———, ed. *Dosgezang fun vilner geto.* Paris, 1947.

———, ed. *Lider fun getos un lagern.* New York, 1948.

Kaganovich, Moshe. *Der onteyl fun yidn in der partizaner bavegung in Sovyet-Rusland.* Rome and New York, 1948.

Kantorowicz, N. *Di yidishe vidershtand-bavegung in poyln beysn 2tn velt-krig (1941–1945).* New York, 1967.

Kaplan, Chaim A. *Scroll of Agony.* New York, 1964.

Kaplan, Israel. *Dos folks-moyl in natsi-klem: reydenishn in geto un katset.* Munich, 1949.

Karski, Jan. *Story of a Secret State.* Boston, 1944.

Kaufmann, Max. *Die Vernichtung der Juden Lettlands: Churbn Lettland.* Munich, 1947.

Klin, David. *Mitn malekh-hamoves untern orem: mayne iberle-*

benishn in poyln beys der natsi-okupatsye 1939–1945. Tel Aviv, 1968.

Korczak, Janusz. *Selected Works.* Warsaw, 1967. (Published for the National Science Foundation, Washington, D.C., and available from the U.S. Department of Commerce, Clearinghouse for Federal Scientific and Technical Information, Springfield, Va. 22151.)

Kruk, Herman, *Togbukh fun vilner geto.* New York, 1961.

Landauer, Georg. *Der Zionismus im Wandel dreier Jahrzehnte.* Edited by Max Kreutzberger. Tel Aviv, 1957.

Lewin, Isaac, ed. *Ele ezkra.* 7 vols. New York, 1956–1972.

Litai, Chaim Lazar. *Muranowska 7: The Warsaw Ghetto Rising.* Tel Aviv, 1968.

Litvin, M., and Lerman, M., eds. *Dos bukh fun lublin.* Paris, 1952.

Mark, Ber, ed. *Dokumentn un materyaln vegn oyfshtand in varshever geto.* Warsaw, 1953.

———. *Khurves dertseyln: dos bukh fun gvure.* Lodz, 1947.

———. *Der oyfshtand in bialystoker geto.* Warsaw, 1950.

———. *Der oyfshtand in varshever geto.* Warsaw, 1955.

———. *Oyfshtand in varshever geto: naye dergentste oyflage un dokumentnzamlung.* Warsaw, 1963.

Meed (Miedzyrzecki), Wladka. *Fun beyde zaytn geto-moyer.* New York, 1948.

———. *On Both Sides of the Wall: Memoirs from the Warsaw Ghetto.* Beit Lohamei Hagettaot, 1972.

Meltzer, Shimshon, ed. *Sefer Horodenka.* Tel Aviv, 1963.

Menczer, Arie, ed. *Sefer Pshemishl.* Tel Aviv, 1964.

Mendelsohn, S. *The Polish Jews Behind the Nazi Ghetto Walls.* New York, 1942.

Michel, Henri. *The Shadow War: European Resistance 1939–1945.* New York, 1972.

Mosse, George L. *Germans and Jews: The Right, the Left, and the Search for a "Third Force" in Pre-Nazi Germany.* New York, 1971.

Mosse, Werner E., and Paucker, Arnold, eds. *Entscheidungsjahr 1932: Zur Judenfrage in der Endphase der Weimarer Republik.* 2nd rev and enl. ed. Tübingen, 1966.

Neustadt, Meilech. *Khurbn un oyfshstand fun di yidn in varshe: Eydes-bleter un azkores.* 2 vols. Tel Aviv, 1948.

Olczak, Hanna. *Mister Doctor, The Life of Janusz Korczak.* London, 1965.

Opoczynski, Peretz. *Reportazhn fun varshever geto.* Warsaw, 1954.

Oshry, Ephraim. *Khurbn lite.* New York, 1951.

———. *Sefer divrei Efraim.* New York, 1949.

————. *Sheelot uteshuvot mimaamakim.* 3 vols. New York, 1963–1968.

Payn un gvure in dem yidishn over in likht fun der kegnvart. Lodz, 1947. (Reprinted from mimeographed original issued Warsaw, July 1940.)

Perlow, Isaac, ed. *Sefer Radom.* Tel Aviv, 1961.

Poor, Harold L. *Kurt Tucholsky and the Ordeal of Germany 1914–1935.* New York, 1968.

Prinz, Joachim. *Wir Juden.* Berlin, 1934.

Reichmann, Eva, ed. *Festschrift zum 80. Geburstag von Rabbiner Dr. Leo Baeck am 23. Mai 1953.* London, 1953.

Reisner, Raphael. *Der umkum fun bialystoker yidntum, 1939–1945.* Melbourne, 1948.

Ringelblum, Emanuel. *Ksovim fun geto.* 2 vols. 2nd rev. ed. Warsaw, 1963.

————. *Notes from the Warsaw Ghetto.* New York, 1958.

Rothenberg, I., ed. *Dos yidishe Radom in khurves.* Stuttgart, 1948.

Rousset, David. *The Other Kingdom.* New York, 1947.

Rudashevski, Yitzhok. *The Diary of the Vilna Ghetto: June 1941–April 1943.* Ghetto Fighters' House, Israel [1972].

Sabotka, H., ed. *Lomzhe: ir oyfkum un unterang.* New York, 1957.

Schindler, Peter. "Responses of Hassidic Leaders and Hassidim During the Holocaust in Europe, 1939–1945, and a Correlation Between Such Responses and Selected Concepts in Hassidic Thought." Doctoral dissertation, School of Education, New York, University, 1972.

Schoeps, Hans Joachim. *Die letzten dreissig Jahre: Rückblicke.* Stuttgart, 1956.

Seidman, Hillel. *Togbukh fun varshever geto.* Buenos Aires, 1947.

Shoshkes, H. *Bleter fun a geto-tog-bukh.* New York, 1943.

Shtrachman, Nahum, ed. *Sefer Lutsk.* Tel Aviv, 1961.

Simon, Ernst. *Aufbau im Untergang: Jüdische Erwachsenenbildung im nationalsozialistischen Deutschland als geistiger Widerstand.* Tübingen, 1959.

Singer, S. D., ed. *Tshenstokhov.* New York, 1958.

Stein, A. S., ed. *Pinkes Bendin.* Tel Aviv, 1959.

Strauss, Herbert A., and Grossman, Kurt R. *Gegenwart im Rückblick: Festgabe für die jüdische Gemeinde zu Berlin 25 Jahre nach dem Neubeginn.* Heidelberg, 1970.

Sudarsky, Mendel, et al., eds. *Lite.* New York, 1951.

Sutzkever, Abram. *Lider fun geto.* New York, 1946.

Tabaksblatt, Israel. *Khurbn lodzh: 6 yor natsi-gehenem.* Buenos Aires, 1946.

Tenenbaum-Tamaroff, Mordecai. *Dappim min hadleka.* Tel Aviv, 1947.

Tramer, Hans, ed. *In zwei Welten: Siegfried Moses zum Fünf-undsiebzigsten Geburtstag.* Tel Aviv, 1962.

Trunk, Isaiah. *Geshtaltn un gesheyenishn.* Buenos Aires, 1962.

———. *Judenrat: The Jewish Councils in Eastern Europe Under Nazi Occupation.* New York, 1972.

———. *Lodzher geto.* New York, 1962.

Turkow, Jonas. *Azoy iz es geven.* Buenos Aires, 1948.

Unger, Menashe. *Sefer kedoshim: rebeyim oyf kiddush-hashem.* New York, 1967.

Varshever geto-oyfshtand: 19ter April 1943–19ter April 1947. Landsberg, 1947.

Weichert, Michal. *Yidishe aleynhilf 1939–1945.* Tel Aviv, 1962.

Wille und Weg des deutschen Judentums. Berlin, 1935.

World Jewish Congress. *Extermination of Polish Jewry: Reports Based on Official Documents.* New York, July–August 1943.

Wulman, L. *In kampf farn gezunt fun yidishn folk (50 yor OSE).* New York, 1968.

Yad Washem. *Blackbook of Localities Whose Jewish Population Was Exterminated by the Nazis.* Jerusalem, 1965.

YIVO Colloquium. *Imposed Jewish Governing Bodies Under Nazi Rule.* New York, 1972.

Zygelboym, Artur Shmuel. *Zygelboym-bukh.* Edited by S. Hertz. New York, 1947.

Zylberberg, Michael. *A Warsaw Diary: 1939–1945.* London, 1969.

APPENDIX A
THE FATE OF THE JEWS IN HITLER'S EUROPE: BY COUNTRY

Braham, Randolph. *The Destruction of Hungarian Jewry: A Documentary Account.* 2 vols. New York, 1963.

Centre de Documentation Juive Contemporaine. *Les Juifs en Europe (1939–1945): rapports présentés à la première conférence européenne des commissions historiques et des centres de documentation juifs.* Paris, 1949.

Chary, Frederick B. *The Bulgarian Jews and the Final Solution.* Pittsburgh, Pa., 1972.

Fried, John H. E. *Anti-Jewish Legislation in Europe and North Africa, Imposed or Inspired by National-Socialist Germany.* Nuremberg, 1947. (Mimeographed)

Knout, David. *Contribution à l'histoire de la résistance juive en France 1940–1944.* Paris, 1947.

Levy, Claude, and Tillard, Paul. *Betrayal at the Vel d'Hiv.* New York, 1969.

Meyer, Peter, et al. *The Jews in the Soviet Satellites.* Syracuse, N.Y., 1953.

Molho, Michal, ed. *In Memoriam: Hommage aux victimes juives des Nazis en Grèce.* 2 vols. Salonika, 1948–1949.

Poliakov, Leon, and Sabille, Jacques. *Jews Under the Italian Occupation.* Paris, 1955.

Presser, Jacob. *The Destruction of the Dutch Jews.* New York, 1969.

Schwarz, Solomon M. *The Jews in the Soviet Union.* Syracuse, N.Y., 1951.

Toynbee, Arnold Joseph, and Toynbee, Veronica, eds. *Hitler's Europe.* London and New York, 1954.

Warmbrunn, Werner. *The Dutch Under German Occupation, 1940–1945.* Stanford, Cal., 1963.

World Jewish Congress. *European Jewry Ten Years After the War: An Account of the Development and Present Status of the Decimated Jewish Communities of Europe.* New York, 1956.

Yahil, Leni. *The Rescue of Danish Jewry.* Philadelphia, 1969.

Index

ABOUT THE AUTHOR

LUCY S. DAWIDOWICZ was educated at Hunter College and Columbia University in New York and studied East European Jewish life at first hand at the Yivo Institute of Jewish Research, formerly in Vilna, Poland. She now teaches modern Jewish history at Yeshiva University, where she holds the Eli and Diana Zborowski Chair in Interdisciplinary Holocaust Studies. She is the author of *The Golden Tradition: Jewish Life and Thought in Eastern Europe* and *Holocaust Reader* (Behrman House).

SPECIAL
MONEY SAVING
OFFER

Now you can have an up-to-date listing of Bantam's *hundreds* of titles plus take advantage of our unique and exciting bonus book offer. A special offer which gives you the opportunity to purchase a Bantam book for only 50¢. Here's how!

By ordering any five books at the regular price per order, you can also choose any other single book listed (up to a $4.95 value) for just 50¢. Some restrictions do apply, but for further details why not send for Bantam's listing of titles today!

Just send us your name and address plus 50¢ to defray the postage and handling costs.